AUTOMATED REASONING

Introduction and Applications

LARRY WOS

ROSS OVERBEEK

EWING LUSK

JIM BOYLE

Argonne National Laboratory
Argonne, Illinois

PRENTICE-HALL, INC.

Englewood Cliffs, New Jersey 07632

Library of Congress Cataloging in Publication Data
Main entry under title:

Automated Reasoning.

Bibliography: p.
Includes index.
1. Automatic theorem proving. 2. Artificial intelli-
gence. 3. Electronic digital computers—Programming.
I. Wos, Larry.
QA76.9.A96A93 1984   001.53'5   83-22968
ISBN 0-13-054453-1
ISBN 0-13-054446-9 (pbk.)

Editorial / production supervision: Nancy Milnamow
Manufacturing buyer: Gordon Osbourne

Printed in the United States of America

10 9 8 7 6 5 4 3 2 1

ISBN 0-13-054453-1
ISBN 0-13-054446-9 {PBK.}

Prentice-Hall International, Inc., *London*
Prentice-Hall of Australia Pty. Limited, *Sydney*
Editora Prentice-Hall do Brasil, Ltda., *Rio de Janeiro*
Prentice-Hall Canada Inc., *Toronto*
Prentice-Hall of India Private Limited, *New Delhi*
Prentice-Hall of Japan, Inc., *Tokyo*
Prentice-Hall of Southeast Asia Pte. Ltd., *Singapore*
Whitehall Books Limited, *Wellington, New Zealand*

To Nan, Joan, Brigid, and Jean

Contents

Contents

13   EXPERT SYSTEMS   371

14   PROLOG: LOGIC AS A PROGRAMMING LANGUAGE   389

Preface

How satisfying it would be if this book showed you how computers can seem to think. They can, you know—that is, if by thinking you mean the ability to solve puzzles, answer open questions in mathematics, prove that computer programs achieve their stated purpose, design electronic circuits, and in general search for information. All of these can be done by the same program—a program that automates the process known as reasoning.

The choice is yours. Here you can learn how to use such a program. Or you can just satisfy your curiosity about how a computer can be programmed to reason.

If you prefer or enjoy a leisurely pace, read the first six chapters in their entirety. If you already know some logic or are somewhat acquainted with automated reasoning, you might begin with Chapter 6 and refer to the earlier chapters only for details and clarification. In Chapter 6, the basic concepts introduced in the first five chapters are briskly reviewed. In the first five chapters, you will be introduced to a language for stating problems to an automated reasoning program and also to many considerations affecting its performance. In addition, you will learn about the different ways such a program reasons and, further, how it is intelligent! The treatment is not particularly formal. Rather, you are introduced to the material by means of various examples. Puzzles are the focus of attention in the early chapters, while later chapters discuss the application of automated reasoning to designing logic circuits, to proving properties of other computer programs, to assisting in research in abstract mathematics and in formal logic, among others. After reading the opening chapters, you can skip to the chapter focusing on your particular interest, for the chapters beginning with Chapter 7 can be read independently. If your particular interest is not specifically covered in one of the chapters, the formal treatment found near the end of the book might enable you to achieve your objective.

Acknowledgements

We acknowledge Steve Winker for his invaluable contributions to the field of automated reasoning and to this book in particular. His research is most pertinent to Chapters 5, 7, 9, 10 and 12–especially the methodology for generating models and the nonstandard uses of demodulation. The previously open questions whose solutions are presented in Chapters 9 and 10 were solved by Winker in collaboration with one of us (Wos).

We acknowledge Brian T. Smith for his work on several automated reasoning programs, for his contribution to Chapter 12, and for his valuable suggestions for the book as a whole.

We are most grateful to Gail Pieper, Rick Stevens, and Robert L. Veroff for their valuable assistance in preparing this manuscript. We also thank Larry Henschen, Bill McCune, Jorg Siekmann, and Susan Gerhart for various suggestions. We are indebted to Argonne National Laboratory, and especially to the Mathematics and Computer Science Division and to Paul Messina, its director, for making possible the writing of this book.

Larry Wos, Ross Overbeek, Ewing Lusk, and Jim Boyle

1

Introduction

What do the following three puzzles have in common?

> There are twelve billiard balls, eleven of which are identical in weight. The remaining ball—the odd one—has a different weight. You are not told whether it is heavier or lighter. You have a balance scale for weighing the balls. Can you find which ball is the odd ball in three weighings, and also find out whether it is lighter or heavier than the others?
>
> There are three missionaries and three cannibals on the west bank of a river. There is a boat on the west bank that can hold no more than two people. The missionaries wish to cross to the east bank. But they have a problem: If on either bank the cannibals ever outnumber the missionaries, those missionaries will be eaten. Is there a way for the missionaries to get their wish—to get to the east bank without losing anyone?
>
> There is a checkerboard whose upper left and lower right squares have been removed. There is a box of dominoes that are one square by two squares in size. Can you exactly cover the checkerboard with the dominoes?

Again, what is common to the three problems? The answer is: They can each be solved with reasoning—logical reasoning. And the answer also is: They have all been solved with the same computer program.

Logical reasoning is not only the key to solving these and many other puzzles, but it is also the key to solving problems in mathematics, to designing electronic circuits, and to answering many everyday questions. Because of the universal importance of reasoning, the natural question is: Can computers be programmed to reason logically? They can be and have been, which brings us to the point of this book—an in-depth discussion of the new field of automated reasoning. Although *automated* reasoning dominates the discussion, the methods and techniques presented here apply even when a computer is not involved.

We begin with examples, some of which are widely known, taken from the world of puzzles. But, while puzzles are the first area for illustration, this book is not merely for the curious. Although the curious will have many of their questions answered, so will those who wish to use an automated reasoning program to assist in diverse investigations, both practical and theoretical. The "real" applications discussed range from the designing and validating of electronic circuits to assisting in mathematical research. These applications require an automated reasoning program to be used in a variety of ways. Therefore, not only will you learn about the expected use of an automated reasoning program for proving that a particular statement is true, but in addition you will see how to use it to find a model having certain desired properties, to generate a counterexample to some conjecture, or simply to obtain general information. You will also learn that such a program can equally well be asked to complete a task on its own or to participate in a dialogue with the investigator.

For each area of application, problems that have actually been solved with an automated reasoning program are selected for illustration. As well as illustrating various techniques and concepts of the field, many of the problems show how an automated reasoning program can be used as an assistant—sometimes an invaluable assistant. In fact, a number of questions whose answers were previously unknown have been answered with such an assistant. Each problem is first stated in its natural language. Thus, for the missionaries and cannibals puzzle, everyday English will suffice. On the other hand, for designing electronic circuits, the language will include statements about "and" gates and "or" gates. The statement of each problem or puzzle is then translated into a single language—one that a reasoning program understands. Since we prefer, when possible, to discuss what has been done rather than what could be done, the illustrations come from actual computer runs.

In these computer runs, all required reasoning steps, including those a person often overlooks, are made explicit. You may be surprised at the number of steps required to answer even the most innocent of questions. In all the problem areas, implicit information abounds—information that a person tacitly assumes but that must be explicitly given to the computer. Being forced to supply such minute and mundane information can certainly be a nuisance. This nuisance is one of the shortcomings of automated reasoning programs, at least in the view of some. But explicitly supplying all information has the advantage of exposing questionable or even incorrect assumptions. Reasoning programs do have two other advantages besides their ability to make explicit every step of reasoning—their ability to reason flawlessly, and their ability to consider many more alternatives than a person would. These advantages have proved to be sufficient incentive for some to rely heavily on the assistance of an automated reasoning program.

To gain the most from the assistance of such a program, good choices must be made from among the ways that it can reason and from among the strategies that it can impose for controlling its reasoning. Thus, besides introducing by example a language understood by a typical automated reasoning program, we shall also cover by example a number of ways the program reasons and a number of ways that reasoning can be controlled. A reasoning program should not simply reason methodically and exhaustively. Intelligence comes into play—intelligence in the form of *strategy*. Strategy is essential. Without the imposition of strategy, an automated reasoning program would attempt to examine exhaustively the set of conclusions that can be drawn from the known set of facts. Exhaustive examination is usually unwise, since there are simply too many possibilities to be considered, even for simple puzzles. The surprising number of steps mentioned earlier is not the cause for needing strategy, but rather the incredible number of fruitless steps that can be taken. An effective reasoning program requires access to strategies for avoiding many of the fruitless paths of inquiry; it also requires strategies for choosing a good move to make next and for discarding useless information.

We discuss each facet of automated reasoning in turn by means of examples, rather than discussing each in terms of the deep logical foundations on which it rests. Nevertheless, to provide you with a means for applying automated reasoning to areas not closely related to those covered in this book, we do include a chapter giving a formal treatment of the logical foundations of automated reasoning. Thus, if the area in which you wish to apply automated reasoning is not covered in one of the chapters, you might read the first six chapters and then read the chapter that gives the formal treatment. Directly or indirectly, we intend to answer questions of a "how to" nature concerning various potential applications.

When your reading is finished, you will understand how an automated reasoning program works and how to have it assist you in some project. You will be able to phrase a wide variety of problems in a language suitable for a reasoning program. You will be in a position to suggest different ways of reasoning that it might try. Finally, you will have a good idea about which choices to make to influence its strategy in attacking a given problem.

Among the applications of automated reasoning, we present a chapter on expert systems and one on Prolog. An expert system is a computer program designed to perform more or less as an expert in a particular field, such as internal medicine. Expert systems, therefore, contain as one of their components a component for reasoning. The Prolog system is a computer program that is on the one hand a programming language, and on the other a reasoning system for solving problems whose solution can be obtained by reasoning in a very algorithmic manner. The chapters on expert systems and Prolog provide an introduction to these two topics, one that is made more accessible in view of the material contained in the early chapters.

1.1 What Is Automated Reasoning?

To understand what automated reasoning is, we must first understand what reasoning is. *Reasoning* is the process of drawing conclusions from facts. For the reasoning to be sound, these conclusions must follow inevitably from the facts from which they are drawn. In other words, reasoning as used in this book is not concerned with some conclusion that has a good chance of being true when the facts are true. Thus, reasoning as used here refers to logical reasoning, not to common-sense reasoning or probabilistic reasoning. The only conclusions that are acceptable are those that follow *logically* from the supplied facts.

The object of *automated reasoning* is to write computer programs that assist in solving problems and in answering questions requiring reasoning. The assistance provided by an automated reasoning program is available in two different modes. You can use such a program in an interactive fashion, that is, you can instruct it to draw some conclusions and present them to you, and then it will ask for further instructions. Or you can use such a program in a batch mode, that is, you can assign it an entire reasoning task and await the final result. In either case, the question is: "How do I instruct an automated reasoning program to carry out a task?"

The first step in instructing a reasoning program is to tell it about the problem to be solved or about the question to be answered. You must supply a set of facts that adequately describes the situation. As you will see in the coming chapters, you must tell it essentially everything, including the simplest and most obvious facts. A reasoning program has very few concepts that it automatically understands. More-over, you must phrase each of the facts in a language that the reasoning program accepts. Everyday language usually does not work, for it is not clear enough and is often ambiguous. Since the program is required to draw only sound conclusions—those that follow inevitably from the given facts—the given facts must not be clouded by ambiguity or a lack of clarity. In Chapter 2, you will learn about a typical language acceptable to a reasoning program.

After being told about the problem, a reasoning program searches for new facts—generates new facts by drawing conclusions from older facts. It obtains the new facts by applying specific types of reasoning, which are called *inference rules*. In the next few chapters, you will see that a number of quite distinct types of reasoning can be applied to a problem. The surprise is that one can identify inference rules that apply in diverse and unrelated areas. But perhaps this fact is not totally surprising, for in arithmetic you learn about rules that apply regardless of where the numbers come from. In reasoning, similar rules exist that apply regardless of where the facts come from. Each type of reasoning is carefully structured to yield conclusions that must follow from the facts it uses. The facts obtained by applying the inference rules are then added to the pool of information or knowledge, depending on various criteria discussed shortly. Exhaustively applying inference rules in an attempt to solve the problem is too naive an approach. The attempt to solve even the simplest of problems or questions or puzzles by exhaustive attack would produce vast amounts of information, much of it irrelevant. Considerable control of the application of reasoning rules is needed.

The need for control is met by having a reasoning *strategy*. In chess, for example, simply playing according to the rules without evaluating the consequences usually loses the game. In poker, betting simply according to the odds usually loses the money. In either game, strategy comes into play and is essential for winning.

Similarly, an automated reasoning program must use strategy if it is to have a chance at solving the problem under attack. Some strategies direct a reasoning program in its choice of information or knowledge on which to focus. Even more vital, some strategies prevent a reasoning program from exploring entire classes of conclusions. Some strategies enable you to convey to a reasoning program your intuition and knowledge about how to solve the problem being studied. An automated reasoning program applies rules of reasoning continually, but subject to various strategies. You will begin to learn of these strategies in Chapter 3.

We commented earlier that a reasoning program adds new facts to the pool of information *only* if certain criteria are satisfied. For example, if the "new" information is actually a copy of already-existing information, then there is no point in keeping the "new" copy. Such duplicate information is in fact discarded immediately upon discovering that it is merely a copy of other information. A more powerful and subtler criterion exists for immediately discarding information: If the "new" information is already captured by an older bit of information—is less general than some fact already present—then the new is discarded. For example, if a reasoning program has available the fact that all fathers are older than their children, then the new fact that "my father is older than I am" is immediately discarded. In Chapter 4, you will learn more fully about this process.

Information that is classed as acceptable and therefore to be retained is not necessarily kept in the form in which it is found by application of one of the rules of reasoning. For example, if you said to someone, "My father's father is coming to visit", your companion might reply, "Oh, your grandfather is coming to see you". An automated reasoning program can take similar action if you provide it with the appropriate rules for rephrasing certain facts. Such rephrasing is vital for many uses of an automated reasoning program. In Chapter 3, for example, a puzzle is solved in which rephrasing plays a role essential to the program's performance.

As a preview of what is to come, we shall briefly show you how an automated reasoning program might solve a puzzle rather simpler than the three puzzles we cited at the beginning of this chapter. You will get a small taste of a language that such a program understands, of a rule it can use to draw conclusions that follow logically, and of a strategy it can apply to control the reasoning. While the full treatment and understanding of these areas of automated reasoning must wait until Chapter 2 and beyond, the following sample provides a hint of what an automated reasoning program can do.

1.2 How Does an Automated Reasoning Program Reason?

A merchant wishes to sell you some fruit. He places three boxes of it on a table. Each box contains only one kind of fruit, apples, bananas, or oranges. As a gesture of good will, the merchant, after asking you to turn your back, selects a piece of fruit from each box and hands you a beautiful apple, a beautiful banana, and a beautiful orange, establishing that each box contains a different type of fruit. You are momentarily puzzled by his request to turn your back, but the reason quickly becomes apparent. The merchant loves to gamble and offers you the chance to win all of the fruit if you can figure out what is in each box. If you lose, you must pay him three times what it is worth. He tells you correctly that each box is mislabeled. Box a is labeled apples, box b oranges, and box c bananas. You accept the bet on the condition that he allow you to look in the box labeled oranges. He agrees, and you look in box b and find that it contains apples. You then turn to him and announce correctly the contents of the other two boxes, and win the fruit. How did you do it?

Your solution might be the following. Since box b contains apples, box a and box c do not. Since box c is labeled bananas, and since the label is incorrect, box c does not contain bananas. So, box c contains oranges, and box a contains bananas.

To present this puzzle to an automated reasoning program, everyday language is not precise enough. Instead, such a program expects the puzzle phrased in a language like the following. For the statement that box b contains apples, we write

(1) CONTAINS(b,apples)

using b for box b. Similarly,

(2) LABEL(a,apples)

(3) LABEL(b,oranges)

(4) LABEL(c,bananas)

tell the program how each box is labeled. To say that each box contains one of the three types of fruit, where "|" represents **or**, we write

(5) CONTAINS(a,apples) | CONTAINS(a,bananas)

    | CONTAINS(a,oranges)

(6) CONTAINS(b,apples) | CONTAINS(b,bananas)

    | CONTAINS(b,oranges)

(7) CONTAINS(c,apples) | CONTAINS(c,bananas)

    | CONTAINS(c,oranges)

which respectively say that box a contains apples or bananas or oranges, and so does box b, and also box c.

At this point, the process of giving all of the facts to a reasoning program becomes slightly more complicated. For example, the fact that "**if** box a contains apples, **then** box b and box c do not" requires some care. Where "¬" represents **not** we write

(8) ¬CONTAINS(a, apples) | ¬CONTAINS(b, apples)

(9) ¬CONTAINS(a, apples) | ¬CONTAINS(c, apples)

(10) ¬CONTAINS(b, apples) | ¬CONTAINS(c, apples)

(11) ¬CONTAINS(a, bananas) | ¬CONTAINS(b, bananas)

(12) ¬CONTAINS(a, bananas) | ¬CONTAINS(c, bananas)

(13) ¬CONTAINS(b, bananas) | ¬CONTAINS(c, bananas)

(14) ¬CONTAINS(a, oranges) | ¬CONTAINS(b, oranges)

(15) ¬CONTAINS(a, oranges) | ¬CONTAINS(c, oranges)

(16) ¬CONTAINS(b, oranges) | ¬CONTAINS(c, oranges)

to cover all the combinations of boxes and fruit. Notice that statement 9 says that box a does not contain apples **or** box c does not contain apples, which is certainly true since they cannot both contain apples. You might wonder at the need to write nine statements to cover this single fact, and you will discover in Chapter 2 that, with a slightly different notation employing variables, only one statement is in fact needed. Variables in a language allow you to talk about "all items having a particular property" without naming each item.

Since we have mentioned variables, let us now give the representation for the fact that every box is mislabeled. That fact can be stated formally as "for every x and every y, x is **not** labeled y **or** x does **not** contain y", which is equivalent to "for every x and every y, **if** x is labeled y, **then** x does **not** contain y". (Such useful equivalences are explained in Chapter 2, which discusses a number of other aspects of logic that also prove to be useful.) We write

(17) ¬LABEL(x, y) | ¬CONTAINS(x, y)

where the variables x and y are interpreted by a reasoning program as "for all x" "for all y". You will learn the full story in Chapter 2.

Given statements 1 through 17, an automated reasoning program can apply a rule for drawing conclusions that would produce the following statements. From 1 and 10, the program concludes

(18) ¬CONTAINS(c, apples)

which says that box c does not contain apples. The reasoning program obtains this conclusion by "canceling" part of 10 against 1. From 4 and 17, the program concludes

(19) ¬CONTAINS(c, bananas)

which says that box c does not contain bananas. Arriving at this conclusion requires a more complex process than arriving at the preceding one does. The program obtains it by in effect replacing the variables x and y in 17 by c and bananas respectively, and then canceling part of the resulting statement against 4. The rule for reasoning logically can then be applied to 18, 19, and 7 simultaneously to give

(20) CONTAINS(c, oranges)

which says that box c contains oranges.

With the contents of box b given and of box c correctly deduced, the reasoning program could then turn to box a. By using 1 again but now with 8, the program concludes

(21) ¬CONTAINS(a, apples)

which says that box a does not contain apples. From 20 and 15, the program then concludes

(22) ¬CONTAINS(a, oranges)

which says that box a does not contain oranges. Finally from 21 and 22 and 5, considered simultaneously, the program concludes

(23) CONTAINS(a, bananas)

which completes the explanation of how you won your bet.

Notice that the conclusions obtained by the reasoning program look very much like your solution, although the steps are not in the same order. What is perhaps more interesting is that an automated reasoning program can use a strategy that decreases its chance of getting lost on the way to solving the puzzle. The conclusions that it draws, statements 18 through 23, are directly or indirectly traceable to statements 1 or 4. In particular, if a reasoning program, or a person for that matter, is prevented from applying rules of reasoning to various pairs of statements unless one of them is directly traceable to statements 1 or 4, then a sharp improvement in effectiveness might result. Such a restriction on reasoning is known as a strategy and is discussed more fully in Chapter 3.

Is the reasoning program being too careful and too pedantic? A variation on this puzzle shows why such care is often needed. In the variation, the merchant does not make the magnanimous gesture of offering you one piece of fruit from each box, but instead correctly tells you none of the boxes is empty. Thus, you cannot assume that each box contains a different type of fruit. If you accept the bet, you will win only if you make the right guesses, for the information given in the variant of the puzzle is insufficient to pin down what is in box a and box c. For example, box a could contain oranges, and box c, like box b, could contain apples. If you had guessed at the contents of boxes a and c, you might have made the wrong guess. You might have assumed that all three types of fruit were contained in the three boxes, and not allowed for two boxes to contain the same type of fruit. Logical reasoning would eventually prove that the puzzle was unsolvable—only guesswork might get you the correct answer. Thus, if the merchant required you to prove that your answers were correct, you would have no chance of winning. An automated reasoning program would not have answered the puzzle incorrectly. In fact, such a program could be used to prove that the correct answers are not deducible. Therefore, for solving the first version or for showing that the second version cannot be solved, an automated reasoning program can provide assistance.

This overview of automated reasoning is now complete. Many details must and will be supplied. Briefly, keep in mind that you supply the description of the problem to a reasoning program and use a language that adds precision to what is being said and removes ambiguity. The program applies various rules of reasoning, subject to your choice, to add to the pool of information or knowledge. The rules that are applied are constrained and directed by various strategies, again subject to your choice. Then, as we shall discuss in detail, the "new" information is processed and filtered to see whether it is worth retaining. If it is deemed worth keeping, then the information is often rephrased before being stored away. A reasoning program continues in this fashion until time runs out, or until space is exhausted, or—and this is the hoped-for result—until it finds the key new fact that in effect says the problem has been solved. To learn how an automated reasoning program knows that the problem has been solved or that the question has been answered, you must wait until you have read Chapter 2. To learn what the book in its entirety is about, you need only read the next section.

1.3 The Map

As with any journey, you can move through the chapters of this book in a number of ways, and yet arrive at the same point. Your choice of routes depends on your preferences, your interests, and your background. To assist in making a good choice, we provide this map of the book, and include certain observations. In particular, the exercises introduce pertinent material, including terminology and information not previously found in the text. They are not included solely to enable you to assess your progress.

For those who wish to travel in a leisurely manner, we suggest beginning with Chapter 2. Since you might have had little or no previous exposure to logic, this chapter provides an introduction to the various logical concepts that are needed. This chapter also introduces a language for communicating with an automated reasoning program. On the other hand, for those who prefer to travel rapidly, we suggest beginning with Chapter 6. In that case, you may find it helpful to consult Chapters 2, 3, and 4 at those points where you desire a detailed explanation. Beginning with Chapter 6 is recommended especially for those who are acquainted with logic and who may already know something about automated reasoning. That chapter provides a review of the basic concepts introduced in Chapters 2 through 5, and the treatment is formal in an informal way. Finally, for those who prefer the very formal approach, we suggest beginning with Chapter 15. If you should choose this route, you might still wish to glance at some of the material in Chapters 3, 4, and 5 before turning immediately to the chapter covering your particular interest.

Chapter 3 builds on what is learned in Chapter 2, introduces new concepts, and applies what you have learned to solving puzzles. First, an automated reasoning program is presented with a simple puzzle about people and jobs. Then the full jobs puzzle is studied. This chapter is recommended to all three classes of traveler. Among the techniques presented there are those for automatically updating information. Thus, even for those quite familiar with automated reasoning, we recommend this chapter.

Chapter 4 focuses on alternative representation of information, and also on certain concepts of automated reasoning not previously covered. In particular, you learn in this chapter that an automated reasoning program can treat the notion of equality as you can—for example, automatically substituting equals for equals. This treatment of equality is a "built-in feature" of various automated reasoning programs. This chapter is recommended to all, with the possible exception of those who are quite familiar with automated reasoning.

Chapter 5 features the study of three classical puzzles. Each is presented to an automated reasoning program, and the corresponding solution is given in detail. Everyone will enjoy this chapter.

Chapter 6 is a summary and review of what has gone before. With this chapter, the introduction to automated reasoning is complete. The chapter can be read, as indicated earlier, in place of much of Chapter 2, and in place of parts of Chapters 3 and 4. This chapter provides useful information whether or not you have begun with Chapter 2.

Chapter 7 focuses on designing logic circuits with the assistance of an automated reasoning program. For those who wish to understand this application but who lack knowledge about circuit design, we begin the chapter with introductory material. Those who are familiar with circuit design may well prefer to skip that material, and immediately turn to the actual use of an automated reasoning program.

Chapter 8 focuses on the use of an automated reasoning program to validate the existing design of a logic circuit. This task is quite different from that of designing the circuit given the specifications.

Chapter 9 studies the successful employment of an automated reasoning program as an automated reasoning assistant in mathematical research. Some of the previously open questions from mathematics that were solved with the aid of an automated reasoning program are discussed. Solving open questions is one of the main activities of mathematicians. The solving of questions whose answers were not previously known until attacked with much assistance from an automated reasoning program provides a concrete illustration of what can be done. This chapter is recommended to mathematicians who might consider using an automated reasoning assistant in their research.

Chapter 10 studies the successful use of an automated reasoning program as an assistant for research in formal logic. Here, as in Chapter 9, previously open questions are featured. Answering such open questions with much assistance from an automated reasoning program provides concrete evidence of what can be done. We recommend this chapter to logicians who might consider using a reasoning program as an automated assistant in their research.

Chapter 11 discusses the use of an automated reasoning program in control systems. We begin with the control of a greenhouse. We then turn to certain control problems that arise in nuclear plants.

Chapter 12 focuses on using an automated reasoning program as a programming assistant. There we discuss both symbolic execution—symbolic testing—of a given program and proving the correctness of—proving that certain properties hold for—a given computer program. We also discuss how the technique of abstract programming can be used to avoid consideration of many of the extremely detailed and uninteresting theorems that are involved.

Chapter 13 provides an introduction to expert systems—computer programs that perform rather like an expert in such areas as medical diagnosis, geological exploration, and chemical analysis. Expert systems depend in part on a reasoning component.

Chapter 14 gives an introduction to Prolog, a programming language that has built-in logical power. Prolog's input language is that of clauses—the language employed throughout this book for communicating to an automated reasoning program.

Chapter 15 presents a formal treatment of many of the concepts on which automated reasoning rests. As commented earlier, we recommend this chapter to those who prefer the formal treatment. We also recommend this chapter to those who wish to consider an application of automated reasoning for which too little information is provided by the other application chapters.

In Chapter 16, we give some guidelines for choosing the representation of information, selecting appropriate inference rules, suggesting effective strategies, and making other decisions. We also give a chapter-by-chapter bibliography to suggest possible material that amplifies the material presented in the book.

2

Learning Logic by Example

Since an automated reasoning program is required to draw conclusions flawlessly, logic plays an essential role in its operation. This chapter is devoted to an introduction to logic.

2.1 and, or, not, if-then

Name a state that begins with a consonant. Pennsylvania will do. Name a state that begins with a vowel **and** ends with a consonant: Arkansas. Name one that begins with a vowel **and** ends with a vowel, **or** begins with a consonant **and** ends with a consonant. Oklahoma is acceptable, but so also is Connecticut. Name one that begins with a vowel **and** does **not** end with a consonant. Oklahoma suffices again.

These illustrations of the *logical operations*—**and**, **or**, and **not**—are reminiscent of their use in everyday language. However, the way **or** is used in everyday language, it often means either is true, but not both. In logic, **or** is true also when both are true. The **and** of two statements is true if and only if both statements are true. The **or** is true if at least one of the statements is true; hence it is true if both statements are true. The **not** of a statement is true if the statement is false, and false if the statement is true.

The definitions, and hence the meanings, of **and**, **or**, and **not** can be conveniently summarized in what are called *truth tables*. Consider the following three truth tables:

and

s1	s2	s1 **and** s2
true	true	true
true	false	false
false	true	false
false	false	false

or

s1	s2	s1 **or** s2
true	true	true
true	false	true
false	true	true
false	false	false

not

s1	**not** s1
true	false
false	true

The first table summarizes the meaning of **and**. Think of the three columns—labeled s1, s2, s1 **and** s2—as standing for three statements that can be true or false. The first row says that, if s1 is true and s2 is true, then s1 **and** s2 must be true. The second row says that, if s1 is true and s2 is false, then s1 **and** s2 must be false. The remaining two rows give the truth value that s1 **and** s2 must have, when s1 is false and s2 true, and when both s1 and s2 are false. The four rows taken together give all possible choices of truth values for s1 and s2, and also give the corresponding truth value forced on s1 **and** s2. The truth table for **or** also has three columns, since **or** connects two statements, just as **and** connects two statements. However, the table for **not** only contains two columns, since **not** acts on a single statement, rather than on a pair of statements. You might wish to study these tables to the point that the logical operations of **and**, **or**, and **not** are very familiar to you. The tables summarize the meanings of **and**, **or**, and **not** as expressed earlier in everyday language.

Now we include a set of exercises. If you have never studied logic before, we strongly recommend that you work out the answers and check them against those found at the end of the chapter.

EXERCISES

1. Which of the following statements are true?
   (a) A minute contains 60 seconds **or** there are 24 hours in a day.
   (b) A minute contains 60 seconds **or** there are 30 hours in a day.
   (c) A minute contains 60 seconds **and** there are 30 hours in a day.
   (d) A minute contains 60 seconds **and** there are 24 hours in a day.
   (e) Two plus two is four **and** eight minus one is six.
   (f) $(2 + 2 = 4)$ **or** $(8 - 1 = 6)$
   (g) **(not** $(2 + 2 = 4)$**) and (not** $(8 - 1 = 6)$**)**
   (h) **not** $((2 + 2 = 4)$ **and** $(8 - 1 = 6))$
   (i) Two plus two is four **and** eight minus six is two **and** 1984 is a leap year.

2. Is there a difference in the meaning of the following two statements?
   George is absent **and** Helen is here.
   Helen is here **and** George is absent.

3. Is there a difference between the following two statements?
   (George is absent **and** Jim is out to lunch) **and** Helen is here.
   George is absent **and** (Jim is out to lunch **and** Helen is here).

4. Is there a difference between the following two statements?
   (George is absent **or** Jim is out to lunch) **and** Helen is here.
   George is absent **or** (Jim is out to lunch **and** Helen is here).

The logical **if-then** is somewhat subtler. Each of the following three statements is an illustration of the everyday use of **if-then**.

If a man is married, **then** he has a wife.

If George has a son named Harry, **then** George and Harry have the same last name.

If today is Monday, **then** tomorrow is Tuesday.

In everyday usage, **if-then** statements are clearly true—and true because the **if** is true and the **then** is true. The **then** part of such statements follows obviously from the **if** part. In everyday usage, you almost automatically assume that an **if-then** statement is true, and not false.

The following **if-then** statements, however, are somewhat less obvious.

If the name of a state begins with the letter "F", **then** the name ends with a vowel.

If it begins with an "I", **then** it ends with a vowel.

If it begins with a "B", **then** it ends with a consonant.

The first of the previous three statements is true, the second false, and the third true. The first is true because there are no exceptions to it; among all the state names, all of those that begin with "F"—Florida—do end with a vowel. The second is false because there is an exception; among all the state names that begin with "I" —Idaho, Illinois, Indiana, and Iowa—there is one that does not end with a vowel. The third is true because there again are no exceptions; no state name begins with a "B", and hence no state begins with a "B" and ends with a vowel. In other words, an **if-then** statement is true when its hypothesis and conclusion are both true, and also true when its hypothesis is false, regardless of the truth or falsity of the conclusion. An **if-then** statement, as with any statement, can be true or false. By definition, the logical **if-then** is false only when the **if** is true and the **then** is false.

If this definition disturbs you, perhaps the truth of the following statement will help. "If the capital of Texas is Dallas, then the state of Texas is in Africa". This statement is true—true because Dallas is **not** the capital of Texas. And, for a subtler example, consider the following statement: "All cookies in this jar are chocolate, and the jar is empty". The way statements are often proved false is by finding a counterexample—an exception. After all, if a statement is false, then there does exist an exception to it—a counterexample. Hence, by proving that no counterexample can exist, a statement can be proved true. Since an empty jar cannot contain a counterexample (a non-chocolate cookie), the statement is true—vacuously true, as mathematicians say. Its relation to **if-then** can be seen by rewriting it as: **If** a cookie is in this empty jar, **then** the cookie is chocolate.

Just as before, we can summarize this entire discussion conveniently with a truth table that precisely states how to determine whether or not "**if** s1 **then** s2" is true:

	if-then	
s1	s2	if s1 **then** s2
true	true	true
true	false	false
false	true	true
false	false	true

EXERCISE

5. Which of the following statements are true?
   (a) **if** $2 + 2 = 4$, **then** $8 - 6 = 6$.
   (b) **if** $8 - 1 = 6$, **then** $2 + 2 = 4$.
   (c) **if not** $(8 - 1 = 6)$, **then** $2 + 2 = 4$.
   (d) **if** $2 + 3 = 5$, **then** 1983 is not a leap year.

(e) **if** $2 + 3 = 5$, **then** 1983 is a leap year.
(f) **if** $((2 + 2 = 4)$ **and** $(8 - 1 = 6))$, **then** $((2 + 3 = 5)$ **or** $(5 - 2 = 3))$.
(g) **if** $2 + 3$ is not equal to 6, **then** $4 + 4 = 7$.
(h) **if** $(2 + 3 = 6)$ **or** $(8 - 4 = 4)$, **then** $(4 - 1 = 3)$ **and** $(8 + 3 = 11)$.

Next note that the **not** of the **not** of a statement is the statement itself. To see this, just apply a true-false test. Suppose the statement is true; then the **not** of it is false. But then the **not** of that new statement is true. On the other hand, suppose the starting statement is false; then the two applications of **not** make it first true, and then false. In other words, in **not** of **not** statements, the two **not**s cancel.

We now come to the first linguistic convention that is observed by most automated reasoning programs. Although the motives for this convention begin to become apparent only when we discuss the different types of reasoning, such programs require statements to be written in terms of **or** and not in terms of **if-then**. This requirement can be imposed without excluding any problems from consideration by a reasoning program, for every **if-then** statement can be translated into an **or** statement. The bridge is the relation between **if-then** and **or**. The bridge allows you to translate from **if-then** to **or** as required by an automated reasoning program, and allows you to translate from **or** to **if-then**, if you wish, to aid readability. As a trivial example, consider: Kim is male **or** Kim is female. This statement is the **or** form of an equivalent statement that can be written in the **if-then** form. This equivalent is: **if** it is **not** the case that Kim is male, **then** Kim is female.

To see that these two statements are equivalent, use the complete true-false test. The complete true-false test consists of considering all combinations of true and false that can be assigned to the parts of the statement. For example, a statement of the form s1 **or** s2 is tested for truth or for falsity by considering four possibilities: that s1 can be true or false and that s2 can be true or false. Similarly, an **if-then** statement is also tested by considering the four possibilities. **If** s1 **then** s2 is false only when s1 is true and also s2 is false. s1 **or** s2 is false only when both s1 and s2 are false. Thus, the **or** form of the statement about Kim is false only when "Kim is a male" is false and "Kim is a female" is false. On the other hand, the **if-then** form is false only when "**not** Kim is male" is true and "Kim is female" is false. But "**not** Kim is male" is true only when "Kim is male" is false, so the **if-then** form and the **or** form are false in exactly the same situations—hence they are equivalent. Symbolically, in the example, s1 stands for "Kim is male" and s2 for "Kim is female". Thus, the possible assignments of true and false to s1 and s2 give the same respective results for the **or** form as for the **if-then** form. Summarizing, s1 **or** s2 is equivalent to **if not** s1 **then** s2.

The complete true-false test amounts to constructing a truth table for the statements. The following truth table summarizes what was stated in the previous paragraph. Notice that the third and fifth columns are identical, which demonstrates the equivalence of s1 **or** s2 and **if** (**not** s1) **then** s2. The third column is included to aid in the examination of the equivalence.

s1	s2	s1 **or** s2	**not** s1	**if** (**not** s1) **then** s2
true	true	true	false	true
true	false	true	false	true
false	true	true	true	true
false	false	false	true	false

Of the five columns in this table, the first two give all possible choices of truth values for s1 and s2. For a particular choice, each row gives the corresponding truth value for s1 **or** s2, **not** s1, and **if** (**not** s1) **then** s2. Since the third and fifth columns are identical, s1 **or** s2 is shown to be logically equivalent to **if not** s1 **then** s2.

Similarly, a statement of the form **if** s1 **then** s2 can be rewritten, without changing its truth, in the **or** form as (**not** s1) **or** s2. When this rule is applied to the given example, the **if-then** form—**if not** s1 **then** s2—becomes (**not not** s1) **or** s2, but the **not**s cancel. We therefore get back the original **or** form of the statement. Now it is clear why we need the rule about **not** of **not** of a statement is the statement itself; that is, the **not**s cancel when you have **not** of **not**. Thus an **if-then** statement, when the **if** portion is sufficiently simple, can be translated into an **or** statement by replacing the **if** with a **not** and by replacing the **then** with an **or**. In certain situations you might prefer reading the **or** form required by a reasoning program as **if-then**—prefer "**if** Ann is a mother, **then** Ann has children" to "Ann is **not** a mother **or** Ann has children".

Of course, the case in which the **if** part is more complicated still has to be covered. For example, the statement "**if** Kim is female **and** a parent, **then** Kim is a mother" requires something additional. In particular, a rule is needed for applying **not** to the **and** of two statements. A rule will also be needed for statements of the form **if** s1 **then** s2 **and** s3. These rules will be discussed in Section 2.3.

EXERCISES

6. Give the **or** form of the following two statements.

    if John is home, **then** Mary is happy.

    if John is not home, **then** Mary is working.

7. Translate

    (**not** Mary is working) **or** (Paul is working)

    to the **if-then** form.

2.2 A Language for Automated Reasoning Programs

We introduce you now to the actual language, or *notation*, that many automated reasoning programs require. This language enables the program to reason very carefully—it allows the program access to various precise ways of reasoning that are exemplified later in this chapter. Notice that, since **if-then** is replaced by **or**, **if-then** is not needed and, in fact, will be avoided.

Here are some statements and their equivalents in the language a reasoning program expects.

Kim is female: FEMALE(Kim)

Kim is male: MALE(Kim)

Florida is a state: STATE(Florida)

Three is less than 5: LESSTHAN(three, five)

The product of a and b is c: PRODUCT(a, b, c)

Kim is not male: ¬MALE(Kim)

The symbol "¬" in the last example stands for **not**. The translations themselves are called *clauses*. Whenever a problem is given to the reasoning program, it must be phrased in the form of clauses.

The clauses just given each consist of a single *literal*. The literal is the entire expression

FEMALE(Kim)

and not just "FEMALE". In contrast to the earlier examples, a clause equivalent consisting of two literals (connected by **or**) is

Kim is female or male:

FEMALE(Kim) | MALE(Kim)

In this book we write many clauses, and we use an abbreviation for the **or** symbol when it occurs in those clauses. The symbol we shall use is the vertical bar, "|". Just think of "|" as standing for **or**. A clause is the **or** of one or more literals. On the other hand, the **and** between clauses is not explicitly written, but is instead present implicitly. Thus,

FEMALE(Kim)

PARENT(Kim)

is interpreted by a reasoning program as, "Kim is female **and** Kim is a parent". Similarly,

YOUNGERTHAN(Kim, Marie)

YOUNGERTHAN(Ann, Kim) | YOUNGERTHAN(Ann, Marie)

says that "Kim is younger than Marie **and** (Ann is younger than Kim **or** Ann is younger than Marie)". Here, two clauses are employed to express the given facts about the relative ages of Kim, Marie, and Ann. The first clause contains a single literal, while the second contains two literals. Literals are called *negative* or *positive* depending on whether or not they are prefixed with a **not** in the form of "¬". Thus in

¬MOTHER(Kim) | HASACHILD(Kim)

¬MOTHER(Kim) is a negative literal, while HASACHILD(Kim) is a positive literal. The ordinary-language equivalent of this clause is: "Kim is **not** a mother **or** Kim has a child", or, recalling the relation between **or**, **not**, and **if-then**, "**If** Kim is a mother, **then** Kim has a child".

As the examples show, you cannot conclude that each statement in a problem translates into one clause. The number of clauses that result depends on the nature of the statement. In any event, the order of the clauses, as well as the order of the literals within a clause, has no effect on their meaning. However, you will see that the order can have an effect in some cases on how efficiently the reasoning program functions.

As you will also see, an automated reasoning program does not in any way understand the actual statements themselves. The only understanding it has is of the **or** represented by the "|" and the implicit **and** and the **not** symbol "¬". In Chapter 4, you will learn that this understanding can be extended to include **equal** when desired.

Thus, when

FEMALE(Roberta)

is encountered by a reasoning program, no meaning is conveyed to the program. To enable a reasoning program to in effect understand the concept of "female", some additional information must be supplied—information in the form of statements called assumptions or axioms, as discussed in a later subsection of this chapter. A concept, such as "female", must be pinned down by adding enough clauses to give its important properties. Only the ensemble of these clauses about "female" has the desired effect of treating the concept appropriately.

EXERCISE

8. Convert the following statements into clauses.
   (a) John is older than Tom or richer than Jim.
   (b) If Jim is at home, then Marty is not.
   (c) Tom is a father and happy.

2.2.1 Predicates and Constants

When properties such as "male" and "parent" and "state" are represented by writing MALE and PARENT and STATE, the words MALE and PARENT and STATE are called *predicates*. In addition, relationships, such as "less than" and "greater than or equal", are also represented in the language under discussion with predicates. A predicate usually has *arguments*. They are written immediately after it, enclosed in parentheses, and separated by commas. For example, Kim and Florida are respectively the only arguments of FEMALE and STATE in

FEMALE(Kim)

STATE(Florida)

On the other hand, the predicate PRODUCT in

PRODUCT(two,three,six)

which says that 2 times 3 is 6, has three arguments: two, three, and six. Technically, Kim and Florida are constant arguments, or just *constants*, because they represent particular individuals rather than classes of objects. Again, in

PRODUCT(two,three,six)

PRODUCT is a predicate, and its arguments are the constants two, three, and six. A predicate may have any fixed number of arguments. Within the clause representation of a single problem, however, each predicate must always be used with the same number of arguments.

2.2.2 Variables

A language containing only predicates and constants can only be used to make statements about individuals. It is not nearly rich enough to express most problems. For example, it can state that a particular person, Kim, has a child if she is a mother.

¬MOTHER(Kim) | HASACHILD(Kim)

but it cannot express the fact that all mothers have a child. So we must extend the class of arguments to include *variables*.

Everyone who is a mother has a child:
¬MOTHER(x) | HASACHILD(x)

Everyone is male or female:
MALE(x) | FEMALE(x)

All numbers are greater than 0, or less than 0, or 0:
GREATERTHAN(x, 0) | LESSTHAN(x, 0) | EQUAL(x, 0)

In this book we shall use the convention that all variables begin with one of the letters u through z, and (with few exceptions) nothing else is allowed to begin with u through z. As the preceding examples suggest, a variable named x in one clause has nothing whatsoever to do with a variable named x in another clause.

Strictly speaking, the translations just given are not flawless. The reason is that a reasoning program treats such statements as

MALE(x) | FEMALE(x)

as meaning "all x are male or female". But, of course, there are objects in the world that are neither male nor female, such as a piano. If this flaw needs to be avoided, write

¬PERSON(x) | MALE(x) | FEMALE(x)

to mean, "**if** x is a person, **then** x is male **or** female". Recall that, in the language of clauses, the "|" represents an **or** between literals of a clause. The previous translation can thus be read, "x is **not** a person, **or** x is male, **or** x is female".

Similarly,

¬NUMBER(x) | GREATERTHAN(x, 0) | LESSTHAN(x, 0)

| EQUAL(x, 0)

is the very careful translation of "all numbers are greater than 0, or less than 0, or 0".

In many contexts, such care is not necessary. As in conversation, a reasoning program can often treat the area under discussion as implicitly agreed upon. Thus,

MALE(x) | FEMALE(x)

often is perfectly acceptable.

Notice that "everyone is male or female" can be written two ways when phrased as **if-then**.

if someone is not male, **then** that person is female.

if someone is not female, **then** that person is male.

Thus, using the **or** form in preference to the **if-then** form has the small advantage of requiring just a single clause. As an aside, the truth of a statement is irrelevant to its representability. For example,

FEMALE(x)

or, strictly speaking,

¬PERSON(x) | FEMALE(x)

is an acceptable translation of the false statement that "everyone is female". In fact, one of the uses of a reasoning program is to assist you in detecting such "false" information by drawing conclusions that you can examine.

Now try translating the statement "**every** parent is a mother **or** a father". You can write "**if** x is a parent, **then** x is a mother **or** a father", or write "x is **not** a parent,

or x is a mother, **or** x is a father". Strictly speaking, you can write "**if** a person is a parent, **then** that person is a mother **or** a father", or you can write "x is **not** a person, **or** x is **not** a parent, **or** x is a mother, **or** x is a father". In clause form, either

$$\neg PARENT(x) \mid MOTHER(x) \mid FATHER(x)$$

or, strictly speaking,

$$\neg PERSON(x) \mid \neg PARENT(x) \mid MOTHER(x) \mid FATHER(x)$$

is the required translation, depending on the needed care and the context.

The previous examples illustrate one more convention of the language used by reasoning programs. Just as a reasoning program (because of the | symbol) automatically treats each clause—each statement in its input language—as having "or" between its literals, it treats each variable x within a clause as "for all x". Technically, each variable in a clause is considered to be *universally quantified*. Variables, denoted by x, y, z, w, and the like, are always treated as signifying "every x" or "for all x". Thus

$$\neg MARRIEDTO(x, y) \mid WIFE(x, y) \mid HUSBAND(x, y)$$

says, "For all x and y, x is **not** married to y, **or** x is the wife of y, **or** x is the husband of y". Equivalently, "For all x and y, **if** x is married to y, **then** x is the wife **or** husband of y".

EXERCISE

9. Translate the following statements into clauses.
   (a) All umpires are strongwilled.
   (b) All integers are either even or odd.
   (c) All old people got sick.
   (d) Only old people got sick.
   (e) No males survived.

2.2.3 Functions

The last example in the preceding section leads naturally to the final concept needed for presenting problems to a reasoning program. The concept, that of *function*, is frequently used by mathematicians, but perhaps not so frequently by others. Just as variables are needed to express "every" or "all" or an implicit "every", functions are needed to express "there exists". (Not all functions that occur in the language of clauses arise from "there exists".)

The relationship that a husband has to his wife can be expressed by using a function. The function "husband" associates Mr. Jones to Mrs. Jones, Mr. Thomas to Mrs. Thomas, and so on. Equally, "wife" can be expressed with a function—one that associates Mrs. Jones to Mr. Jones and so on. The function of "first letter" associates F to Florida, I to Idaho, K to Kim, and d to the word dog.

Why use functions? Can predicates be used in all situations without any harmful effects? Functions can sometimes be replaced with predicates while preserving the integrity of the information. Such a replacement must be made with care, for it can interfere with efficiency and readability, for example. As you will shortly see, functions naturally come into play. The close tie between certain types of reasoning and the notation suggests, in many cases, the choice of functions over predicates. The main difference between functions and predicates is that functions associate a unique object with a particular given object, while predicates do not necessarily do so. The function "husband" associates a specific person with a specific given married woman. The notion of "son", on the other hand, does not pick out a specific person even when the parents are known. Thus, certain concepts are more naturally represented by using a predicate than a function. If married women, for example, had more than one husband, then the relationships would naturally be expressed with the use of a predicate. Such ambiguity does not mesh as naturally with the use of function. Even when the object chosen by the function cannot be clearly identified, as in f(x) for certain functions f, nevertheless a choice of x is intended to point to a unique f(x).

The language we are discussing—the language of *clauses* and the closely related *first-order predicate calculus*—includes functions. They are written in a manner similar to predicates—a name followed by a list of arguments. If "first letter" is abbreviated to "first" and "last letter" to "last", then

Florida begins with an F: IS(first(Florida), F)

This notation can be read, "first of Florida is F". Similarly,

Iowa ends with an a: IS(last(Iowa), a)

Multiplication can be written in terms of a function. Thus

EQUAL(times(two, three), six)

is an alternative way of expressing the fact earlier expressed as

PRODUCT(two, three, six)

(When you use representations such as PRODUCT(two, three, six), then you must include an additional clause to guarantee the uniqueness of product.)

Information that is represented in tabular form is yet another example of the use of function. With a given row and a given column in a table is associated the intersection of that row and column. The intersection is a function of both the chosen row and chosen column.

We shall write functions in lower case—except for the first letter of functions, such as the constant function Florida—and predicates in upper case, regardless of the meaning. Thus we write "times" and "PRODUCT" for the same notion. Since the notion of husband can be treated as a function or as a predicate, it also is written lower case or upper case, depending on its type. For the example of marriage that initiated this discussion of functions, we had

$$\neg\text{MARRIEDTO}(x, y) \mid \text{WIFE}(x, y) \mid \text{HUSBAND}(x, y)$$

This fact could instead be represented with functions as

$$\neg\text{MARRIEDTO}(x, y) \mid \text{IS}(x, \text{wife}(y)) \mid \text{IS}(x, \text{husband}(y))$$

It is read: "**if** x is married to y, **then** x is the wife of y **or** x is the husband of y". How to choose between using a predicate and using a function is not always obvious.

One of the difficulties in formulating a problem for an automated reasoning program is that of making a good choice for the representation of information. A good choice cannot be made solely in terms of notation. Instead, the choice of representation must be closely coupled to both the choice of the type of reasoning and the choice of strategy that controls the reasoning. That they are dependent should not be a surprise, for people often choose a representation for a problem based on the intended method of solution. For example, you might wish to solve a puzzle by making a list of possibilities and then systematically crossing them off. In such a case, a tabular representation of the information is a natural choice.

Finally, we come to the most complicated cause for needing functions. As remarked at the beginning of this discussion of functions, they are needed to express "there exists". "**If** Marie is a wife, **then there exists** a husband of Marie". "**Every** married woman has a husband"; formally: "**there exists** one husband for every married woman". The function husband picks a person, where the choice depends on the woman, and the choice is unique—hence a function.

What is the correct translation into the language of clauses—the language used by the typical reasoning program—of "all married women have husbands"? The suggestion of the clause

$$\neg\text{MARRIED}(x) \mid \text{MARRIED}(x,y)$$

with the intended reading "**if** x is married, **then** x is married to y" has two serious flaws. First, within a problem, a specific predicate cannot simultaneously have one argument and two arguments. Second, all variables that occur in clauses are treated as "for all" by an automated reasoning program, so that the actual reading for the second literal in the preceding clause is "x is married to **every** y".

The solution is to choose two predicates and also to use a function. Let the predicates be MARRIEDWOMAN and MARRIEDTO. Let the function be "husband". The clause

$$\neg\text{MARRIEDWOMAN}(x) \mid \text{MARRIEDTO}(x, \text{husband}(x))$$

says "**for every** x, **if** x is a married woman, **then there exists** a husband of x and x is married to him". In contrast to the earlier example in which "husband" was also used as a function, here the functional dependency is even more visible in the notation husband(x).

Similarly, where the function "first" is used to mean "first letter of",

$\neg$STATE(x) | BEGINSWITH(x, first(x))

says that (the name of) every state begins with a letter. (Formally, the clause states: "**for every** x, **if** x is a state, **then there exists** a letter—call it first(x)—such that x begins with that letter".) And, since, for every number, there is a number bigger than it,

$\neg$NUMBER(x) | GREATERTHAN(successor(x), x)

is one way of expressing this fact. Also,

GREATERTHAN(successor(x), x)

is another way of expressing the fact, where the universe of discourse is implicit.

When a function is employed to express a relation, the corresponding clause, as seen by the examples, may have the functional expression appear before or after that on which it depends. Thus,

MARRIEDTO(Marie, husband(Marie))

says that Marie is married to her husband, while

MARRIEDTO(wife(George), George)

says that George's wife is married to George. Equally,

MARRIEDTO(husband(Marie), Marie)

says that Marie's husband is married to Marie. Functions may depend on one, two, three, or more arguments. Functions, like predicates, once chosen to have a particular number of arguments, must continue to have precisely that same number throughout a problem. As with predicates, once a function symbol has been chosen for a particular purpose in a problem, it cannot also be used for some other purpose. Thus, the use of predicate and function symbols must be consistent throughout a problem—each must have a fixed number of arguments for the problem under consideration and must also stand for the same concept throughout.

The functions used to express **there exists** in the examples just given depend on one or more arguments. The function "husband" depends on one argument, the function "times" on two arguments. In contrast, there are functions used to express **there exists**, but that depend on no arguments. Such functions are denoted by constants, and are technically called *0-ary* functions because they have no arguments. For example, there exists in the alphabet a letter that occurs before any other letter. The clause

EARLIER(a, x)

might seem to be a reasonable translation of this fact into the first-order predicate calculus. It all depends on the meaning of "EARLIER". If EARLIER does not mean strictly earlier—that is, if it means "earlier or equal to"—then the given clause is fine. On the other hand, if EARLIER means strictly earlier, then the clause fails to capture that idea. In that case, the clause

EQUAL(a, x) | EARLIER(a, x)

will suffice. This clause can be read "a equals x **or** a is earlier than x", or can be read "**if** a is not equal to x, **then** a is earlier than x". For the second interpretation of the clause, recall that when a rewording produces **not not**, the **not**s cancel. In fact, the language of clauses prohibits the expression "¬¬".

In the clause

EARLIER(a, x)

the function, a, is a function of no arguments—a 0-ary function. All constants can be thought of as functions of no arguments. If, for example, the problem under study involves the letter that occurs before all others, then that problem is of the form "there exists an x such that for all y". In that case, simply name the letter "a". If the problem involves the number whose product with any other number is 0, name it "0". Such functions that "exist for all elements present"—that are independent of whatever element is chosen and hence do not vary as the chosen element varies—can be named with a constant.

This use of functions—for **there exists** in situations that depend on no arguments—is exemplified by the phrase "there exists an x such that for all y". This situation is in contrast to the situation, "for all y there exists an x", which requires a function of one argument. When the "existence" depends on no arguments, a name suffices.

In Chapter 4, a number of situations are examined, some calling for functional notation and some for predicate notation. Some of the functions that are called for are the result of "existence" that depends on one or more arguments or on none. Also in Chapter 4, we shall see that pitfalls, such as that typified by the alphabetic example with EARLIER and its two possible meanings, abound. There, examples of subtler errors of representation will be given. Guidelines will also be given for detecting errors of representation. Such errors, as well as those in reasoning, occur of course outside of the context of automated reasoning. Automation, in fact, is one way to find and eventually to reduce such occurrences.

EXERCISE

10. Translate the following statements into clauses.
    (a) Every person has a grandmother.
    (b) The sum of two positive numbers is always positive.
    (c) The sum of two positive numbers is greater than either of the numbers.
    (d) Given any integer, you can find another integer that is less than it.
    (e) All people over 80 got sick.
    (f) Only people over 80 got sick.

2.3 Combinations of or with and, Complex if-then, and DeMorgan's Laws

We promised to provide "something additional" to cope with the more complex forms of **if-then** statements. Consider the following translation.

If Kim is female and a parent, then Kim is a mother:

¬FEMALE(Kim) | ¬PARENT(Kim) | MOTHER(Kim)

The question is: How do you get the clause just given from the statement in ordinary language?

The key to the translation into clause form is: **not** of (s1 **and** s2) is logically equivalent to **not** s1 **or not** s2. To prove this, apply a complete true-false test—consider all combinations of true and false for s1 and for s2. The **not** of (s1 **and** s2) is false when both s1 and s2 are true, and true for every other assignment of true and false to s1 and to s2. Similarly, **not** s1 **or not** s2 is false when both s1 and s2 are true, and true for every other assignment. The companion rule is: **not** of (s1 **or** s2) is logically equivalent to **not** s1 **and not** s2. These rules are called *DeMorgan's Laws*.

Thus, given the statement

If Kim is female and a parent, then Kim is a mother

first write it as, **if** (s1 **and** s2) **then** s3. The parentheses say that the **if** covers the entire expression s1 **and** s2. Then apply the rule to convert from **if-then** to **or**. The conversion yields, **not** (s1 **and** s2) **or** s3. Then apply the **not** rule given above, and get **not** s1 **or not** s2 **or** s3. Parentheses are not needed in this last statement because of one of the properties of **or**, namely, the property of *associativity*. Finally, recall that the **or** between literals is replaced by "|", and thus the clause

¬FEMALE(Kim) | ¬PARENT(Kim) | MOTHER(Kim)

is obtained.

Next, we need a rule for statements that can be symbolically represented as **not** s1 **or** (s2 **and** s3). The rule is needed to translate statements such as

If a number is divisible by eight, then the number is divisible by four and by two:

¬DIVISIBLE(x,8) | DIVISIBLE(x,4)

and

¬DIVISIBLE(x,8) | DIVISIBLE(x,2)

The needed rule is that, **not** s1 **or** (s2 **and** s3) is logically equivalent to (**not** s1 **or** s2) **and** (**not** s1 **or** s3). Since **and** between clauses is dropped, while **or** between literals of a clause is replaced, the translation just given can be obtained. The law that is being applied here is known as the distributivity of **or** over **and**. This law, of course, applies to situations similar to the one just covered even when **not** s1 is replaced by s1.

As you perhaps guessed, there is the other distributive law that says **and** distributes over **or**. Thus, s1 **and** (s2 **or** s3) is logically equivalent to (s1 **and** s2) **or** (s1 **and** s3). This law need not be applied, for statements of the form s1 **and** (s2 **or** s3) are already fine as is. In fact, the set of clauses that is given to a typical automated reasoning program is implicitly in this form—the **and** of a collection of statements, each of which is the **or** of its literals.

With the rules given in this subsection, plus those given at the beginning of the chapter, you have all you need to translate statements into clauses—even complex statements. By using a symbolic representation of the type exhibited here—relying on s1, s2, s3, and such for elements of the statement to be translated—the entire process may be made easier.

For example, the logical connective of **equivalent** can be translated using the given rules. The statement that s1 is **equivalent** to s2, or s1 **if and only if** s2, translates into (**if** s1 **then** s2) **and** (**if** s2 **then** s1). Depending on the complexity of s1 and s2, various of the given rules enable you to translate statements in which the logical connective **equivalent** occurs.

EXERCISE

11. Translate the following statements into clauses.
  (a) If Peter drives Tuesday and Mary drives Wednesday, I will drive Thursday.
  (b) If a player is both large and fast, the player is valuable.
  (c) If Peter drives Monday, I will drive Tuesday and Wednesday.
  (d) If Peter drives Monday and Mary Tuesday, I will drive both Wednesday and Thursday.
  (e) If a player is either tired or sloppy, the player will lose.

2.4 Assumptions and Axioms, Types of Reasoning, and Proof

We have now completed the discussion of language—that of the clause language and that of first-order predicate calculus. We have discussed the logical connectives and also the conventions that must be obeyed in the language. Thus the way has been prepared for examining the objectives for using an automated reasoning program and the means for obtaining those objectives. Briefly, the objectives consist of answering questions that range from puzzles to deep mathematical questions. Such questions are answered by starting with some set of assumptions or axioms, applying some types of reasoning that are called *inference rules*, and seeking an answer in the form of a proof. The types of reasoning, inference rules, are the means for drawing conclusions. An automated reasoning program applies various inference rules to various axioms or assumptions taken two at a time or three at a time or ..., and thus finds and retains new facts. Each new bit of information follows logically from its immediate ancestors. The reasoning program proceeds until some termination condition is reached—a condition one fervently hopes is success. The most common successful termination takes the form of generating a proof.

2.4.1 Assumptions and Axioms

The bits of knowledge given to a reasoning program at the start of a problem are called *assumptions* or *axioms*. Facts, definitions, properties, and relationships are all, as far as the reasoning program is concerned, assumptions or axioms. A reasoning program knows nothing at the beginning of a problem other than what it is told. Moreover, it cares nothing about the truth or correctness of what it is told. If it is given incorrect information, it cannot tell that the information should be disregarded. When incorrect information is given, the person using the program can tell often that something is wrong by examining the conclusions that the program draws. As input,

$\neg IS(first(x), F) \mid VOWEL(last(x))$

$\neg IS(first(x), I) \mid VOWEL(last(x))$

$\neg IS(first(x), B) \mid CONSONANT(last(x))$

are three possible clauses that can be given to an automated reasoning program. Assuming that x ranges over possible states in the United States, we have the example that was used at the beginning of this chapter on logic, where the topic of **if-then** is introduced: If a state name begins with F, then it ends with a vowel; if it begins with an I, it ends with a vowel; if it begins with a B, it ends with a consonant.

The first of the three clauses represents good information, for it is true for all x —for all states of the United States. Its truth as a clause can be simply tested by exhaustive examination. For each value of x—for each state—either it is not the case that x begins with an F or it is the case that x ends with a vowel.

The third clause also represents good information as can be seen by applying the same test. For each value of x, either x does not begin with a B or x ends with a consonant. The test comes out true merely because of the first literal, since no value of x begins with the letter B.

For the second clause to be true, it must also be true for each value of x. For Florida, it is true since Florida does not begin with an I. For Idaho, it is true since, although Idaho begins with an I, which makes the first literal false, Idaho ends with a vowel, which makes the second literal true. On the other hand, Illinois is a problem. Since it begins with an I, the first literal comes out false. In order for the clause to be true, the second literal must then come out true for this value of x. But it does not. So the clause represents incorrect information. Incidentally, you cannot simply assume a conclusion to be incorrect merely because one of its premises is suspect, for the conclusion might be true in spite of the underlying assumptions. (In logic, the hypotheses from which a conclusion is drawn are technically called *premisses*, and the word premisses is spelled in this odd fashion.) For example, the program would conclude that the state name Idaho ends with a vowel, since it begins with an I—a correct conclusion based on a faulty assumption, that all states beginning with an I end with a vowel.

Nevertheless, if an automated reasoning program were given all three clauses as input, it would proceed to draw conclusions from them. The conclusions would be logically sound—they would follow logically from their premises or ancestors. But the conclusions would be suspect since some of the starting assumptions are incorrect.

All assumptions or axioms must be given. If Roberta is a character in a puzzle under consideration, and you expect the program to use the fact that "Roberta" is a female name, then the fact that Roberta is a female

FEMALE(Roberta)

must be supplied. The fact that people are male or female

MALE(x) | FEMALE(x)

must be supplied. A reasoning program makes no assumptions, and can deduce no information other than that which can be obtained by applying logical reasoning.

Definitions, and also relationships and properties of objects, that specify the area of interest are all assumptions or axioms. When mathematicians study a field, they define it by giving an appropriate set of axioms. Thus, in a sense, those who use an automated reasoning program must behave as mathematicians. The puzzle solved in Chapter 3 provides ample illustration of what has to be done in presenting a problem to a reasoning program. The hazard, or at least one of the hazards, is the implicit information that people use, not all of which is good information. It is very easy to omit information when presenting a problem to a reasoning program—information such as "Roberta is female". Such information is implicit—is contained in the name Roberta. On the other hand, errors that a person makes in drawing conclusions can sometimes be traced to some implicit bit of information, some implicit assumption that is not justified.

2.4.2 Types of Reasoning, Inference Rules

Fact: All married men have a wife:

$\neg$MARRIED(x) | HASWIFE(x)

Fact: George is married: MARRIED(George)

Conclusion: George has a wife: HASWIFE(George)

Fact: Father and son have the same last name:

$\neg$SON(x, y) | SAMELAST(x, y)

Fact: Harry is the son of George: SON(Harry, George)

Conclusion: Harry and George have the same last name:

SAMELAST(Harry, George)

Fact: All numbers divisible by four are divisible by two:

$\neg$DIVISIBLE(x, 4) | DIVISIBLE(x, 2)

Fact: The number 63 is not divisible by two:

$\neg$DIVISIBLE(63, 2)

Conclusion: 63 is not divisible by four:

$\neg$DIVISIBLE(63, 4)

Drawing conclusions from given facts such as these is one of the main activities of an automated reasoning program. To get an idea of exactly how the program reaches such conclusions, let us study the last example. The program might examine the two given facts and note that they are closely related, especially if x in the first clause is thought of as the constant 63. In that case the first clause becomes

$\neg$DIVISIBLE(63, 4) | DIVISIBLE(63, 2)

Since the first clause is assumed to be true for any value of x, it will be true for this particular value. There is only one way for both this instance of the first fact and also the second fact to be true, namely,

$\neg$DIVISIBLE(63, 4)

must be true.

Such a program never questions the accuracy of the given information. Its job is to be logical—to draw conclusions that follow logically from the facts it is given. Thus, in the previous three examples, a reasoning program would conclude first that George has a wife, second that Harry and George have the same last name, and third that 63 is *not* divisible by four. Even if George were not married, the program, given the false information, would conclude that he had a wife. In the same spirit, consider

Fact: All numbers divisible by three are also divisible by two:

$\neg$DIVISIBLE(x, 3) | DIVISIBLE(x, 2)

Fact: 21 is divisible by three: DIVISIBLE(21, 3)

Conclusion: 21 is divisible by two: DIVISIBLE(21, 2)

The conclusion is obviously nonsense, but it does follow logically given the two facts about "three". A reasoning program can be counted on to be flawlessly logical, and thus, if given misleading information, it can do no better than a person who is given misleading information.

Another feature of a reasoning program you can count on is its ability to recognize patterns. The examples just given all exhibit a common pattern—a single pattern that can be generalized to a type of reasoning, technically called *UR-resolution*. (This type of reasoning is called UR-resolution because a successful application of it produces a *unit clause*, a clause containing exactly one literal, hence Unit-Resulting-resolution.) This type of reasoning is one of the types that an automated reasoning program can use. Each type of reasoning is called an inference rule.

A different type of reasoning—different inference rule—is seen in the following example.

Fact: A sister and brother have the same father:

$\neg$SISTER(x, y) | $\neg$FATHER(z, y) | FATHER(z, x)

Fact: Rita is Harry's sister: SISTER(Rita, Harry)

Fact: George is Harry's father: FATHER(George, Harry)

Conclusion: George is Rita's father:

FATHER(George, Rita)

This example exhibits a pattern somewhat different from the previous three examples. This pattern, when generalized, is technically known as *hyperresolution*. In the previous three examples, the object was to draw a conclusion of a very simple structure, namely, a conclusion that contains exactly one literal. In the example just given, although the clause representing the conclusion happens to contain one literal, the actual objective is to draw a conclusion that has no **not** signs in it. The conclusion

Conclusion: George is Rita's father:

FATHER(George, Rita)

in this example also could have been obtained with the first type of reasoning, *UR-resolution*. The reverse is not true for the third example above. The conclusion

Conclusion: 63 is not divisible by four:

$\neg$DIVISIBLE(63, 4)

of the third example could not be obtained by this second type of reasoning, by using *hyperresolution*, for it contains a **not** sign. As you will learn from various illustrations, there are applications of hyperresolution that cannot be replaced by applications of UR-resolution, so both inference rules—both ways of reasoning—are valuable. For example, to satisfy your curiosity immediately,

a person's child is that person's daughter or son:

$\neg$CHILD(x, y) | DAUGHTER(x, y) | SON(x, y)

Kim is Rita's child:

CHILD(Kim, Rita)

therefore

Kim is Rita's daughter or Rita's son:

DAUGHTER(Kim, Rita) | SON(Kim, Rita)

illustrates a conclusion that is obtainable with hyperresolution but not with UR-resolution. The conclusions obtained by using either type of reasoning are equally sound. Each conclusion made by a reasoning program, regardless of the type of reasoning, follows inevitably from the facts from which it is drawn.

An automated reasoning program has access to many types of reasoning. Each type of reasoning, inference rule, is keyed to a pattern based on the structure of the clauses and the structure of the intended conclusion. For example, a reasoning program can reason from simple facts to simple facts, from complex facts to complex facts, from complex facts to simple facts, from positive assertions to positive assertions. A reasoning program even has access to an inference rule, discussed in Chapter 4, that treats equality as "built in"—treats the equality predicate as meaning equal, as understood by a person. The vital property of any inference rule is that the conclusion follows logically from the assumptions from which it is drawn.

In the succeeding chapters, examples will be given that illustrate the different types of reasoning. You will learn how to choose among the ways of reasoning. Different problems and different formulations of the same problem call for particular choices of inference rule. If the representation emphasizes equality, then the better choice usually is that inference rule that "builds in" equality. Since the inference rules are the means for drawing conclusions, and since different choices yield conclusions of a certain structure, the choice of how to reason can sharply affect the chances of achieving the sought-after goal.

You will also learn how the various types of reasoning are controlled—controlled by strategy. But strategy is not a topic for the chapter on logic, and so must wait until later chapters. Briefly, strategy must be chosen to reflect the choice of inference rule, and the choice of inference rule must reflect the choice of representation. Furthermore, since the three function as a unit and they affect each other in many ways, the choices of representation, inference rule, and strategy cannot simply be made in that order, but must be considered as an ensemble.

2.4.3 Proof

Fact: Harry's father is George.

Fact: Harry's sister is Rita.

Fact: Rita has never married.

Claim: Harry and Rita have the same last name.

How can an automated reasoning program be asked to prove this claim? In fact, what is meant by "prove"? Before giving a proof of the claim—a proof of the type an automated reasoning program might find—let us stop to answer the two questions.

For example, if a reasoning program is given clauses that say that all states whose names begin with an F also end with a vowel,

$\neg$IS(first(x), F) | VOWEL(last(x))

and the program is asked to prove that Florida ends with a vowel, the usual approach is to assume that Florida does *not* end with a vowel.

$\neg$VOWEL(last(Florida))

a proof can be found, provided the necessary information is present. For the needed information, we must add

IS(first(Florida),F)

which states that Florida begins with an F. An inference rule, as discussed in the preceding subsection, exists that takes the first two of the three clauses and obtains

¬IS(first(Florida), F)

which states that Florida does **not** begin with an F. This new fact directly contradicts the meaning of the third clause. These four clauses constitute a proof—a proof by contradiction. From the assumption that Florida does not end with a vowel—an assumption that arises by assuming the sought-after fact is false—and from information about states in general and Florida in particular, a reasoning program can find a new fact to prove the claim about Florida. The resulting contradiction establishes that Florida *does* end with a vowel.

A very common way to ask a reasoning program to prove some claim is to ask it to find a contradiction. A proof by contradiction consists of a set of steps that starts with some facts, finds and adds new information by applying inference rules, and stops with a contradiction. Among the starting assumptions and facts is the assumption that the claim to be proved is false. By including this "false" assumption, a reasoning program is able eventually to find a proof by contradiction—if the included assumption is in fact false.

Now let us prove that Harry and Rita have the same last name. Assume the claim is false, and thus that Harry and Rita do *not* have the same last name. As indicated, such a move is typical when submitting a problem to an automated reasoning program. If the claim follows from the given facts, then the assumption that it is false will lead eventually to a contradiction. The path to the contradiction consists of new facts that are each obtained by applying some type of reasoning—some inference rule as discussed in the preceding subsection.

First translate the three given facts—Harry's father is George, Harry's sister is Rita, and Rita has never married. We get

  (1) FATHER(George, Harry)
  (2) SISTER(Rita, Harry)
  (3) NEVERMARRIED(Rita)

as clauses to be given to the program.

Then we must supply clauses that give information about relationships of sister, father, son, and others. Such information includes, among others, the fact that a person has the father's last name if that person has never married.

  (4) ¬NEVERMARRIED(x) | ¬FATHER(y, x) | SAMELAST(y, x)
  (5) ¬SISTER(x, y) | ¬FATHER(z, y) | FATHER(z, x)
  (6) ¬SAMELAST(x, y) | ¬SAMELAST(y, z) | SAMELAST(x, z)
  (7) ¬FATHER(x, y) | ¬MALE(y) | SON(y, x)
  (8) ¬SON(x, y) | SAMELAST(x, y)
  (9) MALE(Harry)

Finally, we translate the assumed falseness of the claim, getting

(10)   ¬SAMELAST(Harry, Rita)

which will eventually lead to a contradiction.

The first conclusion the program might draw is that George is Rita's father. This conclusion follows from the specific facts that Rita is Harry's sister and that George is Harry's father, and the general fact that a sister and brother have the same father.

Let us look at just how a program makes this deduction. Remember that the clause

(5)   ¬SISTER(x, y) | ¬FATHER(z, y) | FATHER(z, x)

is a way of saying

"For any x, y, and z, if x is the sister of y, and z is the father of y, then z is the father of x".

Since this statement is true for all values of the variables x, y, and z, it is true when we substitute Rita for x, Harry for y, and George for z. Then it becomes

"If Rita is the sister of Harry, and George is the father of Harry, then George is the father of Rita".

Since clauses 2 and 1 say exactly that Rita is the sister of Harry and that George is the father of Harry, we conclude that George is the father of Rita. We write

From clauses 2, 1, and 5:

(11)   FATHER(George, Rita)

Notice that the negative literals in clause 5 are matched with the literals of clauses 2 and 1. The matching looks like this:

Literal in clause 2: SISTER(Rita, Harry)
Literal in clause 5: ¬SISTER(x, y)
Literal in clause 1: FATHER(George, Harry)
Literal in clause 5: ¬FATHER(z, y)

Once the "appropriate" values for the variables are substituted for the variables, the paired literals are identical except for the fact that one is positive and the other one negative. This matching process is called *unification*. When a literal is unified with another literal in another clause that contains only one literal, it is removed from the original clause. That is where clause 11 comes from; the first two literals of clause 5 are removed after unification. The job of the reasoning program is to find the pairs of literals that can be unified and figure out the substitutions of values for variables so that the unification can occur.

Next, the program can conclude that George and Rita have the same last name. This conclusion follows from the specific fact that Rita has never married, the deduced fact that George is Rita's father, and the general fact that a person who has never married has the same last name as the person's father.

From clauses 3, 11, and 4:

(12)   SAMELAST(George, Rita)

Since George is Harry's father, and since Harry is male, Harry is George's son.

From clauses 1, 9, and 7:

(13)   SON(Harry,George)

So Harry and George have the same last name.

From clauses 13 and 8:

(14)   SAMELAST(Harry,George)

Finally, since Harry and George have the same name, and since the program was told that Harry and Rita do *not* have the same last name, the program can conclude that George and Rita do not have the same last name.

From clauses 14, 10, and 6:

(15)   ¬SAMELAST(George, Rita)

The program has obtained a contradiction between 12 and 15, for 12 says that George and Rita have the same last name while 15 says that they do not. A reasoning program immediately detects such obvious contradictions. (In later chapters, the derived contradiction will sometimes be somewhat more general. For example, if the program has among its clauses

Harry is the father of no one: ¬FATHER(Harry, y) and

Harry is the father of Ken: FATHER(Harry, Ken)

then it will immediately detect a contradiction. This contradiction can be reduced to the more obvious kind by simply replacing the variable y by Ken.)

Thus we have a proof that Harry and Rita have the same last name. The assumption that Harry and Rita do not have the same last name enabled the reasoning program to find a contradiction. Without this assumption, and hence without the corresponding clause, the reasoning program would be unable to reach a contradiction. Therefore, the assumption that the claim is false is the key, and the claim is proved.

If the facts were slightly changed, then the outcome would be correspondingly changed. For example, if Rita were married, then it would be incorrect—not logical —to claim that she and Harry have the same last name. And, in fact, the program would not draw this false conclusion. In particular, 12 would not have been found, for 3 would not have been available.

Similarly, 12 would not have been found if clause 3 had simply been over-looked, and hence omitted from the set of clauses given to the reasoning program. Such omissions can easily occur, especially with information that is implicit—as with Roberta being female. This Harry/Rita problem illustrates the need to convey various types of information that a person automatically knows, but that a reasoning program does not. As we said earlier, a program knows only what you tell it, and you must often tell it obvious information to capture an idea. Clause 5, for example, contains information about the notion of father, but supplemental information as contained in 4 and 7 must also be supplied. Otherwise the concept of father is inadequately defined for the program. Only through the ensemble of clauses does a concept begin to take shape.

Using an automated reasoning program guarantees that the conclusions that are drawn really do follow from the facts, but it does not protect you totally from error. If we had carelessly added the clause that says that a brother and sister have the same last name, then the program could produce false information—even if Rita were married, the program would conclude that she and Harry had the same last name. Such a conclusion is in general false, except for the accidental case in which she and her husband happened to have the same last name before marriage. With respect to finding bad information, the program is not different from a person who has accepted bad information; that is, starting with bad information can lead to bad information. While a person can question information that is given, an automated reasoning program cannot.

This process of determining what is to be proved, and then assuming it false and hence that it cannot be proved, is not as arbitrary as you might think. The process produces a set of clauses that is inconsistent, which in turn provides a convenient termination condition for a reasoning program's attempt to solve a given problem. Convenience of termination is, as you will see in later chapters, far from the complete story. By having available a clause or clauses that correspond to the assumed falseness of the conclusion, a reasoning program has access to a very powerful strategy that sharply increases its chances of success. Briefly, reasoning backward from the "false" information avoids exploring many fruitless paths. We shall give examples of this valuable avoidance property, as well as various other properties of strategy, with puzzles much more challenging than that for Harry and Rita.

For example, of a more interesting nature is the missionaries and cannibals puzzle. For this puzzle, the reasoning program is given various facts about crossing a river and the capacity of the boat and such. The program is also told the—what is hoped to be—false information that no sequence of trips will allow the missionaries to get across the river safely. As will be seen in Chapter 5, the program derives a contradiction. Thus, there is a sequence of trips that gets the missionaries safely to their destination after all.

Since the basic approach consists of applying some set of inference rules repeatedly to some starting set of assumptions or axioms with the notion of eventually arriving at a contradiction, some tricks will be required to achieve certain goals. For example, in the puzzle that is the chief focus of attention in the next chapter, no obvious conclusion exists to be assumed false. Thus it becomes necessary to view the puzzle in a way that permits a false assumption to be made—a false assumption that in turn leads to a proof. The view that permits making the needed false assumption is, of course, closely connected to the object of the puzzle. Nevertheless, the assumed false conclusion is clearly a trick—a trick that could easily be overlooked. Such tricks should not be surprising, for people use them often.

EXERCISES

In this set of problems, we consider a situation in which a number of towns are connected by roads. Trucks are allowed to drive on some of the roads, but not on all of them. The object is to deduce answers to questions about whether or not you can go by truck from one particular town to another. To start off, here is axiom 1 in clause form

Ax1. ¬CONNECTED(x, y, z) | ¬TRUCKSOK(z) | GETTO(x, y)

This clause is the translated version of "If town x is connected to town y by highway z, and trucks are allowed (ok) on z, then you can get to y from x by truck".

12. Translate the following axioms into clauses, where Ax. is an abbreviation for axiom.

    Ax. 2: If town x is connected to y by z, then y is connected to x by z.

    Ax. 3: If you can get to y from x, and you can get to z from y, then you can get to z from x.

    Ax. 4: Leadville is connected to Gorm by the Woodland Path.

    Ax. 5: Gorm is connected to Lewistown by the Kings Highway.

    Ax. 6: Leadville is connected to Lewistown by the Main Pike.

    Ax. 7: Lastchance is connected to Astor by the Mudpath.

    Ax. 8: Lastchance is connected to Gorm by Miles Road.

    Ax. 9–11: Trucks are allowed on the Mudpath, the Main Pike, and Miles Road.

    Ax. 12: Trucks are always allowed on either the Kings Highway or the Woodland Path. In other words, each day it may be different, but one of the two roads is always usable.

    Ax. 13: Leadville and Astor are not connected by the Main Pike.

13. What can be concluded from axioms 1, 7, and 9?

14. Can GETTO(Gorm, Lastchance) be concluded from axioms 1, 8, and 11?

15. What can be concluded from clauses 1, 5, and 12? Is the conclusion deducible with UR-resolution, hyperresolution, or both?

16. What can be deduced from clauses 2 and 13? Is it deducible with UR-resolution, hyperresolution, or both?

17. Give a proof showing that you can get from Astor to Gorm.

18. Construct a proof that you can get from Astor to Lewistown.

2.5 Summary

Before beginning the next chapter and giving the puzzle on which it centers, let us review the contents of this chapter. By including this chapter, we have provided information that may well be missing from your experience. Among the topics that were discussed are the meaning of **or, and, not, if-then**, and **equivalent**. Since automated reasoning programs usually rely on **or** rather than on **if-then**, the needed bridge for converting **if-then** statements to **or** was provided. Since most automated reasoning programs require problems to be phrased in the language of clauses, we focused on that language.

The discussion of language then naturally led to the discussion of assumptions and axioms. Assumptions and axioms are the material that a reasoning program uses to begin its search for new information. Since new information is obtained by applying various types of reasoning, we discussed inference rules. Then, after covering the topics of representation of information, of how a reasoning program begins, and of how it progresses, we turned to how it knows it has succeeded. Success is signaled by proof, and the form of proof on which we focused is that of proof by contradiction.

2.6 Answers to Exercises

1. The answers to the problems at the end of Section 2.1 are the following.
   (a) True. Since both of the statements connected by the **or** are true, the entire statement is true.
   (b) True, again. The **or** is true if either or both of the connected statements is true.
   (c) False. The **and** is true only when both connected statements are true.
   (d) True.
   (e) False. For (statement 1) **and** (statement 2) to be true, both statement 1 and statement 2 must be true. In this case, "eight minus one is six" is false, so the entire statement must be false.
   (f) True. The entire statement is true, if either side is true. Since $2 + 2 = 4$, the left side is true.
   (g) False. This one is a little more complicated. We added parentheses to make clear what was meant. First, note that $2 + 2 = 4$ is true. Therefore, **not** $(2 + 2 = 4)$ must be false. Since (a false statement) **and** (any statement) is always false, you do not need to check **not** $(8 - 1 = 6)$.
   (h) True. Previously, we saw that $(2 + 2 = 4)$ **and** $(8 - 1 = 6)$ was false. Therefore, **not** of that statement must be true.
   (i) True. This problem is ambiguous. You might have interpreted it as (Two plus two is 4 **and** eight minus 6 is 2) **and** 1984 is a leap year, or you might instead group the rightmost substatements. Either way evaluates to true.

2. Well, yes, there is the obvious difference in that the right and left sides are reversed. The real question is: Does that matter? The answer is no. You can determine for yourself by making a truth table for s1 **and** s2 and also for s2 **and** s1.

3. These statements are the same, too. It turns out that any number of statements connected by **and**s can be grouped in any order.

4. Consider the case in which George and Helen are both absent. Then the first statement is false, but the second is true.

5. The answers to the problems involving the **if-then** are the following.

   (a) False. Remember that the **if-then** is false exactly when the hypothesis is true and the conclusion is false.

   (b) True. Since $8 - 1 = 6$ is false, you do not need to check the conclusion.

   (c) True. This one is slightly more complex. Since $8 - 1 = 6$ is false, **not** of it is true. Hence, the hypothesis is true. But so is the conclusion. In fact, since the conclusion is true, it really does not matter whether or not the hypothesis is true.

   (d) True. Both the hypothesis and the conclusion are true.

   (e) False. The hypothesis is true, but the conclusion is false.

   (f) True. The hypothesis is false.

   (g) False.

   (h) True. Both the hypothesis and the conclusion are true.

6. The first statement is equivalent to (**not** (John is home)) **or** (Mary is happy). The second is a little more complex. You might translate it to (**not** (John is not home)) **or** (Mary is working). However, one is certainly tempted to simplify this to (John is home) **or** (Mary is working). The presentation of logic we use is very informal. At the level we are now studying the subject, either form is an acceptable answer.

7. Actually, there are two reasonable answers to this question.

   if Mary is working, **then** Paul is working

   if not (Paul is working), **then** (**not** Mary is working)

8. When you are converting ordinary-language statements into clauses, you are forced to select which predicates you are going to use. This, of course, can lead to a variety of equally acceptable answers. The answers for these problems are the following.

   (a) OLDER(John, Tom) | RICHER(John, Jim)

   (b) ¬ATHOME(Jim) | ¬ATHOME(Marty)

   (c) This statement can be converted into two clauses.

   FATHER(Tom)
   HAPPY(Tom)

9. Again, there are many legitimate translations. If your answers differ from the ones we give here, they may still be correct. However, you might carefully examine such differences.

   (a) ¬UMPIRE(x) | STRONGWILLED(x)

   (b) ¬INTEGER(x) | EVEN(x) | ODD(x)

   (c) ¬PERSON(x) | ¬OLD(x) | GOTSICK(x)

   (d) This one is a bit ambiguous. We chose to convert it to two clauses.

   ¬GOTSICK(x) | PERSON(x)
   ¬GOTSICK(x) | OLD(x)

   (e) ¬SURVIVED(x) | ¬MALE(x)

10. For this set there are so many ways to translate the statements, that your choices probably do not agree with the ones we give here. You might carefully study the ones we give.

   (a) ¬PERSON(x) | GRANDCHILD(x, grandmother(x))

   (b) ¬POSITIVE(x) | ¬POSITIVE(y) | POSITIVE(sum(x, y))

   (c) This can be represented by two clauses.

   ¬POSITIVE(x) | ¬POSITIVE(y) | LESSTHAN(x, sum(x, y))
   ¬POSITIVE(x) | ¬POSITIVE(y) | LESSTHAN(y, sum(x, y))

   (d) ¬INTEGER(x) | LESSTHAN(asmaller(x), x)

    (e) ¬PERSON(x) | ¬GREATERTHAN(age(x), 80) | GOTSICK(x)

    (f) ¬GOTSICK(x) | PERSON(x)

       ¬GOTSICK(x) | GREATERTHAN(age(x),80)

11. These exercises get progressively harder. For each one, we shall show the steps required to reach the final clause form.

    (a) One possible translation of the sentence is,

       if (DRIVES(Monday, Peter) **and** DRIVES(Tuesday, Mary))
       then DRIVES(Wednesday, me)

    This can be converted to

       not (DRIVES(Monday, Peter) **and** DRIVES(Tuesday, Mary))
       or DRIVES(Wednesday, me)

    This can be converted to the final clause

       ¬DRIVES(Monday, Peter) | ¬DRIVES(Tuesday, Mary)
       | DRIVES(Wednesday,me)

    (b) The sentence

       if (PLAYER(x) **and** LARGE(x) **and** FAST(x))
       then VALUABLE(x)

    can be rewritten as

       not (PLAYER(x) **and** LARGE(x) **and** FAST(x))
       or VALUABLE(x)

    Now note that **not** (s1 **and** (s2 **and** s3)) is rewritten to **not** s1 **or** (**not** (s2 **and** s3)), which is rewritten to (**not** s1) **or** (**not** s2) **or** (**not** s3). Thus, the clause that we finally obtain is

       ¬PLAYER(x) | ¬LARGE(x) | ¬FAST(x) | VALUABLE(x)

    (c) The sentence

       if Drives(Monday, Peter)
       then (DRIVES(Tuesday, me) **and** DRIVES(Wednesday, me))

    is represented by the pair of clauses

       ¬DRIVES(Monday, Peter) | DRIVES(Tuesday, me)
       ¬DRIVES(Monday, Peter) | DRIVES(Wednesday, me)

    (d) The sentence

       if (DRIVES(Monday, Peter) **and** DRIVES(Tuesday, Mary))
       then (DRIVES(Wednesday, me) **and** DRIVES(Thursday, me))

    becomes

       not (DRIVES(Monday, Peter) **and** DRIVES(Tuesday, Mary))
       or (DRIVES(Wednesday, me) **and** DRIVES(Thursday, me))

    This leads to the two clauses

       ¬DRIVES(Monday, Peter) | ¬DRIVES(Tuesday, Mary)
       | DRIVES(Wednesday, me)

    and

       ¬DRIVES(Monday, Peter) | ¬DRIVES(Tuesday, Mary)
       | DRIVES(Thursday, me)

    (e) This problem is moderately difficult. One way to approach it is to think of it as making two statements.

       If a player is tired, the player will lose

and

If a player is sloppy, the player will lose.

Each of these is represented easily by a single clause. You can convert the entire expression

if PLAYER(x) **and** (TIRED(x) **or** SLOPPY(x))
then LOSER(x)

directly into the same two clauses, but it must be done carefully. You might try it with a glass of wine.

12. The following translation uses the same predicates as axiom 1.

Ax. 2: ¬CONNECTED(x, y, z) | CONNECTED(y, x, z)

Ax. 3: ¬GETTO(x, y) | ¬GETTO(y, z) | GETTO(x, z)

Ax. 4: CONNECTED(Leadville, Gorm, WoodlandPath)

Ax. 5: CONNECTED(Gorm, Lewistown, KingsHighway)

Ax. 6: CONNECTED(Leadville, Lewistown, MainPike)

Ax. 7: CONNECTED(Lastchance, Astor, Mudpath)

Ax. 8: CONNECTED(Lastchance, Gorm, MilesRoad)

Ax. 9: TRUCKSOK(Mudpath)

Ax. 10: TRUCKSOK(MainPike)

Ax. 11: TRUCKSOK(MilesRoad)

Ax. 12: TRUCKSOK(KingsHighway) | TRUCKSOK(WoodlandPath)

Ax. 13: ¬CONNECTED(Leadville,Astor,MainPike)

13. You can deduce GETTO(Lastchance, Astor). To see this, rewrite axiom 1 with x replaced by Lastchance, y replaced by Astor, and z replaced by Mudpath. Then, because axioms 7 and 9 are assumed to be true, it must be the case that the third literal in the instance of axiom 1 is true.

14. No, but you can deduce

GETTO(Lastchance, Gorm)

In order to deduce

GETTO(Gorm, Lastchance)

you must first deduce

CONNECTED(Gorm, Lastchance)

This can be done using axioms 2 and 8.

15. You can deduce

GETTO(Gorm, Lewistown) | TRUCKSOK(WoodlandPath)

This is deduced with hyperresolution. It cannot be deduced with UR-resolution. For now you may determine which inference rule is needed by the following simple rules.

Hyperresolution is used to derive clauses that contain only positive literals. A literal is positive if it does not begin with "¬".

UR-resolution is used to derive clauses that have only one literal.

Thus, if a result is a clause with a single positive literal, then it may be deducible with either UR-resolution or hyperresolution, providing that the appropriate conditions are satisfied. These concepts will be clarified and the precise definitions of the inference rules will be given in a later chapter.

16. You can deduce

¬CONNECTED(Astor, Leadville, MainPike)

using UR-resolution. Since the result contains a negative literal, it could not be deduced with hyperresolution.

17. The proof is the following.

Assume the falseness of the claim:

(14) ¬GETTO(Astor, Gorm)

From axioms 2 and 7:

(15) CONNECTED(Astor, Lastchance, Mudpath)

From axioms 1 and 9, and clause 15:

(16) GETTO(Astor, Lastchance)

From axioms 1, 8, and 11:

(17) GETTO(Lastchance, Gorm)

From axiom 3, and clauses 16 and 17:

(18) GETTO(Astor, Gorm)

This last clause contradicts clause 14, so the proof is complete.

18. The proof is the following.

Assume the falseness of the claim.

(14) ¬GETTO(Astor, Lewistown)

Clauses 15 through 18 are identical to those generated in the last problem.

From axioms 2 and 4:

(19) CONNECTED(Gorm, Leadville, WoodlandPath)

From axiom 1, clause 19, and axiom 12:

(20) GETTO(Gorm, Leadville) | TRUCKSOK(KingsHighway)

From axiom 3, and clauses 18 and 20:

(21) GETTO(Astor, Leadville) | TRUCKSOK(KingsHighway)

From axioms 1, 6, and 10:

(22) GETTO(Leadville, Lewistown)

From axiom 3, and clauses 21 and 22:

(23) GETTO(Astor, Lewistown) | TRUCKSOK(KingsHighway)

From clauses 14 and 23:

(24) TRUCKSOK(KingsHighway)

From axiom 1, axiom 5, and clause 24:

(25) GETTO(Gorm, Lewistown)

From axiom 3, and clauses 18 and 25:

(26) GETTO(Astor, Lewistown)

Finally, since clauses 14 and 26 contradict each other, the proof by contradiction is complete.

3

Puzzles

THE JOBS PUZZLE

There are four people: Roberta, Thelma, Steve, and Pete.
Among them, they hold eight different jobs.
Each holds exactly two jobs.
The jobs are: chef, guard, nurse, telephone operator,
police officer (gender not implied), teacher, actor, and boxer.
The job of nurse is held by a male.
The husband of the chef is the telephone operator.
Roberta is not a boxer.
Pete has no education past the ninth grade.
Roberta, the chef, and the police officer went golfing together.

Question: Who holds which jobs?

Puzzles are a source of entertainment and challenge. But they are also often abstractions of real problems. For example, puzzles that require determining who must go where at what time are like problems in everyday scheduling. The problem of tiling a modified checkerboard with dominoes can be viewed as an abstraction of similar problems in circuit layout design.

Puzzles are a convenient way of illustrating the various ways an automated reasoning program draws conclusions from facts, and also of illustrating how the program can be intelligent in its attempt to solve problems. As promised in the introduction, each puzzle that we solve will be stated in its original form, and then stated in a form suitable for submitting it to an automated reasoning program.

Here are some questions we hope to answer by exploring an increasingly difficult set of puzzles in this and the next few chapters.

1. How can a computer be programmed to reason?

2. Can a program be written to be so general that it can be used to solve puzzles, but also to assist in, for example, both mathematical research and applications such as logic circuit design?

3. How does a reasoning program know what the problem is about?

4. How can its attack be varied according to the type of problem under study?

Some might answer the first of the four questions by saying that, since people can reason, a computer can be programmed to reason by programming it to imitate a person. Although this answer is interesting and conceivable, it is not the way an automated reasoning program works. And perhaps it is not wise to have the computer program imitate a person, for too often a person's reasoning only approximates *logical* reasoning. Too often "conclusions" are drawn from a set of facts when they do not in fact follow from the facts. We are not saying that people cannot think, nor are we saying that the computer is always better at such tasks. What we are saying is that the computer can, for example, stick strictly to the rules that are given and be, therefore, completely logical and thus avoid certain kinds of error. In Chapter 2 you learned something about how a computer can be programmed to reason or, more precisely, how a reasoning program works. In this chapter you will actually see the steps taken by an automated reasoning program at work on a problem of some difficulty.

As for the second of the four questions, yes—programs can and have been written that can both solve puzzles and be used in research and in various application areas. While in this chapter you will only learn about using a reasoning program to solve a puzzle, in later chapters you will learn of various uses that range from abstract mathematics to expert systems.

To show how a reasoning program knows what the problem under study is about, and thus answer the third question, is another of the objectives of this chapter. As we focus on different aspects of the "jobs puzzle", we shall point out the need for various clauses. You will learn, by example, how the meaning of concepts is pinned down, what tests can be applied to suggest that something is missing from the problem description, and what means can be used to state the objective of the problem to a reasoning program. In this chapter, and in succeeding chapters, a variety of representations will be given and a number of "tricks" will be used. Some of the tricks are quite reminiscent of tricks that a person might use in trying to solve a problem.

The last of the four questions is answered by examining problems that are selected from widely differing areas. You will learn how to vary a reasoning program's attack on a problem—by choosing an appropriate representation, a particular type of reasoning, and a strategy reflecting your knowledge.

An automated reasoning program can provide valuable assistance in carrying out reasoning tasks just as the pocket calculator provides assistance in carrying out arithmetic tasks. Like the calculator, a reasoning program must be given accurate instructions based on the problem to be solved. The first phase of the instruction requires representing the problem to the program. You can, for example, use the language discussed in Chapter 2.

3.1 The Jobs Puzzle in Miniature

Rather than immediately tackling the "jobs puzzle" found at the beginning of this chapter, we first focus on a miniaturized—even trivial—version of that puzzle. By doing so, the task of giving a virtually complete treatment of its representation is made much easier.

> Roberta and Steve hold, between them, two jobs.
> Each has one job.
> The jobs are teacher and nurse.
> The job of nurse is held by a male.
>
>   Who holds which job?

Of course, Roberta is a teacher and Steve a nurse. This spontaneous answer is almost a reflex, and appears to require virtually no reasoning. If forced to justify the answer, you might give the following explanation.

Roberta must be a female. Therefore, Roberta must not be a male. Since in this minipuzzle the job of nurse is held by a male, Roberta must not be the nurse. Since each of the two people holds a job, Roberta must be the teacher. This leaves the job of nurse for Steve.

The justification takes five steps, while it might have appeared that only one is required to give the reasoning behind the answer. If this minipuzzle were given to a reasoning program, the program would find the answer and also take five steps to get it. A reasoning program leaves no steps to the imagination, but instead makes every step explicit.

Let us look at exactly how we get an automated reasoning program to solve this puzzle.

3.1.1 Representation of the Miniature Jobs Puzzle

The first task is that of representation.

The program must be told that each person is employed. The clauses

(1) HASAJOB(Roberta, nurse) | HASAJOB(Roberta, teacher)

(2) HASAJOB(Steve, nurse) | HASAJOB(Steve, teacher)

say that each of the two people is employed either as a nurse or as a teacher. Recalling that the symbol $\neg$ is read as **not**,

(3) $\neg$HASAJOB(Roberta, nurse) | $\neg$HASAJOB(Roberta, teacher)

(4) $\neg$HASAJOB(Steve, nurse) | $\neg$HASAJOB(Steve, teacher)

rule out the possibility that one person holds both jobs.

Similarly, we must have clauses that state that each job is held by Roberta or Steve, but not by both. The needed clauses can be patterned after the four clauses just given. We get

(5) HASAJOB(Roberta, teacher) | HASAJOB(Steve, teacher)

(6) HASAJOB(Roberta, nurse) | HASAJOB(Steve, nurse)

(7) $\neg$HASAJOB(Roberta, teacher) | $\neg$HASAJOB(Steve, teacher)

(8) $\neg$HASAJOB(Roberta, nurse) | $\neg$HASAJOB(Steve, nurse)

as four clauses that suffice.

To say that the job of nurse is held by a male, we write

(9) $\neg$HASAJOB(x, nurse) | MALE(x)

This clause can be read, "**for every** x, x does **not** have the job of nurse **or** x is male". Equivalently, it can be read as, **for every** x, **if** x has the job of nurse **then** x is male.

Surely now everything that is needed must be present. After all, haven't all of the pieces of the puzzle been translated into clauses? Yes, but . . . information is missing, implicit information. For example, a piece of information implicitly available to a person solving this puzzle is that every person is female or male, but not both. As before, the translation of this startling information can be patterned after the similar translation just given. The clauses

(10) FEMALE(x) | MALE(x)

(11) $\neg$FEMALE(x) | $\neg$MALE(x)

will do.

Can the discussion now be turned finally to the actual method of solution? Not until clauses are given that state that Roberta is female and Steve is male, information implicit in their respective names. Without additional information about names, an automated reasoning program in no way would deduce this mundane bit of information. Adding the clauses

(12) FEMALE(Roberta)

(13) MALE(Steve)

finally completes the task of representing the miniature puzzle in clause form.

3.1.2 Choosing the Type of Reasoning

The next task is that of choosing the type of reasoning—the inference rule—to apply to the minipuzzle. There are many types of reasoning we can employ. Rather than describe them all here, we prefer to introduce them as we need them. You have already seen *hyperresolution* in Chapter 2. In this problem we are going to use *UR-resolution*, a rule designed to deduce simple facts. When this type of reasoning is employed, all derived clauses contain exactly one literal. Such clauses are called *unit clauses*. Thus the *UR* in *UR-resolution* stands for *Unit-Resulting*. In later chapters you will learn how to predict that this choice is a reasonable one for this puzzle.

3.1.3 Solution of the Miniature Jobs Puzzle

The program might begin its attack on the minipuzzle by focusing on Roberta. Since Roberta is female, the reasoning program might deduce

From clauses 12 and 11:

(14) ¬MALE(Roberta)

which says that Roberta is not male. Then, since the job of nurse is not held by a male, the program could deduce

From clauses 14 and 9:

(15) ¬HASAJOB(Roberta, nurse)

Roberta does not hold the job of nurse. But she is the nurse or the teacher, so

From clauses 15 and 1:

(16) HASAJOB(Roberta, teacher)

Roberta has the job of teacher.

With Roberta's job determined, the reasoning program could turn to determining Steve's. Clause 15 turns out to be useful again, even as it was for pinning down Roberta's job.

From clauses 15 and 6:

(17) HASAJOB(Steve, nurse)

says that Steve is the nurse.

This derivation is essentially the same as that given earlier—the justification a person might give for the spontaneous answer to the question about who holds which job. In this puzzle we simply derived new facts from the ones we were given and noticed when we had the facts we were looking for. In some situations this is fine, but in many others we need a clearer notion of exactly what the program is to look for and how it is to know when it is done. In Chapter 2, you learned that the preferred style of proof is by contradiction. No contradiction occurred in the given proof. What does a proof by contradiction for the minipuzzle look like?

As discussed in Chapter 2, a proof by contradiction starts with—what is hoped to be—false information. What false information is available? In particular, what is the right answer—the answer that we can assume false? A good candidate is, "Steve is the nurse". After all, a person might easily say, "since the job of nurse is held by a male, and since Steve is male, Steve is the nurse". This answer is far from a proof, much less a proof by contradiction, for it contains no hint about what new facts are derived from which older facts. Nevertheless, the answer does suggest a good starting point. We could, for example, begin by assuming that Steve is not the nurse, which we shall do.

Before doing so, however, notice that the original question—who holds which job?—provides no clue to seeking a proof by contradiction. The question contains nothing to falsify, as recommended in Chapter 2. So a "trick" has been uncovered—a trick similar to ones that a person might use. The idea is to replace the original goal with a very closely related one. The new goal is that of deciding between the two possible jobs for Steve and the two for Roberta. You could thus claim that Steve is the nurse, or claim that Steve is the teacher, for example. And that is the trick—replacing the original goal with a claim that leads to a statement that can be assumed false. Since the new claim (for Steve) is that Steve is the nurse, or that Steve is the teacher,

¬HASAJOB(Steve, nurse)

¬HASAJOB(Steve, teacher)

can be used as clauses to represent the assumed falseness of the claim. Of course, only one of these clauses will lead to a contradiction since Steve only holds one job. For example, assuming Steve is not the teacher will, in this problem, lead nowhere—for he is not the teacher. But assuming he is not the nurse is precisely what is needed to determine his job, and we are back to the good starting point.

For the proof by contradiction, we again use clauses 1 through 13 above, augmenting them with

(18) ¬HASAJOB(Steve, nurse)

which is the clause that represents the assumed falseness of the claim. Such a clause is known as *the denial of the claim*, or as *the denial of the theorem*. This denial clause sets everything in motion. Since the job of nurse is held by Roberta or Steve, and since (by assumption) Steve is not the nurse,

Roberta is the nurse, from clauses 18 and 6:

(19) HASAJOB(Roberta, nurse)

But if Roberta is the nurse, and the job of nurse is held by a male,

Roberta is male, from clauses 19 and 9:

(20) MALE(Roberta)

Then

Roberta is not female, from clauses 20 and 11:

(21) ¬FEMALE(Roberta)

since male implies not female. We have arrived at a contradiction—a contradiction between 21 and 12. Clause 21 says that Roberta is not female, while clause 12 says she is. Thus the assumed fact that Steve is not a nurse has, through a sequence of derived facts, led to a contradiction, and the program has proved that Steve is a nurse.

In a similar fashion, by assuming that

Roberta is not a teacher:

(22) ¬HASAJOB(Roberta, teacher)

a reasoning program would eventually conclude that again Roberta is not female. Since this fact contradicts the given one that she is, the program would prove that Roberta is a teacher.

EXERCISES

In this set of exercises we explore the basic method of deducing new clauses.

At the start of this section, it was pointed out that clause 14 could be deduced from clauses 11 and 12. The deduction consists of the following steps.

(a) First, choose an instance of clause 11 such that the first literal is identical, except for sign, with the literal in clause 12. This instance is

¬FEMALE(Roberta) | ¬MALE(Roberta)

(b) Then, since

FEMALE(Roberta)

is true, and the instance of clause 11 is true,

¬MALE(Roberta)

must be true.

This process of picking the right instance of clause 11 is accomplished by *unifying* the first literal in clause 11 with the literal in clause 12. In particular, you must choose an instantiation of the variables that makes the two literals identical (except that their signs are opposite).

1. For each of the following pairs of clauses, choose an instantiation of the variables that allows a deduction to be made, and give the deduced clause. You may think of FATHER(x,y) as asserting that x is the father of y.

   (a) ¬FATHER(George, x) | WEALTHY(son(x))
   FATHER(George, Mike)
   (b) ¬FATHER(George, x) | WEALTHY(son(x))
   FATHER(George, brother(Jim))
   (c) ¬FATHER(George,x) | WEALTHY(son(x))
   ¬WEALTHY(son(brother(Mike)))
   (d) EQUAL(sum(minus(x), x), 0)
   ¬EQUAL(sum(minus(4), y), z) | EQUAL(sum(z, 4), y)
   (e) EQUAL(sum(minus(x), x), 0)
   ¬EQUAL(sum(minus(4), x), y) | EQUAL(sum(y, 4), x)

2. Would a reasoning program deduce

   GRANDFATHER(Bob, Jim)

from

   FATHER(Bob, Marty)

and

   FATHER(Marty, Jim)

3. What new clauses can be deduced from the following four clauses?

   PLAYER(Bob)
   PLAYER(Mary)
   MOTHER(Sue, Mary)
   ¬PLAYER(x) | ¬PLAYER(y) | PAIR(x, y)

4. Consider the following two clauses.

   EQUAL(times(x, x), square(x))
   ¬EQUAL(times(y, z), z) | EQUAL(y, 1) | EQUAL(z, 1)

Can any clauses be deduced from these two parent clauses?

3.1.4 Discussion of the Formulation and Proof

At this point, you might suspect that a reasoning program works in an unnatural and unintelligent fashion. After all, the minipuzzle is trivial and the program's solution surprisingly long. What makes the solution so long is that a reasoning program does not leave out steps. When we tackle the full "jobs puzzle", you will see how intelligent a reasoning program can be. For example, you will learn how it can use hints to sharply increase its effectiveness.

Even this minipuzzle contains information that could have been used to give a hint to a reasoning program. In this problem, one clause—one fact—stands out, namely, the job of nurse is held by a male. It stands out because it is the one fact about who holds which job; the other clauses are about the situation in general. This fact is a big hint to the puzzle's solution, for a person or for a program. You could tell the program to key on this fact, at least at the start. A mechanism—technically known as *weighting*—exists within the program for instructing it to consider certain concepts, and hence certain facts, more important than others. So you could hint to the program that the concept of nurse, and therefore the general clause about nurse, is rather important. Hints like this one are much more important in solving deeper problems, and they will be given much more attention in later chapters.

Next, you might wonder about the wisdom of solving the minipuzzle backward —the wisdom of adding the false information and then seeking a contradiction. A move of this type has various advantages. As remarked in the preceding chapter, seeking a contradiction gives the program a convenient termination condition. When using an automated reasoning program, you often desire that the program stop as soon as it has solved the problem. Finding a contradiction causes it to do just that.

But there are other advantages to adding a *denial* clause. The presence of such a clause, or of such clauses, gives a reasoning program access to a very powerful strategy. In the introduction, you were told that you would learn how a reasoning program can be intelligent. The key to intelligent pursuit of a solution to a problem is *strategy*. In most cases, a reasoning program should not be asked to systematically search through all the possible derivable information. In this problem, such a request would not be particularly harmful, but in most problems the request would produce a disaster. There are entirely too many irrelevant but derivable facts for even the most innocent of problems.

There is a strategy, called the *set of support strategy*, which is illustrated by the contradiction proof above. It keys on the *denial* clause or clauses. The advantage of using this strategy is that, to some extent, it forces a reasoning program to concentrate on the problem rather than wandering around somewhat aimlessly. As we discuss the solution of problems from other areas of interest, it will become very evident that, without strategy, a reasoning program can easily wander away from the goal. In fact, just reasoning forward from the general facts in a problem can easily cause a reasoning program to begin to develop the entire theory on which the problem rests, rather than sticking to the point.

Examination of the proof by contradiction, and in fact of the entire process for submitting this minipuzzle to an automated reasoning program, might easily convince you that you are much better at solving puzzles than such a program. For this minipuzzle, you are. But for rather deeper puzzles, as you may come to agree later, a reasoning program can be an invaluable assistant. A crossover point exists—a point at which the problem is sufficiently hard that automated assistance is perhaps required. Examples, taken from actual computer runs, will be given of hard problems that were solved in extremely short times by a reasoning program. Such examples are not evidence that a reasoning program can replace a person, but rather that it can assist and supplement a person's reasoning power. You, in turn, can assist it by choosing a good representation for the problem, by employing tricks of the kind given above, by choosing well the type of reasoning to be employed, and finally by choosing a good strategy.

Before turning to the more interesting puzzle found at the beginning of this chapter, let us examine the need for all 13 clauses in the minipuzzle. To make the discussion easier to follow, we repeat them here.

    (1) HASAJOB(Roberta, nurse) | HASAJOB(Roberta, teacher)

    (2) HASAJOB(Steve, nurse) | HASAJOB(Steve, teacher)

    (3) ¬HASAJOB(Roberta, nurse) | ¬HASAJOB(Roberta, teacher)

    (4) ¬HASAJOB(Steve, nurse) | ¬HASAJOB(Steve, teacher)

    (5) HASAJOB(Roberta, teacher) | HASAJOB(Steve, teacher)

    (6) HASAJOB(Roberta, nurse) | HASAJOB(Steve, nurse)

    (7) ¬HASAJOB(Roberta, teacher) | ¬HASAJOB(Steve, teacher)

    (8) ¬HASAJOB(Roberta, nurse) | ¬HASAJOB(Steve, nurse)

    (9) ¬HASAJOB(x, nurse) | MALF(x)

  (10) FEMALE(x) | MALE(x)

  (11) ¬FEMALE(x) | ¬MALE(x)

  (12) FEMALE(Roberta)

  (13) MALE(Steve)

The two clauses

    (1) HASAJOB(Roberta, nurse) | HASAJOB(Roberta, teacher)

    (2) HASAJOB(Steve, nurse) | HASAJOB(Steve, teacher)

give the possible jobs for a specific person, Roberta or Steve. After seeing these two clauses, you might easily guess that clauses that give the possible people that can hold a specific job are needed. If you think not, consider the situation in which both Roberta and Steve are teachers. Without the clauses

    (5) HASAJOB(Roberta, teacher) | HASAJOB(Steve, teacher)

    (6) HASAJOB(Roberta, nurse) | HASAJOB(Steve, nurse)

this possibility cannot be ruled out. In fact, without the clauses that force each of the two jobs to be held by Roberta or Steve, a reasoning program could never discover Steve's job. Thus we have clauses that hold the person fixed while varying the job that can be held by that person, and clauses that vary the person while holding the job fixed.

    We have here an illustration of the ease of overlooking what must be done—what is required to completely define the problem. The fact that eight clauses are required to state the relation of the two people to the two jobs perhaps points out the difficulty of avoiding logical errors that frequently occur when solving a problem. Often a person jumps to conclusions that do not follow from the facts. For example, in a similar puzzle, but without sufficient care, you could very easily overlook the possibility that both Roberta and Steve are the teacher. Equally, a solution can be overlooked because a path to that solution is not seen. The making of logical errors on the one hand, and the missing of hidden paths on the other, can be avoided by using an automated reasoning program.

You might wonder about the possibility that, among the first eight clauses, perhaps redundant information is present. Are the first eight clauses independent of each other? The answer is "no, they are not". For example, the fourth clause can be deduced from the first, seventh, and eighth. Redundancy and dependency are present. As is true for a person, redundancy, or dependency, is often a contributor to efficient reasoning by the program. It is often better to have a fact present, rather than being forced to deduce it.

The fact that eight clauses were used to pin down the relation of the two people to the two jobs brings up yet one more question. Suppose we have the results of a run that has not succeeded. Are there tests that we can apply to learn that something is missing in the problem description? One of the most useful tests is simply to look for obvious facts that are missing from the program's reasoning. For example, in the minipuzzle, an important and yet trivial fact is that Roberta is not male. This fact connects the fact that Roberta is female to the conclusion that Roberta is not the nurse. If the program were not asked to reason backward, it should find this connection very easily. On the other hand, if it were reasoning backward from the assumed falseness of the goal, it would first conclude that Roberta is male, which in turn would ordinarily then imply that Roberta is not female. If this conclusion—that Roberta is not female—is not found, then you might look for something missing. The missing something might be

(11) $\neg$FEMALE(x) | $\neg$MALE(x)

that says that a person who is male is not female. This test for missing clauses can often point to easily overlooked or implicit information.

3.1.5 Recapitulation

Examination of the proof of the minipuzzle brings out a number of points that will continually recur. Clauses 14 and 20 are simple illustrations of the basic process that an automated reasoning program uses to draw conclusions from facts. In both cases, a specific fact was coupled with a general fact to yield a specific fact. In effect, the general fact was made specific in such a way as to enable a form of cancellation—a cancellation of components from the two statements, where the components must be opposite in sign. But notice that the specific instance of the general fact did not appear in either proof. A reasoning program does not, as was evident in Chapter 2, bother with the specific instance, but instead combines this instantiation or particularization with the cancellation in a single step. By combining the two processes in one, the effectiveness of a reasoning program is greatly enhanced. Besides seeing the basic process for drawing conclusions, you saw examples of implicit information that must be included, of information that might be viewed as pedantic that had to be included, and of a type of reasoning known as UR-resolution in action.

What you did not see is the more general representation of the minipuzzle that could have been used. The first eight clauses could have been replaced by fewer and more general clauses. If we had included instead

HASAJOB(x, nurse) | HASAJOB(x, teacher)

HASAJOB(Roberta, y) | HASAJOB(Steve, y)

then the assumption that Steve is not the teacher would have yielded immediately the following two clauses.

HASAJOB(Steve, nurse)

HASAJOB(Roberta, teacher)

The first new clause would have resulted from particularizing or instantiating the variable for the person holding a job. The second would have instantiated the variable for the job being held. Searches for the key information needed to solve a problem are often made up of such closely related moves.

3.2 The Jobs Puzzle in Full

There are four people: Roberta, Thelma, Steve, and Pete.
Among them, they hold eight different jobs.
Each holds exactly two jobs.
The jobs are: chef, guard, nurse, telephone operator,
police officer (gender not implied), teacher, actor,
and boxer.
The job of nurse is held by a male.
The husband of the chef is the telephone operator.
Roberta is not a boxer.
Pete has no education past the ninth grade.
Roberta, the chef, and the police officer went golfing together.

Question: Who holds which jobs?

This puzzle has been given to intelligent sixth graders, some of whom have solved it. If you cannot solve it, it may just prove that you are not an intelligent sixth grader, and nothing is wrong with not being classed as a sixth grader.

Those who are good at solving puzzles often use powerful strategies, even when they cannot state them explicitly. In this section of the chapter, we introduce you more fully to strategy. We show you how an automated reasoning program can be quite intelligent in its attack on a problem. Although imitation of a person's reasoning is not the goal, you will also learn how methods that you might employ can be used successfully by a reasoning program.

One way of attempting to solve this "jobs puzzle" is to make a table of the possible people and the possible jobs they might hold. The rows could be labeled with the names of the jobs, while the columns are labeled with the people. An x can be used to show that the possibility is still in doubt.

	Roberta	Thelma	Steve	Pete
chef	x	x	x	x
guard	x	x	x	x
nurse	x	x	x	x
operator	x	x	x	x
police	x	x	x	x
teacher	x	x	x	x
actor	x	x	x	x
boxer	x	x	x	x

The idea is to fill in the squares with yes or no as the conclusions are drawn. For example, when and if it is determined that Roberta is not the nurse, then a no is put in the square where the column labeled Roberta intersects the row labeled nurse. If the plan succeeds, each column will contain exactly two instances of yes when finished, while each row will contain exactly one instance of yes. For each of the four people in the puzzle, one proceeds by crossing off possibilities until only two remain. At that point, the remaining two squares can be immediately filled in with yes.

This puzzle abounds with implicit information, some obvious and some somewhat subtle. For example, obviously Roberta and Thelma are female, while Steve and Pete are male. All eight jobs are filled, that is, are held by one of the four people. No job is held by more than one person. And, as will be seen, the puzzle contains some rather hidden information besides. If the hidden information is not uncovered, and if the implicit information is not used, the puzzle cannot be solved.

3.2.1 The Solution by Person or Persons Unknown

What might a person's solution look like?

A reasonable strategy a person might use is first to concentrate on Roberta's two possible jobs, for more is known—at least implicitly—about Roberta than is known about anyone else in the jobs puzzle. Roberta is not the boxer—that fact is given in the puzzle. To learn more about Roberta and the jobs she holds, we must make some assumptions that are based on common usage of everyday language. The puzzle says that the nurse is male. Since Roberta is female—a fact implicit in her name—we may conclude that she is not the nurse. (The puzzle is subtly designed, for if the four names did not clearly imply the sex of the people, it would be impossible to solve.) We also know that she is not the actor. Why? Because everyday language distinguishes members of this profession based on sex—actor and actress. (Notice, however, that we cannot assume that the police officer is male, for the job is labeled police officer and not policeman.)

The puzzle says that Roberta, the chef, and the police officer went golfing together. This statement is rich in "hidden" facts, for in normal usage it means that three distinct people went golfing. Thus, we know that Roberta is neither the chef nor the police officer.

The husband of the chef is the telephone operator. Coupled with the implicit fact that husbands are male, this fact tells us that Roberta is not the telephone operator. This leaves the jobs of guard and teacher for Roberta. The other six jobs have been crossed off of her list—"no" can be placed in the corresponding squares in her column.

Notice that even though the reasoning that Roberta is not the telephone operator seems explicit—perhaps even painfully so—another bit of implicit information has been used in reaching that conclusion. Females are not males—if you are female then you are not male—is also needed. As in solving the minipuzzle, such a fact must be given to a reasoning program, and it will be when we come to the program's solution of this jobs puzzle.

More squares can immediately be filled in. The puzzle says that there are four people, eight jobs, and that each person holds exactly two jobs. Implicit in these facts, as remarked earlier, is the fact that no job is held by two people. Thus the jobs of guard and teacher can be crossed off the list of possible jobs for each of Thelma, Steve, and Pete. Doing so leaves six possible jobs for the three remaining people—18 squares still to be filled in—and everything is fine. The check that there are enough jobs left for the remaining people in the puzzle is an example of a useful process. Such checks are valuable in puzzle solving, whether the solving is done by a person or by a program.

With Roberta's jobs determined, the person on whom to focus is Thelma. The choice of Thelma is consistent with the strategy that first pointed to Roberta. Although it might appear that we know no more about her than we do about Pete, it is not true. Implicit in her name is the fact that she is female. Some of the arguments used to determine Roberta's jobs therefore apply to Thelma. Thelma cannot be the nurse, the actor, or the telephone operator—those jobs are held by a male. Moreover, since the puzzle says that the chef has a husband, since husbands are male, and since Thelma is the only female left, she is the chef.

Since they went golfing together, the chef and the police officer are not the same person. So Thelma is not the police officer. The jobs of guard and teacher have already been crossed off her list. So she is the chef and—surprise—the boxer. (Nowhere was it implied that the boxer is male.)

The jobs for Steve and Pete can be quickly determined now. The puzzle says that Pete has no education past the ninth grade. To use this information, we must employ some deeply hidden assumptions—some that depend on our knowledge of jobs in our culture. In the United States, in the 1980s, the jobs of nurse, police officer, and teacher each require more than a ninth-grade education. Thus, Pete cannot be the nurse or the police officer. So Pete is the actor and the telephone operator. These jobs can be crossed off the list for Steve. Then the remaining two jobs, nurse and police officer, must be held by Steve.

This puzzle, like so many, is much more easily solved if a good strategy is used. The strategy used here is to concentrate on the person about whom we know the most but for whom the jobs are not yet determined. An automated reasoning program can be made to use this strategy, as you will see in this and in later chapters. The mechanism used to do so is known as *weighting*.

Another feature of this solution to the puzzle is rather interesting. Not only did we learn who held which jobs, but we learned also that Pete and Thelma were married. Finding such extra information is common in people's attempts at solving puzzles, and it is also common in a reasoning program's attempts. If too much extra information is found, the puzzle never gets solved—by a person or by a program. Thus, one of the important items you need to learn to use a reasoning program is how to curtail the finding of extra information. Providing various ways to reduce exploration of fruitless paths is one of the powerful features of an automated reasoning program. Such features will be thoroughly discussed in later chapters.

3.2.2 The Solution by Program or Programs Known

The full jobs puzzle can be and was solved by an automated reasoning program. The solution obtained by the reasoning program is quite like that just given—that which a person might find. To present the solution, we must first give the clauses that a reasoning program could use to attempt to solve the puzzle.

3.2.2.1 The puzzle in clause form.   Ignoring to some extent the order of the statements of the puzzle, let us instead begin with the information that is easiest to represent in clause form. The clauses

(1) FEMALE(Roberta)

(2) FEMALE(Thelma)

(3) MALE(Steve)

(4) MALE(Pete)

give the sex for each of the four people in the puzzle. The clauses

(5) FEMALE(x) | MALE(x)

(6) ¬FEMALE(x) | ¬MALE(x)

say that everyone is female or male, but not both. Then

(7) ¬HASAJOB(Roberta, boxer)

says that Roberta is not the boxer. Next

(8) ¬HASAJOB(x, nurse) | MALE(x)

(9) ¬HASAJOB(x, actor) | MALE(x)

respectively say that the job of nurse is held by a male and that the job of actor is held by a male. These nine clauses take care of some of the implicit information, and are the translations that are the easiest to make.

Next we come to the introduction of functions—functions as discussed in Chapter 2. What are the clauses that are needed for "every person has two jobs" and for "every job is held by a person"? The clauses

(10) HASAJOB(x, job1(x))

(11) HASAJOB(x, job2(x))

(12) HASAJOB(jobholder(y), y)

suffice. Rigorously, the first of these three clauses says that, for every person x, there exists a job, namely job1(x), that x holds, where job1(x) expresses the fact that the job held by x depends on the value of x. Similarly for the second of the three clauses. The third says that, for every job y, there exists a person who holds that job, where jobholder(y) means that the person who holds job y depends on the value of y. It is typical to use such functions when we must express the idea of "existence". Morcover, it is necessary to use the given form—a function of one argument—when there is a corresponding dependence as exhibited in this puzzle.

Next, try translating, "the husband of the chef is the telephone operator". Writing

(13) ¬HUSBAND(x, jobholder(chef)) | HASAJOB(x, operator)

(14) ¬HASAJOB(x, operator) | HUSBAND(x, jobholder(chef))

is a correct answer. Because of this statement about the chef having a husband, we have a closely related fact that can be added.

(15) FEMALE(jobholder(chef))

This clause says that the job of chef is held by a female. Still we are not finished with this clue in the puzzle, at least as far as a reasoning program is concerned. As we continually point out, an automated reasoning program knows no terms or concepts. Thus we must add more facts about "husband". We add

(16) ¬HUSBAND(x, y) | MALE(x)

(17) ¬HUSBAND(x, y) | FEMALE(y)

which say that husbands are male, and their wives are female.

Then there is the clue that Pete has no education past the ninth grade. We have

(18) ¬GREATERTHAN(education(Pete), 9)

For the remaining information about education,

(19) ¬HASAJOB(x, nurse) | GREATERTHAN(education(x), 9)

(20) ¬HASAJOB(x, police) | GREATERTHAN(education(x), 9)

(21) ¬HASAJOB(x, teacher) | GREATERTHAN(education(x), 9)

as the clauses that state which jobs require education past the ninth grade.

Perhaps the most interesting clue in the puzzle is, "Roberta, the chef, and the police officer went golfing". From this clue, a person knows that Roberta is neither the chef nor the police officer, but also knows that the holder of one of those two jobs cannot hold the other. The clauses

(22) ¬HASAJOB(Roberta, chef)

(23) ¬HASAJOB(Roberta, police)

(24) ¬HASAJOB(x, chef) | ¬HASAJOB(x, police)

express this information. In particular, clause 24 says that, for any x (person), x is not the chef or x is not the police officer. If one of the four people, say Roberta, is neither chef nor police officer, this clause is still true for x set to the value "Roberta". Keep in mind that a variable x appearing in a clause means for all x. So the clause must be written to reflect correctly the information, in this case, that none of the four people can be both chef and police officer. The possibility that some persons hold neither job must be covered. Also notice throughout this translation of the puzzle, including the implicit information, that the HASAJOB predicate always has its first argument position a person and its second a job.

At this point, some tedious but necessary items must be translated. Then we can get to the simulation of the crossing off of possibilities, and the technique for having a reasoning program do so—a technique that will be shown to be extremely powerful. As for the necessary items: First, clearly the four people in the puzzle are distinct people.

(25) ¬EQUALP(Roberta, Thelma)

(26) ¬EQUALP(Roberta, Steve)

(27) ¬EQUALP(Roberta, Pete)

(28) ¬EQUALP(Thelma, Steve)

(29) ¬EQUALP(Thelma, Pete)

(30) ¬EQUALP(Pete, Steve)

We did not use EQUAL but instead used EQUALP since equality of people is the concern and not equality in general.

The clause

(31) ¬EQUALJ(job1(x), job2(x))

says that the two jobs a person holds are distinct. Again, we must be very careful to use EQUALJ rather than EQUAL or EQUALP, since we are talking about equality of jobs and not about general equality or equality of people. The other variations of clause 31 that might occur to you are not necessary. This is in part because of the way in which the various EQUAL-type predicates can be treated by a reasoning program. The ability to "build in" equality into an automated reasoning program will also be discussed in Chapter 4.

Since equality has now been added to the concepts given to the program, other clauses must be added. In particular,

(32) EQUALP(x, x)

(33) EQUALJ(x, x)

(34) EQUAL(x, x)

give one of the fundamental properties that any equality-like relation has—anything is equal to itself. This property, known as *reflexivity*, is but one of the properties that one would ordinarily find it necessary to give to a reasoning program to pin down equality. As you will see, the other properties can be omitted if the appropriate type of reasoning, or inference rule, is used. Incidentally, we have also now introduced, in clause 34, the notion of general equality. This notion will shortly be relied on heavily.

You might be appalled at the fact that such mundane information must be present. What you will discover is that frequently a task is completed when a reasoning program discovers that something is not equal to itself—a contradiction of the obvious.

Clauses are also needed to further pin down some of the relationships in this puzzle, and to connect the various notions.

(35) ¬HASAJOB(x, y) | EQUALJ$(y, job2(x))$

   | EQUALJ$(y, job1(x))$

(36) EQUALP(x, z) | ¬HASAJOB(x, y) | ¬HASAJOB(z, y)

The first of these two clauses says that **if** a person holds a job, and **if** that job is **not** equal to the second job held by the person, **then** it is equal to the first job held by the person. Notice that again the **not** of **not** rule applies, and the **not**s cancel. Thus, if Roberta is the teacher, and the job of teacher is not her second job, it is her first. Clause 35 also suffices for the situation in which the job of teacher is not her first job, that is, it then forces the job of teacher to be her second. The convention of requiring clauses to be in the **or** form allows one clause to serve for the two situations. The **or** form has the convenient interpretation: x does not have job y, **or** y is x's second job, **or** y is x's first job.

Clause 36, the second of the two, says that, for any two distinct people, if one of them has a particular job, then the other does not. This clause is used as part of the mechanism to remove a job from another person's list once you know who holds it. A number of additional clauses are needed for that purpose, and we shall shortly turn to those.

Two additional clauses are of use.

(37) ¬FEMALE$(jobholder(y))$ | HASAJOB$(Roberta, y)$

   | HASAJOB$(Thelma, y)$

(38) ¬MALE(jobholder(y)) | HASAJOB(Steve, y)

    | HASAJOB(Pete, y)

These two clauses allow a reasoning program to add information based on facts such as "a particular job is held by a female other than Roberta".

3.2.2.2 Table simulation.

We remarked earlier that an automated reasoning program could conduct its attack on the jobs puzzle in a manner similar to that of the person or persons unknown. The solution given there was aided by a table whose columns are labeled with the four people and whose rows are labeled with the eight jobs. Clauses can be written to simulate the use of this table. Some simulate the table (and its labels). Others enable the program to cross off possibilities and to, in effect, fill in the squares. First we write clauses that fix a person and vary the possible jobs the person might hold. Each of the resulting four clauses lists eight jobs for the particular person. The expression pj(x,y) can be read as "the possibility that person x has job y". The function l is a "list" that gives a job as one of its arguments, and the remaining sublist as the other. The four clauses act like the four columns of the table given earlier. They list the possible pairings of people with jobs.

(39) POSSJOBS(l(pj(Roberta, chef), l(pj(Roberta, guard),

    l(pj(Roberta, nurse), l(pj(Roberta, operator),

    l(pj(Roberta, police), l(pj(Roberta, teacher),

    l(pj(Roberta, actor), l(pj(Roberta, boxer), end)))))))))

(40) POSSJOBS(l(pj(Thelma, chef), l(pj(Thelma, guard),

    l(pj(Thelma, nurse), l(pj(Thelma, operator),

    l(pj(Thelma, police), l(pj(Thelma, teacher),

    l(pj(Thelma, actor), l(pj(Thelma, boxer), end)))))))))

(41) POSSJOBS(l(pj(Steve, chef), l(pj(Steve, guard),

    l(pj(Steve, nurse), l(pj(Steve, operator),

    l(pj(Steve, police), l(pj(Steve, teacher),

    l(pj(Steve, actor), l(pj(Steve, boxer), end)))))))))

(42) POSSJOBS(l(pj(Pete, chef), l(pj(Pete, guard),

    l(pj(Pete, nurse), l(pj(Pete, operator),

    l(pj(Pete, police), l(pj(Pete, teacher),

    l(pj(Pete, actor), l(pj(Pete, boxer), end)))))))))

Similarly, we have eight clauses that hold the job fixed and vary the people who might hold it. These clauses are like the rows of the table.

(43) POSSPPL(l(pj(Roberta, chef), l(pj(Steve, chef),

l(pj(Thelma, chef), l(pj(Pete, chef), end)))))

(44) POSSPPL(l(pj(Roberta, guard), l(pj(Steve, guard),

l(pj(Thelma, guard), l(pj(Pete, guard), end)))))

(45) POSSPPL(l(pj(Roberta, nurse), l(pj(Steve, nurse),

l(pj(Thelma, nurse), l(pj(Pete, nurse), end)))))

(46) POSSPPL(l(pj(Roberta, operator), l(pj(Steve, operator),

l(pj(Thelma, operator), l(pj(Pete, operator), end)))))

(47) POSSPPL(l(pj(Roberta, police), l(pj(Steve, police),

l(pj(Thelma, police), l(pj(Pete, police), end)))))

(48) POSSPPL(l(pj(Roberta, teacher), l(pj(Steve, teacher),

l(pj(Thelma, teacher), l(pj(Pete, teacher), end)))))

(49) POSSPPL(l(pj(Roberta, actor), l(pj(Steve, actor),

l(pj(Thelma, actor), l(pj(Pete, actor), end)))))

(50) POSSPPL(l(pj(Roberta, boxer), l(pj(Steve, boxer),

l(pj(Thelma, boxer), l(pj(Pete, boxer), end)))))

In Chapter 4, we shall discuss other ways of representing information, including alternatives for clauses 39 through 50. Make no mistake, the representation of the problem to an automated reasoning program is sometimes difficult and sometimes tedious. The reward is the assistance of a reasoning program in completing various tasks. Once one problem in an area of interest has been translated into clause form, that information can be used repeatedly with what often turn out to be small additions and modifications to reflect a new problem. The care required to get it right is nontrivial. However, the process sometimes leads to the discovery of hidden assumptions, some of which turn out to be questionable or false. As you read the succeeding chapters, you will discover other valuable properties of using an automated reasoning program as an assistant. For example, you will learn not only how it avoids keeping duplicate information—not much of a feat—but how it can determine that new information is already covered by existing information. In the dominoes-and-checkerboard puzzle discussed in Chapter 5, you will see how a reasoning program can detect the irrelevance of and then discard most of the paths that must be examined to solve the puzzle.

3.2.2.3 Crossing off and preparing for contradiction.   We now need the clauses that describe the crossing off process. First we need a clause that converts the conclusion that a particular person does not hold a particular job into a statement that says that combination can be crossed off.

(51) HASAJOB(x, y) | EQUAL(pj(x, y), crossed)

Then we need a clause to actually do the crossing off, both from the person's list of possible jobs and from the list of possible people that can hold a job.

(52) EQUAL(l(crossed, x), x)

This clause enables the program in effect to put a "no" in the corresponding square of the table, or specifically, to cross off that combination of person and job. Clause 52 is just what is needed with clauses 39 through 50. It allows, because of the particular use of the function l, the removal of a person/job combination no matter where in the list it occurs.

The mechanism for automatically applying an equality of the form

EQUAL(pj(Roberta, nurse), crossed)

is called *demodulation*. The procedure of demodulation has many uses besides this specific trick. As you will see, demodulation is used primarily to rewrite information to some predetermined desirable form. For example, a reasoning program will automatically rewrite

AGEOF(Father(Father(Fred)), 90)

to

AGEOF(Grandfather(Fred), 90)

in the presence of the demodulator

EQUAL(Father(Father(x)), Grandfather(x))

But you will learn much more about demodulation in later chapters. For now, merely note that a process exists within an automated reasoning program to automatically apply equality statements if told to do so. Such applications take place immediately—as soon as the demodulator is deduced. Thus, in the case in which it is determined that Roberta is not the nurse, the job of nurse will be immediately crossed off the various lists as soon as the program deduces

EQUAL(pj(Roberta, nurse), crossed)

From clause 51.

When a person's two jobs have been determined, that person's list will contain exactly the two jobs. The program must be in a position to convert that information to a form that permits appropriate crossing off.

(53) ¬POSSJOBS(l(pj(x, y), l(pj(x, z), end))) | EQUALP(x, w)

      | EQUAL(pj(w, y), crossed)

(54) ¬POSSJOBS(l(pj(x, y), l(pj(x, z), end))) | EQUALP(x, w)

   | EQUAL(pj(w, z), crossed)

When a person's two jobs have been determined, a clause will exist that can be used against the first literal of each of clauses 53 and 54. By also using the clauses that express the inequality (as people) of the four persons in the puzzle, two facts are found. The two facts enable immediate crossing off of various combinations. For example, once we know that Roberta's jobs are teacher and guard, we can cross these jobs off the list of possible jobs for the other people. We thus have an illustration of how all the clauses work together. This process of crossing things off a list, of course, is done almost without thinking by a person. Rather than showing how unfortunately detailed a reasoning program must be, it shows how careful such a program is.

The program must be able to convert one form of information to another form of that same information because of the presence and form of various clauses. Thus we also need

(55) ¬POSSJOBS(l(pj(x, y), l(pj(x, z), cnd))) | HASAJOB(x, y)

(56) ¬POSSJOBS(l(pj(x, y), l(pj(x, z), end))) | HASAJOB(x, z)

These two clauses permit a statement to be made in the HASAJOB predicate of which two jobs have been found for whom. Similarly, we need a clause that directly connects a person to a job when the other possible people who could hold that job have been eliminated. We thus have the clause

(57) ¬POSSPPL(l(pj(x, y), end)) | HASAJOB(x, y)

We come now to yet another trick. As we have commented, a reasoning program usually proceeds by seeking a proof by contradiction. In the minipuzzle we gave a mechanism for replacing the original question by one that in turn led to a formulation yielding a contradiction. For the full jobs puzzle, we present another mechanism. Our intention is to continually present alternative methods and various tricks so that, when working on some particular problem, you will be able to imitate one of them.

Since there are four people whose jobs are to be determined, we write a clause that lists that goal.

(58) STILLTODO(l(jobsof(Roberta), l(jobsof(Steve),

   l(jobsof(Thelma), l(jobsof(Pete), end)))))

Just as with the clauses that list the possible jobs for a person, we intend to remove each of the persons from this clause once that person's two jobs have been determined. Usually, when a person's two jobs have been determined, a unit POSSJOBS clause exists with exactly two jobs on the contained list. Thus we need a clause to convert the POSSJOBS information into some information permitting that person to be removed from the STILLTODO clause. The clause

(59) ¬POSSJOBS(l(pj(x, y), l(pj(x, z), end)))

| EQUAL(jobsof(x), crossed)

is just such a clause. The resulting information is used via demodulation to place "crossed" in the STILLTODO clause, thus permitting clause 52 to come into play. And that leaves the problem of knowing that a contradiction has been reached— reached when the STILLTODO clause is reduced to containing only "end". The clause

(60) ¬STILLTODO(end)

is just perfect.

You might ask: What happens if the reasoning program finds the two jobs of a person, but in terms of HASAJOB? Since the idea is then to cross that person off the STILLTODO clause, isn't a conversion clause necessary? Two different approaches could be used. The first approach, which is the one we shall use, depends on the following clause to derive a demodulator—a clause for converting information from one form to another.

(61) ¬HASAJOB(x, y) | EQUAL(pj(x, y), j(x, y))

The demodulator derived from clause 61 converts information expressed in the function pj to information expressed in the function j. When information is expressed in the function j, it means that a job has been paired with a person. Information in this form will eventually occur in clauses using POSSJOBS. Since we wish an automated reasoning program to know that the two jobs have been determined within POSSJOBS clauses, we add clauses that enable the program to collect such information at the left of the appropriate POSSJOBS clauses. We use the following demodulator to sort the information and force that expressed in the function j to the left.

(62) EQUAL(l(pj(x, y), l(j(x, z), w)), l(j(x, z), l(pj(x, y), w)))

If and when the two jobs for a person are determined and expressed in the function j, they will appear as the left two elements of a list in a clause involving POSSJOBS. The remaining possible jobs—expressed by use of the function pj—can be removed by the following clause.

(63) EQUAL(l(j(x, y), l(j(x, z), l(v, w))), l(j(x, y), l(j(x, z), end)))

To enable the program to cross a person off the STILLTODO list of tasks,

(64) ¬POSSJOBS(l(j(x, y), l(j(x, z), end)))

| EQUAL(jobsof(x), crossed)

is used.

Since a reasoning program can discover a person's jobs either directly in terms of HASAJOB or by eliminating jobs, a clause is needed to cope with this situation. If, for example, one of a person's jobs is discovered directly and the other by elimination, the information will be in POSSJOBS but partly in the function j and partly in the fact that the possible jobs list has been reduced to two elements. The clause

(65) $\neg$POSSJOBS(l(j(x, y), l(pj(x, z), end))) | HASAJOB(x, z)

is used to cope with this possibility. When this situation occurs, clause 59 will not be enough. But clause 65 can be used to derive the fact that the second job (z) is known, expressing it in terms of HASAJOB.

If you find this trick too complicated, or if you just do not like it, a second approach is given in Chapter 4. Instead, 28 clauses using $\neg$EQUALJ could be added, expressing the distinctness of the eight jobs.

EXERCISES

5. In this section, the concept of demodulation was introduced. The following problems are included to further your understanding of the concept.

   (a) Give the demodulator—unit equality clause—that could be used to cause a clause such as

   EQUAL(a, sum(4, sum(10, minus(10))))

   to be rewritten as

   EQUAL(a, sum(4, 0))

   Give the demodulator that might be used to cause this to be rewritten as

   EQUAL(a, 4)

   (b) Suppose that you represent a list of people with a term like

   l(Bob, l(Mary, l(Jim, end)))

   Further suppose that you wish such a term to be rewritten as

   notacceptable

   if the list contains Mary. For example,

   REPRESENTS(Edison, l(Bob, l(Mary, l(Linda, l(Jim, end)))))

   should be rewritten as

   REPRESENTS(Edison, notacceptable)

   Give the demodulators that could be used to make the rewriting occur.

6. Demodulation is frequently used to simplify a newly generated clause. Thus, as each new clause is deduced, it is simplified before any attempt is made to determine whether or not the clause represents significant new information. What unit clauses will be generated from

$$\text{EQUAL}(\text{sum}(a, \text{sum}(\text{times}(2, b), 4)), 0)$$

$$\text{EQUAL}(\text{sum}(\text{minus}(a), \text{sum}(b, \text{minus}(4))), 0)$$

$$\neg\text{EQUAL}(\text{sum}(x1, \text{sum}(y1, z1)), 0)$$

$$| \ \neg\text{EQUAL}(\text{sum}(x2, \text{sum}(y2, z2)), 0)$$

$$| \ \text{EQUAL}(\text{sum}(\text{sum}(x1, x2), \text{sum}(\text{sum}(y1, y2), \text{sum}(z1, z2))), 0)$$

assuming that the demodulators

$$\text{EQUAL}(\text{sum}(x, 0), x)$$

$$\text{EQUAL}(\text{sum}(0, x), x)$$

$$\text{EQUAL}(\text{sum}(x, \text{minus}(x)), 0)$$

$$\text{EQUAL}(\text{sum}(\text{minus}(x), x), 0)$$

are used to simplify the result?

3.2.2.4 Some of an automated reasoning program's proof.   What does the proof look like—a proof obtained by an automated reasoning program? Rather than give the entire proof, we give the fraction that finds Roberta's jobs, and leave the remainder as an exercise. The part of the proof given here is taken from an actual run of an automated reasoning program.

Before any new information is found by the reasoning program, it already knows that Roberta is not the boxer, nor the chef, nor the police officer. These clauses are used by the program to cross off certain possibilities from Roberta's list of jobs. For example,

From clauses 7 and 51:

(66) EQUAL(pj(Roberta, boxer), crossed)

which in effect says that the possibility of Roberta being a boxer can begin to be crossed off. We say "begin" because this equality must be used in turn to rewrite the list of Roberta's jobs, where the rewriting is by means of the process known as *demodulation*. What happens is that the possibility of Roberta being a boxer is first replaced by "crossed" in her list.

66 applied to 39:

(67a) POSSJOBS(l(pj(Roberta, chef), l(pj(Roberta, guard),

l(pj(Roberta, nurse), l(pj(Roberta, operator),

l(pj(Roberta, police), l(pj(Roberta, teacher),

l(pj(Roberta, actor), l(crossed, end)))))))))

But 67a is not actually kept as new information, for it immediately is further transformed by another equality through demodulation.

52 applied to 67a:

(67) POSSJOBS(l(pj(Roberta, chef), l(pj(Roberta, guard),

l(pj(Roberta, nurse), l(pj(Roberta, operator),

l(pj(Roberta, police), l(pj(Roberta, teacher),

l(pj(Roberta, actor), end))))))))

Clause 67 is an updated list of the possible jobs for Roberta. The job of boxer has truly been crossed off; that is, even the "crossed" expression has been removed. Clause 39 is then discarded by the reasoning program, since that clause has been outdated. If clause 39 were kept, then it would be around to be processed for other applications of reasoning and for other applications of rewriting by demodulation. Thus it is efficient to discard this old information, and replace it with the new updated clause 67.

Similarly, the job of chef is crossed off in two steps.

From clauses 22 and 51:

(68) EQUAL(pj(Roberta, chef), crossed)

From clause 67:

(69) POSSJOBS(l(pj(Roberta, guard),

l(pj(Roberta, nurse), l(pj(Roberta, operator),

l(pj(Roberta, police), l(pj(Roberta, teacher),

l(pj(Roberta, actor), end)))))))

Clause 69 is obtained from clause 67 by applying the demodulators 68 and 52, that is, by rewriting 67 with the aid of the equalities 68 and 52. As was the case in producing clause 67, the initial rewrite with clause 68 produces the following intermediate clause, clause 69a, which is not actually kept.

From clause 67:

(69a) POSSJOBS(l(crossed, l(pj(Roberta, guard),

l(pj(Roberta, nurse), l(pj(Roberta, operator),

l(pj(Roberta, police), l(pj(Roberta, teacher),

l(pj(Roberta, actor), end))))))))

Then, clause 69a is immediately rewritten using clause 52 to yield clause 69, the clause that is actually kept. Just as clause 67 forced clause 39 to be discarded in its favor, now clause 69 replaces clause 67. Clause 69 is a further updating of Roberta's possible jobs.

When the reasoning program then takes into account that Roberta cannot be the police officer, it obtains clause 70.

From clauses 23 and 51:

(70) EQUAL(pj(Roberta, police), crossed)

It then obtains clause 71, which replaces 69.

From clause 69:

(71) POSSJOBS(l(pj(Roberta, guard),

l(pj(Roberta, nurse), l(pj(Roberta, operator),

l(pj(Roberta, teacher),

l(pj(Roberta, actor), end))))))

At this point in the reasoning program's attack on the problem, the table of possibilities for all four people is the following, where an x indicates that the corresponding possibility is still in doubt.

	Roberta	Thelma	Steve	Pete
chef	no	x	x	x
guard	x	x	x	x
nurse	x	x	x	x
operator	x	x	x	x
police	no	x	x	x
teacher	x	x	x	x
actor	x	x	x	x
boxer	no	x	x	x

So far the reasoning program has been finding positive clauses, clauses that assert something is true. Now it finds negative clauses, clauses that assert something is **not** true.

From clauses 1 and 6:

(72) ¬MALE(Roberta)

From clauses 72 and 8:

(73) ¬HASAJOB(Roberta, nurse)

From clauses 72 and 9:

(74) ¬HASAJOB(Roberta, actor)

Since Roberta is female, she is not male, which in turn says she cannot be the nurse and cannot be the actor.

Clause 72, although exceedingly mundane, has further use.

From clauses 72 and 16:

(75) ¬HUSBAND(Roberta, y)

Roberta is nobody's husband. Since the variable y in clause 75 as always means for all y, y implicitly ranges over all people in the puzzle. In particular, clause 75 is true for the value of y that is the jobholder(chef). Clause 75 thus leads to

from clauses 75 and 14:

(76) ¬HASAJOB(Roberta, operator)

which, along with clauses 73 and 74, will be used to remove jobs from Roberta's list. First, the three are used to yield clauses 77 through 79 (not actually given here) that are similar to 66, 68, and 70. Then, 77 through 79 are used, as well as 52, to finally reduce Roberta's list to two jobs. We have

from clause 71:

(80) POSSJOBS(l(pj(Roberta, guard), l(pj(Roberta, teacher), end)))

which says that Roberta is the guard and the teacher.

Since the program has now discovered which two jobs Roberta holds, it should deduce information about which jobs are not held by Thelma, Steve, and Pete. It does. By using combinations of 53, 54, 25, 26, and 27 with 80, the program deletes various possible jobs from Thelma's, Steve's, and Pete's list of possible jobs. For example,

from clauses 80, 53, and 25:

(81) EQUAL(pj(Thelma, guard), crossed)

In this manner six clauses are obtained. Each of these clauses becomes a demodulator. And each of these demodulators then, with the help of 52, updates the remaining three job lists. Here is the corresponding table.

	Roberta	*Thelma*	*Steve*	*Pete*
chef	no	x	x	x
guard	yes	no	no	no
nurse	no	x	x	x
operator	no	x	x	x
police	no	x	x	x
teacher	yes	no	no	no
actor	no	x	x	x
boxer	no	x	x	x

Notice that the table still has 18 undecided combinations in it. The number 18 comes from the fact that there are three people whose jobs are still to be determined, and six possible jobs for each. The clauses reflect the 18 possibilities. The four original clauses that respectively gave the eight possible jobs for the four people (clauses 39 through 42) have now been replaced with clause 80 and the corresponding clauses for the other three people. One of the new clauses in the predicate POSSJOBS has two possibilities left on it, and so it will not be replaced by a later updated version. The other three each list six possibilities. Similarly, the original eight clauses giving the possible people that might hold a job have been replaced. Two of them now list a single possible jobholder for the job, while the other six each list three possibilities. Examination of the various clauses listing the various possibilities reveals the correctness of what is happening for the jobs puzzle. On the other hand, had we made a mistake, this same examination might uncover a flaw in the process, and thus point to some erroneous information given to the reasoning program at its start.

With one exception, the remainder of the proof is left for you. Clause 80 and clause 59 taken together yield

from clauses 80 and 59:

(82) EQUAL(jobs(Roberta), crossed)

which says in effect that Roberta's jobs have been determined, or, more to the point, that she is not a problem any more. Clause 82 becomes a demodulator, and

from clause 58:

(83) STILLTODO(l(jobsof(Steve), l(jobsof(Thelma), l(jobsof(Pete), end))))

results. Clause 83 replaces 58, as is typical of demodulation. In other words, 58 has been updated to 83, stating that only three people are left whose jobs need to be determined.

When you have filled in the rest of the proof that the reasoning program might find, you will have the clause

STILLTODO(end)

which contradicts clause 60. At that point in time, clauses will exist that contain the required information. In particular, the four clauses that list the possible jobs for the four people will each contain exactly two possibilities. You will have seen how an automated reasoning program's proof by contradiction looks in its entirety. You will have learned about the value of demodulation, that process that automatically rewrites and updates expressions. Such automatic updating contributes to efficiency by removing unneeded information, but also contributes by doing the updating immediately rather than waiting its turn—waiting until the reasoning program applies some inference rule. A reasoning program applies various criteria to decide which clause to focus on next—a topic we shall cover in the next chapter. This brings us to the discussion of the inference rule that was used throughout this proof by contradiction.

3.2.2.5 An inference rule.   Precisely what type of reasoning was in use throughout the preceding subsection? The rule, *UR-resolution*, requires that a set of simple facts called unit clauses be used to yield a unit. A *unit clause* is a clause that contains exactly one literal, while a *nonunit clause* contains more than one literal. For example, clauses 1, 2, and 7 are *unit* clauses, while clauses 9, 37, and 51 are *nonunit* clauses. Notice that the sign—the presence or absence of "¬"—is irrelevant to whether or not a clause is a unit clause or a nonunit clause.

UR-resolution considers a set of clauses simultaneously. One of the clauses must be a nonunit, while the remaining must each be a unit. Clause 73 is an example of an application of UR-resolution, but so is clause 81. The inference rule of UR-resolution only requires that the resulting new information be a unit clause, and cares nothing about the sign of the result.

In later chapters, you will learn about other inference rules such as *hyperresolution*—a rule that requires that the new information contain no **not** symbols. In contrast to UR-resolution, hyperresolution has no requirement about the number of literals in the result of application. You will also learn of an inference rule, *paramodulation*, that cares neither about the sign nor the number of literals in the result of application. This rule instead concentrates on treating various equality relations as "built in", and thus has other advantages than those of the preceding two inference rules.

EXERCISES

7. In this set of exercises we explore the differences between some of the common inference rules.

   (a) Consider the following two parent clauses.

   FATHER(Bob, Tom) | FATHER(Bob, John)
   ¬FATHER(Bob, Tom) | ¬MOTHER(Mary, Bob) | SISTER(Linda, Bob)

   The clause

   FATHER(Bob, John) | ¬MOTHER(Mary, Bob) | SISTER(Linda, Bob)

   must be a true statement, if the first two are true. Notice that it was formed by "canceling" the first literals in each of the parent clauses. Give an argument showing why the third clause (called a *resolvent*) must be true, if the parents are true.

   (b) Now consider the clauses

   ¬FATHER(x, y) | ¬FATHER(y, z) | GRANDFATHER(x, z)
   FATHER(Bob, John) | FATHER(Bob, Tom)

Give an argument to show that, if these two parent clauses are true, the resolvent

¬FATHER(Tom, z) | GRANDFATHER(Bob, z) | FATHER(Bob, John)

formed by unifying the first literal of the first parent with the second literal of the second parent, and then canceling the unified literals, must be true.

(c) Now, consider the following two clauses.

¬LESSTHAN(x, y) | ¬LESSTHAN(y, z) | LESSTHAN(x, z)
LESSTHAN(x, y) | EQUAL(x, y) | LESSTHAN(y, x)

Give an argument that the following clause must be true, if both of these parents are true.

¬LESSTHAN(y, z) | LESSTHAN(x, z) | EQUAL(x, y) | LESSTHAN(y, x)

(d) Calculate the resolvent that can be formed from the following two clauses.

LESSTHAN(distance(x, y), 2) | FAR(x, y)
¬LESSTHAN(distance(home, y), x)
   | ¬GREATERTHAN(distance(school, y), x)
   | CLOSER(y, home)

8. In the answers to problem 7 it was stated that parent clauses should not contain the same variable names. If they do contain the same names, might the resulting resolvent fail to always be true (assuming that the parent clauses are true) or might you fail to deduce a legitimate resolvent?

9. All of the problems above involve binary resolvents; that is, only two parent clauses are used to form the resolvent. The same techniques are used when hyperresolvents or UR-resolvents are formed. Before considering these inference rules in detail, let us divide all clauses into five classes.

   (1) Those clauses that are composed of a single positive literal assert that some basic statement is true. We call such a clause a positive unit.

   (2) Those clauses that are composed of a single negative literal assert that some basic statement is not true. Such a clause is called a negative unit.

   (3) A clause that contains more than one positive literal and no negative literals asserts that one of several properties must be true, no matter how the variables in the clause are instantiated. We call such a clause a positive nonunit clause. You may think of this clause as specifying a "case-analysis". In effect, such a clause asserts that one of several cases must be true.

   (4) A clause with both positive and negative literals is called a mixed clause. If you think of a mixed clause as converted from the *if-then* form, you may think of the negative literals as specifying conditions that, if satisfied, permit you to deduce the **or** of the corresponding instantiation of the positive literals. For example,

¬LESSTHAN(x, y) | ¬LESSTHAN(y, z) | LESSTHAN(x, z)

may be thought of as the translated form of

if LESSTHAN(x, y) **and** LESSTHAN(y, z)

then LESSTHAN(x, z)

This may be thought of as saying

> For all x, y, and z, if x is less than y, and if y is less than z, you may deduce that x is less than z.

(5) A clause with more than one literal but all of whose literals are negative literals is called a negative nonunit clause.

Using the five classes just given, classify each of the following clauses.

(a) $\neg$FATHER(x, y) | $\neg$FATHER(y, z) | GRANDFATHER(x, z)

(b) MOTHER(Mary, Linda) | SISTER(Mary, Linda)

(c) $\neg$FATHER(Bob, John)

(d) LESSTHAN(a, b) | LESSTHAN(b, c)

(e) LESSTHAN(0, distance(home, school))

(f) LESSTHAN(x, y) | LESSTHAN(y, x) | EQUAL(x, y)

(g) $\neg$LESSTHAN(x, 0) | GREATERTHAN(square(x), x)

(h) $\neg$ISFATHER(John) | $\neg$ISMOTHER(Linda)

10. Now we can study how hyperresolvents are formed. A single mixed clause, along with one or more positive clauses (unit or nonunit) are used to form the hyperresolvent. (The mixed clause can be replaced by a negative clause, unit or nonunit, but we are considering here the most typical case.) Remember that the negative literals in the mixed clause specify the conditions under which the positive literals can be deduced. Each positive clause either says that some condition is true (if the positive clause is a unit), or says that either the condition is true or another case must be considered (if the positive clause is a nonunit). To see this, consider the following set of clauses.

(1) $\neg$LESSTHAN(x, y) | $\neg$LESSTHAN(y, z) | LESSTHAN(x, z)

(2) LESSTHAN(a, b)

(3) LESSTHAN(0, a)

(4) LESSTHAN(b, 14) | LESSTHAN(c, b)

Consider the clause formed by unifying clause 3 with the first literal in clause 1 and 2 with the second literal in 1. The resulting clause is

> LESSTHAN(0, b)

In this case, the condition literals—the first two of clause 1—are satisfied with positive unit clauses. On the other hand, if clause 2 is unified with the first literal of clause 1 and the first literal of clause 4 is unified with the second literal in clause 1,

> LESSTHAN(c, b) | LESSTHAN(a, 14)

is deduced. By definition, each hyperresolvent contains only positive literals. It will be a unit, if there is only one positive literal in the mixed parent and each positive parent is a unit. Show which hyperresolvents can be formed from the following set of clauses.

(1) EMPLOYEE(Bob)

(2) EMPLOYEE(Joan)

(3) EMPLOYEE(Margo)

(4) OWNSCAR(Joan, 45312)

(5) OWNSCAR(Joan, 16289)

(6) OWNSCAR(Margo, 56283)

(7) TICKET(16289, $25, '11/16/82')

(8) TICKET(65302, \$15,'10/23/82')

(9) ¬OWNSCAR(Bob, 65302)

(10) ¬EMPLOYEE(xname)
| ¬OWNSCAR(xname, xlicense)
| ¬TICKET(xlicense, xamount, xdate)
| MUSTPAY(xname, xamount, xdate)

(11) ¬OWNSCAR(xname, xlicense)
| ¬TICKET(xlicense, xamount, xdate)
| GOTTICKET(xname)

(12) ¬GOTTICKET(Margo)

(13) OWNSCAR(Bob, 65302) | OWNSCAR(Margo, 65302)

11. UR-resolvents are formed by using one nonunit parent, and simultaneously canceling all but one literal in the nonunit parent against unit clauses. Thus, the deduced UR-resolvent must be a unit. What UR-resolvents can be generated from the set of clauses in problem 10?

3.2.2.6 Strategy.
How might an automated reasoning program attack the jobs puzzle intelligently? *Strategy.* What does strategy mean? Can the user be of any help to the program in planning the attack on the problem or puzzle?

An automated reasoning program can be intelligent by avoiding many fruitless paths. The way to avoid many of those paths is by using strategy. A strategy exists for a reasoning program that blocks its examination of various combinations of facts, and thereby blocks many paths of inquiry. This strategy, known as the *set of support strategy*, can be used very profitably in the jobs puzzle. In particular, it will block the program from looking at combinations of general facts, and instead force it to look at facts that are specific to the puzzle. Clauses 6 and 16 are general facts, while clause 7 is a fact specific to the jobs puzzle. Technically, the set of support strategy has you choose, from among the input clauses, some that you consider special. Since one is looking for a contradiction, the special clauses often involve the denial of the statement to be proved. You can think of the program as marking the special clauses with a star. With the set of support strategy, an automated reasoning program is not allowed to apply an inference rule to a combination of clauses unless at least one of them has a star. The new clauses that are deduced using this strategy are also given stars. More will be learned about this strategy in later chapters.

There are other strategies that are available to a reasoning program. For now, we shall discuss only the additional one known as *weighting*. With weighting, you can assist the reasoning program by contributing some of your experience, or by using your intuition, to give the program hints. Weighting in effect means assigning "weights" to various concepts. The lighter the weight, the sooner the program will look at the clause. For example, in the jobs puzzle, a good hint is to first concentrate on Roberta. This hint can be given to a reasoning program by setting the *weight* of Roberta smaller than the weight of any other person or job or concept. The program will then concentrate on Roberta and on facts involving Roberta in preference to anything else. What was actually done with an automated reasoning program to obtain a proof of the jobs puzzle was to assign Roberta the lowest weight, Thelma the next, Steve the next, and Pete the next. The other concepts in the puzzle were assigned higher but varying weights to reflect their conjectured importance to the puzzle's solution. The strategy of using weighting to assist and direct a reasoning program's attack on a problem will be illustrated again and again.

EXERCISES

12. Let us reconsider clauses 1 through 13 in problem 10. Suppose that only clause 8 is in the set of support. Give a proof, using hyperresolution constrained by this set of support, that the set of 13 clauses leads to a contradiction. Suppose that only clause 12 were in the set of support. Could a proof be generated using hyperresolution with this set of support?

13. Give a proof that the 13 clauses are contradictory using UR-resolution, and assuming that only clause 12 is in the set of support. Can you give a proof assuming that only clause 8 is in the set of support using UR-resolution? Can you give a proof assuming that only clause 13 is in the set of support?

3.2.3 Summary

So many clauses are necessary to represent the information in this puzzle because a number of interrelated concepts are involved. They include, female, male, husband, nurse, teacher, various people, and connections between them. In addition, a number of clauses are given that aid in the analog of crossing off elements from a list. Common knowledge allows much of that which was made explicit to occur, for a person, automatically—without thinking. Although it is somewhat tedious to be forced to write down so much common knowledge, once it is written it can be used repeatedly. Other and much deeper problems are covered in later chapters with the surprising property that many fewer clauses suffice. The number of clauses required to pin down the area of interest varies widely.

You were shown various processes that are available to an automated reasoning program. Demodulation, the process that automatically rewrites expressions by applying various equalities, was one key to the reasoning program's solution to the puzzle. Demodulation has many and varied uses, and is a rather complex process to grasp. In the succeeding chapters, many examples will be given to familiarize you with the mechanism and to demonstrate its value. Each illustration is intended to provide a template for use in problems only distantly related to the particular one under discussion. The uses found in this chapter are quite different from the later ones, and are given to suggest what can be done.

An application of weighting was discussed in this chapter. Weighting is a very general process that allows you to assign different degrees of significance to different concepts. By judicious assignments, you can help an automated reasoning program immensely, for an automated reasoning program's search is keyed to the weights assigned to the concepts. You can impose your intuition and/or experience on its attempt to find the solution to the problem. Weighting is also a very complex process and will be treated in ever-increasing detail in the succeeding chapters.

The inference rule employed in this chapter is *UR-resolution*. This inference rule requires that the reasoning program consider a set of clauses selected from all available clauses, all but one of which are unit clauses—all but one contain exactly one literal. The remaining clause contains a number of literals equal to one more than the number of unit clauses being used to draw the conclusion. UR-resolution requires that the conclusion be itself a unit clause—contain but one literal—and that the conclusion be obtained in one step by simultaneously considering the selected clauses. As you will learn, there are a number of other inference rules that the program sometimes employs. Each rule has its particular advantages.

Strategy was introduced, at least that of weighting and that of the set of support strategy. Only a hint was provided, an introduction to strategy. In the next chapter, the topic is covered more fully. Strategy is the key to an automated reasoning program attacking problems intelligently. We shall illustrate in the next chapter what can happen if strategy, such as the set of support strategy, is not used.

Both the minipuzzle and the full jobs puzzle might well be revisited. Each illustrates the way knowledge is given to an automated reasoning program, how such a program can reason from facts to conclusions, how a proof is obtained, and how the program can be intelligent.

3.3 Answers to Exercises

1. **(a)** x is replaced with Mike, giving

    WEALTHY(son(Mike))

    as the deduced clause.
    (b) Here x is replaced with brother(Jim), giving

    WEALTHY(son(brother(Jim)))

    as the deduced clause.
    (c) This time the second literal in the first clause is removed after instantiating x to brother(Mike). This gives

    ¬FATHER(George, brother(Mike))

    as the deduced clause.
    (d) In this case x is instantiated to 4, y to 4, and z to 0. This gives

    EQUAL(sum(0, 4), 4)

    as the deduced clause.
    (e) In this problem the two parent clauses have a variable with the same name. This is not desirable. Since the variables in a clause can be renamed without changing the logical meaning of the clause, this should be done first. When a clause is rewritten

with new names for its variables, the copy is called a *variant* of the original clause. Once a variant has been made, the same clause as in part (d) can be deduced.

2. No, the clause would not be deduced. Remember that the program does not have any idea what the symbols in a clause really mean. You must supply a clause like

$$\neg FATHER(x, y) \mid \neg FATHER(y, z) \mid GRANDFATHER(x, z)$$

to allow such a deduction to be made. You must realize that even with this added clause the program "knows" very little about the notion of "grandfather". For example, it does not know that a grandfather must be a male. It does not even know that a grandfather must be a person. So that you will always be aware of the fact, we continually warn you that the program must be told every significant detail about the meaning of a symbol, otherwise some deductions that you might wish to occur will not occur.

3. This is a reasonably complex problem, so let us take some time to answer it carefully. First, note that if x is instantiated to Bob, then

$$\neg PLAYER(y) \mid PAIR(Bob, y)$$

could be deduced from the first and fourth clauses. If y were instantiated to Bob, then

$$\neg PLAYER(x) \mid PAIR(x, Bob)$$

could be deduced (again using the first and fourth clauses as parents). Two similar clauses,

$$\neg PLAYER(y) \mid PAIR(Mary, y)$$

$$\neg PLAYER(x) \mid PAIR(x, Mary)$$

can be deduced from the second and fourth clauses. Still another clause,

$$PAIR(Bob, Bob)$$

can be deduced by instantiating both x and y to Bob. What is the justification for the claim that this last clause must be true, assuming that the first and fourth clauses are true? Similarly,

$$PAIR(Mary, Mary)$$

can be deduced from the second and fourth clauses. Now, if x is instantiated to Bob and y to Mary, you can form the hyperresolvent

$$PAIR(Bob, Mary)$$

from the first, second, and fourth clauses. Finally, by instantiating x to Mary and y to Bob, you can deduce

$$PAIR(Mary, Bob)$$

from the same three clauses. Since the predicate of the literal in the third clause does not match the predicate in any other literal, you could immediately determine that it could not be used to deduce any new clauses.

4. The answer is no. You may know that 1 times 1 is equal to the square of 1, but that cannot be logically deduced from the two parent clauses. There is no instantiation of x, y, and z that unifies the first literal of the second clause with the literal in the first clause. This is really not obvious, so notice what happens: x, y and z must all be made identical (all equal to x, for example) to make the first arguments of the literals identical. But then you reach the position that x (the instantiated value of z) must be made the same as square(x), an impossible feat.

5. The required demodulators are the following.
   (a) The clause

   $$EQUAL(sum(x, minus(x)), 0)$$

   should be used to make the first simplification. You could, of course, use

   $$EQUAL(sum(10, minus(10)), 0)$$

   but the more general clause is the preferable one. In the cases in which you would use such a demodulator, you would probably include

   $$EQUAL(sum(minus(x), x), 0)$$

   as well. The demodulator to simplify addition of 0 is

   $$EQUAL(sum(x, 0), x)$$

   Again, you would normally include the second demodulator,

   $$EQUAL(sum(0, x), x)$$

   to simplify addition of 0 on the left.
   (b) The three demodulators that are needed to collapse such a list are

   $$EQUAL(l(Mary, x), notacceptable)$$

   $$EQUAL(l(notacceptable, x), notacceptable)$$

   $$EQUAL(l(x, notacceptable), notacceptable)$$

6. Here the first unit clause that would be deduced is

   $$EQUAL(sum(sum(a, minus(a)), sum(sum(times(2, b), b), sum(4, minus(4)))), 0)$$

   This would simplify (by demodulation) to

   $$EQUAL(sum(times(2, b), b), 0)$$

   Similarly,

   $$EQUAL(sum(b, times(2, b)), 0)$$

   $$EQUAL(sum(sum(a, a), sum(sum(times(2, b), times(2, b)), sum(4, 4))), 0)$$

   $$EQUAL(sum(sum(minus(a), minus(a)), sum(sum(b, b), sum(minus(4), minus(4)))), 0)$$

   would also be produced after demodulation.

7. This problem is included to clarify why deducing resolvents leads to more true statements.
   (a) To show that the resolvent must be true (assuming that the parents are true), consider that FATHER(Bob, Tom) must be either true or false. If it is true, then the first literal

of the second clause must be false. In that case we know that the second or third literal of the second clause must be true—either ¬MOTHER(Mary, Bob) is true, or SISTER(Linda, Bob) is true. On the other hand, if FATHER(Bob,Tom) is false, FATHER(Bob,John) must be true; otherwise the first parent would be false. Thus, we can conclude that either

> One of the last two literals in the second parent is true

or

> The second literal in the first parent is true.

This is, of course, exactly what the resolvent means—one of the three literals must be true. In general, if you can find two clauses that contain literals that are identical, except that their signs are opposite, you may deduce the clause formed by collecting all of the other literals in the two clauses into one clause. Such a clause is called a *binary resolvent*.

(b) This problem is a more complex version of the preceding problem. First, note that unifying the two literals causes x to be instantiated to Bob, and y to be instantiated to Tom. Thus, the instance of the first parent that we need to look at is

$$\neg\text{FATHER}(\text{Bob}, \text{Tom}) \mid \neg\text{FATHER}(\text{Tom}, z) \mid \text{GRANDFATHER}(\text{Bob}, z)$$

Now this instance must be true, since an instance of a true statement is true. Now if the first literal of this instance and the second literal of the second parent clause are canceled, the resulting resolvent must be true based on an argument similar to the one we used in part (a).

(c) When you are forming a resolvent using two parent clauses that contain variables, you must rename the variables so that no variable occurs in both parents. After all, a variable only has relevance to the clause in which it occurs. In other words, the variables that occur in one clause should be given different names from those that occur in the other clause. To force this to be the case, you may have to create a variant (a copy with variables renamed) of the second clause. In this example, it turns out by accident that you get the same result, whether or not a variant of the second clause is used. You can argue as in part (b) to show that the resolvent follows from its parents. For any choice of the variables in the resolvent—for x, y, and z—either LESSTHAN(x, y) or ¬LESSTHAN(x, y) must be true. If LESSTHAN(x, y) is true, then either ¬LESSTHAN(y, z) or LESSTHAN(x, z) must be true. On the other hand, if ¬LESSTHAN(x, y) is true, then either EQUAL(x, y) or LESSTHAN(y, x) must be true. Thus, no matter what instantiation of x, y, and z is chosen, one of the literals in the resolvent must be true.

(d) This problem, unlike the last, requires that you compute a variant of the second clause before looking for a substitution that unifies the literals. If you do rename the variables in the second clause, say to x2, y2, and z2, you can obtain a resolvent similar to

> FAR(home, y2)
>
> | ¬GREATERTHAN(distance(school, y2), 2)
>
> | CLOSER(y2, home)

Of course the clause that you computed might be a variant of the one just given. Remember, two clauses that are the same, except that the variables have been renamed, are logically equivalent. Note, however, that the variables must be renamed consistently. In other words, all occurrences of a variable must be renamed to the same new name.

8. You will not be able to deduce a resolvent that might be false, while the parent clauses are true (assuming that you unify the literals that are canceled). However, if you fail to use a variant to keep the variable names distinct, you may not be able to deduce legitimate resolvents (as in problem 7).

9. (a) This is a mixed clause, since it has both positive and negative literals.
   (b) This is a positive nonunit clause. Notice that it represents a "case analysis"—either it is the case that Mary is Linda's mother, or Mary is Linda's sister.
   (c) This is a negative unit clause.
   (d) This is a positive nonunit clause.
   (e) This is a positive unit clause.
   (f) This is a positive nonunit clause.
   (g) This is a mixed clause.
   (h) This is a negative nonunit clause.

10. The hyperresolvents that can be formed are

From clauses 2, 5, 7, and 10:

(14) MUSTPAY(Joan, $25, '11/16/82')

From clauses 5, 7, and 11:

(15) GOTTICKET(Joan)

From clauses 1, 8, 10, and 13:

(16) OWNSCAR(Margo, 65302) | MUSTPAY(Bob, $15, '10/23/82')

From clauses 3, 8, 10, and 13:

(17) OWNSCAR(Bob, 65302) | MUSTPAY(Margo, $15, '10/23/82')

From clauses 8, 11, and 13:

(18) OWNSCAR(Margo, 65302) | GOTTICKET(Bob)

From clauses 8, 11, and 13:

(19) OWNSCAR(Bob, 65302) | GOTTICKET(Margo)

From clauses 9 and 13:

(20) OWNSCAR(Margo, 65302)

From clauses 9 and 17:

(21) MUSTPAY(Margo, $15, '10/23/82')

From clauses 9 and 19:

(22) GOTTICKET(Margo)

Notice that 22 contradicts a preceding clause, clause 12, so a contradiction results from assuming that clauses 1 through 13 are true.

11. Clauses 14, 15, and 20 from the set of hyperresolvents are also UR-resolvents. In addition

From clauses 8, 11, and 12:

(24) ¬OWNSCAR(Margo, 65302)

is a UR-resolvent that contradicts 20.

12. Assuming that only clause 8 is in the set of support, the proof is the following.

From clauses 8, 11, and 13:

(14) OWNSCAR(Bob, 65302) | GOTTICKET(Margo)

From clauses 9 and 14:

(15) GOTTICKET(Margo)

Now 15 contradicts 12. There is no solution, assuming that only clause 12 is in the set of support (using hyperresolution). In fact, no hyperresolvents can be generated.

13. The proof using UR-resolution with clause 12 as the only clause in the set of support is the following.

From clauses 12, 8, and 11:

(14) ¬OWNSCAR(Margo, 65302)

From clauses 14 and 13:

(15) OWNSCAR(Bob, 65302)

This clause contradicts clause 9. The proof, assuming that clause 8 is the only clause in the set of support, is identical. The proof, assuming that clause 13 is the only clause in the set of support, is the following.

From clauses 13 and 9:

(14) OWNSCAR(Margo, 65302)

From clauses 14, 8, and 11:

(15) GOTTICKET(Margo)

Clause 15 contradicts clause 12.

4

Alternative Representation

and Equality

PUZZLE OF 15

1	2	3	4
5	6	7	8
9	10	11	12
13	14	15	hole

Fifteen tiles, numbered from 1 through 15, rest in a four by four tray. The tiles can be slid up, down, left, or right, provided that the "hole" allows the move. If the numbered tiles are in a scrambled arrangement, can they be slid up, down, left, right until they are back in order as shown in the diagram?

Representing puzzles or problems to an automated reasoning program presents a paradox. On the one hand, the rules given in Chapter 2 are fairly rigid. You might therefore conclude that representing a problem would be easy—a unique representation would follow from applying the rules. On the other hand, as we saw in the representation of the jobs puzzle discussed in Chapter 3, there are in fact many alternative ways of representing information even within the constraints imposed by the rules. If you thought about the representation of the jobs puzzle as a model you could follow to represent your own puzzle or problem to an automated reasoning program, many of those decisions must have seemed arbitrary. How can you decide among these alternatives?

In this chapter we pause to give some information that will help you make such decisions. Unfortunately, we cannot give a simple algorithm for representing problems. Nor can we give ones for the representation-related issues of choosing a type of reasoning and picking a good strategy. For one thing, the field of automated reasoning is young, and many answers are therefore not yet available. For another, reasoning is so complicated that no pat way exists to cope with many situations. This latter observation is perhaps not surprising in view of the variety of problems that can be solved by automated reasoning programs.

However, we can illustrate various alternative forms of representation. Having seen these, you will be in a better position to invent your own. Solving new problems requires such invention. By comparing the advantages of one representation with those of another, you will see how to make an appropriate choice when confronted with more than one way of giving a problem to a program. In the final analysis, some of these choices are arbitrary, and one person may prefer one alternative while another prefers another. Having discussed some of the alternatives for representing the jobs puzzle, and having discussed the puzzle given at the beginning of this chapter, we return in Chapter 5 to the solution of additional puzzles.

4.1 Generality

In Section 3.1.5, we mentioned that the following eight clauses from the minipuzzle about jobs could be replaced by more general ones.

(1) HASAJOB(Roberta, nurse) | HASAJOB(Roberta, teacher)

(2) HASAJOB(Steve, nurse) | HASAJOB(Steve, teacher)

(3) ¬HASAJOB(Roberta, nurse) | ¬HASAJOB(Roberta, teacher)

(4) ¬HASAJOB(Steve, nurse) | ¬HASAJOB(Steve, teacher)

(5) HASAJOB(Roberta, teacher) | HASAJOB(Steve, teacher)

(6) HASAJOB(Roberta, nurse) | HASAJOB(Steve, nurse)

(7) ¬HASAJOB(Roberta, teacher) | ¬HASAJOB(Steve, teacher)

(8) ¬HASAJOB(Roberta, nurse) | ¬HASAJOB(Steve, nurse)

These eight clauses together say that Roberta and Steve are each a nurse or a teacher. These clauses prevent either person from holding more than one job, and force each to hold one of the two jobs.

This information could have been written in a more general form.

(9) HASAJOB(x, nurse) | HASAJOB(x, teacher)

(10) ¬HASAJOB(x, nurse) | ¬HASAJOB(x, teacher)

(11) HASAJOB(Roberta, y) | HASAJOB(Steve, y)

(12) ¬HASAJOB(Roberta, y) | ¬HASAJOB(Steve, y)

These four clauses together say that, for every person in the puzzle, the person is a teacher or a nurse. And they also say that, for every job in the puzzle, that job is held by Roberta or Steve. The four clauses also prevent anyone from holding more than one job, and prevent any job from being held by more than one person. Of course, which persons are involved in the puzzle is no longer explicit in clauses 9 and 10, as it is in clauses 1 through 8. No information is lost, however. What is perhaps more significant, no information is gained either. The only explicit constants that will ever be substituted for the variable x are those that appear somewhere in the clauses that represent the problem. As we shall see shortly, these constants are just Steve and Roberta.

You may have noticed that the case of two jobs and two people is particularly simple. As a result, the clauses 9 through 12 are deceptively similar. What do the clauses look like that express that there are three jobs and three people, each holding one and only one job? Even though such a statement does not directly play a role in either the minipuzzle or the full jobs puzzle, it is interesting to see the clauses and how they are derived.

The general statement that any of three people has one of the jobs nurse, teacher, or chef is still straightforward. It can be expressed formally as: **for every** person in the puzzle, that person has the job of nurse **or** that person has the job of teacher **or** that person has the job of chef

(9a) HASAJOB(x, nurse) | HASAJOB(x, teacher) | HASAJOB(x, chef)

Expressing that each of the three has only one of the jobs is more interesting. Part of this fact can be stated formally as: **for every** person in the puzzle, **if** that person has the job of nurse, **then** that person does **not** have the job of teacher **and** that person does **not** have the job of chef. This statement can be converted to clauses using the rules of Chapter 2 for both **if-then** and for how to handle the **and** in the **then** (distributive laws). The result is two clauses

(10a) ¬HASAJOB(x, nurse) | ¬HASAJOB(x, teacher)

(10b) ¬HASAJOB(x, nurse) | ¬HASAJOB(x, chef)

The rest of the fact can be expressed formally by two other **if-then** statements with teacher and chef as the job held, respectively. Each of these yields a pair of clauses similar to 10a and 10b, for example,

(10a) ¬HASAJOB(x, teacher) | ¬HASAJOB(x, nurse)

(10c) ¬HASAJOB(x, teacher) | ¬HASAJOB(x, chef)

Although there are two clauses labeled 10a whose difference is the order of their literals, their meanings are the same because of a fundamental property of the operator **or**. The logical operator of **or** (likewise the logical operator of **and**) is *commutative*—the order of literals connected by **or** is irrelevant to meaning in logic. And so it is in automated reasoning programs. The order of the literals in a clause can have a small effect on efficiency.

The third **if-then** statement yields two further clauses, but this time both are redundant. Thus, only three clauses involving negative HASAJOB predicates are needed, because of the symmetry of the **or** formulation discussed in Chapter 2. We can obtain clause 11a and clauses 12a, 12b, and 12c corresponding to clauses 11 and 12, respectively, in a similar fashion.

Note the asymmetry evident in formulating this fact. The statement that each person has one of the jobs, which is naturally an **or** statement, produces one clause, whereas the statement that each person has *only* one of the jobs, which is naturally three **if-then** statements, produces six clauses (three of which are redundant), because of the **and**s in the conclusions.

Incidentally, you can double-check this formulation by thinking about the conclusions that can be drawn from the clauses and comparing them with your intuition about the problem. Whatever job a person is determined to hold, it must be possible to conclude that the person does not hold the other two. A moment's thought shows that clauses 10a through 10c are adequate for this task. It is always worthwhile to think in this way about the clauses you are writing. Doing so will help to protect you from omitting some clauses, and hence some information needed to pin down a concept. Another test for such an omission is to examine the output from a reasoning program to see if some obvious conclusions are absent. Obviously, when we formulate a problem, we wish the set of clauses we write to be adequate to draw all needed conclusions. Unfortunately, there is no way to formalize the idea of "all necessary conclusions".

Returning to the discussion of clauses 9 through 12, let us see how the general information contained in them makes the specific information contained in clauses 1 through 8 superfluous. What a reasoning program can do with the specific, it can do with the general. This point can be illustrated by revisiting the minipuzzle and by concentrating on the first proof for finding Roberta's and Steve's jobs, this time using clauses 9 through 12. From the minipuzzle, we add the information needed to complement them (clauses 9 through 13 from Section 3.1.1).

(13) $\neg$HASAJOB(x, nurse) | MALE(x)

(14) FEMALE(x) | MALE(x)

(15) $\neg$FEMALE(x) | $\neg$MALE(x)

(16) FEMALE(Roberta)

(17) MALE(Steve)

With 9 through 17, an automated reasoning program could find the following facts.

From clauses 16 and 15:

(18) ¬MALE(Roberta)

From clauses 18 and 13:

(19) ¬HASAJOB(Roberta, nurse)

From clauses 19 and 9:

(20) HASAJOB(Roberta, teacher)

From clauses 19 and 11:

(21) HASAJOB(Steve, nurse)

Again, as in Chapter 3, a reasoning program has found that Roberta is the teacher and Steve is the nurse. In fact the two deductions look very much alike, except that the role of 1 is played by 9 and that of 6 by 11. Clauses 9 and 11 are, respectively, more general than 1 and 6. These two more general clauses serve just as well as their more specific counterparts. Thus, as far as a reasoning program is concerned, nothing is lost by replacing the specific with the general. Actually, generality in clauses is preferable.

The preference for generality is based on efficiency. In order to reason, both a person and a reasoning program must search among the facts at hand to find those that go together to yield conclusions. When a general fact can be used to replace several specific ones, there are fewer facts to be searched. Thus, the fewer the facts, the quicker the needed facts will be found.

Additional efficiency is gained because of the way an automated reasoning program manages information. At each reasoning step, an automated reasoning program prefers to keep general information rather than specific, when the general information covers the specific. For example, if a reasoning program found clause 9 during a search for a solution to a problem, and then found clause 1, it would immediately discard clause 1. Equally, if it found clause 1 first and then 9, it would again discard clause 1. The justification for discarding clause 1 in favor of clause 9 is that 1 can be obtained from 9 merely by replacing the variable x in 9 by Roberta. In other words, 1 is an *instance* of 9. A reasoning program discards all *instances* of existing or new information, retaining the more general fact. This is reminiscent of a person's remembering a general rule, and not bothering about remembering individual applications of it. Thus, including a general fact in preference to specific ones may permit more information to be discarded during reasoning, thereby further reducing the facts at hand and the search time.

The means for discarding less general information in preference to more general is a process called *subsumption*. Clause 9 *subsumes* clause 1. But the process of subsumption is more general than just discarding specific instances. An automated reasoning program can use subsumption not only to discard instances but also to discard other information that is less general than some retained fact. For example, in solving the minipuzzle it immediately discards clauses 3 and 8

(3) ¬HASAJOB(Roberta, nurse) | ¬HASAJOB(Roberta, teacher)

(8) ¬HASAJOB(Roberta, nurse) | ¬HASAJOB(Steve, nurse)

when it finds

from clauses 18 and 13:

(19) ¬HASAJOB(Roberta, nurse)

Can you guess what the justification for discarding both 3 and 8 in favor of 19 is?

The answer is that 3 and 8 are weaker statements than 19. Clause 19 says (with certainty) that Roberta is not the nurse, while the others just admit this as a possibility. In particular, 3 and 8 can be true because of the other literal—the one different from ¬HASAJOB(Roberta, nurse). More information is contained in the statement that Roberta is not the nurse than in the statement that she is not the nurse or not the teacher, for example. (In the formal section later in this book, we shall explain why, under most circumstances, subsumption is *complete*—why using it does not block finding the solutions to problems. Automated reasoning relies on an abundance of strategies and—no surprise to some—there are combinations of strategies and inference rules in which one cannot cavalierly use subsumption without encountering incompleteness.)

Since we wish to give an automated reasoning program as much power as possible, and since reducing the number of facts at hand tends to increase its power, it makes sense to discard the less informative statements. The process of subsumption thus, in most cases, enables a reasoning program to discard weaker or less general information in favor of stronger or more general. In particular, the process purges duplicate information. Subsumption is yet one more powerful process resulting in increased effectiveness of automated reasoning programs.

There is another process that purges duplicate information, but information that is duplicated within a single clause, not between two clauses. In ordinary everyday language, you do not say "Roberta is a teacher or a nurse or a nurse" The repetition of "or a nurse" serves no purpose. All of the information contained in this absurd sentence is contained in "Roberta is a teacher or a nurse". In automated reasoning, the same applies. If a literal occurs more than once in a clause, the extra copies are automatically deleted from the clause, by a process called *collapsing duplicate literals*. The extra copies, if kept, would simply contribute to inefficiency and to drawing conclusions that serve no purpose.

In any event, the rule for choosing between a general and a specific representation for facts is simple: Choose the general representation. Reject clauses 1 through 8 in favor of 9 through 12. Simply having fewer clauses is not nearly the whole story —there is power in generality. As compared with the more specific clauses, the more general ones allow the discarding, by means of subsumption, of more information.

EXERCISES

Because of the importance of the concept of subsumption, we include a number of exercises illustrating its various uses and aspects.

1. For each of the following pairs of clauses, determine whether or not one of the pair of clauses subsumes the other and, if subsumption does occur, which subsumes which.
   (a) EQUAL(Sum(1, minus(1)), 0)
       EQUAL(Sum(x, minus(x)), 0)
   (b) EQUAL(Sum(1, minus(1)), 0)
       EQUAL(Sum(minus(x), x), 0)
   (c) FATHER(Tom, Bob) | FATHER(Jim, Bob)
       FATHER(Jim, Bob)
   (d) FATHER(Tom, Bob) | FATHER(Jim, Bob)
       ¬FATHER(Jim, Bob)
   (e) FATHER(Tom, Bob) | FATHER(Jim, Bob)
       FATHER(Jim, Bob) | FATHER(Ron, Bob) | FATHER(Tom, Bob)
   (f) FATHER(Tom, Bob) | FATHER(Jim, Bob)
       FATHER(Ron, Bob) | FATHER(Bob, Mary) | FATHER(Tom, Bob)

2. Having presented a number of specific cases where one clause is more "powerful" than another, we now give a more precise definition of subsumption. A clause C1 subsumes another clause C2 if you can instantiate the variables in C1 in such a way that the resulting literals all occur in C2. Thus,

   LE(x, y) | LE(y, x)

   subsumes

   LE(a, b) | LE(b, a)

   since instantiating x to a and y to b makes the two clauses identical. Perhaps less obvious is the fact that the first clause subsumes

   LE(2, 2)

   That this is the case can be seen by instantiating x and y both to 2, making both of the literals identical to LE(2,2). Do you see why the given definition captures all of the cases of "more powerful" that we have discussed so far? For the following pairs of clauses, determine which subsumes which.
   (a) CONNECTED(x, power) | CONNECTED(power, y) | DISCONNECTED(y, x)
       CONNECTED(w, power) | CONNECTED(power, z) | DISCONNECTED(w, z)
   (b) CONNECTED(x, power) | CONNECTED(power, y) | DISCONNECTED(y, x)
       CONNECTED(a, power) | DISCONNECTED(b, a) | CONNECTED(power, b)
   (c) CONNECTED(x, power) | CONNECTED(power, y) | DISCONNECTED(y, x)
       CONNECTED(a, power) | DISCONNECTED(b, a)

    (d) CONNECTED(x, power) | CONNECTED(power, y) | DISCONNECTED(y, x)
        DISCONNECTED(power, power) | CONNECTED(power, power)
    (e) M(a) | M(b) | M(c)
        M(c) | M(a)

4.2 Tricks versus the Straightforward Approach

To aid in solving the full jobs puzzle in Chapter 3, we showed how to get an automated reasoning program to "cross off" possibilities from a list. The method is based on a "trick"—on using equality in a somewhat nonstandard way. We used a similar trick to allow the program to figure out that the jobs for all four persons had been determined. As in the other trick, equality plays a key role. In both cases, the equalities are used as demodulators. A reasonable question is: Can the problem be solved without using the tricks—can it be solved directly with some inference rule, without using demodulation and the associated equalities? Second, assuming it can be solved, which way should you prefer, the straightforward way or the trick? And third, should one representation be used at one time, and the other at another time?

    To see how to avoid the tricks and obtain a straightforward representation, first look closely at what the full jobs puzzle says. It says that there are eight jobs and each person holds two of them. An immediate consequence is that once we know six particular jobs that a person does not hold, we know the two jobs that person does hold. Moreover, as they are used here, the words imply that each job is held by some person. Thus, the puzzle also says that we know a particular person holds a particular job once we have proved that the other three people do not hold that job. The second of these two facts is the easier to represent.

    (1) HASAJOB(Roberta, nurse) | HASAJOB(Thelma, nurse)

        | HASAJOB(Steve, nurse) | HASAJOB(Pete, nurse)

This clause says that one of the four people holds the job of nurse. If an automated reasoning program finds that Roberta is not the nurse, that Thelma is not the nurse, and that Pete is not the nurse,

    (2) ¬HASAJOB(Roberta, nurse)

    (3) ¬HASAJOB(Thelma, nurse)

    (4) ¬HASAJOB(Pete, nurse)

then the program can remove them from the possible jobholders of nurse, obtaining

    (5) HASAJOB(Steve, nurse)

as the result of applying UR-resolution to clauses 1 through 4.

If you take the approach to representation exemplified by clause 1, you must supply seven other clauses to a reasoning program. Each of the required clauses holds a job fixed and varies the person who might hold it. Since there are eight jobs, there are eight such clauses. However, as we discussed in the preceding section, it is preferable to make use of generality. A clause can be written that is more general than each of the eight and that captures precisely what is needed.

(6) HASAJOB(Roberta, y) | HASAJOB(Thelma, y)

| HASAJOB(Steve, y) | HASAJOB(Pete, y)

Clause 6 says that for any job in the puzzle—any of the eight—the job is held by one of the four named people. Notice that clause 6 subsumes clause 1 and each of the variants of 1 that would be needed for the other seven jobs.

Clause 1 holds a job fixed and varies the person who might hold it, as we said. So also does clause 6. What might be confusing about clause 6 is that a variable appears in the position of the job that is held fixed. But notice that the *same* variable appears in each literal, thus fixing the same job throughout the clause when it is instantiated.

This more general clause performs the function of the less general one when an inference rule is applied. From clause 6 and clauses 2 through 4, UR-resolution again yields clause 5. What happens is that the variable y in 6, in order that 6 and clauses 2 through 4 can be used together to yield a conclusion, is instantiated or replaced by nurse.

With the one fact in the puzzle taken care of—the fact that says that every job is held by a person among the four—let us consider the other fact. The translation into clauses of that fact—the fact that the elimination of six jobs for a person implies that the person holds each of the other two—can be accomplished by a number of steps. We shall illustrate the translation schematically, by giving a pattern for it. First, temporarily "number" the eight jobs job1 to job8, to make them easier to keep track of. Second, state the fact more formally: **if** a person does **not** have job1 **and** does **not** have job2 **and** does not have ... job6, **then** the person has job7 **and** job8. Third, convert this statement to clauses using the rules of Chapter 2 for both **if-then** and for how to handle the **and** in the **then**. This step produces two pattern clauses

(7) HASAJOB(x, job1) | HASAJOB(x, job2) | HASAJOB(x, job3)

| HASAJOB(x, job4) | HASAJOB(x, job5) | HASAJOB(x, job6)

| HASAJOB(x, job7)

(8) HASAJOB(x, job1) | HASAJOB(x, job2) | HASAJOB(x, job3)

| HASAJOB(x, job4) | HASAJOB(x, job5) | HASAJOB(x, job6)

| HASAJOB(x, job8)

They have only positive literals because **not** of **not** cancels. Notice that we have gone immediately to the general form, rather than listing a particular person. The variable x means for any person—any of the four in the puzzle. Fourth, in the two pattern clauses 7 and 8, replace jobs 1 through 8 consistently by the actual jobs in the puzzle —nurse, teacher, and so on.

Conceptually, the given steps must be repeated for all subsets of six jobs from the set of eight. Since there are 28 such subsets, there would be 56 clauses. However, careful inspection of the 56 clauses shows that only eight distinct clauses result—each clause appears seven times. As in the discussion in Section 4.1 of the three people and three jobs, the seven clauses would not have the literals in the same order, but they do have the same meaning. Thus, even if all 56 were included, subsumption would discard all but eight. One might as well write only those eight to begin with. From a more intuitive view (as well as from the symmetry apparent in clauses 7 and 8), a total of eight clauses is all that you might expect—order is unimportant and each omits exactly one of the eight jobs in the puzzle.

We have now shown how to replace the "crossing-off" trick relying on a list function and on demodulation by a straightforward representation relying on standard clauses and on the standard inference rule of UR-resolution. We are left with the problem of replacing the trick used to inform the program that it has solved the puzzle. We are, of course, also left with the problem of making certain changes to other clauses to match the change in representation as compared with that of Chapter 3.

Since the object of the puzzle is to determine which two jobs are held by each of the four people, we can use the predicate HASTWOJOBS.

(9) $\neg$HASTWOJOBS(Roberta, x1, x2) | $\neg$HASTWOJOBS(Thelma, x3, x4)

| $\neg$HASTWOJOBS(Steve, x5, x6) | $\neg$HASTWOJOBS(Pete, x7, x8)

| SOLVED(puzzle)

This clause says that, if for any eight jobs x1 to x8 you know that Roberta has two and Thelma has two and Steve has two and Pete has two, then the puzzle is solved.

Since the predicate in this clause is HASTWOJOBS, we need a clause to connect the information in HASAJOB to information in HASTWOJOBS. For example, if we know that Roberta HASAJOB of teacher and HASAJOB of guard, we need a clause to convert this information to HASTWOJOBS of teacher and guard. We must be careful that the conversion only takes place after two *distinct* jobs have been found. Of course, we prefer to write a single clause to cover all four people.

(10) $\neg$HASAJOB(x, y) | $\neg$HASAJOB(x, z) | EQUALJ(y, z)

| HASTWOJOBS(x, y, z)

This clause is perfect. Notice the literal EQUALJ(y, z). That literal has no **not** sign because the clause says, **if** a person x has a job y **and** has a job z **and** y is **not** equal to z, **then** the person x has the two jobs y and z. Again, the **not** of **not** canceling rule comes into play. By having this equality literal present, the program is protected from mistakenly concluding that a person's two jobs are known when only one is known.

Naturally, using this clause forces us to include clauses that specifically state that the various jobs taken two at a time are different from each other. Two such clauses are

(11) ¬EQUALJ(nurse, teacher)

(12) ¬EQUALJ(chef, nurse)

Since there are eight jobs to be separated, we need 56 such pairs of clauses to state all the differences. Of course, we know that equality relationships are *symmetric*—that if EQUAL(a, b), then EQUAL(b,a) and vice versa. If the program has symmetry of equality built in, and if it can be extended to the EQUALJ predicate, then just 28 individual clauses will suffice.

One last task remains. With the various inequality clauses and the clauses to convert from HASAJOB to HASTWOJOBS, the program is in a position to deduce the unit clause that says that the puzzle is solved

SOLVED(puzzle)

When a reasoning program finds this clause, it should know that the problem has been completed. Thus, we must include

(13) ¬SOLVED(puzzle)

to enable the reasoning program to signal "contradiction". When this contradiction has been found, all four people will have had their jobs determined. Inspection of the output of the program will quickly tell you who holds which jobs. Simply search for the unit clauses that involve the predicate HASTWOJOBS.

In this section, you have learned of a straightforward way to represent certain information for the full jobs puzzle, avoiding the tricks used in Chapter 3. There, tricks using lists and demodulation were employed to automatically cross off combinations of jobs and persons who were known not to hold that job. Here, you learned that such tricks are not required to solve this problem with an automated reasoning program—that suitable clauses and the standard inference rule of UR-resolution can be used to cross off the various combinations.

Why were both approaches discussed? What are the advantages of each? How should you choose between them, especially when confronted with a new puzzle or problem?

The most obvious difference between the two approaches is the number of clauses that must be written if the straightforward is chosen over the tricky. In more complex puzzles or problems, you may find it most unpleasant to write the extra clauses, for their number can be prohibitive when compared to employing tricks of the kind used in Chapter 3. In the straightforward approach, even if symmetry of equality is built into the reasoning program, 28 clauses are required to express the fact that the eight jobs are distinct jobs. If there were 20 jobs, then 190 such clauses would be needed. (If symmetry of equality is not built in, expressing distinctness requires 56 and 380 clauses, respectively.) The inconvenience of preparing so many clauses can be overwhelming.

The inclusion of many extra clauses in order to avoid using a trick has a side effect. The extra clauses reduce the effectiveness and efficiency of a reasoning program. Their presence affects various processes negatively. For example, the process of subsumption, which removes redundant information, is forced to compare each new item of information to all of the clauses that might be relevant. Extra clauses slow up this process. Also, any of the extra clauses may become the focus of the reasoning program's attention, delaying its focusing on those that are the key to the problem. One of the key processes that affects the performance of a reasoning program is the process that chooses the clause on which to focus next. Even if the extra clauses are relegated to lesser importance and thus never become the object of direct focus, they still are present to participate in many paths of inquiry. The more clauses that are available for that purpose, the greater the potential that the reasoning program will explore extraneous paths.

The argument is, however, far from being one-sided. For the person formulating the problem, the straightforward approach is easier to prepare and follow, is less prone to some errors of formulation, is easier to modify, and is easier to control (although less complete control can be exercised) than the tricky one. For example, the conclusions made by a reasoning program employing the straightforward approach are more obvious, thus making it easier to detect that something has been left out of the original statement of the problem.

Nevertheless, we recommend the approach of Chapter 3. The basis for the recommendation is scheduling and separation of tasks. The order in which a reasoning program selects facts on which to focus has an overwhelming effect on its probability of success in reaching the objective. Some tasks are best done as asides, as automatic so that they do not interrupt the main search for important information. When you work with pencil and paper on a puzzle like the full jobs puzzle, you update your information by simply placing appropriate marks in the various squares to indicate who has which job and who cannot have which job. Such updating is often done automatically by a person, as an aside without thought. An automated reasoning program, as you learned in Chapter 3, can do the same thing if you choose an appropriate representation of the problem. By taking advantage of demodulation, we can make the crossing-off tasks, which might be regarded as "housekeeping" operations, happen without interfering with the rest of the reasoning process. The program automatically keeps a current record of information, and, more important, it is less distracted from the real problem of finding new facts.

Insight is required to replace the straightforward approach with the appropriate demodulators, but a sharp increase in reasoning efficiency results. The gain in efficiency comes from the fact that the updating does not have to wait its turn to be carried out by the inference mechanism. A reasoning program chooses in order, according to some rules, each new fact on which to focus. With the straightforward approach, each updating fact must take its turn for consideration by the inference rule(s) being used. With the tricky approach, demodulation automatically uses the new information to update at the end of each inference.

To summarize, a trade-off exists between the two approaches. In the straight-forward, some control is easier to exercise, but overall less control exists than with the one that relies on tricks. With the approach that relies on tricks, more effort and more insight are required in the formulation, but more effectiveness results. In choosing the tricky, there is in some sense also a trade-off of more complexity within clauses for having fewer clauses.

4.3 Equality

We have just shown why you might choose to employ an approach to representation that deemphasizes the straightforward. We now show you why you might choose a representation that emphasizes the natural. In Chapter 3, a mechanism depending on equality was used to automatically cope with tasks that a person might treat as asides. That mechanism, demodulation, permits an automated reasoning program to rephrase information by substituting one expression for another. In the full jobs puzzle, we instruct the program to substitute the expression exp for the expression l(crossed,exp), whenever l(crossed,exp) occurs and regardless of the form of exp. The instruction takes the form of supplying clause 52

(52) $EQUAL(l(crossed, x), x)$

as a demodulator. Since a demodulator automatically rephrases a statement when the demodulator is applicable, and since a variable x in a clause is interpreted as "for all x", clause 52 is what is needed.

Such automatic substitutions frequently occur in problem solving. While in the full jobs puzzle such substitutions occur as asides, they can also occur as key steps in the reasoning. For example, from the fact that Ted's sister's husband is Bob, and from the fact that Ted's sister is Mary, you can conclude that Mary's husband is Bob. The conclusion is obtained simply by substituting Mary for Ted's sister. In clause form, we have

EQUALP(husband(sister(Ted)), Bob)

EQUALP(sister(Ted), Mary)

EQUALP(husband(Mary), Bob)

where the third clause is obtainable from the first two. Although demodulation could be used to produce the third clause, a more general mechanism is needed when the following situation occurs.

From the fact that a person's father is older than the person, and from the fact that Jack's father is Ralph, you can immediately conclude that Ralph is older than Jack. An automated reasoning program can draw the same conclusion if given the following clauses and if the appropriate inference rule is employed.

Fact: A person's father is older than the person

OLDERTHAN(father(x), x)

Fact: Jack's father is Ralph

EQUALP(father(Jack), Ralph)

Conclusion: Ralph is older than Jack

OLDERTHAN(Ralph, Jack)

Since demodulation does not have the power to cope with this situation, a new inference rule is needed. But why is demodulation not sufficient?

Demodulation is not the mechanism that enables a reasoning program to draw the conclusion, for demodulation applies a more general fact to a less general fact. To draw the conclusion that Ralph is older than Jack requires the reverse. The variable x in the term father(x), as well as all other occurrences of x, must be first replaced by Jack to then permit the substitution of Ralph for father(Jack). Thus, if a reasoning program is to draw such conclusions, a mechanism other than demodulation is needed.

The needed mechanism is the inference rule called *paramodulation*. Conclusions that require substituting one expression for another can be made by using paramodulation. Even further, as in the preceding example, conclusions that require variables to be replaced to then permit a substitution can be made with paramodulation. On the one hand, demodulation requires that the variable replacement paving the way for the substitution take place only in the demodulator and not in the expression for which substitution takes place. On the other hand, paramodulation allows variable replacement in either or both the equality and the expression to which the equality is being considered for application. As the following example shows, this extra freedom enables a reasoning program using paramodulation to draw surprisingly strong conclusions in one step.

For example, from the clauses

EQUAL(sum(0, x), x)
EQUAL(sum(y, minus(y)), 0)

paramodulating *from* the first *into* the second yields

EQUAL(minus(0), 0)

as the (commonly used) result. A somewhat more complex illustration is provided by applying paramodulation to the clauses

EQUAL(sum(x, minus(x)), 0)
EQUAL(sum(y, sum(minus(y), z)), z)

where the first clause is the *from* clause, and the second the *into*. The result of the paramodulation

EQUAL(sum(y, 0), minus(minus(y)))

is a clause that says that $y + 0 = -(-y)$. Do you see how this third clause is obtained from the preceding two—what the variable replacement is that, when made, causes $sum(x, minus(x))$ in the first clause to become identical with $sum(minus(y), z)$ in the second? Do you also see what term in the second clause is being substituted for? The variable replacement that unifies these two terms consists of replacing x by $minus(y)$, and replacing z by $minus(minus(y))$. The third clause is then obtained by replacing $sum(minus(y),minus(minus(y)))$ by 0 in the second (modified) clause and, of course, replacing z by $minus(minus(y))$ also.

The clause containing the equality literal that justifies the substitution is called the *from* clause. The clause containing the literal that contains the expression being substituted for is called the *into* clause. As with demodulation, paramodulation can act directly on an expression regardless of how deeply it occurs in a literal. In the preceding example, the expression, $sum(minus(y), z)$, being replaced is a subargument of the first argument of the literal in question. The capacity to substitute directly deep inside some literal is one of the reasons for recommending the use of this inference rule over other inference rules. As with any inference rule, you will learn in the next section that paramodulation is not automatically applied to every expression as demodulation is. Rather it must wait its turn, or, more accurately, each clause must wait its turn to be chosen based on various criteria. One other essential difference between demodulation and paramodulation is that the former only retains the final form of the information, while the latter does not discard the original clause into which the substitution has occurred.

We now turn to the puzzle given at the beginning of this chapter to illustrate the value of paramodulation. In that puzzle, you are presented with a scrambled set of 15 numbered tiles within a four by four tray. The tiles are numbered from 1 through 15, which leaves space for one more tile—hence a hole exists. You are allowed to slide the tiles up, down, left, or right, with the goal of eventually putting them in order.

Puzzle of 15

1	2	3	4
5	6	7	8
9	10	11	12
13	14	15	hole

For example, you might be presented with the following configuration of tiles.

Puzzle of 15

1	6	2	4
5	hole	3	8
9	10	7	11
13	14	15	12

To submit this type of puzzle to an automated reasoning program, the starting configuration must be represented. Next, the possible moves of the hole must be represented, for moving a tile in effect moves the hole. The representation of moves must not allow the hole to move out of the tray. Thus, for example, if in some configuration on the way to achieving the ordered goal the hole is placed on the righthand edge, only three moves must be permitted from this state. If the hole is in a corner, then only two moves are permissible. Finally, we must provide a means for the reasoning program to know when the puzzle has been solved.

4.3.1 The Puzzle in Miniature

As we did in Chapter 3 with the full jobs puzzle, let us begin with a much simpler version. We are presented with a two by two tray in which three consecutively numbered tiles are in a scrambled arrangement. Let us take the case in which the first row consists of the hole followed by the 1 tile, and the second consists of the 3 tile followed by the 2 tile. As with the full jobs puzzle, we use the list function l, and list the tiles in order from left to right starting with row 1. We write

(1) STATE(l(hole, l(n(1), l(end, l(n(3), l(n(2), end))))))

to represent the initial state of the tray of tiles. We use the expression "end" as usual to mark the end of the list, but also to mark the end of a row of tiles. The second usage of "end" prevents the reasoning program from making an illegal move. Expressions such as n(1) can be read "numbered 1". Use of the function n will be seen to enable the program to avoid considering certain moves.

Similarly, we can immediately use this notation to provide the program with a means for determining that the puzzle has been solved.

(2) ¬STATE(l(n(1), l(n(2), l(end, l(n(3), l(hole, end))))))

Clause 2 gives the state that is desired—that all tiles are in order, and the hole is in the bottom righthand corner—and also says that it cannot be reached. More precisely, clause 2 represents the denial of the theorem that the program can reach the desired state. If the program generates a clause that is identical to clause 2 except that no "¬" sign is present, then a proof by contradiction will have been found.

The remaining task is that of representing moves of the tiles, and of discussing how the moves are actually made by a reasoning program. The simpler move is the move of a tile right or left.

(3) EQUAL(l(hole, l(n(x), y)), l(n(x), l(hole, y)))

Clause 3 says that a sequence of tile positions can be replaced by another sequence in which two adjacent expressions are interchanged, provided that certain criteria are met. Notice that it permits interchange of the hole only with a numbered tile, not with the "end" marker. This would not be true if we represented an arbitrary tile by x instead of n(x).

To see how clause 3 is used, let us consider clause 3 with clause 1, and let us use paramodulation as the inference rule. Paramodulation selects either argument of clause 3, and seeks an expression in clause 1 that can be unified with it. The first argument of clause 3 begins with "l(hole,", and therefore only certain expressions are acceptable from clause 1 for attempting to find an appropriate variable replacement to complete a successful unification with the first argument. In fact, the only acceptable expression in clause 1 begins with "l(hole,", namely, the entire first argument of clause 1. Clause 5—clause 4 will be discussed shortly—is the result of applying paramodulation to clauses 1 and 3.

(5) STATE(l(n(1), l(hole, l(end, l(n(3), l(n(2), end))))))

Clause 5 says that the state of the tray is such that the first row (now) consists of tile 1 followed by hole. The fact that clause 5 comes from clauses 3 and 1 can be interpreted as saying that the new state can be reached from the older state by moving the hole to the right. The variable y in both arguments of clause 3 is used to keep the rest of the state of the tray untouched. Were it not for "end" marking the separation of rows of tiles, clause 3 could be used with a clause representing a state in which the hole was at the end of a row. The resulting clause would in effect have moved the hole from the righthand end of one row to the lefthand end of the next, certainly an illegal move. If the number of a tile were not enclosed in the function n, then clause 3 would be forced to dispense with that function. In that case, again a clause such as clause 5 could be used to move the hole from the righthand end of one row to the lefthand end of the next. Such would then be possible because "end" could be matched with the first occurrence of x in clause 3, permitting a corresponding unification.

For moving the tile left, no additional clause is required. Clause 3 suffices. The difference is that the paramodulation is from the second argument of 3, not from the first.

The clause we skipped, clause 4, is that needed for moves of tiles up and down.

(4) EQUAL(l(hole, l(x, l(y, l(n(z), w)))), l(n(z), l(x, l(y, l(hole, w)))))

The structure of clause 4 is explained by the fact that moving the hole down, for example, means moving the hole from one point in the list to another, having to move past "end" marking the end of a row. The hole must be moved past the intervening expressions in the list, among which are the end of a row and the tiles on the next row and to the left of the current position of the hole. In the simplified puzzle, the number of such intervening expressions is two. Examination of clause 4 reveals that the move switches two tile positions, the hole and the one under it, or the hole and the one above it. The remaining tile positions are left untouched, which explains the presence of the other variables not prefixed by the function n. The hole cannot be moved past the bottom (or top) of the tray by the reasoning program employing paramodulation because the corresponding unification involves more terms than are present in a clause representing a state in which the hole is in the bottom (or top) row. The move of the hole down is affected by applying paramodulation to the first argument of clause 4 with the appropriate term in the *into* clause. Similarly, a move up is affected by concentrating on the second argument of clause 4.

Applying paramodulation to clauses 4 and 5 yields clause 6.

(6) STATE(l(n(1), l(n(2), l(end, l(n(3), l(hole, end))))))

Clauses 6 and 2 contradict each other, and therefore clauses 1 through 6 give a proof by contradiction. When clause 6 is found, a reasoning program has solved the puzzle of moving the tiles from the given scrambled state to the desired state, at least for the two by two tray.

Of course, not all of the possible scrambled states lead to the ordered state for the two by two puzzle, or for that matter for the puzzle of 15. Which scrambled states can be rearranged to produce the ordered state, and which of them cannot? What would be the result if one of the tile arrangements that cannot lead to the ordered arrangement were submitted to an automated reasoning program? Would the program succeed in proving the given scrambling impossible to appropriately rearrange, and, if so, how would it do so? Further, if the program did not itself prove the impossibility, could you examine its work to deduce that the given arrangement was impossible to appropriately rearrange?

4.3.2 The Full Puzzle of 15

We are now ready for the puzzle in full. Recall that the scrambled state has the first row consisting of tile 1, tile 6, tile 2, and tile 4, in that order. Starting with a new clause 1 that gives the scrambled state, let us begin again and produce the needed clauses.

(1) STATE(l(n(1), l(n(6), l(n(2), l(n(4), l(end, l(n(5),

l(hole, l(n(3), l(n(8), l(end, l(n(9), l(n(10), l(n(7), l(n(11),

l(end, l(n(13), l(n(14), l(n(15), l(n(12), end)))))))))))))))))))))

We also have

(2) ¬STATE(l(n(1), l(n(2), l(n(3), l(n(4), l(end, l(n(5),

l(n(6), l(n(7), l(n(8), l(end, l(n(9), l(n(10), l(n(11), l(n(12), l(end,

l(n(13), l(n(14), l(n(15), l(hole, end)))))))))))))))))))))

as the analogue to clause 2 for the simplified version, but with the list of tiles numbered from 1 through 15. Clause 3, surprisingly, is the same as clause 3 of the simplified version.

(3) EQUAL(l(hole, l(n(x), y)), l(n(x), l(hole, y)))

No change is necessary because of the role that the variables play. On the other hand, the needed clause 4 is substantially more complicated in appearance when compared with the preceding clause 4. The principle used in determining the preceding clause 4 applies here also. The move of the hole down must allow for all intervening terms in the list, in this case four.

(4) EQUAL(l(hole, l(x, l(y, l(z, l(u, l(n(w), v)))))),

l(n(w), l(x, l(y, l(z, l(u, l(hole, v)))))))

As an exercise, show how an automated reasoning program could use paramodulation to find the clauses that correspond to the moves of the tiles leading from the given scrambled state to the desired ordered state.

A puzzle of this type illustrates the value of paramodulation in its capacity to produce a new clause that results from a substitution of one expression for another deep inside a literal. For example, at one point in solving the given puzzle, the hole can be found in the spot that tile 11 eventually is to occupy. The corresponding clause has the term "hole" deep within a nested set of occurrences of the function l. However, applying paramodulation to this clause and clause 3 moves the hole to the right and the 11 tile to its proper place, and in one step.

So far, the discussion has been in terms of moves that interchange the hole with a tile. A person, however, working on the given scrambled state might immediately note that a complex move could be made, a move that simultaneously changes the position of the hole and that of two of the tiles. For example, in what amounts to a diagonal move, the hole could be moved up and to the right in the starting scrambled state, thus moving tile 6 down to its intended position and also moving tile 2 left to its intended position. The discovery of such moves demonstrates insight and, more important, often greatly reduces the effort required to solve a puzzle. Can an automated reasoning program make such moves? Even further, can a reasoning program discover that such moves can be made?

Of course a reasoning program can make such moves. Simply supply the program with the appropriate clause that says the hole can be moved up and to the right in one step, provided that the move is legal. Perhaps more interesting and surprising, the program can in fact generate the appropriate clause by using paramodulation. For this puzzle, applying paramodulation to clauses 3 and 4 yields the desired clause. This application illustrates the value of the property of paramodulation that allows a nontrivial variable replacement in both the *from* and the *into* clause when completing the corresponding unification. Specifically, the desired clause is obtained by paramodulating *from* the entire first argument of clause 3 *into* the entire first argument of clause 4.

To see what happens, we first rename the variables in clause 3. (Operationally, when applying an inference rule, always rename the variables so that no two clauses have a variable in common. The exception to this is the inference rule *factoring* that is discussed in Chapter 6.)

(3) EQUAL(l(hole, l(n(x7), x8)), l(n(x7), l(hole, x8)))

Then we take clause 4

(4) EQUAL(l(hole, l(x, l(y, l(z, l(u, l(n(v), w)))))),

l(n(v), l(x, l(y, l(z, l(u, l(hole, w)))))))

and seek the variable replacement that, if applied, causes the first argument of clause 3 and the first argument of clause 4 to become identical. The unification succeeds when x is replaced by n(x7), and x8 by l(y, l(z, l(u, l(n(v), w)))). Next, we make this variable replacement uniformly in clauses 3 and 4, getting temporarily clauses 3′ and 4′. Then we substitute the second argument of clause 3′ for the first argument of clause 4′. We obtain

EQUAL(l(n(x), l(hole, l(y, l(z, l(u, l(n(v), w)))))),

l(n(v), l(n(x), l(y, l(z, l(u, l(hole, w)))))))

after renaming the variable x7 to x. If paramodulation is applied to this last clause and any STATE clause, the attempt either will fail or will succeed and produce a new STATE clause. If the paramodulation involves the first argument of this last clause and succeeds, the new STATE clause will have the hole moved down one row and left one column. If the paramodulation involves the second argument and succeeds, the hole will be moved up one row and right one column.

To produce this last equality clause by paramodulation, a reasoning program is required to make a nontrivial replacement in both clauses 3 and 4. The variable x8 in clause 3 and x in clause 4 are each replaced nontrivially. Such an action is not permitted with demodulation, and thus the use of paramodulation, especially when equality is naturally present in the problem under study, provides the needed power to draw conclusions. Further paramodulations of the type just discussed produce clauses that enable a reasoning program to make even more complex moves.

Two remarks complete the treatment of this puzzle. First, and here we answer some of the questions posed at the end of Section 4.3.1, note that half of the scrambled arrangements never lead to the ordered state. In the two by two case in which the first row consists of the hole followed by tile 2 and the second row consists of tile 3 followed by tile 1, we have a state that never leads to the ordered state. An automated reasoning program confronted with such a state will, given sufficient time, exhaust all distinct states, discarding those that duplicate existing ones. Such discarding, by means of subsumption, sharply reduces the number of sequences of states to be examined. In the four by four case, however, that number is still exceedingly large, which brings us to the second remark. We know of no strategy for reducing the number of states sufficiently to make an arbitrarily selected problem in the four by four case solvable in reasonable time. In fact, finding such a strategy, if it were to generalize to a larger class of problems, represents a valuable contribution to the field of automated reasoning.

Employment of paramodulation can produce a far shorter proof than that obtained with some other inference rule, and can sharply increase the effectiveness of an automated reasoning program. The improvement results from the property of paramodulation that allows focusing directly on an expression even when the expression occurs deep within a literal.

4.4 Order of Operations in a Reasoning Program

You might be curious at this point about the order of the various processes that a typical reasoning program might use. By understanding the order, you can see what actions force other actions.

The first operation of many reasoning programs, after analyzing the information that you supply, is that of choosing the information on which to focus. The choice is dictated by the weighting process and by the strategy being employed. If the set of support strategy is in use, then only the clauses in the set of support can be chosen. If not, all of the clauses are allowed to be the choice. In either case, the allowed clauses are considered in the order of increasing weight. Of course, in the case in which the set of support strategy is being used, the remaining clauses are used to complete the application of various inference rules. After the input clauses have been the focus of attention, the choice is made from among the new clauses—those clauses that have been generated and retained because they represent new information that is deemed acceptable. That choice is again dictated by the weighting process for, when the set of support strategy is in use, clauses that are generated and retained are automatically given support. With weighting, you can supply various criteria for defining interesting and for defining complex information. The criteria are used to determine the "weight" of each clause. Based on the weights, the reasoning program then chooses from among the new information that which you deem to be the most interesting. For example, you can force a reasoning program to concentrate on Roberta before all other persons in the puzzle, until nothing more can be concluded about her. On the other hand, you could assign weights so that Roberta is of least interest to a reasoning program. Thus, by appropriately choosing weights for the various concepts, you can impose your will, your intuition, and your knowledge on a reasoning program's search for information.

Once a clause or new fact has been generated or found, the first important process that is applied is demodulation. This process is applied first because it yields the final way of expressing information—its canonical form—which is the key to making various tests. After all, a reasoning program attempts to have information in one form dictated by the various constraints placed on the form by the presence of various demodulators. For example, with the demodulator

EQUALP(father(father(x)), grandfather(x))

the newly deduced fact

AGE(father(father(John)), 60)

would immediately be rewritten as

AGE(grandfather(John), 60)

For the given demodulator to represent a true equality, grandfather here means paternal grandfather.

Then a reasoning program tests the new information to see if it is more complex than desired. When you use a reasoning program, you can instruct it to discard any and all information that is more complex than some maximum level of complexity you deem necessary. For example, if you believe that information that is more complex than child(child(x)) is unimportant and unneeded, and if you have so instructed the program,

AGE(child(child(child(John))), 9)

will be immediately discarded. The method for discarding such information is to inform the reasoning program that, in effect, great-grandchild information is to be thrown away. Weighting is the process that enables a reasoning program to do so.

The next process that is applied is the more powerful complete subsumption check. Here, a reasoning program tests to see if a fact more general than the newly deduced fact is available. If so, the new fact is discarded. For example, the program throws away

EQUALP(father(father(John)), grandfather(John))

if it already has

EQUALP(father(father(x)), grandfather(x))

A more interesting example is the discarding of

HASAJOB(Roberta, teacher) | HASAJOB(Roberta, nurse)

when

HASAJOB(x, nurse) | HASAJOB(x, teacher)

is present. Finally,

HASAJOB(Roberta, teacher) | HASAJOB(Roberta, nurse)

is discarded by using subsumption when

HASAJOB(Roberta, teacher)

is present, as we discussed earlier.

The final test is for the number of literals in the new information. You can instruct a reasoning program to keep information only if the number of literals in the clause is less than a chosen number. For example, you might force a reasoning program to keep only unit facts, or only facts that contain two or fewer literals.

Once it has been decided to keep the new information, two additional procedures are applied. The first, called *back subsumption*, removes existing clauses that are less general than the new clause. The second, called *back demodulation*, seeks to add and apply new demodulators discovered during the attempt to solve the given problem. If the new clause is a unit equality clause that meets various criteria required for it to become a demodulator, then it is applied to existing clauses, and the results are completely demodulated using all demodulators.

EXERCISES

3. There are many strategies employed by different automated reasoning programs. The basic algorithm described in this chapter is amplified to give the following.
   (1) Read in three lists of clauses—the general-axiom list, the set-of-support list, and a list of demodulators. Initially, the have-been-given list is empty.
   (2) While the program has not yet reached a proof and there are still clauses in the set-of-support list, perform the following steps.
   (3) Select a clause from the set-of-support list and call it the "given clause". A number of methods may be used for selecting the next given clause. However, the technique of assigning "weights" to clauses, and then selecting the "lightest" clause, is one effective method.
   (4) Draw all conclusions that can be obtained, using some specified set of inference rules. Each deduced clause must have the given clause as one parent, and all other parent clauses must be selected from the general-axiom list or the have-been-given list. For each deduced clause, perform the following steps.
      (a) Simplify the clause, using the available demodulators.
      (b) Test the clause to see if it is subsumed by an existing clause. If not, add the new clause to the set-of-support list.
      (c) If the new clause subsumes any existing clauses, delete them from whatever lists contain them.
   (5) Move the given clause from the set-of-support list to the have-been-given list.
   To become familiar with precisely how this algorithm works, consider the following small problem. The problem stated in everyday language is the following.

   > On a certain island the inhabitants are partitioned into those who always tell the truth and those who always lie. You land on the island and meet three inhabitants, A, B, and C. You ask A, "Are you a truth-teller or a liar?" He mumbles something that you cannot make out. You ask B what A said. B replies, "A said he is a liar". C then volunteers, "Don't believe B, he's lying!" What can you tell about A, B, and C?

   Before immediately reading the formulation in clauses that we give, see what clauses you would give first. We formulate the problem using a single predicate that is used to indicate that a given statement is true. Thus,

   (1) TRUE(t(x)) | TRUE(l(x))

   means that either the statement t(x) is true or the statement l(x) is true or both are true.

l(x) represents the statement "x is a liar", while t(x) represents the statement "x is a truthteller". We also add

(2) ¬TRUE(t(x)) | ¬TRUE(l(x))

to pin down that everyone is either a liar or a truthteller, but not both. Now we need the axioms that describe exactly what it means to be a truthteller or a liar. We first give the clauses in their **if-then** form.

if TRUE(t(x)) **and** TRUE(said(x, y)) **then** TRUE(y)
if TRUE(l(x)) **and** TRUE(said(x, y)) **then** ¬TRUE(y)
if TRUE(y) **and** TRUE(said(x, y)) **then** TRUE(t(x))
if ¬TRUE(y) **and** TRUE(said(x, y)) **then** TRUE(l(x))

Here, said(x, y) represents the statement that "x said y". The **if-then** clauses are converted into the following clauses.

(3) ¬TRUE(t(x)) | ¬TRUE(said(x, y)) | TRUE(y)

(4) ¬TRUE(l(x)) | ¬TRUE(said(x, y)) | ¬TRUE(y)

(5) ¬TRUE(y) | ¬TRUE(said(x, y)) | TRUE(t(x))

(6) TRUE(y) | ¬TRUE(said(x, y)) | TRUE(l(x))

The remaining two clauses simply give the events that we know occurred.

(7) TRUE(said(b, said(a, l(a))))

(8) TRUE(said(c, l(b)))

(Recall that, in the language of clauses as used in this book, constants and functions must be written in lower case; thus we represent A by a in clauses.) Using the eight clauses, apply the basic algorithm to see exactly how a reasoning program might solve the puzzle. Place the first six clauses in the general-axiom list, and place the last two in the set-of-support list. There are no demodulators for this problem.

Select the given clause using the following method of calculating weights: make the weight of a clause equal to the number of symbols in the clause, excluding commas and parentheses. Thus, the weight of clause 7 is 7, and the weight of clause 8 is 5 ("TRUE" counts as a single symbol). Now apply the algorithm and compute the generated clauses, the results of subsumption, the selection of the given clause, and whatever else is produced with the algorithm. Use hyperresolution as the inference rule.

4. Consider the following two clauses for application of the inference rule of paramodulation.

(1) EQUAL(f(x, y),f(y,x))

(2) EQUAL(f(f(x, y), z), f(x, f(y, z)))

To obtain a paramodulant by paramodulating from clause 1 into clause 2, you first rename the variables in one of the two clauses so that they do not share a variable. Then you unify one of the arguments of clause 1 with a term in clause 2. Then you replace the term in clause 2 with the other argument of clause 1, and instantiate the result with the substitution obtained from the unification. For example, first we can rename the variables in clause 1 giving

(1') $EQUAL(f(x1, y1), f(y1, x1))$

Now, if we unify $f(x1, y1)$ from clause 1' with $f(x, y)$ in clause 2, we find that replacing x1 with x and y1 with y unifies the terms. Now we form the paramodulant by replacing $f(x,y)$ with $f(y1, x1)$ and instantiating the result to

(3) $EQUAL(f(f(y, x), z), f(x, f(y, z)))$

Similarly, if we paramodulate from $f(y1, x1)$ in clause 1' into the second occurrence of y in 2, we get

(4) $EQUAL(f(f(x, f(y1, x1)), z), f(x, f(f(x1, y1), z)))$

Give all of the clauses that can be obtained by paramodulating from clause 1 into clause 2.

5. To this point we have only discussed paramodulating from either argument of a positive unit equality clause. Let us now consider the case in which the from clause contains more than one literal. For example, consider the following two clauses.

(1) $\neg EQUAL(\$div(x, y), f(x, y)$

| $EQUAL(\$div(\$mult(x, z), y), \$mult(z, f(x, y)))$

(2) $EQUAL(u, 0)$

| $EQUAL(\$mult(\$div(v, u), w), \$div(\$mult(w, v), u))$

You may think of the first clause as saying that **if** $(x/y) = f(x, y)$, **then** $((x * z)/y) = (z * f(x, y))$. In other words, if you knew that $(x/y) = f(x, y)$, then you could make substitutions based on the fact that $((x * z)/y) = (z * f(x, y))$. Or, if you take some known fact and perform a substitution based on the conclusion literal, then either the result must be true, or the antecedent literal must be false. For example, if we paramodulate from the first argument of the second literal in clause 1 into $\$div(v, u)$ in clause 2, the result is

(3) $\neg EQUAL(\$div(x, y), f(x, y))$ | $EQUAL(y, 0)$

| $EQUAL(\$mult(\$mult(z, f(x, y)), w), \$div(\$mult(w, \$mult(x, z)), y))$

What is the clause that results from paramodulating from the first argument of the second literal of clause 2 into $\$mult(z, f(x, y))$ in clause 1?

4.5 Extra Care

In both the minipuzzle and the full jobs puzzle, we were content with using a representation that was not fully classified—in some sense, not fully specified. For example, the HASAJOB predicate tacitly assumes that the classification of its first argument is person and that of its second is job, while the predicates MALE and FEMALE each tacitly assumes that the classification of its argument is person. If you wish to be extremely careful, then you must replace most clauses by others that are fully classified. For example

(1) ¬PERSON(x) | FEMALE(x) | MALE(x)

says that if x is a person, then x is female or male. Omitting the literal
¬PERSON(x) makes the class of the variable x implicit. Similarly, to each of
the clauses (16 and 17, Section 3.2.2.1)

(2) ¬HUSBAND(x, y) | MALE(x)

(3) ¬HUSBAND(x, y) | FEMALE(y)

we must add two literals, ¬PERSON(x) and ¬PERSON(y), in order to make them
fully classified. If these additions are not made, again the facts that x and y are of
class person is implicit. Finally, the clause (clause 51, Section 3.2.2.3)

HASAJOB(x, y) | EQUAL(pj(x, y), crossed)

must be replaced with

¬PERSON(x) | ¬JOB(y) | HASAJOB(x, y) | EQUAL(pj(x, y), crossed)

which pins down the class of x and that of y. This version forces x to be a person,
and y to be a job.

By exercising such care and including the necessary additional literals, the
likelihood of error—a person's error in formulating a problem, not an automated
reasoning program's error in solving it—is reduced. The conclusions drawn by a
reasoning program are always logically correct; that is, they follow from the given
facts. But if the facts are in error—such as happens when the representation of the
problem is faulty—then the conclusions are suspect. By including the extra literals
to fully classify each clause, a person is less likely to use predicates in more than one
way. For example, HASAJOB, like all predicates in a problem, must be used in a
consistent fashion—the first argument referring to a person, and the second to a job.

On the other hand, including the additional class-specification literals does
have a negative effect on the performance of an automated reasoning program. Just
as in everyday language, such extra literals can be cumbersome. They make the
individual clauses longer. Moreover, including them also entails adding extra clauses
to specify the classes of the constants in the problem. Thus both reasoning steps and
the search for relevant facts take longer in the presence of class-specification literals.

What is perhaps most annoying about including class-specification literals is
that they contribute nothing during the reasoning steps that solve a problem. If the
formulation contains no errors, the classification literals just clutter up the reasoning.
On the other hand, if the inclusion of the classification literals avoids an error during
reasoning, that error can be detected by simply examining the input clauses. For
these reasons, we recommend that the classification literals not be written in the
clauses of the problem formulation, but that, if you are trying to be very careful,
class checking be done before attempting the solution of the problem.

4.6 Answers to Exercises

1. Here are the answers to the first set of exercises on subsumption.
   (a) The second clause subsumes the first since the first clause is just an instance of the second (with x set to 1).
   (b) Neither clause subsumes the other. Certainly the statements are related. But without knowing that you can reverse the arguments being added, neither statement captures the other.
   (c) The second clause subsumes the first. The second clause states with certainty that Jim is Bob's father, while the first states that either Tom or Jim is Bob's father. Hence, the second clause conveys more information.
   (d) Neither clause subsumes the other. However, it is true that you can deduce
       FATHER(Tom, Bob)
       which will subsume the first clause.
   (e) In this case, the first clause subsumes the second. The first clause narrows the choice for the father to Tom or Jim, while the second only narrows the choice to three possible fathers. However, that would not be enough for subsumption to occur. Subsumption occurs because the two choices given by the first clause are both contained in the second.
   (f) In this case, neither clause subsumes the other.

2. Here are the answers to the second set of questions on subsumption.
   (a) Neither clause subsumes the other.
   (b) The first clause subsumes the second. To see this, let x be set to a and y be set to b.
   (c) Neither clause subsumes the other. The first clause does not subsume the second, because no instance of the second literal occurs in the second clause.
   (d) In this case, the first clause does subsume the second. It is unusual for one clause to subsume another clause with fewer literals. This can occur only if more than one literal in the subsumer can be instantiated to the same literal in the subsumed clause. In this case, the first and second literals in the first clause can both be instantiated to the second literal in the second clause.
   (e) The second clause subsumes the first.

3. Step 1 first causes the clauses to be read into the appropriate lists—clauses 1 through 6 into general-axiom, and clauses 7 and 8 into set-of-support. Step 3 causes a given clause to be selected; in this case it will be clause 8 since 8 is lighter than 7. Step 4 will cause four new clauses to be generated. They are

   From clauses 8, 3, and 1, weight = 7, (count the "|"):

   (9) TRUE(l(b)) | TRUE(l(c))

   From clauses 8, 4, 1, and 1, weight = 7, (use clause 1 twice):

   (10) TRUE(t(c)) | TRUE(t(b))

   From clauses 8, 5, and 1, subsumed by clause 10:

   TRUE(t(c)) | TRUE(t(b))

   From clauses 8 and 6, subsumed by clause 9:

   TRUE(l(b)) | TRUE(l(c))

Step 5 now causes clause 8 to be moved from the set-of-support to the have-been-given list. Now it is time to select a new given clause. Since all three clauses left on the set-of-support weigh 7, we will just choose the first one that was put on the list (clause 7). Step 4 now causes the following clauses to be generated.

From clauses 7, 3, and 1, weight = 9:

(11) TRUE(said(a, l(a)) | TRUE(l(b))

From clauses 7 and 6, subsumed by clause 11:

TRUE(said(a, l(a)) | TRUE(l(b))

After these clauses are generated, clause 7 is moved to the have-been-given list. Then it is time to pick a new given clause. This time it will be clause 9. The clauses that are generated with 9 as the given clause are the following.

From clauses 9, 2, and 1, subsumed by clause 9:

TRUE(l(c)) | TRUE(l(b))

From clauses 9, 4, 1, and 8, subsumed by clause 1:

TRUE(l(c)) | TRUE(t(c))

From clauses 9, 4, 9, and 8, subsumed by clause 9:

TRUE(l(c)) | TRUE(l(b))

From clauses 9, 5, and 8, subsumed by clause 1:

TRUE(l(c)) | TRUE(t(c))

From clauses 9, 2, and 1, subsumed by clause 9:

TRUE(l(b)) | TRUE(l(c))

From clauses 9, 4, 8, and 1, subsumed by clause 1:

TRUE(l(b)) | TRUE(t(b))

From clauses 9, 4, 8, and 9, subsumed by clause 9:

TRUE(l(b)) | TRUE(l(c))

Sometimes the same clause is generated several times, using different parents. Sometimes it can even be generated several times using the same parents, but unifying different literals in the clauses.

In any event, clause 9 is now moved to the have-been-given list, and clause 10 becomes the given clause. The next set of generated clauses is

From clauses 10, 2, and 1, subsumed by clause 10:

TRUE(t(b)) | TRUE(t(c))

From clauses 10, 2, and 9, subsumed by clause 1:

TRUE(t(b)) | TRUE(l(b))

From clauses 10, 3, and 8, subsumed by clause 1:

TRUE(t(b)) | TRUE(l(b))

From clauses 10, 2, and 1, subsumed by clause 10:

TRUE(t(c)) | TRUE(t(b))

From clauses 10, 2, and 9, subsumed by clause 1:

TRUE(t(c)) | TRUE(l(c))

From clauses 10, 3, and 7, weight = 9:

(12) TRUE(t(c)) | TRUE(said(a, l(a))

Then clause 10 is moved to the have-been-given list, and clause 11 is selected as the next given clause. The following clauses will be generated using clause 11 as the given clause.

From clauses 11, 3, and 1, weight = 7:

(13) TRUE(l(b)) | TRUE(l(a))

From clauses 11, 4, 1, and 1, weight = 7:

(14) TRUE(l(b)) | TRUE(t(a))

From clauses 11, 4, 1, and 7, subsumed by clause 1:

TRUE(l(b)) | TRUE(t(b))

From clauses 11, 4, 9, and 7, subsumed by clause 9:

TRUE(l(b)) | TRUE(l(c))

From clauses 11, 4, 11, and 7, subsumed by clause 11:

TRUE(l(b)) | TRUE(said(a,l(a))

From clauses 11, 5, and 1, subsumed by clause 14:

TRUE(l(b)) | TRUE(t(a))

From clauses 11 and 6, subsumed by clause 13:

TRUE(l(b)) | TRUE(l(a))

From clauses 11, 5, and 7, subsumed by clause 1:

TRUE(l(b)) | TRUE(t(b))

From clauses 11, 2, and 1, subsumed by clause 11:

TRUE(said(a, l(a))) | TRUE(l(b))

From clauses 11, 2, and 10, subsumed by clause 12:

TRUE(said(a, l(a))) | TRUE(t(c))

From clauses 11, 4, 7, and 11, subsumed by clause 11:

TRUE(said(a, l(a))) | TRUE(l(b))

From clauses 11, 4, 1, and 8, subsumed by clause 12:

TRUE(said(a, l(a))) | TRUE(t(c))

From clauses 11, 4, 9, and 8, subsumed by clause 11:

TRUE(said(a, l(a))) | TRUE(l(b))

From clauses 11, 5, and 8, subsumed by clause 12:

TRUE(said(a, l(a))) | TRUE(t(c))

Then clause 11 is moved to the have-been-given list, and clause 13 becomes the given clause. The following clauses are generated with clause 13 as the given clause.

From clauses 13, 2, and 1, subsumed by clause 13:

TRUE(l(a)) | TRUE(l(b))

From clauses 13, 2, and 10, weight = 7:

(15) TRUE(l(a)) | TRUE(t(c))

From clauses 13, 4, 7, and 11, subsumed by clause 13:

TRUE(l(a)) | TRUE(l(b))

From clauses 13, 4, 1, and 8, subsumed by clause 15:

TRUE(l(a)) | TRUE(t(c))

From clauses 13, 4, 9, and 8, subsumed by clause 13:

TRUE(l(a)) | TRUE(l(b))

From clauses 13, 5, and 8, subsumed by clause 15:

TRUE(l(a)) | TRUE(t(c))

From clauses 13, 2, and 1, subsumed by clause 13:

TRUE(l(b)) | TRUE(l(a))

From clauses 13, 4, 11, and 1, subsumed by clause 14:

TRUE(l(b)) | TRUE(t(a))

From clauses 13, 4, 11, and 13, weight = 3:

(16) TRUE(l(b))

Clause 16 subsumes clauses 9, 11, 13, and 14

Note that clause 16 represents some significant knowledge—we now know that B is a liar. Clause 13 does not actually get moved to the have-been-given list, since clause 13 was subsumed by clause 16 and, hence, deleted. Clause 16 becomes the next given clause and produces the following three clauses.

From clauses 16, 2, and 1, subsumed by clause 16:

TRUE(l(b))

From clauses 16, 2, and 10, weight = 3:

(17) TRUE(t(c))

Clause 17 subsumes 10, 12, 15

From clauses 16, 5, and 8, subsumed by clause 17:

TRUE(t(c))

After moving clause 16 to the set-of-support, only clause 17 remains. It can be used to generate the following clauses.

From clauses 17, 2, and 1, subsumed by clause 17:

TRUE(t(c))

From clauses 17, 3, and 8, subsumed by clause 17:

TRUE(t(c))

Since there are no more clauses in the set-of-support, processing stops. What have we learned? The answer, of course, is given in clauses 16 and 17; B is a liar, and C is a truthteller. Do we know anything about A? The answer is no. In fact you could try two more runs—one denying that a is a liar, and one denying that a is a truthteller. In neither case could a proof be obtained, so nothing can be determined about A. Note that this run did not contain the denial of a theorem. It was more of a "fishing expedition". We used the program to learn which statements followed from those that we already knew were true.

If you found the computations somewhat tedious, you will see why it is so convenient to have an automated reasoning program around to help. In this run we had no demodulators, and the subsumption checks were all straightforward. In many of the more difficult problems solved with an automated reasoning program, thousands of clauses are generated, and each clause is simplified using as many as several hundred demodulators. By working through this example by hand, you can see exactly how the steps are executed.

This might be a good place to illustrate what happens when less effective inference rules and strategies are employed. Suppose that we had not used the set of support strategy, but had allowed all possible deductions to be made, including those involving only clauses in the given axiom list. Furthermore, suppose we had used binary resolution instead of hyperresolution. What would have happened?

Very many more clauses would have been derived. Here are just a few of them.

¬TRUE(says(x, t(y))) | ¬TRUE(t(z))

| ¬TRUE(says(z, t(x))) | ¬TRUE(says(y, v)) | TRUE(v)

¬TRUE(says(x, says(c, l(b)))) | ¬TRUE(t(y))

| ¬TRUE(says(y, l(x)))

¬TRUE(says(x, y)) | ¬TRUE(y) | ¬TRUE(t(z))

| ¬TRUE(t(v)) | ¬TRUE(t(w))

| ¬TRUE(says(w, says(v, says(z, l(x)))))

These clauses are undesirable because, although they are true, they do not seem to be contributing to solving the problem. The first clause is easier to understand if we reorder its literals and then convert it to the **if-then** form.

> **if** z is a truthteller
> **and** z says that x is a truthteller
> **and** x says that y is a truthteller
> **and** y says v
> **then** v is true

This statement is quite true, and follows from the axioms about truthtellers and liars. You can think of it as an extension of the *theory* of truthtellers and liars. It says nothing about A, B, and C, the subjects of the problem. The objective of using the set of support strategy is precisely to avoid such deducing of consequences of the axioms at the expense of focusing on the problem at hand. The second of the given clauses does mention B and C, but the clause is simply too weak a statement to be very useful. It does not contain even one positive literal. The third clause suggests that, as more clauses are generated, things seem to be getting worse instead of better.

These clauses are not necessary for solving the problem, as we have seen. Use of hyperresolution and the set of support strategy avoids them altogether.

4. There are 10 distinct terms contained in the arguments of clause 2. Let us list them from the inside terms to the outside terms to have an explicit list. In the first argument we have x, y, $f(x,y)$, z, and $f(f(x,y),z)$. In the second argument we have x, y, z, $f(y,z)$, and $f(x,f(y,z))$. Each of these 10 terms unifies with either of the two arguments of $(1')$. Hence, there are 20 possible paramodulants that can be formed. We list them in the following order: First we give the 10 paramodulants formed by unifying $f(x1,y1)$ with the 10 terms, using the order in which we listed the occurrences of those terms. Then we list the 10 formed by matching $f(y1,x1)$ with the 10 terms.

(1) EQUAL($f(f(f(y1,x1),y),z), f(f(x1,y1),f(y,z))$)

(2) EQUAL($f(f(x,f(y1,x1)),z), f(x,f(f(x1,y1),z))$)

(3) EQUAL($f(f(y,x),z), f(x,f(y,z))$)

(4) EQUAL($f(f(x,y),f(y1,x1)), f(x,f(y,f(x1,y1)))$)

(5) EQUAL($f(z,f(x,y)), f(x,f(y,z))$)

(6) EQUAL($f(f(f(x1,y1),y),z), f(f(y1,x1),f(y,z))$)

(7) EQUAL($f(f(x,f(x1,y1)),z), f(x,f(f(y1,x1),z))$)

(8) EQUAL($f(f(x,y),f(x1,y1)), f(x,f(y,f(y1,x1)))$)

(9) EQUAL($f(f(x,y),z), f(x,f(z,y))$)

(10) EQUAL($f(f(x,y),z), f(f(y,z),x)$)

(11) EQUAL($f(f(f(x1,y1),y),z), f(f(y1,x1),f(y,z))$)

(12) EQUAL($f(f(x,f(x1,y1)),z), f(x,f(f(y1,x1),z))$)

(13) EQUAL($f(f(y,x),z), f(x,f(y,z))$)

(14) $EQUAL(f(f(x, y), f(x1, y1)), f(x, f(y, f(y1, x1))))$

(15) $EQUAL(f(z, f(x, y)), f(x, f(y, z)))$

(16) $EQUAL(f(f(f(y1, x1), y), z), f(f(x1, y1), f(y, z)))$

(17) $EQUAL(f(f(x, f(y1, x1)), z), f(x, f(f(x1, y1), z)))$

(18) $EQUAL(f(f(x, y), f(y1, x1)), f(x, f(y, f(x1, y1))))$

(19) $EQUAL(f(f(x, y), z), f(x, f(y, z)))$

(20) $EQUAL(f(f(x, y), z), f(f(y, z), x))$

What can be learned by examining all of these paramodulants? First, note that, once variables are renamed, several of the clauses are derived more than once. Several of the paramodulants are essentially identical. Usually, unrestricted paramodulation is too prolific. The rule has advantages in that it allows the program to generate many desirable clauses in just a few steps and applies at the term level rather than only at the argument level. However, its use can produce a great many uninteresting clauses very quickly. Thus, much of the research focusing on paramodulation has sought strategies to restrict its use in such a way that a higher percentage of the generated clauses are "interesting". Strategies such as "Never paramodulate into a variable" and "Never paramodulate from a variable" are normally applied. At this point, you have learned to compute paramodulants. You have also learned of the power of this rule, and that its use can quickly produce many new clauses.

5. The unification requires that z be instantiated to $div(v, u)$, and w to $f(x, y)$. The resulting paramodulant includes the instantiated versions of the first literal of clause 2, the first literal of clause 1, and the instantiated version of the second literal of 1 that results after making the substitution. The result is

$EQUAL(u, 0) \mid \neg EQUAL(\$div(x, y), f(x, y))$

$\mid EQUAL(\$div(\$mult(x, \$div(v, u)), y), \$div(\$mult(f(x, y), v), u))$

5

Harder Puzzles

We now come to three puzzles, each of which is somewhat harder than the "jobs puzzle" of Chapter 3. Each of these puzzles was solved by an automated reasoning program. Each represents a class of problems that includes "real" problems—ones that occur in, for example, logic circuit design. Thus, the solutions given in this chapter can be used as illustrations of how to attack related problems. While the jobs puzzle illustrates how to state and solve problems whose goal is obtaining information about various people, the three puzzles of this chapter illustrate how to state and solve problems of a quite different nature. The puzzles in this chapter are examples of "state-space problems".

5.1 The Checkerboard and Dominoes Puzzle

There is a checkerboard whose upper left and lower right squares have been removed. There is a box of dominoes that are one square by two squares in size. Can you exactly cover the checkerboard with the dominoes? (See the checkerboard on the next page.)

Does this puzzle remind you of any real problems? For example, consider a real estate developer who owns land that he intends to sell in lots. Including two portions owned by the school district, the shape of the land happens to be a perfect square. Unfortunately, from the developer's viewpoint, the school district refuses to sell its land. The two missing pieces are, respectively, the upper left and lower right squares. So the developer has decided that each lot will also be a square. A market

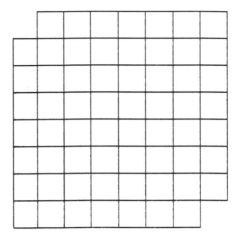

survey has uncovered a potential obstacle to his plan of selling all of the land he owns. The buyers are not interested in single lots, but instead each wishes to purchase two adjoining lots. Can the developer arrange the lots to permit all of them to be sold?

We shall first show how this puzzle—checkerboard or real estate—might be solved by a person. Then we shall show how an automated reasoning program can successfully attack such puzzles.

This puzzle is known to researchers in the field of artificial intelligence as "a tough nut to crack". When the puzzle was suggested in the middle 1960s by John McCarthy, the notion was that a computer program would be hard pressed to solve it. In particular, it was felt that a computer program would be very unlikely to find the solution that a clever person might. The word "solution", by the statement of the puzzle, means an answer to the question "Can the modified checkerboard be covered precisely?", not necessarily a sequence of plays of dominoes that in fact does precisely cover the modified board. Here is a solution that an inventive person might give—the solution that McCarthy was challenging a computer to find.

5.1.1 Solution by Person or Persons Unknown

Before the two squares are removed from the checkerboard, the board contains 32 black and 32 white squares—the number of black squares equals the number of white. However, after removing the upper left and lower right, the number of white squares is 30—two less than the number of black. Each play of a domino covers one black and one white square. Thus, each play leaves the board still unbalanced—leaves two more black than white squares to be covered. When the white squares have all been covered, two black squares still remain uncovered. In other words, no sequence of plays of dominoes exists that precisely covers the modified checkerboard.

The key to finding this solution is the word "checkerboard". The notion of a checkerboard suggests, to a person, black and white squares. If the puzzle had instead been stated as the problem of a real estate developer, the likelihood of finding the black-and-white argument would be small. If the checkerboard had two squares removed, but squares of opposite color, the black-and-white argument would be of no use. If ten squares were removed, the black-and-white argument might not help. The solution given in this chapter—that employed by an automated reasoning program—does not rely on the black-and-white argument. The color of the squares on the board has, of course, nothing to do with the fact that the board can be covered or that it cannot. The solution given here can easily be modified to solve similar puzzles with other squares removed. In fact, without modification, the method given here found a covering for the board with two adjacent squares removed from the first row.

5.1.2 Representing the Puzzle to an Automated Reasoning Program

To have an automated reasoning program attack this puzzle, we must represent various facts about the state of the checkerboard—about which complete coverings and which partial coverings are achievable. At the beginning of the puzzle, the modified checkerboard is empty; no dominoes have been played. All squares are "not covered", except for two squares which have been "removed". After a domino has been played, two squares which were "not covered" are now "covered", and the remaining squares stay as they were. To represent the state of row 1 of the board at the beginning of the puzzle, we write

(1) ACHIEVABLE(row(1), squares(r, n, n, n, n, n, n, n))

which says that row 1 has its first square removed, and its remaining squares not covered. The predicate ACHIEVABLE has two arguments, one that points to the row under discussion and one that gives the state of the squares in that row. The first argument of ACHIEVABLE is the function "row" having one argument, the actual row number. The second argument of ACHIEVABLE is the function "squares" of eight arguments—the eight squares each with its respective state, not covered, covered, or removed. A square that is not covered is denoted by "n", one that is covered by "c", and one that is removed by "r". Clause 1 thus says that (at the beginning) row 1 has its first square removed, and the remaining not covered. This state of the modified board is achievable.

If a domino is played in the seventh and eighth squares of row 1,

ACHIEVABLE(row(1), squares(r, n, n, n, n, n, c, c))

represents the new state of the board—an achievable state. Notice that the state of the board is all that counts as far as the puzzle goes; that is, the particular arrangement of the dominoes does not matter at all. To decide where the next domino can be played, all that counts is which squares are covered, which not covered, and which removed. This observation is extremely important to solving the puzzle, either for a person or for a reasoning program. Because of it, neither we nor the program need consider all the different arrangements of dominoes that might conceivably cover the board. For example, we can select a method for playing dominoes, and concentrate on which partial coverings of the board can be achieved. If we were to consider all possible sequences of plays, we or the program would be forced to examine more than six trillion sequences. By choosing an order in which to play the dominoes, and by also ignoring duplicate paths to the same partial covering, fewer than 500 partial coverings result.

What type of duplication are we trying to avoid? The first two rows, except for the first square in each, can be covered in various ways. For example, number the squares from left to right in each row 1 through 8. For a first covering of rows 1 and 2, excluding square 1 in each, play seven dominoes vertically. Each of the seven dominoes covers one square in row 1 and one in row 2. For a second covering, play three dominoes horizontally in each of rows 1 and 2 in such a way that squares 2 through 7 are covered. Then play a domino vertically to cover the eighth squares of the first two rows. As far as attempting to precisely cover the checkerboard with the two missing squares goes, the two given coverings of the first two rows are equally good. The important points for the two different ways of playing the dominoes are that square 1 of row 1 has not been touched, and that square 1 of row 2 still needs to be covered. This observation also applies to the various other ways of covering the first two rows where the first square in each is ignored.

The rule for playing dominoes that we shall have the reasoning program observe is that a row will not be left until all of its available squares have been covered. Further, all horizontal plays that the program wishes to make must precede any vertical play. Finally, when a vertical play is made, the remaining squares are simultaneously covered by vertical plays. Of course, this rule allows dominoes to be played vertically and thus cover a square in the next row. But the rule does not allow us to play, for example, a domino horizontally in a row unless all of the previous rows have had their available squares covered. This rule can be obeyed by, for example, playing dominoes horizontally in a row as far as possible, and then playing vertically if necessary into the next row. We also add the rule of starting at the top of the board, with row 1 in which the square on the left has been removed. Restricting the play in this way is beneficial regardless of whether a person or an automated reasoning program is attempting to prove that the modified checkerboard cannot be covered.

Although we have not yet shown how the reasoning program actually considers the horizontal and vertical plays, the restriction on play has an immediate effect on the meaning of a unit clause in the predicate ACHIEVABLE. A unit clause—a clause that contains one literal—such as

ACHIEVABLE(row(2), squares(n, n, n, n, n, c, c, c))

means that the sixth, seventh, and eighth squares of row 2 are covered, while the remaining five are not covered. This clause also means that all squares of row 1 that are to be covered are in fact covered. This clause also means that no square of row 3 through row 8 has yet been covered. This last condition follows from the requirement of making all vertical plays that affect a row simultaneously.

Such a partial cover can be achieved, for example, by placing dominoes horizontally in row 1 to cover squares 2 through 7, placing a domino vertically to cover the eighth squares of rows 1 and 2, and placing a domino horizontally in row 2 to cover the sixth and seventh squares. Restricting the play of the dominoes so that the available squares of a row must be all covered before work commences on the next row blocks many paths from being explored. For example, the clause

ACHIEVABLE(row(2), squares(c, c, n, n, n, n, n, n))

cannot be generated. If it were, its meaning would be that the first two squares in row 2 are covered, the remaining squares in row 2 are not, the seven squares to be covered in row 1 are in fact covered, and the squares of rows 3 through 8 are completely uncovered. But this cannot happen, given the restriction on play. Do you see why this cannot happen?

First, since square 1 of row 1 is unavailable for it has been removed, and since square 1 of row 3 is not covered, square 1 of row 2 must be covered with a domino played horizontally. Second, this domino also covers square 2 of row 2. Third, since all remaining squares of row 2 are not covered, all covered squares of row 1 must have been covered by dominoes played horizontally. But there are seven such squares, requiring $3\frac{1}{2}$ dominoes, which is not allowed.

What would you conclude from finding the clause

ACHIEVABLE(row(2), squares(n, c, c, c, c, c, c, c))

The fact that the first argument of squares in this clause is n says that the first square is not covered. Thus, because of the meaning of ACHIEVABLE, all squares of rows 3 and greater are not covered. But all available squares, 2 through 8, of row 1 are covered. What this clause does not tell you is how the dominoes were played to achieve this state. For example, playing seven dominoes vertically or playing six horizontally and one vertically would each achieve this state, and hence cause this clause to exist. Whichever sequence of plays occurred has no effect on the next play, and no effect on proving that the modified checkerboard cannot be precisely covered. Therefore, only the state of the board is recorded, not the particular way it was achieved by playing dominoes. Thus, since we need consider only the partial covering that can be achieved and not the particular play of dominoes that achieves it, we discard, through the use of *subsumption*, all but one of the paths to each achievable partial cover. If this were not done, even with the restricted rule of play, there would be far too many sequences of plays to consider—more than 100,000.

We are now ready for the clauses that enable an automated reasoning program to play dominoes, either horizontally or vertically. Recall that clause 1 gives the initial condition of row 1 before any dominoes have been played.

(1) ACHIEVABLE(row(1), squares(r, n, n, n, n, n, n, n))

If a domino is played horizontally, two adjacent squares are changed from not covered to covered, and the remaining squares stay as they are.

(2) ¬ACHIEVABLE(row(x), squares(n, n, y3, y4, y5, y6, y7, y8))

| ACHIEVABLE(row(x), squares(c, c, y3, y4, y5, y6, y7, y8))

Clause 2 says that, if the state in which the first two squares of a row are not covered can be achieved, then the state in which those same two squares is covered can be achieved, and without affecting the state of the other six squares. In other words, a domino can be played horizontally in the first two squares, when those two squares are not covered.

Notice that in clause 2 we write row(x) to take advantage of "generality" as discussed in Chapter 4. Thus the clause applies to any of the rows of the checkerboard. We do this rather than writing a clause to cover each row, and thus contribute somewhat to the efficiency of a reasoning program and to the ease of its use. The remaining six squares are each marked with a variable to cause the board, after the play of a domino horizontally, to maintain the state as is—except, of course, for the two squares that have just been covered. Can you supply the other clauses that are needed to permit horizontal plays of dominoes?

(3) ¬ACHIEVABLE(row(x), squares(y1, n, n, y4, y5, y6, y7, y8))

| ACHIEVABLE(row(x), squares(y1, c, c, y4, y5, y6, y7, y8))

(4) ¬ACHIEVABLE(row(x), squares(y1, y2, n, n, y5, y6, y7, y8))

| ACHIEVABLE(row(x), squares(y1, y2, c, c, y5, y6, y7, y8))

(5) ¬ACHIEVABLE(row(x), squares(y1, y2, y3, n, n, y6, y7, y8))

| ACHIEVABLE(row(x), squares(y1, y2, y3, c, c, y6, y7, y8))

(6) ¬ACHIEVABLE(row(x), squares(y1, y2, y3, y4, n, n, y7, y8))

| ACHIEVABLE(row(x), squares(y1, y2, y3, y4, c, c, y7, y8))

(7) ¬ACHIEVABLE(row(x), squares(y1, y2, y3, y4, y5, n, n, y8))

| ACHIEVABLE(row(x), squares(y1, y2, y3, y4, y5, c, c, y8))

(8) ¬ACHIEVABLE(row(x), squares(y1, y2, y3, y4, y5, y6, n, n))

| ACHIEVABLE(row(x), squares(y1, y2, y3, y4, y5, y6, c, c))

Clauses 3 through 8 permit a reasoning program to play dominoes horizontally beginning, respectively, in square 2 of the row under consideration. Seven clauses are used to make horizontal plays because there are eight squares in a row, each domino covers two squares, and no domino is allowed to protrude past the edge of the board.

With the horizontal moves taken care of, we need a clause, or perhaps more than one clause, for the vertical moves. If you can supply this clause(s), you have in effect conquered a starred exercise. Since you are learning how to represent information to a reasoning program, let us consider the properties that must be captured by a clause(s) for vertical plays. Listing the properties to be captured is one way of working toward needed clauses in any problem. A vertical play must start with an achievable state and yield an achievable state. A domino played vertically covers one square in each of two adjacent rows, and the squares have the same number between 1 and 8. If a square is covered or removed in the row under consideration, then a domino cannot be played vertically starting with that square. These properties suggest that the predicate ACHIEVABLE be used again, that a mechanism be found to advance the row number by 1, and that another mechanism be found to give the condition of each square in the new row based on the condition of the square above it.

The needed clause(s) can have the same form as clauses 2 through 8—two literals in the predicate ACHIEVABLE, one negative and one positive. This form is suggested by **if** one state is achievable, **then** another is achievable. Of the mechanisms to advance the row number by 1, we choose a function that performs certain arithmetic functions automatically. The function $sum automatically adds two numbers and yields their sum. (Functions preceded by "$" are functions that build in certain operations. Such functions have meaning built into them. They are not available in all automated reasoning programs.) The mechanism for forcing the correct state of a square to be computed based on the square above it is that of complementation. The complement, denoted by compl, of covered is not covered, of not covered is covered, and of removed is not covered. Notice that compl captures the idea that, if a square is covered then the one below it cannot be covered by a vertical play, if not covered then it and the square below it can be covered by a vertical play, and if removed then the one below it cannot be covered.

Relying on the analysis of the situation,

(9) ¬ACHIEVABLE(row(x), squares(y1, y2, y3, y4, y5, y6, y7, y8))

| ACHIEVABLE(row($sum(x, 1)), squares(compl(y1), compl(y2),

compl(y3), compl(y4), compl(y5), compl(y6), compl(y7), compl(y8)))

is perhaps the clause you expected. Clause 9 is the one we shall use. Its use requires certain additional clauses, for we wish to have information about the state of a row maintained directly in terms of the constants r, n, and c rather than in terms of compl. Thus we must provide a means for a reasoning program to rewrite expressions in compl to ones in the constants r, n, and c. In Chapter 3, you were introduced to a mechanism for automatically rewriting information—for transforming information from one form to another. The mechanism, *demodulation*, comes into play here as it did in the jobs puzzle. Can you write down the needed *demodulators* to be used in connection with clause 9?

The idea is the standard one—imitate in a general way what has gone before. This is the idea for doing new problems, ones not covered here. In the jobs puzzle, we wished "crossed" to be automatically removed. The demodulator

$$EQUAL(list(crossed, x), x)$$

was employed to automatically remove "crossed" from any point in a list. Similarly, the demodulators

(10) $EQUAL(compl(c), n)$

(11) $EQUAL(compl(n), c)$

(12) $EQUAL(compl(r), n)$

automatically replace expressions in the function compl by the appropriate value.

Although clause 9, with the aid of clauses 10 through 12, is just what is needed to enable a reasoning program to make vertical plays, a problem does exist. Without anything additional, dominoes could be played vertically to extend into the nonexistent row 9. To prevent such an occurrence, we rely on the mechanism known as *subsumption*. In Chapter 4, subsumption was introduced and shown to be a means for discarding information that is less general than already existing information. As usual, we wish to encourage you to think of the tricks to come, and thus learn to invent your own when new problems are encountered. With this motivation, imagine the kind of clauses that can occur—that can express the play of dominoes that intrude on the nonexistent row 9, and hence must be immediately discarded. For example,

$$ACHIEVABLE(row(9), squares(c, c, c, n, n, n, c, c))$$
$$ACHIEVABLE(row(9), squares(c, n, n, n, c, c, c, c))$$

are two clauses that might occur if no precaution is taken. The object is to supply a clause to the program that is general enough to immediately subsume the two clauses —to immediately classify the two clauses as less general than itself, and thus discard them. This general clause must be able to subsume any other clause like the two just given. The clause

(13) $ACHIEVABLE(row(9), squares(y1, y2, y3, y4, y5, y6, y7, y8))$

will suffice.

Notice that this clause is not as general as possible. For example, the subexpression row(9) could be replaced by row(x), yielding an even more general clause. But this clause is not a good choice. The problem with it is that it would subsume valuable clauses that contain information about rows other than row 9. Thus, in using such a trick, you must find a clause that is general enough to subsume clauses that you wish the program to discard, and not so general that it subsumes and hence discards clauses that the program had better keep. This subsumer clause 13 must not be allowed to participate in the search for new information. Its existence is solely for the purpose of discarding unwanted information. To block clause 13 from participation, clause 13 is placed on a special list that is kept separate from those clauses that are consulted by the inference rules.

The final task of representation is that required to enable the program to find a contradiction, if one can be found. The puzzle simply asks you to determine if the modified checkerboard can be precisely covered with the dominoes. So, as stated, no obvious conclusion is present to assume false, which in turn would prepare the way for finding a contradiction. Examination of the clauses given so far suggests that expected clauses take the form of positive unit clauses—clauses with one literal and without a **not** sign. Thus a good guess at the form of the contradiction leads to the notion that a negative unit clause is needed. From a different viewpoint, and reminiscent of the jobs puzzle, you might deliberately assume that a precise cover of the modified checkerboard exists—that a certain state is achievable. If achievable,

$$\text{ACHIEVABLE}(\text{row}(8), \text{squares}(c, c, c, c, c, c, c, n))$$

is a clause that you would expect a reasoning program to find. Notice that the eighth square in the eighth row is designated in this clause by n and not by r. This results from the form of the clauses that enable the program to make horizontal and vertical plays, and hence the form that the clauses found by a reasoning program will take. In particular, the representation being used here will produce n or c for the state of various squares, and will not produce r. Of course a way exists for expressing the fact that this square is removed rather than not covered, but, since contradiction is the goal, this form is desirable. We thus add

$$(14)\quad \neg\text{ACHIEVABLE}(\text{row}(8), \text{squares}(c, c, c, c, c, c, c, n))$$

as the assumed denial that the board can be covered—the denial that this state can be achieved. Both ways of looking at the problem—the mechanistic and the imitation of the technique illustrated in Chapter 3—suggest a clause like 14. Corroboration of this kind is one check of the accuracy of representation.

5.1.3 Choosing the Inference Rule

The representation phase of this puzzle is the hardest part. As for choosing an inference rule or type of reasoning, first note that the object is to find achievable states. Each such state is represented by a positive unit clause. Thus two inference rules immediately come to mind. The first, *UR-resolution*, takes a set of clauses all but one of which are unit clauses and yields a unit clause. The clauses yielded with this inference rule may be positive or negative. The second choice is *hyperresolution* which takes a set of clauses all but one of which are positive clauses and yields a positive clause. A clause yielded by this inference rule may have one or more literals. Ordinarily, you might think that a combination of the two rules is needed. Such a combination is available to an automated reasoning program. But, in this case, hyperresolution is fine. The reason is that, because of the structure of the clauses in this problem, the only positive clauses that can be yielded by hyperresolution contain exactly one literal.

5.1.4 Strategy for Attacking the Puzzle

Since we wish the reasoning program to concentrate on moving from the original totally uncovered board to the contradiction, if one exists, we employ the strategy known as *set of support*. Use of this strategy allows you to choose from among the clauses for a problem, and designate one or more as the key(s). Employment of the set of support strategy causes a reasoning program to classify newly generated clauses also as keys to permit them in turn to be used. The strategy then forbids a reasoning program from ever applying an inference rule to a set of clauses that fails to have one of the key clauses present. In this puzzle, for example, clause 1 or clauses 1 and 14 can be chosen as the key clause or key clauses. By making either of these choices, a reasoning program using the *set of support strategy* will concentrate on moving forward from the initial state of the modified board. With hyperresolution, clause 14 will come into play only when and if a contradiction has been found.

5.1.5 Properties and Results of the Given Approach

With clauses 1 through 14 as input, an automated reasoning program solved the puzzle in less than 9 seconds on an IBM 3033. Fewer than 500 clauses were needed to complete the analysis. The program found that there is no covering of the modified checkerboard with the dominoes. No "proof by contradiction" was found, for a contradiction would have established the reverse—that a covering does exist. The program instead exhausted all of the possible achievable states—exhausted all of the sequences of plays restricted by the ordering rules, given earlier, of what is an acceptable play. Since the ordering restrictions do not rule out any covering, if one were to exist, the conclusion that no covering exists is correct.

Since the achievable partial coverings are the key, and not the particular play of dominoes that obtain the partial covering, subsumption proved invaluable. Subsumption discarded, for each partial covering, all but one of the ways to reach that partial covering. In other words, subsumption enables a reasoning program to recognize that a partial covering has been obtained by one sequence of plays, and that any other sequence producing the same partial covering is unneeded. This move sharply reduces the combinatorics of the problem. If subsumption were not used, a reasoning program or a person even with the benefit of the restricted rule of play of this chapter would be forced to examine more than 100,000 sequences of plays.

The method given here was successfully applied to other modified checkerboards—ones that could be covered. A cover was found in approximately 3 seconds. The method is one that generalizes to consideration of boards with various squares removed in various combinations. Thus, the method is much more general than the black-and-white argument that a person might properly give for the original puzzle as stated.

The puzzle represents various problems, such as that cited for a mythical real estate developer or such as that of placement of furniture in a room. Similar problems exist for laying pipes or for laying out the wires for a circuit.

While clauses 2 through 8 are used in effect to play one domino at a time, clause 9 plays a number at a time. For example, if clause 1 and clause 9 are considered with hyperresolution, the resulting clause states that seven dominoes have been played vertically, covering squares 2 through 8 of rows 1 and 2. On the other hand, clause 2 and clause 1 do not yield a clause, which is as it should be. After all, clause 2 is for plays in squares 1 and 2 of a row, and square 1 is unavailable in row 1 because of being removed.

If a modified board is studied that can in fact be covered by playing dominoes, the actual plays that achieve the covering can be retrieved. The retrieval is accomplished by tracing the proof to see which clauses were used at which times. A proof will have been found if the modified board is coverable. The clauses that were used allow you to know which dominoes were played horizontally and vertically and on which squares. In retrieving the actual play of the dominoes, keep in mind that a vertical play can play a number of dominoes simultaneously.

Thus, the method can be used for both sides of the question, for proving that a modified board cannot be covered and for finding the cover of a board that can be covered. The method can be used for boards modified by removing various squares of the same or of different colors, whether two squares or ten are removed. Partial coverings, covering an equal number of black and of white squares, of the first three rows that at first might seem achievable were found by an automated reasoning program to be unachievable. Can you give a partial covering of the first three rows—one that covers an equal number of black and of white squares—that cannot be achieved by playing dominoes horizontally and vertically?

Here is one.

```
r   c   c   c   c   c   c   c
c   c   c   c   c   c   c   c
n   c   n   n   c   n   c   n
```

Can you prove that this covering cannot be achieved?

Here is a proof. The first two squares of row 2 must be covered by a domino played horizontally. The second square of row 3 must be covered by a domino played vertically. That vertically played domino must cover the second square of row 2, but that square is already covered by the horizontally played domino. Thus, assuming that such a partial covering is achievable leads to a contradiction.

The black-and-white argument would not help you with this particular problem. Such problems can occur, for example, in laying out a circuit with the constraint of not having wires cross.

EXERCISES

The basic technique described for solving the domino problem can be extended in several ways. In these problems we consider a few of the possible extensions.

1. One essential feature of the approach is that of proceeding methodically, covering the rows strictly in order. However, no ordering is imposed on the horizontal play of dominoes within a single row. For example, if three dominoes are to be played horizontally in a single row to cover six given squares, the program would generate states based on playing them in each of the six possible sequences of plays. Suppose that

    ACHIEVABLE(row(3), squares(c, n, n, n, n, n, n, c))

    is one achievable state, which can occur, for example, if the modified board has squares 1 and 8 missing from the first row. Suppose also that three dominoes are to be played horizontally. The clauses given earlier for playing dominoes horizontally can be used to deduce each of the following six intermediate states.

    ACHIEVABLE(row(3), squares(c, c, c, n, n, n, n, c))
    ACHIEVABLE(row(3), squares(c, n, n, c, c, n, n, c))
    ACHIEVABLE(row(3), squares(c, n, n, n, n, c, c, c))
    ACHIEVABLE(row(3), squares(c, c, c, c, c, n, n, c))
    ACHIEVABLE(row(3), squares(c, c, c, n, n, c, c, c))
    ACHIEVABLE(row(3), squares(c, n, n, c, c, c, c, c))

    The fourth, fifth, and sixth of these clauses can each be obtained in two ways from the preceding three clauses by playing an additional domino horizontally. In particular, if not prevented from doing so, a reasoning program will duplicate each of the last three clauses. Show how the program can be prevented from this duplication by being forced to play dominoes from left to right in any given row.

2. To this point, we have considered checkerboards that are only slightly modified. Suppose now that we wish to consider covering a checkerboard that may have a number of its squares missing. Give at least one way to represent such a problem.

3. Now that you have considered how to cover an arbitrarily modified board with one-by-two dominoes, we turn to the consideration of other shapes. To begin with, show how to handle problems involving one-by-three dominoes.

4. Next, consider the problem of covering a modified checkerboard consisting of exactly 26 squares. You have seven one-by-two dominoes and four one-by-three dominoes. Given one such checkerboard—for example, one consisting of the first three complete rows along with the leftmost two squares of the fourth row—what clauses are sufficient to find a covering, if one exists.

5.2 The Missionaries and Cannibals Puzzle

There are three missionaries and three cannibals on the west bank of a river. There is a boat on the west bank that can hold no more than two people. The missionaries wish to cross to the east bank. But they have a problem: If on either bank the cannibals ever outnumber the missionaries, the outnumbered missionaries will be eaten. Is there a way for the missionaries to get their wish—to get to the east bank without losing anyone?

This puzzle is vaguely reminiscent of scheduling problems. For example, a number of meetings must be held, some of which must run in parallel. Various constraints exist on scheduling all the meetings. Some must precede others, while some must not be held in parallel. Certain speakers have prior travel arrangements, and so must give various talks consistent with their prior plans. The question is: With all of the constraints, does a schedule exist that conforms to the requirements?

5.2.1 Representing the Puzzle to a Reasoning Program

As in the modified checkerboard puzzle, we must represent the situation that exists at the beginning of the puzzle. Then, clauses must be found to enable an automated reasoning program to move missionaries, cannibals, and the boat from one bank of the river to the other and back. The program must be able to cope with the problem of keeping the missionaries alive. Finally, the reasoning program must be able to tell when the puzzle has been solved, or determine if possible that it cannot be solved. If the puzzle is solvable, then there is an arrangement in which the three missionaries are on the east bank of the river. If the puzzle is not solvable, then every sequence of boat trips results at some point in the cannibals having a feast, or a sequence of boat trips that simply results in repeating some arrangement of missionaries and cannibals. For example, one cannibal could take the boat from one bank to the other and back, forever.

We can start by borrowing the predicate ACHIEVABLE from the modified checkerboard puzzle. The general idea is to start with an achievable arrangement of missionaries, cannibals, and boat and deduce other achievable arrangements. Recalling that the key components of achievable states in the preceding puzzle are the row and the squares, you might attempt to parallel the previous solution by listing the key components of achievable states for this puzzle. The list might consist of three items: the number of missionaries and cannibals on the west bank, the position of the boat, and the number of missionaries and cannibals on the east bank. Using these three components, does a glance at clause 1 of the preceding puzzle suggest an acceptable clause 1 for this puzzle?

Clause 1 for this puzzle must give the starting state—three missionaries, a boat, and three cannibals on the west bank of a river.

(1) ACHIEVABLE(west(m3, c3), boatonwest, east(m0, c0))

Notice that, while the predicate ACHIEVABLE in the checkerboard puzzle has two arguments, ACHIEVABLE for this puzzle has three. The three arguments here correspond to the three components of an achievable state. The first argument gives the number of missionaries and cannibals on the west bank—three of each. The second argument gives the position of the boat—on the west bank. The third argument gives the number of missionaries and cannibals on the east bank—zero of each.

Next, clauses are needed to move missionaries and/or cannibals from the west bank to the east bank, and back. After all, the boat holds no more than two, so a number of trips will be necessary—if the puzzle can be solved at all. Again, as is typical of what you will likely do when a new problem is encountered but not covered in the book, imitate what has gone before. In the checkerboard puzzle, clauses were given to enable the program to play dominoes, and similar clauses can be given to enable the program to move people. What are the possible initial moves —the boat trips that make the missionaries' wish have a chance of coming true? Moving one person across is pointless, for that person must just bring the boat back. Moving two missionaries across with the hope of getting their wish quickly is unthinkable, for the missionary left on the west bank will become a meal. Either two cannibals can take the boat to the east bank, or one missionary and one cannibal can.

(2) $\neg$ACHIEVABLE(west(m3, c3), boatonwest, east(m0, c0))

| ACHIEVABLE(west(m3, c1), boatoneast, east(m0, c2))

(3) $\neg$ACHIEVABLE(west(m3, c3), boatonwest, east(m0, c0))

| ACHIEVABLE(west(m2, c2), boatoneast, east(m1, c1))

Clauses 2 and 3, respectively, enable a reasoning program to start with the people on the west bank and move some of them to the east bank without endangering the missionaries. If hyperresolution is applied to clauses 1 and 2, the program gets

(4) ACHIEVABLE(west(m3, c1), boatoneast, east(m0, c2))

which gives the state after moving two cannibals to the east bank. Recall that the type of reasoning or inference rule known as hyperresolution will suffice here because we are starting with a clause with only positive literals, and intending to deduce a clause with only positive literals. To be more precise, we are starting with a positive unit clause—a clause with one positive literal—and aiming at producing a positive unit clause, since we wish to find additional achievable states. Since such achievable states take the form of positive unit clauses, we might under other conditions be forced to ask for more than hyperresolution, for that inference rule does not force the conclusion to consist of one literal. But in this puzzle, the nature of the clauses forces conclusions obtained with hyperresolution to have but one literal.

If hyperresolution is applied to clauses 1 and 3,

(5) ACHIEVABLE(west(m2, c2), boatoneast, east(m1, c1))

is the result. Since neither we nor a reasoning program necessarily knows which trip, if either, is the first of a sequence of good trips for getting the missionaries their wish, both clauses 4 and 5 must be kept. In addition, both 4 and 5 must be used to explore further trips for the same reason. Thus, clauses must be added to continue the trips started by clause 4 and by clause 5, respectively. Can you give the clauses that continue the trips started by clause 4 and started by clause 5?

(6) $\neg$ACHIEVABLE(west(m3, c1), boatoneast, east(m0, c2))

| ACHIEVABLE(west(m3, c2), boatonwest, east(m0, c1))

(7) $\neg$ACHIEVABLE(west(m2, c2), boatoneast, east(m1, c1))

| ACHIEVABLE(west(m3, c2), boatonwest, east(m0, c1))

Clause 6 is the only acceptable one that continues the trip represented by clause 4, since there is no point in having both cannibals return to the west bank. Clause 7 is the only acceptable continuation of 5, since bringing both people back is pointless, and having the cannibal return results in a feast that prevents the missionaries from getting their wish.

So far, the clauses to be given to the reasoning program are 1, 2, 3, 6, and 7. Clauses 4 and 5 are found by such a program and are given here as part of the analysis that shows what other clauses are necessary. With the same technique—that of attempting to continue the various trips in progress—clauses are needed to extend the trip in which the boat is on the west bank and all but one cannibal are also there. The clause

(8) $\neg$ACHIEVABLE(west(m3, c2), boatonwest, east(m0, c1))

| ACHIEVABLE(west(m3, c0), boatoneast, east(m0, c3))

is the only clause to consider for moving people in this situation.

From a general viewpoint, this approach to presenting the missionaries puzzle to an automated reasoning program consists of determining which arrangements of missionaries and cannibals and boat can occur. Both banks of the river must be considered, and clauses must be provided to enable the program to move the boat and no more than two people at a time from one acceptable state to another. Care must be taken not to overlook a possible state and a possible trip from a state to another state. Equally important, care must be taken not to permit a state to occur in which the missionaries' wish is not granted, unless of course their desire is hopeless.

Can you give the needed remaining clauses to complete this approach to presenting the missionaries and cannibals puzzle to an automated reasoning program? Be sure to give the clause that assumes the missionaries cannot get safely across, and is therefore usable by a reasoning program to find a contradiction.

5.2.2 A Sophisticated Representation

The approach to representation that we have just discussed is reasonably straightforward. Unfortunately, it is fraught with various dangers. The dangers are not possible errors that can be made by an automated reasoning program, but are instead errors that can be made by a person submitting the puzzle to such a program. The chances are greater than you might think, and might like, of a person overlooking some sequence of trips that might get the missionaries safely across. In addition, the risk of a person allowing a trip in which the cannibals get their secret wish is not minimized by the approach. Finally, you might say that the puzzle as given has not been presented to a reasoning program, for too much reasoning by a person has been necessary to present just the right clauses—those that represent acceptable trips. In a certain sense, you were required to solve too much of the puzzle in order to give appropriate clauses to a reasoning program. You had to protect the program from making an unwise boat trip, for example. If these last remarks reflect your position, you find us in complete agreement. The approach of the preceding subsection is too dangerous, and too much reasoning outside the program takes place. So we now give a representation that is closer to the actual puzzle, and places the burden of rejecting bad boat trips on an automated reasoning program.

Rather than figuring out which trips are to be avoided and which trips imply further trips, we instead consider the puzzle directly from its description. The boat holds no more than two people. Obviously, a number of trips are necessary, and the boat therefore can at various times be on either side of the river. The possible trips that must thus be considered are: one missionary, one cannibal, one of each, two missionaries, and two cannibals. Each such trip can be from the west bank to the east, or from the east to the west. In further contrast to the preceding, more straightforward approach, we do not wish to list each specific possible combination of missionaries and cannibals that might occur on some bank of the river. Instead, we write a clause that simultaneously covers a number of cases. For example, we write a clause that represents a boat trip that moves one cannibal from the west to the east bank, whether the west bank contains, say, three missionaries and three, two, or one cannibal. The clauses we write are in terms of the combination of people taking a boat trip, and not in terms of the arrangement of people on either side of the river.

The clause

(1) ACHIEVABLE(west($m(s(s(s(0))))$, $c(s(s(s(0))))$), boatonwest,

   east($m(0), c(0)$))

is the clause used to give the situation at the start of the puzzle. This clause 1 is rather like clause 1 of the preceding subsection, except that the number of missionaries and cannibals on each side of the river is denoted with a different representation. In the preceding version, for example, m3 and c0 were used respectively for three missionaries and zero cannibals. In this version, zero missionaries is denoted by $m(0)$, one missionary by $m(s(0))$, two cannibals by $c(s(s(0)))$, and so on. You are correct—the number of occurrences of the function s before a zero represents the number of missionaries or cannibals, as indicated by the function m or c. The function s acts like a function known as the successor function— a function that has a value of one greater than its argument. Thus, the successor of zero is 1, of 1 is 2, and of 2 is 3. Therefore, $s(s(0))$ acts like the number 2.

Clause 1 thus says that three missionaries and three cannibals are on the west bank, and zero of each on the east. How can this choice of representation be extended to the clauses needed to enable a reasoning program to study various boat trips? Let us carefully examine the process that might lead to finding the needed clauses.

For the first such clause—that which takes one cannibal from the west to the east bank—the plan is to have it suffice regardless of how many cannibals, other than zero, are on the west bank. The conclusions derived from the clause in question should, if possible, also record the fact that the number of missionaries on each side of the river has not changed. And the conclusions obtained by its use should record the facts that the number of cannibals on the west bank has been reduced by one, while the number on the east bank has increased by one. This clause, which will be clause 2, must in particular combine with clause 1 under, say, hyperresolution to yield a clause that says that the west bank now has three missionaries and two cannibals there, while the east now has zero missionaries and one cannibal. From clause 2, a reasoning program also should, if possible, deduce the fact that three missionaries and zero cannibals are left on the west bank and zero missionaries and three cannibals are on the east, when presented with the appropriate fact. The appropriate fact is that three missionaries and one cannibal are on the west bank. Finally, clause 2 must not combine with a fact that states that zero cannibals are on the west bank. The key is the use of variables, and thus again the power of the underlying language comes into play.

The clause

(2) $\neg$ACHIEVABLE(west(m(x), c(s(y))), boatonwest, east(m(z), c(w)))

| ACHIEVABLE(west(m(x), c(y)), boatoneast, east(m(z), c(s(w))))

is the one we are after. Notice that in clause 2 the variables x and z will, when its negative literal is matched by hyperresolution with some fact, catch and retain the status quo of the number of missionaries on the west and east banks. On the other hand, the expressions involving the variables y and w in the positive literal will, when hyperresolution is successful, have an occurrence of s removed from one and added to the other. For example, what happens when hyperresolution is applied to clauses 1 and 2 of this subsection?

ACHIEVABLE(west(m(s(s(s(0)))), c(s(s(0)))), boatoneast, east(m(0), c(s(0))))

is yielded, stating that the boat is on the east bank with zero missionaries and one cannibal, while three missionaries and two cannibals are on the west bank. When clause 2 is used, the variable y is replaced by one less than the number of cannibals on the west bank, while the variable w is replaced by the number on the east bank before the boat arrives. Thus, when hyperresolution succeeds in yielding a new fact, everything works just right—the number of cannibals on the east bank is increased by one, for example.

For the boat trip that takes one cannibal and no missionaries from the east bank to the west bank, the needed clause can be obtained by applying an analysis similar to the one that produced clause 2. However, take into account that the number of cannibals on the west bank must increase, while the number on the east bank decreases. The clause

(3) ¬ACHIEVABLE(west(m(x), c(y)), boatoneast, east(m(z), c(s(w))))

| ACHIEVABLE(west(m(x), c(s(y))), boatonwest, east(m(z), c(w)))

is the result.

As commented earlier, we are not building into the clauses that correspond to the possible boat trips protection against trips that cost the missionaries their chance. The needed protection will come later. We must first finish with the clauses that correspond to possible boat trips. Thus, we must have clauses for the remaining possible trips—those in which two people are taken from the west to the east or from the east to the west bank, and those that take one missionary in either direction. Can you supply the remaining eight clauses for these trips?

Two missionaries are taken from the west bank to the east:

(4) ¬ACHIEVABLE(west(m(s(s(x))), c(y)), boatonwest, east(m(z), c(w)))

| ACHIEVABLE(west(m(x), c(y)), boatoneast, east(m(s(s(z))), c(w)))

Two missionaries from east to west:

(5) ¬ACHIEVABLE(west(m(x), c(y)), boatoneast, east(m(s(s(z))), c(w)))

| ACHIEVABLE(west(m(s(s(x))), c(y)), boatonwest, east(m(z), c(w)))

One missionary and one cannibal from west to east:

(6) ¬ACHIEVABLE(west(m(s(x)), c(s(y))), boatonwest, east(m(z), c(w)))

| ACHIEVABLE(west(m(x), c(y)), boatoneast, east(m(s(z)), c(s(w))))

One missionary and one cannibal from east to west:

(7) ¬ACHIEVABLE(west(m(x), c(y)), boatoneast, east(m(s(z)), c(s(w))))

| ACHIEVABLE(west(m(s(x)), c(s(y))), boatonwest, east(m(z), c(w)))

One missionary from west to east:

(8) ¬ACHIEVABLE(west(m(s(x)), c(y)), boatonwest, east(m(z), c(w)))

| ACHIEVABLE(west(m(x), c(y)), boatoneast, east(m(s(z)), c(w)))

One missionary from east to west:

(9) ¬ACHIEVABLE(west(m(x), c(y)), boatoncast, cast(m(s(z)), c(w)))

| ACHIEVABLE(west(m(s(x)), c(y)), boatonwest, east(m(z), c(w)))

Two cannibals from west to east:

(10) ¬ACHIEVABLE(west(m(x), c(s(s(y)))), boatonwest, east(m(z), c(w)))

   | ACHIEVABLE(west(m(x), c(y)), boatoneast, east(m(z), c(s(s(w))))))

Two cannibals from east to west:

(11) ¬ACHIEVABLE(west(m(x), c(y)), boatoneast, east(m(z), c(s(s(w))))))

   | ACHIEVABLE(west(m(x), c(s(s(y)))), boatonwest, east(m(z), c(w)))

Clauses 2 through 11 cover the possible boat trips from west bank to east, and back. By relying on variables, no mention need be made of the actual number of people on either side of the river. By employing the notation relying on the function s and on the constant 0, the clauses prevent, for example, attempting to take a missionary from the west bank to the east when no missionaries are on the west bank. To see that such a trip cannot occur, try applying hyperresolution to a pair of clauses, one that takes at least one missionary from west to east and one that states that no missionaries are on the west bank. What happens is that the attempt to make the negative literal identical to the fact stating that no missionaries are on the west bank fails—fails because the symbols s and 0 are forced to be placed opposite each other, establishing that no substitution exists that makes them identical. Do you see a simple relationship that, when applied, yields the clauses for the east to west trips from the clauses for the west to east?

The relationship, or rule, for getting the east to west correspondent from the west to east is the following. Simply change the signs on the two literals of the west to east clause, making the negative one positive and the positive one negative. If desired, then interchange literals to produce a clause of a similar form. The trip east and the trip west are inverses of one another.

The clause that permits one missionary to travel alone from the west bank to the east is used in just two situations. It is used when three missionaries and two cannibals are on the west bank, and is used when one of each is on the west bank. The remaining situations do not call this clause into play because they correspond to situations in which the cannibals get their way—feast. These situations, as will immediately be seen, are blocked from doing damage by the use of one of the features of an automated reasoning program. But they are allowed to be considered by a reasoning program since we wish the program to recognize bad trips from good rather than being explicitly given the classification of each trip. We prefer to place as much burden as possible on a reasoning program—the burden of accepting or rejecting various situations.

To complete this representation, clauses are needed to block certain damaging boat trips—those that place more cannibals on one side of the river than missionaries. Also, clause(s) are needed to enable the reasoning program to find a contradiction. Let us first consider the second of the two needs, since it is the easier to satisfy.

The puzzle asks whether there is a way to get the missionaries across without losing any of them to the cannibals. As usual, we can either assume there is a way, or assume there is not a way. If we wish to attempt to prove that there is a way for the missionaries to get safely across, then we assume that it cannot be done and seek a contradiction. To assume it cannot be done amounts to assuming that a certain state or arrangement of people is not achievable, at least in the context of the preceding discussion. Although the puzzle (as stated here) asks only about the missionaries getting across, let us seek to prove that all six people can get across without a feast taking place. After all, that version of the puzzle is the more commonly quoted one —that which asks for all six to cross the river safely. What is the state, and the corresponding clause, that must thus be unachievable?

The clause

$$(12) \quad \neg\text{ACHIEVABLE}(\text{west}(m(0), c(0)), x, \text{east}(m(s(s(s(0)))), c(s(s(s(0))))))$$

expresses the unachievable state that corresponds to assuming the puzzle unsolvable. (Technically, the puzzle would also be solved if you prove that no way exists for the missionaries to get their wish, but we are using solvable here to mean that they do get their wish.) Notice that the clause expresses no interest in where the boat ends up, for a variable x is found in the position for the boat. Of course, if the six get to the east bank, the boat will be there, but clause 12 covers that case as well as the case in which the boat is miraculously back on the west bank also. Notice that you are not forced to decide where the boat must be in order to supply clause 12, for that part of the reasoning can be left to the program. If the six people get there safely, then

$$\text{ACHIEVABLE}(\text{west}(m(0), c(0)), \text{boatoneast}, \text{east}(m(s(s(s(0)))), c(s(s(s(0))))))$$

will be deduced, and will contradict clause 12. What does happen in the puzzle? If the puzzle is solvable, can you trace the solution to it in clauses? What clause could be added in place of 12 to correspond to the missionaries getting across safely, yet expressing no interest in what happens to the cannibals?

We come to the final task, that of enabling an automated reasoning program to block the trips that result in distress to the missionaries. Have you guessed what mechanism, among those you have already seen in action, is used? It is subsumption. Recall that subsumption discards unwanted clauses as soon as they are generated—discards them before they can be added to the retained information, and hence before they can be used. Rather than blocking the bad trips, clauses are used to immediately discard the results of a bad trip—before the missionaries are harmed.

As for determining the form of the clauses that are used, list in clause form the arrangements of people to be avoided. For example, two missionaries and three cannibals on the west bank must be avoided. One missionary and either two or three cannibals on the west bank must be avoided. Similar conditions on the east bank must be avoided. After listing all of the arrangements to be avoided, notice that they can be characterized by the difference between the number of missionaries and the number of cannibals. There are four such arrangements—differences of one and of two for either bank of the river. Rather than listing each specific arrangement to be avoided, we again use the power of variables as we did in clauses 2 through 11.

(13) ACHIEVABLE(west(m(s(x)), c(s(s(x)))), y, east(z, w))

(14) ACHIEVABLE(west(m(s(x)), c(s(s(s(x))))), y, east(z, w))

(15) ACHIEVABLE(west(x, y), z, east(m(s(w)), c(s(s(w)))))

(16) ACHIEVABLE(west(x, y), z, east(m(s(w)), c(s(s(s(w))))))

Clauses 13 through 16 suffice. If any bad trip is taken resulting in an excess of cannibals over missionaries on either side of the river, the results are immediately subsumed by one of 13 through 16, and hence discarded. Of course, 13 through 16 are not allowed to participate in the inference mechanism, in the search for achievable arrangements. They are simply placed on a list that is consulted for the purpose of discarding less general information than is present; hence subsumption comes into play. Again, in 13 through 16, a variable occupies the position of the boat, for it does not matter where the boat is if and when an excess occurs.

EXERCISES

5. What clauses might be used to see whether or not four missionaries and four cannibals can get across?

6. Formulate the problem of five missionaries and five cannibals with a boat that will hold three people.

7. Determine whether or not five missionaries and five cannibals can get across with a boat that will hold three people, and, if they can, give the solution.

8. Can you reformulate the missionaries and cannibals problem in such a way that a single transition axiom suffices? In other words, can you find a formulation in which only one rule is used to represent trips from one side of the river to the other?

9. There is a classical problem in artificial intelligence called the "monkey and bananas" problem. In this problem a monkey is in a room with some bananas hanging from the ceiling. The room contains a box. The monkey can reach the bananas only if he stands on the box. Think of a state as characterized by the position of the monkey, the position of the box, whether or not the monkey is on the box, and whether or not he has the bananas. The position of the bananas is some constant. An initial state is given by the following clause

(1) ACHIEVABLE(monkeypos, boxpos, no, no)

stating that the monkey is at monkeypos, the box is at boxpos, the monkey is not on the box, and the monkey does not have the bananas. Suppose that the bananas are at bananaspos.

(a) What clause denies that the monkey can get to the bananas?

(b) What clause can be used to say that the monkey can move anywhere, if he is not on the box?

(c) What clause indicates that the monkey can move the box anywhere if he is not on the box and is at the same position as the box?

(d) With the foregoing as background, what additional clauses are required to complete the problem?

10. Using the clauses from problem 9, give a proof relying on hyperresolution as the inference rule that the monkey can get the bananas.

5.3 The Billiard Balls and Balance Scale Puzzle

There are twelve billiard balls, eleven of which are identical in weight. The remaining ball—the odd one—has a different weight. You are not told whether it is heavier or lighter. You have a balance scale for weighing the balls. Can you find which ball is the odd ball in three weighings, and also find out whether it is lighter or heavier than the others?

This puzzle presents obstacles similar to those encountered when planning a trip that must be completed in a specified amount of time. For example, if you wish to visit two people who live in different sections of the same city but no constraint is placed on when you meet each person, you have one problem to solve. If, however, your first visit cannot end before 2:00 in the afternoon while your second must begin before 3:30, you have quite another problem. In the second case, often you must make a series of choices among possible routes, where some of the choices depend on what the traffic is like at different intersections. You can, of course, discard some choices immediately because you know that the corresponding route will require entirely too much time. The better choices maximize the time left to complete the remainder of the trip.

In the billiard ball puzzle, if you were simply asked to find the odd ball with no restriction on the number of weighings, you would have no difficulty in doing so. You could begin by weighing the first ball against the second. If the scale did not balance, then you would know that one of the two was the odd ball. In that case, at most one more weighing would find the odd one and would also establish whether it was lighter or heavier. On the other hand, if the first weighing resulted in a balanced scale, you could select the first of the two balls just weighed to be then used in succeeding weighings. You would know that the selected ball was of standard weight, and you could, with as many as ten more weighings, find the odd ball and determine its heavier or lighter status. But in this puzzle you must find the odd ball in three weighings, or admit defeat. Thus each weighing must be chosen to give you as much information as possible, just as each choice in your trip must leave as much remaining time as possible. In particular, certain weighings can be eliminated immediately because of the possibility that the outcome will leave too many balls from which to make the desired determination.

How can an automated reasoning program solve this puzzle, if there is a way to find the odd ball in three weighings? How can it determine that a particular weighing is not worth considering because it gives too little information? How can it discard such useless weighings? Finally, for the most obvious question, how can it make weighings at all?

5.3.1 Representing the Puzzle

This puzzle is substantially more difficult to solve than either of the preceding two. The representation of the procedure for solving it is far more complex than what you have seen to this point. The fault is not with the choice of representation but is instead a reflection of the nature of the puzzle. You may find some of the clauses given in this section very taxing. Nevertheless, the effort required to master them may be rewarded by sharply increasing your understanding of various aspects of representing information. In addition, you will learn of techniques for automatically discarding unwanted information—techniques based on evaluation rather than on subsumption. With this warning, we now turn to the puzzle.

As in the preceding two puzzles, the notion of "state" is the key to this puzzle. For the dominoes and checkerboard puzzle, a state consists of the list of squares (in the row under examination) that are removed, those that are covered, and those that are uncovered. We use "transition" axioms to pass from one "achievable" state to another. A transition axiom for that puzzle plays dominoes, horizontally one at a time, vertically many at a time. With few exceptions, the reasoning program examines only achievable states. The exceptions are those that attempt to play a domino in the ninth row. The modified checkerboard is proved uncoverable by examining all distinctly different achievable states and showing that, by exhaustive analysis, a covering of the checkerboard does not exist. In contrast to the missionaries and cannibals puzzle, no moves are made and then rejected because of being bad moves. Were a covering to exist, the number of dominoes to produce it is known, 31. The notion of getting as much out of a single play, because some time limit or its equivalent exists, is not present. We merely begin with the initial state, and apply transition axioms until all achievable states are examined.

In the missionaries and cannibals puzzle, we also begin with the initial state and apply various transition axioms to pass from one achievable state to another. A transition axiom for that puzzle moves some combination of missionaries, cannibals, and the boat from one bank of the river to the other. Application of a transition axiom produces a new state from an older state, resulting in a rearrangement of missionaries, cannibals, and the boat. Although again no attempt is made to get as much as possible out of a move—a boat trip—in contrast to the domino puzzle a number of states are obtained and then rejected. The rejection is to protect the missionaries from disaster and is effected by means of subsumption. Since no limit is placed on the number of boat trips that may be needed to get the missionaries their wish, no information of the type is kept as part of the state. On the other hand, as you will see, a state for the billiard ball puzzle does keep information about how many weighings remain. Again, except for the situation that results in disaster, a number of sequences of boat trips are pursued, since it is not known which will terminate with success.

The billiard ball puzzle differs sharply from the two preceding puzzles because a move—a weighing—to increase the chance of finding the odd ball must add as much information as possible. For example, weighing one ball against another does not add much information. We have to get as much information out of each weighing as we can since the number of weighings we are allowed is so limited. The concept of state, therefore, must take into account the number of weighings that remain. To see what else must be reflected in a state, and also as an illustration of how you can assist an automated reasoning program, notice that the use of a balance scale says that any ball of "standard" weight is as good as any other of standard weight. The assistance takes the form of using the knowledge of what a balance scale is and then imparting that knowledge in the representation of the problem. In particular, a billiard ball need not be numbered with a number from 1 through 12, but can instead be identified by what is known about it. Each ball, at any given time, is in one of four classes. As we learn the results of weighings, a ball may change from being in one class to being in another. Each ball, after a weighing, is known to be of standard weight, light or standard, heavy or standard, or heavy or light or standard weight. For example, if one ball is weighed against another and the scale tips to the left—the left side goes down, and the right side goes up—then the ball on the left is among the heavy or standard weight balls and the one on the right is among the light or standard. Obviously, each weighing may change the classification of the balls that are being weighed. In the initial state, all balls are in the heavy or light or standard class—nothing is known about any of them.

Thus, each state is represented by five numbers, the first four of which, in the representation we shall use, are for the four classes of balls just discussed and the fifth for the number of weighings that remain. For example, if we were not concerned with readability, the clause

ACHIEVABLE(12, 0, 0, 0, 3)

could be used to say that the initial state is achievable. However, since readability is important, we use five functions to indicate the meaning of each of the five numbers. These five functions, therefore, are present only for clarity. For example, hls(12) means that there are 12 balls in the heavy-light-standard class. As a reminder that this group of five numbers is a state, and because we wish to reason about this state, we introduce a "state" function to group these numbers together. Using the abbreviations of hls for heavy or light or standard, hs for heavy or standard, ls for light or standard, s for standard, and rem for remaining weighings, the initial state is given with the clause

ACHIEVABLE(state(hls(12), hs(0), ls(0), s(0), rem(3)))

The transition axioms for this problem are substantially more complex than those for the domino puzzle or the missionaries puzzle. The added complexity arises from the fact that application of a transition axiom, a weighing, in this puzzle can produce three results: the scale may tip to the left, may balance, or may tip to the right. In contrast, in the two preceding puzzles, the application of a transition axiom produces one result. In the missionaries and cannibals puzzle, if a sequence of applications of transition axioms—a sequence of boat trips—leads to a state in which the missionaries have safely reached the east bank of the river, then the puzzle has been solved. In contrast, the billiard ball puzzle requires that a sequence of weighings, regardless of which of the three outcomes may occur at each weighing, leads to a determination of which is the odd ball. It is not enough that one or two of the three possible outcomes leads to a situation in which the odd ball can eventually be found. The idea is that of choosing a weighing so well that each of the three outcomes leads to the next weighing, where the next weighing is based on which of the three outcomes actually has occured. The next weighing must also have this same property of leading to good weighings. Finally, the last weighing must be such that the odd ball has been identified. A state is called "solvable" if it is one of the type just described. It is unsolvable if, for example, the number of balls that remain containing the odd one is too many for the number of weighings that remain. Such occurs when the first weighing weighs one ball against another, and they balance. As you will shortly see, some states can be immediately classed as unsolvable, while others must wait for classification until the reasoning program has finished with the puzzle. The puzzle thus asks whether or not the initial state is solvable. For a state to be called solvable, we also include the requirement of determining whether the odd ball is heavy or light.

Three states can be immediately classed as solvable. In one, no weighings remain, eleven of the billiard balls are known to be of standard weight, and one is known to be heavy or standard. Since the puzzle says eleven are identical and one is odd, we know that the heavy or standard weight ball is in fact heavy. A second solvable state is the counterpart to this one but with the twelfth ball known to be light or standard. A third state in which all twelve billiard balls are known to be of standard weight is solvable, but this state of course says that the puzzle was incorrectly given. Nevertheless, the clause corresponding to this third solvable state will turn out to be useful.

The basic idea for solving this puzzle is first to take the initial state and, using transition axioms, obtain additional achievable states. Since a transition axiom corresponds to a weighing, and since a weighing can produce three possible outcomes—the scale tips to the left, tips to the right, or balances—three achievable states are obtained from one. Since we are interested only in solvable states, we shall discard some of the achievable states or, more precisely, prevent them from being found. The prevention is by means of a numerical computation to be discussed. The generation of three achievable states from one achievable state is a two-step process. The first step generates a clause that "records" together the three resulting states. The second step generates each of the resulting three from the "record" statement.

The reasoning program proceeds in this fashion of generating a "record" statement from which achievable states are derived. They in turn lead to additional "record" statements. Finally, a "record" statement together with certain of the known solvable states discussed earlier enables the reasoning program to expand the number of solvable states. A state is proved solvable if a weighing starting with that state leads to three solvable states. Thus the plan is to take the given solvable states and work backward, expanding the set of solvable states until the initial state is finally included among the solvable states. The process we are about to present can, therefore, be described as proceeding in a forward direction, generating achievable states until the three weighings have been made. At that point, the program then proceeds in reverse, adding to the solvable states until the initial state has been proved solvable. Actually, the forward and reverse processes are not completely separated, nor need they be. Depending on the clause on which the program is currently focusing, the program may be reasoning in either direction.

Since a simple yes or no answer to a puzzle of this type is far from satisfactory —the precise weighings that find the odd ball should be accessible—the clauses contain appropriate information to recover the weighings that lead to the solution.

To complete the background for presenting the transition axioms, let us first discuss the numerical computation promised earlier that leads to classifying certain states as unsolvable, and hence not worth pursuing. The test consists of comparing the number of possible solutions—the number of possibilities for the odd ball—with the number of possible outcomes that can occur for the remaining weighings. The number of possibilities for the odd ball is twice the number of balls in the class of heavy or light or standard plus the number in the class of heavy or standard plus the number in the class of light or standard. (The first of these three numbers must be doubled because the odd ball may be light or heavy if it is among the balls of the first class.) The number of outcomes that can occur when there are n weighings remaining is 3^n. The justification is that each weighing can produce three outcomes. If the number of possibilities for the odd ball is greater than the number of outcomes, then the situation is hopeless. In that case, the state is known to be unsolvable. Put another way, if the first number exceeds the second, then the number of outcomes is insufficient to guarantee determination of the odd ball. Since making a transition to an unsolvable state is pointless—further transitions that build on that unsolvable state are a waste of time—we build a test into the appropriate transition axiom to avoid such states. The test we apply is the one just given. Of course, this test does not identify all unsolvable states, but it does eliminate quite a few.

We can immediately verify that the initial state passes the test. The calculation yields 24 as the number of possibilities for the odd ball: each of the twelve may be the odd one and may either be heavy or light. The calculation yields $3^3 = 27$ for the number of possible outcomes for the three remaining weighings. So we cannot rule out the solvability of the puzzle just on these grounds.

The first transition axiom also is designed to reflect the observation that there is no point in putting standard balls in both the left pan and the right pan. Such an action merely duplicates another weighing in which the smaller number of standard balls in the two pans is removed from both. By convention, no standard balls are ever placed in the left pan.

As we remarked, the object of applying the transition axioms is to obtain a "record" clause that collects together the possible three outcomes of the weighing. Each of the three outcomes is itself a state. Such a "record" clause was not used in the two preceding puzzles because each action led to a single result, not to a set of possible results.

We now come to the first transition axiom, and state it first in everyday language. The statement is quite complex, for it contains various conditions that must be satisfied for a weighing to make sense. We shall take the approach that the odd ball is only slightly different in weight from the standard balls, so that it only makes sense to weigh the same number of balls in each pan of the balance scale. This means that there will never be more than 6 balls in one pan. We assume that none of the balls are weightless, so we shall not consider weighings in which one of the pans is empty. The number of balls selected for the right pan plus the number selected for the left pan, say from the heavy-standard set, must be less than or equal to the number that are available for selection. Here is the axiom in the **if-then** form. Since the axiom must apply to various situations, we use variables to make this possible. Recall that, with few expectations, all expressions beginning with u through z are variables. The variables beginning with x are for the sets of balls from which the selection is made and for the number of weighings remaining, those beginning with y for those selected for the right pan, and those beginning with z for the left pan.

if

(1) we have reached an achievable state with xhls balls in the heavy-light-standard class, xhs balls in the heavy-standard class, xls balls in the light-standard class, xs balls in the standard class, and xrem weighings remain, **and**

(2) you pick yhls balls from the heavy-light-standard class to put in the right pan of the balance scale, **and**

(3) you pick yhs balls from the heavy-standard class to put in the right pan of the balance scale, **and**

(4) you pick yls balls from the light-standard class to put in the right pan of the balance scale, **and**

(5) you pick ys balls from the standard class to put in the right pan of the balance scale, **and**

(6) the total number of balls in the right pan (yhls + yhs + yls + ys) is less than or equal to 6, **and**

(7) the total number of balls in the right pan (yhls + yhs + yls + ys) is greater than 0, **and**

(8) you pick zhls additional balls from the heavy-light-standard class to put in the left pan of the balance scale, **and**

(9) you pick zhs additional balls from the heavy-standard class to put in the left pan of the balance scale, **and**

(10) you pick zls additional balls from the light-standard class to put in the left pan of the balance scale, **and**

(11) the number of balls in each pan is the same, (yhls + yhs + yls + ys) = (zhls + zhs + zls), **and**

(12) the scale tipping to the left is acceptable, meaning that the resulting state cannot be termed unsolvable according to the numerical test given earlier, **and**

(13) the scale tipping to the right is acceptable, meaning that the resulting state cannot be termed unsolvable according to the numerical test given earlier, **and**

(14) the scale balancing is acceptable, meaning that the resulting state cannot be termed unsolvable according to the numerical test given earlier,

then

record the transition. In other words, deduce the clause that records the transition that in turn can be used to deduce the resulting three achievable states.

Before giving the exceedingly long clause that corresponds to this axiom, we supply other needed items. We need clauses that permit a reasoning program to "pick" balls from the various classes.

PICK(0)
PICK(1)
PICK(2)
PICK(3)
PICK(4)
PICK(5)
PICK(6)

These unit clauses are used when the program "picks" balls from the classes. Since we are using a balance scale, and since there are twelve balls, the picking is restricted to values from 0 through 6. The value 0 is included since we need not weigh balls of every class in each weighing.

The next needed item focuses on the result of applying the transition axiom given earlier in everyday language. The clause must compute the new states from the given state, so must compute the effect on each of the classes of billiard balls. Let us first examine what conclusions should be drawn if the scale balances. Before the transition axiom is applied—before the weighing—the number of balls that is in the heavy-light-standard class is xhls. If the scale balances, then we know all the balls we have just weighed are standard. So those selected from among the xhls balls and put in the two pans are now known to be standard, and thus must be subtracted from xhls. Thus, the number of heavy-light-standard balls in the resulting state is xhls − (yhls + zhls). Similarly, the number in the heavy-standard class in the new state is xhs − (yhs + zhs). The number in the light-standard class is xls − (yls + zls).

Finally, the number of standard balls in the new state includes those that were already known to be standard plus those that were in the two pans for the current weighing but whose status was not already established as being of standard weight. Therefore, the number of standard class balls in the resulting state when the scale balances is xs + yhls + zhls + yhs + zhs + yls + zls.

When the scale tips left, no balls remain in the heavy-light-standard class. Those in the left pan are now known to be heavy-standard, those in the right pan light-standard, and those that were previously heavy-light-standard but not used in the weighing are now known to be standard. Thus, in the resulting state, the number in the heavy-light-standard class is zero, the number in the heavy-standard class is zhls + zhs, the number in the light-standard class is yhls + yls, and the number in the standard class is xs + zls + yhs + (xhls − yhls − zhls) + (xhs − yhs − zhs) + (xls − yls − zls).

A similar analysis applies when the scale tips right. The number in the heavy-light-standard is zero, the number in the heavy-standard is yhls + yhs, the number in the light-standard is zhls + zls, the number in the standard is xs + yls + zhs + (xhls − yhls − zhls) + (xhs − yhs − zhs) + (xls − yls − zls).

The final item to be discussed before giving the clause for the complex transition axiom is that of function evaluation. As promised earlier, some clauses are discarded by means of evaluation rather than by subsumption. In the clause to be given, we employ a number of "built-in" functions and predicates. For example, the function $sum automatically adds two expressions if they are both numbers. Similarly, the functions $diff, $prod, and $power perform corresponding arithmetic operations. The predicates $LE, $GT, and $EQ are also "built in" to automatically force certain evaluations. For example, $LE automatically compares its two arguments when they are numbers, and then evaluates the result to "true" or "false". If the literal ¬LE(s,t) for some numbers s and t evaluates to "false", then that literal is automatically removed. This occurs when s is less than or equal to t. If it evaluates to "true", then the attempt to apply hyperresolution, the inference rule we shall employ, is immediately terminated because, in effect, that literal cannot be removed from the clause so completion of the application of the inference rule is not possible. Similar actions are taken with $GT and $EQ. In contrast, the function "action" is not a built-in function, but is present in the transition axiom to retain a history of what the precise nature of the weighing is.

The following clause corresponds to the transition axiom given earlier in everyday language.

¬ACHIEVABLE(state(hls(xhls), hs(xhs), ls(xls), s(xs), rem(xrem)))

   | ¬PICK(yhls)

   | ¬PICK(yhs)

   | ¬PICK(yls)

   | ¬PICK(ys)

   | ¬$LE(yhls, xhls)

| ¬$LE(yhs, xhs)

| ¬$LE(yls, xls)

| ¬$LE(ys, xs)

| ¬$GT($sum(yhls, $sum(yhs, $sum(yls, ys))), 0)

| ¬$LE($sum(yhls, $sum(yhs, $sum(yls, ys))), 6)

| ¬PICK(zhls)

| ¬PICK(zhs)

| ¬PICK(zls)

| ¬$LE($sum(zhls, yhls), xhls)

| ¬$LE($sum(zhs, yhs), xhs)

| ¬$LE($sum(zls, yls), xls)

| ¬$EQ($sum(yhls, $sum(yhs, $sum(yls, ys))),
    $sum(zhls, $sum(zhs, zls)))

| ¬$LE($sum($sum(zhls, zhs), $sum(yhls, yls)),
    $power(3, $sum(xrem, − 1)))

| ¬$LE($sum($sum(zhls, zls), $sum(yhls, yhs)),
    $power(3, $sum(xrem, − 1)))

| ¬$LE($sum($prod(2, $sum(xhls, $minus($sum(yhls, zhls)))),
    $sum($sum(xhs, $minus($sum(yhs, zhs))),
    $sum(xls, $minus($sum(yls, zls))))),
    $power(3, $sum(xrem, − 1)))

| RECORD(parent(state(hls(xhls), hs(xhs), ls(xls), s(xs), rem(xrem))),

  action(putleft(hls(zhls), hs(zhs), ls(zls)),
      putright(hls(yhls), hs(yhs), ls(yls), s(ys))),

  left(state(hls(0), hs($sum(zhls, zhs)), ls($sum(yhls, yls)),
      s($sum($sum(xhls, $minus($sum(yhls, zhls))), $sum($sum(xhs,
      $minus(zhs)),
      $sum($sum(xls, $minus(yls)), xs)))), rem($sum(xrem, − 1)))),

  right(state(hls(0), hs($sum(yhls, yhs)), ls($sum(zhls, zls)),
      s($sum($sum(xhls, $minus($sum(zhls, yhls))), $sum($sum(xhs,
      $minus(yhs)),
      $sum($sum(xls, $minus(zls)), xs)))), rem($sum(xrem, − 1)))),

balance(state(hls($sum(xhls, $minus($sum(yhls, zhls)))),

    hs($sum(xhs, $minus($sum(yhs, zhs)))),

    ls($sum(xls, $minus($sum(yls, zls)))),

    s($sum(xs, $sum(yhls, $sum(zhls, $sum(yhs, $sum(zhs,

    $sum(yls, zls)))))))),

    rem($sum(xrem, − 1)))))

This transition axiom collects together the three states that result from a weighing, given a state as input to the weighing. The various literals containing the built-in functions automatically block certain transitions because they would produce a set of three states, at least one of which is provably unsolvable by the numerical rule given earlier. Three clauses are then used to separate the three resulting states. They convert the "record" clause into three clauses giving achievable states.

¬RECORD(parent(xp), left(xl), right(xr), balance(xbal))

    | ACHIEVABLE(xl)

¬RECORD(parent(xp), left(xl), right(xr), balance(xbal))

    | ACHIEVABLE(xr)

¬RECORD(parent(xp), left(xl), right(xr), balance(xbal))

    | ACHIEVABLE(xbal)

These three transition axioms together with the very long transition axiom are used with the PICK clauses to produce achievable states from an achievable state.

Since the plan calls for expanding the set of solvable states, starting with three known ones, until the initial state is proved solvable, we need the clauses relevant to that aspect. The three known solvable states are given with the following three clauses.

SOLVABLE(state(hls(0), hs(1), ls(0), s(11), rem(0)))

SOLVABLE(state(hls(0), hs(0), ls(1), s(11), rem(0)))

SOLVABLE(state(hls(0), hs(0), ls(0), s(12), rem(0)))

This last clause, representing the state in which all balls are known to be standard, looks a little strange. It is required because we are saying that a state is solvable if each of the three possible states that result from a weighing are solvable. Some cases arise in which one of the possible states resulting from a weighing is impossible unless there is no odd ball, contrary to the statement of the problem. Rather than complexify the definition of SOLVABLE to reflect this situation, we simply define the (impossible) case to be solvable.

To connect the clauses in RECORD with those in SOLVABLE and thus provide a bridge for expanding the class of solvable states, we add the following clause.

¬RECORD(parent(xp), left(xl), right(xr), balance(xbal))
   | ¬SOLVABLE(xl) | ¬SOLVABLE(xr) | ¬SOLVABLE(xbal)
   | SOLVABLE(xp)

As is typical of problem solving with an automated reasoning program, we now supply a clause that denies that the initial state is solvable.

¬SOLVABLE(state(hls(12), hs(0), ls(0), s(0), rem(3)))

This clause is the one that enables a reasoning program to know that the puzzle has been solved. It is used to establish a "proof by contradiction".

The approach we choose for the reasoning program to attempt to solve the puzzle employs the inference rule of hyperresolution. The chosen strategy is the set of support strategy. The only clauses that are placed in the set of support are the clause that gives the initial state and the one that denies that the initial state is solvable. The program is now in a position to attempt to solve the puzzle. When and if a proof by contradiction is found, the puzzle is solved. If the program is instructed to continue—and this is a surprise—many additional solutions are found. There are more than 40 nontrivially distinct solutions for the billiard ball puzzle. (One automated reasoning program solved this puzzle, obtaining all of the nontrivially distinct solutions, in less than 22 seconds on an IBM 3033.)

The following three points summarize the approach to solving problems of this type. First, the concept of state is intended to contain the information required to keep track of what stage a reasoning program or a person is at in the problem. Second, whenever possible, you should avoid making transitions to states that are known to be unproductive and uninteresting. Third, clauses are needed to enable a reasoning program to know when a solution has been obtained.

5.4 Answers to Exercises

1. There are several ways to achieve the desired result. Perhaps the simplest is to add an extra argument to the ACHIEVABLE predicate. This argument gives a column number that gives the minimum value for a column in which a horizontal domino is played. Thus no horizontal domino can be played to the left of this column. Then the initial state is given with

   ACHIEVABLE(row(1), squares(r, n, n, n, n, n, n, n), 1)

   The first two axioms that indicate how horizontal dominoes can be played would then be

   ¬ACHIEVABLE(row(x), squares(n, n, y3, y4, y5, y6, y7, y8), 1)
      | ACHIEVABLE(row(x), squares(c, c, y3, y4, y5, y6, y7, y8), 3)
   ¬ACHIEVABLE(row(x), squares(y1, n, n, y4, y5, y6, y7, y8), xcol)
      | ¬$LE(xcol, 2)
      | ACHIEVABLE(row(x), squares(y1, c, c, y4, y5, y6, y7, y8), 4)

The axiom for playing vertical dominoes would then be

¬ACHIEVABLE(row(x), squares(y1, y2, y3, y4, y5, y6, y7, y8), xcol)
   | ACHIEVABLE(row($sum(x, 1)), squares(compl(y1), compl(y2),
        compl(y3), compl(y4), compl(y5), compl(y6),
        compl(y7), compl(y8)), 1)

The axiom to subsume states in the ninth row and the axiom that the board can be covered must also then include the added third argument.

Here, \$LE is a special predicate that some automated reasoning programs recognize. The use of this predicate permits a program to automatically remove a literal such as

¬\$LE(1, 2)

during the formation of a hyperresolvent justified by noting that the literal must be *false*. If the program does not have this feature, then the third argument can employ values such as 0, s(0), s(s(0)), s(s(s(0))), ... to represent numbers. In addition, the axioms

\$LE(x, s(x))
\$LE(x, s(s(x)))
\$LE(x, s(s(s(x))))
\$LE(x, s(s(s(s(s(s(s(s(x))))))))))

would then be needed. Clearly, the "built-in" predicate is a more convenient approach.

2. There are several ways to solve this problem. The one that we propose may not be the simplest, but it does allow generalizations that are useful. The notion here is based on thinking of the board as a list such as

l(n,l(n,l(n,l(n,l(n,l(n,l(n,l(n,l(c,l(end,
l(n,l(n,l(n,l(n,l(n,l(n,l(n,l(n,l(n,l(end,
     .
     .
     .

)))))))...)

Here we show only two rows in their initial state, where the first row is uncovered except for the rightmost square. The end of each row is marked by the constant "end". Thus, an arbitrarily modified board can easily be represented by one of these huge terms. We employ the convention that any leading arguments that are "c" or "end" are removed. This means that the initial argument will be an "n" as long as at least one uncovered square remains on the board. We shall rely on demodulators to remove undesirable leading arguments in deduced clauses and thus "trim" the clauses. The following clauses suffice.

EQUAL(trim(l(c, x)), trim(x))
EQUAL(trim(l(end, x)), trim(x))
EQUAL(trim(l(n, x)), l(n, x))
EQUAL(trim(end), end)

The two clauses for playing dominoes are the following.

¬ACHIEVABLE(l(n, l(n, xrest))) | ACHIEVABLE(trim(xrest))

¬ACHIEVABLE(l(n, l(y2, l(y3, l(y4, l(y5, l(y6, l(y7, l(y8, l(y9, l(n, xrest)))))))))))
   | ACHIEVABLE(trim(l(y2, l(y3, l(y4, l(y5, l(y6, l(y7, l(y8, l(y9, l(c, xrest)))))))))))

The first clause enables a reasoning program to make horizontal plays of a domino, while the second is for vertical plays. The initial state is given by

ACHIEVABLE(⟨initial-board⟩)

where ⟨initial-board⟩ is the representation of the arbitrarily modified board. The denial that a covering is achievable is given by

¬ACHIEVABLE(end)

Since this solution is rather complex, do not be discouraged if you were not able to obtain it or if you find it difficult to follow.

3. The solution to problem 2 can be extended quite easily to the situation for one-by-three dominoes. Only the two clauses for playing dominoes need modification. If they are replaced by the following two clauses, the problem of representation is solved.

¬ACHIEVABLE(l(n, l(n, l(n, xrest)))) | ACHIEVABLE(trim(xrest))

¬ACHIEVABLE(l(n, l(y2, l(y3, l(y4, l(y5, l(y6, l(y7, l(y8, l(y9,
    l(n, l(y11, l(y12, l(y13, l(y14, l(y15, l(y16, l(y17, l(y18, l(n, xrest)))))))))))))))))))
   | ACHIEVABLE(trim(l(y2, l(y3, l(y4, l(y5, l(y6, l(y7, l(y8, l(y9,
    l(c, l(y11, l(y12, l(y13, l(y14, l(y15, l(y16, l(y17, l(y18, l(c, xrest)))))))))))))))))))

4. This problem can be solved by extending the ideas used to solve problems 2 and 3. We add two arguments to the ACHIEVABLE predicate. These arguments give the number of unplayed one-by-two and one-by-three dominoes. Thus, the initial state is represented with

ACHIEVABLE(7, 4, ⟨initial-board⟩)

The clauses for playing one-by-two dominoes for this problem are

¬ACHIEVABLE(xn1, xn2, l(n, l(n, xrest))) | ¬$GT(xn1, 0)
   | ACHIEVABLE($sum(xn1, −1), xn2, trim(xrest))

¬ACHIEVABLE(xn1, xn2, l(n, l(y2, l(y3, l(y4, l(y5, l(y6, l(y7, l(y8, l(y9, l(n, xrest)))))))))))
   | ¬$GT(xn1, 0)
   | ACHIEVABLE($sum(xn1, −1), xn2, trim(l(y2, l(y3, l(y4, l(y5, l(y6,
    l(y7, l(y8, l(y9, l(c, xrest)))))))))))

The clauses for playing the one-by-three dominoes are similar. This ends the discussion of extensions to the basic notion of how covering problems can be investigated.

5. The "sophisticated representation" can be used almost as is to attempt to solve this problem with an automated reasoning program. The only required changes are to represent the fact, both in the initial and final states, that the problem is about four

missionaries and four cannibals, and to add the two additional subsumer clauses

ACHIEVABLE(west(m(s(x)), c(s(s(s(s(x)))))), y, east(z, w))

ACHIEVABLE(west(x, y), z, east(m(s(w)), c(s(s(s(s(w)))))))

6. To have a reasoning program consider this problem, besides the two subsumption axioms added for problem 5, you must add two additional subsumption axioms. You must also modify the initial and final states to reflect the presence of five missionaries and five cannibals, and you must include some clauses for moving groups of three people across the river in the boat. The extra clauses for crossing the river are for three missionaries, three cannibals, and two missionaries with one cannibal. If you also mistakenly include a clause for moving two cannibals and one missionary, the missionary will perish.

7. The ten people can get across the river in the following way.
   (1) First three cannibals cross, and one returns.
   (2) Then two more cannibals cross, and one returns.
   (3) Then three missionaries cross, and one missionary and one cannibal return.
   (4) Then three missionaries cross, and one cannibal returns.
   (5) Finally, the three cannibals cross.

8. To represent the problem using a single transition axiom, you must modify the arguments in the ACHIEVABLE predicate. You can use

ACHIEVABLE(same(m(x1), c(x2)), xside, other(m(x3), c(x4)))

to mean that the boat is on xbank of the river, that x1 missionaries and x2 cannibals are on the same bank as the boat, and that x3 missionaries and x4 cannibals are on the other bank. The transition axiom then becomes

¬ACHIEVABLE(same(m(x1), c(x2)), xside, other(m(x3), c(x4)))

| ¬PICK(xm)

| ¬PICK(xc)

| ¬$LE(xm, x1)

| ¬$LE(xc, x2)

| ¬$LE($sum(xm, xc), 2)

| ¬$EQ(sideok($diff(x1, xm), $diff(x2, xc)), true)

| ¬$EQ(sideok($sum(x3, xm), $sum(x4, xc)))

| ACHIEVABLE(same(m($sum(x3, xm)), c($sum(x4, xc))), reverse(xside), other(m($diff(x1, xm)), c($diff(x2, xc))))

We need three axioms giving the acceptable values to pick.

PICK(0)

PICK(1)

PICK(2)

In addition, we need demodulators for the functions sideok and reverse.

EQUAL(sideok(0, x), true)

EQUAL(sideok(x, y), $ge(x, y))

EQUAL(reverse(west), east)

EQUAL(reverse(east), west)

The initial state is given by

ACHIEVABLE(same(m(3), c(3)), west, other(m(0), c(0)))

The denial of the theorem is then

¬ACHIEVABLE(same(m(3), c(3)), east, other(m(0), c(0)))

Here we have made a number of assumptions about how an automated reasoning program would process these clauses. First, we assume that $ge is a built-in function such that $ge(t1, t2) evaluates to true or false, whenever t1 and t2 evaluate to integers. Thus, $ge(2, 1) would automatically be rewritten as true. Further, we assume that literals that have the special predicates $LE and $EQ are evaluated whenever their arguments can be evaluated as integers. Many programs have such features, and many do not. For reasoning programs that do have such features, relying on a single transition axiom is rather elegant.

9. The answers to the monkey-and-bananas problems are the following.

(a) The clause denying that the monkey can get the bananas is

(2) ¬ACHIEVABLE(bananaspos, bananaspos, yes, yes)

For this problem, we assumed that the positions determine a position on the floor. This clause says that the monkey cannot be on the box holding the bananas at position bananaspos.

(b) The clause that gives the monkey movement is

(3) ¬ACHIEVABLE(x, y, no, z) | ACHIEVABLE(xnew, y, no, z)

(c) The clause that allows the monkey to move the box is

(4) ¬ACHIEVABLE(x, x, no, y) | ACHIEVABLE(xnew, xnew, no, y)

(d) You also need

(5) ¬ACHIEVABLE(x, x, no, y) | ACHIEVABLE(x, x, yes, y)

which says that the monkey can get on the box, and

(6) ¬ACHIEVABLE(bananaspos, bananaspos, yes, no)

| ACHIEVABLE(bananaspos, bananaspos, yes, yes)

which says that he can grab the bananas if he is on the box in the correct location. You should also include

(7) ¬ACHIEVABLE(x, x, yes, y) ACHIEVABLE(x, x, no, y)

which says that he can get off the box.

10. The proof that the monkey can get the bananas is the following.

From clauses 1 and 3:

(8) ACHIEVABLE(x, boxpos, no, no)

From clauses 8 and 4:

(9) ACHIEVABLE(x, x, no, no)

From clauses 9 and 5:

(10) ACHIEVABLE(x, x, yes, no)

From clauses 10 and 6:

(11) ACHIEVABLE(bananaspos, bananaspos, yes, yes)

This last clause contradicts clause 2, and the proof is complete. Problems similar to this one often are substantially more complex. For example, the room might contain many objects, some limiting the monkey's movements. Although the discussion of such complexities is not appropriate at this point in the book, some of the techniques presented in later chapters might shed some light on what could be done to cope with them.

6

Summary and Partial Formalization

With this chapter, we complete the introduction to automated reasoning. In the succeeding chapters, we discuss various applications of the techniques covered in the preceding chapters. Thus, to prepare the way for the transition from the introduction to the applications, we review what has already been presented. We discuss here the highlights and key features that can be found in an automated reasoning program. For those who might wonder about the actual existence of such a program, we include a brief discussion of the automated reasoning program that has been used to obtain the results presented in this book. We shall focus on some of the special features found in the program, features that are not always present in other reasoning programs. Finally, we include a detailed discussion of an inference rule that "builds in" equality. The rule, *paramodulation*, is employed in Chapter 4 and is heavily used, for example, for various applications covered in Chapter 9. This "building in" of equality illustrates yet another dimension of automated reasoning programs.

In addition to providing a review of the preceding material for those who have read the first five chapters, we have a second motive in including this chapter. As remarked in Chapter 1, some who read this book are already familiar with the basic elements of logic and, therefore, Chapter 2 in part presents information that is already known. Other readers of the book may know a little about automated reasoning and, therefore, find that other parts of Chapter 2 and some of Chapter 3 cover familiar ground. Because of these considerations, this chapter proceeds at a rather brisk pace, especially compared to Chapter 2 and to parts of Chapter 3. If you find that you are one of those who know logic and who perhaps also know something about automated reasoning, or if you simply prefer a faster pace, you can begin with this chapter rather than with Chapter 2. Since we shall be somewhat formal in this chapter, and since we include less explanatory material, consult the earlier chapters when and if some point is unclear. The early chapters contain more explanatory material and more detailed examples.

6.1 Logic

Automated reasoning is concerned with programs that aid in solving problems and in answering questions where reasoning is required. The reasoning referred to here is *logical reasoning*, not common-sense or probabilistic reasoning. The conclusions must follow inevitably from the facts from which they are drawn. To see how an automated reasoning program works, you must first be familiar with certain elements of logic.

The *logical* operators are **and, or, not, if-then**, and **is-equivalent-to**. These operators are used to produce "new" statements from given statements. By definition, **not** is applied to a single statement, and the remaining operators are applied to pairs of statements. The truth or falsity of the "new" statement depends of course on the truth or falsity of the statement(s) to which the operator is applied.

6.1.1 and

The **and** of two statements is true if and only if both statements are true. For example, the statement that Arkansas begins with a vowel **and** ends with a consonant is true because the two statements to which **and** is applied are each true. On the other hand, if Arkansas is replaced by Ohio, the statement is false because one of the two component statements is false—"Ohio ends with a consonant" is false.

6.1.2 or

The **or** of two statements is true if and only if at least one of the statements is true; hence it is true if both statements are true. For example, the statement that (Oklahoma begins with a vowel **and** ends with a vowel) **or** (begins with a consonant **and** ends with a consonant) is true. Although the second half of the statement is false, the statement is true because the first half is true. For another example, the statement that mothers are older than their children or fathers are older than their children is true. In this example, both substatements are true, thus their **or** is true. In everyday language, as opposed to logic, (usually) the **or** of two statements is true when exactly one of them is true.

6.1.3 not

The **not** of a statement is true if and only if the statement is false, and false if and only if the statement is true. For example, the statement that Oklahoma does **not** end with a consonant is true. Its truth follows from the fact that the statement that Oklahoma ends with a consonant is false. Similarly, the statement that mothers are **not** older than their children is false, because they are.

To determine the truth of compound statements involving **not** and some other operator, you simply apply the rules for each operator. For example, the statement that Oklahoma begins with a vowel **and** does **not** end with a consonant is true. Can you now see what the rule is for the **not** of the **not** of a statement? The rule simply is that the **not**s cancel. A statement is true if and only if the **not** of the **not** of it is true, and a similar comment can be made for false.

6.1.4 if-then

An **if-then** statement is false if and only if both the **if** component is true and the **then** component is false. In all other cases, **if-then** statements are true. Notice that this usage—the logical usage—is different from everyday language. In everyday language, **if-then** statements are often assumed true. In fact, typically the **if** is assumed true with the further assumption that this forces the **then** to be true. From a logical viewpoint, what is the truth of the following statement? If mothers are younger than their children, then all children are 20 years old. This statement is true from a logical viewpoint since the **if** component is false. A related example is the statement that if a state name (in the United States) begins with a B, then it ends with a vowel. To prove this statement false, you would have to give a state whose name begins with a B and does not end with a vowel. Since no state exists with a name beginning with a B, the **if-then** statement is true. Such statements are called vacuously true, and do occasionally come into play.

6.1.5 is-equivalent-to

For statements P and Q, P **is-equivalent-to** Q is false if and only if one of P and Q is true while the other is false. The statement that P **is-equivalent-to** Q can be rewritten as (**if** P **then** Q) **and** (**if** Q **then** P). The operator **is-equivalent-to** comes into play in statements of the form P if and only if Q. Although **is-equivalent-to** is barely discussed in Chapter 2, it can be understood in terms of the discussion found there for **if-then** and **and**.

6.1.6 Relationships and Laws in Logic

The operators of **if-then** and **is-equivalent-to** can be replaced by using **or**, **not**, and **and**. The most common replacement or translation that you make when using an automated reasoning program is that of translating **if-then** to **or** and **not**. The rule is, (**if** P **then** Q) translates to ((**not** P) **or** Q). Thus, the statement that Kim is male **or** female is a correct translation of the statement, **if** Kim is **not** male **then** Kim is female. But it is also a correct translation of the statement, **if** Kim is **not** female **then** Kim is male.

Next, we have the distributive laws, stated in the manner in which they are applied for producing information in the form required by the language that we shall discuss. First, (P **and** Q) **or** (P **and** R) translates to P **and** (Q **or** R). Second, P **or** (Q **and** R) translates to (P **or** Q) **and** (P **or** R).

Finally, we have DeMorgan's laws. First, **not** (P **and** Q) translates to (**not** P) **or** (**not** Q). Second, **not** (P **or** Q) translates to (**not** P) **and** (**not** Q).

The distributive laws and DeMorgan's laws are used for translating complex statements into a form in which every pair of statements is joined with an **and**, while the only operators that occur within a statement are **not** and **or**. For example, **if** (P **and** Q) **then** R translates to (**not** P) **or** (**not** Q) **or** R.

EXERCISES

1. Which of the following statements is true?
   (a) $(2 + 4 > 6)$ **and** $(0 + 1 < 2)$
   (b) $(2 + 4 < 8)$ **or** $(3 - 1 > 0)$
   (c) **not** $((1 - 1 = 0)$ **and** $(3 - 2 = 2))$
   (d) **if** $(1 - 1 = 0)$ **then** $(2 - 2 = 0)$
   (e) **if** $(1 - 2 = 0)$ **then** $(2 - 2 = 0)$
   (f) **if** $(1 - 2 = 0)$ **then** $(2 - 1 = 0)$
   (g) $(1 - 1 = 0)$ **is-equivalent-to** $(2 - 2 = 0)$
   (h) $(1 - 2 = 0)$ **is-equivalent-to** $(2 - 2 = 0)$
   (i) $(1 - 2 = 0)$ **is-equivalent-to** $(2 - 1 = 0)$

2. Which of the following translations can be made?
   (a) **not** (**not** $(1 + 2 = 3))$ to $(1 + 2 = 3)$
   (b) **not** (**not** $(1 + 2 = 3))$ to $(2 + 1 = 3)$
   (c) **not** (**not** (**not** $(1 + 2 = 3)))$ to **not** $(1 + 2 = 3)$
   (d) **not** (**not** (**not** $(1 + 2 = 3)))$ to $(1 + 2 = 3)$
   (e) **if** $(8 < 9)$ **then** $(8 < 9 + 1)$ to **not** $(8 < 9)$ **or** $(8 < 9 + 1)$
   (f) **if** $(8 < 9)$ **then** $(8 < 9 + 1)$ to $(8 < 9 + 1)$ **or** (**not** $(8 < 9))$
   (g) **not** (**if** $(2 + 1 = 3)$ **then** $(1 + 2 = 3))$ to $(2 + 1 = 3)$ **and** (**not** $(1 + 2 = 3))$
   (h) **not** (**if** $(2 + 1 = 3)$ **then** $(1 + 2 = 3))$ to $(1 + 2 = 3)$ **and** (**not** $(2 + 1 = 3))$
   (i) **not** (**if** $(2 + 1 = 3)$ **then** $(4 / 2 = 2))$ to $(2 + 1 = 3)$ **and** (**not** $(2 / 4 = 2))$

6.2 A Language Understood by an Automated Reasoning Program

The language used throughout this book to describe the problem under investigation to an automated reasoning program consists of clauses. A *clause* is a statement that is the **or** of its literals. A *literal* is a well-formed formula that consists of an n-ary predicate symbol, possibly preceded by the **not** symbol "¬", followed by its n arguments. The language does not allow **not** of **not**, and simply cancels the two **nots**. A *predicate symbol* is a symbol that denotes a relation. The arguments of a predicate can be variables, constants, or functions with their arguments. The arguments of a function can be variables, constants, or functions with their arguments. All variables that occur in a clause are implicitly treated as *universally quantified*, and therefore to be read as "for all" or as "for each". An implicit **and** occurs between clauses. For most practical problems, this language of clauses is sufficiently powerful for attempting to solve them.

A literal prefixed with a **not** symbol is called a *negative literal*. A literal that is not so prefixed is called a *positive literal*. All literals are classed as negative or positive literals. A clause containing only positive literals is called a *positive clause*. A clause containing only negative literals is called a *negative clause*. A clause containing at least one positive and at least one negative literal is called a *mixed clause*. A clause containing exactly one literal is called a *unit clause*. If the literal in a unit clause is positive, then the clause is called a *positive unit* clause. A *negative unit* clause contains one negative literal. A clause containing more than one literal is called a *nonunit clause*.

For examples of the terminology, consider the following problem. What is a correct translation of, "The job of nurse is held by a male."? More precisely, let the statement to be translated read, "For all x, if x holds the job of nurse, then x is male."

A correct translation is

$\neg$HASAJOB(x, nurse) | MALE(x)

where "|" is the symbol for **or**. This statement is a nonunit clause, and the clause contains two literals, one negative and one positive. The predicates that occur in this clause are HASAJOB and MALE. The variable x is to be read as "for all x". The predicate HASAJOB has two arguments, while MALE has but one.

The clause

EQUALP(Pete, husband(Thelma))

is a positive unit clause, one of whose arguments is the function husband that in turn has the argument Thelma. This clause exhibits one of the few "built-in" concepts available to an automated reasoning program, namely, equality. While almost all concepts must be carefully specified for such a program, since reasoning programs must be given all of the properties that pin down a concept, for equality such is not always necessary. Some reasoning programs can be instructed to interpret a predicate beginning with the letters EQUAL to be treated as you would treat equality.

To state that Thelma is female, **and** Steve is male, **and** everyone is male **or** female, you write the following clauses.

FEMALE(Thelma)

MALE(Steve)

MALE(x) | FEMALE(x)

The **and** is implicit, while the **or** is represented with "|". As pointed out in Chapter 4, if you were being very careful, you would replace the last clause with

$$\neg PERSON(x) \mid MALE(x) \mid FEMALE(x)$$

to state that the variable x in this clause ranges over people.

By convention, duplicate literals in a clause are always removed automatically. In addition, the order of the literals within a clause as well as the order of the clauses themselves has no effect on the meaning or information conveyed to a reasoning program. The order of either can, however, affect the efficiency with which a reasoning program attacks a problem.

6.2.1 Variables

Variables in the language used throughout the book are *universally quantified* and are therefore to be interpreted as "for all". A *name* is a sequence of characters, all of which are letters or numerals. A *variable* is a name beginning with one of the letters between lowercase u and lowercase z, inclusive. With few exceptions, a name beginning with a letter between lowercase u and lowercase z, inclusive, is a variable.

Rather than employing *existentially quantified* variables—for example, there exists an x—the language requires their replacement by functions. The statement that each married woman has a husband can be rigorously phrased as "for each married woman, there exists a husband of that woman who is married to her". In clause form, this statement becomes

$$\neg MARRIEDWOMAN(x) \mid MARRIEDTO(x, husband(x))$$

with the function "husband" replacing the existentially quantified variable that could have been employed.

The rule is that existentially quantified variables are replaced by functions, where the function has as its arguments all universally quantified variables that appear before the existentially quantified variable. In the preceding example—for all x there exists a y such that if x is a married woman, then x is married to y—the function husband must, therefore, have as its argument the variable x. Existentially quantified variables that depend on no universally quantified variables translate into constants. In the alphabet, there exists a letter denoted by the variable y such that, for all letters denoted by the variable x, y occurs earlier in the alphabet than x. In this example, the variable y is an existentially quantified variable depending on no universally quantified variables. Thus, y can be replaced with a constant, say a.

$$EARLIER(a, x)$$

Thus, we have a crucial difference between "for all x there exists a y" and "there exists an x for all y". In the first case, the corresponding clause (or clauses) contains a function of one variable, while in the latter a constant is employed.

The final point to note about variables is that their meaning is relevant only to the clause in which they occur. Thus, if the variable x occurs in two different clauses, no implied connection between the clauses exists because of sharing a variable. In other words, the "for all" that is to be read for the variables in a clause governs only that one clause.

EXERCISES

3. Convert the following statements to clauses:
   (a) **if** MOTHER(Mary, Sam) **and** SISTER(Mary, Linda) **then** AUNT(Linda, Sam)
   (b) **if** MOTHER(x, y) **and** SISTER(x, z) **then** AUNT(z, y)
   (c) **if** MOTHER(x, y) **and** (**not** SISTER(x, z)) **then** (**not** AUNT(z, y))
   (d) **if** MOTHER(x, y) **or** FATHER(x, y) **then** PARENT(x, y)
   (e) **not** (POSITIVE(x) **and** NEGATIVE(x))
4. How would the following statements appear in clause form?
   (a) For any x, there exists a y such that GREATERTHAN(y, x)
   (b) There exists an x such that for all y GREATERTHAN(y, x)
   (c) For any x and y, there exists a z such that $(z = x + y)$
   (d) For any x, there exists a y, such that for all z (**if** $(x < z)$ **then** $(y < z)$)
   (e) There exists an x, such that for all y, there exists a z such that $(y + z > x)$ **or** $(y + z = x)$
   (f) There exists an x, such that for all y, there exists a z such that $(y + z > x)$ **and** $(y - z < x)$

6.3 Submitting a Problem to a Reasoning Program

An automated reasoning program begins its attack on a problem with the information you supply. You pick the problem, you tell it what you wish it to know, and you give it instructions about how to proceed—instructions discussed later.

6.3.1 Assumptions and Axioms

To use an automated reasoning program, you must supply it with various clauses. One set of clauses corresponds to the general information and description of the problem domain. The information that these clauses correspond to includes the assumptions or *axioms* of the problem domain. Also included in this set of clauses are those that correspond to useful, general information.

For example, if the puzzle is about jobs people might hold, the clause

MALE(x) | FEMALE(x)

corresponds to an axiom about people—all of them are male or female. The clause

FEMALE(Roberta)

gives useful information about Roberta. Since an automated reasoning program knows nothing about a problem unless you tell it the information, the set of clauses that corresponds to the assumptions and axioms must contain enough to pin down the various concepts relevant to the problem.

6.3.2 Special Facts and the Special Hypothesis

Another set of clauses that you supply to an automated reasoning program is called the *special hypothesis*. The special hypothesis of a problem is that which narrows the study to a particular question. For example, in the jobs puzzle of Chapter 3, the additional information about Roberta that says she is not the boxer and that she and the chef and the police officer went golfing is special to the puzzle. In the domino and checkerboard puzzle of Chapter 5, the starting position is special, the knowledge that two squares are missing from the standard board.

6.3.3 Denial of the Goal or Theorem

The final set of clauses that ordinarily is given to an automated reasoning program corresponds to assuming that the goal cannot be reached or, equivalently, that the conclusion is false. The clause or these clauses are called the *denial* of the goal or the theorem. Recall, as discussed in Chapter 2, that the usual procedure in using an automated reasoning program to prove some statement is to assume the statement is false. If, in fact, the statement does follow from the remaining facts and properties of the problem, then assuming it false leads eventually to a contradiction. The inclusion of such a statement(s) provides a very convenient means for an automated reasoning program to test for completion of the task. When we said "ordinarily is given", we had in mind that some uses of a reasoning program are simply for finding information, and so no particular result is being sought. Thus, when simply seeking additional information, nothing exists on which to key for seeking a contradiction.

However, the typical use of a reasoning program is that of proving some particular fact or of answering some specific question. For example, if in the jobs puzzle of Chapter 3 you were trying to prove that Roberta is the teacher, you would typically assume that she is not the teacher. You would include the clause

$\neg$HASAJOB(Roberta, teacher)

as the *denial* of the goal or theorem. As a trickier example, in the full jobs puzzle of Chapter 3, no specific goal exists to provide in a straightforward manner clauses for the denial. In that puzzle, you were asked to find out who held which jobs. The denial consisted, in effect, of assuming that the task of finding the two jobs for each of the four people could not be completed. Nevertheless, although far from straightforward, a denial set was used to enable the program to determine that the problem had been solved.

EXERCISES

5. Consider the following problem (quoted from Lewis Carroll).
(1) The only animals in this house are cats.
(2) Every animal is suitable for a pet, that loves to gaze at the moon.
(3) When I detest an animal, I avoid it.
(4) No animals are carnivorous, unless they prowl at night.
(5) No cat fails to kill mice.
(6) No animals ever take to me, except what are in this house.
(7) Kangaroos are not suitable for pets.
(8) None but carnivora kill mice.
(9) I detest animals that do not take to me.
(10) Animals, that prowl at night, always love to gaze at the moon.
The problem is to prove that "I always avoid a kangaroo".

First, write the assumptions of the problem in clause form. To do this, use predicates that specify classes of animals. For example, the first statement, in clause form, is

$\neg$INHOUSE(x) | CAT(x)

Then write clauses that correspond to the denial of the statement to be proved.

6. What clauses would you write for problem 5 if a single predicate ISA(x, y) were used, where ISA(x,y) is taken to mean that "x is a member of the group y"?

6.4 Inference Rules

An *inference rule* is an algorithm that, when successfully applied to some given set of hypotheses or premises, yields a conclusion that follows inevitably and logically from the premises. (The words "premiss" and "premisses" are technical terms in logic, and thus the unusual spelling.) Inference rules—types of reasoning—are the means for yielding possibly new information from given information. The conclusion obtained by applying some inference rule may, of course, not be new because that information may already be present.

6.4.1 Unification

Two literals can be *unified* if there exists a replacement for the variables in both such that, after the replacement, the resulting literals are identical except possibly for the sign. The replacement of course substitutes the same term for all occurrences of a given variable. The procedure of *unification* is the means for unifying two literals. Unification is also used to unify two terms, as occurs in demodulation and also occurs in the inference rule paramodulation discussed later in this chapter. The unification procedure always obtains the most general replacement that can be found, if one exists, for the two expressions to make them identical. When unification is attempted for two given literals, the fact that either is negative or positive is ignored. However, for most of the inference rules, a pair of literals is considered only when they are opposite in sign—one negative and one positive.

For example, the clauses

FEMALE(Roberta)

$\neg$MALE(x) | $\neg$FEMALE(x)

contain literals that can be unified, yielding

$\neg$MALE(Roberta)

stating that Roberta is not male. The unification procedure finds that a replacement of the variable x by Roberta is required. The two literals that are unified are FEMALE(Roberta) and $\neg$FEMALE(x).

A somewhat subtle point in unification is exhibited by the following example.

GE(sum(x, sum(y, minus(x))), y)

$\neg$GE(sum(x, x), y) | ACCEPTABLE(pair(x, y))

The first clause says that x + (y − x) is greater than or equal to y. The second clause says that, if x + x is greater than or equal to y, then the pair x,y is acceptable. Do you see why the two literals in the predicate GE cannot be unified? Even better, do you understand the basic rule that describes such situations that cannot be successfully unified?

The two literals cannot be unified because no (uniform) replacement of variables exists that yields two new and identical (except for sign) literals. (The fact that the same variable x appears in both clauses is not relevant, for recall that a variable only has meaning for the clause in which it appears. Thus, to attempt to unify the two literals from the two clauses, you must in effect rename the variables before making the attempt so that no variables are shared by the two clauses.) As for the principle explaining such failures, note that unification can be attempted by a left-to-right symbol matching. Before applying the algorithm to literals from different clauses, the variables must be renamed so that no variable is shared. In this example, the first step of this matching process dictates replacing the variable that first occurs in each literal by a common variable, say z. The next matching step attempts to then match the new variable z from the second clause with the term sum(y,minus(z)) from the first clause. Thus we have failure since unification does not succeed if at some point in the matching process a variable is matched with a term that already contains that variable. Of course, successful unification requires that the predicates be the same, when applied to two literals.

6.4.2 Binary Resolution

The object of an application of *binary resolution* is to produce a new clause from two existing clauses each of which happens to contain an appropriate literal. Formally, *binary resolution* is that inference rule that takes two clauses, selects a literal in each of the same predicate but of opposite sign, and yields a clause providing that the two selected literals unify. The result of a successful application of binary resolution is obtained by applying the replacement that unification finds to the two clauses, deleting from each (only) the descendant of the selected literal, and taking the **or** of the remaining literals of the two clauses. Of course in practice, to apply binary resolution to a pair of clauses, the variables in the two clauses are renamed so that no variable is shared.

Binary resolution is a generalization of the inference rule that yields (Q **or** R) from (P **or** Q) and ((**not** P) **or** R). Equivalently, binary resolution is a generalization of the inference rule that yields (Q **or** R) from (**if** P **then** Q) and (**if** (**not** P) **then** R). The generalization allows Q or R (or both, see Section 6.5) to be empty. The generalization also allows for unification to be required to produce the required P and ¬P. From a more classical viewpoint, binary resolution is a generalization of both modus ponens and syllogism.

For example, binary resolution applied to the two clauses

¬HASAJOB(x, nurse) | MALE(x)

¬MALE(x) | ¬FEMALE(x)

yields

¬HASAJOB(x, nurse) | ¬FEMALE(x)

as the result. Binary resolution places no restrictions on either of the two clauses to which it is being applied, and no restriction on the resulting clause.

6.4.3 UR-resolution

The object of an application of *UR-resolution* is to produce a new unit clause from a set of clauses one of which is a nonunit clause while the remaining are unit clauses. Formally, *UR-resolution* is that inference rule that applies to a set of clauses one of which must be a nonunit clause, the remaining must be unit clauses, and the result of successful application must be a unit clause. Furthermore, the nonunit clause must contain exactly one more literal than the number of (not necessarily distinct) unit clauses in the set to which UR-resolution is being applied. In addition, except for one literal, the literals of the nonunit clause must be paired with the unit clauses such that each literal has the predicate of its paired unit clause, the two members of a pair are opposite in sign, and the members of a pair unify. For UR-resolution to succeed, a simultaneous replacement of all variables in all clauses in the set under consideration must exist that, when applied to each pair, makes the pair identical except for sign. The result of a successful application is obtained by applying the most general replacement that exists and that satisfies the given criterion, and canceling all but the one literal of the nonunit clause after the replacement has been made in it.

A successful application of UR-resolution can be viewed as a sequence of binary resolutions in which each is required to involve exactly one unit clause. However, what is required is that all such binary resolutions occur simultaneously, thus yielding no intermediate clauses. For example, UR-resolution applied to the clauses

> ¬MARRIEDTO(x, y) | ¬MOTHER(x, z) | FATHER(y, z)
> MARRIEDTO(Thelma, Pete)
> ¬FATHER(Pete, Steve)

yields

> ¬MOTHER(Thelma, Steve)

as the result. In practice, of course, to attempt an application of UR-resolution, the variables in the set of clauses under consideration are renamed so that no variable appears in more than one clause in the set. The name UR-resolution is derived from "unit resulting", since the object of using the rule is to produce unit clauses.

6.4.4 Hyperresolution

The object of an application of *hyperresolution* is to produce a positive clause from a set of clauses one of which is negative or mixed while the remaining are positive clauses. Formally, *hyperresolution* is that inference rule that applies to a set of clauses one of which must be a negative clause or a mixed clause, the remaining must be positive clauses and their number must be equal to the number of negative literals in the negative or mixed clause, and that requires the result of successful application to be a positive clause. The positive clauses are called *satellites*, while the clause with the negative literals is called a *nucleus*. The number of negative literals in the nucleus must equal the number of satellites, which are not necessarily distinct clauses. The literals of the nucleus must be paired with a literal in the corresponding satellite such that each negative literal has the predicate of its paired literal and such that each literal unifies with its paired literal. For hyperresolution to succeed, a simultaneous replacement of all variables in all clauses in the set under consideration must exist that, when applied to each pair, makes that pair identical except for sign. The result of a successful application is obtained by applying the most general replacement that exists and that satisfies the given criterion, canceling all of the negative literals and their counterparts in the positive clauses, and taking the **or** of the remaining literals, after the replacement of variables has been made, in all clauses.

A successful application of hyperresolution can be viewed as a sequence of binary resolutions in which each is required to involve exactly one positive clause. However, what is required is that all such binary resolutions occur simultaneously, thus yielding no intermediate clauses. For example, hyperresolution applied to the clauses

> ¬MARRIEDTO(x, y) | ¬MOTHER(x, z) | FATHER(y, z)
> MARRIEDTO(Thelma, Pete) | OLDERTHAN(Thelma, Pete)
> MOTHER(Thelma, Steve)

yields

    FATHER(Pete, Steve) | OLDERTHAN(Thelma, Pete)

as the result.

The need for hyperresolution is explained by the fact that hyperresolution can yield a positive nonunit clause, while UR-resolution can yield only unit clauses. On the other hand, UR-resolution can yield negative clauses, while hyperresolution cannot. In some cases, hyperresolution and UR-resolution produce the same clause. In practice, of course, to apply hyperresolution to a set of clauses, the variables in the clauses are renamed so that no variable appears in more than one clause. The name hyperresolution indicates that more is occurring than occurs in (ordinary) binary resolution, for hyperresolution combines the actions of a number of binary resolution steps into one step.

6.4.5 Paramodulation

The object of an application of paramodulation is to cause an equality substitution to take place from one clause into another. *Paramodulation* is that inference rule applied to a pair of clauses and requiring that at least one of the two contains a positive equality literal, and yielding a clause in which the equality substitution corresponding to the equality literal has occurred. The clause containing the equality literal is called the *from* clause, and the clause into which the equality substitution is made is called the *into* clause. A successful application of paramodulation requires the selection of a positive equality literal (by convention one whose predicate begins with "EQUAL") in the *from* clause, the selection of one of its two arguments, the selection of a term in the *into* clause, and the successful unification of the selected argument and the selected term. Obtaining the result of a successful application of paramodulation first requires applying to each of the two clauses the replacement of variables dictated by the successful unification of the selected argument and term. Second, for the selected term that has the variable replacement applied to it, paramodulation requires substituting the other argument of the selected equality literal after applying the variable replacement. Finally, the inference rule requires deletion of the selected positive equality literal and forming the **or** of the remaining literals in the *from* clause and all the literals in the *into* clause that result after applying the preceding steps. Paramodulation is a generalization of equality substitution.

For example, paramodulation applies in the following situation and with the following result.

    Fact: A person's father is older than the person:

        OLDERTHAN(father(x), x)

    Fact: Jack's father is Ralph:

        EQUALP(father(Jack), Ralph)

Conclusion: Ralph is older than Jack:

OLDERTHAN(Ralph, Jack)

The first of the three clauses is the *into* clause, the second the *from* clause, and the third the result of a successful application of paramodulation. Paramodulation also includes ordinary equality substitution, as exhibited by the following example.

Fact: Ted's sister's husband is Bob:

EQUALP(husband(sister(Ted)), Bob)

Fact: Ted's sister is Mary:

EQUALP(sister(Ted), Mary)

Conclusion: Mary's husband is Bob:

EQUALP(husband(Mary), Bob)

The first clause is the *into* clause, the second the *from* clause, and the third the result of successfully applying paramodulation.

As the first example shows, paramodulation goes beyond equality substitution and even includes the case, illustrated with the next example, in which variables must be replaced in both the *from* and the *into* clauses before the substitution can take place. This case occurs when the required unification forces a nontrivial replacement of variables simultaneously in both the *from* and the *into* clause. Thus, paramodulation can yield clauses that might not otherwise be obtained by ordinary equality substitution. For example, from the clauses

EQUAL(sum(0, x), x)

EQUAL(sum(y, minus(y)), 0)

paramodulating *from* the first *into* the second yields

EQUAL(minus(0), 0)

as the result. A somewhat more complex illustration is provided by applying paramodulation to the clauses

EQUAL(sum(x, minus(x)), 0)

EQUAL(sum(y, sum(minus(y), z)), z)

where the first clause is the *from* clause, and the second the *into*. The result of the paramodulation is a clause that says that $y + 0 = -(-y)$. The actual detailed paramodulation is left as an exercise for you. An additional example, concerning relationships between people, that illustrates the value of permitting nontrivial variable replacement in both the *from* and the *into* clauses can be found in Section 6.10. In practice, of course, to apply paramodulation, the variables in the two clauses are renamed so that no variable appears in both clauses. The name "paramodulation" is derived from the close relationship of the inference rule to demodulation, a concept discussed in Section 6.7.

6.4.6 Other Inference Rules

Negative hyperresolution is that inference rule that interchanges the roles of positive and negative in hyperresolution. *Unit resolution* is that restriction of binary resolution that requires that at least one of the two clauses be a unit clause. *Factoring* is that rule that takes a single clause, selects two of its literals that are alike in predicate and in sign, attempts to unify the two literals, and applies the replacement of variables that corresponds to a successful unification to produce the new clause. While most inference rules operationally require that the variables be renamed in all of the clauses being considered by the rule so that no two clauses have a variable in common, factoring requires that the variables be left as is. The preceding three inference rules are additional examples of what is offered by an automated reasoning program. An automated reasoning program can make available other combinations and variations, such as requiring that the result of hyperresolution be restricted to be a unit clause. Such a restriction combines some of the properties of hyperresolution with some of those of UR-resolution. A similar restriction that can be imposed on various inference rules is that the result of a successful application be accepted only if the number of literals in the conclusion is less than some fixed number. Thus, rather than being forced to choose from among the inference rules given here, you can mix and match according to what you suspect might aid a reasoning program in its attempt to answer a question or solve a problem. The choice of inference rule can have an overwhelming effect on the performance of a reasoning program. By providing many possible inference rules, a reasoning program offers you the chance of sharply increasing the effectiveness of using such a program.

6.5 The Empty Clause

The *empty clause* is that clause that contains no literals. If a reasoning program finds this clause, then the program has found a *contradiction*. In this book, we in general do not have need of the empty clause, for contradiction is found usually when two unit clauses are obtained that are alike in predicate, opposite in sign, and are unifiable. When such a condition has been obtained, *unit conflict* has been found. By definition, the empty clause is a positive clause, but is also a negative clause. The empty clause is needed in connection with some applications of hyperresolution.

For example, if a reasoning program obtains clauses that say that Steve is strictly older than Pete and that Pete is strictly older than Steve, then rather quickly a contradiction is found. In such a problem, the key clause is

$\neg$OLDER(x, y) | $\neg$OLDER(y, x)

With hyperresolution as the sole rule of inference, an automated reasoning program will, in the presence of the clauses

>   OLDER(Steve, Pete)
>
>   OLDER(Pete, Steve)

deduce the empty clause. Such a deduction informs a reasoning program that a contradiction has been found and, therefore, that the answer to the corresponding question has been obtained.

6.6 Proof by Contradiction

A *proof by contradiction* consists of a number of steps, starting with a given set of facts and properties, such that each step that is not a given step follows from earlier steps and is obtained by applying a specific inference rule, and such that the final step is in direct contradiction with an earlier step. This definition can be modified to cover the case in which the final step is the empty clause, but typically the contradiction is between two unit clauses.

By far the most common termination condition for a reasoning program that succeeds in the assigned task is that of finding a proof by contradiction. The usual way of using a reasoning program to prove that some property follows from a given set of properties, facts, and definitions is to assume the desired conclusion false. If the desired conclusion does follow from the remaining clauses, then assuming it false must in principle eventually lead to a contradiction. Although the precise discussion of this topic is left for Chapter 15, the following example illustrates what can go wrong.

Let us assume that you have chosen binary resolution as your standard approach to attacking a new problem, and that in fact it is the only inference rule being employed. Let us also assume that you are asked to demonstrate the usefulness of an automated reasoning program to a new user, and that the new user has selected a problem that, with a straightforward approach to representation, yields the following clauses.

> $P(x) \mid P(y)$
>
> $\neg P(x) \mid \neg P(y)$

Although this set of clauses is inconsistent—a proof by contradiction can be obtained starting with the set and using the appropriate inference rules—a reasoning program will not find a proof of the inconsistency under the given conditions. (A set that is inconsistent is technically called an *unsatisfiable* set.) The failure to find a proof is caused by the omission, for this problem, of a needed second inference rule. Without the second inference rule, a reasoning program will simply deduce clauses such as

> $P(y) \mid \neg P(z)$

and quickly exhaust the set of (distinct) deducible clauses. To complete the task of finding a proof, and thus provide the desired demonstration, the inference rule of factoring is needed. Do you see what results with that addition?

What happens is that a reasoning program yields

$$P(x)$$

from the first of the two clauses, and

$$\neg P(x)$$

from the second. As defined in this book, a proof is thus obtained.

6.7 Demodulation

Demodulation is the process of rephrasing or rewriting or canonicalizing expressions by automatically applying unit equality clauses designated for this purpose. A unit equality that is designated to be used with demodulation is called a *demodulator*. Typically, all terms of all newly generated clauses are examined for possible demodulation. A term is demodulated if a demodulator exists such that one of the arguments of the demodulator can be unified with the term without replacing any of the variables in the term. A common convention is to consider only the first argument of the demodulator for unification with the term under consideration. The demodulated term is obtained by replacing the term by the second argument of the demodulator after the variable replacement is applied corresponding to the success-ful unification. Then the original version of the clause is replaced by the demod-ulated version. (This replacement, and hence the discarding of the original version of the clause, is one difference between demodulation and paramodulation. The other important difference is, of course, that demodulation permits variable substitution—when unification is being attempted—only in the equivalent of the "from" clause.) When a new demodulator is found by a reasoning program, depending on the instructions given to the program, all clauses that have been previously retained are examined for possible demodulation with the new demodula-tor. Such a process is called *back demodulation*. Typically, one successful application of demodulation is followed immediately by further attempts to apply other demod-ulators.

For example, in the full jobs puzzle of Chapter 3, the discovery of a fact such as "Roberta is not the nurse" yields the demodulator

EQUAL(pj(Roberta, nurse), crossed)

that is then used to remove the possibility that Roberta is the nurse. Specifically, the term pj(Roberta, nurse) that is at one stage of the problem found on the list of possible jobs that Roberta might hold is replaced by the term "crossed". This action is immediately followed by another application of demodulation in which "crossed" is removed.

As a second example, in the presence of the demodulator

EQUALP(brother(father(x)), uncle(x))

the clause

AGE(brother(father(John)), 55)

is immediately rephrased as

AGE(uncle(John), 55)

before being considered for retention as new information.

To succeed, demodulation requires that the variables of the term under consideration for demodulation remain as they are. Thus,

EQUALP(father(Pete), Steve)

demodulates no term in the clause

OLDER(father(x), x)

since the variables of the second clause would be affected nontrivially by the results of any unification. Paramodulation would, however, yield

OLDER(Steve, Pete)

if applied to the two clauses and, of course, without deleting a clause.

Demodulation has a close relationship to paramodulation both in origin and in purpose. Each, if successful, causes an equality substitution to take place. While demodulation requires the equality literal to be in a unit clause, paramodulation does not. Another vital difference is that, while demodulation allows a nontrivial variable replacement only in the argument of the equality literal, paramodulation allows a nontrivial replacement of variables in both the argument of the equality literal and in the term into which the substitution is being attempted. Two additional differences have already been mentioned. First, while demodulation discards the original version of the clause if demodulation is successful, with paramodulation both the original version and the new clause are kept. Second, one successful application of demodulation immediately triggers further attempts at demodulation, while paramodulation stops after a single application of equality substitution.

6.8 Subsumption

Subsumption is the process for discarding a clause that duplicates or is less general than another clause available to a reasoning program. One clause *subsumes* a second clause if the variables in the first can be replaced in such a manner that the resulting clause is a (not necessarily proper) subclause of the second. Thus,

OLDER(father(x), x)

subsumes

OLDER(father(Ann), Ann)

On the other hand,

¬WIFE(Kim, Bob) | FEMALE(Kim)

does not subsume

¬WIFE(x, y) | FEMALE(x)

for the second of these two clauses is more general than the first, so the test for the first subsuming the second fails. Note that the second clause, on the other hand, does subsume the first.

A different example is provided by

¬WIFE(Kim, Bob) | FEMALE(Kim)

FEMALE(Kim)

in which the second clause subsumes the first. One clause can subsume another regardless of the number of literals in either. When a newly generated clause is discarded because a previously retained clause subsumes it, then the process for doing so is called *forward subsumption*. When a newly generated clause is used to discard previously retained clauses by subsumption, the process is called *back subsumption*.

6.9 Strategy

Strategy is a means for guiding an automated reasoning program's attack on a problem. Some strategies, called *ordering strategies*, direct a reasoning program in its choice of which clause to focus on next. Other strategies, called *restriction strategies*, require a reasoning program to avoid ever considering certain combinations of clauses. In addition, processes such as subsumption can be considered *pruning strategies*, while processes such as demodulation can be considered *canonicalization strategies*. Without strategy, an automated reasoning program would usually, even for the simplest of problems, generate too many conclusions to be effective.

6.9.1 The Set of Support Strategy

The *set of support* strategy prohibits application of an inference rule to a set of clauses unless at least one of the clauses *has support*. A clause *has support* if it is an input clause and has been designated as having support, or if it is obtained by application of an inference rule to a set of clauses one of which has support. In other words, having support is inherited in the sense that in each step of the derivation of the clause, at least one of the clauses participating in the step has support.

Technically, therefore, it is the occurrence of a clause that has support, for a clause may be deduced in more than one way.

The recommended choices for the set of support are either the set of clauses that comprise the special hypothesis and also those that comprise the denial, or simply those that comprise the denial. Notice that either of these choices has the property that the complement is expected to be a consistent set of clauses. (A consistent set of clauses is technically called a *satisfiable* set.) By constraining a reasoning program from applying inference rules to sets of clauses completely contained in this consistent set, a reasoning program is prevented from exploring the domain of inquiry as a whole. From an intuitive viewpoint, the set of support strategy restricts a reasoning program from simply expanding a set of consistent clauses, a move that makes sense since (usually) a proof by contradiction is being sought. Thus, the strategy takes advantage of the satisfiability of the set of clauses comprising the complement of the typically chosen set of support. Should the set of support be chosen unwisely, then all proofs might be blocked. This topic is reserved for Chapter 15. The set of support strategy is a restriction strategy.

6.9.2 Weighting

Weighting is the process for assigning priorities to terms, clauses, and concepts. Weighting can be used to reflect your knowledge and intuition about how a reasoning program should proceed. For example, by choosing the appropriate weights, you can cause a reasoning program to focus on one person in a puzzle such as the jobs puzzle. You can assign a weight to Roberta in such a way that the program will always choose a clause in which the term "Roberta" occurs in preference to any other clause. On the other hand, you can assign a weight to Roberta so that every clause containing the term Roberta is given the merest of consideration, or even immediately discarded as undesirable. Weighting is both an ordering and a restriction strategy.

6.9.3 Unit Preference Strategy

Briefly, the *unit preference* strategy is the strategy that causes an automated reasoning program to prefer for application of an inference rule a set of clauses one of which is a unit clause. Further, if a unit clause is found, an automated reasoning program employing this strategy seeks a clause with the fewest possible literals and containing a literal that unifies with the unit clause but is of opposite sign. If no such sets exist, then the unit preference strategy causes a reasoning program to prefer a set in which one of the clauses has a number of literals as few as possible. The motivation for the unit preference strategy is the seeking of unit clauses, and especially of unit conflict. Since applying the strategy when using binary resolution, for example, to a pair of clauses one of which is a unit clause must yield a shorter clause than the participating nonunit, a reasoning program employing the unit preference strategy is proceeding in the direction of generating unit clauses. Unit clauses play an extremely important role in automated reasoning, independent of their potential for establishing proof by contradiction.

For example, with the unit preference strategy, if binary resolution is the only inference rule being used, then the first pairs of clauses to be examined (if such pairs exist) are those in which at least one of the clauses is a unit clause. Within that set of pairs, the strategy prefers a pair in which the nonunit clause has two literals rather than one in which the nonunit clause has three. If no unit clauses are available, then a reasoning program using this strategy will seek a clause with two literals. If a clause with two literals is found, the strategy prefers that the other nonunit clause also have two literals rather than say three or more. Finally, when new unit clauses are deduced and retained, again pairs including one of the unit clauses will be preferred. The unit preference strategy is an ordering strategy.

6.10 An Automated Reasoning Program in Action

We can now illustrate with one mundane example a number of the concepts that have been discussed in this chapter, and also show how you might use an automated reasoning program. Let us assume that certain specific and certain somewhat general facts are available, selected from some hypothetical database of knowledge about relationships. For example, suppose that one of the somewhat general facts is that, if someone is Brian's sibling, then the father of that person and Brian have Brian's last name.

(1) ¬SIBLING(x, Brian)

| EQUAL(last(father(x, Brian)), last(Brian))

Suppose another of the somewhat general facts is that, if Rick is someone's sibling, then the father of Rick and that person have Rick's last name.

(2) ¬SIBLING(Rick, y) | EQUAL(last(father(Rick, y)), last(Rick))

Among the specific facts, we have that Brian is Rick's sibling.

(3) SIBLING(Brian, Rick)

Of course, we know that Brian and Rick have the same last name, but how might an automated reasoning program prove it?

First, you ordinarily would write a clause that amounts to assuming the conclusion false, that says that Brian and Rick do not have the same last name.

(4) ¬EQUAL(last(Brian), last(Rick))

After all, since a proof is the objective, and since proof by contradiction is the usual form of proof, clause 4 is a good beginning.

Next, we come to hidden information, or easily overlooked information. As we have commented in earlier chapters, all potentially useful properties of concepts in the problem must be supplied to a reasoning program. In the problem at hand, a property of sibling that we might need is that if x is the sibling of y, then y is the sibling of x. Therefore, we add the following clause.

(5) $\neg$SIBLING(x, y) | SIBLING(y, x)

The value of this clause can be quickly seen. The literal of the unit clause 3 and the first literal of clause 2 share the predicate SIBLING. However, the argument Rick appears as the second argument in the one clause, and the first argument in the other. Noticing this potential difficulty points to the need for an additional clause, one that permits a reasoning program to cope with the differing position of the argument Rick. The predicate SIBLING is symmetric, and clause 5 will suffice. Clause 6

(6) $\neg$EQUAL(x, y) | EQUAL(y, x)

also is a candidate for a clause that might well be needed. Clause 6 is suggested by the fact that clause 4 is likely to participate in the final step of unit conflict, and the other participant may not have the arguments in the required order to match clause 4.

Since equality literals are present, you might correctly conjecture that paramodulation is one of the inference rules to be employed. Since clause 3 gives information specific to the problem, and since clause 3 would interact with clause 5 were the appropriate inference rule present, a clue exists for choosing another inference rule to employ. Clauses 3 and 5 will produce new information if considered by binary resolution, by UR-resolution, or by hyperresolution. A further clue is provided by the presence of clause 4. Clause 4 is present as the denial of the desired result, and clause 4 would interact with clause 6 were the appropriate inference rule present. Clauses 4 and 6 produce new information either with binary resolution or with UR-resolution as the inference rule, but not with hyperresolution. So hyperresolution can be at least temporarily eliminated from consideration. Binary resolution is eliminated because the object of the problem suggests that a specific unit clause is being sought, and because of being too productive of information. Binary resolution is an inference rule we suggest avoiding in most cases, for conclusions produced from its application often correspond to steps that are smaller than necessary. Finally, we prefer to use as few inference rules as possible to increase the effectiveness of an automated reasoning program's attack on a problem. Thus, UR-resolution is the choice for the moment.

With the choice of representation and of inference rule made (at least for the moment), the question of strategy arises. In general, without strategy an automated reasoning program wanders from the goal. The recommended approach with this example is to use the set of support strategy. Clauses 3 and 4 are placed in the set of support, 3 because it is "special" to the problem, and 4 because it is the "denial" of the conclusion. The remaining four clauses are not placed in the set of support because they are general information.

An automated reasoning program employing the chosen set of support, paramodulation, and UR-resolution and starting with clauses 1 through 6 might obtain the following proof by contradiction.

From clauses 4 and 6:

(7) ¬EQUAL(last(Rick), last(Brian))

From clauses 3 and 5:

(8) SIBLING(Rick, Brian)

From clauses 8 and 1:

(9) EQUAL(last(father(Rick, Brian)), last(Brian))

From clauses 8 and 2:

(10) EQUAL(last(father(Rick, Brian)), last(Rick))

From clauses 10 and 9 (by paramodulation):

(11) EQUAL(last(Rick), last(Brian))

From clauses 11 and 7, unit conflict

The given approach is successful in proving that Rick and Brian have the same last name, which was the goal. Further, we have demonstrated an intuitive method for choosing representation, inference rules, and strategy.

We can use this simple example to illustrate two additional points brought out in this chapter. If paramodulation is applied to clause 2 as the *from* clause with clause 1 as the *into* clause, the result

   ¬SIBLING(Rick, Brian) | EQUAL(last(Rick), last(Brian))

is obtained. First, note that this last application of paramodulation requires a nontrivial variable replacement in both the *from* and the *into* clauses. Second, note that the resulting clause exhibits the collapsing of identical literals. Although we recommend in most cases avoiding paramodulation from nonunit clauses into nonunit clauses, occasionally a reasoning program must consider such applications.

We make one final observation. As you may have surmised, once paramodulation is chosen for use, clause 6 is not needed, for paramodulation builds in equality. Of course, although we did not include it in this simple illustration, EQUAL(x,x) should be included whenever equality is present in a problem. Many proofs are completed by discovering clauses such as

   ¬EQUAL(a, a)

where a is some constant in the problem. If clause 6 were not present, can you complete the proof that Rick and Brian have the same last name?

6.11 An Existing Automated Reasoning Program

An automated reasoning program, AURA (for automated reasoning assistant), does exist that makes available to the user the features discussed in this book. This reasoning program, designed at Argonne National Laboratory and at Northern Illinois University, is the program that was used to obtain the results extracted from the various computer runs and in effect quoted here. With much assistance from AURA, open questions in mathematics and in formal logic were answered, circuits were designed and validated, various puzzles were solved, and assorted tasks were completed.

In addition to the language of clauses, the use of AURA can require setting many flags, choosing various values for a number of control parameters, and complying with various other conventions. One feature that makes AURA quite different from the generic automated reasoning program discussed in this book is its capacity to perform as a set of reasoning programs. Each such reasoning program, called an *environment*, can function quite independently from the others. For example, one inference rule can be used for one task in one environment, while a different inference rule is used for a different task in a separate environment. In the full jobs puzzle of Chapter 3, one task is that of updating the lists of possible jobs still remaining for each individual, while another task is that of finding properties that connect or disconnect various people with certain jobs. The first of these tasks is accomplished with demodulation, while the second relies on various inference rules.

AURA has evolved over a 12-year period and is essentially a computer program for research. Written in IBM 360/370 Assembly Language and PL/I, the program is not portable. In response to this lack of portability, and because of the increasing number of potential applications for an automated reasoning program, the system LMA (Logic Machine Architecture) has been designed and implemented in Pascal. The LMA system is itself not an automated reasoning program, but is a set of procedures for producing reasoning programs tailored to the user's specifications. LMA provides the user with both an aid to research for the development of additional inference rules and strategies, for example, as well as permitting the user to produce a special-purpose reasoning program. Reasoning programs produced with LMA have been run on a number of different machines, including relatively inexpensive ones.

The first major reasoning system implemented within the LMA framework is ITP, an interactive system supporting all of the reasoning mechanisms described in this book, as well as many other features. It can accept a wide variety of input languages, one of which is the one used throughout this book, and includes an integrated Prolog subsystem (see Chapter 14). ITP and LMA together form a large system, consisting of approximately 60,000 lines of Pascal. Both LMA and ITP are in the public domain.

Shortly, automated reasoning programs should be available on many machines and accessible to many users. In fact, LMA and ITP are already being distributed to a number of researchers. The LMA system makes it possible to test new research ideas very quickly, especially those in automated reasoning, and to experiment in turn with those ideas for various possible applications.

EXERCISES

7. Consider the twelve clauses that were produced in problem 5, found before Section 6.4.
   (a) Give a proof using hyperresolution as the only inference rule.
   (b) Give a proof using UR-resolution as the only inference rule.
   (c) Give a proof using binary resolution alone that is distinct from both of your preceding two proofs.

8. BNF grammars are occasionally used to describe the structure of sentences. For example,

   ⟨sentence⟩ :: = ⟨noun-phrase⟩⟨verb-phrase⟩".".

represents a rule that states that a ⟨sentence⟩ can be formed by a ⟨noun-phrase⟩, followed by a ⟨verb-phrase⟩, followed by a period. Similarly,

   ⟨noun-phrase⟩ :: = ⟨noun⟩ | ⟨article⟩⟨noun⟩

describes the possible ways to form a valid ⟨noun-phrase⟩. Here the vertical bar separates the two alternatives. Thus, a ⟨noun-phrase⟩ can simply be ⟨noun⟩, or it can be formed by an ⟨article⟩ followed by a ⟨noun⟩. The possible replacements for ⟨noun⟩ might be given by

   ⟨noun⟩ :: = "cat" | "dog" | "man"

We can complete this simple grammar with the following rules.

   ⟨article⟩ :: = "a" | "the"
   ⟨verb-phrase⟩ :: = ⟨verb⟩ | ⟨verb⟩⟨noun-phrase⟩
   ⟨verb⟩ :: = "walks" | "runs"

Now consider the sentence "the man walks the dog". You can show that the sentence can be formed using the rules in this simple grammar.

   the man walks the dog.   [Given sentence]
   ⟨article⟩ man walks the dog.
   ⟨article⟩ ⟨noun⟩ walks the dog.
   ⟨noun-phrase⟩ walks the dog.
   ⟨noun-phrase⟩ ⟨verb⟩ the dog.
   ⟨noun-phrase⟩ ⟨verb⟩ ⟨article⟩ dog.
   ⟨noun-phrase⟩ ⟨verb⟩ ⟨article⟩ ⟨noun⟩.
   ⟨noun-phrase⟩ ⟨verb⟩ ⟨noun-phrase⟩.
   ⟨noun-phrase⟩ ⟨verb-phrase⟩.
   ⟨sentence⟩

Here, each step consists of a single replacement that can be made according to the rules of the grammar. The problem of finding the structure of a sentence can be described in the following way.

(a) Encode a sentence as a list of symbols. Thus, the short sentence above would be encoded as

l("the",l("man",l("walks",l("the",l("dog",".")))))

(b) We add a clause that indicates that anything that can be rewritten to the symbol "sentence" is a valid sentence.

(1) VALID(sentence)

(c) The substitution rules can be specified by equality clauses in the following way.

(2) EQUAL(l(nounphrase, l(verbphrase,".")),sentence)

(3) EQUAL(noun, nounphrase)

(4) EQUAL(l(article, l(noun, x)), l(nounphrase,x))

(5) EQUAL("cat", noun)

(6) EQUAL("dog", noun)

(7) EQUAL("man", noun)

(8) EQUAL("a", article)

(9) EQUAL("the", article)

(10) EQUAL(verb, verbphrase)

(11) EQUAL(l(verb, l(nounphrase, x)), l(verbphrase, x))

(12) EQUAL("walks", verb)

(13) EQUAL("runs", verb)

(d) The denial of the statement that the sentence is valid is

(14) ¬VALID(l("the", l("man", l("walks", l("the", l("dog", ".")))))))

The problem is now to find a contradiction by showing that

¬VALID(sentence)

can be deduced from clauses 2 through 14. The inference rule to be used in such a case is paramodulation. First, using paramodulation, give the sequence of clauses that can be deduced to arrive at the contradiction. Next, show how the clause

EQUAL(l(article, l(noun, l(verbphrase, "."))),sentence)

can be deduced using paramodulation.

9. This problem uses the notions developed in problem 8. Here we wish to formulate the problem of determining whether or not a sequence of symbols represents a valid arithmetic expression. Suppose that the following expressions are valid.

$$a + b, \ (a + b), \ (a + - b), \ (a - b), \ +a, \ (a*a), \ - - b$$

Suppose that the following expressions are not well-formed.

$$a**b, \ (*b), \ a \ a, \ (+ *b)$$

Write a simple grammar that describes valid expressions. Formulate in clauses the problem of showing that $(a*b - + a)$ is valid.

10. Can we avoid using paramodulation and simply use demodulation as an inference rule for problems 8 and 9?

11. Twelve clauses were used in the answer to problem 5. According to the recommendations in Section 6.9.1, which of those clauses should be put into the set of support? Which of the proofs given in the answer to problem 7 could be produced using the specified set of support?

12. Both of the last two proofs given in the answer to problem 7 are proofs using binary resolution. Which of these satisfies the requirements of the unit preference strategy?

6.12 Answers to Exercises

1. The first set of exercises tests your ability to evaluate expressions using logical operators.
   (a) This statement is false, since $(2 + 4 > 6)$ is false.
   (b) This statement is true. P **or** Q is true when both P and Q are true and, of course, if just one of the two is true.
   (c) This statement is true. Since $(3 - 2 = 2)$ is false, the **and** of it with anything must be false. **not** of a false statement is true.
   (d) The statement is true. Note that, at least here, no attempt is made to determine whether the conclusion must be true *because* the hypothesis is true. No causal connection is implied.
   (e) The statement is true because the hypothesis $(1 - 2 = 0)$ is false.
   (f) This statement is also true. When the hypothesis is false, it does not matter whether or not the conclusion is true.
   (g) This statement is true, since both sides have the same value, namely, true.
   (h) This statement is false.
   (i) This statement is true since both sides have the same value, false.

2. Here are the answers to the question on which translations can be made.
   (a) Yes, this translation follows from **not** (**not** (x)) translates to x.
   (b) This translation is not permitted, although both expressions evaluate to true. Here, we are interested in translations that do not depend on the truth or falsity of the atomic propositions, where we are calling expressions such as "$(1 + 2 = 3)$" atomic. The stand taken here is quite arbitrary, since both expressions represent the same value, namely, true. The intent is merely to give you experience with translations that work, even when you cannot determine the truth or falsity of the atomic propositions.
   (c) This translation can be made using the **not** (**not** (x)) translates to x rule.
   (d) This translation cannot be made.

(e) This translation can be made using the rule: (**if P then** Q) may be translated to (**not** P) **or** Q.

(f) This translation can also be made, but it requires two steps. The first is the one given in the part (**e**). The second is based on the rule that (P **or** Q) may be translated to (Q **or** P).

(g) This translation can be made. The statement is of the form **not** (**if P then** Q). This translates to **not** ((**not** P) **or** Q), which translates to (**not** (**not** P)) **and** (**not** Q). Finally, canceling the double negation gives the final form.

(h) Again, although both expressions evaluate to false, the translation cannot be made (independent of knowing how the atomic propositions evaluate).

(i) Here there is no question—the translation cannot be made.

3. In the following answers, the order of the literals is, of course, irrelevant.

(a) ¬MOTHER(Mary, Sam) | ¬SISTER(Mary, Linda) | AUNT(Linda, Sam)

(b) The use of variables (which are assumed to be universally quantified) does not change things.

¬MOTHER(x, y) | ¬SISTER(x, z) | AUNT(z, y)

(c) In this one, do not be misled by the fact that the statement, given the normal interpretation of the symbols, is not true. It still can be translated to

¬MOTHER(x, y) | SISTER(x, z) | ¬AUNT(z, y)

which is not always true.

(d) This statement can be represented with two separate clauses.

¬MOTHER(x, y) | PARENT(x, y)

and

¬FATHER(x, y) | PARENT(x, y)

(e) This translates to

¬POSITIVE(x) | ¬NEGATIVE(x)

4. The following answers all deal with removing an existential quantifier by introducing a function.

(a) GREATERTHAN(f(x), x)
(b) GREATERTHAN(y, a)
(c) EQUAL(f(x, y), $sum(x, y))

Here the EQUAL and $sum are just the symbols that we have been using for equality and addition. Any others would be just as acceptable.

(d) ¬$LT(x, z) | $LT(f(x), z)

(e) $GT($sum(y, g(y)), a) | EQUAL($sum(y, g(y)), a)

(f) In this case, two clauses are produced by the translation.

$GT($sum(y, g(y)), a)

and

$LT($diff(y, g(y)), a)

Again, the $diff is just the name that we chose to represent subtraction.

5. The clauses that result from the assumptions are

(1) ¬INHOUSE(x) | CAT(x)

(2) ¬GAZER(x) | SUITABLEPET(x)

(3) ¬DETESTED(x) | AVOIDED(x)

(4) ¬CARNIVORE(x) | PROWLER(x)

(5) ¬CAT(x) | MOUSEKILLER(x)

(6) ¬TAKESTOME(x) | INHOUSE(x)

(7) ¬KANGAROO(x) | ¬SUITABLEPET(x)

(8) ¬MOUSEKILLER(x) | CARNIVORE(x)

(9) TAKESTOME(x) | DETESTED(x)

(10) ¬PROWLER(x) | GAZER(x)

The denial of the theorem—the denial of what is to be proved—is represented with two clauses.

(11) KANGAROO(a)

(12) ¬AVOIDED(a)

6. You can use ISA by simply changing CLASS(x) to ISA(x, class). Thus, the first clause would be

(1) ¬ISA(x, inhouse) | ISA(x, cat)

The differences in the two formulations are just cosmetic.

7. The three proofs are the following.
(a) By hyperresolution:

From clauses 3 and 9:

(13) TAKESTOME(x) AVOIDED(x)

From clauses 13 and 12:

(14) TAKESTOME(a)

From clauses 14 and 6:

(15) INHOUSE(a)

From clauses 15 and 1:

(16) CAT(a)

From clauses 16 and 5:

(17) MOUSEKILLER(a)

From clauses 17 and 8:

(18) CARNIVORE(a)

From clauses 18 and 4:

(19) PROWLER(a)

From clauses 19 and 10:

(20) GAZER(a)

From clauses 20 and 2:

(21) SUITABLEPET(a)

Now clauses 21, 7, and 11 taken together are contradictory. Specifically, the empty clause (see Section 6.5) can be derived from these three clauses by using hyperresolution.

(b) By UR-resolution, we can deduce the following proof.

From clauses 12 and 3:

(13) ¬DETESTED(a)

From clauses 13 and 9:

(14) TAKESTOME(a)

The rest of the proof is similar to the proof by hyperresolution. The only difference is now that

From clauses 21 and 7:

(22) ¬KANGAROO(a)

can be deduced, which with clause 11 gives unit conflict and the desired contradiction.

(c) A proof by binary resolution is the following.

From clauses 1 and 5:

(13) ¬INHOUSE(x) | MOUSEKILLER(x)

From clauses 13 and 8:

(14) ¬INHOUSE(x) | CARNIVORE(x)

From clauses 14 and 6:

(15) ¬TAKESTOME(x) | CARNIVORE(x)

From clauses 9 and 3:

(16) TAKESTOME(x) | AVOIDED(x)

From clauses 15 and 16:

(17) CARNIVORE(x) | AVOIDED(x)

From clauses 4 and 10:

(18) GAZER(x) | ¬CARNIVORE(x)

From clauses 17 and 18:

(19) GAZER(x) | AVOIDED(x)

From clauses 19 and 12:

(20) GAZER(a)

From clauses 20 and 2:

(21) SUITABLEPET(a)

From clauses 21 and 7:

(22) ¬KANGAROO(a)

Here clauses 22 and 11 are contradictory. Of course, there are many different ways to construct such a proof using binary resolution.

Note that none of these proofs make use of the fact that a cat is not a kangaroo. But that was not given to you in the problem!

8. The proof proceeds exactly as the nine-step derivation given in the statement of the problem does. For example, the first derived clause is

(15) ¬VALID(l(article, l("man", l("walks", l("the", l("dog", "."))))))

and is obtained by paramodulating from clause 9 into clause 14. The remaining steps are left to you to see that the derivation works.

Note that we are using the concept of equality in a somewhat strange way. Essentially, equality is used here as an equivalence relation. All derivable sentences are "equal" under this interpretation of the symbol. Similarly, "a" and "the" are equal, since they are both equal to article. We do not include an in-depth discussion of the logical foundations for different uses of equality. Simply take note of the different meanings of EQUAL(x, y) throughout. The clause

EQUAL(l(article, l(noun, l(verbphrase, "."))), sentence)

can be derived by paramodulating from clause 2 into clause 4.

9. Several possible grammars would be considered correct. The one that we choose is

$\langle expr \rangle ::= \langle expr \rangle \langle bop \rangle \langle expr \rangle \mid \langle uop \rangle \langle expr \rangle$
   $\mid \langle letter \rangle \mid ``(" \langle expr \rangle ``)"$
$\langle letter \rangle ::= ``a" \mid ``b"$
$\langle bop \rangle ::= ``+" \mid ``-" \mid `` *"$
$\langle uop \rangle ::= ``+" \mid ``-"$

The clauses to represent the given problem are simply

(1) VALID(l(expr, end))

(2) EQUAL(l(expr, l(bop, l(expr, x))), l(expr, x))

(3) EQUAL(l(uop, l(expr, x)), l(expr, x))

(4) EQUAL(letter, expr)

(5) EQUAL(l(``(", l(expr, l(``)", x))), l(expr, x))

(6) EQUAL(``a", letter)

(7) EQUAL(``b", letter)

(8) EQUAL(``+", bop)

(9) EQUAL(``-", bop)

(10) EQUAL(`` *", bop)

(11) EQUAL(``+", uop)

(12) EQUAL(``-", uop)

(13) ¬VALID(l(``(", l(``a", l(`` *", l(``b", l(``-", l(``+", l(``a", end)))))))))

Notice the use of "cnd" to mark the end of the list.

10. No. Demodulation discards the "into" parent. Hence, if there are multiple ways to rewrite a term, only one will be chosen. In each of the problems, there are points where multiple rewrites could occur, and each of the possibilities must be considered. Demodulation should be restricted (normally) to just simplification and normalization. However, in some places we do use it to perform well-defined computations such as counting symbols or sorting a list. Demodulation is not an inference rule as discussed in Chapter 2, for discarding one of the parents as is done with demodulation is not a feature of our treatment of inference rules.

11. In this problem, clause 11 is the "special" hypothesis, and clause 12 denies the conclusion. Hence, the set of support would normally contain either clauses 11 and 12, or just clause 12. The proof by UR-resolution is the only one that conforms to the set of support strategy.

12. The proof by UR-resolution conforms to the unit preference strategy, but the third proof does not.

7

Logic Circuit Design

A CIRCUIT DESIGN PUZZLE

Using as many AND and OR gates as you like, but using only two NOT gates, can you design a circuit according to the following specification? There are three inputs, i1, i2, and i3, and three outputs, o1, o2, and o3. The outputs are related to the inputs in the following simple way:

o1 = not(i1)   o2 = not(i2)   o3 = not(i3).

Remember, you can use only two NOT gates!

In this chapter we shall see how to use an automated reasoning program to design a circuit that meets these requirements.

The design of electronic circuits is a problem that requires various types of reasoning. In this chapter we demonstrate a number of different ways in which an automated reasoning program can be applied to various aspects of this problem. First we review briefly what it means to design a circuit according to given specifications and discuss desirable features of solutions. Later in the chapter we shall examine two distinctly different ways to formulate a circuit design problem for an automated reasoning program. We discuss the advantages and disadvantages of each of the two methods. Finally, in the context of multivalued logic, we introduce more advanced techniques.

7.1 Introduction to Logic Circuit Design

For those who already know about circuit design, the material of Section 7.1 can be skipped. We include it because many reading this book may wish to understand this application of automated reasoning, but lack the required basic knowledge about circuit design.

7.1.1 Components of Logic Circuits

In this section we discuss how to represent to an automated reasoning program the properties of basic circuit components.

7.1.1.1 AND, OR, and NOT gates.   The simplest kind of electronic component is called a *gate*. Here is an example of a gate, called an OR gate:

This OR gate has two input wires, labeled i1 and i2, and one output wire, labeled o1. Each wire carries a voltage, or current, that represents either 0 or 1. The function of an OR gate is to cause the output signal o1 to depend on the input signals i1 and i2 in exactly the following way.

OR		
i1	i2	o1
0	0	0
0	1	1
1	0	1
1	1	1

Thus, for example, when i1 and i2 are both 0, o1 is 0; when i1 is 0 and i2 is 1, then o1 is 1. Strictly speaking, we should say "when i1 is carrying a voltage representing 0" instead of "when i1 is 0", but it is not necessary.

It is easy to see why this gate is called an OR gate. If you compare the given table with the one for the logical **or** in Chapter 2, you see that they look very similar. The only differences are that "true" and "false" have been replaced by 1 and 0 respectively, and that the rows have been presented in reverse order. Other gates exist that correspond to other logical functions. Here is an AND gate:

From its name you can guess that the table describing its behavior is this one.

AND		
i1	i2	o1
0	0	0
0	1'	0
1	0	0
1	1	1

Here is the table for a NOT gate.

NOT	
i1	o1
0	1
1	0

And here is its symbol.

AND, OR, and NOT gates are readily available components. A typical circuit design problem is to use these components to construct a "box" that functions like a gate, but a gate that is not readily available. For example, suppose that we wish to use AND, OR, and NOT gates to make a component with the following table.

???		
i1	i2	o1
0	0	1
0	1	1
1	0	0
1	1	1

We could do so by connecting available gates in the following way.

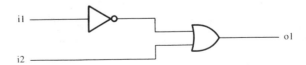

The verification that this circuit does indeed implement the preceding table is left as an exercise.

7.1.1.2 Other basic components.   AND, OR, and NOT gates are not the only basic components one can buy "off the shelf". Two other basic ones are the NAND and the NOR gates, which have the following tables.

NAND				NOR		
i1	i2	o1		i1	i2	o1
0	0	1		0	0	1
0	1	1		0	1	0
1	0	1		1	0	0
1	1	0		1	1	0

NAND gates have the useful property that any circuit that can be made using ANDs, ORs, and NOTs can be made entirely with NANDs. This makes the NAND a sort of "universal" gate. NOR gates have this property as well. Later in this chapter we show how to make an OR gate from NAND gates, and discuss a way an automated reasoning program can figure out how to also. Can you solve this problem now, as an exercise?

7.1.2 Specifications

In the preceding section, we discussed the starting point of circuit design—the basic components a designer has at his disposal. Here we describe the ending point—the specification of the desired circuit's behavior. You must tell a reasoning program about both the components and the specifications, and the specifications come in several forms.

One way to describe a circuit is with a sentence using ordinary, everyday language. An example is: "If both of the inputs are 1, the output must be 0; otherwise the output must be 1". The advantage of the ordinary sentence specification is that often it explicitly uses logical connectives such as **and, or,** and **not,** which we can translate directly into the corresponding gates. The word "if" also has a translation in terms of **and, or,** and **not,** so, for examples of the type just cited, we can "rewrite" an everyday-language description of what we wish the circuit to do directly as a circuit design. The rewriting can be done in an automated way using demodulation, and we shall show how to do this shortly.

For some circuits, there are more concise ways of expressing the relationship between the inputs and outputs of a proposed circuit. Sometimes the best way is by means of functions that are already known. For example, the specification might be expressed in the following way, "Design a circuit with inputs i1 and i2 and output o1 such that

$$o1 = and(i1, i2)".$$

(This specification would be easy if you were allowed the use of an AND gate, but not quite as easy if you were restricted to using NOR gates in the design.) A more complex specification might have the form: "Design a circuit, using only NAND gates, such that

    $o1 = or(i2, and(not(i1), i2))$".

Compared to descriptive sentences or functions, the table is a more general mechanism for expressing the relationship required between the inputs and outputs. We have used tables to describe how the basic components behave, and tables are also useful as a means for describing how the circuits we are trying to design *would* behave if we could only manage to design them. For example, here is the table describing a circuit representing the sum digit of a full binary adder.

SUM

i1	i2	i3	o1
0	0	0	0
0	0	1	1
0	1	0	1
0	1	1	0
1	0	0	1
1	0	1	0
1	1	0	0
1	1	1	1

Part of the specification for a circuit design is a restriction of some type. The most common type of restriction is a limitation on the kinds of components to be used. Indeed, if there were no restriction of this type, then the easy way to obtain a circuit meeting the given specifications would be to buy one!

Other types of restriction might be on the total number of components used or, as in the case of the puzzle that introduces this chapter, on the number of some particular kind of component. A more complex restriction might be a limit on the total cost of the circuit, where the cost of each of the individual components and connections is known. Still different restrictions are introduced by other circuit technologies. VLSI design introduces even more. At this point we are merely introducing the notion of restricting a design.

7.1.3 Problems for the Circuit Designer

The basic problem of circuit design is to describe a way to connect the available components in such a way that both the overall circuit behaves in the desired way, and yet none of the restrictions are violated. This by itself can be a difficult problem, one for which an automated reasoning program can provide valuable assistance.

Finding one solution to the problem is often not enough, however. Typically, there are many solutions, and the designer is interested in finding the best one. What does "best" mean? It may mean "using the smallest number of components" or "having the smallest number of interconnections" or "least expensive" or best in some other way. An automated reasoning program can also provide assistance in this area.

7.2 Circuit Design Using Demodulation

In this section, we begin with simple problems. We assume that the only objective is to find a solution to a given circuit design problem, and that we do not care about its being a "best" solution. We introduce some notation that will be useful in the later sections, and we use a very straightforward approach to constructing the circuits, namely, demodulation. We discuss several examples, differing from one another primarily in the way we describe each to an automated reasoning program in order to have the program assist in the design of the circuit.

7.2.1 Designing from Functional Specifications

The first observation concerns how much circuit design is made obvious by the fact that gates exist to implement certain common logical functions. For example, suppose that we wish to construct a simple circuit with inputs i1 and i2 and output o1 such that

   o1 = or(i1, not(i2)).

To construct this circuit, we merely use available OR and NOT gates dictated by simply glancing at the equational description.

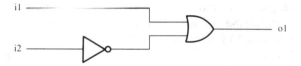

This method (actually no method at all) works as long as the circuit is described in terms of certain primitive building-block functions (such as "and", "or", and "not") *and* we have access to physical components (such as AND, OR, and NOT gates) with which to implement the design. We see in this section that the better the match between the language we use to describe the circuit and the availability of the components we wish to use, the easier the design process is. In the case we are considering, the match is perfect.

   Here is a more complex example of the same type. Suppose we wish to design, in terms of AND, OR, and NOT gates, a circuit described by the equation

   o1 = and(or(i1, not(i2)), not(and(i1, i3))).

Again we could simply look at the equation and immediately draw the circuit.

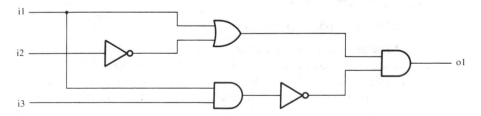

Now let us suppose that the match between the descriptive language and the available gates is not perfect. For example, suppose that instead of AND, OR, and NOT gates, we have only NAND gates to build the circuit with, and we wish to build the following simple circuit cited earlier.

o1 = or(i1, not(i2))

Since the NAND is a universal gate, we know we can build the circuit by using only NAND gates, but we do not know precisely how.

One way to do this simple circuit—others will be discussed later—is to use demodulators to "rewrite" the circuit as it is described into a form that has only "nand"s in it. We start with a unit clause representing the description of the circuit to be designed. In the example we are considering, the clause is

CKT(or(i1, not(i2)))

where CKT means the circuit can be described in this manner. The plan is to demodulate this clause to

CKT(⟨expression⟩)

where the only function symbols in ⟨expression⟩ are "nand"s. What demodulators will we need?

The goal is to replace any expression containing "and"s, "or"s, and "not"s with one containing "nand"s only. First, to eliminate "or", we supply a demodulator that replaces each occurrence of "or" with a logically equivalent expression containing no "or"s.

EQUAL(or(x, y), nand(not(x), not(y)))

Next, we can eliminate "and"s using the following demodulator.

EQUAL(and(x, y), not(nand(x, y)))

Finally, we replace each "not" using

EQUAL(not(x), nand(x, x))

We thus have a set of demodulators that together replace all occurrences of "and", "or", and "not", producing an expression using only "nand". We also use a type of simplification similar to

EQUAL(not(not(x)), x)

The "nand" form of this is

EQUAL(nand(nand(x, x), nand(x, x)), x)

Now let us solve the problem at hand. We place in the set of support a clause containing the specification of the circuit to be designed. (Note that we are proceeding differently here than we did in various examples in the early chapters. There we denied that the goal is reachable, and, therefore, placed the denial in the set of support.)

(1) CKT(or(i1, not(i2)))

We add the demodulators for converting expressions to ones relying exclusively on "nand", and for simplifying expressions.

(2) EQUAL(or(x, y), nand(not(x), not(y)))

(3) EQUAL(and(x, y), not(nand(x, y)))

(4) EQUAL(not(x), nand(x, x))

(5) EQUAL(nand(nand(x, x), nand(x, x)), x)

We treat demodulation as an inference rule here and in certain later examples. Specifically, an input clause in the set of support is chosen and all the demodulators are applied to it. Only the final, fully demodulated version is kept, as well as the original input clause.

   Suppose that the automated reasoning program we are using applies demodulators to terms inside out, starting at the righthand end of the term. In particular, this means that all subterms of a term are demodulated before the term itself is demodulated. We start with clause 1 since it is the only clause in the set of support. The first term examined is i2, the rightmost term. No demodulators apply to it, so the next term considered is not(i2), which clause 4 rewrites to nand(i2, i2). No demodulators apply to nand(i2, i2), or to the next term, i1. So next the reasoning program considers the entire term or(i1, nand(i2, i2)). Clause 2 applies to this term, replacing it with

nand(not(i1), not(nand(i2, i2)))

In determining whether we can further demodulate this term, we again start with the rightmost term. Skipping the subterms to which no demodulators apply, we see that clause 4 replaces not(nand(i2, i2)) with nand(nand(i2, i2),nand(i2, i2)), which is then simplified by clause 5 to just i2. Finally, clause 4 applies to the term not(i1), and the final form is obtained, which is

CKT(nand(nand(i1, i1), i2))

This clause corresponds to the following circuit.

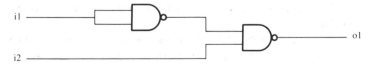

This completes the task of designing the simple circuit. We have rewritten the expression or(i1,not(i2)) in terms of the "nand" function only, so that it is obvious how to implement the circuit in terms of NAND gates.

To apply this technique to the more complex example discussed at the beginning of this section, we use the same set of demodulators, but start with the clause

CKT(and(or(i1, not(i2)), not(and(i1, i3))))

Applying the given demodulators, inside out as before, in the order 3, 4, 4, 5, 4, 2, 4, 5, 4, 3, 4, we get

CKT(nand(nand(nand(nand(i1, i1), i2), nand(i1, i3)),
    nand(nand(nand(i1, i1), i2), nand(i1, i3))))

This circuit need not contain as many NAND gates as there are "nand"s in the given expression. In particular, the expression nand(x,x), where x is a complex subcircuit, does not actually require duplicating all the *gates* in x, merely the output of the subcircuit x, which can be done by splitting a wire. We can use the automated reasoning program to identify instances of nand(x,x) in the given expression. If we subject the expression to rewriting with the demodulator

EQUAL(nand(x, x), splitnand(x))

we get

CKT(splitnand(nand(nand(splitnand(i1), i2), nand(i1, i3))))

which represents the circuit

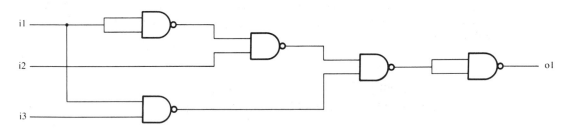

EXERCISES

1. Give an expression, using only the **nor** operator, that is equivalent to **not**(x). Similarly, show how (x **or** y) can be converted to an equivalent expression using only the **nor** operator.

2. In this section, the or(i1,not(i2)) was demodulated to a representation using only the **nand** operator. Show how the expression could be demodulated to an expression that uses only the **nor** operator. Similarly, show what

CKT(and(or(i1, not(i2)), not(and(i1, i3))))

demodulates to, using only the **nor** operator.

7.2.2 Designing from Descriptive Sentences

In the preceding section, each circuit design problem began with a description given in terms of the "and", "or", and "not" functions. Suppose instead that we described the circuit in the following way: "I wish the output of the circuit to be 1 if the inputs are both 0, and 0 otherwise". To convey a circuit description of this type to an automated reasoning program, we use a function of three arguments, called "if". The value of if(x,y,z) is y when x is 1 and z when x is 0. The "if" function behaves like "if x then y else z", where x is thought of being true if it has the value 1. For the moment we assume that x can only have the values 0 and 1. Thus the function "if" works like a "selector" circuit,

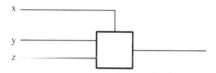

a circuit whose output is the same as one of its inputs y or z, and exactly which one of the two is determined by the value of x. (The given picture depicts an elementary form of a "T-gate". We shall study T-gates in more detail later in this chapter.)

Now let us see how to use this new "if" function to express the requirement that the circuit has output 1 if the inputs are both 0, and 0 otherwise. The key is to make the first argument, x, a function of the second two, y and z. The function or(y,z) is 0 exactly when y and z are both 0. So the function

   if(or(i1, i2), 0, 1)

has the value 1 if i1 and i2 are both 0, since then or(i1, i2) is 0, and 0 otherwise, since then or(i1,i2) is 1.

To design the circuit that has been expressed in terms of "if," we need only design an implementation of the "if" function in terms of whatever components we have at hand. If we have the elementary T-gate above at our disposal, then there is little left to do. If not, however, we can reduce the problem to one we have already solved by converting the expression containing "if" to one involving and, or, and not functions. Recalling from Chapter 2 that "**if** P, **then** Q" can be replaced by "(**not** P) **or** Q", we introduce the demodulator

   EQUAL(if(x, y, z), and(or(not(x), y), or(x, z)))

This demodulator automatically replaces an expression containing "if" with one containing "and", "or", and "not", and then, if we were designing with NAND gates only, the set of demodulators from the preceding section would produce a circuit employing only NAND gates.

7.2.3 Designing from Tables

One of the easiest ways to describe the behavior of a complicated circuit is by means of a table that says what the output is for any combination of inputs. In this section, we describe a method for converting tabular descriptions into the forms we have already treated. Here is a simple table.

		i1	
		0	1
i2	0	0	0
	1	1	0

The table says that the output of the circuit is to be 1 if i1 is 0 and i2 is 1, and 0 otherwise. This has a familiar ring to it, doesn't it? Since what a table says can be described with an "if" statement, we can use the trick from the preceding section for circuits whose specifications are given in tabular form. Let us see how to have demodulation do all of the work.

We use a new function, called "tab", to describe tables. The function tab(x, y, z) gives, for an input x, the output y if x is 0 and z if x is 1. A simple inverter—NOT gate—can be described by the tab function as tab(i1, 1, 0). Because we have used a function rather than a predicate, we can nest occurrences of the tab function when we must consider more than one input. The table given at the beginning of this section can be represented as

tab(i2, tab(i1, 0, 0), tab(i1, 1, 0))

Note that the rows of the table appear in order in this expression, which makes it easy to look at a table and write down the corresponding "tab" expression for it.

To use demodulation to design a circuit expressed in this notation, we add to the collection of demodulators one whose purpose is to translate "tab" to "if". The description of tab says that it should be

EQUAL(tab(x, y, z), if(x, z, y))

Finally, let us use the technique to design, in terms of NAND gates, the circuit described by the given table. We add to the original set of demodulators the new ones

EQUAL(tab(x, y, z), if(x, z, y))
EQUAL(if(x, y, z), and(or(not(x), y), or(x, z)))

We also add demodulators to evaluate "and", "or", and "not" functions. These demodulators are the following.

EQUAL(not(0), 1)
EQUAL(not(1), 0)

EQUAL(and(x, 1), x)

EQUAL(and(1, x), x)

EQUAL(and(x, 0), 0)

EQUAL(and(0, x), 0)

EQUAL(or(x, 1), 1)

EQUAL(or(1, x), 1)

EQUAL(or(x, 0), x)

EQUAL(or(0, x), x)

EQUAL(and(x, not(x)), 0)

EQUAL(and(not(x), x), 0)

EQUAL(or(x, not(x)), 1)

EQUAL(or(not(x), x), 1)

The possibility of replacing almost half of these with the commutativity demodulators

EQUAL(and(x, y), and(y, x))

EQUAL(or(x, y), or(y, x))

is treated in the next chapter.

We now ask the program to demodulate the clause

CKT(tab(i2, tab(i1, 0, 0), tab(i1, 1, 0)))

We obtain, after first applying the given demodulators to change "tab" to "and", "or", and "not" and to simplify the result, and then applying the demodulators that translate the simplified result into "nand" form, the clause

CKT(splitnand(nand(nand(i2, i1), i2)))

which corresponds to the desired circuit.

7.2.4 Advantages and Disadvantages of the Demodulation Approach

The demodulation approach to circuit design described in this section is quite straightforward. In using an automated reasoning program to assist in circuit design, the user takes a description of the desired circuit, described in any one of several ways, and simply "rewrites" the description into a circuit design that uses the prescribed components. The demodulation approach is fast as well as straightforward and only one clause is produced.

The method also has disadvantages. One disadvantage is that only one circuit is produced, whereas several solutions may exist. The one solution produced by demodulation may not be the most desirable solution, in terms of some measure like number of gates. In the remainder of this chapter, we study additional techniques for having an automated reasoning program assist in the design of circuits. Each technique has a different set of advantages and disadvantages.

EXERCISES

3. Consider the following table.

		i1	
		0	1
i2	0	0	1
	1	1	0

With the techniques described in this section, show how to construct a circuit, using only NOR gates, that implements the circuit whose specifications are given in this table.

4. If you could build the circuit using both NOR gates and NOT gates, how would your approach be modified?

7.3 Circuit Design Using Hyperresolution

In this section, we take a completely different approach to circuit design. Instead of rewriting the circuit description into a design, we instruct the reasoning program to deduce which circuits can be constructed that satisfy the constraints we impose. When the program finds one we are looking for, it notifies the user. It is possible to have it look for multiple solutions and evaluate alternative designs. The disadvantage of this approach is that the reasoning program may need sophisticated guidance from the designer to tell it what kinds of circuits to build as subcircuits of the circuit being sought. Without such guidance, a reasoning program may get lost, and spend much time building subcircuits that are of no interest.

7.3.1 The OUTPUT Predicate

In this section, we introduce a new notation for specifying the circuit we are seeking. Although tabular in form, the notation is different from the one used in the demodulation section in that it uses columns to contain both input and output values. For example, a NAND gate with the new notation is described by the table

i1	i2	Output
0	0	1
0	1	1
1	0	1
1	1	0

All of the key information in this table is contained in the column headed "Output". In fact, all tables of this form are identical except for the "Output" column. We encode this information with the OUTPUT predicate. The literal

OUTPUT(x1, x2, x3, x4)

says that we can construct a circuit whose table is

i1	i2	Output
0	0	x1
0	1	x2
1	0	x3
1	1	x4

7.3.2 Construction Rules

Let us suppose that we are designing circuits employing AND, OR, and NOT gates. If we can construct a circuit, say C1, with some output pattern, and if we can construct another circuit C2 with another output pattern, then, since we can employ AND gates in the circuit, we can connect the outputs of C1 and C2 to the inputs of an AND gate. The output pattern of the result would be, for each value of i1 and i2, the result of applying the "and" function to the outputs of C1 and C2. We can state this more clearly in the following way: if we construct a circuit with output pattern (x1, x2, x3, x4) and another circuit with output pattern (y1, y2, y3, y4), then by connecting the two outputs to an AND gate, we can construct the circuit with output pattern

(and(x1, y1), and(x2, y2), and(x3, y3), and(x4, y4))

Stated as a clause, this rule becomes

(1) ¬OUTPUT(x1, x2, x3, x4) | ¬OUTPUT(y1, y2, y3, y4)

    | OUTPUT(and(x1, y1), and(x2, y2), and(x3, y3), and(x4, y4))

The corresponding clauses for OR and NOT gates are

(2) ¬OUTPUT(x1, x2, x3, x4) | ¬OUTPUT(y1, y2, y3, y4)

    | OUTPUT(or(x1, y1), or(x2, y2), or(x3, y3), or(x4, y4))

(3) ¬OUTPUT(x1, x2, x3, x4)

    | OUTPUT(not(x1), not(x2), not(x3), not(x4))

What OUTPUT clauses do we have to begin building circuits from? The input signals themselves correspond to the clauses

(4) OUTPUT(0, 0, 1, 1)

(5) OUTPUT(0, 1, 0, 1)

In addition to the information contained in the first five clauses, we must also tell the program how to evaluate the "and", "or", and "not" functions. The following are taken from the tables at the beginning of this chapter. We combine various bits of information contained in those tables into a single demodulator. For example, since we know that both and$(0,0) = 0$ and that and$(1, 0) = 0$, we can write and$(x, 0) = 0$ to represent both of these facts. Recalling that the variable x in a clause is implicitly treated as "for all values of x"—in this case 0 and 1—we have the demodulators

(6) EQUAL(and$(x, 0), 0$)

(7) EQUAL(and$(x, 1), x$)

(8) EQUAL(or$(x, 1), 1$)

(9) EQUAL(or$(x, 0), x$)

(10) EQUAL(not$(0), 1$)

(11) EQUAL(not$(1), 0$)

7.3.3 Examples

We can illustrate this method by using it to design the same circuit we designed in the preceding section, namely, the one described by

OUTPUT(0,1,0,0)

All we have to do is to deny to the program that this circuit can be constructed. If the program finds a contradiction, its proof will contain a construction of the desired circuit. In this case we add the clause

(12) $\neg$OUTPUT$(0, 1, 0, 0)$

to the given set of clauses. The clauses in the set of support are clauses 4 and 5. Some of the clauses then derived are, where the numbers are those taken from an actual computer run to show how many additional clauses were kept but not used in the proof,

From clauses 4 and 3, with demodulators 11, 11, 10, and 10:

(15) OUTPUT$(1, 1, 0, 0)$

From clauses 15, 1, and 5, with demodulators 6, 6, 7, and 7:

(24) OUTPUT$(0, 1, 0, 0)$

This last clause provides the contradiction, for it contradicts clause 12. We can construct the desired circuit by carefully examining the proof and noting which gates are used at each step. Use of clause 1 corresponds to using an AND gate, clause 2 to using an OR gate, and clause 3 to using a NOT gate. The resulting circuit is

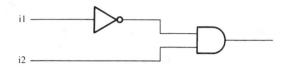

Another way of capturing the design of the circuit is to change the axioms slightly so that each clause contains a history of how it was derived, stored as an argument. Suppose that we replace clauses 1, 2, and 3 with

(1) $\neg$OUTPUT(x1, x2, x3, x4, u) | $\neg$OUTPUT(y1, y2, y3, y4, v)

| OUTPUT(and(x1, y1), and(x2, y2), and(x3, y3), and(x4, y4),

andgate(u, v))

(2) $\neg$OUTPUT(x1, x2, x3, x4, u) | $\neg$OUTPUT(y1, y2, y3, y4, v)

| OUTPUT(or(x1, y1), or(x2, y2), or(x3, y3), or(x4, y4), orgate(u, v))

(3) $\neg$OUTPUT(x1, x2, x3, x4, u)

| OUTPUT(not(x1), not(x2), not(x3), not(x4), notgate(u))

We illustrate how this last approach works by showing how to prove that the NAND and the NOR are universal gates. All we have to do is show how to make AND, OR, and NOT gates out of NANDs and NORs. We show how to make an OR out of NANDs; the other problems are similar.

Since the only gate we are allowed to use is a NAND, we have only one "constructibility" axiom.

(1) $\neg$OUTPUT(x1, x2, x3, x4, u) | $\neg$OUTPUT(y1, y2, y3, y4, v)

| OUTPUT(nand(x1, y1), nand(x2, y2), nand(x3, y3),

nand(x4, y4), nandgate(u, v))

We have the usual input-wire clauses in the set of support.

(2) OUTPUT(0, 0, 1, 1, i1)

(3) OUTPUT(0, 1, 0, 1, i2)

We use demodulators to give the rules for simplifying clauses with "nand"s in them.

(4) EQUAL(nand(0, x), 1)

(5) EQUAL(nand(x, 0), 1)

(6) EQUAL(nand(1, 1), 0)

Finally, we add to the clauses the denial of the statement that an OR gate is constructible.

(7) $\neg$OUTPUT$(0, 1, 1, 1, x)$

The contradiction is derived in the following way. Again the clauses are taken directly from a computer run, which explains the numbering and shows how many additional clauses were kept but not used in the proof.

From clauses 2, 1, and 2, with demodulators 6, 6, 4, and 4:

(8) OUTPUT$(1, 1, 0, 0, \text{nandgate}(i1, i1))$

From clauses 3, 1, and 3, with demodulators 6, 4, 6, and 4:

(10) OUTPUT$(1, 0, 1, 0, \text{nandgate}(i2, i2))$

From clauses 10, 1, and 8, with demodulators 4, 4, 5, and 6:

(26) OUTPUT$(0, 1, 1, 1, \text{nandgate}(\text{nandgate}(i1, i1), \text{nandgate}(i2, i2)))$

Clause 26, which contradicts clause 7, contains in its last argument the circuit we are seeking, which is

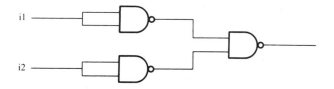

This diagram shows an implementation of an OR gate in terms of NAND gates.

EXERCISE

5. Using the technique described in this section, show how an AND gate can be constructed in terms of NOR gates.

7.3.4 Achievable Signals and the OUTPUT Predicate

Notice how similar the design technique under discussion is to the notion of achievable state discussed in Chapter 5. The OUTPUT predicate says that a particular pattern of output signals is achievable. In other words, the OUTPUT predicate asserts that one can build a circuit whose output is as stated. Unless the "history" argument is present, it does not assert the constructibility of a specific circuit. This distinction, between the constructibility of a specific circuit and the constructibility of *some* circuit having a specific output, will be more significant in the next section.

Recall that in using an automated reasoning program to solve puzzles like the domino problem, subsumption plays a major role. Essential to the use of subsumption in such puzzles is the fact that we do not keep track of all of the possible ways of placing the dominos, but only note the squares of the board that have been covered. The same principle applies in the case of the OUTPUT predicate. If it represents only a constructible *signal*, rather than a specific *circuit*, the derivation of two clauses representing the same signal pattern achieved by two different gate configurations causes subsumption to remove one of them. This process reduces the size of the clause space, resulting in greater efficiency.

7.4 Solution to the Two-Inverter Puzzle

Next we show how to do the puzzle that introduced this chapter. We use the hyperresolution approach of the preceding section, augmented with some new techniques introduced in this section. Recall that the object of the puzzle is to design a circuit with three inputs, i1, i2, and i3, and three outputs, o1, o2, and o3, such that

$$o1 = not(i1)   o2 = not(i2)   o3 = not(i3).$$

The challenge is to use only two NOT gates in the entire circuit.

We give three clause formulations for this puzzle. The first one introduces most of the notation and is sufficient for an automated reasoning program to solve the puzzle, given enough time. In the second formulation, we introduce some ideas that enable a reasoning program to solve the puzzle more efficiently. The third formulation introduces an approach that provides even greater efficiency.

7.4.1 Some New Complexities

The problem we are about to tackle, in addition to being substantially harder than the design problems we have considered so far, introduces several obvious new complexities.

The first is that the circuit has three inputs instead of two, which has the effect of expanding the number of arguments of the OUTPUT predicate. The literal

$$OUTPUT(x1, x2, x3, x4, x5, x6, x7, x8)$$

means that we can construct a circuit with the following output signal pattern.

i1	i2	i3	o1
0	0	0	x1
0	0	1	x2
0	1	0	x3
0	1	1	x4
1	0	0	x5
1	0	1	x6
1	1	0	x7
1	1	1	x8

A second complexity is that we, and hence the program, must keep track of how the inverters are used, since we are allowed the use of only two. We do this with a list notation similar to the one used in Chapter 3 to keep track of lists of jobs. Instead of the end marker, however, we shall use a variable. This enables short lists to subsume longer lists, which is desirable in this problem. (If we can construct a signal pattern using a small number of inverters, then we do not care if we later learn that we can construct the same pattern using more inverters.) For example, we know that we can construct the pattern $(0, 0, 0, 0, 1, 1, 1, 1)$ with no inverters, since it is one of the input signals. We represent this fact by the clause

$$\text{OUTPUT}(0, 0, 0, 0, 1, 1, 1, 1, v)$$

If we invert this signal, we add one inverter to the list, obtaining

$$\text{OUTPUT}(1, 1, 1, 1, 0, 0, 0, 0, l(\text{invtab}(1, 1, 1, 1, 0, 0, 0, 0), v))$$

The inverter is represented by the "invtab" term, which captures the signal pattern at the output of the inverter. If we were to apply another inverter to the resulting signal pattern, we would get

$$\text{OUTPUT}(0, 0, 0, 0, 1, 1, 1, 1,$$
$$l(\text{invtab}(0, 0, 0, 0, 1, 1, 1, 1), l(\text{invtab}(1, 1, 1, 1, 0, 0, 0, 0), v))))$$

This clause would be immediately subsumed by the first of the preceding two clauses because the first clause has the same pattern but has only a variable for its (empty) inverter list.

The third new complexity is that the circuit we are looking for in this puzzle has three outputs instead of one. The problem does not reduce to three separate problems, for we are not looking for three separate circuits. Instead, we expect much of the circuit that carries the three input signals to the three outputs to be shared. We are trying to prove that we can produce all three output patterns with one circuit. Therefore the denial is a three-literal clause stating that at least one of the three desired patterns cannot be constructed.

$$\neg\text{OUTPUT}(1, 1, 1, 1, 0, 0, 0, 0, v)$$
$$| \ \neg\text{OUTPUT}(1, 1, 0, 0, 1, 1, 0, 0, v)$$
$$| \ \neg\text{OUTPUT}(1, 0, 1, 0, 1, 0, 1, 0, v)$$

Note that the last argument of each of the three literals is identical. The fact that the three last arguments are identical is what forces the key condition—that, in order to solve the puzzle, we must construct all three of these OUTPUT patterns with exactly the same use of the inverters.

7.4.2 The First Formulation

The first two axioms are the constructibility axioms corresponding to the use of AND and OR gates. In order to prevent the proliferation of output patterns, we shall impose a restriction on the use of these gates. We shall apply them only to signals resulting from circuits that share whatever inverters have been used. Specifically, the two OUTPUT clauses to which we apply these constructibility axioms must have related last arguments—one of the two lists recording the number of inverters used must be a sublist of the other. Here are the constructibility axioms for AND and OR gates.

(1) $\neg$OUTPUT(x1, x2, x3, x4, x5, x6, x7, x8, v)

  | $\neg$OUTPUT(y1, y2, y3, y4, y5, y6, y7, y8, v)

  | OUTPUT(and(x1, y1), and(x2, y2), and(x3, y3), and(x4, y4),

  and(x5, y5), and(x6, y6), and(x7, y7), and(x8, y8), v)

(2) $\neg$OUTPUT(x1, x2, x3, x4, x5, x6, x7, x8, v)

  | $\neg$OUTPUT(y1, y2, y3, y4, y5, y6, y7, y8, v)

  | OUTPUT(or(x1, y1), or(x2, y2), or(x3, y3), or(x4, y4),

  or(x5, y5), or(x6, y6), or(x7, y7), or(x8, y8), v)

When we use a NOT gate, we add the resulting signal, which we capture as an "invtab" term, to the list of inverter output signals already used in the construction of the signal patterns we are inverting. For reasons that we discuss later, we add the invtab term at the end of list rather than at the beginning. To do this, given the representation we have chosen for lists, requires a little trickery, which we can accomplish with demodulation. The clause that computes the new output and adds the invtab information is

(3) $\neg$OUTPUT(x1, x2, x3, x4, x5, x6, x7, x8, v)

  | OUTPUT(not(x1), not(x2), not(x3), not(x4), not(x5),

  not(x6), not(x7), not(x8), addinv(v, invtab(not(x1),

  not(x2), not(x3), not(x4), not(x5), not(x6),

  not(x7), not(x8))))

The result is then rewritten to the standard form (with a list in the last argument) by the demodulators

  EQUAL(addinv(l(x, y), z), l(x, addinv(y, z)))

  EQUAL(addinv(x, y), l(y, x))

The first of these recursively converts the expression to list notation; the second, which applies only when the first does not, accomplishes the last step of moving the variable marking the end of the original list to the end of the new one. The effect of all this is that, when we apply a NOT gate to an existing output, we note that the outcome is the result of using an inverter. Then every OUTPUT literal that says that a particular output pattern is constructible also contains a list of the intermediate output patterns coming out of any inverters that are used.

The set of support contains the statements that the input signals are constructible.

(4) OUTPUT(0, 0, 0, 0, 1, 1, 1, 1, v)

(5) OUTPUT(0, 0, 1, 1, 0, 0, 1, 1, v)

(6) OUTPUT(0, 1, 0, 1, 0, 1, 0, 1, v)

We deny that the puzzle can be solved. The denial says that at least one of the desired output patterns cannot be constructed.

(7) ¬OUTPUT(1, 1, 1, 1, 0, 0, 0, 0, v) | ¬OUTPUT(1, 1, 0, 0, 1, 1, 0, 0, v)

      | ¬OUTPUT(1, 0, 1, 0, 1, 0, 1, 0, v)

The set of demodulators contains, as usual, the clauses that define the meanings of the functions we are using.

(8) EQUAL(and(x, 0), 0)

(9) EQUAL(and(x, 1), x)

(10) EQUAL(or(x, 1), 1)

(11) EQUAL(or(x, 0), x)

(12) EQUAL(not(0), 1)

(13) EQUAL(not(1), 0)

We add the demodulators that enable the reasoning program to add an invtab at the end of a list.

(14) EQUAL(addinv(l(x, y), z), l(x, addinv(y, z)))

(15) EQUAL(addinv(x, y), l(y, x))

The requirement that only two inverters be used is not enforced explicitly. Therefore, we assign priorities, by using weighting, so that circuits with two inverters are constructed before those with three, and see whether we get a solution with only two inverters.

In order to see how this set of clauses works, let us examine the derivation of some clauses. For example, from clauses 4 and 3 we get

OUTPUT(not(0), not(0), not(0), not(0), not(1), not(1),

    not(1), not(1), addinv(v, invtab(not(0), not(0), not(0),

    not(0), not(1), not(1), not(1), not(1))))

Demodulators 12 and 13 evaluate all the "not"s, so that we get

OUTPUT(1, 1, 1, 1, 0, 0, 0, 0, addinv(v, invtab(1, 1, 1, 1, 0, 0, 0, 0)))

Demodulator 15 then puts this in standard form.

(16) $OUTPUT(1, 1, 1, 1, 0, 0, 0, 0, l(invtab(1, 1, 1, 1, 0, 0, 0, 0), v))$

From clauses 16, 1, and 5 we derive, with help from demodulators 8 and 9,

(50) $OUTPUT(0, 0, 1, 1, 0, 0, 0, 0, l(invtab(1, 1, 1, 1, 0, 0, 0, 0), v))$

This corresponds to applying an AND gate—since clause 1 was used—to the input signal represented by clause 5 and the output of the inverter we installed in the preceding step. We can add another inverter by using clause 50 with clause 3 to get

(310) $OUTPUT(1, 1, 0, 0, 1, 1, 1, 1,$

$$l(invtab(1, 1, 1, 1, 0, 0, 0, 0), l(invtab(1, 1, 0, 0, 1, 1, 1, 1), v)))$$

This clause represents an output signal we can build with two inverters, and it keeps track of how the inverters were used to produce it. Notice that the new inverter has been added to the end of the list of inverters. What this does, in conjunction with the practice of marking the end of the inverter list with a variable, is make the longer inverter list an *instance* of the shorter one. This means that clauses 50 and 310 can be used together with clause 2, for example, even though they do not contain identical inverter lists.

   Proceeding in this way, we can exhaustively construct all the possible output patterns that can be constructed, subject to the restriction imposed by the form of clauses 1 and 2, and maintain for each one a list of how the inverters are used in its construction. If the puzzle is solvable in this fashion, then the program will eventually obtain a contradiction by simultaneously considering clause 7 together with the unit clauses that contain the three output patterns we are seeking and that have the two inverters used exactly the same way in each of the three subcircuits.

   Unfortunately, while in search of the proof, the reasoning program will generate an inconveniently large number of clauses. Not only are there 256 possible output patterns to generate, but we are keeping distinct clauses to represent the same pattern but constructed with inverters used in different places in the circuit. A more sophisticated approach is needed.

7.4.3 Reversions

The sophisticated formulation of the problem, designed to guide the generation of new signal patterns toward the ones we are seeking, is based on the notion of *reversion*. A circuit may have one or more reversions. A *reversion* is a pair of sets of input values, differing on one of the three input wires, that causes one of the outputs of the circuit to differ "in the opposite direction". For example, suppose that the output o1 is 1 for the input pattern $(0, 0, 1)$ and 0 for the input pattern $(0, 1, 1)$. In other words, a change from 0 to 1 on input wire i2 produces a change from 1 to 0 on the output wire o1. This counts as one reversion.

Now let us consider the circuit we are trying to design. It has quite a few reversions—twelve of them to be precise. This is the way to count them. First we note that there are four possible sets of input values for i1 and i2 together. Each set gives rise to a reversion, since changing i3 from 0 to 1 changes o3 from 1 to 0. Similarly, there are four reversions associated with fixing i1 and i3 while letting i2 change from 0 to 1, and four more from fixing i2 and i3. Thus there are twelve in all.

The strategy in this problem, since we are aiming for a circuit with a large number of reversions, is to introduce demodulators that allow the reasoning program to keep track of the reversions. Then we use the weighting mechanism to favor the circuit with the greatest number of reversions when the program is deciding which clause to focus on next. We count reversions at the time we introduce an inverter into the circuit. This means that we replace the clause 3 we have been using with one whose positive literal is not an actual OUTPUT literal, but rather a literal that captures the number of reversions that would result from applying an inverter to the output pattern being considered. Let us call the predicate for such a literal TEST. The arguments for TEST include the information that we need to construct the corresponding OUTPUT clause if we decide to do so, plus an argument whose function is to count the reversions in the resulting output pattern.

We replace clause 3 with

(3) $\neg$OUTPUT(x1, x2, x3, x4, x5, x6, x7, x8, v)

| TEST(not(x1), not(x2), not(x3), not(x4), not(x5), not(x6),

not(x7), not(x8), addinv(v, invtab(not(x1), not(x2),

not(x3), not(x4), not(x5), not(x6), not(x7), not(x8))),

makerevlist(l(invtab(not(x1), not(x2), not(x3), not(x4),

not(x5), not(x6), not(x7), not(x8)), v)))

All that remains is to define the "makerevlist" function so that it keeps track of the number of reversions in the list of signals represented by the list of invtabs. This is accomplished with demodulators that recognize reversions and make a list of them. The first step is to convert the "makerevlist" term to a list of possible reversions to be tested. The possible reversions are terms of the form

possrev(name, x, y)

where "name" is the name of a possible reversion and x and y are 0 or 1 depending on the signal pattern being examined. Here is how we name the possible reversions for a circuit with three inputs. Each reversion corresponds to a pair of rows in the eight-row table of possible combinations of the three inputs. For example, we can give the name "R00m" to the potential reversion corresponding to the first two rows of the table, in which i1 and i2 are both 0 and i3 is the bit which changes from 0 to 1 in these two rows. If the output changes from 1 to 0 as we change i3 from 0 to 1, then R00m is an actual reversion; otherwise that particular reversion is not present.

The "m" in the name "R00m" represents the fact that the third bit is the one modified in that particular reversion. Now we are ready to define the "makerevlist" function.

To make it easier to see what variables from the invtab are associated with each potential reversion, we rename the variables in such a way that the name reminds you of the input pattern of 0's and 1's in the row for which that variable is the output.

EQUAL(makerevlist(l(invtab(x000, x001, x010, x011,

   x100, x101, x110, x111), v)),

 lr(possrev(R00m, x000, x001),

 lr(possrev(R01m, x010, x011),

 lr(possrev(R10m, x100, x101),

 lr(possrev(R11m, x110, x111),

 lr(possrev(R0m0, x000, x010),

 lr(possrev(R0m1, x011, x001),

 lr(possrev(R1m0, x100, x110),

 lr(possrev(R1m1, x101, x111),

 lr(possrev(Rm00, x000, x100),

 lr(possrev(Rm01, x001, x101),

 lr(possrev(Rm10, x010, x110),

 lr(possrev(Rm11, x011, x111),

 makerevlist(v)))))))))))))))

This demodulator changes a list of signal patterns generated at the outputs of a list of inverters—a list of invtabs—into a list of terms representing possible reversions. For the case of an empty list, we need one additional demodulator.

EQUAL(makerevlist(v), end)

In order to evaluate the list, we must evaluate each possible reversion to see whether it is an actual reversion or not. Then we will sort the list of actual reversions to remove duplicates. The evaluation is accomplished with the following demodulators.

EQUAL(possrev(xname, 1, 0), xname)

EQUAL(possrev(xname, 0, 1), notrev)

EQUAL(possrev(xname, x, x), notrev)

These replace a reversion test term with "notrev" unless the output is changed from 1 to 0 by changing the modified bit from 0 to 1, as required in the definition of a reversion. We then remove these terms from the list with the following demodulator.

EQUAL(lr(notrev, x), x)

In order to ensure that we do not count a reversion more than once, we sort the resulting list. It makes no difference what order the sort produces; the important point is to bring two occurrences of the same reversion together in the list so that one copy can be removed. The demodulator

EQUAL(lr(x, lr(y, z)), lr(y, lr(x, z)))

sorts the list because it applies only when whatever is substituted for y precedes whatever is substituted for x in some ordering of the reversion names. Once the duplicates are brought together in the list, the demodulator

EQUAL(lr(x, lr(x, y)), lr(x, y))

removes the duplicate. After all of these demodulators have been applied, we shall have in the TEST clause a list of the reversions present in the list of inverters that results from adding a new inverter. We can then instruct the reasoning program to prefer TEST clauses that contain long reversion lists when deciding which TEST clause to convert into a regular OUTPUT clause so that the resulting signal pattern can be combined with others using AND and OR gates. The clause that does so is

¬TEST(x1, x2, x3, x4, x5, x6, x7, x8, v)

| OUTPUT(x1, x2, x3, x4, x5, x6, x7, x8, v)

Here is an illustration of the reversion-counting mechanism in action. Two of the OUTPUT clauses corresponding to signal patterns that can be produced without the use of any inverters are

(32) OUTPUT(0, 1, 1, 1, 0, 1, 1, 1, v)

(35) OUTPUT(0, 1, 0, 1, 0, 1, 1, 1, v)

When these signals are inverted, the resulting clauses are

(47) TEST(1, 0, 0, 0, 1, 0, 0, 0, l(invtab(1, 0, 0, 0, 1, 0, 0, 0), v),

lr(R1m0, lr(R0m0, lr(R10m, lr(R00m, end)))))

(50) TEST(1, 0, 1, 0, 1, 0, 0, 0, l(invtab(1, 0, 1, 0, 1, 0, 0, 0), v),

lr(Rm10, lr(R1m0, lr(R10m, lr(R01m, lr(R00m, end))))))

The reversion list in clause 50 is longer than that in clause 47. Thus it is selected before clause 47 as a TEST clause to be converted to an OUTPUT clause. In fact, the problem is solved before the program ever considers clause 47.

7.4.4 Solving the Puzzle Faster

In solving this problem, a typical automated reasoning program adds more than five hundred clauses to the clause space, each representing a signal pattern that can be constructed using inverters in specific ways. Far more clauses are generated but are immediately subsumed. These subsumed clauses represent signal patterns that the program already knows how to construct, using the inverters in the same way, but with a different arrangement of AND and OR gates. We allow them to be subsumed because they do not represent information we need to solve the problem. Is there a way to save computer time by avoiding the generation of such clauses, rather than subsuming them? After all, subsumption can be very time-consuming.

To answer this question, let us examine what occurs when an automated reasoning program attempts to design a circuit. We base the examination and discussion on one of the possible algorithms that an automated reasoning program can employ in processing clauses. (We assume that the set of support strategy is being used, and thus a set of clauses is chosen from among the input clauses and designated the initial set of support.) With this algorithm, all retained clauses are divided into three sets, each resulting in the corresponding list of clauses. The first set is the set of support, a set that includes the chosen input clauses that comprise the initial set of support as well as the clauses that are generated and retained during the run. The second set, called the axiom set, is comprised of the input clauses that are not in the initial set of support. The third set, called the have-been-given set, is comprised of the clauses that were once in the set of support but have been already chosen as the focus of attention for deducing additional clauses. A clause in the have-been-given set may have been an input clause or a generated clause. It is placed in that set when no more clauses are yielded by focusing on it.

The reasoning program chooses a clause on which to focus from among those in the set of support, where the choice is based on various criteria such as the weight of the clause. Let us call the chosen clause "the given clause". The algorithm under discussion permits the given clause to be considered by whatever inference rules are being used, where the remaining clauses required by the inference rule are selected from the axiom set or the have-been-given set, but not from the set of support. The generated clauses that pass the various tests (discussed in Chapter 4) of subsumption and weighting and that have been fully demodulated are then added to the set of support. When no additional clauses can be deduced with the given clause as one of the immediate ancestors, the given clause is removed from the set of support set and placed in the have-been-given set. A new clause is then selected from the set of support, and the cycle is repeated. This completes the overview of the basic algorithm.

Since we are discussing how to avoid the generation of vast numbers of unneeded and unwanted clauses, let us examine what happens in the two-inverter problem when an OUTPUT clause is chosen as the given clause. It can be unified with both of the negative literals in clauses 1 and 2 and also with the negative literal in clause 3. For each OUTPUT clause on the have-been-given list, two clauses can be generated from clause 1 by unifying the given clause with each of the two negative literals, two additional clauses from clause 2, and one additional clause from clause 3. As the pool of OUTPUT clauses grows, a steadily increasing percentage of the generated clauses will be subsumed. When a clause is subsumed, the time required to generate it is wasted.

With the algorithm in hand and with the review of what can occur, we can now present a method for reducing the number of generated clauses. We maintain two pools of OUTPUT-type clauses. The first we designate with the usual OUTPUT predicate. The second we designate with the predicate BOUTPUT (for Basic OUTPUT) in place of OUTPUT. The meaning of the BOUTPUT predicate is the same as that of the OUTPUT predicate. Thus, at any point in the run, the reasoning program has access to two pools of clauses, OUTPUT clauses and BOUTPUT clauses. A clause in either pool describes a constructible signal with specific uses of inverters. Next we need to explain how the two pools of clauses grow and how they interact.

Here are the rules governing their growth and their interaction, which we give shortly in clause form.

1. The input signals are BOUTPUTs.
2. The result of applying an AND gate to two BOUTPUTs is a BOUTPUT. (We never apply AND gates to OUTPUTs.)
3. Whenever we use a BOUTPUT, we create an OUTPUT duplicate of it.
4. The result of applying an OR gate to a BOUTPUT and an OUTPUT is an OUTPUT. (We never apply an OR gate to either two OUTPUTs or two BOUTPUTs.)
5. We construct TEST clauses from OUTPUT clauses. TEST clauses are converted to BOUTPUT clauses. (We do not apply inverters to BOUTPUT clauses.)
6. The denial is still stated as a disjunction of OUTPUT literals.

The clauses that implement these rules are merely slight modifications of the clauses given in the preceding section.

(1) $\neg$BOUTPUT(x1, x2, x3, x4, x5, x6, x7, x8, v)

   | $\neg$BOUTPUT(y1, y2, y3, y4, y5, y6, y7, y8, v)

    | BOUTPUT(and(x1, y1), and(x2, y2), and(x3, y3), and(x4, y4),

       and(x5, y5), and(x6, y6), and(x7, y7), and(x8, y8), v)

(2) $\neg$BOUTPUT(x1, x2, x3, x4, x5, x6, x7, x8, v)

   | $\neg$OUTPUT(y1, y2, y3, y4, y5, y6, y7, y8, v)

    | OUTPUT(or(x1, y1), or(x2, y2), or(x3, y3), or(x4, y4),

       or(x5, y5), or(x6, y6), or(x7, y7), or(x8, y8), v)

(3) $\neg$OUTPUT(x1, x2, x3, x4, x5, x6, x7, x8, v)

　　| TEST(not(x1), not(x2), not(x3), not(x4), not(x5), not(x6),

　　　　not(x7), not(x8), addinv(v, invtab(not(x1), not(x2),

　　　　not(x3), not(x4), not(x5), not(x6), not(x7), not(x8))),

　　　　makerevlist(l(invtab(not(x1), not(x2), not(x3),

　　　　not(x4), not(x5), not(x6), not(x7), not(x8)), v)))

(3a) $\neg$TEST(x1, x2, x3, x4, x5, x6, x7, x8, v, xrevlist)

　　| BOUTPUT(x1, x2, x3, x4, x5, x6, x7, x8, v)

(3b) $\neg$BOUTPUT(x1, x2, x3, x4, x5, x6, x7, x8, v)

　　| OUTPUT(x1, x2, x3, x4, x5, x6, x7, x8, v)

(4) BOUTPUT(0, 0, 0, 0, 1, 1, 1, 1, v)

(5) BOUTPUT(0, 0, 1, 1, 0, 0, 1, 1, v)

(6) BOUTPUT(0, 1, 0, 1, 0, 1, 0, 1, v)

(7) $\neg$OUTPUT(1, 1, 1, 1, 0, 0, 0, 0, v) | $\neg$OUTPUT(1, 1, 0, 0, 1, 1, 0, 0, v)

　　| $\neg$OUTPUT(1, 0, 1, 0, 1, 0, 1, 0, v)

Let us see how the use of the clauses corresponding to the given rules affects the generation of clauses. The idea is to permit the pool of BOUTPUT clauses to grow, but to control the growth of the number of OUTPUT clauses. When a new BOUTPUT clause is generated and retained, as before, it can unify with two literals in clause 1 to generate additional BOUTPUT clauses. However, such a newly retained clause can unify with only one literal in clause 2, which leads to far fewer clauses being generated. In particular, if the have-been-given list contains few OUTPUT clauses, then few clauses will be generated using clause 2. A further improvement in efficiency results from the fact that the newly generated BOUTPUT clause cannot unify with the negative literal in clause 3. Of course, because of one of the rules, the new BOUTPUT clause immediately causes the generation of an OUTPUT clause that is its duplicate. However, that new OUTPUT clause, since it is in the set of support, is not available to complete the application of an inference rule such as hyperresolution until it has been chosen as the given clause. The choice of such a new OUTPUT clause as the given clause can be delayed by using weighting appropriately.

Weights of predicates can be assigned so that a reasoning program always prefers focusing on a BOUTPUT clause in the set of support in preference to an OUTPUT clause in that set. Thus, the program will choose an OUTPUT clause as the given clause only when no BOUTPUT clauses remain on the set of support. When this occurs, a large number of clauses will be generated using clause 2. However, none of them will be moved to the have-been-given list until they have been chosen as the given clause, which often occurs much later. The new OUTPUT clause will generate no clause from clause 1, but will generate one TEST clause.

Thus we see that maintaining the two pools of clauses and restricting their interaction—BOUTPUTs can be ANDed but not ORed, and OUTPUTs are only ORed with BOUTPUTs—reduces the number of clauses generated from each given clause. Of course, this approach dramatically improves the time required to find the circuit in question only if the program is not forced to consider too many given clauses. The potential for increased effectiveness is a consequence in part of fewer paths of unification. More important is the truncation of trees of clauses that can result by retaining unneeded clauses. Such unneeded clauses lead to the deduction of additional unneeded clauses, and the cycle can continue.

We are making certain bets when we use this approach to solving the two-inverter puzzle. For example, we are betting that it is not necessary to connect the output of an OR gate to the input of an AND gate to find a circuit of the desired type, since the revised set of axioms does not allow this. We are also betting that the difficult phase of solving the problem is to find and retain a sufficiently rich set of signal patterns with a small number of 1's in them—ANDing two signal patterns, which we allow freely, does not increase the number of 1's—and that a relatively small pool of OR outputs will provide enough building blocks to solve the problem. The effectiveness of this approach can be measured only by looking at the statistics on generated, subsumed clauses for runs made both with and without the technique described in this section. When such a test is made, the solution is reached both with the formulation using BOUTPUT and with the formulation which does not use it. However, when the BOUTPUT trick is used, only 3,635 clauses are generated before the solution is found, whereas when BOUTPUT is not used, 19,902 clauses are generated before the solution is found. In both cases, most of the clauses generated are subsumed.

The circuit designed using this technique, which is a solution to the puzzle that opened the chapter, is shown on the next page.

7.5 Multivalued Logic Design Using Negative Hyperresolution

In this section, we introduce additional circuit design techniques. For a change of scene, we now turn to the area of multivalued logic. Problems in this area differ from the logic design problems of the preceding sections in that the signal that can be carried on a single wire can have more than two values. In a corresponding way, the components we use are different. Instead of AND, OR, and NOT gates, we use "T-gates". A T-gate is to multivalued logic design as the NAND gate is to binary logic design, namely, a universal gate.

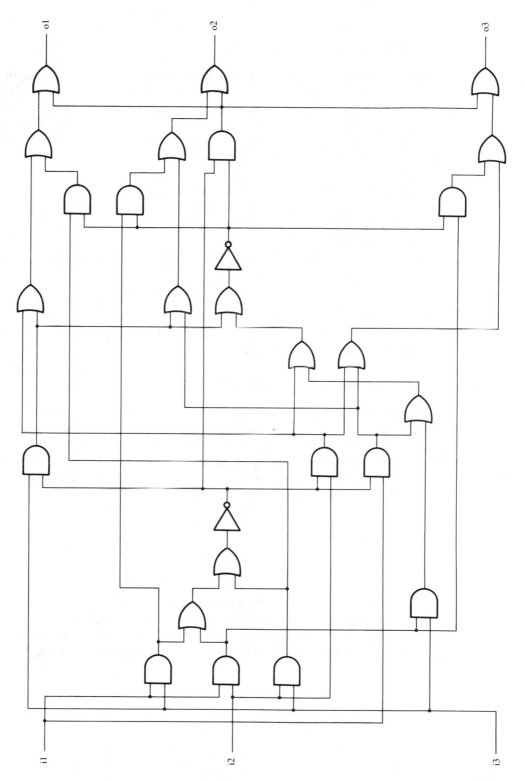

7.5.1 T-gates

Let us consider the case in which the voltages in the circuits can be represented by three different values, say 0, 1, and 2. We are thus discussing *three-valued logic*. A *T-gate* for three-valued logic has four inputs and one output. One of the inputs can be thought of as the "control input" or "selector" which selects as the output of the circuit one of the other three inputs, where the selection mechanism acts like an index. Specifically, if the value of the selector input is 0, then the first of the other three inputs is selected to be the output; if the value of the selector is 1, then the second input is selected; if the value is 2, then the third input is selected. Thus, if the value of the selector input is 2, and the values of the other inputs are 2, 1, and 0, respectively, then the output of the T-gate is 0. A T-gate is a generalization of a multiplexer in the world of binary logic.

T-gates can also be thought of as generalizations of familiar gates in binary logic in the following way. A T-gate in binary logic would have three inputs and one output. We can construct an ordinary AND gate out of such a gate by maintaining a constant 0 on one of the noncontrol inputs and by having it selected by a 0 on the control input. Thus the T-gate has only two free inputs, and functions exactly like an AND gate since its output is 1 only when both of its free inputs—the control input and the other noncontrol input—are 1.

7.5.2 Representation of Multivalued Logic Functions

To represent the functions that occur in multivalued logic design, we use a simple extension of the "tab" function that we used earlier in this chapter. In the present context, "tab" has four arguments instead of three, but it is interpreted in much the same way as before. Here, tab(w, x, y,z) gives, for an input w, the value x if w is 0, y if w is 1, and z if w is 2. In other words, "tab" acts like an indexing function. A function of one variable, given by the table

i1	f(i1)
0	2
1	1
2	0

can be expressed using the "tab" function as tab(i1, 2, 1, 0).

Just as in the case of the "tab" function in binary logic, the notation permits nested occurrences of "tab" to represent functions of more than one variable. For example, we can represent the function of two variables given by the table

		i1		
		0	1	2
	0	0	1	0
i2	1	1	2	1
	2	0	1	0

with the expression

$$\text{tab}(i2, \text{tab}(i1, 0, 1, 0), \text{tab}(i1, 1, 2, 1), \text{tab}(i1, 0, 1, 0))$$

We use a predicate "CKT" to mean that a circuit described in this notation is constructible, and thus use CKT in a slightly different manner than earlier in this chapter. Thus, $\text{CKT}(\text{tab}(i1, 2, 1, 0))$ means that a circuit implementing the function presented in the first of the two tables can be constructed.

Finally, we must define what a T-gate is in the formal language of clauses. The standard notation represents a T-gate with its control input written last. For example, $\text{tgate}(2, 1, 0, i1)$ represents an implementation of a function using one T-gate. With the representation for truth tables using the "tab" function, it is easy to express the relationship between the description of a function (using "tab") and its implementation in terms of T-gates (using "tgate").

$$\text{EQUAL}(\text{tab}(w, x, y, z), \text{tgate}(x, y, z, w))$$

7.5.3 Construction Rules

As in preceding sections, we need clauses that express the fact that new circuits can be constructed from existing circuits by connecting the outputs of already constructed circuits to the inputs of basic components. Since here we are using only one basic component, the T-gate, we have the constructor clause

$$\neg\text{CKT}(x) \mid \neg\text{CKT}(y) \mid \neg\text{CKT}(z) \mid \text{CKT}(\text{tgate}(x, y, z, w))$$

This clause says that we can connect any three constructible circuits to the noncontrol inputs of a T-gate, resulting in a new constructible circuit. By using only this constructor clause, we are implementing a restriction that only inputs to the circuit we are trying to design can be connected to the control inputs of the T-gates in the circuit.

7.5.4 Negative Hyperresolution

Negative hyperresolution is an inference rule that acts like the reverse of (positive) hyperresolution. Its intuitive meaning is "given an if-then statement, if the conclusion is false, then one of the hypotheses must be false". Formally, negative hyperresolution behaves like hyperresolution but with the roles of positive and negative interchanged. Starting with a clause that has at least one positive literal, all of the positive literals must be removed by unifying them with literals from other clauses containing only negative literals, yielding a clause with only negative literals. For example, from the clauses

$$\neg P(x) \mid \neg Q(y) \mid R(x, y)$$
$$\neg R(a, b) \mid \neg S(a)$$

we can conclude, using negative hyperresolution,

$\neg$P(a) | $\neg$Q(b) | $\neg$S(a)

Negative hyperresolution is useful when we wish to reason backwards, as we do in this section. We shall use this inference rule to conclude that, if a certain circuit is not constructible using T-gates, then certain subcircuits must not be constructible. This is the reverse of the way we reasoned about circuits earlier in this chapter.

7.5.5 An Example

Let us try to synthesize the example circuit previously described—the one described by the table

		i1		
		0	1	2
	0	0	1	0
i2	1	1	2	1
	2	0	1	0

We assert that a T-gate implementation of this function is not constructible, and eventually arrive at a contradiction. The design we are seeking is extractable from the proof. What clauses do we need?

Most of them have been given already. First we have the constructor clause

(1) $\neg$CKT(x) | $\neg$CKT(y) | $\neg$CKT(z) | CKT(tgate(x, y, z, w))

Next, we have clauses that assert that we can construct constant functions.

(2) CKT(0)

(3) CKT(1)

(4) CKT(2)

We deny that the desired circuit is constructible.

(5) $\neg$CKT(tab(i2, tab(i1, 0, 1, 0), tab(i1, 1, 2, 1), tab(i1, 0, 1, 0)))

Finally, we add a demodulator that expresses the relationship between the "tab" we use to express the specifications for the circuit and the "tgate" we use to construct circuits.

(6) EQUAL(tab(w, x, y, z), tgate(x, y, z, w))

We use negative hyperresolution as the inference rule and employ the set of support strategy with the set of support consisting of clause 5 after it has been rewritten, using clause 6 to

(7) ¬CKT(tgate(tgate(0, 1, 0, i1), tgate(1, 2, 1, i1),
          tgate(0, 1, 0, i1), i2))

The following clauses are among those deduced by an automated reasoning program.

From clauses 7 and 1:

(8) ¬CKT(tgate(0, 1, 0, i1)) | ¬CKT(tgate(1, 2, 1, i1))

From clauses 8 and 1:

(9) ¬CKT(tgate(1, 2, 1, i1)) | ¬CKT(0) | ¬CKT(1)

From clauses 9 and 1:

(11) ¬CKT(0) | ¬CKT(1) | ¬CKT(2)

From clauses 11 and 2:

(14) ¬CKT(1) | ¬CKT(2)

From clauses 14 and 3:

(17) ¬CKT(2)

Clauses 17 and 4 contradict each other, proving that the circuit is constructible. As before, we find the circuit we are looking for by examining the proof. The first deduced clause, clause 8, actually contains all the information we need. It represents a decomposition based on values of i2, and specifies the T-gate outputs to be used as inputs to the final T-gate. Thus the circuit we are looking for is

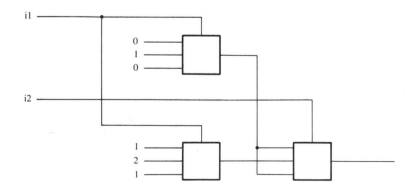

EXERCISE

6. Construct the circuit described by the following table, using T-gates.

		i1		
		0	1	2
	0	1	2	2
i2	1	0	1	0
	2	2	0	1

7.6 Answers to Exercises

1. The first part of this problem is quite simple: **not**(x) is equivalent to (x **nor** x). Now, since we know how to convert **not**, the conversion of **or** becomes easier. Since (x **or** y) is equivalent to **not**(x **nor** y), it must also be equivalent to ((x **nor** y) **nor** (x **nor** y)).

2. We shall use the same technique, but we must replace clauses 2 through 5 with versions that express and(x, y), or(x, y), and not(x) in terms of the nor operator. These clauses are the following.

   (2) EQUAL(and(x, y), nor(not(x), not(y)))

   (3) EQUAL(or(x, y), not(nor(x, y)))

   (4) EQUAL(not(x), nor(x, x))

   Finally, we can use

   (5) EQUAL(nor(x, x), splitnor(x))

   (6) EQUAL(splitnor(splitnor(x)), x)

   If you now demodulate clause 1, you get

   CKT(splitnor(nor(i1, splitnor(i2))))

   Similarly, if you demodulate

   CKT(and(or(i1, not(i2)), not(and(i1, i3))))

   you get

   CKT(nor(nor(i1, splitnor(i2)), nor(splitnor(i1), splitnor(i3))))

3. In order to do the design in terms of NOR gates, you can use the demodulators from problem 2, along with

   (7) EQUAL(not(0), 1)

   (8) EQUAL(not(1), 0)

   (9) EQUAL(or(x, 1), 1)

   (10) EQUAL(or(x, 0), x)

   (11) EQUAL(and(x, 0), 0)

(12) EQUAL(and(x, 1), x)

(13) EQUAL(nor(x, 1), 0)

(14) EQUAL(nor(x, 0), not(x))

(15) EQUAL(tab(x, y, z), if(x, z, y))

(16) EQUAL(if(x, y, z), and(or(not(x), y), or(x, z)))

In addition, you will have to cope with the fact that the two-place operators are commutative—or(x, y) evaluates to the same result as or(y, x). This entire topic is covered in more detail in Chapter 8. For the purposes here, we can simply add the following demodulators.

(17) EQUAL(or(1, x), 1)

(18) EQUAL(or(0, x), x)

(19) EQUAL(and(0, x), 0)

(20) EQUAL(and(1, x), x)

(21) EQUAL(nor(1, x), 0)

(22) EQUAL(nor(0, x), not(x))

When they are applied to CKT(tab(i2, tab(i1, 0, 1), tab(i1, 1, 0))), the result is

CKT(nor(nor(splitnor(i2), splitnor(i1)), nor(i2, i1)))

which corresponds to the desired circuit.

4. In the case in which NOT gates can also be used, you can delete the clause that rewrites not(x) to nor(x,x). Similarly,

EQUAL(nor(x, x), splitnor(x))

should be replaced with

EQUAL(nor(x, x), not(x))

and

EQUAL(splitnor(splitnor(x)), x)

should be replaced with

EQUAL(not(not(x)), x)

With these changes, the clause demodulates to

CKT(nor(nor(not(i2), not(i1)), nor(i2, i1)))

5. Using the approach described in this section, we would use the following clauses.

(1) ¬OUTPUT(x1, x2, x3, x4, u) | ¬OUTPUT(y1, y2, y3, y4, v)

| OUTPUT(nor(x1, y1), nor(x2, y2), nor(x3, y3), nor(x4, y4), norgate(u, v))

(2) OUTPUT(0, 0, 1, 1, i1)

(3) OUTPUT(0, 1, 0, 1, i2)

(4) EQUAL(nor(1, x), 0)

(5) EQUAL(nor(x, 1), 0)

(6) EQUAL(nor(0, 0), 1)

(7) ¬OUTPUT(0, 0, 0, 1, x)

The contradiction is reached in the following way.

From clauses 1, 3, and 3:

(8) OUTPUT(1, 0, 1, 0, norgate(i2, i2))

From clauses 1, 2, and 2:

(9) OUTPUT(1, 1, 0, 0, norgate(i1, i1))

From clauses 1, 9, and 8:

(10) OUTPUT(0, 0, 0, 1, norgate(norgate(i2, i2), norgate(i1, i1)))

Clauses 7 and 10 contradict one another. Thus, the circuit that we are looking for is

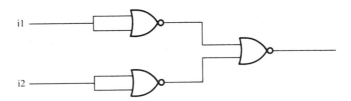

6. To submit this problem to an automated reasoning program, we simply replace clause 5 from the example in Section 7.5.5 with

(5) ¬CKT(tab(i2, tab(i1, 1, 2, 2), tab(i1, 0, 1, 0), tab(i1, 2, 0, 1)))

The proof that results with negative hyperresolution is then the following.

From clause 5 demodulated using 6:

(7) ¬CKT(tgate(tgate(1, 2, 2, i1), tgate(0, 1, 0, i1), tgate(2, 0, 1, i1)))

From clauses 7 and 1:

(8) ¬CKT(tgate(1, 2, 2, i1)) | ¬CKT(tgate(0, 1, 0, i1)) | ¬CKT(tgate(2, 0, 1, i1))

From clauses 8 and 1:

(9) ¬CKT(tgate(0, 1, 0, i1)) | ¬CKT(2, 0, 1, i1) | ¬CKT(1) | ¬CKT(2)

From clauses 9 and 1:

(10) ¬CKT(tgate(2, 0, 1, i1)) | ¬CKT(1) | ¬CKT(2) | ¬CKT(0)

From clauses 10 and 1:

(11) ¬CKT(1) | ¬CKT(2) | ¬CKT(0)

From clauses 11 and 3:

(12) ¬CKT(2) | ¬CKT(0)

From clauses 12 and 4:

(13) ¬CKT(0)

Clause 13 contradicts clause 2. The circuit can be constructed then by using the technique described in this chapter. The result is the following.

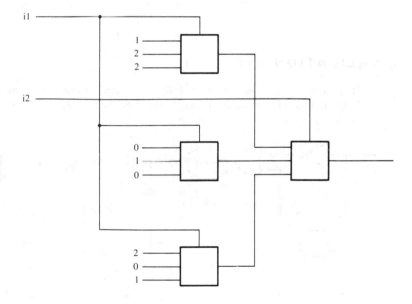

8

Logic Circuit Validation

A VALIDATION PROBLEM

Does the pictured circuit satisfy the following specifications? Given input signals i1 and i2 with i1 above i2, return as output i1 and i2 but with i2 above i1 and without crossing wires.

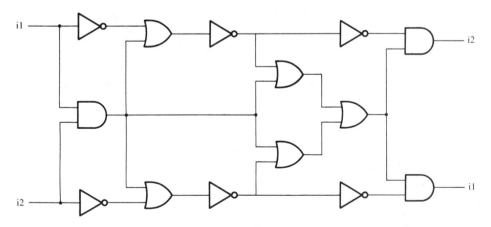

8.1 What Is Validation?

In this chapter, we consider the problem that is in a certain sense opposite to the design problem of Chapter 7. In Chapter 7, we were given specifications for a circuit and asked to design one meeting those specifications. In this chapter, we are given the circuit already designed as well as the specifications it supposedly satisfies, and asked to prove that the design in fact meets the specifications.

8.2 A Simple Example

Let us consider the following simple problem. In Chapter 7, we designed an OR gate using only NAND gates. Of course we are confident that the design is correct because it was produced by an automated reasoning program, but let us suppose that we wished an independent proof that the design is correct. Here is the design we (with the help of an automated assistant) obtained in Chapter 7.

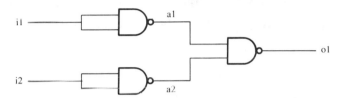

In order to study the behavior of this circuit, we label the segments of wire between the gates. We thus label the signal patterns being carried on the wires as functions of the inputs i1 and i2. The gates in the diagram then control the way in which these functions are related. In the example we are considering, let us call the two segments leading into the rightmost NAND gate a1 and a2. Then the inputs i1 and i2 and the output o1 can be related through the intermediate signals a1 and a2 in the following way.

(1) EQUAL(o1, nand(a1, a2))

(2) EQUAL(a1, nand(i1, i1))

(3) EQUAL(a2, nand(i2, i2))

These demodulators are used merely to represent the diagram. Since the specification of the circuit is that o1 is actually or(i1,i2), the hope is that this fact can be deduced from the given clauses describing how o1, a1, a2, i1, and i2 are related, and the definition of nand.

How would we represent this problem so that an automated reasoning program could attempt to solve it? Here is one plan.

We begin with a clause whose sole function is to contain the term o1, on which we intend to operate. This clause is

CKT(o1)

Then we add demodulators that rewrite the o1 term in two phases. In the first phase, we use the demodulators that define the circuit itself—clauses 1 through 3 relating o1 to a1 and a2, and relating a1 and a2 to i1 and i2—to expand o1 to a complex expression with several occurrences of the nand function in it. Then we use a set of demodulators, defining nand and other logical functions, to simplify this complex expression. We hope that it simplifies to

CKT(or(i1, i2))

since that is the function the circuit is designed to implement.

As we shall see later in this chapter, the choice of demodulators to do this simplification can be a difficult problem, but for the moment we shall simply pick some equality clauses that look like they suffice for this example. Here they are.

(4) EQUAL(nand(x, y), not(and(x, y)))

(5) EQUAL(and(x, x), x)

(6) EQUAL(and(not(x), not(y)), not(or(x, y)))

(7) EQUAL(not(not(x)), x)

Now we take the clause

(8) CKT(o1)

and apply all of these demodulators to it. In the first phase, the demodulators 1, 2, and 3 apply to expand it to the following complex expression in terms of nand.

CKT(nand(nand(i1, i1), nand(i2, i2)))

Then this clause is rewritten using demodulators 4 through 7 to get the clause

(9) CKT(or(i1, i2))

Actually, in the interest of efficiency, the two phases are combined, and the terms are demodulated in order from right to left, with each resulting term redemodulated from right to left. We shall illustrate this process in detail for this simple example; it would be cumbersome to do it for more complicated examples. Here is the sequence of terms with exactly one demodulation leading from each one to the next.

CKT(o1)	(What we start with)
CKT(nand(a1, a2))	from 1
CKT(nand(a1, nand(i2, i2)))	from 3
CKT(nand(a1, not(and(i2, i2))))	from 4
CKT(nand(a1, not(i2)))	from 5
CKT(nand(nand(i1, i1), not(i2)))	from 2
CKT(nand(not(and(i1, i1)), not(i2)))	from 4
CKT(nand(not(i1), not(i2)))	from 5
CKT(not(and(not(i1), not(i2))))	from 4
CKT(not(not(or(i1, i2))))	from 6
CKT(or(i1, i2))	from 7

What we have just accomplished is to verify that the circuit under consideration does indeed implement the "or" function, as desired.

EXERCISES

1. Consider the following diagram.

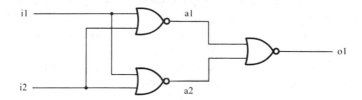

   Use the techniques described in Section 8.2 to verify that this circuit functions as an OR gate.
2. Will your approach to solving problem 1 work if i1 and i2 are interchanged as inputs to the lower NOR gate? If not, what would be required to make it work?

8.3 Important Features of the Example

Having presented a simple example, we now examine some of its features.

8.3.1 Validation as Language Translation

You can view the type of validation we just discussed as a translation between languages. Gates and their connections are part of the language used to express the design of the circuit. This language is well understood by the person who is going to build the circuit with physical components. That person, in fact, does not even need to know what logical function is implemented by the circuit. The person who is going to use it, however, has just the opposite viewpoint. The user of the circuit does not care how it is built, but instead simply relies on it to perform its function—in this case, as the logical **or**. The validation consists of proving that the two expressions

        nand(nand(i1, i2), nand(i2, i2))

and

        or(i1, i2)

are equivalent, where the first expression is in the builder's language and the second is in the user's language. There are several ways to do this. One is to translate the gate-level language into the logical-level language, which is the way we treated the previous example. Another is to translate the logical-level language into the gate-level language. (This second approach was used as a circuit design method in the first part of Chapter 7.) A third possibility is to translate both languages into a third one, and see whether we get the same result from each of the two expressions. We shall illustrate this method later in this chapter.

8.3.2 Canonicalization

Suppose that in the given example, when we were trying to prove that the circuit constructed out of NAND gates implemented the function or(i1, i2), we had translated it instead to or(i2, i1). The unit conflict signaling that we had completed the validation would not have occurred. But the design would be valid on the grounds that or(i2, i1) is obviously the same as or(i1, i2). We could tell this to an automated reasoning program by giving it the demodulator

$$EQUAL(or(x, y), or(y, x))$$

This is a very dangerous demodulator. What makes it dangerous is that it can be applied to or(i1, i2) to yield or(i2, i1), then to or(i2, i1) to give or(i1, i2) back again, and so on forever. Clearly, some mechanism is needed to control such demodulators.

Probably what comes to mind first is a restriction on the number of times a demodulator can apply. For example, we might give the reasoning program the rule that no demodulator is allowed to apply more than once to the same term. This turns out to be too simple a rule, because sometimes we do not wish such a demodulator to apply at all! To see why this is, let us take a closer look at the example.

What we actually need is a way for the program to recognize that or(i1, i2) and or(i2, i1) are effectively the same. One way is to pick some standard form for an expression with "or" in it, and apply

$$EQUAL(or(x, y), or(y, x))$$

only if the expression is not in the standard form. For example, we could decree that the two arguments of an "or" should be in alphabetical order. Then the demodulator

$$EQUAL(or(x, y), or(y, x))$$

would leave the term or(a, b) untouched, but would rewrite or(b, a) to or(a, b). With this decree, we say that or(a, b) is the *canonical* form for both or(a, b) and or(b, a). An important part of the circuit validation process is to use demodulation to rewrite expressions into a canonical form.

8.3.3 Simplification

One type of demodulator we used in the verification of the NAND gate implementation of the "or" function can be called a *simplifier*. Two examples are the clauses

   EQUAL(and(x, x), x)

   EQUAL(not(not(x)), x)

If we had not used the first of these in that problem, we would have reduced the original expression in nand only to

   CKT(or(and(i1, i1), and(i2, i2)))

which is indeed the same as

   CKT(or(i1, i2))

but not sufficient to produce unit conflict, hence not sufficient to signal that the task has been completed. Although we classify the given demodulators as simplifiers as opposed to canonicalizers, sometimes it is difficult to distinguish between the two classes. (After all, shouldn't we consider i1 to be simply the canonical form of and(i1, i1)?) Nonetheless, we shall discuss the two classes of demodulators separately. Interaction between canonicalizing and simplifying demodulators turns out to pose special problems, which for the moment we defer.

8.3.4 Commutativity-Type Demodulators and Lexical Ordering

We return now to the problems caused by demodulators like

   EQUAL(or(x, y), or(y, x))

Notice that the two arguments of this equality, or(x, y) and or(y, x), are essentially the same except for the names of the variables. Demodulators that have this property are called *commutativity-type* demodulators, named for the preceding demodulator which expresses the property of "or" called commutativity. Another example of a commutativity-type demodulator is

   EQUAL(or(or(x, y), z), or(or(x, z), y))

Commutativity-type demodulators all share the danger of potentially causing infinite looping. To prevent looping, we impose a restriction on their application similar to the "alphabetical-order" mechanism discussed earlier. This imposition simply amounts to giving an automated reasoning program a definition of alphabetic order. For example, if we specify the following ordering of symbols,

   or, b, a, not

in the presence of the commutativity-type demodulators

   (1) EQUAL(or(x, y), or(y, x))

   (2) EQUAL(or(or(x, y), z), or(or(x, z), y))

then the term

   or(a, or(not(a), b))

will be rewritten as follows, applying demodulators 1 and 2 on subterms from right to left,

or(a, or(not(a), b))	(start)
or(a, or(b, not(a)))	from 1, since b precedes not
or(or(b, not(a)), a)	from 1, since or precedes a
or(or(b,a),not(a))	from 2, since a precedes not

Demodulation now stops because all instances of the left sides of the demodulators, such as or(b,a), are in the canonical order.

We call the order we assign to the nonvariable symbols the *lexical ordering* of those symbols. Lexical ordering is always an important consideration when commutativity-type demodulators are present.

8.4 A More Complex Example

In this section, we shall validate the circuit that was pictured at the beginning of this chapter. The circuit design purports to interchange the values of its inputs without having any wires cross. We can see by merely inspecting it that the wires do not cross. But does the circuit meet the specifications given for it?

We have a two input, two-output circuit that we represent with the clause

(1) CKT(i1, i2, o1, o2)

As is typical, we begin by denying that the outputs are just the inputs reversed.

(2) ¬CKT(i1, i2, i2, i1)

We add demodulators that express the outputs in terms of the inputs, thus describing the circuit as pictured at the beginning of this chapter. If canonicalization and simplification then cause the first clause to be rewritten as

CKT(i1, i2, i2, i1)

which means that the circuit behaves as required, we get unit conflict with clause 2.

The first set of demodulators, the ones describing the circuit, are obtained by assigning labels to the wires, as in the first example in this chapter.

(3) EQUAL(o1, and(a1, a3))

(4) EQUAL(o2, and(a2, a3))

(5) EQUAL(a1, not(c1))

(6) EQUAL(a2, not(c2))

(7) EQUAL(a3, or(b1, b2))

(8) EQUAL(b1, or(c1, c3))

(9) EQUAL(b2, or(c2, c3))

(10) EQUAL(c3, e3)

(11) EQUAL(c1, not(d1))

(12) EQUAL(c2, not(d2))

(13) EQUAL(d1, or(e1, e3))

(14) EQUAL(d2, or(e2, e3))

(15) EQUAL(e1, not(i1))

(16) EQUAL(e2, not(i2))

(17) EQUAL(e3, and(i1, i2))

Next, we have some commutativity-type demodulators.

(18) EQUAL(or(x, y), or(y, x))

(19) EQUAL(or(or(x, y), z), or(or(x, z), y))

(20) EQUAL(and(x, y), and(y, x))

(21) EQUAL(and(and(x, y), z), and(and(x, z), y))

Since we have commutativity-type demodulators, we must carefully specify the lexical ordering of the symbols. We choose

or, and, o1, o2, a1, a2, a3, b1, b2, c1, c2, c3, d1, d2, e1, e2, e3, i1, i2, not, 0, 1

as the ordering.

Why did we pick this particular order? At this stage, much of the ordering is arbitrary, but once it is picked, one must be aware of it when choosing other demodulators. An example of the relationship among commutativity-type demodulators, lexical ordering, and other demodulators is given by considering the associativity demodulator. At first glance, it looks like we can choose either or(x, or(y, z)) or or(or(x, y), z) as the canonical form for the "or" of three terms. But we must be careful. If we were to decide on the first of these two forms as the canonical one, we would add the demodulator

EQUAL(or(or(x, y), z), or(x, or(y, z)))

Consider what would then happen to a term like or(or(a1, b1), c1). First the associativity demodulator would rewrite it as or(a1, or(b1, c1)). But since "or" precedes "a1" in the lexical ordering, clause 18 would replace it with or(or(b1, c1), a1). Then associativity would again apply, giving or(b1, or(c1, a1)). Now c1 and a1 are out of lexical order as arguments of "or", so 18 applies again, this time to give or(b1, or(a1, c1)). Since "or" precedes "b1" in the lexical ordering, this demodulates to or(or(a1, c1), b1), and so on. Thus an infinite loop would result from introducing the wrong form of associativity. Therefore, the form of associativity we should introduce is

$$EQUAL(or(x, or(y, z)), or(or(x, y), z))$$

Note that clauses 18 and 19 transform $or(a1, or(b1, c1))$ into $or(or(a1, b1), c1)$ in three steps, so we do not actually need the associativity demodulator to cause this term to left-associate, but without the associativity demodulator, the program would not be able to canonicalize $or(or(a1, b1), or(c1, d1))$ into its completely left-associated form $or(or(or(a1, b1), c1), d1)$.

To return to the problem we are considering, we add as canonicalizers the associativity demodulators

(22) $EQUAL(or(x, or(y, z)), or(or(x, y), z))$

(23) $EQUAL(and(x, and(y, z)), and(and(x, y), z))$

We have thus decided that sequences of terms connected by "or" and "and" will be associated to the left. Clauses 18 through 21 will also sort such sequences into lexical order. Other canonicalizing decisions we make are to move all "not"s to the inside of expressions.

(24) $EQUAL(not(and(x, y)), or(not(x), not(y)))$

(25) $EQUAL(not(or(x, y)), and(not(x), not(y)))$

We also canonicalize to the "sum-of-products" form by pushing all occurrences of "and" inside all occurrences of "or".

(26) $EQUAL(and(or(x, y), z), or(and(x, z), and(y, z)))$

Note that we need only this form of the distributive law and not its counterpart

$$EQUAL(and(x, or(y, z)), or(and(x, y), and(x, z)))$$

because, unless x instantiates to a complex expression beginning with "or", clause 20 will modify $and(x, or(y, z))$ to $and(or(y, z), x)$, permitting clause 26 to apply. If x is a complex expression beginning with "or", then clause 26 will apply directly. Note that this analysis relies on the given choice of the lexical ordering for "and" and "or".

Now we turn to the simplifying demodulators. The first two are concerned with "canceling".

(27) $EQUAL(or(x, not(x)), 1)$

(28) $EQUAL(and(x, not(x)), 0)$

We rely on canonicalization performed by the earlier demodulators to manipulate terms such as $and(not(a1),a1)$. By the choice of lexical ordering, clause 20 will rewrite this term to and(a1,not(a1)) so that clause 28 applies. In general, when adding simplifiers, we must be aware of how the canonicalizing demodulators will apply, which in turn is affected by the choice of lexical ordering. The left arguments of simplifying demodulators should always be in canonical form; otherwise, canonicalizing demodulators may prevent simplification.

Even so, canonicalization may block simplification. Consider the term

$$and(and(a1, b1), not(b1))$$

It is in canonical form, yet it should be simplified to 0. The demodulator

$$EQUAL(and(x, not(x)), 0)$$

is in some sense the "reason" for such a simplification, but it does not apply to the given term. What we do in this situation is recognize that when we add

$$EQUAL(and(x, not(x)), 0)$$

we should also add some other demodulators that are logically related to it. For the time being we shall add

(29) $EQUAL(or(or(x, y), not(y)), 1)$

(30) $EQUAL(or(or(x, y), not(x)), 1)$

(31) $EQUAL(and(and(x, y), not(y)), 0)$

(32) $EQUAL(and(and(x, y), not(x)), 0)$

and postpone discussion of other possible demodulators.

Other simplifying demodulators are

(33) $EQUAL(or(x, x), x)$

and

(34) $EQUAL(and(x, x), x)$

As earlier, when we add these demodulators, we should also add the related demodulators

(35) $EQUAL(or(or(x, y), y), or(x, y))$

(36) $EQUAL(and(and(x, y), y), and(x, y))$

Why isn't

$$EQUAL(or(or(x, y), x), or(x, y))$$

necessary? We do need to add the simplifying demodulator

(37) $EQUAL(not(not(x)), x)$

We also add some rather subtler demodulators, again to perform simplifications that can be blocked by canonicalization—in this case, by the canonicalization to sum-of-products form.

(38) EQUAL(or(and(x, y), and(x, not(y))), x)

(39) EQUAL(or(and(x, y), and(y, not(x))), y)

Both left arguments are in canonical form and will not be altered by any of the existing demodulators.

Finally, we add the "evaluation" demodulators, which describe how to treat the logical constants 1 and 0.

(40) EQUAL(or(x, 0), x)

(41) EQUAL(or(x, 1), 1)

(42) EQUAL(and(x, 0), 0)

(43) EQUAL(and(x, 1), x)

(44) EQUAL(not(0), 1)

(45) EQUAL(not(1), 0)

Since 0 and 1 are last in the lexical ordering, we do not need to consider a term such as or(0,x) because it will be rewritten by other demodulators.

This set of demodulators is sufficient for validating the circuit under study. In fact, not all of the given demodulators are needed. (This problem illustrates some of the subtleties of choosing a set of demodulators.) If we submit this set of clauses to an automated reasoning program with clause 1 in the set of support and forward demodulation as the inference rule, clause 1 is demodulated (in 147 steps!) to

(46) CKT(i1, i2, i2, i1)

which conflicts with clause 2.

What we have shown is that the statement given by clause 1 can be translated into clause 46, thus proving that the outputs of the circuit are indeed the inputs reversed.

EXERCISE

3. Consider the 46 clauses given to solve the problem in Section 8.4. Why are the clauses

    EQUAL(or(or(x, y), x), or(x, y))

    EQUAL(and(and(x, y), x), and(x, y))

   not required?

8.5 Validating an Adder

In this section, we show how an automated reasoning program can be used to validate the design of an adder. The discussion touches on some of the deeper issues in the use of demodulation to simplify and canonicalize expressions.

8.5.1 The One-Bit Full Adder

We begin by considering a one-bit full adder. This circuit has three inputs, called a, b, and carryin, and two outputs, called sum and carryout. Multiple-bit adders can be constructed from a sequence of these one-bit adders by connecting the carryout signal from one to the carryin input of the next. Later in this chapter we shall consider validating such a circuit. The output called "sum" represents the sum digit, either 0 or 1, resulting from adding the three input digits a, b, and carryin, while "carryout" represents the carry digit. A table for this circuit is

a	b	carryin	sum	carryout
0	0	0	0	0
0	0	1	1	0
0	1	0	1	0
0	1	1	0	1
1	0	0	1	0
1	0	1	0	1
1	1	0	0	1
1	1	1	1	1

Let us suppose that we wish to prove that the following circuit implements this table.

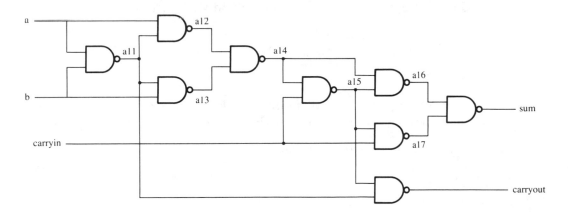

We can use the techniques of the previous sections to analyze this circuit, using demodulation to simplify and canonicalize it. We shall compare the result to the

specification. An automated reasoning program can do this if the specification is expressed in the same language as the circuit, in this case "and"s, "or"s, and "not"s.

Let us take the sum output first. One way in which it can be conveniently expressed is with a logical function we have not used before, the "exclusive or". Its table is

i1	i2	eor(i1, i2)
0	0	0
0	1	1
1	0	1
1	1	0

This table has the same pattern as the first four rows of the sum digit in the specification of the adder, and in fact we can express the sum digit as

$$sum(x, y, z) = eor(eor(x, y), z)$$

The advantage of this representation is that exclusive or also has a representation in terms of "and", "or", and "not". The expression x **eor** y means x **or** y but not both. So we can translate eor into more familiar terms with the demodulator

$$EQUAL(eor(x, y), or(and(x, not(y)), and(y, not(x))))$$

Now let us look at the carry bit. We would like to express its specification in terms of "and", "or", and "not", because we shall translate the NAND gate form of the circuit into these terms. If we examine the table, we see that the column for "carryout" has a 1 in it for all of the rows containing at least two 1's in the input pattern. So we can specify carryout by saying

$$EQUAL(carryout(x, y, z), or(or(and(x, y), and(y, z)), and(x, z)))$$

We are now ready to represent the validation problem.

We have one clause representing the circuit that is being validated.

$$CKT(s1, c1)$$

The demodulators to be given will rewrite this clause into a form in terms of "and", "or", and "not". We deny that this satisfies the specifications for a one-bit adder

$$\neg CKT(sum(a, b, carryin), carryout(a, b, carryin))$$

where the specifications are expressed by the given demodulators.

$$EQUAL(sum(x, y, z), eor(eor(x, y), z))$$
$$EQUAL(carryout(x, y, z), or(and(x, or(y, z)), and(not(x), and(y, z))))$$

In addition to the demodulators we used in the previous sections, we must add the one that defines eor.

EQUAL(eor(x, y), or(and(x, not(y)), and(y, not(x))))

We then put the two CKT clauses in the set of support, choose forward demodulation as the inference rule, and instruct the reasoning program to rewrite the two CKT clauses. If demodulation produces unit conflict, then we have validated the adder circuit. Because of the way we have formulated the problem, a successful validation will be signaled by unit conflict between the two CKT clauses. Note that we do not care about which expressions appear in the argument of the CKT predicate when the unit conflict occurs, but only care that the arguments of CKT and of ¬CKT unify.

Here are the clauses that describe the adder as it is built using NAND gates.

EQUAL(a11, not(and(a, b)))

EQUAL(a12, not(and(a11, a)))

EQUAL(a13, not(and(a11, b)))

EQUAL(a14, not(and(a12, a13)))

EQUAL(a15, not(and(a14, carryin)))

EQUAL(a16, not(and(a14, a15)))

EQUAL(a17, not(and(a15, carryin)))

EQUAL(s1, not(and(a16, a17)))

EQUAL(c1, not(and(a11, a15)))

Because this problem is more complex than the previous one, we need to expand the set of demodulators and give more thought to the order in which they are applied. Therefore the set of demodulators for simplifying and canonicalizing expressions in "and", "or", and "not" is larger.

These demodulators move not symbols inside, simplify not(not(x)) to x, and do no other processing:

EQUAL(not(and(x, y)), or(not(x), not(y)))

EQUAL(not(or(x, y)), and(not(x), not(y)))

EQUAL(not(not(x)), x)

This set of demodulators commutes and and or arguments and moves ands inside ors:

EQUAL(and(x, y), and(y, x))

EQUAL(or(x, y), or(y, x))

EQUAL(and(or(x, y), z), or(and(x, z), and(y, z)))

EQUAL(or(or(x, y), z), or(or(x, z), y))

EQUAL(and(and(x, y), z), and(and(x, z), y))

Evaluators of pairs of terms:

EQUAL(and(x, 0), 0)
EQUAL(and(x, 1), x)
EQUAL(and(x, not(x)), 0)
EQUAL(or(x, 0), x)
EQUAL(or(x, 1), 1)
EQUAL(or(x, not(x)), 1)
EQUAL(not(0), 1)
EQUAL(not(1), 0)
EQUAL(and(x, x), x)
EQUAL(or(x, x), x)

Evaluators of lists of three terms:

EQUAL(and(and(x, y), not(y)), 0)
EQUAL(and(and(x, y), not(x)), 0)
EQUAL(or(or(x, y), not(y)), 1)
EQUAL(or(or(x, y), not(x)), 1)
EQUAL(and(and(x, y), y), and(x, y))
EQUAL(or(or(x, y), y), or(x, y))

Simplifiers for products of four terms:

EQUAL(and(and(and(x1, x2), x3), not(x1)), 0)
EQUAL(and(and(and(x1, x2), x3), not(x2)), 0)

Subsumption-type demodulators:

EQUAL(or(and(x, y), y), y)
EQUAL(or(and(x, y), x), x)
EQUAL(or(or(and(x, y), z), y), or(z, y))
EQUAL(or(or(x, and(y, z)), z), or(x, z))

This set of demodulators corresponds to the Karnaugh map technique for simplification:

EQUAL(or(and(x, not(y)), y), or(x, y))
EQUAL(or(and(not(x), not(y)), y), or(y, not(x)))

Karnaugh simplifier inside a product:

EQUAL(or(and(and(x, y), not(z)), and(x, z)), or(and(x, y), and(x, z)))

8.5.2 Combining Validated Subcircuits

Now that we have validated the one-bit adder, we can treat it like a "black box". This means that we can forget about its internal design in terms of NAND gates and use it as a basic component to construct larger circuits. For example, we can construct a two-bit adder by connecting two one-bit adders A1 and A2 in the following way.

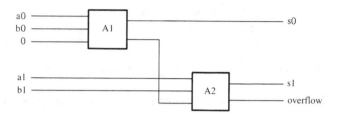

In this picture, we are adding two two-bit numbers a and b to get their sum s. The inputs a0 and a1 represent the low-order bit and the high-order bit of a, respectively; similarly for b and s. The high-order bit of the sum s is obtained, as in the case of decimal addition, by adding the high-order bits of a and b to the carry bit from the addition of the low-order bits of a and b. That explains why we connect the carryout output of adder A1 to the carryin input of adder A2. Since there are only two bits in the sum, a nonzero carry out of A2 represents an overflow condition—the numbers a and b are too large for their sum to be represented as a two-bit number. When this circuit is being used to add two numbers, the carryin input of A1 will be set to 0. Thus the two-bit adder is a four-input, three-output circuit.

The method for validating the two-bit adder is exactly the same as the method we used for the one-bit adder: we match the specifications of the circuit against its physical implementation. The implementation is in terms of one-bit adders, however, instead of directly in terms of NAND gates. The clause that describes the circuit as we have constructed it is

CKT(s0, s1,overflow)

where

EQUAL(s0, sum(a0, b0, 0))

EQUAL(s1, sum(a1, b1, carryout(a0, b0, 0)))

EQUAL(overflow, carryout(a1, b1, carryout(a0, b0, 0)))

and sum and carryout are defined as they were for the one-bit adder.

The clause that denies that this circuit meets its specifications can be written in several ways, depending on how we represent the specifications. Let us treat it the same way we did the one-bit adder, using exclusive or as a way to describe the sum.

For the specification of the sum bits s0 and s1, we then have

s0 = eor(a0, b0)
s1 = eor(eor(a1, b1), carryout(a0, b0, 0))

We then must specify the overflow bit. When should it be set to one? It should be set to one (overflow occurs) when the real sum of a and b is greater than three, the largest binary number that can be stored in two bits. There are two cases. One is when both a and b are at least two, which is when a1 and b1 are both one, and the other is when both a0 and b0 are one, causing a carry of one from adder A1, and at least one of a1 and b1 is one. Therefore, we can describe the overflow output by

or(and(a1, b1), and(and(a0, b0), or(a1, b1)))

So finally we have the clause that denies that the circuit meets its specifications.

¬CKT(eor(a0, b0),
    eor(eor(a1, b1), carryout(a0, b0, 0)),
    or(and(a1, b1), and(and(a0, b0), or(a1, b1))))

We use the same set of demodulators as for the one-bit adder, augmented by the given demodulators that define s0, s1, and overflow.

This technique, of validating subcircuits and then using them in the construction of more complex circuits, is very powerful. For example, now that we have validated a two-bit adder, we can combine two of them to make a four-bit adder, and so on.

8.6 Answers to Exercises

1. If you apply the approach used for the example in Section 8.2, you get the following clauses.

(1) EQUAL(o1, nor(a1, a2))

(2) EQUAL(a1, nor(i1, i2))

(3) EQUAL(a2, nor(i1, i2))

(4) EQUAL(nor(x, y), and(not(x), not(y)))

(5) EQUAL(and(x, x), x)

(6) EQUAL(and(not(x), not(y)), not(or(x, y)))

(7) EQUAL(not(not(x)), x)

The object is then to show that CKT(o1) demodulates to CKT(or(i1,i2)). The steps in detail are the following.

CKT(o1)

CKT(nor(a1, a2))

CKT(nor(a1, nor(i1, i2)))

CKT(nor(a1, and(not(i1), not(i2))))

CKT(nor(a1, not(or(i1, i2))))

CKT(nor(nor(i1, i2), not(or(i1, i2))))

CKT(nor(and(not(i1), not(i2)), not(or(i1, i2))))

CKT(nor(not(or(i1, i2)), not(or(i1, i2))))

CKT(and(not(not(or(i1, i2))), not(not(or(i1, i2)))))

CKT(and(not(not(or(i1, i2))), or(i1, i2)))

CKT(and(or(i1, i2), or(i1, i2)))

CKT(or(i1, i2))

2. The approach in problem 1 does not work. Using the same set of demodulators, you would derive

   CKT(and(or(i1, i2), or(i2, i1)))

   Section 8.3 discusses how to solve such a problem. You need to add a commutativity-type demodulator

   EQUAL(or(x, y), or(y, x))

   to make sure that or(i1, i2) and or(i2, i1) canonicalize to the same term. The term i1 should precede i2 in the lexical ordering; otherwise, the final result would be

   CKT(or(i2, i1))

3. The clauses are not required since clauses 18 through 23 have the effect of associating to the left and sorting the arguments. Thus, any term of the form or(or(t1, t2), t1) demodulates to either or(or(t2, t1), t1) or or(or(t1, t1), t2). In either case, the existing demodulators are permitted to apply, giving either or(t1, t2) or or(t2, t1), depending on the lexical order of t1 and t2.

9

Research in Mathematics

What do the following three theorems have in common?

In a group, if the square of every element is the identity, the group is commutative.

In a ring, the product of x and 0 is 0.

In set theory, intersection distributes over union.

The common feature of these theorems is that each can be and has been easily proved with an automated reasoning program. A mathematician would have little trouble proving any of the three theorems and would call them neither hard nor deep. You might wonder, therefore, what is significant about the fact that all three can be proved by an automated reasoning program.

First, rather than requiring separate computer programs, all three are provable by a single reasoning program—a general-purpose program not designed with any specific theorem in mind. Second, each can be proved by following the process discussed in the first few chapters of this book—to use an automated reasoning program the mathematician does not have to be a computer programmer. And third and most significant, the ease with which each of the three theorems can be proved hints at the possible value of using an automated reasoning program to assist in research in mathematics.

This hint is not misleading, for a number of previously open questions in mathematics have been answered with much assistance from an automated reasoning program.

Of the five axioms for a ternary Boolean algebra, which, if any, are dependent axioms?

Does there exist a finite semigroup that admits a nontrivial antiautomorphism but that does not admit any nontrivial involutions?

If one or more such semigroups exist, what is the order of the smallest?

How many nonisomorphic semigroups of minimal order exist admitting a nontrivial antiautomorphism, but admitting no nontrivial involutions?

Each of these previously open questions was answered with the assistance of an automated reasoning program. Some of the questions were answered by the program's supplying a proof, some by its generating a finite model, and some by its finding a counterexample. The two aspects—proof and counterexample—are vital to research in mathematics. Later in this chapter, we shall touch on some of the features that enabled an automated reasoning program to be of great assistance in solving the open questions. We shall also give the answers to the questions but omit the corresponding proofs. Since certain previously open questions have been answered with the assistance of a reasoning program, and since the two complementary aspects of such questions have been attacked, the combination of mathematical research and automated reasoning appears promising.

9.1 A Simple Example

For the first illustration of the use of an automated reasoning program in mathematics, we consider a classroom exercise in group theory.

In a group, if the square of every element is the identity, the group is commutative.

This theorem, although very easy to prove, is sufficient to illustrate various features provided by an automated reasoning program.

As in the early chapters of the book, we must devise a representation for the axioms required to solve the problem. We shall consider two rather different representations, as well as considering the appropriate inference rules to be employed with each. For the first representation, we shall use a three-place predicate P for product. The statement "$P(x, y, z)$" will mean that the product of x and y is z, in the group being studied. For the axioms of left and right identity, we thus have

(1) $P(e, x, x)$

and

(2) $P(x, e, x)$

where e stands for the identity element of the group.

Next, we need clauses for the axioms of left and right inverse. Since the inverse of an element depends on the element—is a function of the element—we use the function g for inverse. We thus add

(3) $P(g(x), x, e)$

and

(4) $P(x, g(x), e)$

as the needed clauses.

Associativity is more complicated. It is most easily expressed using the equality predicate, and we shall use that particular representation in the second formulation of this problem, given in Section 9.2. Since we are using the predicate P in this section, we need to write associativity in terms of P. What we are trying to express is that the product of x, y, and z is the same, regardless of whether we multiply x and y together, and then multiply the result by z, or multiply x by the product of y and z. To represent this relationship, we introduce names for the intermediate expressions xy and yz. We let $u = xy$ and $v = yz$. We also introduce a name for the entire product, namely, w. Then the associativity axiom becomes:

$uz = w$ if and only if $xv = w$.

The "if and only if" is represented with two clauses, one for the "if" part and one for the "only if" part. As will be seen, the first clause says

if $uz = w$, then $xv = w$.

The second clause says

if $xv = w$, then $uz = w$.

What we really mean is that these statements are true if u and v have the meanings we just assigned to them. To express the definition of u and v, we add their definitions to the hypothesis part of this statement, which now becomes:

if $xy = u$ and $yz = v$ and $uz = w$ then $xv = w$.

The "only if" part is similar:

if $xy = u$ and $yz = v$ and $xv = w$ then $uz = w$.

These two sentences then translate easily into the clauses

(5) $\neg P(x, y, u) \mid \neg P(y, z, v) \mid \neg P(u, z, w) \mid P(x, v, w)$

(6) $\neg P(x, y, u) \mid \neg P(y, z, v) \mid \neg P(x, v, w) \mid P(u, z, w)$

Before giving the remaining clauses that would ordinarily be present for a study of group theory, let us turn immediately to the theorem to be proved. We must add clauses to state that the group has exponent 2—the square of every element is the identity—and write

(7) $P(x, x, e)$

as the needed clause. Since we wish to prove such groups commutative, but also wish to obtain a proof by contradiction, we write clauses that state that two elements exist which do not commute.

(8) $P(a, b, c)$

and

(9) $\neg P(b, a, c)$

We are, of course, simply naming the two noncommuting elements a and b and the product c.

A detailed mathematical proof might be the following. Since $ab = c$, we can multiply on the right by b, getting $cb = (ab)b = a(bb) = ae = a$. Multiplying next on the left by c, we have $ca = c(cb) = (cc)b = eb = b$. Finally, multiplying on the right by a, we have $ba = (ca)a = c(aa) = ce = c$. Since ba was assumed not to equal c, we have a contradiction.

An automated reasoning program, given these nine clauses, can obtain a proof that mirrors the mathematical one just given. What inference rule should we choose? Clues exist in the mathematical proof. If the justification of each equality in each step were explicitly given, it would be in terms of reliance on an axiom or the added hypothesis of exponent 2. The corresponding clauses are each positive clauses. Next, each step relies on reassociation, hence on the clauses that correspond to associativity. Finally, the conclusion of each step in clause form is also positive. Since an inference rule exists that takes a set of positive clauses against a clause with negative literals and yields positive clauses, and since the clauses for associativity contain negative literals, the choice of inference rule is strongly suggested. The inference rule that we use is hyperresolution.

We can actually map the mathematical proof directly into a proof, employing hyperresolution, that could be obtained by a reasoning program. Let us give a detailed account of the first set of equalities that leads to the conclusion that $cb = a$. Which of clauses 5 and 6 is the required nucleus for hyperresolution that produces the first step of the given proof? Step 1 of the given proof focuses on reassociating (ab)b, and that suggests that the substitution performed on the selected clause replaces x with a, y with b, and z with c. Further, $ab = c$ is used in that first step, and that in turn suggests that c is substituted for u. Since the result is that $cb = a$, we can use this fact and the given substitutions to see which of 5 and 6 will suffice. The positive literal of 5 has the variable x in the first position, and thus, if it were the choice, the result of applying hyperresolution would be the product of a with something. On the other hand, the first argument of the positive literal of clause 6 is u, and the choice of clause 6 matches that which has so far been observed. In fact, clause 6 is the required nucleus for hyperresolution to yield cb = a,

P(c, b, a)

Closer examination of the first step of the mathematical proof enforces the choice of clause 6. In that step, bb = e is implicitly used with the justification that the square of every element is the identity. Then, ae = a is implicitly used with the justification of right identity. Finally, the first part of the step relies on ab = c, part of the assumed falsity of the theorem. The hyperresolution step in fact does pair clause 8 with the first literal of clause 6, 7 with the second, and 2 with the third.

From clauses 6, 8, 7, and 2:

(10) P(c, b, a)

A similar detailed analysis yields the mapping of the remaining steps into the corresponding hyperresolution steps.

From clauses 5, 7, 10, and 1:

(11) P(c, a, b)

From clauses 6, 11, 7, and 2:

(12) P(b, a, c)

Clauses 12 and 9 provide the contradiction.

As promised, we now give the full set of axioms for a group, employing the predicate P for product, the predicate EQUAL for equal, the function f for product, the function g for inverse, and the constant e for the identity element. The last six of these axioms express the fact that if two expressions are equal, then one can be substituted for the other in any argument position of any predicate or function.

Left identity:

(1) P(e, x, x)

Right identity:

(2) P(x, e, x)

Left inverse:

(3) P(g(x), x, e)

Right inverse:

(4) P(x, g(x), e)

Associativity:

(5) $\neg P(x, y, u) \mid \neg P(y, z, v) \mid \neg P(u, z, w) \mid P(x, v, w)$

(6) $\neg P(x, y, u) \mid \neg P(y, z, v) \mid \neg P(x, v, w) \mid P(u, z, w)$

Closure:

(7) $P(x, y, f(x, y))$

Well-definedness of multiplication:

(8) $\neg P(x, y, u) \mid \neg P(x, y, v) \mid EQUAL(u, v)$

Reflexivity:

(9) $EQUAL(x, x)$

Symmetry:

(10) $\neg EQUAL(x, y) \mid EQUAL(y, x)$

Transitivity:

(11) $\neg EQUAL(x, y) \mid \neg EQUAL(y, z) \mid EQUAL(y, z)$

Equality substitution:

(12) $\neg EQUAL(u, v) \mid \neg P(u, x, y) \mid P(v, x, y)$

(13) $\neg EQUAL(u, v) \mid \neg P(x, u, y) \mid P(x, v, y)$

(14) $\neg EQUAL(u, v) \mid \neg P(x, y, u) \mid P(x, y, v)$

(15) $\neg EQUAL(u, v) \mid EQUAL(f(u, x), f(v, x))$

(16) $\neg EQUAL(u, v) \mid EQUAL(f(x, u), f(x, v))$

(17) $\neg EQUAL(u, v) \mid EQUAL(g(u), g(v))$

Analyses of the kind just given can be used to aid in choosing the appropriate inference rule or rules. Similar analyses, coupled with intuition and knowledge, can also be used to provide important guidance to an automated reasoning program. As you will see later in this chapter, many considerations are present when relying on the assistance of a reasoning program. Both intuition and knowledge and understanding of a field and proofs of the theorems of the field can all be employed to increase the effectiveness of conducting research with a reasoning program as a colleague.

9.2 A Simple Example Revisited

Again we focus on the simple classroom exercise.

In a group, if the square of every element is the identity, the group is commutative.

We continue to use the function f for product, g for inverse, e for the identity, but replace the predicate P with the predicate EQUAL to express equality. We have

Left identity:

(1) EQUAL(f(e, x), x)

Right identity:

(2) EQUAL(f(x, e), x)

Left inverse:

(3) EQUAL(f(g(x), x), e)

Right inverse:

(4) EQUAL(f(x, g(x)), e)

Associativity:

(5) EQUAL(f(f(x, y), z), f(x, f(y, z)))

Reflexivity:

(6) EQUAL(x, x)

as clauses to represent the usual axioms for a group.

To express the fact that the square of every element is the identity—the exponent 2 property—we have

(7) EQUAL(f(x, x), e)

as the clause for the hypothesis of the theorem. Finally, we need a clause or clauses to state the conclusion of the theorem under discussion.

Commutativity can be stated as

EQUAL(f(x, y), f(y, x))

However, as you learned in the early chapters, a reasoning program usually seeks proof by contradiction. Such a move is, of course, very familiar to a mathematician. So, as in Chapter 3, for example, we assume the statement of the purported theorem to be false—we negate it. We therefore assume that the group is not commutative—that there exist elements a and b such that ab ≠ ba. The clause

(8) ¬EQUAL(f(a, b), f(b, a))

is the needed clause.

The following typical mathematical proof will not quite be duplicated by an automated reasoning program, but the proofs obtained by such a program are nonetheless satisfactory. A mathematician might begin with, $(yz)(yz) = e$. So, $zyz = y$. Therefore, $yz = zy$. A typical automated reasoning program does not suddenly say, $(yz)(yz) = e$, with the justification that $xx = e$. Of course, this step could result from instantiating clause 7. Instead, a typical reasoning program only substitutes terms for the variables in a clause when another clause causes the substitution. An inference rule that simply substitutes terms for variables in a clause to directly obtain an instance of the clause is generally not employed, nor is such a rule necessary. (Moreover, if the instantiation step under discussion did occur as the result of some sequence of steps, the resulting clause

$$EQUAL(f(f(y, z), f(y, z)), e)$$

would immediately be subsumed—discarded—as an instance of clause 7. Suppressing subsumption is unwise, for in problems of this type, it is not unusual for subsumption to eliminate 5000 or more generated clauses. Thus, subsumption is essential for using an automated reasoning program for research in mathematics, as well as for many other uses of such a program.)

The following proof is typical of that obtained by reasoning programs. The proof employs paramodulation, discussed in Chapters 4 and 6. (We explain the inference rule and the reasoning steps in more detail shortly.)

From clause 5 into clause 7:

(9) $EQUAL(f(x, f(y, f(x, y))), e)$

From clause 7 into clause 5, with demodulation by 1:

(10) $EQUAL(f(x, f(x, z)), z)$

From clause 9 into clause 10, with demodulation by 2:

(11) $EQUAL(f(y, f(x, y)), x)$

From clause 11 into clause 10:

(12) $EQUAL(f(x, y), f(y, x))$

Clause 12 contradicts clause 8.

Notice that, although the precise operations are far from transparent, the steps themselves of this proof are very familiar mathematically. In fact, the latter two are the same as those given for the mathematician's proof.

Since we are providing an illustration of how an automated reasoning program finds proofs, we had best examine in detail the proof consisting of clauses 9 through 12. The inference rule that justifies each of the steps is paramodulation—a generalization of equality substitution. Paramodulation has been discussed in detail in Chapter 4 and in Chapter 6. Roughly, it works in the following way. In ordinary equality substitution, you substitute *from* one expression *into* another. For example, in the presence of

$$EQUAL(f(e, x), x)$$

and

$$EQUAL(f(x, f(x, z)), f(e, z))$$

paramodulation yields

   EQUAL(f(x, f(x, z)), z)

In unification, variables are replaced in the two expressions being unified, if possible, so that they become identical. In many unifications, only the variables in one expression need be replaced to obtain identical expressions. Thus, in the obvious combination of unification and equality substitution, only the variables in one of the two expressions—the *from* or the *into* expression—need be replaced in order to make the substitution justified by the equality. For example, from

   EQUAL(f(x, e), x)

and

   EQUAL(f(f(a, e), b), c)

the deduction of

   EQUAL(f(a, b), c)

is not surprising. Nor is it much of a generalization of equality substitution. After all, a reasoning program that makes this deduction is simply saying that, knowing that xe = x and that (ae)b = c, the conclusion that ab = c follows.

   Paramodulation, however, is more complex. In contrast to this example and to the obvious use of equality substitution, paramodulation permits replacement of the variables in *both* expressions in order to apply equality substitution. A case in point is clause 9.

   To arrive at clause 9, some variables in each of 5 and 7 must be replaced in order to prepare the way for an equality substitution. To see precisely what is required, first rewrite 7 as 7a.

   (7a) EQUAL(f(w, w), e)

Next, find the replacement, if one exists, for the variables in 7a and in

   (5) EQUAL(f(f(x, y), z), f(x, f(y, z)))

that causes the same expression to appear as the first argument of each of the clauses. The sought-after replacement consists of replacing w by f(x,y) and z by f(x,y), thereby making the first arguments of the two EQUAL predicates identical. The clauses

   (7b) EQUAL(f(f(x, y), f(x, y)), e)

and

   (5a) EQUAL(f(f(x, y), f(x, y)), f(x, f(y, f(x, y))))

result. The obvious equality substitution replaces the first argument of 7b with the second argument of 5a to yield clause 9. In contrast to ordinary equality substitution, the inference rule of paramodulation yields clause 9 from clauses 7 and 5 in a single step, without producing the intermediate clauses 7a, 7b, and 5a.

9.2.1 The Set of Support Strategy and the Simple Example

Does an automated reasoning program, when given the problem of the preceding section, simply set to work? Is there a means for such a program to find the proof consisting of clauses 8 through 11 without investigating group theory as a whole? Specifically, can such a program deduce clauses 9 through 12 without deducing many additional clauses?

With respect to the first question, a program certainly can be used in this fashion by simply choosing an inference rule and exercising no other controls. However, mathematical theories are so rich that this approach is almost certainly doomed to failure. With this naive approach, a reasoning program will begin developing the entire theory, rather than concentrating on the theorem under study. The theorem will be proved essentially by accident, only when the appropriate clauses have been found by mere chance.

For the second question, a strategy—the *set of support strategy*—was formulated precisely for the purpose. It was discussed less formally in the early chapters, and is discussed quite formally in Chapter 15. Employing the set of support strategy prevents an automated reasoning program from exploring a theory randomly. It is designed to cause a reasoning program to concentrate on the theorem under investigation. The proof consisting of steps 9 through 12 is an example of a proof found by a reasoning program whose search is constrained by the set of support strategy.

What happens when a reasoning program is not restricted or constrained by such a strategy? With an unrestricted approach, a reasoning program will very quickly find clauses that are either totally trivial and are discarded by subsumption, or it will find clauses that are trivial and unnecessary lemmas. For example, assume that paramodulation is the chosen rule of inference, as in the proof given earlier. If unrestricted, a reasoning program will deduce clauses like the following.

From clause 1 into clause 2:

$EQUAL(e, e)$

From clause 3 into clause 5:

$EQUAL(f(e, z), f(g(y), f(y, z)))$

The first of the two clauses, $e = e$, is discarded because it is an instance of reflexivity, and subsumption comes into play. (The axiom of reflexivity

(6) $EQUAL(x, x)$

is a clause that should always be included when submitting a problem that involves equality to an automated reasoning program. Quite often, a proof is completed by deducing a clause such as

$\neg EQUAL(a, a)$

for some specific a. Omission of a clause expressing reflexivity would often prevent a reasoning program from realizing that a proof has been found. A mathematician would, of course, consider the deduction of

$$\neg EQUAL(a, a)$$

as completing the proof by contradiction. With the axiom of reflexivity, an automated reasoning program functions similarly.)

The second of the two clauses

$$EQUAL(f(e, z), f(g(y), f(y, z)))$$

would in a typical use of a reasoning program be immediately transformed to

$$EQUAL(z, f(g(y), f(y, z)))$$

even before it was considered for possible retention. This transformation, well known to the mathematician, is carried out by demodulation. The transformed clause says that z is equal to the product of the inverse of y with yz, an obvious fact in group theory. Lemmas of this type abound. A mathematician does not simply randomly prove such lemmas, nor should an automated reasoning program be allowed to prove them. Rather, only lemmas that seem to be relevant to the purported theorem should be proved. The set of support strategy tends to restrict the program's attention to proving lemmas germane to the purported theorem.

If the set of support strategy restricts a reasoning program from examining certain paths of inquiry, does its use prevent a proof from being found? Put differently, does there exist a theorem that could be proved when the strategy is not imposed, but which is not provable with it? The answer is no, not if the strategy is used properly. (The formal treatment of this topic is found in Chapter 15.) When properly used, you will see that the strategy possesses a property that is both surprising and powerful.

The set of support strategy, as discussed in the early chapters, requires you to choose a subset of clauses from among the set S of clauses that represent the problem under study to the reasoning program. Let T be the nonempty subset of S that is chosen. By definition, the clauses in T *have support*, while those in S-T do not. Recall that most inference rules are applied to sets consisting of two or more clauses. The set of support strategy permits their application to such a set of premises only if at least one of them has support. And, it gives support to any clause deduced with the set of support strategy. Because it restricts the application of inference rules, the set of support strategy is known as a *restriction* strategy. Restriction strategies are essential to effective automated reasoning.

In the example consisting of clauses 1 through 8 given in the preceding section, let T be comprised of clauses 7 and 8. Then clauses 7 and 8 have support by definition, and clauses 1 through 6 do not. Clauses 9 and 10 also have support, for each has one of its premises in T. Further, clauses 11 and 12 also have support since each is deduced from premises at least one of which has support. On the other hand, the clause discussed earlier in connection with unrestricted inference

from clause 3 into clause 5:

$$EQUAL(f(e, z), f(g(y), f(y, z)))$$

does not have support, for its immediate premises are in S-T and neither, therefore, has support. In fact, the proof given in the preceding section is obtainable within the constraints of the set of support strategy, while clauses like that just cited are not. Thus, the strategy permits a reasoning program to find the proof it is after, and prevents it from proving many of the spurious lemmas irrelevant to the purported theorem's proof.

Now we can explain what is meant by proper usage of the strategy. Proper usage means choosing the subset T—the set of support—in such a way that the choice does not prevent a proof from being obtained when one is in fact obtainable without the strategy. If T is chosen so that its complement S-T is satisfiable and hence consistent, depending on the choice of inference rule(s) (discussed in Chapter 15), nothing can go wrong. (A set is satisfiable if a model exists for the set, see Chapter 15.) Such a choice for the set of support does not prevent a proof from being found. For example, notice that the choice of T that consists of clauses 7 and 8 is such that its complement—the set consisting of clauses 1 through 6—is satisfiable. Similarly, the choice of T as clause 8 alone also has the same property. That clauses 1 through 6 form a consistent set is proved by the fact that they axiomatize a group, and hence a model exists for them. (For this set, a simpler proof of its satisfiability can be given. The fact that no negative literals occur in the set forces it to be satisfiable under the assignment of "true" to all positive literals, which is more fully discussed in Chapter 15.) In general, for a problem of this type, we recommend the choice of clauses 7 and 8 for T. The justification, intuitively, is that the added hypothesis that the square of every element is the identity should be a key to proving the theorem under consideration. Such is usually the case—the clauses that we designate as the *special hypothesis* usually play a vital role in the proof of the sought-after theorem.

(The surprise is that, although an appropriately chosen set of support prevents various basic lemmas from being deduced, proofs relying on those lemmas are still obtained with the strategy. Succinctly, the reason that the set of support strategy, when properly used, does not block all proofs is that deductions can generally be inverted. If a given deduction relies on reasoning forward from the axioms and thus relies on some basic lemma to prove some theorem, then that deduction usually can be used to yield a deduction that reasons backward from the denial of the theorem. To better understand the spirit of the set of support strategy and also why the preceding claim holds, we make the following remarks. Briefly, although the lemmas themselves do not occur directly in the proof, an analysis of the proof often demonstrates that they do play a role. To see which basic lemmas are indirectly used in the proof of a theorem, first note that every proof not relying on equality-based inference rules pairs all literals involved in the proof. A study of the unifications that lead to a proof shows that for every positive literal that is involved, a negative literal is present that pairs with it, and conversely. A typical process for recovering the statement of the lemma consists of, first, tracing the proof back to the use of some nonunit axiom. Next, note which axioms are paired against the literals of that nonunit clause, excluding the literal that paired directly with a literal from the actual proof. Then, unify those axioms with the literals of the nonunit clause dictated by the preceding step to yield some instance of the remaining literal. That instance in general will be the lemma that played an implicit and disguised role in the proof. For equality-based inference rules, an analogous set of steps can be taken, with term-pairing replacing literal-pairing.)

We recommend the following general choices for the set of support. Let the term "special hypothesis" denote the set of clauses that are present in the description of the problem, but that are not axioms or basic lemmas of the theory. Clause 7 is such a clause. The special hypothesis consists of the clauses that correspond to the hypothesis of the theorem under study. We suggest choosing for the set of support either the join of the special hypothesis with the set of clauses that correspond to the denial of the conclusion of the theorem, or just the denial of the conclusion of the theorem alone. In the example from group theory, the suggestion thus says either choose clauses 7 and 8 as the set of support, or choose clause 8. Summarizing, a judicious choice for the set of support permits an automated reasoning program to find proofs in all cases where it otherwise would, while at the same time avoiding many paths of inquiry not germane to the attempt at finding a proof.

9.2.2 Weighting Applied to the Example

Using the set of support strategy enables one to prevent an automated reasoning program from wandering aimlessly. Moreover, the strategy can be used with almost no thought, except for following the recommendation. Are there techniques for directing the search for a proof based on your intuition or knowledge? After all, research in mathematics depends heavily on both intuition and knowledge, so a reasoning program would do well to provide a means for relying on either.

Of course a strategy of the desired type exists. In fact, there are a number of them. Such strategies are called *directive* or *ordering* strategies, for they inform a reasoning program how to choose the fact it should consider next. An ordering strategy can be based on the number of symbols in the clause, the number of literals in the clause, or the particular symbols themselves, for example. The last of these three is the basis for the strategy we focus on in this section, the strategy of *weighting*.

The strategy of weighting allows you to assign values, or *weights*, to the various symbols present in the clauses, where these weights indicate the importance of the various symbols. By assigning appropriate weights to the symbols, you assign the relative importance to the corresponding concepts. For example, in the preceding illustration from group theory, you could instruct a reasoning program to consider the function f of greater importance than the function g. You might do this if your intuition suggested that inverse was not particularly relevant to finding a proof of the theorem. The given proof, in fact, does not rely on the function inverse. By assigning a relatively large weight to the concept of inverse, you cause a reasoning program to defer consideration of any clause containing the function g that stands for inverse.

Moreover, you can choose the importance, or weight, of a symbol so that clauses containing the symbol are actually discarded immediately upon generation. Thus, weighting can be used as an ordering strategy, but it can equally be used as a restriction strategy. By discarding clauses based on weight, you can make a reasoning program much more effective than it would be if it kept all clauses. Just as a mathematician or a graduate student can be hampered by having at hand too many lemmas that are irrelevant to the search for a proof, so also is a reasoning program. A mathematician automatically discards lemmas of various types based on their structure. Weighting is a means for having a reasoning program do the same.

For example, a mathematician can immediately give or prove a variety of lemmas concerning inverse in a group. Depending on the nature of the theorem under study and on intuition, many such lemmas are totally ignored, or at least put aside to be used only when all else fails. Weighting can be used so that an automated reasoning program proceeds as the mathematician would. Clauses such as

$$EQUAL(f(f(x, g(z)), z), f(x, e))$$

$$EQUAL(f(f(x, z), g(z)), f(x, e))$$

could either be retained but weighted so that they received little attention, or simply discarded. If the former, then weighting would play the role of an ordering strategy; if the latter, weighting would play the role of a restriction strategy. Of course, the two clauses represent acceptable conclusions, but a mathematician might wish to have a reasoning program treat inverse as being of little importance or even of no importance.

Weighting allows you to impose more complicated priorities on clauses. Clauses such as

$$EQUAL(f(f(x, y), f(z, f(x, f(y, z)))), e)$$

are derivable from clause 8 above coupled with associativity. In this clause, product occurs five times. If a mathematician believes that products of no more than four elements are of interest, weighting could be used to discard this last clause. An interesting observation is that this clause is derivable even with the chosen set of support, and hence weighting provides added power not provided by the set of support strategy.

Far more exotic uses of weighting exist, uses that enable you to impose extremely complex priorities on the conclusions drawn by a reasoning program. Consider the case in which you wish to seek an alternative proof, and hence wish to avoid certain expressions (as is the case in Chapter 10). Or consider the case in which the presence of certain expressions, if allowed to interact with other expressions, will cause a reasoning program to stray from the type of proof your intuition suggests can be found. For example, suppose that the product of the inverse of xy with z,

$$f(g(f(x, y)), z)$$

is an expression you wish to have a reasoning program bypass at all times. A weight can be assigned to this undesired expression in such a manner that any clause containing it will be immediately purged. The obvious weight assignment will not affect expressions that are proper instances of this expression, only alphabetic variants of this expression. You may also wish to avoid any instance of such an expression. For example,

$$f(g(f(a, b)), z)$$

and

$$f(g(f(g(g(w)), c), b)$$

are instances of

$$f(g(f(x, y)), z)$$

that you might also wish a reasoning program to ignore. A weight can be assigned in such a manner that, not only is the expression avoided, but any instance of the expression is avoided. On the other hand, weights can be assigned so that certain instances are treated in one fashion, while the term of which they are instances is treated in another.

By choosing the weights for variables, for functions, and for predicates appropriately, you can force a reasoning program to reflect very closely your knowledge and intuition. The concepts present in the problem will be given priorities according to your instructions. Thus, you can assist a reasoning program that you are in turn using as an automated reasoning assistant.

9.2.3 Demodulation and Canonicalization

Canonicalization of expressions is yet one more process that a mathematician uses in his research. An automated reasoning program relies on canonicalization also. In the proof given in Section 9.2, demodulation was cited in two of the four steps of the proof. In clause 10, left identity was used as a demodulator to remove an unwanted and unneeded occurrence of the identity e.

Before demodulation:

(10a) $EQUAL(f(x, f(x, z)), f(e, z))$

In clause 11, right identity was used similarly.

Before demodulation:

(11a) $EQUAL(f(y, f(x, y)), f(x, e))$

Such automatic removal of symbols, as well as other automatic and implicit operations, is quite common in mathematical proofs. So often a proof contains steps that implicitly replace the inverse of the inverse of x by x, that automatically reassociate (xy)y to x(yy), and that immediately rewrite ab + ac to a(b + c). Omitting such steps from a proof is standard practice, and convenient notationally. What may not be so obvious is that various instances of canonicalization clarify the picture during a study. For example, when a number of functions are present, and when the expression is lengthy, rewriting the expression so that the function symbols all prefix the expression and simultaneously simplifying the expression can point to the heart of a proof. In addition, canonicalization is an aid to retention of the information and to removing paths that are not of interest. For example, forcing all the function symbols to the front of an expression and avoiding those in which they occur elsewhere may eliminate a path deemed uninteresting.

An automated reasoning program also benefits in the corresponding ways by relying heavily on canonicalization. For example,

$$EQUAL(g(g(x)), x)$$

is a demodulator that can be added to the clauses that are given to a reasoning program at the start of a search for a proof. When any clause is generated—when any new fact is found—that contains $g(g(x))$, the program automatically replaces $g(g(x))$ by x if the given demodulator is present. When the demodulator

$$EQUAL(f(f(x, y), z), f(x, f(y, z)))$$

is present, all expressions will automatically be converted to the right associated form. When the demodulator

$$EQUAL(j(f(x, y), f(x, z)), f(x, j(y, z)))$$

is present, where j is read as sum and f as product, a clause of the form

$$EQUAL(j(f(a, b), f(a, c)), d)$$

will be automatically rewritten as

$$EQUAL(f(a, j(b, c)), d)$$

These are only samples of the use of demodulation.

Use of demodulators of the type just given is highly recommended. With such usage, the number of conclusions retained by a reasoning program is drastically reduced, for information that would ordinarily be retained in many different forms is mapped to a single form. For example, a reasoning program with the demodulator for right associating does not retain all of the possibly many associations that can occur in a somewhat complicated expression. By rewriting the distinct forms that can occur without right association into a single form, the feature of subsumption can come into play. Recall that subsumption automatically removes copies of an already existing clause.

The use of demodulation has an additional value. Recall that in an earlier chapter you learned that every new fact obtained by an automated reasoning program is immediately demodulated, rewritten, before any other process is applied. If demodulation were not employed, say for example right associating, then the new fact when kept could eventually be considered by the program, and eventually couple with associativity to produce the right associated form also. However, the new fact would be forced to wait its turn, and its turn might not occur for a long time. By automatically rewriting expressions into a canonical form rather than forcing the program to consider them only when their turn comes, a reasoning program functions more effectively. As was seen in the "full jobs puzzle" in Chapter 3, such tasks as updating a list of possibilities should be treated as asides. Canonicalizing can also be viewed as an aside, and demodulation treats it as such. After all, examination of typical mathematical proofs demonstrates that the main effort is clearly not canonicalization.

9.2.4 Subsumption and Redundancy

Subsumption plays a key role in automated reasoning, regardless of the application. But for research in mathematics, it is essential. Actual computer runs point out the startlingly large number of clauses, for example, that are generated and are merely instances of the axiom of left identity. In a run that found the proof that Boolean rings are commutative, more than 20,000 clauses were discarded by subsumption—clauses that were instances of the various axioms of a ring. Thus, if a mathematician is conducting research with the assistance of an automated reasoning program, and if the option exists for using subsumption, the very strong recommendation is to use it.

EXERCISES

1. Give the clauses that define the axioms for a ring using a three-place predicate P for product, a three-place predicate Q for sum, and the two-place predicate EQUAL for equality. Use 0 as the constant to represent the identity element for addition.
2. Using the axiomatization for a ring from problem 1, give a clause that asserts that the product of any element in the ring with 0 is 0. Now give the clause that denies that theorem.
3. Give the clauses that define the axioms for a ring using only the two-place predicate EQUAL for equality. Use the two-place function symbol j for the sum, and the two-place function symbol f for product. Again, use 0 to represent the identity element for addition.
4. There is a well-known theorem that states that $x + x = 0$ in any ring in which $x \times x = x$. Give the clauses that deny the theorem, using the equality axiomatization. Then give a proof using paramodulation as the inference rule.
5. Consider axioms that define a group using the three-place predicate P defined in this chapter. Give the clause or clauses that deny the theorem that the inverse of the inverse of x is x. Using UR-resolution as the inference rule, prove the theorem.

6. Consider axioms that define a group using the two-place equality predicate. Give the clause or clauses that deny the theorem that the inverse of the inverse of x is x. Using paramodulation as the inference rule, prove the theorem.

7. Which demodulators would you recommend for problems in group theory?

8. In problems 5 and 6, you were asked to give proofs using UR-resolution and paramodulation, respectively. In each case, which input clauses would you recommend for inclusion in the set of support?

9. Alfred Tarski published a paper called "What Is Elementary Geometry?". The axioms that Tarski gives are based on two predicates. $B(x, y, z)$ may be thought of as asserting that "y is between x and z". $L(x1, y1, x2, y2)$ may be thought of as asserting that "the distance from x1 to y1 is the same as the distance from x2 to y2". The following clauses correspond to Tarski's axioms with only one exception. We do not give his full axiom of continuity, which is not easily represented in first-order logic. However, much of the theory can be developed without the use of this axiom.

   Identity axiom for betweenness:

   (1) $\neg B(x, y, x) \mid EQUAL(x, y)$

   Transitivity axiom for betweenness:

   (2) $\neg B(x, y, u) \mid \neg B(y, z, u) \mid B(x, y, z)$

   Connectivity axiom for betweenness:

   (3) $\neg B(x, y, z) \mid \neg B(x, y, u) \mid EQUAL(x, y) \mid B(x, z, u)$
   $\mid B(x, u, z)$

   Reflexivity axiom for equidistance:

   (4) $L(x, y, y, x)$

   Identity axiom for equidistance:

   (5) $\neg L(x, y, z, z) \mid EQUAL(x, y)$

   Transitivity axiom for equidistance:

   (6) $\neg L(x, y, z, u) \mid \neg L(x, y, v, w) \mid L(z, u, v, w)$

   Pasch's axiom (2 clauses):

   (7) $\neg B(x, t, u) \mid \neg B(y, u, z) \mid B(x, f1(t, x, y, z, u), y)$

   (8) $\neg B(x, t, u) \mid \neg B(y, u, z) \mid B(z, t, f1(t, x, y, z, u))$

   Euclid's axiom (3 clauses):

   (9) $\neg B(x, u, t) \mid \neg B(y, u, z) \mid EQUAL(x, u)$
   $\mid B(x, z, f2(t, x, y, z, u))$

   (10) $\neg B(x, u, t) \mid \neg B(y, u, z) \mid EQUAL(x, u)$
   $\mid B(x, y, f3(t, x, y, z, u))$

(11) ¬B(x, u, t) | ¬B(y, u, z) | EQUAL(x, u)

    | B(f2(t, x, y, z, u), t, f3(t, x, y, z, u))

Five-segment axiom:

(12) ¬L(x1, y1, x2, y2) | ¬L(y1, z1, y2, z2) | ¬L(x1, u1, x2, u2)

    | ¬L(y1, u1, y2, u2) | ¬B(x, y, z) | ¬B(x2, y2, z2)

    | EQUAL(x1, y1) | L(z1, u1, z2, u2)

Axiom of segment construction (two clauses):

(13) B(x, y, f4(x, y, u, v))

(14) L(y, f4(x, y, u, v), u, v)

Lower dimension axiom (three clauses):

(15) ¬B(c1, c2, c3)

(16) ¬B(c2, c3, c1)

(17) ¬B(c3, c1, c2)

Upper dimension axiom:

(18) ¬L(x, u, x, v) | ¬L(y, u, y, v) | ¬L(z, u, z, v)

    | EQUAL(u, v) | B(x, y, z) | B(y, z, x) | B(z, x, y)

Weakened continuity axiom (two clauses):

(19) ¬L(u1, x1, u1, x2) | ¬L(u1, z1, u1, z2) | ¬B(u1, x1, z1)

    | ¬B(x1, y1, z1) | L(u1, y1, u1, f5(x1, y1, z1, x2, z2, u1))

(20) ¬L(u1, x1, u1, x2) | ¬L(u1, z1, u1, z2) | ¬B(u1, x1, z1)

    | ¬B(x1, y1, z1) | B(x2, f5(x1, y1, z1, x2, z2, u1), z2)

Equality axioms:

(21) EQUAL(x, x)

(22) ¬EQUAL(x, y) | EQUAL(y, x)

(23) ¬EQUAL(x, y) | ¬EQUAL(y, z) | EQUAL(x, z)

Equality substitution axioms for B:

(24) ¬EQUAL(x, y) | ¬B(x, x2, x3) | B(y, x2, x3)

(25) ¬EQUAL(x, y) | ¬B(x1, x, x3) | B(x1, y, x3)

(26) ¬EQUAL(x, y) | ¬B(x1, x2, x) | B(x1, x2, y)

Equality substitution axioms for L:

(27) ¬EQUAL(x, y) | ¬L(x, x2, x3, x4) | L(y, x2, x3, x4)

(28) ¬EQUAL(x, y) | ¬L(x1, x, x3, x4) | L(x1, y, x3, x4)

(29) ¬EQUAL(x, y) | ¬L(x1, x2, x, x4) | L(x1, x2, y, x4)

(30) ¬EQUAL(x, y) | ¬L(x1, x2, x3, x) | L(x1, x2, x3, y)

Equality substitution axioms for f1:

(31) ¬EQUAL(x, y)

   | EQUAL(f1(x, x2, x3, x4, x5), f1(y, x2, x3, x4,x5))

(32) ¬EQUAL(x, y)

   | EQUAL(f1(x1, x, x3, x4, x5), f1(x1, y, x3, x4, x5))

(33) ¬EQUAL(x, y)

   | EQUAL(f1(x1, x2, x, x4, x5), f1(x1, x2, y, x4, x5))

(34) ¬EQUAL(x, y)

   | EQUAL(f1(x1, x2, x3, x, x5), f1(x1, x2, x3, y, x5))

(35) ¬EQUAL(x, y)

   | EQUAL(f1(x1, x2, x3, x4, x), f1(x1, x2, x3, x4, y))

Equality substitution axioms for f2:

(36) ¬EQUAL(x, y)

   | EQUAL(f2(x, x2, x3, x4, x5), f2(y, x2, x3, x4, x5))

(37) ¬EQUAL(x, y)

   | EQUAL(f2(x1, x, x3, x4, x5), f2(x1, y, x3, x4, x5))

(38) ¬EQUAL(x, y)

   | EQUAL(f2(x1, x2, x, x4, x5), f2(x1, x2, y, x4, x5))

(39) ¬EQUAL(x, y)

   | EQUAL(f2(x1, x2, x3, x, x5), f2(x1, x2, x3, y, x5))

(40) ¬EQUAL(x, y)

   | EQUAL(f2(x1, x2, x3, x4, x), f2(x1, x2, x3, x4, y))

Equality substitution axioms for f3:

(41) ¬EQUAL(x, y)

   | EQUAL(f3(x, x2, x3, x4, x5), f3(y, x2, x3, x4, x5))

(42) ¬EQUAL(x, y)

   | EQUAL(f3(x1, x, x3, x4, x5), f3(x1, y, x3, x4, x5))

(43) ¬EQUAL(x, y)

   | EQUAL(f3(x1, x2, x, x4, x5), f3(x1, x2, y, x4, x5))

(44) ¬EQUAL(x, y)

    | EQUAL(f3(x1, x2, x3, x, x5), f3(x1, x2, x3, y, x5))

(45) ¬EQUAL(x, y)

    | EQUAL(f3(x1, x2, x3, x4, x), f3(x1, x2, x3, x4, y))

Equality substitution axioms for f4:

(46) ¬EQUAL(x, y) | EQUAL(f4(x, x2, x3, x4), f4(y, x2, x3, x4))

(47) ¬EQUAL(x, y) | EQUAL(f4(x1, x, x3, x4), f4(x1, y, x3, x4))

(48) ¬EQUAL(x, y) | EQUAL(f4(x1, x2, x, x4), f4(x1, x2, y, x4))

(49) ¬EQUAL(x, y) | EQUAL(f4(x1, x2, x3, x), f4(x1, x2, x3, y))

Equality substitution axioms for f5:

(50) ¬EQUAL(x, y)

    | EQUAL(f5(x, x2, x3, x4, x5, x6), f5(y, x2, x3, x4, x5, x6))

(51) ¬EQUAL(x, y)

    | EQUAL(f5(x1, x, x3, x4, x5, x6), f5(x1, y, x3, x4, x5, x6))

(52) ¬EQUAL(x, y)

    | EQUAL(f5(x1, x2, x, x4, x5, x6), f5(x1, x2, y, x4, x5, x6))

(53) ¬EQUAL(x, y)

    | EQUAL(f5(x1, x2, x3, x, x5, x6), f5(x1, x2, x3, y, x5, x6))

(54) ¬EQUAL(x, y)

    | EQUAL(f5(x1, x2, x3, x4, x, x6), f5(x1, x2, x3, x4, y, x6))

(55) ¬EQUAL(x, y)

    | EQUAL(f5(x1, x2, x3, x4, x5, x), f5(x1, x2, x3, x4, x5, y))

Prove B(x, y, y); that is, for all points x and y, y is between x and y.

9.3 Answering Open Questions

Is the use of an automated reasoning program for research in mathematics simply a speculation? Can the various features discussed so far in this chapter actually be relied upon to yield new results in mathematics? Both questions can be answered by noting that an automated reasoning program has indeed been used to assist in answering previously open questions, and by noting that the features discussed here were essential. So let us immediately answer the open questions (posed at the beginning of this chapter) by paraphrasing the results so obtained. Then let us discuss some of the salient properties and techniques that were employed in the various investigations.

The first previously open question concerns ternary Boolean algebra. Since such an algebra is not a well-known structure in mathematics, we give the definition here.

(1) $f(f(v, w, x), y, f(v, w, z)) = f(v, w, f(x, y, z))$

(2) $f(y, x, x) = x$

(3) $f(x, y, g(y)) = x$

(4) $f(x, x, y) = x$

(5) $f(g(y), y, x) = x$

A nonempty set satisfying these five axioms is a ternary Boolean algebra. The function f can be thought of as (a three-place) product, while the function g can be thought of as inverse. (From a ternary Boolean algebra, with appropriate definitions of union, intersection, complement, 0, and 1, in terms of the functions f and g, one can produce a Boolean algebra, and conversely.) A set of interesting questions arises from this set of axioms: Which, if any, of the five axioms is dependent on the remaining four? It was known that the fourth and fifth were dependent on the first three axioms. The questions that were open were whether or not each of the first three axioms is independent of the remaining four.

In fact, each of the first three is independent of the remaining four. The independence results were proved by finding appropriate models. The study of this algebra led directly to the formulation of the technique of model generation by an automated reasoning program. This model generation technique is discussed and illustrated in Section 9.4.

Incidentally, although independence and dependence among axioms can be interesting subject for mathematical study, dependent sets of axioms are often more useful than independent ones in finding proofs. Both the mathematician and the automated reasoning program benefit from dependency in the axioms. For example, the study of group theory is made more difficult if you omit the axioms of right identity and right inverse, even though they are derivable from the remaining ones. Just as the mathematician usually assumes their presence, we recommend their inclusion among the clauses given to a reasoning program. Omitting them forces both the mathematician and the reasoning program to derive them if they are required in the proof. If a reasoning program is forced to find a longer proof, then it often finds the task more time-consuming, although not always.

The qualification in the last statement may seem surprising. After all, shouldn't it always require less time to find a shorter proof than a longer one? The answer is no, because the shorter proof may be more difficult to find. The shorter proof may require a reasoning program, or a mathematician, to examine far more intermediate conclusions than the longer version requires.

The study of finite semigroups led to answers to each of the following questions. Does there exist a finite semigroup that admits a nontrivial antiautomorphism but that does not admit any nontrivial involutions? If one or more such semigroups exist, what is the order of the smallest? How many semigroups of the desired type and of smallest order exist?

There exists a semigroup of the desired type. The first found has order 83. There exist semigroups of order 7 with the desired properties, but none of smaller order. There are four nonisomorphic semigroups of the type under discussion among the more than 800,000 semigroups of order 7.

The semigroup of order 83 was found by the model generation technique discussed in Section 9.4, but by employing generators and relations rather than a multiplication table. The nonexistence of a semigroup of the desired type of order less than 7 was established by finding an appropriate proof. Finally, the four distinct semigroups of order 7 were found by again using the model generation technique, but this time both generators and relations, and multiplication tables, were employed.

The fact that these questions were open until an automated reasoning program was brought into the game is proof that the use of such a program is not simply speculation. (Ternary Boolean algebras were invented in 1947 and the questions remained open until they were solved with an automated reasoning program in 1977. The existence questions for semigroups were raised by I. Kaplansky.) An automated reasoning program can provide a surprising amount of assistance and much power. As evidence, note that the two individuals who solved the open questions in both ternary Boolean algebra and finite semigroups were merely conversant with the two fields, and in fact relied heavily on an automated reasoning program. If open questions can be answered by researchers with so little knowledge, then mathematicians with solid credentials in a field might produce truly startling results.

What makes these questions, as well as others that might be attacked, amenable to solution with the assistance of a reasoning program? First, as a simple exercise, you might write the clauses that correspond to the axioms of a ternary Boolean algebra and then those for the axioms of a semigroup. This simple exercise establishes that each of the two domains is easily represented in clause form. Second, we consider the following three clauses.

EQUAL(h(f(x, y)), f(h(y), h(x)))

EQUAL(j(f(x, y)), f(j(y), j(x)))

EQUAL(j(j(x)), x)

If h and j represent mappings and f denotes product, we have the clauses that state the key property of an antiautomorphism h and the key properties of an involution j.

Next comes the representation for a possible semigroup to be studied. As in mathematics, we can either present the entire multiplication table to the reasoning program, or supply appropriate generators and relations. The latter approach was used in answering the questions. Let b, c, d, and e be the generators, and let the defining relations be bbc = dde and the relation that says that all products of four or more elements are identical. Further, let h be a proposed antiautomorphism that cycles b through e. The clauses

$$EQUAL(f(b, f(b, c)), f(d, f(d, e)))$$
$$EQUAL(h(b), c)$$

are some of the clauses that are needed. The clauses needed to complete the definition of h are obvious. But can you give a clause that says that all products of four or more elements are identical?

A clause that works is

$$EQUAL(f(x, f(y, f(w, z))), f(b, f(b, f(b, b))))$$

In effect, this clause defines a canonical representation for all products of four or more elements in terms of the fourth power of b. The value of variables that are treated as meaning *for all* is well illustrated with this clause.

The techniques for actually generating a model with a reasoning program are discussed in Section 9.4, but that discussion focuses on ternary Boolean algebra and not on finite semigroups. The statement that a semigroup is finite cannot be easily stated in the language required by a reasoning program. The methods used to solve open questions that have been sketched here show what can be done with such a program. To gain more insight into what is possible, and also what is difficult if not impossible, we give examples in Section 9.5. At this point, we turn to the general technique for generating models and finding counterexamples with the assistance of an automated reasoning program.

9.4 Model and Counterexample Generation

When a conjecture is made that resists attempts to establish its validity, the possibility that it is false must be considered. Equally, when a purported theorem resists attempts at finding a proof, the suspicion grows that it is in fact not a theorem. In either case, a counterexample in the form of a model is often sought. To find such a counterexample, one might rely on the assistance of an automated reasoning program. The use of a reasoning program to find counterexamples and small finite models is somewhat different from the use to find proofs.

In connection with this observation, and before giving the technique for generating models, we digress slightly to discuss the logical basis for the need for a separate procedure for model generation. Procedures do exist that will, if given an actual theorem expressed in the first-order predicate calculus, always find a proof after some finite amount of time. Is it not then correct to conclude that a procedure exists that can cope with either side of the question—establish which statements are theorems and which are not? Unfortunately, this is not the case. A fundamental theorem of logic establishes that no procedure of the desired type exists. This theorem of logic in effect says that, for any given proof procedure, there exists a nontheorem that will force that procedure to continue indefinitely in its search for a proof. Thus, you cannot simply rely on an automated reasoning program in its proof-finding capacity to answer yes or no to a question of the form: Is the statement under investigation a theorem or not?

When the two observations—that procedures exist that guarantee to find a proof for any statement that is in fact a theorem, and that any given procedure fails to establish for some nontheorem that it is in fact a nontheorem—are taken together, we have the fact that the first-order predicate calculus is *semidecidable*. Although a universal procedure for identifying nontheorems cannot exist, an individual nontheorem nevertheless can be identified by producing a counterexample. Thus, from the viewpoint of using an automated reasoning program to assist in mathematical research, the capacity of such a program to find counterexamples and to generate models proves most valuable. Of course, the theoretical impediment to coping with both sides of the question of being a theorem is certainly of interest, but the practical impediments are what concern the researcher using a reasoning program. In particular, questions of time to obtain the result, space needed to conduct the search for information, and choices for representation, inference rule, and strategy are the real concern. In Chapter 16, we give advice in the form of proverbs for making choices in each of these three areas. In this section, we focus instead on the actual technique for generating counterexamples and models.

As with various other concepts and procedures discussed in this book, we illustrate the technique of model generation with a specific example rather than discussing the technique in general. The example focuses on ternary Boolean algebra. A ternary Boolean algebra is a nonempty set satisfying the following five axioms, where the function f can be thought of as (a three-place) product and the function g as inverse.

(1) $f(f(v, w, x), y, f(v, w, z)) = f(v, w, f(x, y, z))$

(2) $f(y, x, x) = x$

(3) $f(x, y, g(y)) = x$

(4) $f(x, x, y) = x$

(5) $f(g(y), y, x) = x$

Recall that in Section 9.3 we answered without proof the open question concerning the possible independence of axiom 2, raised at the beginning of this chapter. The independence is established by finding a model of axioms 1, 3, 4, and 5 that fails to satisfy axiom 2. The question here is: How can such a model be found?

The sought-after model is found by relying on an automated reasoning program and making a sequence of computer runs. The model takes the form of a table that gives the products and inverses for the elements of the model. The general approach is to choose a small set of elements, and have the program attempt to complete the multiplication table and the inverse table. The entries in the two tables must satisfy axioms 1, 3, 4, and 5 since the model must satisfy those axioms. In addition, at least one of the entries in the multiplication table must fail to satisfy axiom 2, since the model is intended to establish that axiom 2 is independent of the other four axioms. Each of the runs attempts to extend the results of the preceding run, for example, by finding products that were not known or finding inverses that were not known or proving lemmas that might be useful. As is typical in seeking a counterexample or a model, occasionally the results of a run are not extendible in a satisfactory fashion, and thus you must backtrack by returning to an earlier run, and then modify one or more assumptions. This backtracking will not be illustrated in this discussion of ternary Boolean algebra, but in fact it often is necessary.

The first step in the process of seeking a model of the desired type is to have the reasoning program find obvious lemmas that might prove useful. These lemmas fall into two classes. One class consists of lemmas provable from axioms 1, 3, 4, and 5, which therefore must hold in the sought-after model. The elements of this class are of interest because they aid in determining the structure of the model. The second class consists of lemmas whose proof apparently depends on axiom 2. By assuming that elements of this class do not hold in the model under construction, we aid the program's search for a model that violates axiom 2.

To find lemmas deducible from axioms 1, 3, 4, and 5, we give the reasoning program those axioms in clause form. Partly as a mnemonic and partly because of the usefulness of the axiom of reflexivity, x = x, we number the clauses to match the axiom number, with clause 2 the correspondent of reflexivity.

(1) $EQUAL(f(f(v, w, x), y, f(v, w, z)), f(v, w, f(x, y, z)))$

(2) $EQUAL(x, x)$

(3) $EQUAL(f(x, y, g(y)), x)$

(4) $EQUAL(f(x, x, y), x)$

(5) $EQUAL(f(g(y), y, x), x)$

Of course, only four clauses corresponding to four axioms appear since we are specifically avoiding axiom 2.

A computer run with this set of five clauses immediately proves, by using the inference rule of paramodulation, a lemma of the first class that is quite useful. In clause form, the lemma

(6) $EQUAL(f(x, y, x), x)$

is deducible from axioms 1 and 4. As for the second class of elements, the lemma that $g(g(x)) = x$ is provable from axioms 1 through 5, and, in particular, the proof found by the reasoning program relies on axiom 2. Therefore we add

(7) $\neg EQUAL(g(g(a)), a)$

to the input to state that the sought-after model violates that lemma for at least one element of the proposed model. Clause 7 is used to inform the program that the proposed model is consistent with the requirement that $g(g(a))$ be different from a, and the evidence that this requirement has not been fulfilled is signaled by the deduction of unit conflict with clause 7. The elements of the first class of lemmas are used to unearth the structure of the model, while those of the second class are used to suggest what should not be true of the proposed model.

The next step is that of choosing elements for the model. Let a be one such element of the proposed model. Here, a reasoning program can be of immediate assistance. Since the functions g (inverse) and f (product) are present, and since the model must be closed under each, we have the program begin listing the necessary elements. In that regard, we add the clauses

(8) ¬ELEMENT(x) | ELEMENT(g(x))

(9) ¬ELEMENT(x) | ¬ELEMENT(y) | ¬ELEMENT(z)

   | ELEMENT(f(x, y, z))

to the input. Clause 8 says that if x is an element, then g(x) is also. Clause 9 says that if x, y, and z are elements, then f(x, y, z) is an element of the model.

As commented earlier, each run is intended to build on the preceding one, and thus the set of input clauses for a later run usually includes all of the input clauses from the earlier run plus possibly additional ones. (Were backtracking necessary because the partial model being investigated failed to have the desired properties, certain clauses from the input of an earlier run might be deleted or replaced.) We shall number the input clauses as if they were all present and known at the beginning.

The assumption of the existence of the element a results in adding

(10) ELEMENT(a)

as an input clause. When, in the next run, the inference rule of hyperresolution is applied to clauses 8 and 10, the clause

(11) ELEMENT(g(a))

is found. When hyperresolution is then applied to clauses 11 and 8,

(12) ELEMENT(g(g(a)))

is found. Clauses 11 and 12, among others, are found in the same run. Because of 7, g(g(a)) and a are distinct elements. In fact, g(a) is assumed different both from a—otherwise g(g(a)) = a, contradicting clause 7—and from g(g(a)) to provide room in the model. Thus, so far, the partial model contains three elements. Since the lemma stating that g(g(x)) = x is deducible from axioms 1 through 5, assuming g(g(a)) distinct from a contributes to the possibility that the model, when completed, will violate axiom 2.

Since we have the typical desire of keeping the model small to reduce the various calculations, we now add (perhaps temporarily) the assumption

(13) EQUAL(g(g(g(x))), g(x))

to force the proposed model to close with respect to the function g. (Here is an example of employing mathematical intuition to guide an automated reasoning program. In place of clause 13 we could have adjoined

(13a) EQUAL(g(g(g(x))), x)

Clause 13 is preferred over clause 13a because the model is intended to satisfy all but one of the axioms for a ternary Boolean algebra, and the lemma g(g(x)) = x holds in such an algebra. Since the choice of clause 13 weakens this lemma only slightly, intuitively it seems the better choice for models that are intended to be, so to speak, nearly a ternary Boolean algebra.) Clause 13 and clauses 3 through 6 are added to the list of demodulators, and placed in the input for the next run. Thus, in the next run, when hyperresolution is applied to 12 and 8, the clause

ELEMENT(g(g(g(a))))

that is generated is immediately demodulated to

ELEMENT(g(a))

which is discarded by subsumption because it is a copy of clause 11.

The next run, using paramodulation as the inference rule, yields two lemmas that are deducible because of the presence of clause 13. The two lemmas are valuable, first because they help to fully determine the structure of the proposed model, and second because they are valuable in ascertaining that the model has the desired property of satisfying certain of the axioms. We add the two proved lemmas

(14) EQUAL(f(x, g(g(y)), g(y)), x)

(15) EQUAL(f(g(y), g(g(y)), x), x)

to the input for the next run.

At this point, the sequence of runs has yielded certain information for the partially defined model. Since the object is in effect to produce two tables, one for inverse and one for product, we add

(16) ¬ELEMENT(x) | INVERSE(x, g(x))

to the input to first find the values for the table for inverse. Hyperresolution is again applied, this time to clause 16 and to clauses such as 10, 11, and 12 to yield the entries in the table for inverse. Note in particular the result of the program's consideration of clauses 12 and 16. The resulting clause is

INVERSE(g(g(a)), g(a))

because demodulator 13 applies.

To complete the model, we must force it to close under the function f, and we must produce the table for product. Ideally, the model will require the addition of no other elements than a, g(a), and g(g(a)). When and if the model is completed, we must then establish that axioms 1, 3, 4, and 5 hold for the model, but axiom 2 does not hold. We would then have found a counterexample to the assumption that axiom 2 depends on the other four axioms. Clause 9 is one of the keys to completing the model. By applying hyperresolution to clause 9 with various combinations of clauses 10, 11, and 12, we get at least a partial list of elements that must be present because of the function f (product). During this phase of the model generation, clauses 3 through 6 play an important role as demodulators. For example, when clause 10 is used three times as satellite with clause 9 as nucleus, rather than deriving

$$\text{ELEMENT}(f(a, a, a))$$

the program derives

$$\text{ELEMENT}(a)$$

Of course, the key is

$$\text{EQUAL}(f(x, x, y), x)$$

in its role as a demodulator. This latest clause, stating that a is an element, is immediately discarded by subsumption because it is a copy of 10. The clauses that are not subsumed at this point are precisely those for which the products are yet to be determined. For example, $f(a, g(a), g(a))$ is such a product.

Since there are 3 elements in the model, and since the product function f is a three-place function, 27 products must be determined. Of the 27 products, 24 are established as already known by the current run, thus leaving three still to be determined. The 24 are forced because of clauses 3, 4, 5, and clauses 13, 14, and 15. The three that remain are $f(a, g(a), g(a))$, $f(a, g(g(a)), g(g(a)))$, and $f(g(g(a)), a, a)$. The fact that these three are the only as yet undetermined products is firmly established when the product table is being generated. To generate that table, we add

$$(17) \; \neg\text{ELEMENT}(x) \mid \neg\text{ELEMENT}(y) \mid \neg\text{ELEMENT}(z)$$

$$\mid \text{PRODUCT}(x, y, z, f(x, y, z))$$

to the input for the next run to mark the entries in the product table and, in this case, to point to those not yet determined.

As it turns out, the values for the second and third to-be-determined products are forced by the requirement that the proposed model must satisfy axiom 1. The specific values are found in the next run—a run designed to show that axiom 1 is in fact satisfied by the partial model—leaving one entry of the product table yet undetermined. We thus have an illustration of how a run designed to check that the desired properties are still present can in fact yield other information about the proposed model. To check that the proposed partial model does in fact satisfy axiom

1, we add

    (18) ¬ELEMENT(v) | ¬ELEMENT(w) | ¬ELEMENT(x)

          | ¬ELEMENT(y) | ¬ELEMENT(z)

          | EQUAL(f(f(v, w, x), y, f(v, w, z)), f(v, w, f(x, y, z)))

to the input for the next run. When hyperresolution is applied to clause 18 and various combinations of clauses 10, 11, and 12, the program finds that $f(a, g(g(a)), g(g(a))) = a$ and also that $f(g(g(a)), a, a) = g(g(a))$.

For the product $f(a, g(a), g(a))$, the first of the three products that were earlier identified as requiring determination, examination of the output of the program again proves profitable. In the reasoning program's attempt to verify that axiom 1 is satisfied by the proposed partial model, the program finds that $f(f(a,g(a),g(a)),g(g(a)),a) = a$. Although this discovery itself does not determine the final value needed to complete the product table, it leads to a case analysis that does. If $f(a, g(a), g(a))$ were $g(g(a))$, then clause 4 would apply in its role as a demodulator, yielding $g(g(a)) = a$. But this is not allowed, for the model is assumed so far to consist of three distinct elements, and, in particular, $g(g(a))$ is assumed to be distinct from a, as stated in clause 7. Next, if $f(a, g(a), g(a))$ were assigned $g(a)$, that assignment would satisfy axiom 2, but we are attempting to violate axiom 2. Although in fact this assignment is acceptable and we already have a violation of axiom 2 with $f(g(g(a)),a,a) = g(g(a))$, we might as well assign the product to be a, and again violate axiom 2.

With the last three products assigned values, clause 17 can be used to establish that products taken three at a time always evaluate to one of the three elements of the model. Demodulation is relied upon heavily here. Since the product table and the inverse table are complete, and since axiom 2 is not satisfied—the last three products violate it—all that remains is to show that the completed model satisfies axioms 1, 3, 4, and 5. Clauses similar to 18 are adjoined to enable the reasoning program to check that axioms 3, 4, and 5 are satisfied. (As an exercise, can you supply these three clauses?) A final run is then made using hyperresolution as the inference rule. Each of the clauses that are generated by this run and considered for retention demodulates to an instance of reflexivity, $x = x$, and clause 2 finally comes into play. In particular, each of the resulting clauses is subsumed by clause 2. The demodulation that occurs relies in part on clauses 14 and 15, and therefore the lemmas derived from the corresponding paramodulation run are proved valuable. The fact that all resulting clauses are subsumed by clause 2 and hence are instances of reflexivity means, among other things, that no clause of the form EQUAL(a, g(a)), for example, results. Such a clause would certainly signal a problem with the completed model. The use of clause 18, as well as those corresponding to axioms 3, 4, and 5, force the reasoning program to examine all possible and relevant substitutions from among the elements of the model. This fact, coupled with the preceding remarks, shows that the four axioms in question are satisfied by the model, and we have succeeded in proving that axiom 2 is independent of the remaining four.

An illustration of the verification of axiom 3 might be helpful. That axiom must hold when a is substituted for x and g(g(a)) for y, for example. Before demodulation is applied, the result is a clause that says that f(a, g(g(a)), g(g(g(a)))) = a. The first application of demodulation immediately replaces g(g(g(a))) by g(a). This action then causes a demodulation that uses clause 14. The result is a = a, and that instance of axiom 3 is verified.

We can now summarize the process just discussed for finding counterexamples and for generating models. The process consists of making a computer run, examining the results, and then making another run based on the results of the preceding run, until the model is complete. This sequential process illustrates well the assistance that an automated reasoning program can provide, and illustrates the dialogue that in effect takes place between the researcher and the reasoning program.

9.5 Representable Concepts: Easy and Difficult

In order to consider using an automated reasoning program to assist in research in mathematics, you need an understanding of what concepts can and what concepts cannot easily be treated with such a program. Of course, the best situation is that in which the problem can obviously and relatively easily be mapped into the first-order predicate calculus, described informally in Chapter 2 and formally in Chapter 15. For example, the axioms for a group, a ring, a semigroup, a modular lattice, Tarskian geometry, and a field can easily be stated in the first-order predicate calculus. (More accurately, Tarskian geometry is not fully representable because of the axioms for continuity, which do not readily map into the first-order predicate calculus.) Specific mappings and various properties of mappings often can be represented in a straightforward manner. On the other hand, statements that an algebra is finite are essentially not representable in the first-order predicate calculus, and statements that an algebra is infinite can be represented but in a manner that is not of much use. Between the two is a statement such as: The group has order 120. With this statement, the obvious choice is to list 120 distinct constants, and then provide the obvious set of negative equality clauses that say they are distinct. This solution is not very satisfying aesthetically, and it is certainly cumbersome to write and potentially inefficient to use. An alternative is to have a feature in the program that automatically evaluates equality of pairs of elements, and then takes appropriate action.

For statements that focus on "all mappings from G to H", we are essentially helpless at the moment. Even statements such as "there exists a function from G to H" force us to an indirect solution. We borrow from the mathematician, and simply name the function "that exists". For example, in the semigroup problem, the antiautomorphism of interest was simply named h, and its action on the generators was specified. Similarly, were you studying one of the homomorphism theorems in group theory, you would simply name the mapping h whose properties you wished to prove.

Statements that can be represented with equations are no problem. As we have seen, there are inference rules that treat equality as "built in". If the group has exponent 3, that is, the cube of any element is the identity, then

EQUAL(f(x, f(x, x)), e)

serves well. If the statement is that, in a ring, the cube of x is x (for all x),

EQUAL(f(x, f(x, x)), x)

serves similarly. In fact, one of the more difficult problems solved with an automated reasoning program is that of proving that, in a ring, commutativity follows from the fact that the cube of x is x (for all x). A proof of this fact requires at the moment approximately 2 minutes on a large and fast computer. In contrast, the following related problem in group theory requires less than 3 seconds. If the cube of x (for all x) is the identity, then [[x, y], y] = e, where [x, y] is the commutator f(x, f(y, f(g(x), g(y)))), in which f denotes product and g denotes inverse.

Even when a property cannot be directly represented with an equation, there is often no difficulty. For example, the nonzero elements of a field possess multiplicative inverses. Simply write

EQUAL(x, 0) | EQUAL(f(g(x), x), 1)
EQUAL(x, 0) | EQUAL(f(x, g(x)), 1)

as the needed clauses.

The given examples are merely a sample of what can and what cannot be conveniently studied with an automated reasoning program. Perhaps a way will soon be found to represent some of the difficult-to-consider concepts. The field is ever changing. For example, before 1978 how to have a reasoning program assist in finding small finite models and counterexamples was not known.

9.6 Review

Certain differences and certain similarities between proofs given by a mathematician and those obtained with an automated reasoning program become evident. In both, axioms are given to characterize the domain of inquiry. While some of the axioms are implicit for the mathematician, all axioms must be explicit for an automated reasoning program. Hence all axioms that are needed must be explicitly given in the language required by the automated reasoning program in use, thus, for programs of the type discussed in this book, given in the language of clauses. For example, when equality is present, you must either include the axioms of equality and one axiom for each position of substitutivity, or you must rely on an inference rule that treats equality and some of its properties as "built in". If the former, for example, as we saw at the end of Section 9.1, you must include for studies in group theory two axioms that state that substitution is possible in each of the arguments of f, and one that states that substitution is possible for the function g. In addition, if a three-place predicate is present, then three axioms in the form of clauses are needed to enable equality substitution into each of the arguments of the predicate. If the latter, as exemplified in Section 9.2, you must rely on an inference rule like paramodulation. When you rely on an inference rule such as paramodulation, all of the equality axioms except reflexivity can be omitted.

If you studied mathematics in graduate school, you might remember being puzzled about the problem of knowing when you had found a proof. In a mathematical proof, many steps are omitted and assumed to be obvious. In contrast, a proof obtained from an automated reasoning program explicates all steps. Such a proof also gives the justification for each step by listing the immediate premises from which it was derived and by listing all demodulators that were used for canonicalization. In mathematics, the justification of each step is almost never given. Similarly, in mathematical proofs the inference rules used are not explicit. With a reasoning program, the inference rules are explicit and must be deliberately chosen by you or by default.

These differences are cited not for normative reasons but rather to remind you of what you can expect when using an automated reasoning program. Instead of pointing to deficiencies in mathematics, the evidence of this chapter shows how the mathematician can guide an automated reasoning program and in turn receive certain assistance from such a program. To summarize, the proof produced by a mathematician is usually unverifiable algorithmically, while that of a reasoning program can be algorithmically verified. A proof obtained from an automated reasoning program can thus be examined sufficiently to virtually eliminate the possibility of error. Many tales exist of papers that have been published and subsequently been shown to contain an error in one of the proofs. On the other hand, unlike the mathematician, an automated reasoning program has no intuition and no knowledge other than what it is given.

The full explication and algorithmic verifiability are two of the advantages of using an automated reasoning program in mathematical research. Other advantages include the use of subsumption both to automatically prevent the same path in search of a proof from being explored repeatedly and to automatically block the program from reproducing a known proof. This latter property of subsumption was actually used in a study in formal logic, discussed in Chapter 10, in which the goal was to find a shorter proof than the one that was already known. The effort was rewarded—a proof of half the length of the known one was found by a reasoning program. One of the disadvantages of using an automated reasoning program is the need to represent the problem in such detail and the need to supply it with knowledge and guide it with intuition. Nevertheless, to be able to guide it also does have its advantages.

Occasionally, research is now being conducted with the assistance of an automated reasoning program. You may tackle either side of the question—you can seek a proof, or you can seek a small finite model or counterexample. Research in mathematics requires both aspects. Both aspects were necessary for the research briefly discussed in this chapter. What can clearly be said is that various open questions have been answered by using an automated reasoning program very extensively.

EXERCISES

10. Assume that you have a model including tables defining the actions of applying two operators. In particular, by inspecting the tables, you can verify that the operations are closed. Give the clauses that can be used to verify that each operator is associative. Give the clauses that can be used to verify that each operator distributes over the other.

11. Give the clauses that can be used to verify that a proposed finite model is a group. Assume that the tables for addition and inverse are given explicitly. How would you construct the desired group if the tables were incomplete? In particular, you have determined which elements you wish the model to consist of, but have not specified all the table entries.

9.7 Answers to Exercises

1. We need the axioms that state that the ring is a group under addition. These are simply the seventeen axioms given in Section 9.1, but with the identity element represented by 0 and the predicate P replaced with the predicate Q and the function f replaced with the function j. In addition, we need the following axioms.

    Addition is commutative:

    (18) $\neg Q(x,y,z) \mid Q(y,x,z)$

    Associativity of product:

    (19) $\neg P(x,y,u) \mid \neg P(y,z,v) \mid \neg P(u,z,w) \mid P(x,v,w)$

    (20) $\neg P(x,y,u) \mid \neg P(y,z,v) \mid \neg P(x,v,w) \mid P(u,z,w)$

    Product is well defined:

    (21) $\neg P(x,y,u) \mid \neg P(x,y,v) \mid EQUAL(u,v)$

    Closure of product:

    (22) $P(x,y,f(x,y))$

    Equality substitution (for the added predicates and functions):

    (23) $\neg EQUAL(u,v) \mid \neg P(u,x,y) \mid P(v,x,y)$

    (24) $\neg EQUAL(u,v) \mid \neg P(x,u,y) \mid P(x,v,y)$

    (25) $\neg EQUAL(u,v) \mid \neg P(x,y,u) \mid P(x,y,v)$

    (26) $\neg EQUAL(u,v) \mid EQUAL(f(u,x),f(v,x))$

    (27) $\neg EQUAL(u,v) \mid EQUAL(f(x,u),f(x,v))$

Distributivity axioms:

(28) $\neg P(x, y, v1) \mid \neg P(x, z, v2) \mid \neg Q(y, z, v3)$

$\mid \neg P(x, v3, v4) \mid Q(v1, v2, v4)$

(29) $\neg P(x, y, v1) \mid \neg P(x, z, v2) \mid \neg Q(y, z, v3)$

$\mid \neg Q(v1, v2, v4) \mid P(x, v3, v4)$

(30) $\neg P(y, x, v1) \mid \neg P(z, x, v2) \mid \neg Q(y, z, v3)$

$\mid \neg P(v3, x, v4) \mid Q(v1, v2, v4)$

(31) $\neg P(y, x, v1) \mid \neg P(z, x, v2) \mid \neg Q(y, z, v3)$

$\mid \neg Q(v1, v2, v4) \mid P(v3, x, v4)$

2. The clause that says that $x \times 0 = 0$ is

$P(x, 0, 0)$

The denial of the property is given by

$\neg P(a, 0, 0)$

3. As in problem 2, we begin with the first six axioms from Section 9.2, but with the constant e replaced by 0 and the function f replaced by the function j. We do not need to include axioms for symmetry, transitivity, or substitutivity of equality, since we are treating equality here as a "built-in" predicate. Thus, we must add the following axioms.

Addition is commutative:

(7) $EQUAL(j(x, y), j(y, x))$

Product is associative:

(8) $EQUAL(f(f(x, y), z), f(x, f(y, z)))$

Distributivity:

(9) $EQUAL(f(x, j(y, z)), j(f(x, y), f(x, z)))$

(10) $EQUAL(f(j(y, z), x), j(f(y, x), f(z, x)))$

4. The special hypothesis is

(11) $EQUAL(f(x, x), x)$

The denial of the theorem is

(12) $\neg EQUAL(j(a, a), 0)$

The proof of the theorem using paramodulation is the following.

$x(x + y) = x + (xy)$, from clause 11 into clause 9:

(13) $EQUAL(f(x, j(x, y)), j(x, f(x, y)))$

$x(x + x) = x + x$, from clause 11 into clause 13:

(14) $EQUAL(f(x, j(x, x)), j(x, x))$

$x + y = x(x + y) + y(x + y)$, from clause 11 into clause 10:

(15) $EQUAL(j(x, y), j(f(x, j(x, y)), f(y, j(x, y))))$

x + x = (x + x) + x(x + x), from clause 14 into clause 15:

   (16) EQUAL(j(x, x), j(j(x, x)), f(x, j(x, x)))

x + x = (x + x) + (x + x), from clause 14 into clause 16:

   (17) EQUAL(j(x, x), j(j(x, x)), j(x, x)))

(x + x) + y = (x + x) + ((x + x) + y), from clause 17 into clause 5:

   (18) EQUAL(j(j(x, x), y), j(j(x, x), j(j(x, x), y)))

0 = x + x, from clause 4 into clause 18 (then demodulated with 4):

   (19) EQUAL(0, j(x, x))

0 ≠ 0, from clause 19 into clause 12:

   (20) ¬EQUAL(0, 0)

Clause 20 contradicts clause 6. This lemma—that x + x = 0—is ordinarily proved as part of a more difficult problem. The more difficult theorem is to show that, if xx = x for all x, then xy = yx for all x and y. Can you prove the more difficult theorem?

5. Starting with the 17 axioms that are given for a group in Section 9.1, we must add the clause that denies the theorem.

   (18) ¬EQUAL(g(g(a)), a)

The proof by UR-resolution is

From clauses 18, 8, and 1:

   (19) ¬P(e, g(g(a)), a)

From clauses 6, 4, 4, and 19:

   (20) ¬P(a, e, a)

Clause 20 contradicts clause 2.

6. Start with the six axioms for a group given in Section 9.2 and add

   (7) ¬EQUAL(g(g(a)), a)

which denies the theorem. The proof then is the following.

From clause 4 into f(x, y) in clause 5:

   (8) EQUAL(f(e, z), f(x, f(g(x), z)))

From clause 1 into f(e, z) in clause 8:

   (9) EQUAL(z, f(x, f(g(x), z)))

From clause 4 into f(g(x), z) in clause 9:

   (10) EQUAL(g(g(x)), f(x, e))

From clause 2 into f(x,e) in clause 10:

(11) EQUAL(g(g(x)), x)

Clause 11 contradicts clause 7.

7. You will almost always wish to use

EQUAL(f(e, x), x)
EQUAL(f(x, e), x)
EQUAL(f(g(x), x), e)
EQUAL(f(x, g(x)), e)

as demodulators. For various problems, you may wish to add others. Lemmas such as

EQUAL(g(g(x)), x)

can easily be proved, and you will usually wish to add these as demodulators as well.

8. In problem 5, the denial of the theorem works quite well, as long as UR-resolution is used as the inference rule. If hyperresolution were used instead, no clauses could be generated. You will find, in problems like this, that it is often effective to deny the theorem with clauses like

EQUAL(g(g(a)), b)
¬EQUAL(a, b)

Using this form of the denial, a proof can be obtained with hyperresolution. With paramodulation, you cannot get a proof using the set of support strategy with the denial given as the single clause, unless you permit paramodulation from a variable. Can you derive a proof when the denial is given with the two clauses?

9. The denial of the theorem is simply

(56) ¬B(a, b, b)

The proof, using UR-resolution, is the following.

From clauses 56, 2, and 13:

(57) ¬B(a, b, f4(b, b, x1, x2))

From clauses 56, 26, and 13:

(58) ¬EQUAL(f4(a, b, x1, x2), b)

From clauses 57, 2, and 13:

(59) ¬B(b, f4(b, b, x1, x2), f4(a, b, x3, x4))

From clauses 58 and 5:

(60) ¬L(f4(a, b, x1, x2), b, x3, x3)

From clauses 60, 6, and 4:

(61) ¬L(b, f4(a, b, x1, x2), x3, x3)

Clause 61 contradicts clause 14. You might be surprised if you try to prove the related theorem, B(x, x, y). There are an amazing number of such basic lemmas that must be established before any of the more usual theorems of geometry can be attacked. For example, you might also try to show that betweenness is symmetric—show that B(c, b, a) must be true if B(a, b, c) is true.

10. Let us represent the operators with o1 and o2. Then you must add axioms that give the elements. These will be of the form

ELEMENT(a)
ELEMENT(b)
ELEMENT(c)
  .
  .
  .

You also need the clauses that define the tables. They are of the form

EQUAL(o1(a, b), c)

The clauses to test for associativity and distributivity are the following.

¬ELEMENT(x) | ¬ELEMENT(y) | ¬ELEMENT(z)
 | EQUAL(o1(o1(x, y), z), o1(x, o1(y, z)))
¬ELEMENT(x) | ¬ELEMENT(y) | ¬ELEMENT(z)
 | EQUAL(o2(o2(x, y), z), o2(x, o2(y, z)))
¬ELEMENT(x) | ¬ELEMENT(y) | ¬ELEMENT(z)
 | EQUAL(o1(x, o2(y, z)), o2(o1(x, y), o1(x, z)))
¬ELEMENT(x) | ¬ELEMENT(y) | ¬ELEMENT(z)
 | EQUAL(o2(x, o1(y, z)), o1(o2(x, y), o2(x, z)))
¬ELEMENT(x) | ¬ELEMENT(y) | ¬ELEMENT(z)
 | EQUAL(o1(o2(y, z), x), o2(o1(y, x), o1(z, x)))
¬ELEMENT(x) | ¬ELEMENT(y) | ¬ELEMENT(z)
 | EQUAL(o2(o1(y, z), x), o1(o2(y, x), o2(z, x)))

Now, if you put all of these clauses into the set of support and run the program, all of the generated clauses, after demodulation by the equalities that define the tables, should be instances of EQUAL(x,x). If they are not, an error has been detected.

11. If the tables are given explicitly, this problem is the same as problem 10. If they are not, then an iterative approach resembling the ternary Boolean algebra example in the text can be used. Specifically, the program is allowed to proceed. Wherever an equality unit of the form

EQUAL(t1, t2)

is derived that is not an instance of reflexivity, various actions must be taken. If t1 and t2, both elements of the proposed model, are constants, then an error has been detected since, presumably, the model under construction consists of distinct elements. If one of the two terms is a constant and the other is a function of constants, then you have calculated a new table entry. Otherwise, you must add table entries that will assign the complex terms to elements of the group, and iterate. It is this iterative approach to constructing a model that led to the successes described in this chapter.

10

Research in Formal Logic

What is common to the following seven formulas?

$$XJL = e(x, e(y, e(e(e(z, y), x), z)))$$
$$XKE = e(x, e(y, e(e(x, e(z, y)), z)))$$
$$XAK = e(x, e(e(e(e(y, z), x), z), y))$$
$$BXO = e(e(e(e(x, e(y, z)), z), y), x)$$
$$XCB = e(x, e(e(e(x, y), e(z, y)), z))$$
$$XHK = e(x, e(e(y, z), e(e(x, z), y)))$$
$$XHN = e(x, e(e(y, z), e(e(z, x), y)))$$

First, each of the seven is a formula from the equivalential calculus, a field of formal logic concerned with the abstraction of "equivalence". Second, each of the seven, until recently, pointed to an open question in equivalential calculus. Third, each of the seven previously open questions was answered with the assistance of an automated reasoning program. The question is: Which, if any, of the seven is a single axiom for that field of formal logic known as equivalential calculus?

In this chapter, we shall show how questions of this type can be answered by relying on an automated reasoning program. The use of such a program does not require you to be a computer programmer, but rather has you employ various techniques discussed in this chapter and covered in the first six chapters of the book. Although the focus is on the equivalential calculus, the techniques are applicable to other areas of formal logic. The logician expects the use of specific inference rules and the requirement that a proof contain the explicit derivation information for each step of the proof. Before turning to a simple illustration of the use of a reasoning program, we provide the following review.

10.1 The Equivalential Calculus

The equivalential calculus is that field of formal logic concerned with the notion of equivalence. The domain of EC (equivalential calculus) is the set of formulas in the two-place function e and the variables x, y, z, ... The inference rule that is often employed is *condensed detachment*. Condensed detachment considers two formulas of the form e(A, B) and A', respectively, and if successful, yields a formula B''. To apply the rule successfully, A and A' must unify—a substitution must exist that, when applied, causes the resulting subformulas to become identical. For example, if

   e(x, x) and

   e(e(y, y), e(z, z))

are considered with condensed detachment, the formula

   e(e(y, y), e(z, z))

results. A slightly more interesting example is provided by applying condensed detachment to

   e(e(e(x, x), y), y) and

   e(e(x,y),e(y,x))

which yields

   e(x, x).

Definition.   For the two formulas e(A, B) and A', which are assumed to have no variables in common, *condensed detachment* is that inference rule that yields the formula B'', where B'' is the second argument of e(A'', B''), and where e(A'', B'') and A'' are respectively obtained from e(A, B) and A' by the most general possible substitution whose application forces A and A' to become identical. Condensed detachment is denoted by CD.

In the equivalential calculus, the *theorems* are just those formulas in which each variable occurs an even number of times. Thus, for example,

   e(x, x),

   e(e(x, y), e(y, x)), and

   e(e(x, y), e(e(y, z), e(x, z)))

are each theorems in EC. Notice that these three formulas might be read, respectively, as reflexivity, symmetry, and transitivity. These three properties are what you would expect if studying equivalence. The calculus can be axiomatized with these three formulas, but EC can also be axiomatized with certain single formulas. Single axioms exist for EC that contain 11 symbols (excluding commas and grouping symbols), and no shorter formulas are strong enough to serve as a single axiom for the calculus.

With this background, we can now turn to a simple example of studying EC with the assistance of an automated reasoning program.

10.2 A Simple Example

One of the shortest single axioms for EC is denoted by XGK.

$$XGK = e(x, e(e(y, e(z, x)), e(z, y)))$$

To illustrate the use of an automated reasoning program, we prove that $e(x, x)$ is deducible from XGK by applications of CD (condensed detachment). Since XGK is a single axiom for EC, and since $e(x, x)$ is a theorem of EC and hence deducible with CD from XGK, the primary task is that of selecting an inference rule to mirror CD.

Before choosing the inference rule, let us dispense with the question of representation. Since we are using clauses to represent information to a reasoning program, we choose a representation that maps the formulas of EC to expressions in the first-order predicate calculus. The mapping simply prefixes each formula with a predicate symbol. We can use the predicate DEDUCIBLE, and write

$$DEDUCIBLE(e(x, e(e(y, e(z, x)), e(z, y))))$$

when studying the formula XGK with an automated reasoning program. We of course include given formulas for study—actually, given axioms—in the class DEDUCIBLE.

What are the properties of the inferences that are expected by applying CD, and which (if any) of the inference rules exhibited earlier come to mind? Questions of this type can lead you to the information required to use a reasoning program in research. Formulas deduced by a reasoning program employing the given representation will be unit clauses—will contain one literal. These formulas will also be positive clauses. The first of the two properties suggests using the inference rule of UR-resolution, while the second points to hyperresolution. In either case, we must still supply a clause or clauses to permit the reasoning program to mirror CD. The clause

(1) $\neg$DEDUCIBLE(e(x, y)) | $\neg$DEDUCIBLE(x) | DEDUCIBLE(y)

will suffice.

Clause 1 says that, if the formula $e(x, y)$ and the formula x are each deducible, then the formula y is deducible. Recall that CD yields a formula, when applied to a pair of formulas, precisely when a substitution of the appropriate type exists. In particular, if $e(A, B)$ and A' are two such formulas, then CD yields B'' when A and A' can be replaced by related formulas obtained by a substitution for their variables, and when the new formulas are identical. Now notice that UR-resolution applied to clause 1 with two other clauses that correspond to $e(A, B)$ and A' yields a new clause B'' under the same conditions. Also, hyperresolution applies successfully with the same result and under the same conditions. To prepare the way for illustrations of other uses of an automated reasoning program that rely on the employment of lists, we choose here to employ UR-resolution.

Since the goal is that of proving that the formula $e(x, x)$ is deducible with condensed detachment from the formula XGK, we follow the typical procedure used in the early chapters. We attempt to find a proof by contradiction of the result. We thus assume that $e(x,x)$ is not deducible. We have

(2) DEDUCIBLE($e(x, e(e(y, e(z, x)), e(z, y))))$)

(3) $\neg$DEDUCIBLE($e(a, a)$)

in addition to clause 1 as input to the program. The choice of UR-resolution will always use clause 1 as one of the clauses in drawing conclusions. The remaining clauses must all be unit clauses. At the beginning of the attempt to obtain the desired deduction, clauses 2 and 3 are candidates for use as unit clauses. However, since we are forcing the reasoning program to mirror condensed detachment, we must therefore prevent clause 3 from being used to draw conclusions—to produce formulas that are considered deducible by CD. Clause 3 plays only one role: It is present simply to tell the reasoning program that the formula we are after has been deduced. If clause 3 were allowed to participate in a successful application of UR-resolution, the resulting clause would be a negative clause, but the program must find only positive clauses if it is to mirror CD precisely. (If clause 3 were allowed to participate in the search for a proof, and if a proof were found, then of course the desired goal would be proved obtainable. In that event, however, to see exactly which formulas participated in the deduction, one would be forced to invert the resulting proof.) To prevent clause 3 from being used otherwise, it is placed on a separate list that is consulted only to find out if a contradiction has been reached. What we wish to illustrate is this use of lists of clauses that have a specific and special purpose. As will be seen later, placing clauses on various lists allows you to use a reasoning program with greater flexibility.

An automated reasoning program, starting with clauses 1 and 2, will quickly find the desired proof by contradiction.

(1) $\neg$DEDUCIBLE($e(x, y)$) | $\neg$DEDUCIBLE(x) | DEDUCIBLE(y)

(2) DEDUCIBLE($e(x, e(e(y, e(z, x)), e(z, y))))$)

(3) $\neg$DEDUCIBLE($e(a, a)$)

From clauses 2, 2, and 1:

(4) DEDUCIBLE($e(e(x, e(y, e(z, e(e(u, e(v, z)), e(v, u)))))), e(y, x))$)

From clauses 4, 2, and 1:

(5) DEDUCIBLE($e(e(e(e(x, e(y, z)), e(y, x)), e(z, u)), u)$)

From clauses 5, 5, and 1:

(6) DEDUCIBLE($e(x, x)$)

Clause 6 contradicts clause 3.

If hyperresolution were used in place of UR-resolution, the proof would be exactly as given. No special treatment of clause 3 would be required, for it could not be involved in applying hyperresolution until the contradiction had been found. However, we chose UR-resolution to illustrate the use of special lists of clauses for specific purposes. We now give another illustration of the use of special lists of clauses.

10.3 Imposing Knowledge and Intuition

When you are seeking to prove some theorem or disprove some conjecture, you often have some knowledge and/or intuition about how the question should be attacked. If you were working with a colleague, you would share this knowledge and/or intuition. Similar sharing can occur when using an automated reasoning program to assist with research. By supplying such extra information to a reasoning program, you can sharply affect its chances of reaching the sought-after goal.

In the study of equivalential calculus, for example, you might wish a reasoning program to avoid using certain formulas. Such is the case when you are seeking an alternative proof to a theorem, and wish the program to avoid the known proof and instead traverse a different path. To enable a reasoning program to follow your plan, the known proof must be blocked—the program must be prevented from producing that proof. One way to accomplish this is by placing some step of the known proof on a special list of clauses that is classed as unavailable for applications of inference rules. This special list has the additional property of being consulted for classifying generated clauses as already known information, as less general than that already known, or as new information. The procedure of subsumption, discussed in the early chapters, is the key. Recall that subsumption is that process that is used to reject information if it duplicates that already present or if it is less general than that already present. Thus, when an automated reasoning program finds, for example, a step of a known proof and that step has been placed on a list consulted only by subsumption, the second copy of that step is immediately discarded. Such action prevents that step, or a copy of that step, or even an instance of that step, from being used in a possible proof.

In a similar way, your knowledge and intuition can be used to aid a reasoning program in its attempt to reach a desired goal. If you decide that some step or steps are useless, then they can be placed on a special list of clauses consulted only by subsumption. By doing this, you provide the needed information that allows a reasoning program to avoid wasting its time on the corresponding fruitless paths. By removing such steps from consideration, entire paths of inquiry can be blocked. Thus, the use of special lists of clauses can sharply improve a reasoning program's chance of success.

Having shown how a reasoning program can be made to avoid various considerations, what about the other side of the question? Can such a program be instructed to concentrate on some formula, for example? It can, and the process of weighting employed in the early chapters is the means. By way of illustration, assume that you were studying equivalential calculus and, in particular, wished to emphasize the importance of the formula $e(x, x)$. The formula $e(x, x)$ could be placed on a special list of clauses, and the program instructed to continually revisit that list for clauses to participate in the inference mechanism. Or the formula could be assigned a weight that would cause a reasoning program to consider it preferable to all other clauses. In this last case, if $e(x, x)$ were ever found by the program, as occurs in the short proof given earlier, the program would immediately turn its attention to that formula. The assignment of weights assigns priorities to clauses. On one hand, weights can be assigned to give formulas of one structure strong preference, while on the other hand, weights can be assigned to give formulas of another very weak preference. In fact, you can use weighting as a means for instructing a reasoning program to immediately discard information of certain types. You can decide for an automated reasoning program what is to be considered complex and thus, for example, have the program treat short expressions as undesirable.

These techniques are sufficiently effective that an automated reasoning program was used to find an alternative proof for a result proved for EC. Specifically, the problem that was solved was that of finding a shorter proof establishing the formula XGK to be a single axiom for the calculus. The first proof consists of 44 steps and in fact was also obtained with the assistance of an automated reasoning program. The alternative proof that was found consists of 24 steps. This result provides additional evidence of the usefulness and power of an automated reasoning program.

A reasoning program can also be used in a way that is distantly related to that discussed in this section. When you wish to have one formula be the major premiss of all applications of condensed detachment, the notation can be changed to precisely achieve the goal. Simply write instead of clause 1

$$(1') \neg MAJOR(e(x, y)) \mid \neg MINOR(x) \mid MINOR(y)$$

as the clause to be used with either UR-resolution or hyperresolution. All formulas deduced with this clause will be treated as minor premisses and will not be allowed to interact with each other. Maneuvers of this type, as well as those relying on list manipulation, are among the "tricks" that enable you to use more fully an automated reasoning program.

10.4 Solving Open Questions

As stated at the beginning of this chapter, an automated reasoning program can be used to answer open questions in formal logic. At this point, we shall focus on one of the open questions that in fact was answered with the assistance of such a program. The question is: Is the formula XJL strong enough to serve as a single axiom for the equivalential calculus? The formula

$$XJL = e(x, e(y, e(e(e(z, y), x), z)))$$

can be proved to be a single axiom if some known single axiom can be deduced from it by repeated application of condensed detachment. On the other hand, it can be proved too weak by showing that some theorem of equivalential calculus cannot be deduced from it.

If the task were that of proving the formula sufficiently strong, you could proceed as illustrated in Section 10.2. For example, clauses that correspond to denying the deducibility of various known single axioms could be placed on a list consulted only for establishing that a proof by contradiction had been found. In that case, UR-resolution could be the choice for the inference rule to be used. (In practice, allowing such denial clauses to interact with various formulas appears to decrease the effectiveness of an automated reasoning program.) In addition, you would, or might, use some of the techniques described in Section 10.3. If a contradiction were found, then you would have a proof that some known single axiom of EC is deducible from XJL and, therefore, that XJL is a single axiom. The formula

$$PYO = e(e(e(x, e(y, z)), z), e(y, x))$$

is a known shortest single axiom for EC. When its deducibility is denied and the notation of Section 10.1 is used,

$$\neg DEDUCIBLE(e(e(e(a, e(b, c)), c), e(b, a)))$$

is the result. This clause, as well as the corresponding clauses that deny the deducibility of other known single axioms, can be placed on a special list that is consulted only to test for the presence of contradiction. Any known axiom of EC can be employed in this manner. The length of such a formula is not relevant. We mention shortest single axioms simply because they are readily available. The inference rule of UR-resolution could then be used, and you could impose your knowledge and/or intuition on the program's attack.

Rather than discussing the alternative of trying to prove XJL a single axiom, we instead focus on the other alternative, that of proving XJL too weak. We present the approach one might then employ—an approach that we in fact used in 1980 to answer the question, which was at the time still open. Two approaches come to mind. One can try to have a reasoning program assist in finding a model that satisfies XJL but fails to satisfy some known theorem of EC. Or one can attempt to characterize, with the assistance of a reasoning program, all theorems deducible from XJL, and show that some known theorem of EC is absent from that set. At the time we were studying the open question, the methodology for generating models and counterexamples with an automated reasoning program had already been developed. In view of this fact, why not choose the model-generation approach over the apparently more difficult theorem-characterization approach?

We rejected the approach of generating an appropriate model because it was decided that too many models would have to be examined. Thus the choice was to take the second approach. To be careful, the second approach was not directly chosen, but rather the decision was to learn more about XJL with the hope of making some crucial discovery. A brief account of what was actually discovered illustrates the type of invaluable assistance that an automated reasoning program can provide.

10.4.1 Finding Useful Notation

Here are some formulas that are deducible from XJL, and that you might find by having a reasoning program begin a study of XJL.

$$e(x, e(y, e(e(e(z, y), x), z)))$$
$$e(v, e(e(e(w, v), e(x, e(y, e(e(e(z, y), x), z)))), w))$$
$$e(e(e(v, e(x, e(y, e(e(e(z, y), x), z)))), e(x', e(y', e(e(e(z', y'), x'), z')))), v)$$
$$e(e(x, e(y, e(e(e(z, y), x), z))), e(x', e(y', e(e(e(z', y'), x'), z'))))$$

What is common to these four formulas? *Hint:* The variable names have been deliberately chosen to point to some commonality.

Recalling that the first of the formulas is XJL, notice what occurs when XJL and alphabetic variants of XJL are denoted by K.

$$K = XJL = e(x, e(y, e(e(e(z, y), x), z)))$$
$$e(y, e(e(e(z, y), K), z))$$
$$e(e(e(z, K), K), z)$$
$$e(K, K)$$

All four expressions contain, not necessarily as a proper subexpression, a copy of XJL = K. Using the notation of setting XJL to K and also of setting alphabetic variants of XJL to K increases the readability of the formulas. But, as we shall soon see, this replacement does much more.

How can an automated reasoning program be instructed to make such a replacement? Demodulation is the means. Recall that demodulation is that process that enables a reasoning program to automatically rewrite expressions in terms of some given equality or given equalities. To cause a reasoning program to automatically employ the notation, the program is given

$$EQUAL(e(x, e(y, e(e(e(z, y), x), z))), k)$$

and also given the formulas produced by a preceding run and instructed to apply the demodulator to them. (Since in this book we use lower case letters to represent constants when they appear in clauses, K becomes k when we use it in a clause.) Each formula has all occurrences of XJL and of alphabetic variants of XJL thus replaced by K. (The notation was, in fact, discovered by examining the output of a run that deduced a number of formulas, starting with XJL, and noticing that at least some of them contained a copy of XJL itself.)

10.4.2 Suggesting Conjectures

We remarked in the preceding subsection that the replacement of alphabetic variants of XJL by K does much more than add to readability. What occurs when this notation is employed is that a large number of formulas deducible from XJL contain, when examined, K as a subexpression. This observation led immediately to the conjecture that all formulas deducible by repeated application of condensed detachment starting with XJL must contain K. If this conjecture can be proved true, then the status of XJL being a single axiom is established, and the corresponding open question is solved with the assistance of an automated reasoning program. After all, if every theorem deducible from XJL contains a subexpression equal to K, then the theorem $e(x, x)$ is not deducible from XJL, for it does not contain such a subexpression.

With heavy reliance on a reasoning program, the conjecture was proved, and thus XJL was shown to be too weak to be a single axiom for the equivalential calculus. The proof of the conjecture employs a case analysis conducted in terms of schemata, rather than in terms of individual formulas. The schemata themselves and the results of applying CD to pairs of them were discovered with much assistance from a reasoning program. A typical schema that was used in the study of XJL is

$$f(A) = e(y, e(e(e(z, y), A), z))$$

for formulas A. In addition, the entire case analysis was conducted by such a program. Examination of the entire study does yield a characterization of all theorems deducible from XJL, a characterization in terms of the schemata.

Finally, we note that this study led to a general methodology that was used to answer six related open questions in the equivalential calculus and also answer certain comparable questions in related calculi. The method has the pleasing property that it can be used for both establishing weakness of a formula or strength of a formula. In fact, two new shortest single axioms for EC were found employing the method. Of the seven formulas listed at the beginning of this chapter, the first four are each too weak to be a single axiom. In each case, the corresponding proof relies on a finite set of schemata. The fifth also is too weak, but the number of schemata used to establish this fact is infinite. Both XHK and XHN, the sixth and seventh formulas, are each strong enough to serve as a single axiom for EC. The proofs establishing this adequacy are rather complex. One proof consists of 84 condensed detachment steps, including steps that involve formulas containing 71 symbols excluding commas and grouping symbols. The other consists of 159 steps, including steps that involve formulas containing 103 symbols. Such complexity might be beyond that which any logician would find pleasant. Thus, again the value and power of an automated reasoning program are demonstrated.

EXERCISES

In this chapter, we discussed at a general level some of the ways in which an automated reasoning program was used to solve open questions in the equivalential calculus. In the following exercises, we explore in more detail exactly how such a program was used to establish that specified formulas are too weak to be single axioms. The complete proofs are quite complex and well beyond the scope of this work. What we are interested in here is how an automated reasoning program can be used as an assistant in the investigation. Let us consider the formula

$$e(x, e(y, e(e(x, e(z, y)), z)))$$

called XKE. The basic strategy used in the formal proof that XKE is too weak requires several steps. The goal is to obtain a complete characterization of the theorems that are deducible from XKE by condensed detachment, and then show that this set does not include some known theorem of the equivalential calculus. We denote the set of theorems that can be deduced from XKE by repeated use of condensed detachment CL(XKE). Now the question is: Exactly which theorems are in CL(XKE)? This question is quite similar to those that arise when investigating any formal system in which theorems are deduced from a small number of given formulas using specified rules. The first step in analyzing such a question is to look at a few of the theorems that can be deduced. You can do this by manually applying condensed detachment.

1. Which theorems can be deduced from XKE, using as many as three applications of condensed detachment?
   The answer to this exercise leads to two observations. First, the actual computations can be quite complex and prone to error. Second, the formulas become somewhat long and do not easily reveal their general structure. Remember, our first goal is to obtain a characterization of CL(XKE).

2. Use the technique described in Section 10.4.1 to rewrite the theorems deduced in problem 1 in terms of schemata, and thus obtain a more readable notation.

3. By examining the set of theorems produced in solving problem 2, determine a general pattern, or schemata, that characterizes some of the deduced theorems.

4. Another use of an automated reasoning program is to classify deduced formulas. During the study of EC, a method was formulated to assign formulas of EC to specific disjoint classes, and then use those classes to term certain formulas as uninteresting. The intent was to discard a formula if it were classed as uninteresting. In various problems, it is convenient to apply such a classification scheme to formulas. In the case under study, the classification scheme is the following.

   (1) Formulas of the form $e(x, t)$ are in class 1, where x is some variable and t is some expression.
   (2) Formulas that are not in class 1 and are of the form $e(t, x)$ are said to be in class 2.
   (3) Class 3 formulas are of the form $e(e(x, y), t)$, where x and y are (not necessarily distinct) variables.
   (4) Class 4 formulas are formulas not in class 3 and of the form $e(t, e(x, y))$.
   (5) All other formulas are in class 5.

To achieve this classification, we can use the following clause to deduce new formulas.

$$\neg DEDUCIBLE(e(x, y), v) \mid \neg DEDUCIBLE(x, w) \mid DEDUCIBLE(y, class(y))$$

Here class(y) must be made to demodulate to the correct class. Give the demodulators that achieve this. You may assume that demodulators are applied strictly in the order in which they occur. Thus, if two demodulators can be applied to the same term, the first is applied.

5. One of the tasks presented in investigating the equivalential calculus involved searching for shorter derivations. Specifically, you are given a derivation of a formula by condensed detachment, and you are to search for a shorter derivation. We found it useful to employ the concept of the *level* of a formula. The level of each input formula is 0. If f3 is deduced by condensed detachment from f1 and f2, and the level of f1 is l1, and the level of f2 is l2, then the level l3 of f3 is 1 greater than the maximum of l1 and l2. Thus, if l1 were 3 and l2 were 2, l3 would be $4 = 3 + 1$. What is needed is a way for an automated reasoning program to automatically compute the level of each deduced formula, for the level is often closely related to the derivation length. In addition, if a formula is deduced in more than one way, only the occurrence of the formula with the smaller level should be retained. To accomplish this, clauses can be written that contain the formula but also contain the level of that occurrence of the formula. If the form of the clauses is appropriately chosen, subsumption can be used to discard one occurrence of a formula in favor of another occurrence whose level is lower. When the levels are equal, the occurrence that was found later will be discarded by subsumption. Give the clauses that will automatically compute the level and cause the desired subsumption.

10.5 Answers to Exercises

1. The formulas that can be deduced with as many as three applications of condensed detachment from XKE are the following, where 1 in clause form is

    (1) ¬DEDUCIBLE(e(x, y)) | ¬DEDUCIBLE(x) | DEDUCIBLE(y)

If the following formulas are viewed as deduced in the clause representation, then clause 1 is, of course, an ancestor of each. We omit the predicate DEDUCIBLE, and simply give the formulas themselves.

Formula 2 is just XKE itself.

    (2) e(x1, e(x2, e(e(x1, e(x3, x2)), x3)))

From formulas 2 and 2:

    (3) e(x1, e(e(e(x2, e(x3, e(e(x2, e(x4, x3)), x4))), e(x5, x1)), x5))

From formulas 3 and 2:

    (4) e(x1, e(e(e(x2, e(e(e(x3, e(x4, e(e(x3, e(x5, x4)), x5))),

         e(x6, x2)), x6)), e(x7, x1)), x7))

From formulas 3 and 3:

    (5) e(e(e(x1, e(x2, e(e(x1, e(x3, x2)), x3))), e(x4, e(x5, e(e(e(x6,

         e(x7, e(e(x6, e(x8, x7)), x8))), e(x9, x5)), x9)))), x4)

From formulas 3 and 2:

(6) e(e(e(x1, e(x2, e(e(x1, e(x3, x2)), x3))), e(x4, e(x5, e(x6,

e(e(x5, e(x7, x6)), x7))))), x4)

From formulas 4 and 2:

(7) e(x1, e(e(e(x2, e(e(e(x3, e(e(e(x4, e(x5, e(e(x4, e(x6, x5)),

x6))), e(x7, x3)), x7)), e(x8, x2)), x8)), e(x9, x1)), x9))

From formulas 4 and 3:

(8) e(e(e(x1, e(x2, e(e(x1, e(x3, x2)), x3))), e(x4, e(x5, e(e(e(x6,

e(e(e(x7, e(x8, e(e(x7, e(x9, x8)), x9))), e(x10, x6)),

x10)), e(x11, x5)), x11))))), x4)

From formulas 4 and 4:

(9) e(e(e(x1, e(e(e(x2, e(x3, e(e(x2, e(x4, x3)), x4))),

e(x5, x1)), x5)), e(x6, c(x7, e(e(e(x8, e(e(e(x9,

e(x10, c(e(x9, e(x11, x10)), x11))), e(x12, x8)),

x12)), e(x13, x7)), x13)))), x6)

From formulas 4 and 2:

(10) e(e(e(x1, e(e(e(x2, e(x3, e(e(x2, e(x4, x3)), x4))),

e(x5, x1)), x5)), e(x6, e(x7, e(x8, e(e(x7, e(x9, x8)),

x9))))), x6)

From formulas 4 and 3:

(11) e(e(e(x1, e(e(e(x2, e(x3, e(e(x2, e(x4, x3)), x4))),

e(x5, x1)), x5)), e(x6, e(x7, e(e(e(x8, e(x9, e(e(x8,

e(x10, x9)), x10))), e(x11, x7)), x11)))), x6)

From formulas 6 and 2:

(12) e(x1, e(e(e(e(e(x2, e(x3, e(e(x2, e(x4, x3)), x4))),

e(x5, e(x6, e(x7, e(e(x6, e(x8, x7)), x8))))),

x5), e(x9, x1)), x9))

From formulas 6 and 3:

(13) e(e(e(x1, e(x2, e(e(x1, e(x3, x2)), x3))), e(x4,

e(e(e(x5, e(x6, e(e(x5, e(x7, x6)), x7))), e(x8,

e(x9, e(x10, e(e(x9, e(x11, x10)), x11))))), x8))), x4)

From formulas 6 and 4:

(14) e(e(e(e(x1, e(e(e(x2, e(x3, e(e(x2, e(x4, x3)), x4))),

       e(x5, x1)), x5)), e(x6, e(e(e(x7, e(x8,

       e(e(x7, e(x9, x8)), x9))), e(x10, e(x11,

       e(x12, e(e(x11, e(x13, x12)), x13))))), x10))), x6)

From formulas 6 and 3:

(15) e(e(x1, e(x2, e(e(x1, e(x3, x2)), x3))), e(e(x4,

       e(x5, e(e(x4, e(x6, x5)), x6))), e(x7, e(x8,

       e(e(x7, e(x9, x8)), x9)))))

From formulas 6 and 4:

(16) e(e(x1, e(e(e(x2, e(x3, e(e(x2, e(x4, x3)), x4))),

       e(x5, x1)), x5)), e(e(x6, e(x7, e(e(x6,

       e(x8, x7)), x8))), e(x9, e(x10, e(e(x9,

       e(x11, x10)), x11)))))

From formulas 5 and 2:

(17) e(x1, e(e(e(e(e(x2, e(x3, e(e(x2, e(x4, x3)), x4))),

       e(x5, e(x6, e(e(e(x7, e(x8, e(e(x7,

       e(x9, x8)), x9))), e(x10, x6)), x10)))),

       x5), e(x11, x1)), x11))

From formulas 5 and 3:

(18) e(e(e(x1, e(x2, e(e(x1, e(x3, x2)), x3))), e(x4,

       e(e(e(x5, e(x6, e(e(x5, e(x7, x6)), x7))),

       e(x8, e(x9, e(e(e(x10, e(x11, e(e(x10,

       e(x12, x11)), x12))), e(x13, x9)), x13)))), x8))), x4)

From formulas 5 and 4:

(19) e(e(e(x1, e(e(e(x2, e(x3, e(e(x2, e(x4, x3)), x4))),

       e(x5, x1)), x5)), e(x6, e(e(e(x7, e(x8,

       e(e(x7, e(x9, x8)), x9))), e(x10, e(x11,

       e(e(e(x12, e(x13, e(e(x12, e(x14, x13)),

       x14))), e(x15, x11)), x15)))), x10))), x6)

From formulas 5 and 3:

(20) e(e(x1, e(x2, e(e(x1, e(x3, x2)), x3))), e(e(x4,

e(e(e(x5, e(x6, e(e(x5, e(x7, x6)), x7))),

e(x8, x4)), x8)), e(x9, e(x10, e(e(x9,

e(x11, x10)), x11)))))

From formulas 5 and 4:

(21) e(e(x1, e(e(e(x2, e(x3, e(e(x2, e(x4, x3)), x4))),

e(x5, x1)), x5)), e(e(x6, e(e(e(x7, e(x8,

e(e(x7, e(x9, x8)), x9))), e(x10, x6)), x10)),

e(x11, e(x12, e(e(x11, e(x13, x12)), x13)))))

2. The schemata that result after demodulating the clauses are the following.

(2′) K

(3′) e(x1, e(e(K, e(x2, x1)), x2))

(4′) e(x1, e(e(e(x2, e(e(K, e(x3, x2)), x3)), e(x4, x1)), x4))

(5′) e(e(K, e(x1, K)), x1)

(6′) e(e(K, e(x1, e(x2, e(e(K, e(x3, x2)), x3)))), x1)

(7′) e(x1, e(e(e(x2, e(e(e(x3, e(e(K, e(x4, x3)), x4)),

e(x5, x2)), x5)), e(x6, x1)), x6))

(8′) e(e(K, e(x1, e(x2, e(e(e(x3, e(e(K, e(x4, x3)), x4)),

e(x5, x2)), x5)))), x1)

(9′) e(e(e(x1, e(e(K, e(x2, x1)), x2)), e(x3, e(x4,

e(e(e(x5, e(e(K, e(x6, x5)), x6)), e(x7, x4)), x7)))), x3)

(10′) e(e(e(x1, e(e(K, e(x2, x1)), x2)), e(x3, K)),x3)

(11′) e(e(e(x1, e(e(K, e(x2, x1)), x2)), e(x3, e(x4,

e(e(K, e(x5, x4)), x5)))), x3)

(12′) e(x1, e(e(e(e(K, e(x2, K)), x2), e(x3, x1)), x3))

(13′) e(e(K, e(x1, e(e(K, e(x2, K)), x2))), x1)

(14′) e(e(e(x1, e(e(K, e(x2, x1)), x2)), e(x3, e(e(K, e(x4, K)), x4))), x3)

(15′) e(K, e(K, K))

(16′) e(e(x1, e(e(K, e(x2, x1)), x2)), e(K, K))

$(17')$ $e(x1, e(e(e(e(K, e(x2, e(x3, e(e(K, e(x4, x3)), x4)))),$

$\qquad x2), e(x5, x1)), x5))$

$(18')$ $e(e(K, e(x1, e(e(K, e(x2, e(x3, e(e(K, e(x4, x3)), x4)))), x2))), x1)$

$(19')$ $e(e(e(x1, e(e(K, e(x2, x1)), x2)), e(x3, e(e(K, e(x4,$

$\qquad e(x5, e(e(K, e(x6, x5)), x6)))), x4))), x3)$

$(20')$ $e(K, e(e(x1, e(e(K, e(x2, x1)), x2)), K))$

$(21')$ $e(e(x1, e(e(K, e(x2, x1)), x2)), e(e(x3, e(e(K, e(x4, x3)), x4)), K))$

3. By examining clauses 3′ and 4′ from problem 2, you might conjecture that many formulas in CL(XKE) have the form

$\qquad e(x, e(e(A, e(y, z)), y))$

where A conforms to one of the schemata. So far we have only two schemata—K and $e(x, e(e(A, e(y, z)), y))$, which we call f(A). We may find additional schemata. In addition, clauses 5′, 6′, and 8′ might well lead to the conjecture that

$\qquad e(e(B, e(z, A)), z)$

is another such schemata. There exists a general technique for looking for such schemata. First, reformulate the clause to implement condensed detachment in the following way.

$\qquad$ (1) ¬DEDUCIBLE($e(x, y), v$) | ¬DEDUCIBLE(x, w)

$\qquad$ | DEDUCIBLE(y, abr(y))

Here abr(y) means "the abbreviation of y". Then the starting clause for XKE is

$\qquad$ (2) DEDUCIBLE($e(x, e(y, e(e(x, e(z, y)), z)))$,

$\qquad$ abr($e(x, e(y, e(e(x, e(z, y)), z)))$))

In addition, demodulators for the schemata are added. Thus, for the three schemata we have so far, we add

$\qquad$ EQUAL(abr($e(x, e(y, e(e(x, e(z, y)), z)))$), k(abr($x$), abr($y$), abr($z$)))
$\qquad$ EQUAL(abr($e(x, e(e(x1, e(y, z)), y))$), f(abr($x$), abr($x1$), abr($y$), abr($z$)))
$\qquad$ EQUAL(abr($e(e(x2, e(z, x1)), z)$), g(abr($x2$), abr(z), abr($x1$)))

(Recall that the schema K represents a formula with variables in it, so it makes sense to utilize it in the first clause above as if it were a function of three variables.) The variables x1 and x2 are allowed to be instantiated with schema, but the other variables are not. If we now examine the output of the program using these clauses as input, we see the deduced formulas along with their abbreviations. If the function e appears in the abbreviation, then more schemata must be identified. Furthermore, we must scan the arguments in the abbreviation to make sure that the arguments that we expect to be variables—all three arguments of K, all but the second argument of f, and the second argument of g—are of the form abr(v), where v is some variable. If you make this run for XKE, you will find that a schema is missing. The schema $e(A, B)$, where A and B conform to any schema, must be added. Thus,

> EQUAL(abr(e(x1, x2), i(abr(x1), abr(x2))))

should also be added. Once this demodulator is added, further runs indicate that all of the schemata for XKE have been identified. Of course, you cannot be sure of this until a formal proof has been produced. What we are describing is a way to arrive at a reasonable guess as to the structure of CL(XKE).

4. The first point that might be noted is that you need to be able to test a term to see if it is a variable. To do that, you can use the following two demodulators.

> EQUAL(ifvar(e(x, y)), false)
>
> EQUAL(ifvar(x), true)

Note that here we rely on the fact that the second demodulator applies only if the first does not. We then add a demodulator for performing the classification.

> EQUAL(class(e(x, y)), eval(ifvar(x), ifvar(y), e(x, y)))

The function "eval" has three arguments. The first two evaluate to true or false, depending on the arguments of the term to be classified. The third argument is just a copy of the term to be classified. If the first argument of eval is true, then the term is in class 1. If the second argument of eval is true, then the term is in class 2.

> EQUAL(eval(true, v, w), 1)
>
> EQUAL(eval(false, true, w), 2)

Now we must provide for the case in which the term is not in class 1 and is not in class 2.

> EQUAL(eval(false, false, e(e(x1, x2), e(y1, y2))),
>
>   eval2(and(ifvar(x1), ifvar(x2)), and(ifvar(y1), ifvar(y2))))
>
> EQUAL(and(true, x), x)
>
> EQUAL(and(false, x), false)
>
> EQUAL(eval2(true, v), 3)
>
> EQUAL(eval2(false, true), 4)
>
> EQUAL(eval2(false, false), 5)

More complex classification schemes can also be implemented. Note that we rely both on the fact that demodulators are applied strictly in the order in which they occur and on the fact that demodulation proceeds from inside out—subterms are demodulated before terms that contain them.

5. The basic idea that can be used to solve this problem is to add an argument to the DEDUCIBLE predicate. The added argument contains the level of the deduced formula. We represent the levels as x, s(x), s(s(x)), s(s(s(x))), ... This has the effect that higher levels are all instances of lower levels. Thus, the needed clause for deducing new formulas with the corresponding level information is

> ¬DEDUCIBLE(e(x, y), xl) | ¬DEDUCIBLE(x, xl) | DEDUCIBLE(y, s(xl))

Note that having xl as the second argument in each of the first two literals will cause xl to be instantiated to the maximum of the two levels. Now, if we were studying the formulas deducible from XGK = $e(x, e(e(y, e(z, x)), e(z, y)))$, we would use the following input clause.

DEDUCIBLE($e(x, e(e(y, e(z, x)), e(z, y))), xl$)

(The formula XGK is the shortest single axiom for which a shorter proof was found.) Note that the level of a deduced formula does not necessarily equal its derivation length. For example, an occurrence of a clause may be in level 5, but have a much longer derivation length. However, locating the lowest level in which a formula is deduced does aid in locating shorter derivations.

11

Real-Time Systems Control

One goal of this book is to demonstrate that automated reasoning techniques can be applied in a wide variety of common situations. In this chapter we consider a class of problems involving "real-time" control of one or more devices. To illustrate what we mean by real-time control of devices, let us first consider a very simple and common situation.

> You have a workshop with a heater. The heater is controlled by a thermostat. For this discussion, the basic mechanism consists of *sensors* that detect features of the environment and *devices* that can be activated or deactivated. For sensors, we have a thermometer to determine the temperature, a sensor that detects the desired temperature, and a sensor that determines whether or not the heater is on. The heater is the single device.

The type of "reasoning" we are considering is that normally performed by the thermostat. In this situation, of course, the thermostat is a much more practical solution than using a reasoning program to make decisions. For more complex control problems than the one we are discussing, more sophisticated reasoning than a thermostat provides is necessary. For now, let us study this simple situation in order to develop a basic approach to coping with control problems.

11.1 Basic Components of Real-Time Reasoning

In Chapter 5 we introduced the notion of *state* and illustrated how it can be used in solving puzzles. We said the notion of state is at the heart of many problems in which someone must choose an action from a set of possibilities. In this chapter we shall see that the concept of state again plays a central role. In the problem under discussion, controlling the heater to maintain a desired temperature in the workshop, the state of the system is determined by

1. The actual temperature

2. The desired temperature

3. Whether or not the heater is running

The information needed to determine what action should occur consists of the values of the sensors.

We can now give the basic reasoning process. All of the sensors are checked at regular intervals. Each time the sensors are checked, the reasoning component is invoked to determine whether or not any actions are required. If actions are required, the appropriate devices must be turned on or off.

In the case of the heater, the appropriate action is to check the sensors every few minutes. Each time the sensors are checked, the reasoning component determines whether or not the heat has fallen below the desired value. If it has, and if the heater is off, the heater is turned on. On the other hand, if the temperature is above the desired value, and if the heater is on, it is turned off.

Actually, you may not wish always to turn the heater on when the temperature drops below the desired value; instead, you may wish to wait until it drops some designated amount below the desired value, say 1.5 degrees. Similarly, you might wish to turn the heater off only after the temperature rises noticeably above the desired value. These actions prevent the heater from turning on and off almost continuously. For our example, we shall cause the heater to be turned on only if the temperature drops 1.5 degrees below the desired value, and turned off if it goes 1.5 degrees above the desired value.

The construction of real-time control systems presents two fundamentally different, but highly interrelated, problems. First, the construction of sensors and the electromechanical interfaces poses a variety of challenges. The second problem involves implementing the required reasoning component. The second problem is the one which will be considered in this section; we intentionally omit any consideration of the first problem. In many situations, such as this simple heater example, the required reasoning is so simple that almost all of the attention is directed to building appropriate sensors. On the other hand, in very complex situations, the rules needed by the reasoning component may be much more complex than the design of any single sensor. For our purposes, it is necessary to completely divorce the reasoning component from any issues involving electromechanical details of sensing devices. To divorce the two components, we choose the following view of how the reasoning component works.

1. The reasoning component is an automated reasoning program of the sort described in the first part of this book. Initially, the rules that determine which responses are necessary in any given situation are encoded as clauses in the general-axiom list. The set-of-support list is empty. Thus, nothing can be deduced. The system "sleeps" between the periodic sensor checks.

2. When the sensors are checked, a single clause giving the current state of the system is formed and put into the set-of-support list. Then, the reasoning component "wakes up" and begins deducing the actions to be taken. In the case of the example under consideration, a clause of the form

    STATE(68, 66, on)

    is generated, where 68 is the actual temperature, 66 is the desired temperature, and "on" is the status of the heater. The STATE clauses represent sensory input from the outside world.

3. The reasoning component starts deducing the actions to be taken. Whenever a unit clause with the predicate DO is generated, the system causes the indicated action to actually take place. For example, if

    DO(heater, off)

    were generated, the system would cause the heater to be turned off. The DO commands are the mechanism for transmitting instructions from the reasoning component to the devices. To see how this actually works, let us look at the general axioms that would be used for the simple example.

    $\neg$STATE(xtemp, xdesired, off)

    | $\neg$\$LE(\$sum(xtemp, 1.5), xdesired)

    | DO(heater, on)

    $\neg$STATE(xtemp, xdesired, on)

    | $\neg$\$LE(\$sum(xdesired, 1.5), xtemp)

    | DO(heater, off)

    The first clause causes the heater to be turned on, if the workshop gets too cold. The second clause turns the heater off, when the temperature gets 1.5 degrees above the desired value. Here the \$sum function is a special function that is used to add the two arguments. By using \$LE, a special predicate, a reasoning program can immediately make certain evaluations. Whenever a literal with the \$LE predicate becomes ground in the inference process, the literal is immediately evaluated—to true, if the first argument is less than or equal to the second, otherwise to false. If the literal evaluates to true, the inference process is terminated without drawing a conclusion to be considered for addition to the set of existing conclusions; if it evaluates to false, the \$LE literal is removed, and the inference process continues.

4. Finally, when all of the possible conclusions have been made, the set-of-support list is again empty, and the have-been-given list contains all of the

intermediate clauses that were used in the process. The system simply purges the have-been-given list, which returns the system to its initial state, and waits for the arrival of the next STATE clause.

In the next section, we apply these concepts to a significantly more complex problem. Before proceeding, here are some exercises that you might do to ensure that everything is clear so far.

EXERCISES

1. In the simple example, what would occur if the clause generated by checking the sensors were STATE(73, 65, on)?
2. What would occur if the clause were STATE(73, 65, off)?
3. Consider an elevator that services six floors. Suppose that it always goes to the first floor requested that is in the same direction as it has been traveling. A request is issued either by a person in the elevator wishing to get off at a particular floor, or by a person waiting for an elevator on some particular floor. Let us assume that on each floor there is a single button to indicate that you wish to get on the elevator, rather than two buttons, one for each direction. If no request is issued that matches the direction in which the elevator is traveling, then the elevator reverses direction. If there are no requests, it just stops. What determines the state of the elevator? Give the general axioms that could be used to govern the operation of the elevator.

11.2 A More Complex Example

In the preceding section, we introduced the basic concepts for using an automated reasoning program for real-time control. In this section, we apply those concepts to a slightly more complex situation. Consider a greenhouse that is 20 feet wide and 50 feet long. Further, assume there are three sets of windows along the length of the structure, one set near each end and one set in the middle. The windows are controlled by small motors that are interfaced to an automated reasoning program. Inside the greenhouse, there are two heaters, one near each end. The greenhouse has sensors for the actual temperature at each end of the structure, the outside temperature, the windspeed outside, and the desired temperatures at each end of the structure. Sometimes a temporary plastic partition is erected to allow slightly different temperatures to be maintained at each end. A real greenhouse might have numerous other devices to consider, such as fans, misting equipment, and such. However, this simplified situation is sufficient to illustrate the utility of using logic to describe the required reasoning.

First, let us consider what determines the state of the system.

1. The outside environment is represented by the outside temperature and the windspeed.

2. The ends of the greenhouse are each characterized by the status of a heater (on or off), the desired temperature, the actual temperature, and the status of one set of windows (open or closed).

3. Finally, the windows in the middle can be open or closed.

In situations in which a state depends on many variables, it is useful to think of the state of the system as being determined by the states of its subsystems. For this case, we divide the system into four subsystems—the outside, each of the two identical ends, and the middle windows. We base the analysis and the implementation in clauses on this division into subsystems. Thus, rather than a single STATE clause being introduced periodically, several clauses, each giving the state of a subsystem, are introduced. In this greenhouse example, four distinct unit clauses are generated. The formats for the four generated clauses are

STATEOUTSIDE($\langle$windspeed$\rangle$, $\langle$temperature$\rangle$)

STATEEND(1, $\langle$heater-status$\rangle$, $\langle$desired-temp$\rangle$, $\langle$real-temp$\rangle$, $\langle$windows$\rangle$)

STATEEND(2, $\langle$heater-status$\rangle$, $\langle$desired-temp$\rangle$, $\langle$real-temp$\rangle$, $\langle$windows$\rangle$)

STATEMIDDLE($\langle$windows$\rangle$)

where

$\langle$windspeed$\rangle$ is the windspeed in miles per hour,

$\langle$heater-status$\rangle$ is "on" or "off",

$\langle$temperature$\rangle$, $\langle$desired-temp$\rangle$, and $\langle$real-temp$\rangle$ are numeric temperature readings, and

$\langle$windows$\rangle$ is "open" or "closed".

Note that the states of the ends are given by clauses with the same predicate, STATEEND. This allows one to write rules in the form of clauses that can be used to control both ends, rather than separate clauses for each end. For example,

$\neg$STATEEND(xend, xheater, xdesired, xreal, open)

| $\neg$STATEOUTSIDE(xspeed, xouttemp)

| $\neg$\$LE(xreal, xdesired)

| $\neg$\$LE(xouttemp, xdesired)

| DO(windows(xend), close)

applies to either end, and simply causes the windows to close when it is too cold inside and also colder than desired outside.

Now let us consider what rules might be used to govern the heater and the windows.

1. The windows must be closed, if the windspeed exceeds 20 mph.

2. If it is too cold at one end, if the windows are closed, if it is warmer than desired outside, and if the windspeed is acceptable, then open the windows at that end.

3. If it is too warm at one end, if the windows are closed, if it is colder than desired outside, and if the windspeed is acceptable, then open the windows at that end.

4. If the windows are open, if the actual temperature is too low, and if it is colder outside than desired, then close the windows.

5. If the windows are open, if the actual temperature is too high, and if it is warmer outside than desired, then close the windows.

6. If the windows at either end are closed, then the windows in the middle must be closed; else, they must be open.

7. If the windows are closed at one end, if it is too cold, and if the heater is off, then turn it on.

8. If it is too hot, and if the heater is on, then turn it off.

The eight rules seem reasonable, and yet they may still lack something. For example, you cannot open all three sets of windows at one time. Similarly, you cannot close the windows and turn on the heater simultaneously. If the time between checks is not large, these shortcomings should not pose a problem. Nevertheless, the discussion shows that, as situations become increasingly complex, it is useful to be able to experiment with the effects of different rules. The ability to specify rules in a high-level language such as logic makes it much easier to create, read, and maintain the set of rules.

EXERCISE

4. Consider a system in which little robots move around guided by tracks in the floor. Suppose that the robots are used to carry food from the kitchen of a restaurant to tables. To simplify things a bit, suppose that there are just three tables and two robots. The system can be thought of as one point, the kitchen, connected via tracks with three other points, the tables. The kitchen is large enough to hold both robots, but each of the tables is only large enough for a single robot to work at. A track can be used by only one robot at a time. Requests for service come either from the kitchen, requesting that food be taken to a given table, or from a table, requesting that the table be cleared. A robot can be requested to go to some point, or to clear a table. A cook can also request that the next available robot come to the kitchen. A robot can sense when it is carrying food. Thus, when a cook has some food ready to serve, he may request that the next available robot come to the kitchen. When the robot obeys the request, the cook will put food on top of the robot and command the robot to go to the correct table. The robot will wait at the table until it is ordered to come back to the kitchen, which should occur once the robot is free of its load. Assume that all sensors are checked quite frequently, and that the sensors can detect the positions of the robots as well as the direction in which a moving robot is going. Formulate what is meant by the state of such a system, and then give a set of general axioms that could be used to control the system. This problem is intentionally somewhat ambiguous. You will have to make some reasonable design decisions for various aspects of the problem.

11.3 Applications in the Nuclear Power Industry

In the preceding sections, we developed some of the basic ideas that apply to real-time control systems. These same ideas apply to large systems that must be monitored in real time. The specific application that we shall discuss in this section is based on the nuclear power industry. However, all of the general comments apply equally well to monitoring a large assembly line, a steel manufacturing plant, a petroleum distillation plant, or a chemical production system. All of these systems require a large number of sensors to keep track of the state of the system and a mechanism for reacting to abnormal states. All of them may eventually be monitored by computers. In many cases, the master logic will be managed via an automated reasoning system.

The typical production nuclear reactor relies on literally thousands of interacting components. The failure of certain combinations of components may cause a sequence of events that requires a response. Nuclear power plants are designed explicitly with enough safety mechanisms built in to prevent such a single component failure from causing a severe emergency. Even so, such failures of a single component do require a response and action to be taken. In many cases, the extent of damage depends on how quickly and accurately an operator can make the appropriate response and take the appropriate action.

In a large power plant, there are numerous sensing devices that gather data concerning the state of the system. These sensors are controlled by small computers that record data about the state of the system and check for severe abnormalities. If a problem is detected, it must somehow be brought to the attention of the operator. A device for alerting the operator that some problem may exist is called an *annunciator panel*. An annunciator panel is a large panel of lights, each of which is labeled with the type of event that can cause the light to be turned on. When a problem is detected, the corresponding light is turned on and an alarm is sounded. The operator must manually turn off the alarm to indicate an awareness of the problem. If the problem continues for some predetermined interval, the alarm is reactivated. What complicates the situation is that one problem may in turn lead to many more problems. Thus, once a single annunciator light has been turned on, several other lights may turn on shortly thereafter. This cascading effect can continue until a number of lights are on and a number of alarms are sounding. To understand how to react appropriately to the problem, it is useful to know not only what lights are on, but also the order in which they were turned on. In short, emergency situations may require accurate, rapid reasoning under pressure.

The precise role for an automated reasoning program is not yet determined. Should the reasoning program actually activate responses to the emergency, or should it merely make suggestions to the operator for acceptance or rejection? The answer, of course, depends on the level of reliability of the reasoning program, the speed with which responses are required, and the nature of the specific emergency. For many applications, such a program will be used simply as a very knowledgeable advisor. The operator can issue a request both for an analysis of the probable cause of a problem and a suggestion for what action to take. Since a reasoning program can supply the precise details of how conclusions are obtained, the operator can ask the program for the basis for its analysis and its suggestion. With this information, decisions can be reached more quickly and with greater accuracy.

The early versions of programs that diagnose and monitor problems have been programs in which the problem analysis is encoded in a procedural programming language, such as assembler language, FORTRAN, and C. In many cases, hardware constraints and available software forced these choices. In the future, however, hardware prices are expected to drop drastically, and automated reasoning programs will rapidly become widely available. In this changing environment, an emphasis will be placed on ways to formulate the rules for problem analysis in the most convenient language. It will be important that the rules for diagnosing a problem and prescribing a response be readily understandable to nonprogrammers. The ability to easily modify and improve the rules will be more important than questions of hardware/software resources, major constraints in today's environment.

Logical statements offer one reasonable language for expressing such rules. In particular, many of the basic rules for diagnosing problems can naturally be expressed using the **if-then** logical operators. For example,

if

(1) septifoil header low pressure alarm, **and**

(2) D20 leak indicated in -20 or -40 RDZ,

then

D20 leak likely from the septifoil system

is a typical rule used in such cases. In this case, "septifoil header low pressure alarm" is *true* if a specific annunciator light is on. The other condition, "D20 leak indicated in -20 or -40 RDZ", is a condition deducible using other rules. For example,

if

(1) airborne activity sensed at -20 - or -40-ft level
of exhaust stack, **and**

(2) there is an indication of D20 loss,

then

D20 leak indicated in -20 or -40 RDZ

is another rule used for diagnosing such problems. In many cases, thousands of such rules have been carefully specified by plant designers in order to indicate precisely how unusual conditions are to be diagnosed.

By properly encoding the pertinent conditions, these rules can be converted into clauses and made accessible to an automated reasoning program. The main difficulty with using such a reasoning program is the exchange of knowledge between the expert designers of the control system and the reasoning system. A closely related problem involves a convenient interface for the operator using a reasoning program. These problems are receiving increasing attention, and expert reasoning systems will almost certainly become integral parts of future nuclear reactors.

EXERCISE

5. Suppose that you have a miniature annunciator panel that contains only 13 lights labeled in the following way.

Light	Label
1	1260A Sump high-level alarm
2	1260B Sump high-level alarm
3	Stack high activity alarm
4	AC forced cooling required
5	Overflow tank low-level alarm
6	Stack tritium high-activity alarm
7	Septifoil header low-pressure alarm
8	40 ft. exhaust high-activity alarm
9	Reactor D20 coarse level low
10	1260A sump level check shows high
11	1260B sump level check shows high
12	Septifoil header flow normal or high—sensor A
13	Septifoil header flow 5% low—sensor B

Now suppose that you have the following rules given to you from the designer's specifications.

if
    light 1 is on,
then
    there is water in the 1260A sump on the far side

if
    light 10 is on,
then
    there is water in the 1260A sump on the far side

if
    light 1 is off, **and**
    light 10 is off,

then
water is not in the 1260A sump on the far side

if
light 2 is on,
then
there is water in the 1260B sump on the far side

if
light 11 is on,
then
there is water in the 1260B sump on the far side

if
light 2 is off, **and**
light 11 is off,
then
water is not in the 1260B sump on the far side

if
there is not water in the 1260A sump on the far side, **and**
there is water in the 1260B sump on the far side,
then
water is in the 1260B sump on the near side only

if
light 3 is on, **and**
((light 6 is on) **or** (light 8 is on)),
then
airborne activity has been sensed

if
light 5 is on,
then
there is an indication of D20 loss

if
light 9 is on,
then
there is an indication of D20 loss

if
airborne activity has been sensed, **and**
there is an indication of D20 loss,
then
D20 leak indicated in -20 or -40 RDZ

if
light 7 is on, **and**
D20 leak indicated in -20 or -40 RDZ,
then
D20 leak indicated in septifoil system

if
> light 12 is on, **and**
> light 13 is on,

then
> low flow in near side septifoil header only

if
> light 4 is on, **and**
> water is in the 1260B sump on the near side only, **and**
> D20 leak indicated in septifoil system, **and**
> low flow in near side septifoil header only,

then
> spill from near side septifoil header

Describe a system that would notify the operator whenever a spill from the near side of the septifoil header occurred.

11.4 Summary

In this chapter we have attempted to introduce the basic notions that can be used to allow an automated reasoning program to control devices in real time. The idea of periodically introducing the state of the system as a set of unit clauses and accepting DO commands to manipulate devices separates the reasoning component from the electromechanical details of the interface. This allows one to easily create and study alternative sets of rules, encoded as clauses.

We have not examined cost or efficiency issues at all. For many applications, computers and the required interfaces are still much too expensive to use the approach that we have discussed. However, as the price of computer hardware continues to plummet, the number of devices controlled by a mechanism of the sort we described will continually grow. Eventually, heaters, microwave ovens, cars, elevators, assembly lines, security systems, sprinkler systems, electronic tellers, and an endless variety of other electromechanical systems will all be managed via a computer executing some form of an automated reasoning program. In fact, certain copying machines now include a resolution-based reasoning component.

11.5 Answers to Exercises

1. The clause DO(heater, off) would be generated, which should cause the heater to be turned off.

2. Nothing will be generated. The system will purge the STATE clause and wait for the next one to arrive.

3. The state of the system is characterized by the location of the elevator (tacitly assumed to be at one of the six floors), the direction in which it is moving, the status of the six buttons signaling people waiting to get on, and the status of the elevator's six buttons that specify at which floors the elevator must stop to let people get off. Therefore, the generated clauses are of the form

$$\text{STATE}(\langle loc\rangle,\langle direct\rangle,\langle get\text{-}on\text{-}1\rangle,\ldots,\langle get\text{-}on\text{-}6\rangle,\langle get\text{-}off\text{-}1\rangle,\ldots,\langle get\text{-}off\text{-}6\rangle)$$

where

$\langle loc\rangle$ is a value from 1 to 6,

$\langle direc\rangle$ is either "ascending" or "descending",

$\langle get\text{-}on\text{-}1\rangle$ through $\langle get\text{-}on\text{-}6\rangle$ are all either "on" or "off", and

$\langle get\text{-}off\text{-}1\rangle$ through $\langle get\text{-}off\text{-}6\rangle$ are all either "on" or "off".

The axioms to control the elevator are a bit complex. First, we have a set of axioms that convert the information in a state into several clauses. We use the following three demodulators.

EQUAL(checktwo(off, off), off)

EQUAL(checktwo(on, x), on)

EQUAL(checktwo(x, on), on)

These three clauses allow conversion of the settings of the two different sets of buttons—the set of buttons used to signal that someone wishes to get on at a given floor, and the set of buttons used to signal that someone wishes to get off at that floor—into a single setting. We then have six axioms that generate clauses of the form

FLOORSTATE($\langle floor\rangle$, $\langle on/off\rangle$)

to indicate whether a stop is requested at the given floor.

¬STATE(xloc, xdir, xon1, xon2, xon3, xon4, xon5, xon6,
    xoff1, xoff2, xoff3, xoff4, xoff5, xoff6)
| FLOORSTATE(1, checktwo(xon1, xoff1))

¬STATE(xloc, xdir, xon1, xon2, xon3, xon4, xon5, xon6,
    xoff1, xoff2, xoff3, xoff4, xoff5, xoff6)
| FLOORSTATE(2, checktwo(xon2, xoff2))

¬STATE(xloc, xdir, xon1, xon2, xon3, xon4, xon5, xon6,
    xoff1, xoff2, xoff3, xoff4, xoff5, xoff6)
| FLOORSTATE(3, checktwo(xon3, xoff3))

¬STATE(xloc, xdir, xon1, xon2, xon3, xon4, xon5, xon6,
    xoff1, xoff2, xoff3, xoff4, xoff5, xoff6)
| FLOORSTATE(4, checktwo(xon4, xoff4))

¬STATE(xloc, xdir, xon1, xon2, xon3, xon4, xon5, xon6,
   xoff1, xoff2, xoff3, xoff4, xoff5, xoff6)
| FLOORSTATE(5, checktwo(xon5, xoff5))

¬STATE(xloc, xdir, xon1, xon2, xon3, xon4, xon5, xon6,
   xoff1, xoff2, xoff3, xoff4, xoff5, xoff6)
| FLOORSTATE(6, checktwo(xon6, xoff6))

Then we use a single clause that extracts the floor and direction of the elevator.

¬STATE(xloc, xdir, xon1, xon2, xon3, xon4, xon5, xon6,
   xoff1, xoff2, xoff3, xoff4, xoff5, xoff6)
| NEXT(xloc, xdir, xloc, 1)

NEXT(xloc, xdir, xnext, xval) says that the elevator is on the floor xloc, going in a direction given by xdir, the next floor to check is given by xnext, and finally the indication of whether or not all of the floors that are in the same direction is given by xval—1 means that the program is still checking floors in the same direction, and 2 means that the program is now checking floors in the opposite direction. The clauses that actually control the search to find the next floor to stop at are the following.

¬NEXT(xloc, xdir, xnext, xval)
| ¬FLOORSTATE(xnext, on)
| DO(goto, xnext)

¬NEXT(xloc, ascending, xnext, xval)
| ¬FLOORSTATE(xnext, off)
| ¬$LE(xnext, 5)
| NEXT(xloc, ascending, $sum(xnext, 1), xval)

¬NEXT(xloc, ascending, 6, 1)
| ¬FLOORSTATE(6, off)
| ¬$LE(2, xloc)
| NEXT(xloc, descending, $sum(xloc, −1), 2)

¬NEXT(xloc, descending, xnext, xval)
| ¬FLOORSTATE(xnext, off)
| ¬$LE(2, xnext)
| NEXT(xloc, descending, $sum(xnext, −1), xval)

¬NEXT(xloc, descending, 1, 1)
| ¬FLOORSTATE(1, off)
| ¬$LE(xloc, 5)
| NEXT(xloc, ascending, $sum(xloc, 1), 2)

These clauses compute the correct floor to send the elevator to next. We assume that it is valid to tell the elevator to "goto" the floor that it is already at, if someone is holding one of the buttons down. Such a command should be interpreted as holding the elevator at the current location. This completes the solution of the elevator problem.

4. To construct the solution, we made several assumptions. First, whenever we transmit a "cleartable" command to the robot, it will clear the table that it is located at, and then stay where it is because it has been given no command to direct it to its next destination. It will move only after the next periodic check occurs and it is commanded to return to the kitchen. Next, whenever an "acceptfood" command is given to cause a robot to accept an order from the chef, the destination of the food will automatically become the destination of the robot. Similarly, a "servefood" command will cause the robot to serve the food at the table where the robot is standing, and it will cause the destination value to become "nil". This means that the "acceptfood" command should not be issued to the robot until the path to the table is clear—until you are sure that the other robot is not clearing the table. With these comments in mind, we first separate the state of the system into three subsystems, each of the two robots and the requests. The format of a clause giving the state of a robot is

$$\text{STATEROBOT}(\langle num \rangle, \langle loc \rangle, \langle dest \rangle, \langle loaded \rangle)$$

where

$\langle num \rangle$ is a 1 or 2 (the number of the chosen robot),

$\langle loc \rangle$ is the location of the robot,

$\langle dest \rangle$ is the destination of the robot, and $\langle loaded \rangle$ is either "on" or "off" to indicate whether or not the robot is carrying food from the chef.

We name the possible locations and destinations as "kitchen", "table(1)", "table(2)", "table(3)", "path(1)", "path(2)", and "path(3)". The term "path(1)" connects the "kitchen" to "table(1)", and similarly for the other paths. The state of the requests is given by

$$\text{STATEREQUESTS}(\langle kreq \rangle, \langle t1req \rangle, \langle t2req \rangle, \langle t3req \rangle)$$

where $\langle kreq \rangle$ is a number from 1 to 3 to indicate where the chef wishes some food delivered, and the other arguments are either "on" or "off" to indicate whether or not a request to clear the table has been made. The next four clauses simply convert the information in a single STATEREQUESTS clause into four separate clauses.

$\neg$STATEREQUESTS(xk, xt1, xt2, xt3) | STATEREQ(kitchen, xk)

$\neg$STATEREQUESTS(xk, xt1, xt2, xt3) | STATEREQ(table(1), xt1)

$\neg$STATEREQUESTS(xk, xt1, xt2, xt3) | STATEREQ(table(2), xt2)

$\neg$STATEREQUESTS(xk, xt1, xt2, xt3) | STATEREQ(table(3), xt3)

The rules that govern the movements of the robots can now be given. The first clause just says that, if a robot is at a table that has requested clearing, it will clear the table.

$\neg$STATEROBOT(xnum, table(x), xdest, xloaded)

| $\neg$STATEREQ(table(x), on)

| DO(xnum, cleartable)

The next clause says that, if a robot is carrying food and has arrived at the table, then it will put the food on the table.

¬STATEROBOT(xnum, xloc, xloc, on)

| ¬STATEREQ(xloc, off)

| DO(xnum, servefood)

The next clause is used to return a robot to the kitchen after it has cleared a table or served a dish.

¬STATEROBOT(xnum, table(x), nil, off)

| ¬STATEREQ(table(x), off)

| DO(xnum, goto(kitchen))

The goto command activates the robot to return, and sets the destination value to "kitchen", thus automatically setting it to "nil" when the robot arrives at the kitchen. We are now ready for the clauses that assign available robots to handle requests.

We wish to do this in a general way, and thus find an approach that works for any number of robots and tables, as long as there is room in the kitchen for all of the robots. To begin with, a scan is made for the next request. If one is found, a search is made for the next available robot. If one can be found, it is assigned to the task, and the scan for another request begins. As these scans occur, it is necessary for the program to remember its position in both the set of requests and the set of robots in order to avoid assigning two robots to the same request or the same robot to two requests. (Note that this type of problem, being algorithmic, might well be suited to Prolog, a language based on logic and discussed in a separate chapter.) First, we use two clauses that check to see whether or not the kitchen is requesting a robot.

¬STATEREQ(kitchen, xtnum)

| ¬$LE(1, xtnum)

| FINDROBOT(1, 1, kitchen)

¬STATEREQ(kitchen, 0) | FINDTASK(1, 1)

The clause

FINDROBOT(⟨robotnum⟩, ⟨next-table-to-check⟩, ⟨requester⟩)

amounts to starting a search for the first robot with a number greater than or equal to ⟨robotnum⟩ to handle ⟨requester⟩. If one is found, the scan begins at table ⟨next-table-to-check⟩ to look for another request. FINDTASK(⟨next-robot⟩, ⟨next-table-to-check⟩) causes a scan for the next requesting table, starting at table(⟨next-table-to-check⟩). If any more requests are found, available robots are selected from the set with numbers greater than or equal to ⟨next-robot⟩. The clauses that define FINDROBOT are the following.

¬FINDROBOT(xnum, xtable, xrequester)

| ¬STATEROBOT(xnum, kitchen, nil, off)

| ASSIGN(xnum, xrequester)

¬FINDROBOT(xnum, xtable, xrequester)
| ¬STATEROBOT(xnum, kitchen, nil, off)
| FINDTASK($sum(xnum, 1), xtable)

¬FINDROBOT(xnum, xtable, xrequester)
| ¬$LE(xnum, 1)
| ¬NOTAVAIL(xnum)
| FINDROBOT($sum(xnum, 1), xtable, xrequester)

To complete the definition of FINDROBOT, we define ASSIGN and NOTAVAIL. NOTAVAIL(⟨robot⟩) is true exactly when ⟨robot⟩ is not available. ASSIGN causes a robot to be assigned to the designated requester. The definitions for these are the following.

¬STATEROBOT(xnum, xloc, xdest, xloaded)
| ¬$NE(xloc, kitchen) | NOTAVAIL(xnum)

¬STATEROBOT(xnum, xloc, xdest, xloaded)
| ¬$NE(xdest, nil) | NOTAVAIL(xnum)

¬ASSIGN(xnum, xrequester)
| ¬$EQ(xrequester, kitchen)
| ¬STATEREQ(kitchen, xtnum)
| ¬PATHCLEAR(xtnum)
| DO(xnum, acceptfood)

¬ASSIGN(xnum, xrequester)
| ¬$NE(xrequester, kitchen)
| ¬PATHCLEAR(xrequester)
| DO(xnum, goto(xrequester))

The clauses for ASSIGN check to ensure that the path to the appropriate table is clear before assigning a robot. If the path is not clear, the robot is not assigned to another task, but rather waits in order to proceed on the next check of the sensors. The clauses to ensure that a path is clear are the following.

¬STATEROBOT(1, xloc, xdest, xloaded)
| ¬$NE(xloc, path(1))
| ¬$NE(xloc, table(1))
| CHECKPATH(2, 1)

¬STATEROBOT(1, xloc, xdest, xloaded)
| ¬$NE(xloc, path(2))
| ¬$NE(xloc, table(2))
| CHECKPATH(2, 2)

¬STATEROBOT(1, xloc, xdest, xloaded)

| ¬$NE(xloc, path(3))

| ¬$NE(xloc, table(3))

| CHECKPATH(2, 3)

Here CHECKPATH(⟨next-robot-to-check⟩, ⟨table-to-check⟩) checks to see if the path is clear to table(⟨table-to-check⟩). The path is clear if no robots with numbers greater than or equal to ⟨next-robot-to-check⟩ are on path(⟨table-to-check⟩) or at table(⟨table-to-check⟩).

¬CHECKPATH(xnum, xtable)

| ¬$EQ(xnum, 3)

| PATHCLEAR(xtable)

¬CHECKPATH(xnum, xtable)

| ¬STATEROBOT(xnum, xloc, xdest, xloaded)

| ¬$NE(xloc, path(xtable))

| ¬$NE(xloc, table(xtable))

| CHECKPATH($sum(xnum, 1), xtable)

This completes the definition of FINDROBOT. Now let us return to the problem of finding the next requester.

¬FINDTASK(xnum, xtable)

| ¬STATEREQ(table(xtable), on)

| FINDROBOT(xnum, $sum(xtable, 1), table(xtable))

¬FINDTASK(xnum, xtable)

| ¬STATEREQ(table(xtable), off)

| ¬$LE(xtable, 2)

| FINDTASK(xnum, $sum(xtable, 1))

We now have all of the clauses required to control the robots. What is required to handle an arbitrary number of robots and tables? What is required to handle multiple kitchens?

5. The first step is to note that the settings of the 13 annunciator lights determine the state of the system. Then the rules must be converted to clauses. The conversion is rather straightforward, except for the rule for detecting airborne activity, which is converted into two clauses. Once this is done, an extra clause with a DO is needed to say that, if there has been a spill, DO("notify operator"). We thus have a very straightforward, rather simplistic solution. Rules of the sort that say "if 3 out of 5 of the following conditions hold, deduce the following condition" do cause problems when they are converted to clauses. Similarly, when there are hundreds of lights on the annunciator panel, the details of generating new states at rapid time intervals can cause implementation problems. However, if you apply your imagination to finding solutions to such problems, you will find many acceptable solutions.

12

Program Debugging and

Verification

Designing and writing programs—except for the most elementary ones—is a difficult task. Many details must be mastered. They range from details of the problem being solved—how to compute a payroll, format text, or solve a partial differential equation—to details of the programming language and data representations being used—choosing the right limits for indexing loops or avoiding running off the end of a list. Failure to keep track of even one of these details can lead to the occurrence of a "bug"—a failure of the program to execute correctly.

Program bugs can be difficult to locate and correct. For example, does the following fragment that moves array elements contain any bugs? (Assume that $1 \leq I \leq N$ and $1 \leq J \leq N$.)

```
INTEGER A(N)
INTEGER K
. . .


K = I
DO WHILE (K ≤ J)
   A(K − 1) = A(K)
   K = K + 1
END
. . .
```

If so, what are they, and how can they be found? If not, how can you convince yourself there are none?

Certainly reasoning is involved in answering questions such as these. In fact, it is involved in all aspects of programming, from the initial formulation of a problem to the writing, testing, and debugging of the code. On the one hand, the effective solution of a problem may involve inventing and proving, by means of deduction, a new method for its solution. On the other, most programmers use *symbolic execution*, which is a form of algebraic reasoning, to check such program details as whether loop bounds have been chosen correctly.

Since reasoning is involved, you might naturally wonder whether an automated reasoning program can provide assistance in performing any of these tasks. Yes, it can. In this chapter we will explore primarily how a reasoning program can assist a programmer in showing that a given computer program does what it is supposed to do. At least two approaches are possible. One is to have a software system—based on an automated reasoning program—carry out symbolic execution of fragments of a program, or even of entire programs. Symbolic execution can help to verify such details as proper choice of loop bounds, correctness of array subscripts, and validity of list operations. It may also uncover a bug in a program by producing a *counterexample*—a set of input data for which the program executes incorrectly.

The second approach is to use a software system—at the heart of which is again an automated reasoning program—to *verify* that a program has certain required properties. Indeed, if you verify enough properties of a program, you and your colleagues may agree that you have constructed a *proof of correctness* for the program. You must always keep in mind, however, that such proofs are never *absolute*—they are *relative* to some chosen specification of what the program should do. Hence, if you write some specifications for a program—but ones that do not adequately capture your intent—you may find yourself in possession of a program that has been "proved correct" yet does not do what you intended. Thus, whenever we use the term "proof of correctness" in this chapter we do not mean a proof that a program contains absolutely no bugs, but rather a proof that that program does what is claimed for it. (Of course, the correctness of a program is similarly relative to the axioms used to define the semantics of the programming language in which it is written. Should the implementation of that language on some machine be inconsistent with the axioms, then a program that has been proved correct may not do what is claimed for it on that machine.)

In this chapter, we show how automated reasoning techniques can be used to execute a program symbolically (Section 12.1) and how they can be used to prove that a program has certain properties (Section 12.2). We conclude with a discussion of how "abstract programming" can be used to organize and simplify the task of reasoning about programs (Section 12.3). A thorough discussion of these topics could easily fill a book, so that given here is necessarily highly simplified and not at all complete. Nevertheless, it should give you an idea of the applications, both actual and potential, of automated reasoning to computer programming.

As always, one of the central problems is that of *representation*—how to cast a program into clause form so that a reasoning program can operate on it. You will observe that the representation of even a very small program requires many input clauses—many more than are needed for even rather subtle mathematical proofs. In some sense, they reflect the multitude of details that are involved in programming. Because a program requires so many clauses for its representation, one normally uses an *input translator* to automatically generate the clauses from the program and its specification.

Only rarely in reasoning about programs written in the usual programming languages is it necessary to prove a theorem of any depth. Not surprisingly, perhaps, most of the reasoning is shallow. It involves mainly substitution, arithmetic operations, and inequalities. And it is highly specific to a given program—the results are not readily applicable to other, apparently similar, programs. Even though such reasoning is shallow, in practice it is often extraordinarily difficult, whether automated or not. Thus, in some sense, reasoning about programs as they are usually written is not very "rewarding", for much effort is expended to prove results of limited significance.

At the end of this chapter we shall consider how the idea of *abstract programming* might be used to alleviate this problem. When we write an abstract program, we express it in terms of the concepts and notation usually used to describe the problem being solved. Such a program omits many of the specifically computer-oriented details of the solution to the problem. Thus, when we attempt to prove that an abstract program has a certain property, it is likely that we can recognize that the proof depends on significant results from the problem domain—the strictly computer-oriented details that clutter the proof for an ordinary program are absent. For the same reason, it is also likely that a result proved about an abstract program can be used in proofs of related abstract programs. Abstract programming thus raises the level of programming. Such higher-level programming should permit both the program designer and the reasoning program to concentrate on fewer, deeper, and more rewarding properties of programs, rather than on numerous mundane details, as they must now.

We turn now to consider some examples. They are representative of programs that can be written in languages such as Pascal or FORTRAN. We present them in a language that is similar to FORTRAN but that contains structured programming constructs such as if-then-else statements and do-while loops. These constructs probably are familiar to you. If not, their meaning will be made precise by the clauses that represent them.

12.1 Symbolic Execution

Let us begin by considering the simple example of a programmer's use of symbolic execution to conclude that no out-of-bounds subscript references can occur in a program fragment. The example will introduce some ideas about how you can represent a FORTRAN-level program and its meaning to an automated reasoning program, and it will show how such a reasoning program can aid the programmer.

12.1.1 Reasoning about a Program Fragment

The following fragment might be part of a program that does an in-place sort of the elements in an array.

```
INTEGER A(N)
INTEGER K
. . .

K = I + 1
DO WHILE (K ≤ J)
    A(K − 1) = A(K)
    K = K + 1
END
. . .
```

Intuitively speaking, its specification is that it moves the elements numbered $I + 1$ to J one position earlier in the array Λ, so that, say, the element that formerly was at I can be inserted into the position J. How do you convince yourself that, when the do-while loop executes, the subscripts of the array A never lie outside the range 1 to N specified in its declaration?

In order to make any progress in verifying a property of a program, it is necessary to make some *input assumptions*—assumptions that the input to the program must satisfy. With the given specification, it is reasonable to assume that the part of the program ahead of this fragment guarantees that I and J are within the bounds of the array A, that is, that $1 \leq I \leq N$ and $1 \leq J \leq N$. Moreover, in checking for subscript bounds errors, typically we would assume that J is beyond I, that is, $I < J$. If it were not, the loop would not be executed and no array references would be made in this fragment, so, of course, no subscript bounds error could occur.

Often programmers "verify"—that is, check—subscript bounds in a loop by considering a "representative" example. Letting $N = 5$ would seem to provide (for this example) a class of test cases that are general enough to enable us to uncover potential bugs, yet small enough to enable us to work them out in a reasonable time. We might guess from looking at the program that if there is to be any problem with subscript bounds, it will arise when I and J have their extreme values (subject to the input assumptions), namely, $I = 1$ and $J = 5$.

To check the program by hand, we would carry out a symbolic execution. A convenient way to do so is to write down copies of the program statements in the order they are executed and with the actual values of the variables substituted into them. We can use ASSUME statements to represent the input assumptions and

ASSERT statements to represent conditions that are true at the place in the program where they appear. In this example, the ASSERT statements are derived from the condition $K \leq J$ in the do-while loop. Using these ideas, we can write out the symbolic execution of the program in a kind of tableau.

ASSUME (N = 5)

ASSUME (I = 1)

ASSUME (J = 5)

K = 2

ASSERT (2 ≤ 5)

A(1) = A(2)

K = 3

ASSERT (3 ≤ 5)

A(2) = A(3)

K = 4

ASSERT (4 ≤ 5)

A(3) = A(4)

K = 5

ASSERT (5 ≤ 5)

A(4) = A(5)

K = 6

ASSERT (6 > 5)

Having written out the symbolic execution for this test case, we examine it to see if any references to elements of A outside the range $A(1), \ldots, A(5)$ occur. None do. To the extent that this execution is representative of all possible executions, we may conclude that the loop bounds are correct.

Carrying out the symbolic execution, even for this simple case, is tedious. We would like an automated reasoning program to do it.

12.1.2 Representing a Program for Symbolic Execution

There are two parts to solving the problem of representing a program for symbolic execution. One is, of course, to represent the statements that are in the program. The other is to represent the program state—the background information—that is necessary to understand the meaning of the program statements. We shall consider the representation of the state first, since it will be used in the representation of the statements.

12.1.2.1 Representing the program state.   Programs written in languages at the level of abstraction typified by that of FORTRAN describe primarily actions that are performed on the memory of a computer. For example, a reference to a variable on the left of the assignment symbol indicates that a value is to be stored in the memory location associated with that variable. Similarly, a reference to a variable in most other contexts indicates that the value stored at its associated memory location is to be fetched and used in some computation. In order to represent the meaning of such programs, we can use the concept of *program state*. The program state is simply a list of the variables that are modified—assigned to—in the program being represented.

How can we get an automated reasoning program to simulate the changes in a program's state that take place during execution? This problem of simulating changes in state lies at the heart of program verification for languages such as FORTRAN and Pascal. It is all the more interesting because solving it requires us to model time—to model the *sequence* of values that a variable takes on during the execution of a program. Changes in state are really, of course, substitutions of one value for another—the variable K in the given program fragment has the value 2 during the first execution of the loop; just before the beginning of the second execution, the value 3 is substituted for the value 2. An automated reasoning program offers two choices for a technique for carrying out substitution. We can use the substitutions that take place as a result of the unifications that it makes in order to apply inference rules. Or, we can use those that result from applying demodulation—a restricted form of equality substitution.

Here we shall employ an approach based on demodulation. Using demodulation, as you have seen in earlier chapters, often involves using functions. To model the program state, we can define a function—call it lvals—to construct a list of the names and values of the variables in the state. Hence, lvals has three arguments: the name of a program variable, the value of that variable, and the rest of the list of program variables. A constant, nil, can represent the end of the list. If the example program did not modify the array A, its initial state could be represented as

lvals(k, notinit, nil)

Here the constant notinit indicates that the variable has not yet been assigned a value. Later, after K has been assigned the value 2 in the first assignment statement in the fragment, the state would be represented by

lvals(k, 2, nil)

In reality, the example program does make assignments to the array A. As will be seen, arrays require special treatment. Hence the state for the example program has a slightly more complicated representation than that just given. We can use the same trick to represent the elements of the array A that we used to represent the state (after all, the computer memory used to hold the state can be thought of as an array). To construct the list of array elements for a one-dimensional array, we use a function lels1, whose first argument is an array element index, whose second argument is an array element value, and whose third argument is the rest of the list of array elements. Using this function, the state upon entry to (just before executing the assignment K = I + 1 in) the example program fragment can be represented by

lvals(a, lels1(1, 7, lels1(2, 19, lels1(3, 1, lels1(4, 73, lels1(5, 6, nil))))),

lvals(k, notinit, nil))

assuming that elements 1 through 5 of the array A initially contain 7, 19, 1, 73, and 6, respectively.

There is one further item that we should include as part of the state of the program: an indication of the "current" statement being executed.

We can use the predicate PSTATE to represent the full state of the program. PSTATE has two arguments. The first is the name of the statement currently being executed. (In order to avoid ambiguity, we must assign a unique name to each statement in a program fragment to be executed.) The second argument of PSTATE is the lvals list giving the current values of the program variables. If entry is the name given to the first statement in the program fragment we are testing here, we can finally write a clause

(1) PSTATE(entry,

lvals(a, lels1(1, 7, lels1(2, 19, lels1(3, 1, lels1(4, 73, lels1(5, 6, nil))))),

lvals(k, notinit, nil)))

to represent the full state when the fragment is entered.

EXERCISES

1. The concept of program state is basic to the treatment given here. Write the clauses to give the program state in which the variable AMOUNT has the value 10, B(1) has the value 4, B(3) has the value 2, and the current statement is labeled headloop.

2. How would you construct with clauses a list of array elements for a two-dimensional array using a function lels2 that is similar to lels1? Show how to encode a two-dimensional array with the value 10 in the 1,1 position and the value 20 in the 1,3 position.

12.1.2.2 Representing the assignment statement.   The next step in presenting this problem to an automated reasoning program is to write the clause representation for the statements in the program. To do so, we use clauses that are, in effect, axioms for the statements in the programming language in which the program is written. The meaning of programming languages is not usually defined using axioms. And writing axioms for existing languages (defined in some other way) is extremely tricky, for all existing languages have complicated semantics. Nevertheless, given a representation for the program state, it is possible to do so, at least for the types of statement we shall encounter here.

It is convenient to give once and for all a general axiom for each type of statement (such as assignment, do-while, and if-then) in the programming language.

Then we can represent the specific statements that occur in a program economically —with single-literal clauses that connect them to the appropriate general axiom. The general meaning of each type of statement in the language is expressed by an **if-then** of the form: **if** the program is at statement xinstr and has state xstate **and** a statement of this type is executed, **then** the program next executes statement yinstr with (possibly changed) state ystate. For example, for statements of type assignment, the general axiom in clause form is

(2) $\neg$PSTATE(xinstr, xstate)

| $\neg$ASSIGN(xinstr, zassignto, wexpr, yinstr)

| PSTATE(yinstr, store(zassignto, eval(wexpr, xstate), xstate))

The functions store and eval will be defined in Section 12.1.3.

To particularize this general behavior to an assignment statement in the program, say K = I + 1, we write a unit clause describing that assignment. Let us give the statement name entry to this assignment, and the name dows (do-while start) to its successor statement. Then the unit clause is

(3) ASSIGN(entry, pvar(k), sum(pparam(i), pconst(1)), dows)

(Recall that, in the language of clauses as used in this book, constants and functions must be written in lower case; hence, for example, the program variable K is written as k in clauses.) It says that the assignment statement is named entry, K is the program variable assigned to, sum(...) is the expression to be evaluated, and the next statement to be executed is named dows. As we shall see in Section 12.1.3, the functions pvar, pparam, and pconst govern how their arguments are evaluated using the state—pvar(x) is fetched from the state, while pparam(x) and pconst(x) have values that are independent of the state.

The meaning of this particular assignment in any execution of this program (whatever the state) can be obtained by resolving clauses 2 and 3 to get

$\neg$PSTATE(entry, xstate)

| PSTATE(dows, store(pvar(k),

eval(sum(pparam(i), pconst(1)), xstate), xstate))

This clause says that if the program is at the assignment statement entry with any state xstate, it makes a *transition* to statement dows with a new state obtained from updating xstate by storing for the program variable K the result of evaluating the sum of I and 1 using xstate.

Now we can see how such clauses model program execution. The symbolic execution starts with clause 1, which defines the state on entry to the program fragment. Since we have given each statement in the program fragment a unique name, there is only one clause—the preceding one—that contains a negative PSTATE literal with the same statement name as that in the positive PSTATE literal in clause 1. Clause 1 unifies with it to produce a new positive PSTATE literal with the statement name dows. Again there is only one clause with a corresponding negative literal. These transitions from one statement to the next repeat until finally a positive PSTATE containing a statement name with no corresponding clause is produced. Then we say that the symbolic execution has terminated, and we can examine the final state to see the results produced by the test case.

EXERCISE

3. Give the ASSIGN clause corresponding to an assignment of the form I = A + B. Give the clause that results from resolving the ASSIGN clause with clause 2. Assume that the label corresponding to the assignment statement is assgn1 and the label of the next instruction is nextins.

12.1.2.3 A word about side effects.   We must make a side remark—nevertheless an important one—about the axiom for assignment given in clause 2. It specifies that the store function updates the program state (xstate) that existed when execution of the assignment statement started. Thus, if the state is altered during the evaluation of the expression on the right side of the assignment (wexpr), those alterations will be lost. Such alterations, which occur, for example, when a function that is called during evaluation of an expression alters variables in the state, are called *side effects*. We are thus giving axioms for a language without side effects (unlike FORTRAN or Pascal). If we wish to define a language in which side effects are permitted, the definitions for assignment and especially for the function eval (which are given later) become complicated. In particular, eval must return not only the value of the evaluated expression, but also the updated state, which the function store then in turn updates. (Multiple values can be returned by a function by having it return a list of those values.) At that point, we would also have to make a decision about whether the evaluation of subscript expressions for the variable on the left side of the assignment statement is to be performed with the state on entry to the statement, or with the one produced by eval. The axiom for assignment with the environment fully threaded through the evaluations to take account of side effects might look like

$\neg$PSTATE(xinstr, xstate)

| $\neg$ASSIGN(xinstr, zassignto, wexpr, yinstr)

| PSTATE(yinstr, store(zassignto, eval(wexpr, xstate)))

This axiom dictates that the right-side expression be evaluated before the left, since the state that results from evaluating wexpr (returned as part of the result of eval) is passed to store, which will use it to evaluate any subscript expressions that are part of zassignto.

The main point of this discussion is to make you aware that the axioms we give ignore side effects—if they occur, they are discarded. These axioms will work fine with programs that do not cause any side effects, but they could give erroneous results with programs that do. If you wish to be protected, you must accept the additional complication that the possibility of side effects imposes. You can write axioms either to take account of them properly or to cause the symbolic execution or proof to fail for programs that cause side effects. One way to simplify taking proper account of side effects is to transform the program to isolate side-effecting function calls, as we discuss in Section 12.2.6. This approach guarantees that there is only one side-effecting function call per statement, thereby simplifying the axiomatization.

12.1.2.4 Representing other programming language statements.   The meaning of each other type of statement in the language is defined by a general axiom similar to the one given in clause 2 for assignment. Here are the axioms for the statements used in this example program. Notice that none of them alters the program state (provided that we are defining a language without side effects, as discussed earlier). The axiom for the do-while statement is

(4) ¬PSTATE(xinstr, xstate)

| ¬DOWHILE(xinstr, wcond, yinstr, zinstr)

| PSTATE(if(eval(wcond, xstate), then(yinstr), else(zinstr)), xstate)

The function if in this axiom selects one of two alternative successor statements, yinstr or zinstr, depending on the result of evaluating the expression wcond in xstate. The axiom for the END statement is

(5) ¬PSTATE(xinstr, xstate)

| ¬DOEND(xinstr, yinstr)

| PSTATE(yinstr, xstate)

Notice that it specifies no evaluations and no alterations to the input state—it serves only to transfer from one statement name to another. This definition reflects the intuitive notion that the state at the end of executing the body of a do-while loop is the same as the state at the beginning of the next execution. As we shall see in Section 12.2.4, the simplicity of the END statement is important because it facilitates "cutting" loops in proofs of program correctness.

So far, we have said nothing about how array subscripts get checked for being in bounds. Let us add to the programming language a statement for checking for and indicating errors, such as

    IF (expression) ERROR

For its axiom we use

(6) ¬PSTATE(xinstr, xstate)

| ¬IFERROR(xinstr, wexpr, yinstr)

| PSTATE(if(eval(wexpr, xstate), then(error), else(yinstr)), xstate)

In order to use this statement to check subscript bounds, we must first transform the program fragment to introduce explicit subscript checks. The resulting program is

```
INTEGER A(N)
INTEGER K
. . .

K = I + 1
DO WHILE (K ≤ J)
   IF (K − 1 > HB(A, 1)) ERROR
   IF (1 > K − 1) ERROR
   IF (K > HB(A, 1)) ERROR
   IF (1 > K) ERROR
   A(K − 1) = A(K)
   K = K + 1
END
. . .
```

The function HB is intended to give the "high bound" of the array that is its first argument in the dimension that is its second argument. The value of HB for an array is obtained from the bound specified in the declaration for that array.

Transforming a program to facilitate checking some property is frequently part of program verification. Automated program transformation systems can be used to carry out such transformations, as well as to perform ones that simplify the axiomatization of side effects, as mentioned earlier. Moreover, transformation systems can also be used to automate the process of translating the program into clauses.

EXERCISE

4. What program fragment results from transforming the program fragment consisting of the following statement to include subscript checks?

A(J) = C + B(2) − 1

What clauses would be produced to correspond to these checks?

12.1.2.5 Representing the statements in the program. Now that we have the general axioms for statements, translating the program to clauses is fairly straightforward. The statement INTEGER A(N) translates into a demodulator

(7) EQUAL(hb(parr(a), pconst(1)), pparam(n))

since it is nonexecutable and does not need to be linked into the statement sequence. The function parr serves primarily as a reminder to readers that A is an array.

We are now ready to represent the example program with clauses. Let us give the nine executable statements in the transformed program fragment the following names: entry, dows, ife1, ife2, ife3, ife4, asga, asginc, and dowe, and let exit be the name that will cause termination of the symbolic execution—effectively, it is the name of the statement after the do-while loop. Then clause 3, already given, translates $K = I + 1$. The translation of the do-while statement is

(8) DOWHILE(dows, le(pvar(k), pparam(j)), ife1, exit)

The remainder of the statements translate in the following way.

(9)   IFERROR(ife1, gt(diff(pvar(k), pconst(1)), hb(parr(a), pconst(1))), ife2)

(10) IFERROR(ife2, gt(pconst(1), diff(pvar(k), pconst(1))), ife3)

(11) IFERROR(ife3, gt(pvar(k), hb(parr(a), pconst(1))), ife4)

(12) IFERROR(ife4, gt(pconst(1), pvar(k)), asga)

(13) ASSIGN(asga, parr1(a, diff(pvar(k), pconst(1))), parr1(a, pvar(k)), asginc)

(14) ASSIGN(asginc, pvar(k), sum(pvar(k), pconst(1)), dowe)

(15) DOEND(dowe, dows)

Here, the function parr1 is used to represent a reference to a one-dimensional array; its arguments are the array name and the subscript expression. The other functions not already mentioned represent the arithmetic and relational operators occurring in the program.

Roughly, the rules for translating a program statement are the following.

1. Write down the statement type as the predicate, and make the statement name its first argument.
2. Fill in the functional representations of the expressions and left-side variables (where used). In these representations, make each program variable, program array, one-dimensional program array reference, program parameter (named program constant), and program constant the first argument of the function pvar, parr, parr1, pparam, and pconst, respectively.
3. Fill in the name of the successor statement and any alternative successor statements as required by the particular statement-type predicate.

Finally, we must translate the input assumptions about the values of the program parameters N, I, and J. Recall that they are

ASSUME (N = 5)
ASSUME (I = 1)
ASSUME (J = 5)

The corresponding clauses are demodulators.

(16) EQUAL(pparam(n), pconst(5))

(17) EQUAL(pparam(i), pconst(1))

(18) EQUAL(pparam(j), pconst(5))

12.1.3 Demodulators That Model Program Execution

At this point we have given the general axioms for the programming language statements used in the example program, and we have given the clauses that represent this particular example program. Only one task—albeit a large one—remains before we can use an automated reasoning program to symbolically execute the example. We must write the demodulators—equality clauses—to be used with the axioms already given. These demodulators define the functions introduced by the general axioms and enable an automated reasoning program to simulate the execution of a program containing the given types of statement. Throughout, we assume that the demodulators are applied inside out, that is, that the innermost terms are demodulated before terms containing them, as illustrated in Chapter 7 (Section 7.2.1).

12.1.3.1 Demodulators for operators in expressions.   Let us begin with eval, the function that defines the evaluation of expressions, including—and this is the main point for this example—checking that the variables involved are defined and valid in the program state. The following demodulators express the evaluation of the operators that occur in the example program.

(19) EQUAL(eval(sum(x, y), zstate), sum(eval(x, zstate), eval(y, zstate)))

(20) EQUAL(eval(diff(x, y), zstate), diff(eval(x, zstate), eval(y, zstate)))

(21) EQUAL(eval(gt(x, y), zstate), gt(eval(x, zstate), eval(y, zstate)))

(22) EQUAL(eval(le(x, y), zstate), le(eval(x, zstate), eval(y, zstate)))

When other operators occur in a program, similar demodulators must be included for them; we shall add some more (but still far from a complete set) in Section 12.2.2.

These four demodulators have the effect of forcing eval ever deeper into expressions until it surrounds program variables, program array references, program parameters, or program constants. Now, eval applied to a program variable must fetch its value from the current state.

(23) EQUAL(eval(pvar(x), zstate), fetch(pvar(x), zstate))

Similarly, eval applied to a program array reference must evaluate the subscript expression in the current state and fetch the value of the element from the current state.

(24) EQUAL(eval(parr1(x, y), zstate), fetch(parr1(x, eval(y, zstate)), zstate))

(Here, again, this choice of demodulator specifies that side effects that occur during the evaluation of the subscript expression are ignored.) Finally, eval applied to a program constant or parameter must simply produce a valid result independent of the state.

(25) EQUAL(eval(pconst(x), zstate), isvalid(x))

(26) EQUAL(eval(pparam(x), zstate), isvalid(x))

The function isvalid used here will also appear in a number of the following demodulators. Its presence serves as a marker to indicate that the result of a computation has been validated by the demodulators—that the result has been fetched or computed correctly, and is valid for further computation. As will become apparent, the absence of isvalid around a result effectively stops the symbolic execution. Apart from this role as a marker in the demodulation process, isvalid can be thought of as the identity function, that is, it returns the value of its argument, not the values true and false.

The effect of executing the arithmetic and relational operations on validated operands is represented by the demodulators

(27) EQUAL(sum(isvalid(x), isvalid(y)), isvalid($sum(x, y)))

(28) EQUAL(diff(isvalid(x), isvalid(y)), isvalid($diff(x, y)))

(29) EQUAL(gt(isvalid(x), isvalid(y)), isvalid($gt(x, y)))

(30) EQUAL(le(isvalid(x), isvalid(y)), isvalid($le(x, y)))

These four demodulators complement demodulators 19 through 22. Whereas 19 through 22 force the function eval down into the expression until it surrounds program variables and constants, 27 through 30 force the function isvalid up around the expression until it marks the entire expression as being valid.

The functions beginning with "$" used in the demodulators just given are subject to *pseudo-demodulation*. Specifically, if both arguments of a "$" function are constants, the automated reasoning program behaves as if there were a demodulator equating that function with that pair of arguments to its appropriate constant result. (In reality, pseudo-demodulation appeals to the arithmetic and logical operations of the underlying computer to construct the constant result.) If a "$" function has an argument that is not a constant, no pseudo-demodulation occurs, and the "$" function remains in the clause.

The pseudo-demodulators for the functions $gt and $le produce the constants true and false as results. The following demodulators define the behavior of the if function (used in clauses 4 and 6) for these two constant values.

(31) EQUAL(if(isvalid(true), then(x), else(y)), x)

(32) EQUAL(if(isvalid(false), then(x), else(y)), y)

12.1.3.2 Demodulators for fetching from the state.   Having defined the meaning of the functions that represent operations in expressions, we next define the functions that obtain the operands of expressions from the program state.

The function fetch attempts to obtain the value of a program variable or array element from the program state and causes the validity of the value to be checked. Fetch returns either the value from the state or an error indication. For variables, the demodulators are

(33) EQUAL(fetch(pvar(x), lvals(x, xval, zlist)), ckfetch(pvar(x), xval))

(34) EQUAL(fetch(pvar(x), lvals(y, yval, zlist)), fetch(pvar(x), zlist))

(35) EQUAL(fetch(pvar(x), nil), fetcherror(pvar(x), notdef))

If x is the first variable in the program state, get its value and use ckfetch (discussed later) to check its validity. If x is not the first variable in the program state, look for it in the rest of the program state. If the end of the state has been reached, indicate that the variable is not defined (is not in the state).

For arrays, the corresponding demodulators are

(36) EQUAL(fetch(parr1(x, isvalid(y)), lvals(x, xval, zlist)),

ckfetch(parr1(x, isvalid(y)), fetch1(isvalid(y), xval)))

(37) EQUAL(fetch(parr1(x, isvalid(y)), lvals(w, wval, zlist)),

fetch(parr1(x, isvalid(y)), zlist))

(38) EQUAL(fetch(parr1(x, isvalid(y)), nil),

fetcherror(parr1(x, y), notdef))

Note that these demodulators for fetch will apply to fetch an array element value only if a valid subscript value has been computed—only if the subscript expression is an argument to the function isvalid. The function fetch1 retrieves a value from the list for an array by finding a matching subscript. The demodulators for it are

(39) EQUAL(fetch1(isvalid(xsubs), lels1(xsubs, xval, zlist)), xval)

(40) EQUAL(fetch1(isvalid(xsubs), lels1(wsubs, wval, zlist)),

         fetch1(isvalid(xsubs), zlist))

(41) EQUAL(fetch1(isvalid(z), nil), notinit)

(Note that the value fetched by these three demodulators is validated by the ckfetch function introduced by demodulator 36.)

Finally, we complete the definition of evaluation (eval and its related functions) by giving the demodulators for the "check function" ckfetch. This function checks whether the value fetched from the state is valid for further computation. For the present example, the value is valid provided that it is not the constant notinit, which indicates that the variable or array element was not initialized.

(42) EQUAL(ckfetch(x, notinit), fetcherror(x, notinit))

(43) EQUAL(ckfetch(x, y), isvalid(y))

We give no demodulators for the function fetcherror. As remarked earlier, the absence of the function isvalid—the presence of fetcherror—prevents further demodulators from applying to complete the evaluation of an expression. Thus, if demodulation ever introduces fetcherror, it will remain in the clause. Its presence signals that there was a problem fetching a value from the program state. And its arguments give valuable debugging information: the first argument exhibits the variable or array element that was being fetched, and the second exhibits the nature of the problem (undefined variable or uninitialized value).

The order in which the demodulators are given is significant for several groups of these demodulators. For example, demodulator 42 checks for a special case—the second argument of ckfetch being a particular constant notinit. If 42 does not apply, then 43 will, because it contains a variable in the second argument position. When the demodulators are used in order, clause 43 really means "ckfetch(x, y) is equal to (replaced by) isvalid(y), provided that the match for the variable y is not notinit". Similarly, both demodulators 33 and 34 match in the case that the first variable in the program state is the same as the variable that is the argument of pvar. Of course, we intend that the more specific demodulator, 33, be used in that case. Provided that we select the option to apply the demodulators in the order they are presented, clause 33 will, indeed, be used. (See Chapter 16 for a discussion of the question of the logical soundness of ordered demodulators.)

EXERCISE

5. Write the demodulators that would be required to handle two-dimensional arrays. For example, a demodulator similar to clause 24 would be needed to extend the eval function. Similarly, additional clauses to extend the concept of fetch to two-dimensional arrays will be necessary.

12.1.3.3 Demodulators for storing into the state. The only task remaining before we can begin symbolic execution is to define the store function, which places new values into variables in the program state. As we have seen in clause 2, store takes three arguments: the variable or array reference being assigned to, the value to be stored, and the program state. Storing simple variables is fairly straightforward.

(44) EQUAL(store(pvar(xvar), isvalid(yval), lvals(xvar, zval, wlist)),

lvals(xvar, yval, wlist))

(45) EQUAL(store(pvar(xvar), isvalid(yval), lvals(zvar, zval, zlist)),

lvals(zvar, zval, store(pvar(xvar), isvalid(yval), zlist)))

If x is the first variable in the program state, return the state updated by substituting yval for the old value of xvar. If x is not the first variable in the program state, look for it in the rest of the program state. (Another demodulator, 49, is needed to introduce the storeerror function, which gives an error indication when the end of the list is reached without matching a variable name. It can be general enough to apply to both the store of a variable and of an array. Therefore, to keep the demodulators in the correct order we give those for storing arrays first.)

Note that demodulator 44 can be applied only if the function isvalid surrounds the value to be stored, indicating that a valid result has been computed, and that it removes isvalid before placing the value in the state. It thus completes the implementation of the behavior of isvalid discussed in Sections 12.1.3.1 and 12.1.3.2.

Storage into an array element is defined similarly. The first step is to evaluate the array subscript.

(46) EQUAL(store(parr1(x, y), isvalid(w), zstate),

store(parre1(x, eval(y, zstate)), isvalid(w), zstate))

(Here, we have required that the second argument of store have the form isvalid(w) to illustrate one way to force the evaluation of the subscript expression on the left side to follow the evaluation of the right side of the assignment. In the absence of side effects, however, the order of evaluation makes no difference.) Demodulator 46 introduces the function parre1 in place of parr1 to indicate that the subscript expression has been subjected to evaluation. If it did not do so, a demodulation loop could occur if the evaluation of the subscript expression produces an invalid result—if a fetch error occurs in evaluating it. Once the subscript expression is evaluated, demodulators 47 and 48 locate the array in the lvals list as in demodulators 44 and 45 above and pass the list of elements to store1 to perform the actual storage.

(47) EQUAL(store(parre1(xarr, isvalid(yval)), isvalid(wval),

lvals(xarr, lels1(x, y, z), zlist)),

lvals(xarr, store1(isvalid(yval), isvalid(wval), lels1(x, y, z)), zlist))

(48) EQUAL(store(parrel(xarr, isvalid(yval)), isvalid(wval),

lvals(zvar, zval, zlist)),

lvals(zvar, zval, store(parrel(xarr, isvalid(yval)),

isvalid(wval), zlist)))

Finally, we can give the demodulators that treat the case where the variable or array being stored into is not found in the list representing the program state.

(49) EQUAL(store(x, isvalid(yval), nil), storeerror(x, yval, notdef, nil))

(50) EQUAL(lvals(xvar, yval, storeerror(w, vval, vtype, zlist)),

storeerror(w, vval, vtype, lvals(xvar, yval, zlist)))

Demodulator 49 introduces the check function storeerror (analogous to fetcherror) in case the variable is undefined, and demodulator 50 "bubbles" storeerror to the head of the lvals list. (The intent is that, when storeerror is at the head of the lvals list, it prevents further fetching from and storing into the list and leaves behind an indication of the cause of the error, just as does the introduction of fetcherror in place of isvalid. In order to actually stop the reasoning program when a state beginning with storeerror is produced, it is necessary to include a special unit clause, clause 56, as discussed in Section 12.1.5.)

In writing a demodulator like 50 in which the first and second arguments of EQUAL are of essentially the same complexity, we are assuming that demodulators are always applied to replace an instance of the first argument of EQUAL by an instance of the second (left-to-right demodulation). In systems where demodulators are applied in the direction that reduces the complexity of terms, we would have to define complexity so that the second argument of EQUAL in this demodulator is considered less complex than the first. We would also have to take similar care with demodulators 19 through 22 and 27 through 30.

We can summarize the effect of the demodulators for storing as follows. The result of the store function is an updated program state, or an indication of a storage error. In the case in which the first variable in the state list matches the variable being stored, demodulator 44 or 47 produces the list updated with the new value for that variable. Otherwise, demodulator 45 or 48 recursively attempts the store on the remainder of the list. If the end of the list is reached without finding the variable being stored, clause 49 applies to insert the storeerror function. The manner in which variables are used in clauses 49 and 50 makes them sufficiently general to treat properly the storeerror function for both variables and arrays—separate clauses are not required.

When an array element is being stored, clause 47 inserts the function store1 once the array has been located. The demodulators for store1 define storage into the indicated array element. They replace the old value of the element if that element is already in the list. They add that element with its (new) value if it is not already in the list.

(51) EQUAL(store1(isvalid(xsubs), isvalid(w),

   lels1(xsubs, xval, zlist)), lels1(xsubs, w, zlist))

(52) EQUAL(store1(isvalid(xsubs), isvalid(w),

   lels1(zsubs, zval, zlist)),

   lels1(zsubs, zval, store1(isvalid(xsubs), isvalid(w), zlist)))

(53) EQUAL(store1(isvalid(xsubs), isvalid(w), nil), lels1(xsubs, w, nil))

EXERCISE

6. Add the demodulators required to store into a two-dimensional array. To do so, you will need clauses, corresponding to clauses 46 through 53, that use the functions parr2, parre2, and store2, which correspond to the functions for processing one-dimensional arrays.

12.1.4 Symbolic Execution of a Correct Program Fragment

Since we now have the needed clauses and demodulators, we can submit the program fragment for symbolic execution to an automated reasoning program. To do so, we use clauses 2 through 6 and 8 through 15 as axioms (non-set-of-support clauses), clause 1 as the set-of-support clause—it, in effect, starts execution—and clauses 7 and 16 through 53 as demodulators. The demodulators are to be used in the order presented and each demodulator is to be used left to right—always substituting instances of the second argument of EQUAL for those of the first. Hyperresolution is a suitable inference rule, and we ask the automated reasoning program to stop when all possible clauses have been generated.

   The first step in the symbolic execution generates the clause

PSTATE(dows, store(pvar(k), eval(sum(i, pconst(1)),

   lvals(a, lels1(1, 7, lels1(2, 19, lels1(3, 1, lels1(4, 73, lels1(5, 6, nil)))))),

   lvals(k, notinit, nil))),

   lvals(a, lels1(1, 7, lels1(2, 19, lels1(3, 1, lels1(4, 73, lels1(5, 6, nil)))))),

   lvals(k, notinit, nil))))

from clauses 1, 2, and 3 by hyperresolution. This clause then immediately demodulates (with the application of seven demodulators) to

PSTATE(dows, lvals(a, lels1(1, 7, lels1(2, 19, lels1(3, 1, lels1(4, 73,

   lels1(5, 6, nil)))))), lvals(k, 2, nil)))

in which the value of K has been replaced by 2, reflecting the effect of the first assignment statement in the program. In addition, the statement name in PSTATE is dows, indicating that the next statement to be executed is the test at the beginning of the do-while loop.

Let us think a moment about the role of demodulation in deriving this clause. You may recall seeing in earlier chapters that demodulation is often used to perform canonicalization. Even here, demodulation plays the same role. You can think of the result of each hyperresolution step before demodulation as representing the program statement just before its execution begins. In this result, the function eval has been inserted to initiate the execution. But the canonical form of such a statement is its completely executed form—the form in which eval (and its descendants) no longer appears, but isvalid does. The demodulators given in clauses 7 and 16 through 53 define that canonical form by defining properties of eval that allow it to distribute over operations and ultimately to be removed. Once demodulation of the initial result is complete, the statement has been "executed"—more precisely, the meaning of executing it has been determined.

The remainder of the execution of the program fragment proceeds similarly. Each application of hyperresolution yields a new instance of PSTATE with the name of the next statement to be executed and the state to be used. The execution passes through the states ife1, ife2, ife3, ife4, asga, asginc, dowe, and then back to dows. This cycle repeats several times, finally terminating when state dows transfers to state exit (because $K > J$) by producing the clause

$$\text{PSTATE(exit, lvals(a, lels1(1, 19, lels1(2, 1, lels1(3, 73, lels1(4, 6,}$$
$$\text{lels1(5, 6, nil))))), lvals(k, 6, nil)))}$$

At this point, no further clauses can be generated, because no clause contains a negative PSTATE(exit,...) literal.

The fact that execution thus "reaches" statement exit indicates that for this set of test data the program fragment executed correctly. And the value of the second argument of PSTATE in the clause just given is the state containing the final values of the program variables. On the other hand, if the program fragment contains bugs that can be detected by symbolic execution, execution becomes "trapped" and does not reach statement exit, as we shall see in the next section.

12.1.5 Symbolic Execution of an Incorrect Program Fragment

If the original program fragment had contained certain bugs—certain errors—a clause containing the statement name exit would not be among those generated, and one of the error indicators (fetcherror, storeerror, or the error statement name) would be present among the generated clauses. Another indication of error is also possible—for some programs and certain errors, the symbolic execution may continue indefinitely. For example, if the do-while loop had been written with the test $K \neq J$ instead of $K \leq J$, and if the initial value of K were greater than N, then the termination condition for the loop would never be satisfied. Since symbolic execution is normally attempted on "small" examples, it is usually obvious from the number of generated clauses that the execution has "run away".

Let us now return to the example program presented at the beginning of this chapter. It is

```
INTEGER A(N)
INTEGER K
. . .

K = I
DO WHILE (K ≤ J)
  A(K − 1) = A(K)
  K = K + 1
END
. . .
```

After transforming it to include the array bounds checks and representing it using clauses, the representation is the same as that of the original fragment (clauses 3 and 8 through 15), except that clause 3 is replaced by

(54) ASSIGN(entry, pvar(k), i, dows)

If we give the altered set of clauses to an automated reasoning program to carry out the symbolic execution, it terminates almost immediately. A transition to statement name error occurs in the following generated clause.

PSTATE(error, lvals(a, lels1(1, 7, lels1(2, 19, lels1(3, 1, lels1(4, 73,

lels1(5, 6, nil)))))), lvals(k, 1, nil)))

It is easy to figure out why, simply by observing that the value of K in the state in this clause is 1, and the statement name in the PSTATE of the clause from which this one is derived is ife2. Since the statement named ife2 (defined in clause 10) protects against the subscript value K − 1 being less than 1, we conclude that the error in the program is that K − 1 < 1. A little analysis of the program would show that the statement K = I is incompatible with the use of K − 1 as a subscript, so one of them—in this case K = I—must be changed. Of course, choosing the right "test case" for the symbolic execution is important—if we had not chosen one involving the extremes of the range of I and J, we would not have detected this error.

Suppose that your finger had slipped while typing, resulting in the program

```
INTEGER A(N)
INTEGER K
. . .

K = I + 1
DO WHILE (K ≤ J)
  A(K − 1) = A(K)
  L = K + 1
END
. . .
```

After transforming the program to include array bounds checking, its clause representation would be the same as that of the example in Section 12.1.1, except that clause 14 would be replaced by

(55) ASSIGN(asginc, pvar(l), sum(pvar(k), pconst(1)), dowe)

When symbolic execution is started, it produces the clause

PSTATE(dows, storeerror(pvar(l), 3, undefined,

      lvals(a, lels1(1, 19, lels1(2, 19, lels1(3, 1, lels1(4, 73, lels1(5, 6, nil))))),

      lvals(k, 2, nil))))

This clause indicates that an error occurred during a store operation into the program state. The arguments of the storeerror function show what the error was: The program attempted to store the value 3 into the variable L, and L was undefined (not present in the state); the last argument of storeerror gives the program state at the time of the error.

With just the clauses given so far, the automated reasoning program may not stop immediately when a clause containing storeerror (or fetcherror) is generated. If you wish it to stop when a state beginning with storeerror is generated, you can include among the axioms the following clause.

(56) ¬PSTATE(x, storeerror(w, yv, yt, z))

For completeness, you might wish to include also the clause

(57) ¬PSTATE(error, z)

to catch transfer to the statement named error. Normally, these two clauses do not interact with the symbolic execution, because normally a state does not begin with the function storeerror and normally there is no transfer to statement error. When one of these errors does occur, however, including the two clauses permits the automated reasoning program to derive the empty clause, signaling "proof", and hence stopping the execution. These two clauses can be thought of as the denial of the theorem that the symbolic execution completes without a storeerror and without an array bounds error.

Stopping symbolic execution upon generation of a clause that contains the fetcherror function is somewhat more difficult than stopping upon generation of storeerror or upon transfer to error. Unlike storeerror, which occurs in "state" contexts, fetcherror occurs in "value" contexts—wherever the function isvalid can occur. These contexts appear in many demodulators. If you wish to stop execution in the state in which a fetcherror is generated, you first must write a set of demodulators for these contexts that "bubble" fetcherror to be the value of the entire expression. Then you must write several clauses analogous to 56 that catch the appearance of fetcherror in place of isvalid and permit derivation of the empty clause.

As a final example of symbolic execution of programs containing bugs, consider the following program.

```
INTEGER A(N)
INTEGER K
. . .

K = I + 1
DO WHILE (K ≤ J)
   A(K) = A(K − 1)
   K = K + 1
END
. . .
```

After transformation to include array bounds checking, its representation differs from that given in Section 12.1.2 only in the order of the subscript range checks (which is not significant) and in clause 13, which is replaced by

(58) ASSIGN(asga, parr1(a, pvar(k)), parr1(a, diff(pvar(k), pconst(1))), asginc)

The symbolic execution of this program produces no overt indication of an error. It reaches state exit with the clause

PSTATE(exit, lvals(a, lels1(1, 7, lels1(2, 7, lels1(3, 7, lels1(4, 7,
     lels1(5, 7, nil))))), lvals(k, 6, nil)))

However, if we examine the final state, we might think it odd that one value, 7, is propagated throughout the array. From this observation, we might realize that the program contains two complementary (with respect to this test) errors—interchange of the subscripts of A. This example clearly illustrates that your interpretation of the results of a symbolic execution is important in locating errors, and that symbolic execution offers no guarantee that an error will be flagged. If you wish to be assured of finding such errors, you must attempt a proof of correctness for the program.

12.2 Proving Programs Correct

Symbolic execution is, of course, very useful when it finds, and enables us to correct, bugs in a program. Suppose, however, that we run some symbolic executions on a program and find no bugs. How justified are we in concluding that the program is correct?

Not very, as it turns out. The usefulness of symbolic execution in demonstrating correctness is limited by one's ability to choose "representative" test data, just as is ordinary testing of a program. For example, in the first erroneous version of the program discussed in Section 12.1.5, if we had chosen the initial value of I to be 2 instead of 1 in the test data, the symbolic execution would have terminated normally, with no indication of an error. The clause produced using this set of test data is

PSTATE(exit, lvals(a, lels1(1, 19, lels1(2, 1, lels1(3, 73, lels1(4, 6,

lels1(5, 6, nil))))), lvals(k, 6, nil)))

It appears to be a satisfactory result, and in fact it is identical to that produced from the symbolic execution of the correct program on a different set of test data (Section 12.1.4). It would take very careful analysis to learn from this test that there are any bugs in the program. Is there a way to use automated reasoning that avoids the limitations of testing?

The answer is to use the power of universally quantified variables in clauses to prove that the program will execute correctly for all admissible input data—for all data that satisfy the program's input assumptions. As you might already have guessed, proving a program correct is not so easy as it sounds. In order to attempt to prove a program correct, we need a *specification* of its intended meaning. Any proof of correctness for the program is *relative* to this specification—it consists of showing that the program does have the specified behavior.

Producing a suitable specification for a program is difficult for several reasons. First, finding a way to capture the meaning of a program that is independent of the program itself can be difficult. For a function that computes the square root, an excellent specification is

$\neg$GE(x, 0) | PROD(sqrt(x), sqrt(x), x)

where GE is intended to mean "greater than or equal to" and PROD is intended to mean "product" (possibly carried out only to some finite precision). This specification is almost certainly different from the method that will be used to compute the square root in the program, so it provides a very good basis for verifying the program. Such specifications tend to be rare, however.

Second, convincing yourself that a specification really captures the intended meaning of the program, and that it does not admit unintended interpretations, can be difficult. For a program that sorts an array A of N elements, "For every x, if x is between 1 and $N - 1$, $A(x) \leq A(x + 1)$" might seem to be an excellent specification. Unfortunately, the program that always sets the x-th element of A to x, regardless of the original contents of A, satisfies this specification! For a program considered in isolation, this problem of ensuring the *completeness* of the specification requires a great deal of thought. Fortunately, when the program is a submodule of a larger piece of software, incompleteness of its specification usually shows up because the specification is not strong enough to prove the required properties of the larger piece of software.

Most program specifications tend to be complicated, even when the programs themselves appear to be simple. For example, a specification for the program fragment given in Section 12.1.1 is "For every program state z1, if at the beginning of this fragment the state is z1 and z1 contains the variables used in the fragment and $1 \leq I$ and $I \leq N$ and $1 \leq J$ and $J \leq N$, then there exists a program state z2 containing the variables used in this fragment and for every x, if $1 \leq x$ and $x < I$, then A(x) fetched from z2 is equal to A(x) fetched from z1, and if $I \leq x$ and $x < J$, then A(x) fetched from z2 is equal to A(x + 1) fetched from z1, and if $J \leq x$ and $x \leq N$, then A(x) fetched from z2 is equal to A(x) fetched from z1". Not only is this specification complicated, but also it does not differ much from what the statements of the program itself say.

When these difficulties can be overcome, however, a proof of correctness does provide the advantage that the program is guaranteed to meet its specifications for all input data that satisfy its input assumptions. In the following sections you will see how to construct such a proof for a very simple example.

12.2.1 A Simple Program and Its Specification

To illustrate the ideas involved in proving a program correct, let us consider the following simple program.

```
INTEGER K, S
ASSUME (N ≥ 0)
K = 0
S = 0
DO WHILE (K < N)
   K = K + 1
   S = S + 2
END
ASSERT (S = 2 × N)
```

The ASSUME and ASSERT statements give the input assumptions and the output specification for this program in notation similar to that used in the program. Stated more formally, we wish to prove:

> For every initial state zentry, there exists a final state exit such that if zentry is valid (if it contains the program variables) and on entry to the program the program parameter N evaluated in the state zentry is greater than or equal to zero, then on exit from the program the variable S evaluated in the state exit is equal to $2 \times N$ evaluated in the state exit (or in the state zentry, since N does not change).

As you have seen in earlier chapters, to have the automated reasoning program search for a proof, we have it search for a proof by contradiction. Doing so requires that we add the denial of the theorem to the set of support. The set of support thus consists of the clauses that correspond to the special hypothesis of the theorem and those that correspond to assuming the conclusion false. The clauses are

(59) PSTATE(entry, lvals(k, notinit, lvals(s, notinit, nil)))

(60) ¬PSTATE(entry, zentry)

   | EQUAL(eval(ge(pparam(n), pconst(0)), zentry), isvalid(true))

(61) ¬PSTATE(exit, zexit)

   | ¬EQUAL(eval(pvar(s), zexit), eval(prod(pconst(2), pparam(n)), zexit))

The first says that the program is entered at statement entry with a valid state (one that contains the program variables K and S). The second (the input assumption) says that if the program is entered with any state, then the program parameter N is greater than or equal to 0. The third (the denial of the conclusion) says that, for every state, if the program is at statement exit in that state, then S evaluated in that state is not equal to $2 \times N$ evaluated in that state.

    Since the program contains a loop, we cannot prove the theorem directly. The program must be divided into segments of straight-line code, and special techniques are needed to deal with the loop, as we shall see shortly. To begin, we consider proof of correctness for straight-line code.

12.2.2 Proving the Correctness of Straight-Line Code

The initial statements of the example program, up to the beginning of the do-while loop, provide an example of straight-line code.

   K = 0
   S = 0

In order to conduct a proof of correctness, we use the same representation for programs as we did for symbolic execution. Thus, the preceding statements can be represented by the following clauses.

(62) ASSIGN(entry, pvar(k), pconst(0), asgse)

(63) ASSIGN(asgse, pvar(s), pconst(0), dows)

Here dows is the statement name given to the statement that follows S = 0, the do-while statement. With an eye toward proving the correctness of the entire program, we choose the following clauses as the special hypothesis and the denial of the correctness theorem for this code.

(64) PSTATE(entry, lvals(k, notinit, lvals(s, notinit, nil)))

(65) ¬PSTATE(entry, zentry)

   | EQUAL(eval(ge(pparam(n), pconst(0)), zentry), isvalid(true))

(66) ¬PSTATE(dows, zexit)

| ¬EQUAL(eval(pvar(k), zexit), eval(pconst(0), zexit))

| ¬EQUAL(eval(ge(pparam(n), pconst(0)), zexit), isvalid(true))

| ¬EQUAL(eval(ge(pparam(n), pvar(k)), zexit), isvalid(true))

| ¬EQUAL(eval(pvar(s), zexit), eval(prod(pconst(2), pvar(k)), zexit))

The first two clauses are the special hypothesis for the theorem and are the same as the special hypothesis for the correctness theorem for the entire program. Clause 66 denies (among other things) that we arrive at the do-while statement dows after executing the straight-line code and that S has a value that is consistent with its representing twice the value of K.

You may ask: Why prove these particular facts? Why not prove, instead, that K = 0 and S = 0? The answer is that the theorem represented by clauses 64 through 66 is more useful in continuing the proof of the entire program than is the theorem that K = 0 and S = 0. This point illustrates a general fact about proving the correctness of programs and fragments of programs—what you need to prove depends not solely on the program itself but also on the larger context in which that program is to be used.

To prove this theorem, we use the set of axioms represented by clauses 62 and 63 together with clauses 2, 4, and 5 developed in Section 12.1.2 and the following axioms connecting the relational operators treated as functions and the values true and false. (It is convenient to treat the relational operators as functions rather than as predicates so that they can be used in expressions that are evaluated by the demodulators for the function eval. Since the operator " = " is not used that way in this example, it is not necessary to treat it so.)

(67) ¬EQUAL(x, isvalid(true)) | ¬EQUAL(x, isvalid(false))

(68) ¬EQUAL(isvalid($ge(x, y)), isvalid(true))

| EQUAL(isvalid($gt(x, y)), isvalid(true))

| EQUAL(isvalid(x), isvalid(y))

(69) ¬EQUAL(isvalid($gt(x, y)), isvalid(true))

| EQUAL(isvalid($ge(x, $sum(y, 1))), isvalid(true))

(70) EQUAL(x, x)

The first of these clauses says that if an expression demodulates to isvalid(true), then it does not demodulate to isvalid(false), and conversely. The second relates $ge to $gt and EQUAL. The third says that if x > y, then x ≥ y + 1; it is, of course, valid only if x and y are integers, as they are in this program. The fourth is the reflexivity axiom for EQUAL. It plays a vital role in obtaining a contradiction, because demodulation eventually brings the evaluation of S and of $2 \times K$ to the same expression in the negative equality literal, and the use of axiom 70 then completes the proof. (Not all of these additional axioms are used in the proof of the straight-line code; some are used only in the subproofs of this program given in the following sections.)

For demodulators, we can use most of the clauses developed in Section 12.1.3, namely, 19 through 53, plus the following additional ones that define new functions used in this program.

(71) EQUAL(eval(prod(x, y), zstate), prod(eval(x, zstate), eval(y, zstate)))

(72) EQUAL(eval(ge(x, y), zstate), ge(eval(x, zstate), eval(y, zstate)))

(73) EQUAL(prod(isvalid(x), isvalid(y)), isvalid($prod(x, y)))

(74) EQUAL(ge(isvalid(x), isvalid(y)), isvalid($ge(x, y)))

(75) EQUAL($prod(x, $sum(y, z)), $sum($prod(x, y), $prod(x, z)))

(76) EQUAL($prod(x, 1), x)

Demodulators 71 through 74 are modeled on ones in the original set for similar functions. Their order in the set of demodulators is not important, but they could be placed with their corresponding models. Demodulator 75 states that

$$x(y + z) = xy + xz$$

while 76 says that 1 is a right identity for product. Of course, additional demodulators such as these could be included, but these suffice for the proof of this program.

Using an automated reasoning program, the proof can be carried out using unit resolution as the inference rule. (Unit resolution requires one of the two clauses to be a unit clause, and places no requirement on the deduced clause.) Unit resolution is a good rule because the process of simulating the execution of the statements in the program begins with the unit clause 59, and each successive statement "execution" generates another unit clause involving the predicate PSTATE. For this purpose hyperresolution would also suffice, since the resulting unit clause is positive. Using a rule like unit resolution becomes necessary, however, when we arrive at the statement dows, represented by the generated clause

PSTATE(dows, lvals(k, 0, lvals(s, 0, nil)))

It must resolve with clause 66—the denial of the theorem—in order to instantiate the state variable zexit in that clause, which then permits demodulation to simplify the terms in the four negative equality literals. Hyperresolution will not deduce this clause, because the clause has no positive literals in the conclusion. If the clause is not deduced, the simplifications are not made. If the simplifications are not made, this clause cannot participate in hyperresolution, because the unsimplified equality literals do not permit the required unification to complete. Thus the proof is blocked.

Back demodulation—the process of applying a newly deduced demodulator to clauses that already exist—also plays an important role in this proof. Several new equality units are deduced in the course of the proof. They must be allowed to simplify and canonicalize clauses that have already been derived. Otherwise, the success of the proof would depend on the order in which the new equalities are derived.

When a contradiction is obtained, we know that the given program, if started in the entry state with $N \geq 0$, will arrive at the start of the do-while loop with $K = 0, N \geq 0, N \geq K$ and $S = 2 \times K$. Why this result is useful will become clear in the section after the following one.

12.2.3 Proving the Correctness of Conditional Statements

Although the example program given in Section 12.2.1 does not contain any conditional statements, it is worthwhile considering how to prove the correctness of a program consisting of straight-line code and conditional statements. A program with a conditional statement that is closely related to the one in Section 12.2.1 is

```
INTEGER K,S
ASSUME (N ≥ 0 & N ≤ 1)
S = 0
IF (N > 0) THEN
   S = S + 2
END
ASSERT (S = 2 × N)
```

We could easily prove that if $N = 0$, then $S = 0$ on exit, and if $N = 1$, then $S = 2$ on exit. However, the ASSERT statement in the given program suggests a more interesting theorem, namely,

For every N, if $N \geq 0$ and $N \leq 1$, then on exit $S = 2 \times N$.

This statement has the important property that *it is true no matter by what path control reaches the exit of the program*—if $N = 0$, then the if-then statement is not executed, and $S = 0 = 2 \times N$ at the exit, while if $N = 1$, the if-then is executed and $S = 2 = 2 \times N$ at the exit. Statements of this type are called *invariants* and they have exactly the property that they are always true at a particular point in the program, regardless of by what path or how many times control reaches that point. Thus, invariants can be used in proving the correctness of programs involving conditional statements. Moreover, they play a fundamental role in proving the correctness of programs containing loops.

The special hypothesis for the correctness theorem for this program, which was just stated informally, is

(77) PSTATE(entry, lvals(s, notinit, nil))

(78) ¬PSTATE(entry, zstate)

| EQUAL(eval(ge(pparam(n), pconst(0)), zstate), isvalid(true))

(79) ¬PSTATE(entry, zstate)

| EQUAL(eval(le(pparam(n), pconst(1)), zstate), isvalid(true))

The denial of the correctness theorem is

(80) ¬PSTATE(exit, zexit)

| ¬EQUAL(eval(pvar(s), zexit), eval(prod(pconst(2), pparam(n)), zexit))

In order to prove this theorem, the proof must be divided into two cases, corresponding to the two execution paths through this program. To do so, we use the condition in the if-then statement, N > 0, to split the input assumptions into two mutually exclusive and mutually exhaustive classes, represented by the following two clauses.

(81) ¬PSTATE(entry, zstate)

| EQUAL(eval(gt(pparam(n), pconst(0)), zstate), isvalid(true))

(82) ¬PSTATE(entry, zstate)

| EQUAL(eval(le(pparam(n), pconst(0)), zstate), isvalid(true))

For one proof, take as the set of support clauses 77 through 80 together with 81, and for the other, take as the set of support clauses 77 through 80 and 82. Clauses such as 81 and 82 are often called *forcing clauses* because they "force" the program to follow one path or the other. In this case, clause 81 forces the program to execute the statements in the body of the if-then statement, while 82 forces it to skip the body of the if-then statement.

To carry out the two proofs, we can use as axioms the three clauses that describe the program given in this section, together with clauses 2, 4, 5, 67 through 70 and two additional clauses. One of these defines the execution of the if-then statement and is analogous to clause 4. The other relates the functions ge and le and the predicate EQUAL. For demodulators we use the same set as in Section 12.2.2.

Unit resolution is a suitable inference rule, and back demodulation should be used. When we have proved the two cases, we know that the theorem holds and the program is correct relative to that specification.

Some observations about the use of forcing clauses in practice can be made. The introduction of forcing clauses corresponds to performing the proof by case analysis. As in case analysis, it is important that the chosen forcing clauses exhaust all possibilities, for, if they do not, the proof will not be valid. In practice, choosing an exhaustive set of forcing clauses is not a problem, because the information necessary for the split is contained in the if-condition of each if-then statement.

If a program contains a long sequence of straight-line code with several conditional statements in it, the number of forcing clauses (cases) needed grows exponentially in the number of conditional statements. In such cases, you can partition the program into segments each of which contains only one conditional statement by introducing invariants between the conditional statements. Then you can prove each segment separately. Provided that you can find invariants of the type illustrated in this section—ones that state something that is true of both paths rather than just restating the two alternatives—this approach will result in simpler proofs.

With this brief introduction to invariants and forcing clauses, we can return to the task of proving the correctness of the loop in the example program given in Section 12.2.1.

EXERCISES

7. We have seen how clause 2 is used to represent the effects of an assignment statement, and how clause 4 represents the do-while statement. Give the corresponding clause(s) for an if-then statement.

8. Give the axioms that correspond to the executable statements in the program at the beginning of this section.

9. As mentioned earlier, to prove the program with a conditional statement, you will need a lemma relating the functions ge and le to the predicate EQUAL. Supply the required lemma, and give proofs of both cases.

10. Develop the axioms required for an

```
IF (condition) THEN
    statements
ELSE
    statements
END
```
construct.

12.2.4 Proving the Correctness of a Program Loop

In Section 12.2.2, we proved that the example program of Section 12.2.1 is correct up to the beginning of the do-while loop. Now we examine how to show that the do-while loop is correct regardless of the number of times it is executed. Two ideas serve as the foundation for the method of proving loops correct. One is the idea of invariant—in this case the *loop invariant*—that we met in Section 12.2.3. The other is an idea that in its practical application is similar to case analysis, although it is theoretically much more powerful—the principle of *mathematical induction*.

12.2.4.1 Loop invariants.   A loop invariant is a logical statement about a program loop that is, like any invariant, always true—true at the beginning of the body of the loop and again true after the body is executed. At first, the idea of finding such a statement may seem absurd. After all, the purpose of the loop is to compute something, so how can it be that nothing changes? The point is, however, that the statements in the body of a loop do change some things, but then they change other things (often by incrementing the loop variable) so that the invariant is again true for the next execution of the statements of the body.

You can think of a loop invariant as being like watching a person climbing a set of stairs—watching that person through a movable window that gives a view of just one step. You see the person standing on the step that is in view. He raises his leg and moves up out of view onto the next step. Then the window moves up one step, and suddenly everything looks just as it did to begin with—you see the person standing on the step that is in view. Nevertheless, the climber is making progress up the steps.

This idea of loop invariant—the moving window—underlies all correctly written program loops, whether the programmer has stated the invariant explicitly or not. The body of a program loop cannot be considered to have executed successfully unless it has properly set things up for its next execution. Sometimes, however, finding a suitable loop invariant can be difficult.

For the example program, the loop invariant is given by the assert statements that appear in the following fragment of the program.

```
DO WHILE (K < N)
   ASSERT (S = 2 × K)
   K = K + 1
   S = S + 2
   ASSERT (S = 2 × K)
END
```

It is now clear that each execution of the loop entails incrementing the variable K and then adjusting the value of S so that the invariant is again true.

12.2.4.2 Mathematical induction.   It is the principle of mathematical induction that permits use of the invariant to construct a proof that the loop is correct. Induction can also be thought of in terms of the set of stairs analogy. For climbing stairs, induction says: If we are able to show that the climber can step onto the bottom step, and if we can show that if the climber is on some intermediate step then he can climb to the next one, then we can validly conclude that the climber can climb every step. Of course, making this conclusion depends on the invariant that all the steps are exactly alike. (In some proofs, it may be necessary to use the "strong" form of mathematical induction. Instead of assuming that the climber is on some intermediate step to show that he can climb to the next one, strong induction permits assuming that he was able to climb all preceding steps. This distinction is rather subtle.)

In mathematics, induction is usually used to show that something is true of an infinite set of objects—an infinitely long set of stairs. In programming as well as in stair climbing, we are usually interested in a finite process—in showing that the loop or the climb terminates. We shall return to this topic a little later.

Stated a bit more formally, the principle of mathematical induction says the following. Suppose that we have any statement, $S(n)$, that is a function of an integer n. Then if we can prove

$S(m)$ for m = 1 (or m = 0, or any other fixed integer value)

and if we can also prove

if $n \geq m$ and $S(n)$ then $S(n + 1)$

then we can conclude that $S(n)$ is true *for all n* greater than or equal to m. The first step in an induction proof is called the *ground case*, while the second is called the *induction step*. Incidentally, most automated reasoning programs do not contain any inference rule corresponding to mathematical induction—they simply permit you to prove the ground case and the induction step, whereupon you can conclude that the theorem you are proving by induction is valid. A few special-purpose automated reasoning programs do have built-in induction, however.

12.2.4.3 Correctness of the loop.
Loop invariants and mathematical induction provide the basis for proving the correctness of the loop in the example program. The induction is on the loop variable K, and we wish to prove that if $S = 2 \times K$ when the program is at the beginning of the loop the first time (with K = 0), then $S = 2 \times K$ at the beginning of the loop for all values of $K \geq 0$.

First consider proving the ground case. Recall that we gave the do-while statement the name dows. The ground case requires proving that when the program reaches statement dows in a valid state, K = 0 and $S = 2 \times K$, where all variables are evaluated in that state. Now we see why the particular theorem proved in Section 12.2.2 is useful—it guarantees both of these facts, plus two others that are useful in proving the entire program correct. Thus we have proved the ground case of the induction for this loop in Section 12.2.2. In general, to prove a program loop correct, we first must prove that the straight line code preceding it correctly *initializes* the loop, which corresponds to proving the ground case of the induction.

Next we prove the induction step. First we need the clauses for the statements in the loop. They are

(83) DOWHILE(dows, gt(pparam(n), pvar(k)), asgk, exit)

(84) ASSIGN(asgk, pvar(k), sum(pvar(k), pconst(1)), asgs)

(85) ASSIGN(asgs, pvar(s), sum(pvar(s), pconst(2)), dowe)

To prove the induction step, we only need to go around the loop once. Therefore, we "cut" the loop—omit the clause that permits the transition from the END statement back to the top of the loop. It is convenient to make the cut between statements dowe and dows because the transition from dowe to dows does not alter the state. Thus when we state the denial of the theorem for the inductive step, the hypothesis, corresponding to "if $S(n)$" in the description of induction, is stated relative to statement dows. The conclusion, corresponding to "then $S(n + 1)$", is stated relative to statement dowe. The two statements are effectively equivalent, and cutting the loop avoids the ambiguity of having two different program states in statement dows.

The special hypothesis and the denial of the theorem for the induction step are represented by the clauses

(86) PSTATE(dows, lvals(k, kval, lvals(s, sval, nil)))

(87) ¬PSTATE(dows, zstate)

    | EQUAL(eval(ge(pparam(n), pconst(0)), zstate), isvalid(true))

(88) ¬PSTATE(dows, zstate)

    | EQUAL(eval(gt(pparam(n), pvar(k)), zstate), isvalid(true))

(89) ¬PSTATE(dows, zstate)

    | EQUAL(eval(pvar(s), zstate), eval(prod(pconst(2), pvar(k)), zstate))

(90) ¬PSTATE(dowe, zexit)

    | ¬EQUAL(eval(ge(pparam(n), pconst(0)), zexit), isvalid(true))

    | ¬EQUAL(eval(ge(pparam(n), pvar(k)), zexit), isvalid(true))

    | ¬EQUAL(eval(pvar(s), zexit), eval(prod(pconst(2), pvar(k)), zexit))

The last of these is the denial of the theorem. It contains not only the denial necessary for the induction ($S \neq 2 \times K$), but also the denials of two other facts useful in proving the entire program correct. Notice clause 88; it is a *forcing clause* similar to those we encountered in Section 12.2.3. It forces execution to enter the body of the loop for the proof of the inductive step. We shall see the use of its logical complement in the following section.

The proof of the induction step uses the same axioms (except for the substitution of clauses 83 through 85 for clauses 62 and 63), demodulators, and inference rules used in Section 12.2.2. Once it has been proved, the principle of induction permits concluding that the correctness theorem for the loop is valid. In addition, the other literals in the denial of the ground case and in the induction step permit concluding that the loop preserves N.

12.2.5 Proving Correctness on Exit from the Loop

The only subproof now remaining is to show that when the loop terminates—when N > K is no longer true—the program produces the correct value, namely, S = 2 × N. In this example, no actual statements intervene between the end of the loop and the end of the program. Thus clause 83, which specifies the transfer from statement dows to statement exit when the do-while loop test is false, is the only axiom needed. The set of support clauses—the special hypothesis and the denial of the correctness of the program from the loop to the end—are

(91)　PSTATE(dows, lvals(k, kval, lvals(s, sval, nil)))

(92)　¬PSTATE(dows, zstate)

　　　| EQUAL(eval(ge(pparam(n), pconst(0)), zstate), isvalid(true))

(93)　¬PSTATE(dows, zstate)

　　　| EQUAL(eval(ge(pparam(n), pvar(k)), zstate), isvalid(true))

(94)　¬PSTATE(dows, zstate)

　　　| EQUAL(eval(pvar(s), zstate), eval(prod(pconst(2), pvar(k)), zstate))

(95)　¬PSTATE(dows, zstate)

　　　| ¬EQUAL(eval(gt(pparam(n), pvar(k)), zstate), isvalid(true))

(96)　¬PSTATE(exit, zexit)

　　　| ¬EQUAL(eval(pvar(s), zexit), eval(prod(pconst(2), pparam(n)), zexit))

Clauses 91 through 95 represent the special hypotheses. All but one of them are conclusions of the correctness theorem for the loop (clause 90). The exception is clause 95. It is a forcing clause that forces the program to exit the loop, the logical complement of clause 88 used in Section 12.2.4 to force execution to enter the loop.

In contrast to the introduction of a pair of forcing clauses for the conditional statement in Section 12.2.3, the introduction of clause 95 represents an additional hypothesis that we are making. (To see that it really is an additional hypothesis, consider the given program with the statement K = K + 1 omitted from the loop body. We could still prove the part of the conclusion of the theorem that states that N ≥ K, but doing so certainly does not imply that at some point N = K.) We did not prove in Section 12.2.4 that eventually K will not be less than N. Although it is "obviously" true for this loop, in general the problem of proving that a loop does *terminate* is a subtle one. The general approach is to try to find a *well-founded ordering*—some quantity that decreases each time the loop is executed and that has a lower bound that is related to the termination test for the loop. (In this example, the successive values of N − K are a well-founded ordering, since they decrease with each execution of the loop and the loop terminates when N − K reaches 0.) Mathematical induction can also be extended to induction over well-founded orderings by replacing the set of integers by the ordering. This extension is useful in proving programs correct, but we shall not discuss it further here.

In this discussion, we shall be content with simply adding the hypothesis that the loop terminates, without formally proving it. Doing so corresponds to proving what is technically called the *partial correctness* (in contrast to *total correctness*) of the program. The term "partial correctness" is perhaps misleading. It does not mean that the program is only "partly correct". Rather, it means that the program has been proved to produce the (completely) correct result, *if it ever stops executing*—if it ever reaches the exit state. So a partially correct program is guaranteed either to produce the correct result or to execute forever. If we prove the total correctness of a program, on the other hand, we know that it produces the correct result and that it does always terminate.

Clause 96 represents the denial of the conclusion of the theorem. The theorem is proved with the same axioms (suitably changed), demodulators, and inference rules used in the preceding sections.

12.2.6 Correctness of the Program

To see that the program is correct—that we have proved the theorem stated in Section 12.2.1—let us review the hypotheses and conclusions of the subproofs, and the forcing hypotheses. In Section 12.2.2, we proved a theorem about the initial segment of straight-line code, subject only to the hypotheses that the program starts with a valid state and that N ≥ 0. In Section 12.2.4, we proved a theorem about the execution of the loop. Its hypotheses are all conclusions of the theorem for the straight-line code, except for the addition of the forcing clause N > K, which forces execution into the loop. That forcing clause is consistent with the part of the conclusion of the theorem for the straight-line code that says that N ≥ K. Thus the two theorems "fit together"—having proved that if P then Q and if Q' then R (where Q implies Q'), we can conclude if P then R. In a similar vein, in Section 12.2.5 we proved a theorem about the correctness of the exit from the loop. Its hypotheses are all conclusions of the theorem for the execution of the loop, except for the forcing clause that says N ≤ K, which is consistent with the part of the conclusion that says $N \geq K$. Thus these two theorems again fit together, with the additional hypothesis that the loop terminates. The conclusion of the exit theorem is the conclusion of the correctness theorem for the program, so we have proved that the program is correct provided that the loop is entered and terminates.

There is another path through the program. It is taken when $N = 0$. To see that we have proved correctness for this case, we must see if the straight-line code theorem and the exit theorem fit together. All of the hypotheses of the exit theorem are conclusions of the straight-line theorem, except for the forcing clause $N \leq K$, which is again consistent with the conclusion $N \geq K$. Thus we can conclude that the program is correct if the loop is not entered.

Putting these two results together, we can conclude that the program is correct if it is entered with $N \geq 0$ and if the loop terminates, which is what we set out to prove.

This example, then, illustrates the general approach to proving a program correct, which consists of the following steps.

1. Obtain or formulate the specification and input assumptions for the program.
2. Use invariants to divide the program into segments of straight-line code, possibly containing conditional statements, and to cut loop bodies so that they consist of sequences of straight-line, and possibly conditional, code.
3. Formulate and prove the relevant theorems for each code segment and the inductions for the loops.
4. Verify that the conclusions and hypotheses of adjacent subtheorems match along all possible execution paths, identifying hypotheses added to force termination (or confirming that termination has been proved).
5. Conclude that the program has been proved partially (or totally) correct.

What this process amounts to on larger and more complicated programs is the following.

> By using invariants, we divide the program into blocks of code whose correctness theorems are reasonably easy to prove.
>
> We prove the correctness theorems for the "innermost" blocks of code—the innermost loop bodies and conditional statement bodies.
>
> We replace these blocks by their theorems.
>
> We then repeat the preceding two steps until the innermost block is the entire program itself, whereupon the proof is complete.

If the program contains calls to procedures—functions and subroutines—they can be treated in the same way as if they were blocks of code: we prove their correctness theorems and then replace them by their theorems. When functions with side effects, which change the program state, are involved, this replacement is somewhat complicated. As mentioned in Section 12.1.2.3, it may be simplest in this case to transform the program, in a manner similar to that used to insert the array bounds checks in Section 12.1.2.4, so that each such function call occurs in an assignment statement by itself. Thus if we have a program

$$A = B + F(X) \times C$$

we would transform it to

$$TEMP = F(X)$$
$$A = B + TEMP \times C$$

in which it is easier to take account of the altered program state produced by the function F.

EXERCISE

11. Consider the following program segment.

```
INTEGER K, S
ASSUME (N ≥ 0)
K = 0
S = 0
DO WHILE (K < N)
   K = K + 1
   S = S + K
END
ASSERT (S = (N × (N + 1)/2))
```

Show how the proof that this program segment works can be reduced to showing that

$$\frac{K(K + 1)}{2} + K + 1 = \frac{(K + 1)((K + 1) + 1)}{2}$$

Specifically, give the details of how to prove that this program segment works. However, when you reach the point where the preceding identity must be established, you are not being asked to supply the axioms required to prove it.

12.2.7 Proving the Correctness of Programs Involving Arrays

The use of arrays in a program adds a certain amount of complexity to the task of proving it correct. Discussing the proof of the correctness of the example program given in Section 12.1.1 would take too long. Instead, we consider a much briefer example, a program that simply sets one element of an array to twice another.

```
INTEGER A(N)
INTEGER K, J
ASSUME (1 ≤ K & K ≤ N & 1 ≤ J & J ≤ N)
A(K) = 2 × A(J)
ASSERT (A(K) = 2 × A(J)_entry)
```

Here the subscript "entry" in the second ASSERT denotes the value of A(J) taken from the state on entry to the program. The axiom for this program is

(97) ASSIGN(entry, parr1(a, pvar(k)), prod(pconst(2), parr1(a, pvar(j))), exit)

The set of support clauses are

(98) PSTATE(entry, lvals(a, lels(jval, akval, nil),

lvals(k, kval, lvals(j, jval, nil))))

(99) ¬PSTATE(entry, zentry)

| EQUAL(eval(ge(pvar(k), pconst(1)), zentry), isvalid(true))

(100) ¬PSTATE(entry, zentry)

| EQUAL(eval(ge(pparam(n), pvar(k)), zentry), isvalid(true))

(101) ¬PSTATE(entry, zentry)

| EQUAL(eval(ge(pvar(j), pconst(1)), zentry), isvalid(true))

(102) ¬PSTATE(entry, zentry)

| EQUAL(eval(ge(pparam(n), pvar(j)), zentry), isvalid(true))

(103) ¬PSTATE(exit, zexit)

| ¬PSTATE(entry, zentry)

| ¬EQUAL(eval(parr1(a, pvar(k)), zexit),

eval(prod(pconst(2), parr1(a, pvar(j))), zentry))

Notice how the denial is translated, using state zentry for the reference to the value that A(J) had on entry to the program, and notice how zentry is bound to the value of the initial state by including the literal ¬PSTATE(entry, zentry). Using this set of support and the by-now-familiar axioms and demodulators from Section 12.2.2, with clause 97 replacing the program-specific axioms, we obtain a proof by contradiction.

Now suppose that we decide to augment the theorem to prove that A(J) remains unchanged. Then we replace clause 103 by

(104) ¬PSTATE(exit, zexit) | ¬PSTATE(entry, zentry)

| ¬EQUAL(eval(parr1(a, pvar(k)), zexit),

eval(prod(pconst(2), parr1(a, pvar(j))), zentry))

| ¬EQUAL(eval(parr1(a, pvar(j)), zexit), eval(parr1(a, pvar(j)), zentry))

Unfortunately, we also get a proof for this statement—"unfortunately" because if it happens that K = J, it is not a theorem!

What goes wrong? The problem is that when we wrote demodulator 51 for storing into an array element, we assumed that locating the correct array element to store into in the lels1 list could be done by exactly matching the subscript value occurring in the program (the second argument to the parr1 function). And conversely, we assumed that if no such exact match occurred, then a new element of the array was being stored. These assumptions are justified for symbolic execution, because all subscript values (which effectively are names for array elements) are integers. The integers are a unique canonical form for such values, so an identity test is sound.

However, proofs of correctness involve symbolic values for subscripts, and for them there is no unique canonical form to use for the identity test. In its absence, demodulator 51 fails to apply because kval does not exactly match jval, so the array elements are considered to differ, even though jval could be equal to kval. Instead, demodulator 52 applies, in effect tacitly assuming that $K \neq J$. In the treatment given in this chapter, demodulation is employed in part procedurally. The nature of the procedure permits a tacit assumption to be made by the program, an assumption that is not desirable. Such potential unsoundness when using demodulation procedurally is discussed in Chapter 16.

Note however, that none of the proofs in Sections 12.2.2 through 12.2.6 are invalidated by these potentially unsound demodulators, because none of these proofs used arrays.

There are at least two ways to overcome this problem. We could replace the offending demodulators by "conditional demodulators"—axioms that require proving that two subscript values are equal or unequal before the demodulator can be applied. A simpler approach is just to recognize that we must do a case analysis for the theorem. Two cases are possible, $K = J$ and $K \neq J$. For the statement in clause 103, we therefore attempt two proofs, one with each of the following forcing clauses.

(105) ¬PSTATE(entry, zentry)

    | ¬EQUAL(eval(pvar(k), zentry), eval(pvar(j), zentry))

(106) ¬PSTATE(entry, zentry)

    | EQUAL(eval(pvar(k), zentry), eval(pvar(j), zentry))

The proof using 105 goes through as before. Among the generated clauses is the one giving the final state of the program, in which the array element A(K) has been stored.

PSTATE(exit, lvals(a, lels1(jval, akval, lels1(kval, \$prod(2, akval), nil)),
    lvals(k, kval, lvals(j, jval, nil)))))

On the other hand, the proof using clause 106 eventually terminates without contradiction, having exhausted the set of support clauses. The final state of the program is

> PSTATE(exit, lvals(a, lels1(jval, $prod(2, akval), nil),
>   lvals(k, kval, lvals, (j, jval, nil)))))

Examination of this clause reveals that element jval of array A has been altered.

This example thus sounds a cautionary note: *When proving programs involving arrays with symbolic indices, or mixed symbolic and numeric indices, we must properly account for overlapping index values by doing case splitting.* The necessary case analysis does not have to be particularly imaginative, for including a case that specifies that two index values are equal when other facts prevent them from being equal does not prevent finding a contradiction. Of course, the preferred approach is to automate such case analyses without relying on the programmer to supply the needed information.

12.3 Abstract Programming and High-Level Program Proofs

Reflecting on the program proofs given in Section 12.2, we can hardly escape being struck by two factors. First, these program specifications and proofs are extremely detailed and complicated relative to the simplicity of the programs involved. It is hard to imagine writing such specifications and seeking such proofs for real programs of even a few hundred lines. Second, they are extremely low-level. They seldom involve concepts related to the problem the program is trying to solve, but instead deal with strictly programming objects such as arrays and pointers.

Suppose that we wish to prove the correctness of a program that was written to solve a problem in some discipline, say physics. As a result of the two factors, the proof of such a program is carried out at a low level and is rarely concerned with what a physicist or mathematician would call significant results in the discipline. Suppose further that the correctness of the program depends on some such result, say, for example, on the Prime Factorization Theorem from ring theory. It is hard to imagine how we would deduce from a program and proof at the level of those given in the preceding sections that this result is needed. What is required is some method to *raise the level of the proof*—to raise its level of abstraction so that the steps in the proof are phrased in terms of the objects of the problem discipline rather than in terms of strictly computer-oriented objects. If the level of the proof could be so raised, then we might be able to detect that a result like the Prime Factorization Theorem is required.

Much of the programming research undertaken in the last decade, especially in the areas of functional programming, stepwise refinement, abstract machines, layered software development, abstract data types, knowledge-based programming, and program transformation, bears on the solution to this problem. These investigations are far from complete, so we cannot yet present hard and fast results. Nevertheless, some of the outline of a solution is beginning to emerge, as we discuss briefly in the following sections.

12.3.1 The Nature of Abstract Programming

One approach to raising the level of programs and their proofs is to "factor" them along a different dimension than was used in Section 12.2. There the proof was factored—recast into manageable-sized pieces—according to the flow of control in the low-level program. Thus, for the example program in Section 12.2 we factored the proof into subproofs of the initial straight-line code segment, the loop body, and the final (empty) straight-line code segment. Suppose instead that we factored the proof, and hence the programming task, in terms of levels of abstraction.

Factoring the proof in terms of levels of abstraction is a consequence of employing *abstract programming methodology*. Using this approach to programming the solution to a problem, we would actually write a sequence of programs. The sequence would begin with a program written in terms of the concepts and objects of the discipline from which the problem is taken. In the case of a physics program, these objects might be quantum mechanical entities such as charm, color, and the like; in the case of a business program, they might be employees, plants, and the like. In any event, this top-level abstract program and its specification would contain just enough detail—enough and no more—to permit us to show that it does solve the problem at hand. They would thus be remarkable for what they do not say. Typically, they would not say anything about how arrays are indexed, how memory is referenced, or how data are stored. Since such things would not be present in the abstract program, the properties claimed for it, and hence their proofs, would necessarily be independent of them.

We would then seek to prove this top-level abstract program correct. Such a program would be little more than a restatement of the mathematical or other formulation of the problem, and its proof would be correspondingly general and would not depend on irrelevant details. The proof would employ the objects and the notation of the problem discipline. And because it does so, where it depends on fundamental results from the problem discipline would be clear.

Of course, implementation details cannot be ignored forever. The next step would be to *refine* the program, making it somewhat more explicit and including some more details—details not of the problem discipline, but rather of how to solve the problem. For example, the second level of the program might include details related to the numerical method being used to solve the problem. Again, we would prove the program correct at this level—not directly, but rather by showing that the individual implementations of concepts at the preceding level are correct and correctly introduced into the program.

This process of refinement and proof of implementation would continue through several levels. At the lower levels, refinements would include items such as implementing the objects of the problem discipline in terms of computer objects—lists, records, and arrays, for example. Eventually, a program at the level of Pascal, FORTRAN, or even the assembly language of a particular machine would be achieved. *This program would be provably correct, but would not itself have to be proved*, since it would have been correctly derived from a correct program.

In some sense, the downward progression from one level of program abstraction to another corresponds to making and introducing implementation decisions. For example, at some level we might decide to represent the abstract concept of "employee" by a record or structure; similarly, we might decide to implement the abstract concept of "stack" by an array and pointers. Incorporating each of these decisions makes the program less abstract—more concrete—and hence makes progress toward an implementation of it.

Typically, each such implementation decision creates possibilities for optimizing the program at the next level, because making concrete implementation decisions cuts off other possible implementations of the abstract program. Such optimizations can be effected using program transformation techniques. Applying program transformations—substitution rules not unlike demodulators—preserves the correctness of the program if the transformation rules themselves have been proved correct.

Of course, the abstract programming methodology outlined in this section is still in the research stage, particularly with respect to the higher levels of abstraction. Nevertheless, numerous developments in programming research support the idea that it will become practical.

12.3.2 An Abstract Programming Example

We shall briefly sketch an example illustrating how abstract programming could simplify program proofs. In this sketch, we show how the proof factors at the later stages of the refinement—at the more concrete stages. But since the process of refining is essentially the same at all levels—an invariant—this sketch is representative.

12.3.2.1 An abstract program to append lists.

Suppose that we wish to write a program that manipulates lists, say one that appends one list to another, and that the eventual goal is a program at the FORTRAN level in which the lists are implemented using arrays. We could, of course, try to write such a program directly. We are using the abstract programming approach, however, so we define the concept of "list", implement the function append in terms of lists, and then refine that implementation to one in terms of arrays.

To define lists, we give properties of the primitive operations that can be performed on them. For the primitive operations, we choose the following: MakeList(x,y), FirstElement(x), RestList(x), IsEmptyList(x), EmptyList, and Equal-Lists(x,y), which we regard as functions. These functions correspond roughly to cons, car, cdr, null, nil, and equal in the LISP language. (We use functions even for primitives that might naturally be thought of as predicates—IsEmptyList and EqualLists—because they are used in the same manner as functions in programs.) We also assume that there is an unspecified class of "atoms" that can be put in lists, a function IsAtom(x) that distinguishes atoms from lists, and a function EqualAtoms(x, y) for comparing atoms.

A number of axioms are required to state the needed properties of these primitives. In clause form, those needed (apart from defining equality) are

(107) EQUAL(isemptylist(x), true)

  | EQUAL(equallists(makelist(firstelement(x), restlist(x)), x), true)

(108) EQUAL(equallists(firstelement(makelist(x, y)), x), true)

(109) EQUAL(equallists(restlist(makelist(x, y)), y), true)

(110) EQUAL(isemptylist(emptylist), true)

(111) ¬EQUAL(isemptylist(makelist(x, y)), true)

For example, clause 107 says that if a given list is not empty, then reconstructing it from its first element and the rest of it gives back a list that has the relation EqualLists to it. (As we have pointed out before, in the language of clauses as used in this book, constants and functions must be written in lower case; hence, a function such as MakeList is written makelist in clauses.) We also need several clauses, which we shall not give here, specifying the meaning of EqualLists (which in fact can be used for both lists and atoms) recursively. (The two arguments to EqualLists are equal if they both satisfy IsEmptyList, if they both satisfy EqualAtoms, or if their FirstElements both satisfy EqualLists and their RestLists both satisfy EqualLists.)

In some cases, we may also wish to give *type axioms* for use in type checking the program. Examples of type axioms for these primitives are

(112) ¬ISATOM(x) | ¬ISLIST(y) | ISLIST(makelist(x, y))

(113) ¬ISLIST(x) | ¬ISLIST(y) | ISLIST(makelist(x, y))

(114) ISLIST(emptylist)

For example, the first two together say that if x is an atom or a list and y is a list, then Makelist(x,y) is a list. (Unlike in LISP, the second argument of MakeList is not permitted to be an atom.)

Using these primitives, we can write the abstract program for the function append. (We extend the "language" in which we write examples with some constructs from LISP, notably with recursion and with the *conditional expression*, which returns one of two values depending on the result of a test.)

```
FUNCTION append(l1, l2)
LIST l1, l2
    RETURN (IF (IsEmptyList(l1)) THEN l2
        ELSE MakeList(FirstElement(l1), append(RestList(l1), l2))
END
```

Instead of proving the correctness of append—it is not easy to find a suitable specification—we consider proving that it has the property: "for every x, if x is a list and IsEmptyList(x) = false, then EqualLists(FirstElement(x), FirstElement(append(x,y))) = true". We do not give the clauses here, but the proof could proceed in the following way. From the axiom represented by clause 111, we conclude that x = MakeList(z,w) for some z and w. (From here on the proof mainly involves demodulation.) Substituting in the conclusion, we see that

$$FirstElement(x) = FirstElement(MakeList(z,w)) = z$$

and

$$FirstElement(append(x,y)) = FirstElement(append(MakeList(z,w),y))$$

Substituting in the program for append, we get

$$FirstElement(x) = FirstElement(MakeList(FirstElement(MakeList(z,w)),$$
$$append(RestList(MakeList(z,w)),y)))$$

which also simplifies to z using the axiom represented by clause 108 twice. (Although not required to prove this property, *recursion induction*, an analog of induction for loops, would be required to prove many properties.)

12.3.2.2 Implementing the list primitives and append.
The next step in the abstract programming process is to write implementations for the primitive operations in terms of arrays and indices. Then, by substituting the implementations for the functions in the abstract program, we can obtain a program at the next level. One of the many possible implementations is to use integers to represent lists and atoms, and to use two arrays LISTF and LISTR of length N to hold the link information for lists. Then the integer value 0 represents the empty list, integer values between 1 and N represent lists (and are used as indices into LISTF and LISTR), and integer values greater than N represent atoms.

It is convenient to sketch the implementations for the list primitives in the following way. We give some "global" declarations and initializations for the integers and arrays, and then we give each primitive followed by a program fragment (an expression, or one or more statements) that defines it; we use → to mean "is defined to be". Then the implementations are

```
INTEGER LISTF(N), LISTR(N)
INTEGER I
I = 0
. . .
MakeList(x, y) →
   I = I + 1
   IF (I > N) ERROR
   LISTF(I) = x
   LISTR(I) = y
   RETURN (I)
```

FirstElement(x) → LISTF(x)
RestList(x) → LISTR(x)
IsEmptyList(x) → x = 0
EmptyList → 0

According to the outline of the abstract programming methodology given in Section 12.3.1, we need now only prove that these implementations—the program fragments on the right sides of the definitions—are correct. Fortunately, we already have their specifications at hand—the axioms for the list operations exemplified by clauses 107 through 111, plus those for EqualLists. It is not hard, using the techniques presented in Section 12.2, to prove that these fragments satisfy the list axioms. Thus any properties of the program append that we have proved using those axioms will remain true when that program is executed using the preceding fragments to carry out the list operations.

We have deliberately sketched the program fragments implementing the primitives for lists in a way that suggests that they could be substituted into the program. Program transformations—the same mechanism discussed in Section 12.1.2 for introducing statements to check array bounds—can be used to carry out such substitutions. Moreover, they can also be used to simplify (optimize) the resulting code. For the example program append and the preceding definitions of the primitives, the result of such transformation is

```
FUNCTION append(l1, l2)
INTEGER l1, l2
INTEGER temp
  IF (l1 = 0) THEN
    RETURN (l2)
  ELSE
    temp = append(LISTR(l1), l2)
    I = I + 1
    IF (I > N) ERROR
    LISTF(I) = LISTF(l1)
    LISTR(I) = temp
    RETURN (I)
  END
END
```

(We assume that the variables LISTR, LISTF, I, and N are available globally or, in FORTRAN parlance, in COMMON.) This second-level abstract program is closer to the FORTRAN level than is the top-level one. But it is still abstract with respect to FORTRAN, because it employs recursion.

12.3.2.3 Comparing the proofs at the two levels. It is evident that carrying out the proof of the property discussed in Section 12.3.2.1 for the second-level abstract program is more difficult than it is for the top-level abstract program. In the first place, the property can no longer be stated in list terms; it must be phrased in terms of the implementation. It might seem that the property to be proved is "for every x, if x is an integer and x ≠ 0 and x ≤ N, then LISTF(x) = LISTF(append(x, y))". But since the axioms for lists no longer play a role, we must also replace x ≠ 0 and x ≤ N by a statement in terms of the existence of variables z, w, and v such that LISTF(v) = z and LISTR(v) = w. In the second place, the program itself is more complicated than in its list form and now involves the use of the program state, whereas the abstract version does not. These additional complications contribute to making concrete proofs harder than abstract ones.

Returning for a moment to consideration of the proof at the abstract level, notice that the axioms for lists—which can be considered to define lists as an abstract data type—play a role in splitting the proof analogous to that played by the invariants used in Section 12.2. Here, however, the splitting is not in terms of the execution paths, but instead it is in terms of the primitives and their definitions. The execution paths are not inherently interesting, and they are not inherently related to the abstract form of the problem being solved, so it is not surprising that the theorems derived from them are low-level and uninteresting. On the other hand, as the axioms reveal, there is structure to the ensemble of the primitives, so one can expect that a split in this dimension will lead to interesting, higher-level proofs.

Splitting the proof in terms of the primitives has another advantage. Although this brief example does not provide a strong illustration, in typical programs the accessing functions are used many times. Thus the proofs necessary to show that a particular implementation satisfies the axioms for the data type have a high payoff, because the "theorems" are, in effect, used many times. Contrast this with the situation of proving that several fragments of straight-line code satisfy an invariant. In that situation, each of the fragments is unique, and no reuse of the proofs is possible.

Finally, notice that part of the simplification in the proof of the abstract program comes from the fact that it is a *functional program*—one that does not use assignment and does not cause side effects. As remarked earlier, proofs for such programs can be obtained without use of a program state. Also, they involve mainly algebraic substitutions (demodulations), which are a particularly simple method of proof.

12.3.2.4 Yet another level of refinement. To close this discussion of an abstract programming example, we return to the remark that, with respect to FORTRAN, the program for append with lists implemented in terms of arrays is still abstract, for it still includes a recursive call to append. Such calls are not permitted in FORTRAN. Thus at least one more level of refinement is needed to obtain a true FORTRAN program. To obtain this refinement, we consider such items as function arguments, local variables, function calls, and function returns to be abstract. We define implementations for them in terms of arrays, GO TO statements, and computed GO TO statements, proceeding as we did for lists. We prove these implementations to be correct. Then we can obtain, again by program transformation, an even more concrete—and now executable—FORTRAN subroutine for append.

```
      SUBROUTINE APPEND
      . . .
      STACK(IP + 1) = 1
      GO TO 20
   10 CONTINUE
      RETURN
   20 CONTINUE
      IP = IP + 1
      JP = JP − 3
      IF (JP .LE. IP) ERROR
      IF (STACK(JP + 1) .EQ. 0) GO TO 30
         STACK(JP + 2) = STACK(JP)
      GO TO 50
   30 CONTINUE
         STACK(JP − 2) = LISTR(STACK(JP + 1))
         STACK(JP − 3) = STACK(JP)
         STACK(IP + 1) = 2
      GO TO 20
   40    CONTINUE
         STACK(JP + 2) = STACK(JP − 1)
         I = I + 1
         IF (I .GT. N) ERROR
         LISTF(I) = LISTF(STACK(JP + 1))
         LISTR(I) = STACK(JP + 2)
         STACK(JP + 2) = I
   50 CONTINUE
      JP = JP + 3
      IRLAB = STACK(IP)
      IP = IP − 1
      GO TO (10, 40), IRLAB
      END
```

Consider how difficult it would be to prove the program correct at this level!

EXERCISES

12. Give the clauses that characterize a function *count(x)* that evaluates to the length of a list.
13. Give an alternative implementation of the primitive operations for lists.
14. Give a set of primitives appropriate for a sorted list of integers.

12.4 Conclusions

In this chapter, we have discussed the application of automated reasoning techniques to the problem of establishing the reliability of computer programs.

On the one hand, an automated reasoning program can be used to assist you in checking a program and in finding bugs by carrying out symbolic executions of that program. In this use, the automated reasoning program automates a part of the process of desk-checking a computer program. It can carry out the tedious and error-prone simulation of the execution of the program on selected data, and it can provide useful indications of where a bug may lie when the execution is not correct. Of course, executing a program—whether symbolically or by actually running it—will reveal a bug only if the test data selected happen to cause the program to execute a faulty path. Thus no finite amount of such testing can prove a program correct.

If you wish to increase your confidence that your program is correct, an automated reasoning program can provide assistance. You can attempt to prove that your program is correct—to prove that whatever the input data, if the data are valid, then the result of executing the program satisfies some specification. We have illustrated the traditional, or invariant assertion, method of proving programs correct. Such proofs tend to be complicated, and they are difficult to produce correctly by hand. Hence, using an automated reasoning program can be a valuable aid in proving programs correct.

Finally, because proofs of even very simple programs are so complicated, it is natural to look for alternative approaches to proving programs—alternative approaches that might remove some of the complication and raise the level of abstraction. While such approaches are still a topic for research, the technique of abstract programming seems to hold great promise. In it, we use abstract data types and other abstraction mechanisms to write and prove the program at a level close to the statement of the problem. Then we prove that the abstract, problem-oriented entities have been implemented correctly in terms of more concrete programming objects like arrays and pointers. We have given a very simple example of this approach and have remarked upon some of the considerations that make proofs of abstract programs less complicated than those of ordinary concrete ones.

12.5 Answers to Exercises

1. The encoding for the given state is

   PSTATE(headloop, lvals(amount, 10, lvals(b, lels1(1, 4, lels1(3, 2, nil)), nil)))

   The first argument gives the name of the current statement. The second argument is a list that contains entries for the variable AMOUNT and the array B. The value for the array B is given by the list constructed with the lels1 function.

2. You can use a four-place function, lels2, to represent the values in a two-dimensional array. The first two arguments give the subscripts for an element, the third gives the value of the element, and the fourth contains the rest of the list. Thus the required list of elements is

   lels2(1, 1, 10, lels2(1, 3, 20, nil))

3. The ASSIGN clause for I = A + B (here A and B are assumed to be program variables that are not arrays) is

   ASSIGN(assgn1, pvar(i), sum(pvar(a), pvar(b)), nextins)

   After resolving with clause 2, you get

   ¬PSTATE(assgn1, xstate)
   | PSTATE(nextins, store(pvar(i), eval(sum(pvar(a), pvar(b)), xstate), xstate))

4. The subscript checks added for the given statement are

   IF (J > HB(A, 1)) ERROR
   IF (1 > J) ERROR
   IF (2 > HB(B, 1)) ERROR
   IF (1 > 2) ERROR

   (Note that we are assuming here that the array subscripts start from 1, as for simple FORTRAN arrays. If the array subscripts start from 0 (as in the programming language C) or if you can specify the lowest legal subscript, the same approach works, with minor modifications. The function LB can be used to specify the "low bound" of an array in a manner analogous to HB.) The corresponding clauses are

   IFERROR(ife20, gt(pvar(j), hb(parr(a), pconst(1))), ife21)
   IFERROR(ife21, gt(pconst(1), pvar(j)), ife22)
   IFERROR(ife22, gt(pconst(2), hb(parr(b), pconst(1))), ife23)
   IFERROR(ife23, gt(pconst(1), pconst(2)), asg8)

   Here the statement names that occur in the clauses are essentially arbitrary (but must be unique). Thus, ife20 must be a name that does not correspond to more than one statement in the transformed program, and asg8 must be the name of the given assignment statement.

5. The clauses that would have to be added to handle two-dimensional arrays are the following.

EQUAL(eval(parr2(xarr, x1, x2), xstate),
 fetch(parr2(xarr, eval(x1, xstate), eval(x2, xstate)), xstate))

EQUAL(fetch(parr2(xarr, isvalid(x1), isvalid(x2)),
 lvals(xarr, xval, zlist)),
 ckfetch(parr2(xarr, isvalid(x1), isvalid(x2)),
 fetch2(isvalid(x1), isvalid(x2), xval)))

EQUAL(fetch(parr2(xarr, isvalid(x1), isvalid(x2)),
 lvals(w, wval, zlist)),
 fetch(parr2(xarr, isvalid(x1), isvalid(x2)), zlist))

EQUAL(fetch(parr2(xarr, isvalid(x1), isvalid(x2)), nil),
 fetcherror(parr2(xarr, x1, x2), notdef))

EQUAL(fetch2(isvalid(x1), isvalid(x2),
 lels2(x1, x2, xval, zlist)), xval)

EQUAL(fetch2(isvalid(x1), isvalid(x2), lels2(w1, w2, wval, zlist)),
 fetch2(isvalid(x1), isvalid(x2), zlist))

EQUAL(fetch2(isvalid(x1), isvalid(x2), nil), notinit)

6. The clauses that are needed to handle storing into two-dimensional arrays are the following.

EQUAL(store(parr2(xarr, x1, x2), isvalid(w), zstate),
 store(parre2(xarr, eval(x1, zstate), eval(x2, zstate)),
 isvalid(w), zstate))

EQUAL(store(parre2(xarr, isvalid(x1), isvalid(x2)), isvalid(wval),
 lvals(xarr, lels2(xs1, xs2, xv, xr), zlist)),
 lvals(xarr, store2(isvalid(x1), isvalid(x2), isvalid(wval),
 lels2(xs1, xs2, xv, xr)), zlist))

EQUAL(store(parre2(xarr, isvalid(x1), isvalid(x2)), isvalid(wval),
 lvals(zvar, zval, zlist)),
 lvals(zvar, zval, store(parr2(xarr, isvalid(x1), isvalid(x2)),
 isvalid(wval), zlist)))

EQUAL(store2(isvalid(x1), isvalid(x2), isvalid(wval),
 lels2(x1, x2, xval, zlist)),
 lels2(x1, x2, wval, zlist))

EQUAL(store2(isvalid(x1), isvalid(x2), isvalid(wval),
 lels2(z1, z2, zval, zlist)),

lels2(z1, z2, zval, store2(isvalid(x1), isvalid(x2),

isvalid(wval), zlist)))

EQUAL(store2(isvalid(x1), isvalid(x2), isvalid(wval), nil),

lels2(x1, x2, wval, nil))

7. The clause required for if-then statements is the following one.

¬PSTATE(xinstr, xstate)

| ¬IFTHEN(xinstr, wcond, yinstr, zinstr)

| PSTATE(if(eval(wcond, xstate), then(yinstr), else(zinstr)), xstate)

8. There are three executable statements in the program, two assignments and an if-then statement. The clauses corresponding to these statements are

ASSIGN(entry, pvar(s), pconst(0), if1)

IFTHEN(if1, gt(pparam(n), pconst(0)), asgn2, exit)

ASSIGN(asgn2, pvar(s), sum(pvar(s), pconst(2)), exit)

9. The required lemma is

¬EQUAL(isvalid($ge(x, y)), isvalid(true))

| ¬EQUAL(isvalid($le(x, y)), isvalid(true))

| EQUAL(isvalid(x), isvalid(y))

The proof for the first case (N > 0) is the following.

From clauses 77 and 81:

(E1) EQUAL(eval(gt(pparam(n), pconst(0)), lvals(s, notinit, nil)), isvalid(true))

(The first argument demodulates to isvalid($gt(n, 0)).)

From clauses 77, 2, and the first assignment clause in problem 7:

(E2) PSTATE(if2, store(pvar(s), eval(pconst(0), lvals(s, notinit, nil)),

lvals(s, notinit, nil))

(The second argument in clause E2 demodulates to lvals(s, 0, nil).)

From clause E2, the IFTHEN clause from problem 7, and the clause in problem 8:

(E3) PSTATE(if(eval(gt(pparam(n), pconst(0)), lvals(s, 0, nil)),

then(asgn2), else(exit)), lvals(s, 0, nil))

(The first argument demodulates to asgn2, which requires the use of clause E1 among the demodulators.)

From clauses E3 and 2, and the second ASSIGN in problem 7:

(E4) PSTATE(exit, lvals(s, 2, nil))

From clauses 77 and 79:

     (E5)   EQUAL(isvalid($le(n, 1)), isvalid(true))

From clauses E1, E5, and 69:

     (E6)   EQUAL(isvalid($ge(n, 1)), isvalid(true))

From clauses E5 and E6, and the lemma:

     (E7)   EQUAL(isvalid(n), isvalid(1))

From clauses E4 and 80:

     (E8) $\neg$EQUAL(2, 2)

This last clause results from the use of a number of demodulators, including E7. It contradicts clause 70. The second proof is the following.

From clauses 77 and 78:

     (E9)   EQUAL(isvalid($ge(n, 0)), isvalid(true))

From clauses 77 and 82:

     (E10)   EQUAL(isvalid($le(n, 0)), isvalid(true))

From clauses E9 and E10, and the lemma:

     (E11)   EQUAL(isvalid(n), isvalid(0))

(Clause E2 is derived just as in the first proof.)

From clause E2, the IFTHEN clause in problem 7, and the clause in problem 8:

     (E12)   PSTATE(exit, lvals(s, 0, nil))

From clauses E12 and 80:

     (E13) $\neg$EQUAL(0, 0)

Again, this last clause contradicts 70.

10. For every if-then-else construct in a program, two clauses must be used. One is an IFTHEN clause of the sort described in problem 7, where the last argument must be the label corresponding to the first statement in the set following the ELSE). The other is a clause for the ELSE of the form

     $\neg$PSTATE(xinstr, xstate) | $\neg$ELSE(xinstr, yinstr)
     | PSTATE(yinstr, xstate)

Here the branch would be to the first statement following the if-then-else construct. It is simply a branch identical to the one used at the bottom of a loop.

11. To prove that this segment works correctly, we must prove that the initial straight-line segment works correctly, prove that the loop works correctly, and then show that, when these two components of the program work correctly, the entire program works correctly. Let us begin by proving that the straight-line segment composed of the first two assignment statements works correctly. The proof, of course, will be quite similar to the

example given in Sections 12.2.1 and 12.2.2. Since the example and the current problem are quite similar, many of the required clauses are identical. Thus, clauses 59, 60, 62, 63, 64, and 65 will apply with no changes to the current problem. Instead of clauses 61 and 66, we need

(E14) ¬PSTATE(exit, zexit)

> | ¬EQUAL(eval(pvar(s), zexit), eval(div(prod(pvar(n),
>
> sum(pvar(n), pconst(1))), pconst(2)), zexit))

(E15) ¬PSTATE(dows, zexit)

> | ¬EQUAL(eval(pvar(k), zexit), eval(pconst(0), zexit))
>
> | ¬EQUAL(eval(ge(pparam(n), pconst(0)), zexit), isvalid(true))
>
> | ¬EQUAL(eval(ge(pparam(n), pvar(k)), zexit), isvalid(true))
>
> | ¬EQUAL(eval(pvar(s), zexit), eval(div(prod(pvar(k),
>
> sum(pvar(k), pconst(1))), pconst(2)), zexit))

The proof of the straight-line code proceeds similar to the example.

From clauses 2, 59, and 62:

(E16) PSTATE(asge, lvals(k, 0, lvals(s, notinit, nil)))

From clauses 2, 63, and E16:

(E17) PSTATE(dows, lvals(k, 0, lvals(s, 0, nil)))

Using 64 and 65 you can deduce

EQUAL(isvalid($ge(n, 0)), isvalid(true))

which is added as a demodulator. The empty clause can then be deduced from clauses E15, E17, and 70 (after a number of intermediate demodulations).

The proof that the loop works is similar to the example in Section 12.2.4. We shall insert ASSERT statements to give the loop invariant.

```
DO WHILE (K < N)
   ASSERT (S = (K × (K + 1))/2)
   K = K + 1
   S = S + K
   ASSERT (S = (K × (K + 1))/2)
END
```

Again, we can use some of the clauses from that section. In particular, clauses 83, 84, 86, 87, and 88 are used with no change. Clauses 85, 89, and 90 are replaced with

(E18) ASSIGN(asgs, pvar(s), sum(pvar(s), pvar(k)))

(E19) ¬PSTATE(dows, zstate)

    | EQUAL(eval(pvar(s), zexit), eval(div(prod(pvar(k),

      sum(pvar(k), pconst(1))), pconst(2)), zexit))

(E20) ¬PSTATE(dowe, zexit)

    | ¬EQUAL(eval(ge(pparam(n), pconst(0)), zexit), isvalid(true))

    | ¬EQUAL(eval(ge(pparam(n), pvar(k)), zexit), isvalid(true))

    | ¬EQUAL(eval(pvar(s), zexit), eval(div(prod(pvar(k),

      sum(pvar(k), pconst(1))), pconst(2)), zexit))

The proof (at least initially) proceeds much like the example.

From clauses 86 and 87:

(E21) EQUAL(isvalid($ge(n, 0)), isvalid(true))

From clauses 86 and 88:

(E22) EQUAL(isvalid($gt(n, kval)), isvalid(true))

From clauses 86 and 89:

(E23) EQUAL(isvalid(sval),

    isvalid($div($prod(kval, $sum(kval, 1)), 2)))

In the derivation of the last clause, it is assumed that the set of demodulators in the chapter has been extended to handle functions such as div, $div, and the like.

From clauses 86, 83, and 4:

(E24) PSTATE(asgk, lvals(k, kval, lvals(s, sval, nil)))

From clauses E24, 84, and 2:

(E25) PSTATE(asgs, lvals(k, $sum(kval, 1), lvals(s, sval, nil)))

From clauses E25, 85, and 2:

(E26) PSTATE(dowe, lvals(k, $sum(kval, 1),

    lvals(s, $sum(sval, $sum(kval, 1)), nil)))

To proceed, we need a lemma—one that would normally be present. It is

(E27) ¬EQUAL(isvalid($gt(x, y)), isvalid(true))

    | EQUAL(isvalid($ge(x, y)), isvalid(true))

The proof continues.

From clauses E27 and E22:

(E28) EQUAL(isvalid($ge(n, kval)), isvalid(true))

From clauses E26, E28, E20, and 70:

(E29) ¬EQUAL(isvalid($sum($div($prod(kval, $sum(kval, 1)), 2)),

$sum(kval, 1))), isvalid($div($prod($sum(kval, 1),

$sum($sum(kval, 1), 1)), 2)))

At this point, we have reduced the problem of proving that the loop works to deriving a contradiction using clause E29. In some sense, that is the object of studying these rather mechanical rephrasings of problems. The goal is to distinguish between the tedious reasoning involved in simply making the transitions and the deep reasoning at the heart of some of the proofs. Such deep reasoning may involve basic theorems about integers, polynomials, and data structures. A program verification system can be viewed as consisting of two parts: the part that generates all of the required clauses (except the background theory) from the code and proves the trivial theorems, and the part that proves the tougher theorems that are at the heart of the problem.

To complete the proof, we must show that the proofs of the straight-line code and the loop can be used to show that the entire program segment works correctly. Again, we can use clauses from the example. Clauses 91, 92, 93, and 95 can be used along with

(E30) ¬PSTATE(dows, zstate)

| EQUAL(eval(pvar(s), zstate), eval(div(prod(pvar(k), sum(pvar(k), 1)), 2)))

(E31) ¬PSTATE(exit, zexit)

| EQUAL(eval(pvar(s), zstate), eval(div(prod(pparam(n),

sum(pparam(n), 1)), 2)))

This proof is quite similar to the preceding one. Note that we have only sketched a proof of partial correctness; we have not sketched a proof that the loop (and, hence, the program segment) terminates.

Before leaving this problem, we emphasize that we are not proposing that a person should cope with this tedium in order to verify program segments; that is what machines are for. The goal is simply to have the programmer insert the ASSUME and ASSERT statements into the program. From that point on, the complete proofs should be generated by the reasoning program supplemented by special-purpose program verification components.

12. The axioms that characterize count are the following.

¬EQUAL(isemptylist(x), true) | EQUAL(count(x), 0)

¬ISLIST(x)

| EQUAL(isemptylist(x), true)

| EQUAL(count(x), $sum(count(restlist(x)), 1))

13. One closely-related implementation is to use successive elements of one array. In this case, the implementations of the basic operations are the following.

INTEGER LISTARR(N)
INTEGER I
I = 0
. . .
MakeList(x, y) →
  I = I + 2
  IF (I > N) ERROR
  LISTARR(I) = x
  LISTARR(I + 1) = y
  RETURN (I)
FirstElement(x) → LISTARR(x)
RestList(x) → LISTARR(x + 1)
IsEmptyList(x) → x = 0
EmptyList → 0

14. A reasonable set of primitive operations for a sorted list of integers consists of replacing the MakeList function with a function InsertList(x,y), which creates a list in which the integer x is inserted into the correct location in the list y.

13

Expert Systems

What is the common feature of playing chess, checkers, bridge, or go, and practicing medicine, law, or geology? The common feature is, if you are skilled at any of them, you are called an "expert". An expert is required to reason, and often to reason deeply. Since the focus of this book is automated reasoning, a natural question to ask is: Can an automated reasoning program be used to perform as an expert?

The answer is a qualified yes. Systems exist that perform many functions of an expert and in an expert manner—systems that depend in part on automated reasoning. Such systems are called *expert systems*. In this chapter, we discuss expert systems, focusing on the aspects that are directly related to automated reasoning. For this discussion, an *expert* is a person with the appropriate qualifications, while an *expert system* is a program that performs like an expert.

13.1 What Is an Expert System?

An expert system can be loosely thought of as a computer program that performs an intellectually demanding task as well as most actual experts. An activity such as that of multiplying two matrices is normally considered "mechanically" rather than "intellectually" demanding and is, therefore, not the type of activity of interest in this chapter. Instead, a task of the type on which we focus here must be one that requires a professional. The following examples illustrate the difference between "mechanically" and "intellectually" demanding.

1. A program that plays a game, such as checkers, chess, bridge, backgammon, or go, would normally be considered an expert system.
2. A program that can diagnose the cause of a problem, medical or mechanical, would be considered an expert system.
3. In contrast, a statistics package that evaluates complex formulas would normally be considered *not* an expert system.

Expert systems in the first two areas do in fact exist. The goal for certain researchers in artificial intelligence is to design machines or programs to perform many such tasks, once those tasks are thoroughly understood.

Three advantages of such a system—of such an expert system—can be given immediately.

1. An expert system does not die. Normally, such a system is continuously improved, or at least maintains its quality forever. Unfortunately, such is not the case for the expert individual. An expert normally improves for many years, but then gradually loses the requisite skills.
2. An expert system can be replicated for pennies. Suppose for a moment that a program existed that would give even moderately good medical advice. Thousands of copies could be made at very low cost.
3. If several expert systems existed, each performing a distinct type of service, a single system could be created that has the capabilities of all the systems.

This third point brings to mind the science fiction novel that discusses the possibility of a "global human intelligence". In such stories, several individuals develop high levels of mental communication and function as a single, integrated intelligence. While it seems unlikely that such global human intelligences will arise, the correspondent in machine intelligence may eventually appear.

13.2 Expert Systems That Play Games

A number of expert systems have been developed for playing games of strategy. One of the first such programs was a checker-playing program that eventually could match the best players. This naturally led to a great deal of excitement and predictions that similar programs could be created for playing chess.

Unfortunately, the techniques that led to a successful checker-playing program failed to produce a good chess-playing program. However, good chess-playing programs have been produced during the last decade. At this point they play better than the vast majority of people who play chess, but not as well as the best players. The better chess programs all use special-purpose algorithms designed for chess—algorithms that do not seem to generalize to other games.

A good backgammon program has been produced. Although weaker than the best players, the program did beat the world champion in a short match.

Finally, we come to the game of go. The Japanese are planning to devote significant resources to producing a go program. The game of go is one of the more difficult of strategy games, and it will probably be many years before a program will be written that can beat the better go players.

The development of expert systems to play games is interesting for several reasons. The first reason is that no single basic algorithm has been found that provides the basis for a program that plays several different games well. Such an algorithm may eventually be found, but the first programs to beat the best players of chess, backgammon, and go will almost certainly not be based on general algorithms of the sort presented in this book.

A second reason for the development of expert systems being interesting is that the development of expert game-playing programs offers the opportunity to study the stages of development that an expert system might go through. In the case of chess, early programs could be used to perform some of the tedious evaluations such as checking for a two-move mating sequence. Of course, such a program is of limited use. An expert could use the program to help evaluate a position, but these early programs could in no way be classed as expert. Later programs were of greater use. For example, in most situations these later programs could recommend moves that, if not optimal, were at least reasonable. Current programs are still inferior to the best chess players. However, for most players the role of the program has switched from mediocre assistant to superior player. In addition, such programs can be used as teaching devices. They can evaluate a player's moves, recommend alternatives that are better, and offer precise reasons for the choices.

It has been conjectured that programs will outperform the best players of chess, as well as most other games of strategy, within the twentieth century. Whether they do or do not during this century, the probability is high that they will eventually. The role of the expert may change. Experts may instead compete to see who can produce the most powerful programs. The quality of the actual games may consistently exceed that attainable by people who play chess. While these changes in the world of games may not directly affect most people, those discussed in the next section will.

13.3 Expert Systems of Other Types

Researchers are successfully producing expert systems that are actually useful in areas such as medical diagnosis, chemical analysis, and geological exploration. Furthermore, they are based on general techniques. Unlike most of the game-playing programs, the techniques used to create MYCIN, one of the systems for medical diagnosis, are useful for creating expert programs in a number of areas. In fact, the creation of MYCIN led to the design and implementation of a set of software tools, called EMYCIN, that can be used to produce new expert systems. What components are present in an expert system?

Perhaps the best known expert systems are the following:

1. MYCIN, developed to offer consultation in a limited area of medicine
2. DENDRAL, created to aid in analyzing organic chemical compounds
3. PROSPECTOR, programmed to aid in selecting sites for mineral exploration

The basic reasoning component utilized in the typical expert system is not particularly powerful. The critical component in such systems is the user interface. The delay in the development of expert systems was not due to the lack of a sufficiently powerful reasoning component, but rather the result of other missing features. The key missing features were those that permit easy use of such a computer program.

An expert system like MYCIN is composed of three components.

1. The first is a *reasoning component* to direct conversation between the system and its user and to make the appropriate logical deductions.
2. The second is a component for interacting with an expert in order to obtain the expert's knowledge. The component is designed to communicate with an expert even if the expert knows little about programming or computing. The goal is to transfer the facts and rules that are used by the expert to perform the job requiring expertise. Such a component is called the *knowledge acquisition component*.
3. The third is a *user interface* to permit the unskilled user to interact with the program.

13.4 The Reasoning Component

The reasoning component of many expert systems is based on *production rules*. To illustrate what is meant by a production rule, let us consider an example of a production rule used in MYCIN as it is stated in ordinary language:

if

   (1) The infection that requires therapy is meningitis, and

   (2) The patient does have evidence of serious skin or tissue infection, and

   (3) Organisms are not seen on the stain of the culture, and

   (4) The type of the infection is bacterial,

then

   Evidence exists that the organism (other than those seen on cultures or smears) that might be causing the infection is staphylococcus-coag-pos (.75) streptococcus-group-a (.5)

The given rule has several properties worth noting. First, the rule can easily be encoded or captured with two clauses. Two clauses are required since two conclusions can be obtained when the **if** conditions are true. The rule as given has an implied **and** in the **then** condition. Second, the possible conclusions in the **then** condition each have an associated *confidence factor*. Different expert systems deal with uncertainty in different ways—some use conditional probability and Bayes's theorem, while others use more ad hoc techniques. Third, while the rules are kept in an internal format that is normally as complicated as clauses, the external format is surprisingly readable.

What frequently surprises people is the fact that production rules can easily be written as clauses, and that most production rules can be trivially converted to a single clause. In fact, the types of reasoning employed by those current expert systems that use a general reasoning component are strongly related to the types of reasoning used by typical automated reasoning programs and by Prolog. Unfortunately, distinct terminologies have evolved that tend to obscure the fundamental similarities.

The software tool package EMYCIN bases most of its inference mechanisms on back-chaining using production rules. In EMYCIN such rules of inference are called *consequent rules*. Such rules are similar to the inference mechanism utilized by Prolog (see Chapter 14), except that in EMYCIN the order of the rules does not determine the order in which conclusions are drawn. In addition to consequent rules, EMYCIN also utilizes *antecedent rules*. Antecedent rules are used in an activity that is remarkably similar to forming hyperresolvents. In both antecedent rules and hyperresolution, when all of the premises of the rule are known to be true, the conclusion is deduced.

Besides using a small number of inference mechanisms based on production rules, most serious expert systems require some inference mechanism that is domain dependent. In particular, most expert systems require some inference mechanism that is not based on general reasoning processes. In fact, different expert systems can be characterized in terms of the amount of special-purpose reasoning that is required. Expert systems range from those that rely almost exclusively on special-purpose mechanisms to those that rely for the most part on general-purpose algorithms. Chess-playing programs are an example of the first type of expert system, and MYCIN is an example of the second type.

In contrast to the approach exhibited in the early chapters, an issue that many expert systems address is the problem of uncertainty. Assertions cannot always be made with total confidence; some can be made only with a probability that they are true. For example, the expert system PROSPECTOR utilizes Bayesian probability theory, while other systems such as MYCIN use techniques that are normally viewed as ad hoc. While uncertainty is important to some expert systems and not discussed in the early chapters, its presence has no serious impact on the choice of inference rule. No matter which approach is used to compute the certainty of a conclusion based on the certainties of the premises, a similar calculation is easily achieved using standard clause representation and standard automated reasoning techniques. To cope with the presence of degrees of certainty, an extra argument is added to specified predicates to reflect the certainty with which the statement is known. The corresponding argument in the conclusion appears as a function of the certainties of the premisses. If the formula can be calculated using standard arithmetic operators that are built into demodulation, then the certainty of the conclusion will be automatically calculated during demodulation. On the other hand, if operations such as table lookups are necessary to simplify the formula, then the demodulation logic must be expanded. In any event, the changes are minimal. Thus we see that the concept of uncertainty that is needed in various expert systems can in fact be treated within the context of automated reasoning.

To illustrate what can be done, let us investigate the question of translating the MYCIN rule given earlier into clauses. First, we must cope with the issue of uncertainty. In systems based on EMYCIN, the concept of *certainty factor (CF)* is based on two concepts, *measure of belief (MB) in a hypothesis* and *measure of disbelief (MD) in the hypothesis*. MB ranges from 0, no belief, to 1, complete belief. Similarly, MD ranges from 0, no disbelief, to 1, complete disbelief. The formula defining CF is

$$CF = MB - MD$$

Thus, CF ranges from -1 to 1. We encode an extra argument for the CF into any of the required predicates.

One significant use of EMYCIN is to encode/decode between rules in ordinary language and rules in an internal form. To do this, predicates could be designated and mechanisms could be used for translating. Instead, we shall simply choose appropriate predicates. The rule that we shall translate has four antecedent conditions:

1. The infection that requires therapy is meningitis, and
2. The patient does have evidence of serious skin or tissue infection, and
3. Organisms are not seen on the stain of the culture, and
4. The type of the infection is bacterial

The first can be represented as

EQUAL(complaint, meningitis)

which states that the complaint has been identified as meningitis. The second can be represented as

SERIOUSINF(xcf)

and

$GT(xcf, 0)

which states that xcf is the certainty factor of a serious skin or tissue infection, and that xcf > 0. The third antecedent condition can be represented as

NOTSEEN(organism, culturestain)

Finally, the fourth can be represented as

TYPEOFINFECTION(bacterial, 1)

which states that the type of infection is bacterial with a certainty factor of 1. The consequent,

> There is evidence that the organism (other than those seen on cultures or smears) that might be causing the infection is staphylococcus-coag-pos (.75) streptococcus-group-a (.5)

would normally be represented as two literals,

CAUSE(scp, .75)

and

CAUSE(sga, .5)

Employing the given notation, the two resulting clauses are

¬EQUAL(complaint, meningitis)
| ¬SERIOUSINF(xcf)
| ¬$GT(xcf, 0)
| ¬NOTSEEN(organism, culturestain)
| ¬TYPEOFINFECTION(bacterial, 1)
| CAUSE(scp, .75)

and

¬EQUAL(complaint, meningitis)
| ¬SERIOUSINF(xcf)
| ¬$GT(xcf, 0)
| ¬NOTSEEN(organism, culturestain)
| ¬TYPEOFINFECTION(bacterial, 1)
| CAUSE(sga, .5)

Alternative representations in clause form exist that serve equally well.

13.5 A Simple Expert System

The following expert system provides assistance in meal planning and related dietary considerations. We present the system in clause form to illustrate that expert systems can easily be represented in a language well understood by the typical automated reasoning program. We thus show the strong connection that exists between automated reasoning as discussed in this book and that phase of expert systems concerned with reasoning. We shall present only a fraction of the expert system, but enough to give concrete examples of what we have just discussed.

The dietary consultant—the expert system we present here—can be used to keep track of what foods you have in the house, which need to be purchased, what you have eaten so far today, what you have eaten during the last week, whether or not you are getting enough vitamins, and whether or not you are getting the correct number of calories. In addition, it makes recommendations for meals or snacks. Thus, the system combines normal data processing—keeping track of the inventory of food—with some ability to make recommendations.

In this example we focus on the reasoning component of the system. We assume that the knowledge acquisition component has already been created, and facts and rules that the dietary consultant uses have been accepted as correct. The user interface conveys events to the system and displays responses.

The dietary consultant relies on an automated reasoning program to maintain the *state* that is comprised of items of data required to make decisions. Here we are using the word state in a manner similar to that discussed in Chapters 5 and 11. When an event occurs, the expert system we are discussing processes the event, using information from the state of the system, to compute the appropriate response. The consumption of a meal is an event, and the request for a meal suggestion is also an event, for example. Occasionally, an event requires a change of the state.

To implement this expert system, an automated reasoning program processes five lists of clauses.

1. The general-axiom list includes the rules that determine how information should be processed.

2. The state list includes positive unit ground clauses that give the facts that determine the state of the system. For example,

   STATECALORIES(sofar(1345), goal(2200))

   might occur in the state list to convey that 1345 calories have been consumed today, while 2200 is the desired daily goal.

3. The demodulator list, as usual, contains positive equality units that can be used to simplify or normalize deduced clauses.

4. The set-of-support list remains empty until an event occurs. Then the clause corresponding to the event appears as one or more clauses in the set-of-support list.

5. The final list, the have-been-given list, consists of clauses that were at one time on the set-of-support list and have served their purpose and been migrated to this list.

When an event occurs, clauses appear in the set-of-support list. They are selected one at a time as "given clauses", as the clause on which the reasoning program focuses its attention. For each given clause, all of the clauses that can be deduced from the given clause considered with the other clauses required by the inference rule and selected from the general-axiom list, the state list, and the have-been-given list are placed at the end of the set-of-support list. In addition, if any of the deduced clauses is a positive ground unit clause having one of the predicates INVEN, SOFARTODAY, DAILYGOALS, NUTHIST, or MENUHIST, then it immediately replaces the corresponding unit on the state list. Thus, the old unit is deleted in favor of the newly-deduced unit clause.

Having discussed in a somewhat abstract fashion the approach that we are going to use, what clauses do we need in the general-axiom list and the state list? We begin with the clauses that comprise the state list. What data items are relevant to allowing the system to react to events and offer good consultation? In the abbreviated system, we use the following.

(a) A clause of the form

INVEN($\langle$item-number$\rangle$, $\langle$item-desc$\rangle$, $\langle$on-hand$\rangle$, $\langle$min-on-hand$\rangle$)

is used for each basic foodstuff, such as eggs, butter, flour, and such, to keep track of how much is in the pantry and how much should normally be there. The first argument gives the $\langle$item-number$\rangle$, which is simply an arbitrary number used to reference the item. The second argument gives the description; the third argument gives the number of units in stock; and the last argument gives the reorder suggestion—buy some more if the amount in stock falls below this value. If the system were to be expanded to include the ability to make out shopping lists, you might wish to include the best store to purchase replacements from as well.

(b) Clauses of the form

MENUITEM($\langle$item-number$\rangle$, $\langle$item-dec$\rangle$, $\langle$requires-list$\rangle$)

are used to determine the requirements for any menu item. Thus,

MENUITEM(52, 'macaroni-and-cheese', l(63, l(46, l(13, nil))))

is used to say that macaroni and cheese is made from three subitems. In a more complete system, we would include exact amounts and preparation instructions. The preceding example might be thought of as simply saying that milk, macaroni, and cheese are required to make menu item 52. As you see, we are talking about *menu items* and *basic foodstuffs*. Sometimes a single foodstuff can also be a menu item, but normally a menu item is prepared from a number of foodstuffs.

(c) Clauses of the form

NUTRITIONAL($\langle$item$\rangle$, $\langle$calories$\rangle$, $\langle$vit-a$\rangle$, $\langle$vit-b$\rangle$,...)

are used to list the nutritional contents of one serving of the menu item. Here, we only keep track of the number of calories and the number of units of vitamin A, so clauses like

NUTRITIONAL(162, calories(375), a(16))

are used, showing that item number 162 has 375 calories per serving and each serving contains 16 units of vitamin A.

(d) Clauses of the form

SOFARTODAY($\langle$calories$\rangle$, $\langle$vit-a$\rangle$, $\langle$vit-b$\rangle$,...)

are used to record the nutritional value of the items consumed so far today.

(e) Clauses of the form

DAILYGOALS($\langle$calories$\rangle$, $\langle$vit-a$\rangle$, $\langle$vit-b$\rangle$,...)

are used to record the daily goals.

(f) We also record the history for the last week in order both to detect trends in poor nutrition and to avoid menu duplication. To do this, we use two distinct types of clause—one to record the amount of nutrients, and one to record the general categories of food that were eaten. The first type allows the system to check for nutritional deficiencies. The second allows the system to propose menu plans that do not repeat recent fare. The first type is of the form

NUTHIST(avg($\langle$cal$\rangle$, $\langle$vit-a$\rangle$, $\langle$vit-b$\rangle$,...),

l($\langle$day-7$\rangle$, l($\langle$day-6$\rangle$, l($\langle$day-5$\rangle$,....))))))))

Here, the avg(...) gives the average values for caloric and vitamin consumption. The second argument is a list of seven values; each value is of the form day($\langle$cal$\rangle$, $\langle$vit-a$\rangle$,...) and gives the nutritional values for a single day. At the end of a day, the values are shifted, the current day's totals are inserted into the list, and the averages are recomputed. The second type of history is kept in a clause of the form

MENUHIST($\langle$menu-item-list$\rangle$, $\langle$meat-list$\rangle$, $\langle$veg-list$\rangle$)

The clause contains lists of the menu items, meats and vegetables, that have been served during the last week.

To this point, we have discussed the data items that together constitute the state of the system. Now let us discuss the types of *event* that can occur, each of which places a clause on the set-of-support list. In this system, we allow for the following types of event.

(a) The first type of event occurs when a food is eaten. The generated clause is of the form

ATE($\langle$item-number$\rangle$, $\langle$portion-size$\rangle$)

For example,

ATE(92, .5)

is used to indicate that one half of a portion of the menu item numbered 92 has been eaten.

(b) Whenever food is purchased, clauses of the form

BOUGHT($\langle$item-number$\rangle$, $\langle$amount$\rangle$)

are used to indicate that the stock-on-hand values in the INVEN clauses must be incremented.

(c) Whenever any food is used or thrown away, clauses of the following form are generated.

USED($\langle$item-number$\rangle$, $\langle$amount$\rangle$)

(d) The user of the system can request information. To ask whether or not a specific dish is acceptable, given what has already been consumed during the day, the following clause is added.

HOWABOUT($\langle$item-number$\rangle$, $\langle$amount$\rangle$)

To ask the system for a recommendation on what to eat, a clause of the following form is used.

PROPOSE($\langle$type-meal$\rangle$, $\langle$type-meat$\rangle$, $\langle$type-veg$\rangle$)

Here, the $\langle$type-meal$\rangle$ could be "snack", "breakfast", "lunch", or "dinner". The $\langle$type-meat$\rangle$ might be specified as a general class, or left as "unspecified" when any type is acceptable. Similarly, $\langle$type-veg$\rangle$ can be used to restrict the type of vegetable, if desired. Clearly, a comprehensive system could introduce restrictions on far more categories of food, but these are adequate for the illustration.

(e) Finally, a clause of the form

END(day)

is generated at the end of each day.

The specification of the format of the information that constitutes the state of the system, along with the formats of the clauses that represent events, imposes a conceptual structure on the system. However, it is still necessary to give the rules that determine how each event is processed. Let us begin with a simple event. In particular, suppose that

BOUGHT(92, 12)

appears in the set of support. What rule or rules are necessary to process such an event correctly? This is one of the simpler events that can occur. The **if-then** form of the rule is

if

you have purchased n units of item number i,

then

increment the record of the number of units in stock by the value n.

In clause form, the correspondent is

¬BOUGHT(xitem, xamount)
 | ¬INVEN(xitem, xdesc, xonhand, xmin)
 | INVEN(xitem, xdesc, $sum(xonhand, xamount), xmin)

Such processing is trivial. The processing of a used item is slightly more complex—the system must check that the in-stock value does not fall below the desired minimum. This requires the presence of two clauses.

¬USED(xitem, xamount)
 | ¬INVEN(xitem, xdesc, xonhand, xmin)
 | ¬INVEN(xitem, xdesc, $minus(xonhand, xamount), xmin)

¬INVEN(xitem, xdesc, xonhand, xmin)
 | ¬$LT(xonhand, xmin)
 | DO(print, l("Time-to-buy-more", l(xdesc, nil)))

The second of the two clauses simply causes a warning to be printed in the event that the stock in the pantry falls too low.

The logic required to process the other events is significantly more complex. We do not include it here since we are merely illustrating the various properties that can be given to a dietary consultant based on automated reasoning. However, it might prove useful to examine some of the rules required to process a PROPOSE event.

The main rule used to process a PROPOSE is the following.

¬PROPOSE(xtype, xmeat, xveg)
 | ¬GETACCEPTABLE(xtype, xmeat, xveg, xlist)
 | PICKANSWER(xlist)

In **if-then** format the rule is

if

the request is for a meal restricted by the parameters

xtype, xmeat, xveg, **and**

if computing the list of possibilities results in xlist,

then

return a random selection from xlist.

This is not, of course, a particularly profound rule. We now consider the subproblem of computing the list of acceptable solutions. An example of the type of rule that could be used to compute the set of possible choices is the following.

¬BREAKFASTMEATS(xbrklist)

| ¬INSTOCK(xbrklist, xinstock)

| ¬PICKFROM(xinstock, xmeat, xlist)

| GETACCEPTABLE(breakfast, xmeat, unspecified, xlist)

This rule may be thought of as saying "To pick the set of possible breakfast meats, take the set of breakfast meats (xbrklist) and determine the subset that is in stock (xinstock); then pick (subject to possible restrictions) from that set". INSTOCK(xbrklist, xinstock) is true when xinstock is the sublist of xbrklist of elements that are in stock. PICKFROM(xinstock, xmeat, xlist) is true when xlist is the set of acceptable candidate meats chosen from xinstock subject to the restriction specified by xmeat, which was originally acquired from the user in the PROPOSE request. It is assumed that the general-axiom list contains a clause of the form

BREAKFAST(l(11, l(18, l(63, l(82, nil)))))

that lists the types of meat that are acceptable for breakfast, where "sausage" has the item number 11, "ham" has the number 18, "bacon" has the number 63, and "steak" has the number 82. Furthermore,

INSTOCK(list1, list2)

is true exactly when list2 is computed from list1 as the set of elements in list1 that are in stock. The clauses that accomplish this computation are the following.

INSTOCK(nil, nil)

¬INSTOCK(x, y)

| ¬INVEN(xitem, xdesc, 0, xmin)

| INSTOCK(l(xitem, x), y)

¬INSTOCK(x, y)

| ¬INVEN(xitem, xdesc, xamount, xmin)

| ¬$GT(xamount, 0)

| INSTOCK(l(xitem, x), l(xitem, y))

The clauses that define how to pick an acceptable selection from the set of meats in stock are the following.

EQUAL(xmeat, nil)

| ¬INLIST(xmeat, xinstock)

| PICKFROM(xinstock, xmeat, l(xmeat, nil))

INLIST(x, l(x, y))

¬INLIST(x, y) | INLIST(x, l(z, y))

¬MENUHIST(xitems, xmeatlist, xveglist)

| ¬LISTDIFF(xinstock, xmeatlist, xdiff)

| ¬EQUAL(xdiff, nil)

| PICKFROM(xinstock, unspecified, xdiff)

¬MENUHIST(xitems, xmeatlist, xveglist)

| ¬LISTDIFF(xinstock, xmeatlist, nil)

| PICKFROM(xinstock, unspecified, xinstock)

LISTDIFF(nil, x, nil)

¬LISTDIFF(x, y, z) | ¬INLIST(xe, y) | LISTDIFF(l(xe, x), y, z)

¬LISTDIFF(x, y, z) | INLIST(xe, y) | LISTDIFF(l(xe, x), y, l(xe, z))

Here LISTDIFF(x, y, z) is true when z is a list containing exactly those elements that occur in list x but not in list y. Note that these clauses select those meats that are in stock, but have not been recently eaten. If all of the meats that are in stock also have been eaten during the last week, then all of the meats in stock are returned as acceptable.

The clauses that define how to pick from the acceptable set of meats should allow "no meat", when the request is made by a vegetarian, for otherwise every selection would result in an unacceptable breakfast. Note that the clauses do not check for the best choices in terms of calories or vitamins. These checks could easily be included, or simply deferred until the end of the day, when checks occur to produce any required warning messages.

Having given the representation of a small fraction of the expert system that functions as a dietary consultant and meal planner, we simply comment that an inference rule that suffices for drawing conclusions and for processing the clauses is hyperresolution. Of course, for finding certain elements in various lists, demodulation would be needed. What we have here is an expert system defined in terms of a typical automated reasoning system. The expert system uses the clause notation, and relies on inference rules and strategies and various procedures that we have covered in the early chapters of this book.

The complete set of rules for selecting an appropriate choice of food is quite large. In many expert systems, the set of rules contains thousands of clauses. The acquisition of the facts and the rules to manipulate those facts and to answer questions is at least tedious, and sometimes extremely difficult. Once the person who is an expert has supplied that information, the interface to the user must be created. For example, in the given dietary system, to be of much use it must be very convenient for the user to input purchases, uses, and requests. That issue aside, we have shown you how an automated reasoning program may provide assistance in solving an everyday problem.

13.6 The Depth of Reasoning Used in Expert Systems

How powerful will the reasoning component be in future expert systems? The answers to this question vary widely. One popular opinion is that the not-very-powerful reasoning component now in use in systems such as EMYCIN will be adequate. Since we do not share this opinion, let us examine the situation.

For years, work progressed on different types of reasoning programs. Although such programs gradually increased in power, only recently have automated reasoning programs proved useful in solving problems of the level of open questions. The success with such systems as MYCIN, DENDRAL, and PROSPECTOR suggests that much more can be accomplished with reasoning programs. By designing good user interfaces and knowledge acquisition components, extremely useful systems were implemented relying on unsophisticated reasoning components. By improving the user interfaces and knowledge acquisition components, and by making occasional minor additions to the basic reasoning components, it seems likely that a wide variety of expert systems will emerge over the next five years.

Do these facts justify the opinion that the limited reasoning components now in existence will be adequate for the foreseeable future? To answer this question, we give the following rough classification of degrees of reasoning. The classification is gleaned from imagining how a person who is an expert attempts to solve problems.

1. In the first type, an overall plan is conceived. The plan consists of a set of goals that, if each is achieved, solves the problem under study. We call this type of reasoning *strategic reasoning*.

2. Once the major intermediate goals have been selected by some form of strategic reasoning, it is still necessary to work on each of the intermediate problems. Frequently, the highest level work here tends to be relatively *unfocused*. (We shall consider the notion of *focused reasoning* shortly.) In unfocused reasoning, the expert may have some idea about which facts are relevant and which types of conclusions might lead to more information, but no well-defined procedure is known to the expert that can be used to directly yield the answer. Therefore, we call this type of reasoning *relatively unfocused*.

3. In the process of investigating what follows from one or more facts, it is occasionally necessary to temporarily halt the main investigation and compute some needed value. For example, when investigating certain properties about a graph, it might be necessary occasionally to calculate the shortest path between two nodes. This type of reasoning is more *focused* in that a known procedure is used. The procedure may still involve backtracking, but the basic computation is well-controlled. This type of reasoning is best illustrated by the common uses of Prolog. We call this type of reasoning *relatively focused*.

4. Finally, there is totally focused reasoning, by which we mean a computation such as adding two numbers, inverting a matrix, or calculating the orbit of a satellite. This type of reasoning, which could easily be considered as not

warranting the term "reasoning", has received a majority of the study in computer science over the short history of the discipline. Numerous algorithms for performing well-defined computations have been developed and will continue to be developed at an increasing rate.

The last three types of reasoning are distinguished by the degree of "focus" in searching for an answer. Of course, no precise separation exists between focused and unfocused reasoning. Most of the topics covered in this book employ what we are calling relatively unfocused reasoning. In such cases, you cannot say with any certainty which of the possible conclusions will be most productive and will bring you closer to a solution. That is why we have called this type of reasoning unfocused. You may, on the other hand, have a good idea of which steps should be taken next in order to get a solution. The surer you are that you can pick the next step correctly, the more focused the reasoning. In the case of multiplying two matrices, each step that is required can be described before you even begin, which is why we refer to such an activity as totally focused reasoning.

To understand the differences between relatively focused and relatively unfocused reasoning, let us review the basic steps used by most automated reasoning programs that utilize unfocused reasoning. The input to such a program can normally be separated into three classes of statements, and hence into three sets of clauses:

1. General axioms that describe the overall characteristics of the system being explored

2. Set-of-support statements that include both the information that is special to the problem and the statements that amount to assuming the goal unreachable or the conclusion false

3. Demodulators that allow rephrasings based on known equalities

The reasoning program selects a "promising" clause from the set of support, using some heuristic. Then the program deduces the set of new clauses that follow from the selected clause, general axioms, and clauses that have been previously selected from the set of support. Each new clause is simplified, using demodulators and any desired special-purpose simplification algorithms, and then checked with subsumption to see whether or not the new information has already been deduced or captured by a more general piece of information. This process of selecting a clause, generating new clauses, simplifying the new clauses, and finally checking them to see if they should be retained, is a relatively unfocused process.

This type of reasoning is completely appropriate in areas in which no adequate focused approach exists. For example, consider the domino problem presented in chapter 5. In that problem it was not at all clear which moves, if any, might lead to a covering of the checkerboard. Hence, all possibilities (within the given covering scheme) had to be investigated, and intermediate results had to be retained. This type of situation arises in areas in which an investigator has minimal intuition as to exactly how a problem should be attacked, but has some idea about how to recognize potentially useful results.

Focused reasoning, on the other hand, is characterized by a clear idea of exactly how a result can be obtained. Intermediate results are seldom required, removing the often substantial overhead of simplification and subsumption checks. In focused reasoning, backtracking may be necessary, for a clear idea of how to obtain the solution may not point precisely to the required path of reasoning. Focused reasoning is a type of reasoning that is both faster and easier to implement.

The current expert systems use relatively focused reasoning only. Of the four given types of reasoning, Prolog offers a particularly attractive way to implement the last two types of reasoning, although enormous amounts of knowledge concerning the totally focused reasoning has already been encoded in other languages such as FORTRAN and Pascal.

The majority of reasoning by those people classed as expert is probably relatively focused or totally focused. Indeed, frequently the difference between the expert and a novice in any given area is simply that the expert's method of solving the problem is relatively focused, while the novice may fall back on a more general, less directed style of attack.

One mark of progress in a given area is the way standard problems are attacked. The early explorations depend heavily on reasoning of the strategic and relatively unfocused types. Eventually, methods for directly computing solutions are discovered. These methods may work in all cases, or in only a subset of the interesting cases. In any event, they reduce the required effort enormously by being focused and well-controlled. Once good focused techniques are established, the more general and inefficient methods are used only in those cases in which the focused approaches fail to arrive at a desired solution.

Let us return to the question of what types of reasoning will be used in expert systems of the future. Certainly the core reasoning components of such systems will include thousands of focused techniques encoded in some suitable manner. It remains to be seen exactly how much of the focused portion will be special-purpose routines of the sort used in the chess-playing programs. For the next few years, a majority of the work in reasoning components for expert systems will be to encode the focused techniques. Two main tasks exist.

1. First the enormous wealth of encoded algorithms must be made accessible to expert systems. This issue is essentially one of software design, and does not relate directly to the contents of this book.

2. The second task is that of encoding the focused techniques actually utilized by those who are experts. This task is normally referred to as knowledge acquisition. Since this task may present quite a problem, the knowledge acquisition tools that are now being developed (and those that already exist) will be of great importance.

The fact that focused techniques have wide application, however, should not detract from the fact that unfocused reasoning is essential in many fields. The earlier chapters of this book give many examples of problems that require unfocused reasoning. We do not share the view that neither strategic reasoning nor unfocused reasoning will be used in expert systems of the future. In areas in which no effective focused method exists, unfocused reasoning seems both appropriate and required. In many cases, unfocused reasoning has proved to be remarkably productive. To require that expert systems be designed only for areas in which all of the reasoning is focused overlooks many possible applications. Perhaps it is easier to create systems based on focused reasoning, and it may even be the case that the majority of the potential applications will not require unfocused reasoning. Nevertheless, many significant applications will require unfocused reasoning.

In many ways, the question of the need of focused versus unfocused reasoning is reminiscent of what occurred early in the history of computing. When computers were first used for numerical computation, one noted expert stated that there would never be a demand for more than a handful of computers—there was just no need for all of that computational power. Then, as more machines came into existence and software packages for numerical computation began to emerge, many limitations were built into the routines. For example, it was not uncommon to fix the maximum dimension of a matrix to some value, such as 100, with the justification that it would not be necessary to consider matrices any larger. It is still certainly the case that most matrices manipulated by programs fall within the old limits. However, numerous significant applications have arisen that are untenable if such limitations are imposed. Note that the earlier packages with their limitations proved extremely useful and are still being used in many applications. In many cases, however, the earlier routines have proved too restrictive for many unforeseen situations.

13.7 Summary

Research in automated reasoning is very relevant to the design and implementation of expert systems. One of the objectives is, in fact, to produce such systems. This position is acceptable, however, only if the concept of expert system is broadened to include strategic and unfocused reasoning, as well as the focused reasoning that characterizes current systems. The current work in automated reasoning, logic programming—as exemplified by Prolog—and expert systems is highly interrelated. Rather than unrelated efforts, the three represent diverse attacks on the same problem—the problem of reasoning.

14

Prolog: Logic as a Programming Language

In the preceding chapters, you have seen how to present problems from widely different areas to an automated reasoning program. In all cases, the problem description consists of a set of clauses. In this chapter, we focus on a somewhat different use of clauses, namely, the use of clauses as a programming language. The programming language to be discussed is Prolog. Programs written in Prolog are written in clause form. Although the notation is slightly different, clauses have the same meaning in this context as they do in the other chapters of this book.

While sharing essentially the same notation, the use of clauses in a Prolog program differs rather sharply from the use in a typical automated reasoning program. In a Prolog program, clauses are used to express an algorithm chosen to solve some given problem in a very focused fashion—an algorithm intended to compute a solution with very little searching. In contrast, the clauses given to a typical automated reasoning program are used to initiate a less focused search for a solution—less focused in that no precise algorithm is employed to directly compute the solution. Thus, Prolog is recommended for use on problems where you suspect that an algorithm can be programmed to answer a given question without gathering much additional information. When such an algorithm is not known, then the problem calls for assistance from a reasoning program to search for needed missing information. Prolog does not employ such procedures as demodulation or subsumption, for its use is based on executing a very directed approach to solving the problem and thus assumes that little extraneous information will be examined. By dispensing with such procedures, a Prolog program has the potential of being quite efficient when compared with a typical reasoning program.

The effectiveness of a Prolog program depends greatly on the order of the clauses that comprise the program, for the focus of attention is based on that order. In a general reasoning program, on the other hand, the focus of attention is often based on other criteria supplied by the user, criteria such as the weights assigned to various concepts and the clauses placed in the set of support. As with any programming language, each step in a Prolog program is precisely dictated, where the instruction is based on the order of the clauses and on the built-in approach described in this chapter. Of course, the steps taken by an automated reasoning program are in accordance with precise instructions, but the intent is not the execution of a very directed approach to the goal. In Prolog, you hope and often expect to explore one path that starts with the given clauses and terminates with the answer to a question. In a typical reasoning program, you also hope to explore one path, but in fact expect to explore many paths before answering the question. Thus, a trade-off exists in choosing to have a Prolog program assist you over choosing a general reasoning program to assist you. In Prolog, you have the potential of a far faster execution, a potential that is realized on certain classes of problems. That potential is not realized when the algorithm expressed in the given clauses is forced to begin an extensive search. The lack of demodulation and subsumption and access to a wide variety of inference rules and strategies can be very costly. When this occurs, then the question can instead be submitted for assistance to an automated reasoning program that does utilize these added features.

An example of a problem that you might submit to Prolog is that of computing the greatest common divisor of two integers. Just as you might write a FORTRAN program for this task, you can instead write a Prolog program. An algorithm exists that computes that desired result directly without requiring a search for new information. In contrast, the mathematical research discussed in Chapter 9 does require rather extensive searching and, therefore, is not the type of problem to be solved by writing a Prolog program. As we discuss shortly, Prolog offers certain features that other programming languages do not, which is why it is an attractive alternative.

You can view Prolog as employing negative hyperresolution as its sole inference rule. But what corresponds to negative hyperresolution in Prolog does not add new clauses (unless explicitly requested to by the Prolog program). Not adding new clauses contributes to the efficiency of the language and in part explains why demodulation and subsumption are not employed. Even though the language does not actually employ negative hyperresolution, thinking of Prolog's processing of the given clauses in terms of an inference rule that is somewhat familiar gives you a head start. The object of negative hyperresolution is to produce clauses each of whose literals is preceded by the **not** symbol ¬. Recall that such clauses are called *negative* clauses. A *positive* clause contains only positive literals, and a *mixed* clause contains some positive and some negative literals. Negative hyperresolution selects a set of negative clauses, *satellites*, and seeks a positive clause or a mixed clause, a *nucleus*, to be used with the selected clauses. It attempts to find a variable replacement that simultaneously unifies various literals to then yield a negative clause.

Besides the connections of the clause language and of inference rule between a typical reasoning program and Prolog, the connection of strategy exists. The set of support strategy discussed in Chapter 3 and employed in the various other applications is in effect also employed by Prolog. In one common use of this programming language, a question is asked. The question takes the form of a negative unit clause, and is the only clause placed in the set of support.

Because of the connections just discussed, you can view Prolog as an application of automated reasoning. Whereas in many of the chapters of this book we focus on how to solve some class of problems with an automated reasoning program, here we focus on a programming language that is both an application itself and a means for solving certain problems of a "determinate" character.

14.1 An Introduction to Prolog

Prolog is a programming language that employs clauses as the basic form of representation. It differs from other programming languages in that logical power is "built into" the language. In particular, since clauses are the means for giving information to Prolog, statements involving quantified variables are easily made and easily manipulated.

For example, the definition of grandparent is easily conveyed either to the typical automated reasoning program or to Prolog, but the notation is not identical. While for the former, you can write

$$\neg PARENT(z, y) \mid \neg PARENT(x, z) \mid GRANDPARENT(x, y)$$

for the latter you write

$$grandparent(X, Y) :- parent(X, Z),\ parent(Z, Y).$$

In Chapter 2, you learned that the first of these two clauses can be read as, "for *all* z, y, and x, **if** z is the parent of y **and** x is the parent of z, **then** x is the grandparent of y". For Prolog, the second clause can be read the same way. Alternatively, you could read it as "To show that X is the grandparent of Y, first find a Z such that X is the parent of Z, and then show that Z is the parent of Y". Now if you know that Tom is a parent of Bob, and also know that Bob is a parent of Linda, then you can quickly conclude that Tom is a grandparent of Linda.

Fact:

PARENT(Tom, Bob)

Fact:

PARENT(Bob, Linda)

Conclusion:

GRANDPARENT(Tom, Linda)

If Prolog were given these familiar clauses as well as the second version of the definition of grandparent, and if the appropriate question about grandparents were asked, Prolog would immediately correctly answer it. The question would be trivial for Prolog because of its "built-in" treatment of variables and its "built-in" ability to process clauses in a way reminiscent of the inference rule negative hyperresolution.

These built-in features present a sharp contrast to other programming languages. In those languages, you would be forced to program the corresponding treatment of variables and of general information of the "grandparent" variety. Other programming languages do not give you this logical power and, therefore, require much more of you when confronted with various problems of the type just given. What is perhaps surprising is that Prolog gives you this added power and convenience, and yet the price is remarkably small. Implementations exist that are reasonably competitive in terms of speed with various commonly used programming languages.

The first point to note, when integrating an understanding of Prolog into your understanding of automated reasoning in general, is the notational differences between Prolog and the material presented in the other chapters of the book. Although a number of representations are used with Prolog, we give that which is gaining in acceptance. Certain conventions are observed for representing variables and predicates and functions and, of greatest importance, for representing clauses. Rather than employing the first clause given above for the definition of grandparent, the second is the one most commonly used.

grandparent(X, Y) : − parent(X, Z), parent(Z, Y).

Such a clause defines a procedure. Facts, on the other hand, are always positive unit clauses, but not conversely. In other words, there are unit clauses that are not facts, but no nonunit clause is considered a fact. A Prolog program consists of facts and procedures. By considering the facts and, when necessary, executing the procedures, a Prolog program can answer various questions.

To see how Prolog works, let us examine the following set of facts and procedures that form a Prolog program, a program that can be used to answer questions about the relationships between people. Although not all of the facts that we give are needed for the example, the set of these facts illustrates the typical situation that Prolog copes with so well.

There are thirteen people who are related in various ways: Jan, Sally, Linda, Carol, Jenny, Gail, Mary, Tom, Bob, Jim, Dick, Earl, and John. Jan and Tom are parents of Bob, Jim, and Carol. Sally and Bob are parents of Dick and Linda. Earl and Mary are parents of John. Carol and John are parents of Jenny and Gail. This information or collection of facts is represented in Prolog with unit clauses. Notice the familiar situation that occurred in the early chapters, the need to say in clause form who is female and who is male.

(1) female(jan).	(16) parent(jan, jim).
(2) female(sally).	(17) parent(tom, jim).
(3) female(linda).	(18) parent(jan, carol).
(4) female(carol).	(19) parent(tom, carol).
(5) female(jenny).	(20) parent(sally, dick).
(6) female(gail).	(21) parent(bob, dick).
(7) female(mary).	(22) parent(sally, linda).
(8) male(tom).	(23) parent(bob, linda).
(9) male(bob).	(24) parent(earl, john).
(10) male(jim).	(25) parent(mary, john).
(11) male(dick).	(26) parent(carol, jenny).
(12) male(earl).	(27) parent(john, jenny).
(13) male(john).	(28) parent(carol, gail).
(14) parent(jan, bob).	(29) parent(john, gail).
(15) parent(tom, bob).	

Predicates, functions, and constants begin with lower case letters, variables with upper case letters; clauses are terminated with a period.

Next, let us assume that the question to be programmed in Prolog is about grandparents. In that case, a definition is needed for being a grandparent, and the clause given above is it.

(30) grandparent(X, Y) :− parent(X, Z), parent(Z, Y)

As we said, clause 30 defines a procedure. A procedure is a definition, or consists of the steps required to compute some value. Each clause in a procedure begins with a single positive literal called the *head* of the clause, and each procedure is made up of clauses that have the same predicate in the head literal. In a procedure, the single positive literal—the head—always occurs to the left of the :− symbol. The literals to the right of :− are thought of as negative literals. The negative literals are called *subgoals*. The positive literal is the *goal*. In Prolog, the object is to reach the *goal* by satisfying the *subgoals*.

The Prolog meaning of clause 30 is

To show that X is the grandparent of Y, first find a Z such that X is the parent of Z, and then show that Z is the parent of Y.

A more mechanistic way of saying this is:

> To show that X is the grandparent of Y, first go through the input clauses in order, looking for a way to satisfy the first subgoal. In the example that we are considering, this amounts to selecting the first fact (in terms of occurrence within the set of facts) that unifies with the first literal to the right of the $:-$. If there is one, this action will instantiate Z. Now try to unify a fact with the partially instantiated third literal, again going through the set of clauses in order.

The first literal of clause 30 is a goal that can be reached by solving the two subgoals, represented by the negative literals, in order. Prolog always attempts to solve the subgoals in order from left to right.

In the example, clause 30 can be used to answer a question of any of four forms.

> Tom is the grandparent of whom?
>
> Who is the grandparent of Linda?
>
> Who is the grandparent of whom?
>
> Jan is the grandparent of Linda?

You can execute a Prolog program—say that consisting of clauses 1 through 30—by asking a question of one of the given types, for example. No matter which of the four questions you ask, the Prolog program will be executed in the same way, although the outcome will of course be different. So let us ask one of the questions and see exactly what is meant by executing the given Prolog program—see what Prolog actually does.

> Tom is the grandparent of whom?:   grandparent(tom, GC)

When this question is asked, the Prolog program under examination first looks through its facts to see if the answer is already present. If one of the facts in the program answers the question, the program stops with the answer. If not, then a procedure is invoked. Clause 30 comes into play, and its positive literal is partially instantiated by substituting Tom for X. As we said, to reach the goal of answering the question, Prolog attempts to solve the subgoals in order from left to right. To solve the first subgoal, the Prolog program looks through its facts in the order they are given to it, starting with the earliest. A fact is being sought that unifies with the second literal, the first negative literal to the right of $:-$. But the fact must unify with the partially instantiated second literal, for the variable X has been replaced by tom. (Recall that variables must begin with an upper case letter, while constants and functions and predicates must begin with a lower case letter.) If such a fact is found, then the variable Z is instantiated with the value forced on it by the unification with the found fact. When this occurs, the first subgoal has been solved. Then the Prolog program attempts to solve the second subgoal—to find a fact that unifies with the second negative literal that, in this case, is partially instantiated. The second literal has had its occurrence of Z replaced by the value forced on it by the previous solving of a subgoal.

If the second subgoal cannot be solved within the constraints of the given solution of the first subgoal, then a new solution for the first subgoal is sought. If a new solution is found, again the Prolog program attempts to solve the second subgoal, constrained of course by the new solution. This process of seeking a second solution for an earlier subgoal because the first solution does not extend to a solution of later subgoals is called *backtracking*. Prolog will continue attempting to solve the subgoals in order from left to right, backtracking again and again when necessary, until no way to consistently solve the subgoals can be found. (Although not usual, it is possible for the program to continue backtracking forever.)

With the given question, Prolog will use clause 15 to solve the first subgoal, and then use clause 21 to solve the second subgoal. Thus, the answer that is found is that Tom is the grandparent of Dick. If asked, the Prolog program would continue from here to find the other grandchildren of Tom.

Does this description remind you of an inference rule and a strategy, each of which was discussed in the first few chapters? Clauses 30, 15, and 21 taken together yield

GRANDPARENT(Tom, Dick)

by applying the inference rule of hyperresolution. On the other hand, keying on the question in the form, in effect, of a negative literal is reminiscent of the set of support strategy. While a general-purpose automated reasoning program does not have any built-in constraints on the order of actions, a Prolog program does. The negative literals must be considered for unification in the order from left to right. The unification of each must be attempted with the facts taken in the order they are supplied, earliest first. Such constraints and rules for taking action are why the word "procedure" is used. Prolog specifies precisely how grandparents are to be found, and thus "procedure" is an appropriate word. Such procedures or subroutines or subprograms in the form of clauses or sets of clauses are a key concept in Prolog. The given example illustrates that a program is being executed. Thus, Prolog is a programming language and not, in fact, an automated reasoning system. Clause 30 can be thought of as a definition of grandparent, or thought of as a procedure for computing grandparents.

If you had instead asked the question grandparent(X,Dick), the given Prolog program would first find one grandparent of Dick. After printing out the answer, Prolog would pause. You could then have it continue until all four grandparents had been determined by the given program. But you might wonder at this point what it means to program in Prolog, since Prolog is a programming language.

To program in Prolog, you represent in clause form the facts as positive unit clauses. The procedures for using the facts—for computing answers to questions—are programmed by writing the appropriate sets of clauses. All clauses for a specific procedure or subroutine must begin with a positive literal with the identical predicate. Clauses in a procedure are not necessarily nonunit clauses. Finally, the clauses are arranged according to your desire for the execution of the program. The choice of arrangement, as with any programming language, is up to you. Just as you can arrange code, say in FORTRAN, in a number of ways to produce the same result, so also can you arrange the clauses of a Prolog program. The arrangement has an important effect on the efficiency of the program. The arrangement determines what will happen, for the order of solving subgoals and the order of attempting to solve a particular subgoal is predetermined. That is the nature of Prolog.

Although you might feel constrained by the built-in features of Prolog, remember that you are given the choice of the order in which the clauses are placed. As commented earlier, this programming language gives a programmer built-in logical power through its treatment of variables and its treatment of clauses.

As with other programming languages, Prolog permits one procedure or subroutine to call another. This occurs, for example, when the set of given facts is insufficient to solve a subgoal. To illustrate this situation, let us consider some additional procedures.

(31) grandmother(X, Y) : − grandparent(X, Y), female(X).

(32) grandfather(X, Y) : − grandparent(X, Y), male(X).

(33) father(X, Y) : − parent(X, Y), male(X).

(34) mother(X, Y) : − parent(X, Y), female(X).

(35) sibling(X, Y) : − ne(X, Y), parent(P, X), parent(P,Y).

(36) niece(X, Y) : − female(X), parent(X, Z), sibling(Z, Y).

(37) ne(X, Y) : − X = Y, !, fail.

(38) ne(X, Y).

The procedure consisting of clause 31 is a procedure that cannot be executed strictly by using the facts, clauses 1 through 29. The first subgoal—the first negative literal of clause 31—cannot be solved with the given facts. To solve this subgoal, clause 30 must be employed. Put another way, the procedure 31 invokes the procedure 30. Under what condition would clause 31 be executed?

The procedure consisting of clause 31 is executed, for example, when the question is: Who is Gail's grandmother? To ask this question of the Prolog program consisting of clauses 1 through 38, you type

grandmother(GM, gail).

In this clause, GM is a variable for, as required by Prolog, all variables begin with an upper case letter, and expressions that begin with an upper case letter must be a variable. When this question is asked, clause 31 is the only path to be explored, for no other clause has grandmother as a predicate. Prolog first attempts to solve the first subgoal to the right of : −, the first negative literal of clause 31. The facts 1 through 29 are examined in order with the intent of solving that subgoal. No fact in that set of facts has the predicate grandparent, so Prolog then attempts to solve the subgoal by invoking another procedure.

Not only are the facts taken in the order they are given when attempting to solve a subgoal, but the clauses within a procedure to be invoked are also. With this program, clause 30 is the only one to consider since it is the only clause that contains a literal with the predicate grandparent. Using clause 30 in an attempt to find a literal to match the first negative literal of clause 31 is much like invoking a subroutine in one of the more commonly used programming languages. The specific subgoal to be solved is

grandparent(GM, gail)

since the question

grandmother(GM, gail).

instantiates the variables X and Y of clause 31 respectively to GM and gail. When the procedure 30 is invoked by clause 31, the head or main goal of 30 has its variables X and Y respectively instantiated to GM and gail. Clause 30 can be thought of as a subroutine, grandparent, that takes two parameters. In this invocation, the subroutine 30 will assign to GM the name of the first computed grandparent of the second parameter gail.

Clause 30, when invoked, presents two subgoals to be solved. They are solved respectively by clauses 20 and 18, and GM in clause 30 is assigned the constant jan. At that point in the Prolog program, the first subgoal of clause 31 has been solved, and the program then attempts to solve the second subgoal, constrained by the solution to the first. The second subgoal, female(jan), is solved with clause 1, and the question is successfully answered. The program returns the answer jan is the grandmother of gail.

The position in grandparent is saved in case backtracking occurs. Thus, if using the fact that jan is the grandparent does not allow the program to complete, the program will then try tom. The Prolog program, when asked for Gail's grandmother, will try all possibilities until none remain—all possibilities to simultaneously solve both subgoals of clause 31. Such is the typical performance of a Prolog program—a procedure is called, and its subgoals are considered for solution. The solution to each is sought by using the given facts and, if they are insufficient, by invoking other procedures. If the facts and procedures are found lacking, then the program stops with no answer to the given question.

We now come to additional features of the programming language that differ from other programming languages. Among the added features to be discussed, certain of them lack the logical properties that are often demanded in automated reasoning. When these features are encountered, for example, the lack of an "occurs check", we shall clarify this point.

Prolog offers a built-in treatment of equality. Clause 37 illustrates Prolog's treatment.

The first subgoal

X = Y

of clause 37 is automatically solved when the instantiations of X and Y can be unified. When they cannot, the subgoal is automatically considered to fail. Clauses 37 and 38 together define a procedure for determining whether two terms are unequal. The first subgoal of clause 37 is considered for solution. If it is solved—if X and Y are instantiated to the same value—then the second subgoal of clause 37 is considered. The second subgoal, !, is a special Prolog symbol, and by definition always succeeds—always is solved. And here is a feature that alters the normal backtracking algorithm in Prolog.

The ! symbol is called the *cut* symbol. When it is encountered, Prolog's actions are strongly constrained. No backtracking is permitted for subgoals that occur before the cut symbol. All attempts at solving succeeding subgoals must be within the constraints imposed by the instantiations that have occurred up to the cut symbol. Also, no later clauses in the procedure being invoked are examined. Thus, if the ! is reached in clause 37, then clause 38 will not be examined, for clauses 37 and 38 are part of the same procedure since the head literal of each contains the predicate ne. When a ! is reached, alternative instantiations of earlier literals are not permitted. This restriction naturally leads to the question of whether clauses must always have a logical interpretation, or whether they can have either a logical or a procedural interpretation. Clauses 37 and 38 can be interpreted only in a procedural way. In particular, clause 38 cannot be read or interpreted separately; if it were, it would obviously be false. In effect, clauses 37 and 38 are bound together. However, this feature is quite useful when the algorithm being programmed is known to have certain properties.

In clause 37, when the subgoal ! is reached, it is solved automatically. The third subgoal, fail, is also a special Prolog symbol. The subgoal of "fail" automatically fails—cannot be solved. Thus, when the subgoal X = Y succeeds, the procedure does not succeed, for no further instantiation can be tried with clause 37, and clause 38 cannot be examined. On the other hand, if the first subgoal of clause 37 cannot be solved, then clause 38 will be considered. Since clause 38 has no subgoals, it automatically is solved. In that case, the terms in question are determined to be not equal.

Prolog programmers find the cut a convenience, especially when, for example, a procedure is being written to test a condition, and an algorithm is known for showing when the condition does not hold. In that case, a procedure of the form

conditionholds(PARAMETERS) : − notcondition(PARAMETERS), !, fail.
conditionholds(PARAMETERS).

can be used.

Next, we consider a feature of Prolog that lacks a desirable logical property—soundness. In many implementations, no *occurs check* is made during unification. In other words, no test is made during unification to determine whether or not a term substituted for a variable contains that variable. Thus, in principle, an unsound deduction can be made under certain conditions.

Let us now review what we have covered. A Prolog program consists of a set of facts and a set of procedures. A procedure is a set of clauses that together specify how to compute a value or set of values. All clauses in a procedure have the same predicate in the head or first literal. Each clause in a procedure presents a set of subgoals—possibly none—that must be solved in order from left to right to execute the procedure, and thus to compute the value. The subgoals are the literals to the right of :- and can be thought of as negative literals. If all of the subgoals are solved, the computation is said to succeed. If all attempts at simultaneously solving the subgoals fail, the procedure fails. When a subgoal is solved, the solution imposes constraints on later subgoals, for certain of their variables may have been instantiated by the solution. When a later subgoal fails, Prolog backtracks—tries another solution of the previous subgoal.

A subgoal can be solved with facts that are given in the input as part of the Prolog program, or can be solved by invoking another Prolog procedure. Facts and procedures invoked to solve a subgoal must be used in the order they occur in the Prolog program. The example given above for the use of the cut symbol illustrates the importance of choosing an appropriate order.

All clauses in Prolog, with the exception of the questions asked of a Prolog program, must contain exactly one positive literal. In effect, questions take the form of negative unit clauses. Unless specifically requested, no new clauses are created during the execution of a Prolog program. Thus, subsumption and demodulation play no role in Prolog. By retaining no new clauses, by not employing subsumption, and by not employing demodulation, a Prolog program offers the potential for increased efficiency. In many implementations, no *occurs check* is made during unification. Not making such a check adds to the potential efficiency, although it also admits the possibility of making an unsound deduction.

To illustrate the logical power of a Prolog program, we suggest you program in another language the example used here—that of computing a person's grandfathers. In basic, FORTRAN, PL/I, C, or Pascal, you do not have the built-in features that are present in Prolog, such as its treatment of variables and its other aspects.

EXERCISES

1. Write a Prolog program to compute the notion of cousin.
2. What would happen if the first subgoal of clause 35 were eliminated?
3. Give an alternative procedure for calculating grandmother.
4. Give a Prolog procedure to calculate great-grandparents.

5. Give a Prolog procedure to determine whether or not someone has siblings. In particular,

> sibling(p)

succeeds exactly when p has at least one sibling. Then give one that succeeds only when p has no siblings.

14.2 An Example from Nuclear Reactor Design

The design of nuclear plants presents many problems, some of which are quite like those in circuit design. We consider a problem from reactor design to illustrate what can be done with Prolog.

14.2.1 Description of the Problem

The component of nuclear reactors on which we now focus is called the "reactor trip system". Its function is to shut down a reactor in the event of a serious problem. An error in the design of such a system could produce serious consequences. To minimize the likelihood of such an error occurring, much research has ensued in the area of reasoning about the design of such systems. One goal is that of verifying the properties of a design before construction has begun.

The reactor system consists of a set of *components*. Each component has a set of *connection points*. A *connection* runs from a connection point on one component to a connection point on another component. The diagram on the next page is merely an approximation of a section of such a system. The components in the diagram are divided into three categories. The circles on the left represent devices that detect different types of emergency conditions, such as seismic activity, an operator calling for a shutdown, or a powerloss. The rectangles in the middle represent intermediate components that must react to the emergency signals and forward them. Thus, if the *seismic* component detects an emergency, then *emlatch 1, emlatch 2,* and *scramvalve* all receive the signal and must react properly. The diamonds on the right are the *rods* in the core of the nuclear reactor. If two or more rods receive an emergency signal and drop, the reactor is supposed to shut down successfully.

Each type of component has a set of connection points. For example, an *emlatch* has four connection points. Each connection point on a component—at least in the reactor trip system—may be thought of as either an *input* connection point or an *output* connection point. For example, the *seismic* component has three output connection points, while an *emlatch* has three input connection points and one output connection point.

We can easily encode the information in the diagram into four tables. These tables may be thought of as a small database of facts that describe the situation we are considering.

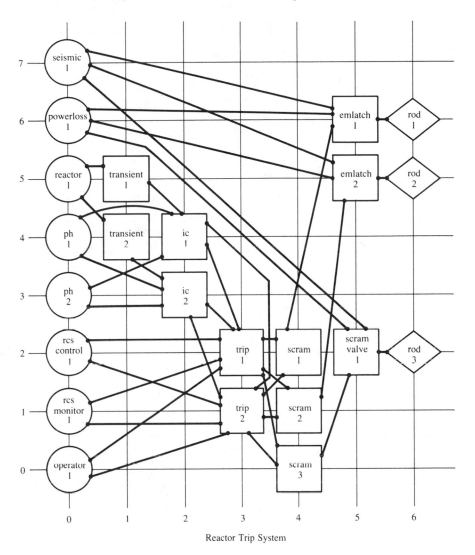

Reactor Trip System

1. The first table describes the types of components in the drawing. For example, an *emlatch* is a type of component.

2. The second describes the attributes of each connection point on a component type.

3. The third describes occurrences of the component types. In the drawing, there are two *emlatches*. Each is an occurrence of the *emlatch* component type.

4. The fourth table describes how the occurrences are connected.

The tabular form of the data in the drawing is the following.

Component Types

Component	Number of Connection Points	Component	Number of Connection Points
seismic	3	transient	2
powerloss	3	ic	5
reactor	2	trip	8
ph	2	scram	3
rcscontrol	2	scramvalve	4
rcsmonitor	2	emlatch	4
operator	2	rod	1

Connection Point Attributes

Type	Connection Point	Attribute	Type	Connection Point	Attribute
seismic	1	output	ic	5	output
seismic	2	output	trip	1	input
seismic	3	output	trip	2	input
powerloss	1	output	trip	3	input
powerloss	2	output	trip	4	input
powerloss	3	output	trip	5	input
reactor	1	output	trip	6	output
reactor	2	output	trip	7	output
ph	1	output	trip	8	output
ph	2	output	emlatch	1	input
rcscontrol	1	output	emlatch	2	input
rcscontrol	2	output	emlatch	3	input
rcsmonitor	1	output	emlatch	4	output
rcsmonitor	2	output	scram	1	input
operator	1	output	scram	2	input
operator	2	output	scram	3	output
transient	1	input	scramvalve	1	input
transient	2	output	scramvalve	2	input
ic	1	input	scramvalve	3	input
ic	2	input	scramvalve	4	output
ic	3	input	rod	1	input
ic	4	output			

Component Occurrences

Type	Occurrence	X-coord	Y-coord	Type	Occurrence	X-coord	Y-coord
seismic	1	0	7	trip	1	3	2
powerless	1	0	6	trip	2	3	1
reactor	1	0	5	scram	1	4	2
ph	1	0	4	scram	2	4	1
ph	2	0	3	scram	3	4	0
rcscontrol	1	0	2	scramvalve	1	5	2
rcsmonitor	1	0	1	emlatch	1	5	6
operator	1	0	0	emlatch	2	5	5
transient	1	1	5	rod	1	6	6
transient	2	1	4	rod	2	6	5
ic	1	2	4	rod	3	6	2
ic	2	2	3				

Connections

Type-1	Occ-1	Conn-pt-1	Type-2	Occ-2	Conn-pt-2
seismic	1	1	emlatch	1	1
seismic	1	2	emlatch	2	1
seismic	1	3	scramvalve	1	1
powerloss	1	1	emlatch	1	2
powerloss	1	2	emlatch	2	2
powerloss	1	3	scramvalve	1	2
reactor	1	1	transient	1	1
reactor	1	2	transient	2	1
ph	1	1	ic	1	2
ph	1	2	ic	2	2
ph	2	1	ic	1	3
ph	2	2	ic	2	3
rcscontrol	1	1	trip	1	3
rcscontrol	1	2	trip	2	3
rcsmonitor	1	1	trip	1	4
rcsmonitor	1	2	trip	2	4
operator	1	1	trip	1	5
operator	1	2	trip	2	5
transient	1	2	ic	1	1
transient	2	2	ic	2	1
ic	1	4	trip	1	1
ic	1	5	trip	2	1
ic	2	4	trip	1	2
ic	2	5	trip	2	2
trip	1	6	scram	1	1
trip	1	7	scram	2	1
trip	1	8	scram	3	1
trip	2	6	scram	1	2
trip	2	7	scram	2	2
trip	2	8	scram	3	2
scram	1	3	emlatch	1	3
scram	2	3	emlatch	2	3
scram	3	3	scramvalve	1	3
emlatch	1	4	rod	1	1
emlatch	2	4	rod	2	1
scramvalve	1	4	rod	3	1

Here each connection is shown just once. In some sense, including two rows for each connection would add no new information, since the second row can be computed from the first by a known rule.

We have given a highly abstracted view of the reactor trip system. In fact this description resembles in many ways a set of connected stereo components or connected integrated circuit chips. The same tabular encoding scheme works for those systems as well.

In the reactor trip system, all input and output values are ON or OFF. At any point in time, the output of the detection devices depends on the external environment. The output values of an intermediate component depend only on its input values. In the reactor trip system, the dependence is very simple: if any input value is ON, all output values are ON; otherwise, all output values are OFF.

The object is to reason about the behavior of the system described by the tables. Consider, for example, the following questions.

> Suppose that all detection devices work correctly and that exactly one nondetection component is broken. Will a signal of ON from one of the detectors necessarily cause at least two rods to drop, resulting in a successful shutdown?

> If one intermediate component and one rod are malfunctioning, will a signal of ON from any detector cause the other two rods to drop?

Such questions are important in determining the safety of any given design. In systems with hundreds or thousands of components, checking all possible cases manually is difficult, if not impossible.

14.2.2 Representation of the Facts in Prolog

Let us now proceed to see how Prolog can be used to answer questions about systems such as the reactor trip system. First, it is necessary to encode the information in the four tables into Prolog facts. You will recall from the brief introduction to Prolog that facts are represented with unit clauses. A natural way to represent the tabular data is to use one Prolog fact for each line in the table. The predicate for a fact is the table name, and the arguments are the column entries. Thus,

(1) type(seismic, 3).

(2) type(powerloss, 3).

(3) type(reactor, 2).

(4) type(ph, 2).

(5) type(rcscontrol, 2).

(6) type(rcsmonitor, 2).

(7) type(operator, 2).

(8) type(transient, 2).

(9) type(ic, 5).

(10) type(trip, 8).

(11) type(scram, 3).

(12) type(scramvalve, 4).

(13) type(emlatch, 4).

(14) type(rod, 1).

represent the information in the first table. The second table encodes into the following clauses.

(15) conpt(seismic, 1, output).

(16) conpt(seismic, 2, output).

(17) conpt(seismic, 3, output).

(18) conpt(powerloss, 1, output).

(19) conpt(powerloss, 2, output).

(20) conpt(powerloss, 3, output).

(21) conpt(reactor, 1, output).

(22) conpt(reactor, 2, output).

(23) conpt(ph, 1, output).

(24) conpt(ph, 2, output).

(25) conpt(rcscontrol, 1, output).

(26) conpt(rcscontrol, 2, output).

(27) conpt(rcsmonitor, 1, output).

(28) conpt(rcsmonitor, 2, output).

(29) conpt(operator, 1, output).

(30) conpt(operator, 2, output).

(31) conpt(transient, 1, input).

(32) conpt(transient, 2, output).

(33) conpt(ic, 1, input).

(34) conpt(ic, 2, input).

(35) conpt(ic, 3, input).

(36) conpt(ic, 4, output).

(37) conpt(ic, 5, output).

(38) conpt(trip, 1, input).

(39) conpt(trip, 2, input).

(40) conpt(trip, 3, input).

(41) conpt(trip, 4, input).

(42) conpt(trip, 5, input).

(43) conpt(trip, 6, output).

(44) conpt(trip, 7, output).

(45) conpt(trip, 8, output).

(46) conpt(emlatch, 1, input).

(47) conpt(emlatch, 2, input).

(48) conpt(emlatch, 3, input).

(49) conpt(emlatch, 4, output).

(50) conpt(scram, 1, input).

(51) conpt(scram, 2, input).

(52) conpt(scram, 3, output).

(53) conpt(scramvalve, 1, input).

(54) conpt(scramvalve, 2, input).

(55) conpt(scramvalve, 3, input).

(56) conpt(scramvalve, 4, output).

(57) conpt(rod, 1, input).

The third table encodes into the following clauses.

(58) occur(seismic, 1, 0, 7).

(59) occur(powerloss, 1, 0, 6).

(60) occur(reactor, 1, 0, 5).

(61) occur(ph, 1, 0, 4).

(62) occur(ph, 2, 0, 3).

(63) occur(rcscontrol, 1, 0, 2).

(64) occur(rcsmonitor, 1, 0, 1).

(65) occur(operator, 1, 0, 0).

(66) occur(transient, 1, 1, 5).

(67) occur(transient, 2, 1, 4).

(68) occur(ic, 1, 2, 4).

(69) occur(ic, 2, 2, 3).

(70) occur(trip, 1, 3, 2).

(71) occur(trip, 2, 3, 1).

(72) occur(scram, 1, 4, 2).

(73) occur(scram, 2, 4, 1).

(74) occur(scram, 3, 4, 0).

(75) occur(scramvalve, 1, 5, 2).

(76) occur(emlatch, 1, 5, 6).

(77) occur(emlatch, 2, 5, 5).

(78) occur(rod, 1, 6, 6).

(79) occur(rod, 2, 6, 5).

(80) occur(rod, 3, 6, 2).

Finally, the last table encodes into the following clauses.

(81) connected(seismic, 1, 1, emlatch, 1, 1).

(82) connected(seismic, 1, 2, emlatch, 2, 1).

(83) connected(seismic, 1, 3, scramvalve, 1, 1).

(84) connected(powerloss, 1, 1, emlatch, 1, 2).

(85) connected(powerloss, 1, 2, emlatch, 2, 2).

(86) connected(powerloss, 1, 3, scramvalve, 1, 2).

(87) connected(reactor, 1, 1, transient, 1, 1).

(88) connected(reactor, 1, 2, transient, 2, 1).

(89) connected(ph, 1, 1, ic, 1, 2).

(90) connected(ph, 1, 2, ic, 2, 2).

(91) connected(ph, 2, 1, ic, 1, 3).

(92) connected(ph, 2, 2, ic, 2, 3).

(93) connected(rcscontrol, 1, 1, trip, 1, 3).

(94) connected(rcscontrol, 1, 2, trip, 2, 3).

(95) connected(rcsmonitor, 1, 1, trip, 1, 4).

(96) connected(rcsmonitor, 1, 2, trip, 2, 4).

(97) connected(operator, 1, 1, trip, 1, 5).

(98) connected(operator, 1, 2, trip, 2, 5).

(99) connected(transient, 1, 2, ic, 1, 1).

(100) connected(transient, 2, 2, ic, 2, 1).

(101) connected(ic, 1, 4, trip, 1, 1).

(102) connected(ic, 1, 5, trip, 2, 1).

(103) connected(ic, 2, 4, trip, 1, 2).

(104) connected(ic, 2, 5, trip, 2, 2).

(105) connected(trip, 1, 6, scram, 1, 1).

(106) connected(trip, 1, 7, scram, 2, 1).

(107) connected(trip, 1, 8, scram, 3, 1).

(108) connected(trip, 2, 6, scram, 1, 2).

(109) connected(trip, 2, 7, scram, 2, 2).

(110) connected(trip, 2, 8, scram, 3, 2).

(111) connected(scram, 1, 3, emlatch, 1, 3).

(112) connected(scram, 2, 3, emlatch, 2, 3).

(113) connected(scram, 3, 3, scramvalve, 1, 3).

(114) connected(emlatch, 1, 4, rod, 1, 1).

(115) connected(emlatch, 2, 4, rod, 2, 1).

(116) connected(scramvalve, 1, 4, rod, 3, 1).

We have given three forms for representing the information—the diagram, the tables, and the unit clauses—to illustrate exactly how a database of facts can be encoded.

14.2.3 A Simple Program to Validate Connection Point Attributes

Once such a database of facts is encoded, we can write Prolog procedures to answer questions about the content. For example, we might wish to verify that each connection connects an input connection point to an output connection point. In a diagram as large as the one we are using, it is quite easy to represent a connection incorrectly. The results could, of course, be disastrous, so any possible cross-checking is desirable. The following Prolog procedure provides one such cross-check.

```
badconnect(TYPE1, OCC1, CONPT1, TYPE2, OCC2, CONPT2) : −
    connected(TYPE1, OCC1, CONPT1, TYPE2, OCC2, CONPT2),
    conpt(TYPE1, CONPT1, ATR1),
    conpt(TYPE2, CONPT2, ATR2),
    ATR1 = ATR2.
```

This procedure finds all bad connections—those that connect two connection points with the same attribute.

EXERCISE

6. Write a Prolog procedure that finds every connection that does not connect an input connection point to an output connection point. The procedure must find, among others, any misspelling of the attribute of a connection point.

14.2.4 Finding Paths

The goal is to write a program to verify that the diagram does have the property that the reactor will shut down in the case of an emergency, even if a single intermediate component or a rod fails. To do this, the program looks for paths between detectors and rods. For example, the program looks for paths that miss some designated component that has failed. The program might be required to determine whether or not a path exists from *ph 1* to *rod 3* without going through *ic 2*. The following procedure checks for such a path.

> ispath(rod, RODNUMBER, RODNUMBER, MISSTYPE, MISSOCC).
>
> ispath(STARTTYPE, STARTOCC, RODNUMBER, MISSTYPE,
>   MISSOCC) : −
>   notsame(STARTTYPE, STARTOCC, MISSTYPE, MISSOCC),
>   connected(STARTTYPE, STARTOCC, SCONPT, XTYPE, XOCC,
>   XCONPT),
>   notsame(XTYPE, XOCC, MISSTYPE, MISSOCC),
>   conpt(STARTTYPE, SCONPT, output),
>   conpt(XTYPE, XCONPT, input),
>   ispath(XTYPE, XOCC, RODNUMBER, MISSTYPE, MISSOCC).
>
> notsame(T1, O1, T2, O2) : − ne(T1, T2).
> notsame(T1, O1, T2, O2) : − ne(O1, O2).

This set of clauses determines whether or not a path exists from any component to a designated rod, without passing through a component that must be skipped. For example, a component must be skipped if it is broken.

14.2.5 Checking Single Component Failure

Taking the preceding Prolog programs into account, we can now write a Prolog procedure to determine whether or not the failure of any intermediate component or rod could prevent a shutdown. The following procedure can be used to answer such questions.

```
systemfail(XTYPE, XOCC) : −
        occur(XTYPE, XOCC, XXCORD, XYCORD),
        notdetector(XTYPE),
        occur(DTYPE, DOCC, DXCORD, DYCORD),
        isdetector(DTYPE),
        occur(rod, ROD1, R1XCORD, R1YCORD),
        occur(rod, ROD2, R2XCORD, R2YCORD),
        ROD1 < ROD2,
        nopath(DTYPE, DOCC, ROD1, XTYPE, XOCC),
        nopath(DTYPE, DOCC, ROD2, XTYPE, XOCC).

isdetector(seismic).
isdetector(powerloss).
isdetector(reactor).
isdetector(ph).
isdetector(rcscontrol).
isdetector(rcsmonitor).
isdetector(operator).

notdetector(TYPE) : − isdetector(TYPE), !, fail.
notdetector(TYPE).

nopath(DTYPE, DOCC, RODNUMBER, MISSTYPE, MISSOCC) : −
        ispath(DTYPE, DOCC, RODNUMBER, MISSTYPE, MISSOCC),
        !, fail.
nopath(DTYPE, DOCC, RODNUMBER, MISSTYPE, MISSOCC).
```

To use this program, a user types the following clause.

```
systemfail(XTYPE, XOCC).
```

The Prolog program tries to find values for XTYPE and XOCC that identify a specific component such that the failure of that component could prevent a shutdown. If Prolog can find such values for XTYPE and XOCC, they will be displayed.

If not, you can conclude that the system is resilient enough to shut down in the presence of the failure of a single component.

The preceding program illustrates what can be done with Prolog.

EXERCISES

7. The Prolog procedure *ispath* relies on the assumption that there were no cycles in the diagram. In particular, it assumes that there could not be a path from a given component back to itself. Give a Prolog program that can be used to detect cycles.
8. Assume that, in the diagram being studied, cycles can legitimately occur. How should the program for *systemfail* be modified to work properly?

14.3 Summary

A number of features of Prolog differ from those of a typical automated reasoning program. An automated reasoning program attacks a given problem by

1. Selecting a clause from which new clauses are generated
2. Simplifying or rephrasing generated clauses
3. Performing subsumption tests on the newly-generated clauses
4. Keeping those clauses that result and that satisfy some given criteria for determining what is or is not potentially useful

This process is quite general and has proven extremely useful in a variety of areas.

In contrast, Prolog utilizes a distinctly different approach. It treats its input either as facts or as procedures for computing values determined by the head literal. Except for questions, which take the form of negative unit clauses, Prolog requires each clause to contain exactly one positive literal. The capacity to generate a clause with two positive literals—probably leading to a case analysis—just does not exist in a Prolog program. Next, many implementations do not use a unification algorithm that checks that the resulting deduction is sound, that the conclusion follows logically. Specifically, in many implementations the "occurs check" is not made—the check that determines whether or not a variable is in effect being replaced by a term containing the variable. The type of problem that is submitted to Prolog is expected not to require this check to be made. The appropriate problem is one in which you know ahead of time what steps are required. Such a problem is called "algorithmic" or "determinate".

Prolog employs a control mechanism in which no choices exist, but instead relies on a specified process for attacking a problem. No new clauses are generated unless specifically requested. The process performs an arbitrary number of unifications to ascertain that the various goals and subgoals have been solved. The process is governed by just two rules:

1. Subgoals in a clause are processed strictly left-to-right
2. Clauses used to solve a subgoal are processed in the order in which they occur in the input

This simple control mechanism is well suited to the specification of many algorithms.

The choice of which to use, a typical automated reasoning program or Prolog, for attempting to solve a specific problem depends on the conjectured properties of the problem. If you suspect that the problem requires exploring possible new facts that in turn may require simplification, then the first choice is the automated reasoning program. If you believe that you can give an algorithm for the required reasoning such that exploration of possibilities is minimal, then Prolog would be the first choice. Prolog does not employ demodulation or subsumption. Problems related to the mathematical research of Chapter 9 are not suitable for attack with Prolog. Such problems require the retention of new clauses, and the solving of them relies heavily on subsumption, demodulation, weighting, and the use of various inference rules.

In actuality, many problems require both approaches, that of exploring many new facts and that of applying an algorithm to compute certain quantities. For example, a problem may require proving a number of new intermediate results and also require factoring some polynomial. If you were presented with such a problem, you might wish access to a program that offers assistance of both kinds. Thus the need exists for a program that integrates an approach similar to that offered by Prolog and the approach offered by a typical automated reasoning program. The program ITP discussed in Chapter 6 is such a program.

14.4 Answers to Exercises

1. The Prolog procedure to compute cousins is the following.

cousin(X, Y) : − parent(PX, X),
        parent(PY, Y),
        sibling(PX, PY).

2. If the first goal of clause 35 were eliminated, a person would be considered a sibling of himself.

3. Another procedure to compute grandmothers is

grandmother(X, Y) : − mother(X, Z), parent(Z, Y).

4. A procedure to compute great-grandparents is the following.

greatgrandparent(X, Y) : − parent(X, Z), grandparent(Z, Y).

5. The clauses required to check for siblings or the absence of siblings are the following.

   hassibling(X) : − sibling(X, Y).

   nosiblings(X) : − hassibling(X), !, fail.
   nosiblings(X).

6. The clauses that might be used to find connections that do not connect an input connection point to an output connection point are the following.

   findbad(TYPE1, OCC1, CONPT1, TYPE2, OCC2, CONPT2) : −
       connected(TYPE1, OCC1, CONPT1, TYPE2, OCC2, CONPT2),
       badcon(TYPE1, OCC1, CONPT1, TYPE2, OCC2, CONPT2).

   goodcon(TYPE1, OCC1, CONPT1, TYPE2, OCC2, CONPT2) : −
       conpt(TYPE1, CONPT1, ATR1),
       conpt(TYPE2, CONPT2, ATR2),
       goodvals(ATR1, ATR2).

   goodvals(ATR1, ATR2) : − ATR1 = input, ATR2 = output.
   goodvals(ATR1, ATR2) : − ATR2 = input, ATR1 = output.

   badcon(TYPE1, OCC1, CONPT1, TYPE2, OCC2, CONPT2) : −
       goodcon(TYPE1, OCC1, CONPT1, TYPE2, OCC2, CONPT2), !,fail.
   badcon(TYPE1, OCC1, CONPT1, TYPE2, OCC2, CONPT2).

7. A short procedure for finding cycles is the following.

   cycle(X) : − connected(X, Y), ispath(Y, X).

8. For a diagram that might include cycles, you can simply reprogram the procedure *ispath*. The new version keeps a list of the points that occur in a path, and avoids visiting a node more than once.

   ispath(X, Y) : − findpath(X, Y, nil).

   findpath(X, Y, Z) : − connected(X, Y).
   findpath(X, Y, Z) : − connected(X, X1),
       notin(X1, Z),
       findpath(X1, Y, l(X1, Z)).

   notin(X, nil).
   notin(X, l(Y1, Y2)) : − ne(X, Y1), notin(X,Y2).

In some of the standard texts on Prolog, you will find that a special notation for processing lists can be used. This notation can be very convenient and significantly improves readability. To see just how complex list expressions can be, again read the domino and checkerboard puzzle discussed in Chapter 5.

15

The Formal Treatment of

Automated Reasoning

In this chapter, we discuss the formal basis for automated reasoning. For those of you who began with Chapter 2, we now answer various questions that may have arisen during your reading. For example, if a strategy such as the set of support strategy is imposed on an inference rule to control its application, does the restriction interfere with an automated reasoning program completing its assignment? For those of you who prefer the academic approach and, as suggested in Chapter 1, might be starting with this chapter as your introduction to automated reasoning, it is here where you will be introduced to the basic aspects of automated reasoning. In particular, we discuss a language commonly used by an automated reasoning program, some of the inference rules that are employed, and certain facets of strategy. For example, we show that the use of the set of support strategy, when the appropriate conditions are satisfied, does not interfere with the capacity for finding a proof. As promised at the beginning of this book, we provide here a mechanism that can be employed to permit you to undertake the study of some domain not specifically covered in another chapter.

15.1 Language

Many automated reasoning programs employ the language of *clauses*, a language closely related to the first-order predicate calculus, for representing a problem under consideration. In an important sense, the language of clauses is far less rich than the language of first-order predicate calculus. Nevertheless, the language of clauses has sufficient logical power for use with an automated reasoning program and, because of its adherence to a normal form, has advantages for formulating various inference rules. To understand the language of clauses, we first briefly discuss the first-order predicate calculus.

The first-order predicate calculus includes propositional calculus as a sublanguage. All of the usual connectives are present, **or**, **and**, **not**, **if-then**, and **is-equivalent-to**. The elements of the language are predicates, functions, and variables. The predicates are the relation symbols. The functions are the familiar functions as occur, for example, in mathematics. The variables are either universally quantified or existentially quantified. For example,

for all x for all y (**if** WIFE(x, y) **then** HUSBAND(y, x))

is a typical statement in the language. Also,

for all x for all y (**if** GRANDFATHER(x, y)

then there exists z such that (FATHER(z, y)))

is a typical statement.

All statements in the first-order predicate calculus can be rewritten in *prenex normal form*, all quantifiers occurring before the statement. Further, the statement within the quantification can then be rewritten into a conjunctive normal form, the **and** of a set of statements each of which is the **or** of its *literals*. A literal is a predicate symbol, possibly preceded by a **not** sign, followed by the arguments of the predicate. The number of such arguments is determined by the predicate. The existentially quantified variables can then be replaced by *Skolem functions*. (We shall shortly discuss this more fully. Note that universal quantifiers distribute across **and**, while existential quantifiers distribute across **or**. If an existential quantifier occurs before the **and** of two statements, then uniformly replacing that existential by a function retains the information that the same existential is present in both statements.) Finally, the quantifiers and the quantified statement can be rewritten, resulting in the **and** of a set of statements each of which is the **or** of its literals, and such that the quantifiers that appear before a member of the set apply only to that member. This final form closely resembles the language of clauses that is employed by many reasoning programs. Certain additional restrictions are present.

The language of clauses does not admit the connectives of **if-then** and **is-equivalent-to**, but relies only on the explicit use of **or** and **not** and the implicit use of **and**. The connectives of **if-then** and **is-equivalent-to** are replaced by the appropriate correspondents using **or**, **not**, and **and**. The replacement is achieved by employing rules such as **if** P **then** Q is equivalent to **not** P **or** Q. In addition, the distributive laws for **and** and **or** and the reduction of **not not** P to P is employed. The objective of applying these rules is to produce a set of statements, each of which is the **or** of its literals, that are connected by **and**. Next, the **and** is removed, and considered present implicitly. As the final step, all quantifiers are dropped from the set of statements. Instead of explicit quantification, all variables that appear in a statement are implicitly treated as universally quantified.

The result of these actions is the conversion from the language of first-order predicate calculus to the language of clauses. The set of clauses thus produced is the implicit **and** of its members. Each clause is the **or** of its literals, where **or** is represented in this book by "|". All variables that occur in a clause are implicitly universally quantified, and the scope of a variable is just that clause in which it occurs. Thus, and this point is crucial, should the variable x occur in two distinct clauses, no implied connection exists as a result—except of course for the implicit **and**. As you will see when we come to inference rules, for most of them you are in effect required to rename the variables so that no two clauses share a variable.

Earlier we promised a discussion of the replacement of existentially quantified variables by Skolem functions. Such a replacement is necessary to eventually produce a set of clauses, for the language of clauses permits only universally quantified variables. Recall that, at the point where existentially quantified variables are to be replaced by Skolem functions, all quantifiers occur before a statement that itself is in conjunctive normal form. The existentially quantified variables are each replaced by a function whose arguments are those universal quantifiers that precede it. Intuitively, this replacement gives a name to that which is said to exist because of the presence of the existential quantifier. For example,

for all x there exists a y such that $P(x, y)$

is replaced with

$P(x, f(x))$

where the function f has not been previously used. Similarly,

for all x for all y there exists z such that (**not** $P(x, y, z)$ **or** $Q(z)$)

is replaced with

$\neg P(x, y, g(x, y)) \mid Q(g(x, y))$

where "$\neg$" stands for **not**, "|" stands for **or**, and the function g has the arguments x and y. In contrast, the statement

there exists x such that for all y $P(x, y)$

is replaced by the clause

$P(a, y)$

where a is a constant (function of no variables) that has not previously been used. Notice the difference that occurs in the clauses in which the existential quantifier follows the universal quantifier as compared with what occurs when the existential quantifier precedes the universal quantifier.

You might well wonder if the given actions of restricting the logical connectives, of rewriting statements into a normal form, and of replacing existential quantifiers with Skolem functions preserve the logical meaning of a statement. They do not. However, as you will see, the actions preserve enough of the logical properties, more accurately, preserve the appropriate property—that of refutation completeness, to be defined later. The precise formulation of what occurs is that the resulting set of clauses is not necessarily logically equivalent to the original statement. The loss of logical equivalence is due to the use of Skolem functions. The essence of the situation is, however, that, if the original statement in first-order predicate calculus is unsatisfiable—inconsistent or self-contradictory—then the resulting set of clauses is also, and conversely.

The language of clauses observes one additional normalization property. While in first-order predicate calculus the statement

for all x (P(x) **or** P(x))

is admissible, its (proposed) correspondent in clause form

P(x) | P(x)

is not. Duplicate literals are not permitted within a clause. Thus, in this case,

P(x)

is the only acceptable translation. On the other hand,

P(x) | P(y)

is acceptable, even though

P(x)

is logically equivalent to it. The clause language does not demand reductions of the last type, but only reductions for logical trivialities as evidenced in the possible presence of duplicate literals.

EXERCISE

1. Convert the following logical expression to the appropriate clauses:

For all x, (**if** P(x) **then** (there exists a y such that (Q(x,y) **and not** Q(y,x))))

15.2 Inference Rules

An *inference rule* is a means for drawing conclusions that follow logically from the given premisses. (Note that the words "premiss" and "premisses" are technical terms, and that the given spelling is that preferred in logic.) Further, an algorithm must exist that permits you to apply the rule—to select appropriate premises, to draw the conclusion(s), and to be able to test that a conclusion is justifiable with the rule. One of the simplest inference rules, *modus ponens*, yields Q from ((**not** P) **or** Q) and P. The algorithm amounts to canceling a literal in the more complex statement against the literal in the less complex statement, when the two literals are opposite in sign. In clause form

    P

    ¬P | Q

allow an automated reasoning program to conclude

    Q

when the appropriate inference rule is applied. The literal P is termed a *positive literal*, while the literal ¬P is termed a *negative* literal.

The slightly more complicated inference rule of *syllogism* yields P **or** R from (P **or** Q) and ((**not** Q) **or** R). The algorithm consists of canceling a literal from each of the two premisses, when the two literals to be canceled are alike in predicate and opposite in sign, and taking the **or** of the remaining literals in the two. In clause form

    P | Q

    ¬Q | R

yield

    P | R

when the appropriate inference rule is applied.

Both the preceding example of modus ponens and the one just given for syllogism are stated here on the propositional level. Additional complexity is introduced when variables are present. Knowing that

    if x is the husband of y, **then** y is the wife of x

and

    Pete is the husband of Thelma

leads to the conclusion that

    Thelma is the wife of Pete

by applying an inference rule that generalizes the modus ponens rule given earlier. In clause form

    (1) ¬HUSBAND(x, y) | WIFE(y, x)

    (2) HUSBAND(Pete, Thelma)

yields

(3) WIFE(Thelma, Pete)

as the conclusion. The propositional form of modus ponens can be applied to yield the desired conclusion after an appropriate *substitution* is first applied.

Definition.   A *term* is a well-formed expression that is either a variable, a constant, or a function symbol followed by its n arguments where n is the number of arguments required by the function. Technically, a constant is a function of zero arguments.

Definition.   A *substitution* is a set of ordered pairs ti/xi, where ti are terms and xi are distinct variables.

Definition.   The clause D is an *instance* of the clause C if D can be obtained from C by applying a substitution.

The substitution, Pete/x,Thelma/y, applied to clause 1 yields clause 1′ as an instance.

(1′) ¬HUSBAND(Pete, Thelma) | WIFE(Thelma, Pete)

Modus ponens applied to clauses 1′ and 2 yields clause 3. We thus have an example of what an automated reasoning program does—finding, if one exists, a substitution that permits a third clause to be obviously obtained from two given clauses. Rather than seeking any such substitution, a reasoning program seeks the most general that suffices.

Definition.   A *most general common instance* MGCI, if one exists, of the literals K and M is a literal L such that L is an instance of both K and M and such that, if L′ is an instance of both K and M, then L′ is an instance of L.

The literals $Q(x, b, y)$ and $Q(w, b, z)$ have as a common instance the literal $Q(x, b, c)$, and as a most general common instance $Q(x, b, y)$. The literals $Q(x, a, z)$ and $Q(b, y, w)$ have a MGCI of $Q(b, a, z)$, but $Q(b, a, c)$ is not a MGCI. On the other hand, the literals $P(x, x)$ and $P(y, f(y))$ have no common instance, and hence no MGCI. No substitution can be found such that, when it is applied to this last pair of literals, the resulting literals become identical.

Earlier we mentioned that the occurrence of x in two distinct clauses does not mean the same x, and that this point is crucial. For example, the literals $P(a, x)$ and $P(x, b)$, respectively, in the clauses

$P(a, x) \mid Q(y)$

$\neg P(x, b) \mid R(w)$

do have a common instance, namely, $P(a, b)$. To find this common instance, rename the variables in the two clauses so that no variable occurs in both of them. Such a renaming is permitted because the scope of a variable is simply the clause in which it occurs. Let the renaming replace x in the second clause by z. Then the substitution that yields the common instance is b/x, a/z. Such renamings are a key to applying most inference rules. Even though a substitution must be applied uniformly—all occurrences of a variable must be consistently replaced by the designated term—the apparent common occurrence of x in the two literals does not prevent the substitution from being applied for the variable x is not the same variable in the two clauses.

Definition.   The literals K and M are said to *unify* if there exists a substitution that, when applied to both K and M, produces K′ and M′, respectively, such that K′ = M′. The literals are then said to be *unifiable*. A substitution that, when applied, yields a MGCI of two unifiable literals is called a *most general unifier* MGU.

The substitution b/x, a/y, z/w is a MGU of Q(x, a, z) and Q(b, y, w), but b/x, a/y, c/w, c/z is not. The number of components in the substitution is not the key, as can be seen by the fact that z/x, z/y is a MGU of the literal pair R(x) R(y), while a/x, a/y is not. Rather, the generality of the substitution is what counts for it to be a MGU. Similarly, whether some of the terms in a MGU are selected from the first literal or from the second of the pair being unified does not matter. Thus R(x) and R(y) have as MGU x/y and also have as MGU y/x. The various most general unifiers for a given pair of literals merely produce alphabetic variants when applied.

15.2.1 Binary Resolution

Definition.   The inference rule *binary resolution* yields the clause C from the clauses A and B (that are assumed to have no variables in common) when A contains the literal K, B contains the literal M, K and M have the same predicate, one of K and M is a positive and the other a negative literal, and except for sign K and M are unifiable. The clause C is termed a *resolvent* of A and B. The clause C is obtained by finding a MGU of K and M, applying the MGU to both A and B to yield A′ and B′, respectively, and forming the **or** of A′ − K′ and B′ − M′. By A′ − K′ we mean the deletion from A′ of just the descendant of K after the substitution is applied, not the deletion of all occurrences of K′. We treat B′ − M′ similarly. (The justification of deleting merely the descendants of the literals being unified will be given shortly.)

Binary resolution is but one of the inference rules we shall discuss. We shall concentrate on that inference rule before discussing others because we can introduce many of the basic notions with it. In particular, as you will see, the key notion of strategy will be discussed mainly in the context of binary resolution. We therefore begin with imparting an understanding of how binary resolution works.

From the clauses

P(a) | Q(x) | R(x)

¬P(y) | ¬Q(b) | S(y)

the resolvents

Q(x) | R(x) | ¬Q(b) | S(a)

P(a) | R(b) | ¬P(y) | S(y)

can be deduced by application of binary resolution. To deduce the first of the two resolvents requires unification of the first literal in each of the two given clauses. To deduce the second resolvent requires unification of the second literals of the two given clauses. The clauses to which binary resolution is applied to yield a resolvent are called the *parents* or *immediate ancestors* of the resolvent.

This definition of binary resolution is not universally employed. The difference between this definition and that used by some is captured by the following example. From the clauses

P(x) | P(a) | Q(a)

¬P(a)

the application of binary resolution in which the first literals are unified yields

P(a) | Q(a)

using the given definition, while in the alternative definition

Q(a)

is the resolvent. The precise point is that, in the given definition, A′ − K′ is not treated settheoretically, nor is B′ − M′. In other words, if the substitution causes literals to become identical in either A′ or B′, that fact is ignored until the **or** is taken. This definition is preferred primarily because of its effect on implementation, which is the promised justification for the interpretation of A′ − K′.

To obtain a resolvent of a pair of clauses by applying binary resolution, a literal in each must be chosen such that they share a predicate, but such that one literal is positive while the other is negative. Next, the variables are renamed so that the two clauses share no variable. Finally, the two literals must be considered for unification. If the unification succeeds, then a resolvent is obtained. If it fails, then no resolvent exists for the particular chosen pair of literals. If a different pair is chosen, a resolvent may be obtained, depending of course on the outcome of the attempt to unify the newly chosen literals.

A number of unification algorithms exist. Perhaps the easiest to understand is that which proceeds left to right, focusing on each symbol as it occurs. The first step is that of separating the variables in the two clauses and hence in the two literals to be considered for unification. This renaming of variables produces two literals that do not share, even syntactically, a variable. The plan is to produce a substitution table for the list of variables that occur after renaming. If the unification is successful, a replacement of the variables in both literals dictated by the substitution table will cause the two literals to become identical, except for sign. Once the unification process has begun, the actual variable names do count. In other words, once the attempt at unification commences, a variable that becomes common to the expressions being unified is the same variable. The algorithm employs the following rules. If the two symbols that are encountered are both variables, then modify the partial substitution table to reflect that one variable is to replace the other. Assume with no loss that, when possible, we are in effect replacing from the second literal into the first. If two function symbols are encountered, or two constants, or a function symbol and a constant, then skip the pair unless they are not identical. In this event—different function or constant symbols—terminate the unification with failure. When one of the symbol pair is a variable and the other not, then modify the substitution table to reflect a replacement of the variable by the entire term begun by the nonvariable element of the pair. Continually update the partial substitution table, obeying the rules just given. For example, if y/x and a/y are entries, modify the table to read a/x, a/y. For another example, if y/x and y/z are entries, modify the table to read y/x, y/z or, equally, to read z/x, z/y.

We are now at the crucial point in the algorithm. If the term to be substituted for a variable contains that variable, then terminate the algorithm with failure. Such a failure is what we had in mind when we said earlier that the variable names count once unification has begun. This situation occurs when applying, for example, the algorithm to the following two clauses.

$$P(x, f(x))$$

$$\neg P(y, y)$$

The predicates satisfy the requirement of being identical, and the algorithm passes to the next symbol pair. The consideration of the first nonpredicate pair by the algorithm adds y/x to the partial substitution table. Consideration of the next pair adds f(x)/y to the table. Then the updating of the table requires y/x to be modified to read f(x)/x, resulting in termination of the attempt at unification with failure. Failure is what is desired in this case, for no consistent replacement of the variables in the two literals in question can make them identical.

Consideration of the following two clauses results in an example of a successful application of the algorithm.

$$P(f(x1), y1, g(f(x3), x3)) \mid Q(y1, x3)$$

$$\neg P(x2, x2, g(y2, a))$$

The given unification algorithm, when applied to these two clauses, yields as the final updated substitution table f(x1)/x2, f(x1)/y1, f(a)/y2, a/x3, which is the substitution that unifies the two literals. The resolvent

$$Q(f(x1), a)$$

results. (You might prefer to determine the outcome of attempting a unification by replacing the process of producing the substitution table by a process that applies each element of the substitution as it is discovered.)

The first question to ask about an inference rule is: Is the inference rule *sound*? Intuitively, an inference rule is sound if the conclusions yielded by it are true when the premises are true. From the opposite viewpoint, a rule is unsound when a model can be found in which the premises hold, but some conclusion yielded by application of the rule to them does not. In other words, a rule is unsound if a counterexample to its soundness can be found, an illustration that the rule can yield a conclusion that does not follow logically. Rather than supplying a proof, we simply remark that binary resolution is a sound inference rule. Thus the new clauses yielded by its application are logical consequences of the premises to which it is applied.

The next question to ask about an inference rule is: Is it *refutation complete*? Before we give the formal definitions upon which this concept rests, note that, intuitively, an inference rule is refutation complete if it is sufficiently powerful that it can be used to establish inconsistency for any inconsistent set of clauses. The property in question is vital to guaranteeing, from the logical viewpoint, that a proof of a claim can be found where a proof is known to exist. Keeping in mind the intuitive definition and the motivation, we now turn to the relevant formal definitions.

EXERCISES

2. Here you are asked to calculate some instances and unifiers.

   (a) Find a MGCI for $PSUM(g(x, y), c, f(y))$ and $PSUM(g(x, y), y, f(x))$.
   (b) Find a MGU for $PSUM(x, g(x, y), y)$ and $PSUM(g(x, y), x, y)$.

3. Let us consider a variety of plausible inference rules and see how they relate to binary resolution. In each case, we give a rule in the if-then format. You are to convert the statements to clauses, and indicate whether or not the corresponding inference can be made with resolution. For example, consider

   From

   if H1 **then** C1

   and

   H1

   conclude

   C1

This rule is simply *modus ponens*. In clause form the rule is

   From

   ¬H1 | C1

   and

   H1

   conclude

   C1

This conclusion can be achieved by performing a single binary resolution.

(a) Consider the rule

   From

   if (H1 **and** H2) **then** C1

and

    H1

conclude

    if H2 **then** C1

(b) Consider the rule

From

    if H1 **then** (C1 **or** C2)

and

    not H1

conclude

    (**not** C1) **and** (**not** C2)

(c) Consider the rule

From

    if (H1 **and** H2) **then** (C1 **or** C2)

and

    not C1

conclude

    if (H1 **and** H2) **then** C2

15.2.2 Refutation Completeness

To prepare the way for the key definitions, we begin with their correspondents for sets of clauses that are on the propositional level only—that contain no variables. The more interesting and by far more relevant case is, of course, that in which variables are present. The definitions that will be needed are generalizations of those we now give.

Definition. A set of variable-free clauses is *truth-functionally satisfiable* if there exists a consistent assignment of true and false to the literals such that the **and** of the clauses is true.

Of course, if true is assigned to the literal K, then false must be assigned to $\neg K$, and conversely. For a set of clauses to be truth-functionally satisfiable, the true-false assignment that establishes this must make each clause true under the assignment.

Definition. An *interpretation* of a variable-free set of clauses is an assignment of true and false to the various literals.

Definition. A set of variable-free clauses is *truth-functionally unsatisfiable* if no interpretation exists that establishes the set to be truth-functionally satisfiable.

Thus, a set of clauses in which variables are absent is truth-functionally unsatisfiable if and only if no assignment of true and false to the literals of the clauses yields true for the **and** of its members. Such a set can be thought of as inconsistent. For example, the set of clauses

P | Q

¬P

¬Q

is truth-functionally unsatisfiable. The question then arises of how to define the analogue for clauses that contain variables.

Definition.   The *Herbrand universe* for a set S of clauses consists of all well-formed terms that can be composed from the function symbols and individual constants that are present in S. When no constants are present, the constant c is supplied.

For example, if S consists of the clauses

P(x)

¬P(f(g(b, c)))

then the Herbrand universe for S contains b, c, f(b), f(c), g(b,c), g(b,b), g(c,c), g(c, b), f(f(b)), f(f(c)), f(g(b,c)), ..., g(f(b),f(b)), ... The elements of the Herbrand universe are called *ground terms*.

Definition.   The clause D is termed a *ground instance* of the clause C if D is an instance of C such that D is variable-free.

The only ground instances that are ordinarily considered for a set S are those obtainable by employing elements of the Herbrand universe.

Definition.   A *Herbrand interpretation* of S is an assignment of true and false to the well-formed expressions that can be composed from the predicates of S and the terms from the Herbrand universe. If true is assigned to a literal K, then false must be assigned to ¬K.

Herbrand's Theorem.   A set S of clauses is unsatisfiable if and only if there exists a finite set of (Herbrand) ground instances of S that is truth-functionally unsatisfiable.

To gain an intuitive understanding of Herbrand's theorem, note that, since each variable in a clause is interpreted as "for all", a domain must exist over which the variables range. The domain can be chosen as the Herbrand universe. If a set S of clauses is satisfiable, then a Herbrand interpretation exists that establishes S to be truth-functionally satisfiable. In other words, if S is replaced by the full set of ground instances over its Herbrand universe, then an assignment of true and false exists that yields true for the set of ground instances. Note that an instance is a logical consequence of the clause of which it is an instance. Looked at from the other side of the issue, if S is unsatisfiable, then no assignment of true and false to the full set of ground instances makes the set evaluate to true. On the other hand, if a finite set of Herbrand ground instances is truth-functionally unsatisfiable, then all extensions to the full set of ground instances are truth-functionally unsatisfiable. Of course, when considering the full set of ground instances of a set S of clauses, you must allow any single clause to produce (by instantiation over the Herbrand universe) the appropriate number of ground clauses.

The significance of the Herbrand theorem is that it provides, at least in principle, an algorithm for establishing the unsatisfiability of a (finite) unsatisfiable set S of clauses. The algorithm consists of considering ever-expanding sets of ground instances over the Herbrand universe—sets obtained from S by starting with those instances yielded by substituting the constants from S for the variables. The set of ground instances is then expanded by substituting Herbrand terms from the next level, where level 1 consists solely of the constants that are present in the members of S. If S is unsatisfiable, eventually the algorithm will produce a finite set of ground instances that is truth-functionally unsatisfiable. Since each instance is a logical consequence of the clause in S from which it was obtained, the truth-functionally unsatisfiable set of ground instances follows logically from S. Therefore, S must have been itself unsatisfiable.

The truth-functional unsatisfiability can be proved with an exhaustive true-false test. Neither the algorithm nor the exhaustive true-false test is particularly pleasing or efficient. From the viewpoint of logic, however, the theorem provides the basis for automated reasoning, and also provides the incentive for seeking an effective way to establish unsatisfiability. The reason for the ineffectiveness of exploring the Herbrand expansion rests with the exponential character of the Herbrand universe and with the exponential increase in complexity of the corresponding truth-functional analysis. A quick calculation shows how large the Herbrand universe gets even by level 4, when but a few constants and functions are present in a set S of clauses.

The question now arises as to how to test for unsatisfiability for sets of clauses that contain variables. What is the analogue of a truth-functional analysis? One answer is suggested by what often occurs in mathematics, namely, obtaining two statements that are obvious contradictions of each other. Thus, if a number of applications of a sound inference rule yields two clauses that obviously contradict each other, then unsatisfiability has been established. For example, the clauses

$$P(x, y)$$
$$\neg P(w, z)$$

contradict each other. The first says that all pairs of elements have the property P, while the second says that all pairs lack the property P. Similarly,

$$P(a, g(b))$$
$$\neg P(x, g(y))$$

contradict each other. The first says that the pair $a, g(b)$ has property P, while the second says that the pair $x, g(y)$ for all x and y lacks property P. The deduction of a contradictory pair of clauses is reminiscent of the mathematician saying, "and thus we have established a contradiction".

Definition.   A clause consisting of a single literal is called a *unit clause*, or simply a *unit*. If the literal is negative, the clause is called a *negative unit*.

Definition.   Two clauses are termed *contradictory unit clauses* if each of the two clauses contains a single literal, if the two are opposite in sign, and if the two literals (ignoring sign) can be unified. When two such clauses have been obtained, *unit conflict* has been found.

Definition.   A *deduction* D (employing binary resolution) of the clause A from the set S of clauses is a finite sequence of clauses A1, A2,..., An such that A = An and such that, for every $1 \leq i \leq n$, Ai is in S or there exist Aj and Ak with j < i and k < i and with Ai a resolvent of Aj and Ak.

If an automated reasoning program applies binary resolution some number of times and obtains the clause A, and if S is the set of clauses that are input to the program, then we say that we have a *proof* of A from S employing binary resolution. In particular, among the clauses that have been obtained, a deduction D exists of A from S. If a reasoning program has deduced contradictory unit clauses—equivalently, found unit conflict—then we have a *proof by contradiction* of the unsatisfiability of S. An alternative definition of a proof by contradiction consists of replacing the requirement of having found unit conflict by having deduced the *empty clause*. The *empty clause* is a clause containing no literals. Since the empty clause cannot be "true" in any interpretation and can be thought of as "false", deducing the empty clause establishes unsatisfiability. In this book, we generally prefer to define "proof by contradiction" in terms of deducing unit conflict, rather than in terms of deducing the empty clause.

A key aspect of studying the possible satisfiability or unsatisfiability of a set S of clauses concerns *undecidability*. Briefly, no algorithm exists that can be fixed and then answer yes or answer no correctly, when presented with a finite set of clauses and asked to determine whether or not S is satisfiable. This result is a very deep and complex result. For any given algorithm, finite sets S exist that are satisfiable, but for which the algorithm will be unable to establish that fact in a finite amount of time. However, as will become clear, automated reasoning rests mainly on that side of the problem concerned with unsatisfiable sets S of clauses. The technical statement is that the property of *semidecidability* is present—algorithms exist that, given a theorem, will always find a proof in a finite amount of time.

Definition.   An inference rule is *refutation complete* if, given an unsatisfiable set S of clauses, the unsatisfiability can be established by recourse solely to the inference rule.

As defined earlier, binary resolution is not refutation complete. The set of clauses

P(x) | P(y)

¬P(w) | ¬P(z)

is unsatisfiable, but binary resolution is not powerful enough by itself to establish the fact. A second inference rule, *factoring*, suffices to bridge the gap.

Definition.   The inference rule *factoring* yields the clause D from the clause C when C contains two literals K and M that have the same sign and that can be unified. The clause D, called a *factor*, is obtained by applying to C a MGU that unifies K and M. In addition, all factors of factors of C are themselves factors of C, and are said to be obtained by factoring.

For example,

P(a) | P(x) | P(y)

has both of the clauses

P(a) | P(y)
P(a)

as factors. Of course, since the scope of variables is the entire clause, variables in the literals being considered for unification are not separated.

The use of factoring is now immediately clear when we again examine the preceding example, which illustrated that binary resolution is not refutation complete.

P(x) | P(y)
¬P(w) | ¬P(z)

With factoring, the clauses

P(x)
¬P(z)

are obtained. These two factors provide a contradiction, since the first says that all x have property P, while the second says that all x lack property P. If binary resolution alone is applied to the example, all clauses that can be obtained contain two literals and are alphabetic variants of one of the two given clauses or of

¬P(x) | P(y)

and therefore no proof of unsatisfiability can be found using binary resolution alone. Specifically, no deduction of unit conflict can be found without factoring, and hence no proof by contradiction. In practice, binary resolution is usually sufficient for finding a proof, and factoring is often not employed in actual problem solving.

The proof that the combination of binary resolution and factoring is refutation complete rests on a lemma called the "lifting lemma", which we state here but do not prove. The proof that the system composed of binary resolution and factoring is refutation complete proceeds by establishing the system to be refutation complete for ground clauses, clauses in which no variables appear. Then the lifting lemma is applied for the case in which variables are present.

Lifting Lemma.   If A′ and B′ are, respectively, ground instances of the clauses A and B (which are assumed to have no variables in common), and if C′ is a resolvent of A' and B', then there exist clauses E and F such that an application of binary resolution to E and F yields a clause C, where C' is an instance of C, and where E = A or is a factor of A and F = B or is a factor of B.

The fact that the combination of binary resolution and factoring is refutation complete provides the basis for a superior approach to proving the unsatisfiability of a set S of clauses that is, in fact, unsatisfiable. Even for a variable-free set S that is unsatisfiable, the use of binary resolution is more efficient than the cumbersome true-false test. (For variable-free sets S, factoring plays no role.) As the size of the set under study grows, the complexity of an exhaustive true-false test increases exponentially. Since the size of the levels of the Herbrand universe also grows exponentially, the need to perform a truth-functional analysis and on a set of clauses obtained from substituting ever-expanding sets of terms from the Herbrand universe makes such an approach highly ineffective. For sets S containing variables, the combination of the two inference rules of binary resolution and factoring is far superior to examining an ever-expanding set of ground clauses obtained from substituting terms from the Herbrand universe. In fact, the two inference rules were formulated to combat the difficulties encountered with an approach based on Herbrand expansion. Although the exponential problem present with a truth-functional examination is essentially simply replaced by a corresponding problem, the exponential problem resulting from instantiation is sharply reduced because of the generality of inference rules like resolution. Such rules yield inferences that capture a number of instances simultaneously, thus improving the situation markedly. However, a potential exponential explosion still exists, which is why even more powerful inference rules are needed and why strategies to control the inference rules are also needed.

EXERCISES

4. Compute the factor(s) of the following three clauses.

  (a) $\neg\$GT(x, 0) \mid \neg\$GT(y, 0) \mid \$GT(\$sum(x, y), 0)$

  (b) $\neg\$GT(x, 0) \mid \neg\$GE(y, 0) \mid \$GT(\$sum(x, y), 0)$

  (c) $\neg Psum(x, y, w) \mid \neg Psum(y, z, v) \mid \neg Psum(w, z, u) \mid Psum(x, v, u)$

5. In this section, the notion of *refutation complete* was developed. Let us consider a somewhat different notion of completeness. Suppose that you have a set of clauses S and another clause C. Further, suppose that C must be true, if all of the clauses in S are true. An inference rule is called *deduction complete* if C can always be deduced by some number of applications of the rule from the clauses in S. Specifically, starting with the clauses in S, you will be able to generate C in a finite number of applications of the inference rule. Is binary resolution with factoring deduction complete?

15.3 Strategy

Employing inference rules such as binary resolution and factoring is far better than relying on an algorithm based on Herbrand expansion and truth-functional analysis. Nevertheless, still more is needed before automated reasoning can be effective. In particular, *strategy* is required. A strategy is a rule or set of rules that governs the use of inference rules. If the strategy dictates where next to apply an inference rule, the strategy is an *ordering strategy*. If it constrains application of an inference rule, then it is a *restriction strategy*. Both types of strategy are necessary for an automated reasoning program to be effective. If a reasoning program is allowed to wander through the space of possible clauses that can be obtained by indiscriminately applying inference rules, the sought-after goal will seldom be reached. Equally, if such a program does not totally avoid considering certain paths through the clause space, the problem under study will seldom be solved. Restriction strategies affect efficiency more than ordering strategies because they provide a means for an automated reasoning program to avoid potentially fruitless paths. Although this discussion will be essentially in terms of the inference rules of binary resolution and factoring, the spirit of what we say is germane to the use of other inference rules.

Perhaps the most powerful restriction strategy is the *set of support strategy*. Intuitively, the set of support strategy forbids a reasoning program from applying an inference rule unless at least one of the potential parents to which it is being applied has been deduced from some specified subset of the input clauses. To employ the set of support strategy when presented with a set S of clauses, first choose a nonempty subset T of S. The subset T is called the set of support, and the members of T are said to *have support* or to be *supported*.

Before giving the formal definition of the set of support strategy, we note that a given clause can be deduced in potentially many distinct ways and often with different immediate ancestors. Because of this fact, we are concerned in the following definition with a specific occurrence of a clause. Two copies of the same clause are considered distinct clauses.

To understand the formal definition of the set of support strategy, it may help to view the strategy in terms of what is not permitted rather than in terms of what is permitted. When the inference rules consist of binary resolution and factoring, the set of support strategy for the choice T for set of support does not permit the resolution of two occurrences C and D of clauses when C and D are in S − T or factors of clauses in S − T. Thus, the set of support strategy is designed to prohibit application of binary resolution, as well as prohibit the application of other inference rules, when the set of clauses being considered for the application is a subset of S − T.

A constructive form of the definition of the set of support is the following.

Definition.   Let I be any inference rule, and let S be any nonempty set of clauses. The *set of support strategy* requires choosing a nonempty subset T of S. Let T0 be the set of all clauses D such that D is in T or D is a factor of a clause C in T. Let T1 be the set of clauses D such that D is deduced by applying I to the set C1, C2,...,Cn with at least one of Cj in T0 and with the

Ck not in T0 being clauses in or factors of clauses in S, or such that D is a factor of a clause in T1. The set T2 is obtained similarly from T1, T3 from T2.... A *T-supported deduction* is a sequence of occurrences of clauses such that every occurrence in the sequence is in Tk for some k or is a clause in or a factor of a clause in S. Clauses in Tk for some k are said to *have T-support* or *be T-supported*. Thus, a T-supported deduction consists of clauses that have T-support or clauses that are in S or factors of clauses in S. The *set of support strategy* prohibits a reasoning program from generating an occurrence of a clause unless it has T-support or is a factor of a clause in S.

Technically, an occurrence of a clause, rather than all occurrences of that clause, inherits support if (recursively) one of its immediate ancestors has support. Thus, each occurrence of a clause must be judged separately. However, the judgment is not made after the clause is deduced, but rather is a restriction placed on the application of an inference rule. The set of support strategy restricts application of an inference rule to those pairs of clauses—in the case of binary resolution—such that at least one of the pair has support. Thus, employment of the set of support strategy with the combination of binary resolution and factoring results in an automated reasoning program generating only (occurrences of) clauses that are T-supported, where T is the chosen set of support, or that are factors of clauses in S − T. Applying the criteria for having support before the application of an inference rule rather than after results in an important gain in efficiency.

The important question to ask is whether or not the use of the set of support strategy results in the loss of the property of refutation completeness. For example, if S consists of the clauses

P(a)

P(x) | Q(y)

¬P(b)

¬Q(c)

while T is chosen to contain only the first of the given clauses, then refutation completeness is lost. This set S is unsatisfiable, but no clauses can be found using the set of support strategy with this choice of T. What is required is adherence to the fundamental theorem for the set of support strategy.

Set of Support Theorem.   If S is an unsatisfiable set of clauses, and if T is a subset of S such that S − T is satisfiable, then the imposition of the set of support strategy on the combination of binary resolution and factoring preserves the property of refutation completeness for that combination.

This theorem says that, if T is appropriately chosen, then the important logical property of refutation completeness, and hence the desired logical power, of the inference rule(s) being employed is not lost. For example, for the preceding set of clauses, if T is chosen to consist of the third and fourth clauses, then binary resolution suffices to establish the unsatisfiability of S. In fact, given an arbitrary unsatisfiable set S of clauses, a simple criterion exists for choosing a subset T such that S − T is satisfiable, and hence such that T can be used as the set of support without losing refutation completeness. If S is an unsatisfiable set of clauses, then T can be chosen to consist of all those clauses containing no positive literals, or all those clauses containing no negative literals. The first choice makes S − T satisfiable since an interpretation, for example, in which all positive literals are assigned true forces all clauses in S − T to be true because each contains at least one positive literal. A similar remark holds for the second choice of T. With either choice for T as the set of support, the set of support strategy preserves refutation completeness for the combination of binary resolution and factoring. However, neither choice for the set of support is recommended for actual use of an automated reasoning program when employing the corresponding strategy. Instead, the recommended choice is based on semantic criteria, and not on syntactic, and we shall discuss such a choice shortly. (The set of support strategy is not compatible with all inference rules. In particular, if the inference rule hyperresolution, to be defined later, is the only rule in use, imposition of the set of support strategy can result in the loss of refutation completeness. For example, you will soon be in a position to prove that there exist sets S of clauses such that, if T is chosen to consist of all clauses that contain no positive literals, then restricting hyperresolution to generating clauses with T-support results in the generation of no clauses.)

The proof that choosing T such that S − T is satisfiable preserves refutation completeness is the following. We assume that the empty clause is not a member of S. If it were, then for S − T to be satisfiable, T must contain the empty clause. A deduction consisting of just the empty clause would then suffice.

Proof of the Set of Support Theorem.   First we prove the theorem for the ground case, where S contains no variables. We call the unsigned literals of S the *atoms* of S, and denote the set by P. If P contains a single element Q, then among the elements of S there exist unit clauses Q and ¬Q. Regardless of the choice for T, T must contain at least one of Q and ¬Q. The 2-line proof

$$Q$$
$$\neg Q$$

suffices. Assume that the result is true when P contains $1 \leq i \leq n$ atoms.

We next argue by induction and assume that P contains exactly $n + 1$ atoms. Let Q be any element of P. Let S1 be that set obtained by deleting from S all clauses containing Q and by deleting ¬Q from the remaining elements of S. Let S2 be obtained from S by deleting all clauses containing ¬Q and by deleting Q from the remaining elements of S. Let T1 and T2 be obtained from T similarly. S1 and S2 are unsatisfiable since S is. S1 − T1 or S2 − T2 or both are satisfiable since S − T is. Assume without loss of generality that S1 − T1 is.

Where the induction hypothesis applies, there exists a deduction of contradiction from S1 with T1 as set of support. (The only case in which it does not apply is that in which ¬Q is a unit clause in S.) Let R and ¬R be contradictory unit clauses contained in that deduction. The corresponding deduction from S has T-support. At best it contains R and ¬R, and the proof of the ground case is complete. At worst the clauses

¬Q | R

¬Q | ¬R

are part of that deduction, and, by adding their resolvent, one has a deduction D1 of ¬Q as a unit clause, and the deduction has T-support. In the case in which the induction hypothesis does not apply, the T-supported deduction D1 of ¬Q consists of the single line ¬Q. Each of the remaining cases can be extended to a deduction D1 with T-support of the unit clause ¬Q.

Similarly, if S2 − T2 is satisfiable, at worst there exists a deduction D2 of Q with T-support. The juxtaposition of D1 and D2 is a deduction D of contradiction.

One case remains—that in which S2 − T2 is unsatisfiable. In that case, let U be the set of those clauses of S2 − T2 which are obtained from S by deleting the literal Q. Since the elements of (S2 − T2) − U are elements of S − T, (S2 − T2) − U is satisfiable. If the induction hypothesis does not hold in S2   T2, then the unit clause Q is a member of S. In that case, form the deduction D by adding the line Q to D1. Such a deduction D is a deduction of contradiction with T as set of support. When the induction hypothesis holds in S2 − T2, there exists a deduction D3 of contradiction with U-support. Let U1 be the set of those clauses of U which appear in D3. Let V be that subset of S from which U is obtained by deletion of the literal Q. Equivalently, the elements of U1 are obtainable by successive resolution of ¬Q with the elements of V. Since ¬Q has T-support, the elements of U1 do also. Therefore, the deduction formed by juxtaposing D1 and V and D3 is a deduction D of contradiction with T-support.

Thus, in all cases we can find a deduction of contradiction with T as set of support. It remains to consider the case in which S contains variables. The lifting lemma comes into play at this point. In addition, we require the observation that, if A' is obtainable from A by instantiation and has strictly fewer literals than A, then there exists a factor B of A such that A' is an instance of B and A' and B have the same number of literals.

From Herbrand's theorem, we know that there exists a finite set H of constants such that, when S is instantiated over H, a set S' of clauses is obtained that is finite, free of variables, and still unsatisfiable. Similarly, T', the instantiation of T over H, is such that S' − T' is satisfiable since S' − T' is contained in the set obtained by instantiating S − T over H. By the ground case given earlier, there exists a deduction D' of contradiction from S' with T'-support.

We now construct a deduction D of contradiction from S with T-support. When A' occurs in D' and is an element of S', either replace A' by A or by the sequence A, B with B a factor of A, depending on the number of literals in A' compared to that in A. When C' appears in D' as the resolvent of A' and B', where A and B are the replacements of A' and B', replace C' by the sequence E, F, C, as dictated by the lifting lemma. If C' has strictly fewer literals than C, replace C by C and the obvious factor of C. Adherence to the given replacement rules produces a deduction D of contradiction from S with T-support, and the refutation completeness of the set of support strategy is proved for the choices of T with $S - T$ satisfiable, which completes the proof.

In practice the set of support T should be chosen on semantic grounds rather than syntactic, to gain the most from the use of the strategy. Two choices are effective. To understand the motivation for each, consider some problem that has been translated into a finite set S of clauses. Since unsatisfiability is one of the key logical properties on which much of automated reasoning rests, it may not be surprising to find that the usual mode of obtaining a proof of some conjecture is proof by contradiction. Thus, assume that the problem is one of finding a proof, and assume further that a proof by contradiction is being sought. In that case, the set S of clauses to be considered is unsatisfiable—if the statement of the problem in fact represents a theorem. In other words, where the original theorem to be proved has the form **if P then** Q, S consists of clauses that correspond to P **and not** Q.

In S, three subsets of clauses can be identified. The first set consists of the axioms or assumptions on which the area of study is based. The second consists of clauses that are "special" to the problem or theorem under consideration. The third set consists of clauses that correspond to the assumed falsity of the result. One effective choice for the set of support T consists of the third subset alone. The other effective choice consists of the union of the second and third subsets.

These choices have the intuitive appeal that the complement of each is prevented from producing clauses based solely on its members. Such prevention avoids exploring the underlying theory from which the theorem or problem was extracted. Further, since a proof by contradiction is the objective, and since reasoning from a consistent set—the set of axioms—simply produces additional consistent clauses, use of the set of support strategy in accordance with the fundamental theorem for the strategy takes advantage of the consistency of the axioms of a theory. In actuality, if all clauses are given support—T is chosen to be S, and in effect the set of support strategy is ignored—the efficiency of a reasoning program is sharply reduced in most cases.

In contrast to restriction strategies—strategies that prevent a reasoning program from applying an inference rule to various subsets of clauses—an ordering strategy dictates where next to focus attention. One of the more powerful ordering strategies is that of *weighting*. With this strategy, priorities for variables, function symbols, and predicate symbols are assigned by the user. Thus, the user informs the program about which concepts are thought to be keys to solving the problem at hand. These priorities or *weights* are relied upon to direct a reasoning program in its choice of the next clause on which to focus. An automated reasoning program employing weighting chooses the clause with the most favorable weight. If the set of support strategy is also in use, then the choice is constrained to those clauses having support. The weighting strategy can be imposed regardless of the combination of inference rules being employed. Using weighting in this manner imposes an ordering strategy on the program's processing of clauses. In contrast, weighting also permits a threshold to be assigned that in turn causes the deletion of clauses whose weight exceeds that threshold. Used in this manner, weighting imposes a restriction strategy on the processing of clauses. Whether used as an ordering strategy or as a restriction strategy, weighting can interfere with refutation completeness. As a restriction strategy, the loss of refutation completeness results from the possibility of discarding a necessary clause because its weight exceeds the chosen threshold. As an ordering strategy, the loss of refutation completeness results from the possibility that the program will continue to retain (new) clauses of a small enough weight that the needed clause is never examined. Of course, if no weighting threshold is employed and the reasoning program exhausts all possible conclusions without finding a proof, then the set of clauses under study is proved to be satisfiable, assuming that no other interference with refutation completeness is present.

15.4 Other Inference Rules

Although the formulation and use of binary resolution with its companion of factoring improves the effectiveness of an automated reasoning program, and although still further improvement results from the imposition of strategy on those inference rules, more powerful inference rules are desired and needed. Some of the rules emphasize the role of positive clauses, some the role of negative clauses, some the role of unit clauses, and some the role of the equality predicate. Certain of these rules consider simultaneously three or more clauses, rather than making deductions from a pair of clauses. The object of these inference rules is to increase the effectiveness of an automated reasoning program.

Definition.   The inference rule *hyperresolution* considers simultaneously a clause N that contains at least one negative literal and a set of clauses Ai, each of which contains only positive literals, and yields when successful a clause B containing only positive literals. The clause B is obtained by finding a MGU that simultaneously unifies one positive literal in each of the Ai with a distinct negative literal in N, applying the MGU to yield N' and Ai', and taking the **or** of all literals in the Ai' and in N' that do not participate in the unification. The clauses N and Ai are assumed pairwise to have no variables in common. The clause N is termed the *nucleus* and the clauses Ai the *satellites* for the application of hyperresolution. The clause B is termed a *hyperresolvent*.

For example, from

$\neg P(x) \mid \neg Q(y) \mid R(x, y)$
P(a)
Q(b)

an application of hyperresolution yields

R(a, b)

in a single step. Similarly, from

¬P(a) | ¬Q(b)

P(x)

Q(b)

hyperresolution yields the empty clause. This last example illustrates why the empty clause must be employed in certain discussions and why unit conflict does not suffice in all cases. As a third example, from

¬P(a) | Q(b)

P(a) | R(c)

hyperresolution yields

Q(b) | R(c)

as the hyperresolvent.

When negative and positive are interchanged in the definition of hyperresolution, the definition of *negative hyperresolution* results. When, instead, the satellites are required to be unit clauses, the nucleus only constrained to have one more literal than the number of satellites, and the result is required to be a unit clause, the definition of *UR-resolution* results. The inference rule UR-resolution derives its name from the fact that unit clauses result from its use.

While the previously described inference rules can be thought of as distinct and new inference rules, the following can be classed as restrictions on existing inference rules. When binary resolution is restricted to require that at least one of the two clauses to which it is applied be a unit, then the resulting inference rule is called *unit resolution*. When the unit restriction is replaced by the requirement that at least one of the two clauses be an input clause, the result is *input resolution*. When the requirement is that one of the two clauses be a positive clause, then *P1-resolution* is the inference rule. Hyperresolution can be thought of as the simultaneous application of a set of P1-resolutions. Similarly, UR-resolution can be thought of as the simultaneous application of the appropriate unit resolutions.

With each inference rule, the question again arises about the presence of refutation completeness, especially when coupled with various strategies. For example, hyperresolution is refutation complete when unrestricted, but refutation completeness may be lost when hyperresolution is constrained by the set of support strategy. When the subset T of the unsatisfiable set S is chosen to consist of the clauses containing only negative literals, then often no applications other than that which would immediately yield the empty clause are possible. Since many unsatisfiable sets S require a number of applications of hyperresolution before the empty clause is deduced, such a choice for the set of support may lose the refutation completeness of the inference rule. In fact, the combination of hyperresolution and the set of support strategy may result in the deduction of no additional clauses.

Unit resolution and input resolution are refutation complete when the set S of input clauses consists of *Horn clauses*—clauses containing at most one positive literal. In fact, a unit refutation exists if and only if an input refutation exists. Since many areas of interest can be represented with Horn clauses, unit resolution and input resolution are not as restrictive as they might seem. Obviously, unit resolution is not refutation complete, and, not so obviously, neither is input resolution. To see what the problem is, merely consider

P(a) | Q(a)

¬P(a) | Q(a)

P(a) | ¬Q(a)

¬P(a) | ¬Q(a)

for the set S of clauses.

The final inference rule to be discussed in this chapter is that of *paramodulation*. Paramodulation is a generalization of equality substitution in that it combines in a single step the seeking of a variable replacement that permits an equality substitution and the equality substitution itself. While the other inference rules discussed here are oriented to the literal level, this rule is oriented to the term level.

Definition.   An *equality literal* is a literal whose predicate is to be interpreted as meaning "equal". The inference rule of *paramodulation* yields the clause C from the clauses A and B that are assumed to have no variables in common when A contains a positive equality literal and B contains a term that unifies with one of the arguments of that equality literal. Assume without loss of generality that the chosen equality literal has the form EQUAL(r, s) for terms r and s, and that the first argument is that which is being unified with the chosen term in B. The clause C is obtained from A and B by first finding a MGU for the argument of the positive equality literal in A and the term in B. Second, the MGU is applied to A and B to yield, respectively, A' and B'. Third, where K' of the form EQUAL(r', s') is the correspondent to the chosen positive equality literal K of the form EQUAL(r, s) for terms r and s in A, and where t' is the correspondent to the chosen term t in B, replace t' by s'. Finally, form the **or** of A' − K' and B", where B" is obtained from B' by the replacement of t' by s'. The clause A' − K' here means the complement in A' of K', not the set-theoretic difference, for we wish only to remove the one literal from those to which **or** is applied. Clause A is called the *from clause*, clause B the *into clause*, and clause C a *paramodulant*.

For example, from

EQUAL(a, b)

Q(a)

the clause

Q(b)

is obtained by an application of paramodulation. From

EQUAL(sum(x, 0), x)

P(sum(sum(a, 0), b)), c)

paramodulation yields

> P(sum(a, b), c)

as a paramodulant. From

> Q(g(f(g(x))))
> EQUAL(g(a),b)

the clause

> Q(g(f(b)))

is deducible. A somewhat more complex illustration is provided by applying paramodulation to the clauses

> EQUAL(sum(x, minus(x), 0))
> EQUAL(sum(y, sum(minus(y), z)), z)

where the first clause is the *from* clause, and the second the *into*. The result of one possible paramodulation is

> EQUAL(sum(y, 0), minus(minus(y)))

This clause says that $y + 0 = -(-y)$. In this last example, the unification requires a nontrivial variable replacement in both of the terms being unified. Those of you who are familiar with the procedure known as demodulation—that procedure used to automatically simplify and canonicalize—will note certain differences between it and paramodulation. Those who are unfamiliar with demodulation will shortly see the differences.

Although paramodulation is refutation complete when unrestricted by strategy, certain modifications are necessary to preserve refutation completeness when used with the set of support strategy. In particular, the *functional reflexive* axioms must be adjoined to the input clauses, if refutation completeness is to be guaranteed. The functional reflexive axioms are just those instances of reflexivity—EQUAL(x, x) —that can be obtained by instantiating the variable x with the terms f(y), g(y, z), h(w, y, z),..., where the functions f, g, and h are present in the input set S and are one-place, two-place, and three-place. The given method for proving that the set of support strategy preserves refutation completeness of binary resolution coupled with factoring fails to apply here. The reason is that the lifting lemma does not hold. Consider

> EQUAL(a, b)
> Q(x)

and their instances

> EQUAL(a, b)
> Q(f(a))

and the paramodulant

$Q(f(b))$

of the instances. Paramodulation applied to the two clauses before instantiation does not yield a clause that captures the given paramodulant as an instance. Despite this anomaly, when using the set of support strategy, an effective practice is to omit the functional reflexive axioms. In most cases, their inclusion merely interferes with the program's search for the desired answer to the question under study.

EXERCISES

6. Much of the early work in theorem proving dealt with problems in formal areas of mathematics. One reason is that the axioms required to formulate such problems were well understood. A great many of the early problems were from group theory. A group is a set together with a binary operator, which we designate as " $*$ ". The axioms for a group are the following.

   (1) For any two elements a1 and a2 in the group, there exists a third element a3 such that $a1 * a2 = a3$. This is called the *closure axiom*.

   (2) There exists in the group an element e, called the *identity element*, such that $a1 * e = a1$ and $e * a1 = a1$ for any element a1 in the group.

   (3) For any element a1 in the group, there exists an element a2 in the group such that $a1 * a2 = e$, and $a2 * a1 = e$. The element a2 is called the *inverse* of a1.

   (4) For any three elements a1, a2, and a3 in the group, $a1 * (a2 * a3) = (a1 * a2) * a3$. This states that the operator $*$ is *associative*.

These axioms can be written as clauses using a three-place predicate P, where $P(a, b, c)$ may be taken to mean that $a * b = c$. Some of the clauses that result are the following (see Chapter 9 for the complete set).

The closure axiom:

   (1) $P(x, y, f(x, y))$

e is the identity:

   (2) $P(e, x, x)$

   (3) $P(x, e, x)$

Each element has a two-sided inverse:

   (4) $P(g(x), x, e)$

   (5) $P(x, g(x), e)$

The operator is associative:

(6) $\neg P(x, y, u) \mid \neg P(y, z, v) \mid \neg P(u, z, w) \mid P(x, v, w)$

(7) $\neg P(x, y, u) \mid \neg P(y, z, v) \mid \neg P(x, v, w) \mid P(u, z, w)$

One simple theorem in group theory is the following:

If $x * x = e$ for all x in the group, then $x * y = y * x$ for any two elements in the group.

First, give a set of two clauses that together denies the theorem. Next, give a set of three clauses that denies the theorem, and such that the Skolem function "f" (for product) is not used in any of the three clauses. For each of the two formulations, which clauses should be in the set of support, assuming that hyperresolution is used as the inference rule.

7. Prove that hyperresolution is refutation complete for sets of ground clauses.

8. What else is required to show that hyperresolution is refutation complete for arbitrary sets of clauses?

9. As stated in the section, a Horn clause contains at most one positive literal. Show that unit resolution is refutation complete for a set of ground Horn clauses.

10. Both hyperresolution and UR-resolution are much more effective than binary resolution. Binary resolution generates too many intermediate clauses—clauses that correspond to small steps occurring between the clauses in focus and the conclusions to be obtained. Generating all possible binary resolvents usually results in very poor performance. It is very important to drastically reduce the set of generated clauses by employing a strategy such as the set of support strategy. An analogous situation exists for paramodulation. Paramodulation is powerful enough to arrive at the desired results; however, the steps are frequently too small, and restrictions are highly desirable. This desire has led to a number of general strategies such as "Do not paramodulate into or from a variable". Let us first search for a rule analogous to hyperresolution.

   (a) In problem 6, you were asked to give two formulations of the denial of the theorem. Give a proof by hyperresolution using the second formulation.

   (b) If the problem is reformulated using just the equality predicate, the axioms become

   Equality is reflexive:

   (E1) EQUAL(x, x)

   There exists an identity:

   (E2) EQUAL$(f(e, x), x)$

   (E3) EQUAL$(f(x, e), x)$

   Each element has an inverse:

   (E4) EQUAL$(f(g(x), x), e)$

   (E5) EQUAL$(f(x, g(x)), e)$

   The operator is associative:

   (E6) EQUAL$(f(x, f(y, z)), f(f(x, y), z))$

The square of every element is the identity:

(E8) EQUAL(f(x, x), e)

Denial of the theorem:

(E9′) EQUAL(f(a, b), c)

(E9″) ¬EQUAL(f(b, a), c)

Give a proof using paramodulation that follows the same basic steps as the hyperresolution proof. Assuming the first step in the hyperresolution proof is to deduce P(a, c, b), start by deducing EQUAL(f(a, c), b).

(c) Can you formulate an inference rule that is to paramodulation as hyperresolution is to binary resolution?

(d) One restriction that can be imposed on the formation of paramodulants is that the variables in the into clause cannot be instantiated to anything but variables and constants. This restriction is called "noncomplexifying paramodulation". Does the proof in part b) employ noncomplexifying paramodulation?

(e) Suppose that you have an equation represented in clause form. For example,

EQUAL($sum($power($sum(g(x), b), 2), $sum(g(x), b)), $sum(x, 4))

can be used to represent $(g(x) + b)^2 + (g(x) + b) = x + 4$. Assume, in addition, that you have the clause

EQUAL($sum(g(x), x), $power(x, .5))

and wish to use the second clause to instantiate and simplify the first. Formulate an inference rule that is an extension of paramodulation and that can be used in such situations.

15.5 Subsumption

Even with the improvement in performance derived from the use of both ordering and restriction strategies, an automated reasoning program faces serious difficulties when attempting to reach a given goal. Among those difficulties is the generation of many copies of the same clause. Another closely related problem is the generation of clauses that are either proper instances of already existing clauses or the reverse. For example,

EQUAL(minus(minus(a)), a)

EQUAL(minus(minus(x)), x)

can be generated in either order. Whichever occurs, from the viewpoint of usefulness, the second of the two clauses is preferable to the first. For almost all problems and with almost any combination of inference rules and strategies, what an automated reasoning program can do with the first clause it can do with the second. The second clause has more logical power than the first. Thus a procedure is needed to purge the first in favor of the second, regardless of the order in which they occur. The needed procedure is called *subsumption*.

Definition.   The clause A *subsumes* the clause B when there exists an instance of A that is a subclause of B.

The clause

P(x)

subsumes the clause

P(a)

obviously. Of the clauses

P(x)
P(a) | Q(b)

the first subsumes the second. An example that might be unexpected consists of

P(a, b)
P(a, x) | P(y, b)

in which the second clause subsumes the first. This type of subsumption is not always advantageous for it causes unit clauses to be deleted, and unit clauses are often one of the intermediate objectives of a search being conducted by a reasoning program.

Employing subsumption to prune clauses from the space of kept clauses does not, in most cases, have an effect on refutation completeness. Removing a clause that is subsumed by another clause does not affect the satisfiability or unsatisfiability of a set of clauses. When clause A subsumes clause B, ordinarily clause A can be used where clause B would have been used. One of the exceptions is provided by the conflict that can occur when employing the set of support strategy. A clause B with support can be subsumed by a clause A without support, and the needed step of a deduction may then not be permitted. However, if clause A is given support when this happens, then the needed step will be permitted.

15.6 Demodulation

In the hunt for power and efficiency, one more procedure has been formulated. This procedure, called *demodulation*, is designed to enable an automated reasoning program to simplify and canonicalize information. By doing so, clauses that represent information that is in a sense semantically redundant, although not syntactically redundant, can be purged. For example,

EQUAL(sum(sum(x, 0), sum(y, z)), sum(sum(x, y), z))

contains the information that

$$\text{EQUAL}(\text{sum}(x, \text{sum}(y, z)), \text{sum}(\text{sum}(x, y), z)))$$

contains. With demodulation and the appropriate demodulator, the first of these two clauses would be rewritten as the second.

Definition.   A *demodulator* is a positive unit clause with an equality predicate that has been designated to be used to rewrite expressions. A demodulator C of the form $\text{EQUAL}(r, s)$ for terms r and s applies to a term t if and only if t is an instance of r or t is an instance of s. When t is an instance of r, the result of applying the demodulator C to a clause D replaces D by a demodulant E, obtained by replacing t by s', when $r' = t$. In particular, $\text{EQUAL}(r', s')$ is that instance of $\text{EQUAL}(r, s)$ that results from unifying say r with t. When t is an instance of r, the corresponding demodulant is obtained.

In practice, a choice is made between left-to-right and right-to-left applications of demodulators. Ordinarily, when demodulation is in use, a term is treated to as many demodulations as apply. Only the final demodulant is retained. When newly adjoined clauses are designated as demodulators and are applied to already retained clauses, the process is termed *back demodulation*. Employment of demodulation can result in the loss of refutation completeness. Nevertheless, demodulation is heavily used for many problem domains by many automated reasoning programs.

Several important differences exist between demodulation and paramodulation. Briefly, with demodulation the unification is constrained to making nontrivial variable replacements only in the analogue of the "from" clause. Also, demodulation requires that the equality literal reside in a (positive) unit clause. Finally, demodulation discards that clause into which the substitution takes place, while paramodulation retains the clauses before and after substitution.

EXERCISE

11. Give an example of a set of clauses for which binary resolution is sufficient to lead to a proof were it not for the presence of certain demodulators. In particular, give a set of clauses S, a set of support T, and a set of demodulators such that a proof can be obtained with binary resolution if and only if the demodulators are not used to "simplify" the generated clauses.

15.7 Answers to Exercises

1. The expression

   For all x, (**if** P(x) **then** (there exists a y such that (Q(x,y) **and** not Q(y,x)))) is first converted to prenex form:

> For all x, there exists a y such that
> **(if** P(x) **then**
>   (Q(x, y) **and not** Q(y, x)))

Then it is rewritten into conjunctive normal form:

> For all x, there exists a y such that
> ((**not** P(x) **or** Q(x,y)) **and**
> (**not** P(x) **or not** Q(y, x)))

Then a Skolem function is introduced to remove the existentially quantified variable:

> For all x,
> ((**not** P(x) **or** Q(x, f(x))) **and**
> (**not** P(x) **or not** Q(f(x), x)))

Thus, the clauses that result are

> (1) $\neg$P(x) | Q(x, f(x))
>
> (2) $\neg$P(x) | $\neg$Q(f(x), x)

2. Remember to rename variables before attempting to unify two literals.
  (a) The MGCI is Psum(g(c, c), c, f(c)).
  (b) There is no MGU for the two literals.

3. (a) This inference rule when converted into clauses says that from

> (1) $\neg$H1 | $\neg$H2 | C1
>
> (2) H1

you can conclude

> (3) $\neg$H2 | C1

This again is just an instance of binary resolution.
  (b) When you convert this rule to clauses you get

From

> (1) $\neg$H1 | C1
>
> (2) $\neg$H1 | C2
>
> (3) $\neg$H1

Conclude

> (4) $\neg$C1

and

> (5) $\neg$C2

The conclusions cannot be obtained using binary resolution. This is quite reasonable, since the inference rule is not sound—the conclusions yielded by it do not always follow logically, so you should avoid using it.

(c) When you convert this rule to clauses you get

From

(1) ¬H1 | ¬H2 | C1 | C2

(2) ¬C1

Conclude

(3) ¬H1 | ¬H2 | C2

The conclusion is again just a binary resolvent of clauses 1 and 2.

4. (a) There is one factor of this clause.

¬$GT(x, 0) | $GT($sum(x, x), 0)

(b) There are no factors of this clause.

(c) There are three factors of this clause.

¬Psum(x, x, w) | ¬Psum(w, x, u) | Psum(x, w, u)

¬Psum(x, y, x) | ¬Psum(y, y, v) | Psum(x, v, x)

¬Psum(x, y, y) | ¬Psum(y, z, v) | Psum(x, v, v)

5. No, binary resolution is not deduction complete. Let S contain the single clause

P(a)

Then let C be the clause

Q(b) | ¬Q(b)

The clause C clearly must be true if the single clause in S is true, for it is always true. However, C cannot be deduced from S using binary resolution and factoring.

6. The first formulation uses the following two clauses.

(8) P(x, x, e)

(9) ¬P(a, b, f(b, a))

The second formulation replaces clause 9 with

(9′) P(a, b, c)

(9″) ¬P(b, a, c)

If hyperresolution is chosen for the inference rule, then for the first formulation both clauses 8 and 9 should be in the set of support. If clause 9 alone is in the set of support, no clauses will be generated. On the other hand, if the second formulation is used, clause 8 can be omitted from the set of support. In either formulation, you cannot be assured of a proof unless all of the clauses are in the set of support. However, if you do include all of the clauses in the set of support, the generated clauses will include numerous lemmas from group theory, and the reasoning program will not focus well on the problem at hand. In the second formulation, you should seek a proof with just clauses 9′ and 9″ in the set of support. If none can be found, again seek a proof, but put clause 8 in the set of support as well. If that fails too, put all of the clauses into the set of support. Hyperresolution tends to determine the consequences of the positive clauses in the set of support. If lemmas must be generated from the general axioms alone, a proof will not be obtained. Hence, some researchers have experimented with performing a limited number of hyperresolutions with the general axioms alone to prove and retain a pool of lemmas; then the resulting pool is used as the general axiom set with all of its members excluded from the set of support. Thus, the problem is attacked in stages—first lemmas are proved, and then an attempt is made to reason from the specific assumptions of the problem to arrive at a contradiction.

7. To show that hyperresolution is refutation complete, we must show that if S is an unsatisfiable set of ground clauses then the empty clause is deducible using hyperresolution. The proof that we give here is due to Anderson and Bledsoe. If a clause contains n literals, we shall say that it contains $n - 1$ *excess literals*. For any set of clauses, the number of excess literals in the set is just the sum of the number of excess literals in the individual clauses, which is equal to the total number of literal occurrences minus the number of clauses in the set. The proof is by induction on the number of excess literals in S. Suppose that S contains no excess literals. Then, since S is unsatisfiable by assumption, there must be conflicting unit clauses in S. Hence, a hyperresolvent can be formed from these units, producing the empty clause. Now let us suppose that hyperresolution is refutation complete for any ground set of clauses containing k or fewer excess literals. Then let us consider the case in which S contains $k + 1$ excess literals. First try to find a clause C that is not a unit clause and contains at least one positive literal L. If no such C exists—if all clauses containing a positive literal are unit clauses—then there must be a negative clause in which each literal conflicts with a positive unit clause. If this were not the case, S would be satisfiable. In this case, the empty clause can again be produced as a single hyperresolvent (of the negative nucleus and the conflicting positive satellite clauses). Therefore, let us consider the case in which such a C can be found. In this case, define C1 as the clause formed from C by omitting the literal L. Define C2 as the positive unit clause containing L. Let S1 be obtained from S by replacing C with C1. Let S2 be obtained from S by replacing C with C2. Since S is unsatisfiable, both S1 and S2 must be unsatisfiable. Furthermore, since both S1 and S2 contain k or fewer excess literals, hyperresolution can be used to deduce the empty clause from either S1 or S2. Now consider the deduction of the empty clause from S1. If we were to compute all of the corresponding hyperresolvents from clauses in S, they would be identical to those in S1—except that some of them might include the literal L. In particular, either the empty clause or C2 will be deduced. But in the case in which C2 is deduced, the empty clause can be deduced by computing the same hyperresolvents used to show that S2 is unsatisfiable. This completes the proof.

8. You need to prove a lifting lemma similar to the one stated in Section 15.2.2, except that binary resolution is replaced with hyperresolution. Note that hyperresolution, as defined in section 15.4, is not refutation complete. Hyperresolution together with factoring is refutation complete. That factoring is needed can be seen by examining the example given to show its need for the refutation completeness of binary resolution.

9. The proof here can be based on the fact that hyperresolution is refutation complete for sets of ground clauses. If S is an unsatisfiable set of ground Horn clauses, then there exists a deduction of the empty clause using hyperresolution. However, since all of the

clauses are Horn clauses, all of the satellite clauses used in forming a hyperresolvent must be unit clauses. Hence, each hyperresolvent can be deduced by a sequence of unit resolutions. This completes the proof.

10. (a) The proof using hyperresolution is the following.

From clauses 6, 8, 9′, and 2:

(10) $P(a, c, b)$

From clauses 7, 10, 8, and 3:

(11) $P(b, c, a)$

From clauses 6, 8, 11, and 2:

(12) $P(b, a, c)$

From clauses 9″ and 12:

unit conflict and proof by contradiction

Note that here the nucleus is specified first, followed by the satellites (in the same order as the literals in the nucleus that they conflict with).

(b) First, the hyperresolvent clause 10 is formed by unifying three literals in clause 6 with three positive units. We can form a correspondence between literals in clause 6 and the terms in clause E6. The term $f(x, y)$ in clause E6 corresponds to the first literal in clause 6, the term $f(y, z)$ in clause E6 to the second literal in clause 6, the term $f(f(x, y), z)$ to the third literal in 6, and $f(x, f(y, z))$ to the fourth literal in 6. Since clause 10 is formed by unifying clause 8 with the first literal in clause 6, let us begin by paramodulating from clause E8 into $f(x, y)$ in clause E6. If we then paramodulate from clause E9′ into the term deduced from $f(y, z)$ in clause E6, and finally from clause E2 into the entire right argument, the clause

(E10) $EQUAL(f(a, c), b)$

results. If we give the proof one step at a time, it is the following.

Into $f(x, y)$ in clause E6 from clause E8:

(E10a) $EQUAL(f(x, f(x, y)), f(e, y))$

Into $f(x, y)$ in clause E10a from clause E9′:

(E10b) $EQUAL(f(a, c), f(e, b))$

Into $f(e, b)$ in clause E10b from clause E2:

(E10) $EQUAL(f(a, c), b)$

The correspondence between the literals in clause 7 and the terms in clause E6 is the following: the first literal corresponds to $f(x, y)$, the second literal to $f(y, z)$, the third literal to $f(x, f(y, z))$, and the fourth literal to $f(f(x, y), z)$. Using this correspondence the remainder of the proof is the following.

Into $f(x, y)$ in clause E6 from clause E10:

(E11a) $EQUAL(f(a, f(c, x)), f(b, x))$

Into $f(c, x)$ in clause E11a from clause E8:

(E11b) EQUAL$(f(a, e), f(b, c))$

Into $f(a, e)$ in clause E11b from clause E3:

(E11) EQUAL$(a, f(b, c))$

Into $f(x, y)$ in clause E6 from clause E8:

(E12a) EQUAL$(f(x, f(x, y)), f(e, y))$

Into $f(x, y)$ in clause E12a from clause E11:

(E12b) EQUAL$(f(b, a), f(e, c))$

Into $f(e, c)$ in clause E12b from clause E2:

(E12) EQUAL$(f(b, a), c)$

Unit conflict has been obtained.

(c) Such a rule is merely suggested by an exercise such as the one just given. The variants of such a rule are germane to a current research topic. Certainly, one approach is to designate certain input clauses as "nuclei". Then within the nuclei certain terms can be designated to be paramodulated into by "satellites". The result of paramodulating into all of the designated terms is a new satellite. The intermediate clauses formed in the sequence to produce a new satellite are discarded. Such a rule captures the spirit of hyperresolution. There are a number of complexities that are beyond the scope of this work—complexities such as how to choose the nuclei and the designated terms. Nevertheless, knowing of such rules and possible variations might cause you to formulate other interesting options.

(d) Yes, the preceding proof was by noncomplexifying paramodulation. There is one detail of noncomplexifying paramodulation that is worth mentioning: if a variable occurs in the into clause only in the term being paramodulated into, it can be instantiated to anything. In effect, although the variable is instantiated to a more complex term, the added complexity is not reflected in the generated paramodulant.

(e) In cases like this, you probably wish to replace all occurrences of the term being paramodulated into. In this example, both occurrences of $sum(g(x), b)$ should be replaced with $power(b, .5)$. This would normally require two applications of paramodulation. However, a natural extension of paramodulation is to generate the clause formed by replacing not only the into term, but all occurrences of the term. As far as we know, no one has experimented yet with this extension.

11. Consider the following set of clauses.

(1) $\neg Q(x, y) \mid P(y, g(x))$

(2) $Q(a, b)$

(3) $\neg P(x, g(y)) \mid P(y, x)$

(4) $\neg P(a, b)$

(5) EQUAL$(g(a), b)$

If clause 5 is used as a demodulator, no proof is obtainable using hyperresolution. If clause 5 is not used as a demodulator, a proof can easily be produced. The problem arises because the first literal in clause 3 looks for a property that holds between two elements, x and g(y), where the second element has a specified structure that is arrived at by applying the function g to a third element. In other words, g(a) and b are the same element, but the name g(a) conveys the added information that the element can be obtained by applying the function g to the element a.

16

The Art of Automated Reasoning

Reasoning is an art and not a science. This aphorism applies as well to people as it does to computer programs designed to automate reasoning. The use of such a program is an art, even though an automated reasoning program employs an unambiguous and exacting notation for representing information, precise inference rules for drawing conclusions, and carefully delineated strategies to control those inference rules. Thus, by reasoning we mean more than the process called deduction. The good artist carefully chooses a style, a medium, and a subject, and demonstrates an inventiveness and flair. In using an automated reasoning program, the analogue consists of making good choices for representation, for inference rules, and for strategies. A good choice for representation includes a notation that increases the chance of solving the problem and includes information that, though not necessary, is helpful. A good choice for inference rules is one that meshes well with the chosen representation. A good choice for strategies is one that controls the inference rules in a manner that sharply increases the effectiveness of the reasoning program. But what are the rules for making good choices in these three areas?

Rules we cannot give, just proverbs. Unfortunately, precise rules do not as yet exist for using an automated reasoning program; instead, only hints and imprecise suggestions can be given. For every well thought out suggestion for how to use an automated reasoning program, an exception can be found. Nevertheless, we can give guidelines—suggestions based on thousands of experiments with various automated reasoning programs. Where we can, we provide intuitive justification for making the recommendations. We include warnings of various kinds, for problem solving is tricky and difficult, even when aided by a reasoning program.

For those who wish to delve into the literature, we include a chapter by chapter set of references to various papers and books. The references cover the salient points and represent, but by no means exhaust, the research on which this book is based.

16.1 Proverbs

The following imprecise rules can be treated as proverbs. They summarize our recommendations. They are not meant to be followed without thought, but are merely guidelines. Fuller explanations follow in Sections 16.2 through 16.4.

For the representation of a problem to an automated reasoning program, we recommend the following.

1. Use unit clauses in preference to nonunit clauses.
2. Employ equality predicates.
3. Rely on shorter clauses in preference to longer.
4. Depend on implicit argument typing in preference to literal typing.
5. Include dependent information.

For choosing inference rules, we give these suggestions.

1. Use paramodulation when equality units are present.
2. Use UR-resolution when unit clauses are present or when unit clauses are being sought.
3. Use hyperresolution when positive clauses are being sought.
4. Avoid binary resolution.

For choosing strategies, we recommend the following.

1. Rely on the set of support strategy, with the choice for the set of support the clauses that comprise the special hypothesis and the clauses that comprise the denial.
2. Weight functions and predicates to reflect your knowledge and intuition about how the problem being studied might be solved.
3. Include in the input demodulators that simplify and canonicalize.
4. Employ the unit preference strategy, if you need to employ binary resolution.

Although the use of an automated reasoning program may be difficult at first, practice and experience will increase your skill. You are not required to be an expert in automated reasoning to have such a program assist you in solving problems of various kinds. We use such a program as an automated assistant and a colleague. The open questions cited in Chapters 9 and 10 would most likely not have been answered were it not for heavy reliance on an automated reasoning program.

16.2 Representation of Information

The art of translating a problem into an effective set of clauses is subtle and sometimes complex. Nevertheless, we can provide some hints and some intuitive guidelines for making various choices. The abundance of choices is one of the reasons representing a problem to an automated reasoning program is termed an art. Given one representation of a problem, a reasoning program may solve it in a few seconds. Given another, a few minutes might be required, or even hours, or the choice of representation might even result in failure to reach any solution. Thus, when using an automated reasoning program to assist in solving a particular problem, your choice of representation can play an essential role in its chance of succeeding.

A second reason for terming problem representation as art is the difficulty of characterizing the concepts that are present—the difficulty of supplying enough information to pin down the concepts. We can give no test for determining that a concept has been sufficiently delineated. On the other hand, the output of a single run of a reasoning program does provide useful clues to what might be missing, if something is in fact missing. For example, you can examine the output to see if some obvious conclusion is absent even though the program has already focused on the relevant information. Such an absence is often due to a missing clause, such as the fact that being a sibling is symmetric.

$$\neg SIBLING(x, y) \mid SIBLING(y, x)$$

Ordinarily, you would expect a reasoning program to conclude that Rick lives in Canada, if it knows that Brian's siblings live in Canada and that Rick is one of Brian's siblings. However, the only relevant clauses available might be the following.

$$\neg SIBLING(x, Brian) \mid LIVEIN(x, Canada)$$

$$SIBLING(Brian, Rick)$$

If this were the case, the reasoning program would conclude nothing from the two given clauses. The clause

$$\neg SIBLING(x, y) \mid SIBLING(y, x)$$

provides the required link.

A third reason for saying "the art of translating a problem" rests with the interconnection of good choices for representation with good choices for inference rule and then in turn with good choices for strategy. As we justify the proverbs given earlier, you will quickly see how intertwined these three areas are.

We are not implying with the discussion of representation that no procedure exists for producing clauses to represent a problem once given the statement in first-order predicate calculus. Algorithms exist that perform a sequence of transformations that eventually produce from such a statement a set of clauses in which variables that say "there exists" are replaced by functions. Unfortunately, such algorithms provide merely a beginning. They shed no light on questions about preference for nonunit clauses over unit clauses, preference for avoiding equality predicates over their use, or preference for predicates over functions. Precise answers to such questions do not yet exist, only suggestions based on experience and intuition.

16.2.1 Unit Clauses

The presence of unit clauses, everything being equal, increases the effectiveness of a reasoning program. After all, most successful uses of such a program terminate with unit conflict—with finding two unit clauses that contradict each other. Therefore, in a simplistic sense, the more unit clauses that are present, the more likely that unit conflict will be found within the retained set of clauses. Do we therefore recommend that all information, if possible, be represented with unit clauses? Are there any harmful consequences of doing so? Besides, how can a concept that naturally is represented with a nonunit clause be instantly transformed into a unit clause?

Let us take these three questions in the reverse order. The *or* function can be employed to instantly convert many nonunit clauses to unit clauses. For example, merely replace the clause

$$MALE(x) \mid FEMALE(x)$$

by the clause

$$TRUE(or(male(x), female(x)))$$

(We say many clauses can be converted in this manner, but not all. To convert the remaining, the *not* function must also be used.) Such replacements are not to be made lightly. Various basic research questions in automated reasoning are yet to be answered before much can be said. We recommend the use of the *or*, the *not*, and the *and* functions to permit a representation that replaces a nonunit clause with a unit clause or that replaces a set of clauses with a single unit clause only for a person who is an expert in automated reasoning.

A second approach to replacing nonunit clauses with unit clauses involves use of functions and of an equality predicate. For example, the fact that a person's father's brother is that person's paternal uncle can easily be represented (in part) without function symbols and by avoiding an equality predicate, or it can easily be represented with function symbols and an equality predicate.

$$\neg FATHER(y, z) \mid \neg BROTHER(x, y) \mid UNCLE(x, z)$$

$$EQUALP(brother(father(x)), uncle(x))$$

While the second of these two clauses is sufficient for reasoning from the fact that Ralph is Jack's father's brother to the fact that Ralph is Jack's uncle and conversely, the first is not. If a program is to be able to reason in both directions and is also using the first of the two choices for representation, then two additional clauses are needed, which explains why we said "(in part)" above.

$\neg$UNCLE(x, z) | FATHER(f(x, z), z)

$\neg$UNCLE(x, z) | BROTHER(f(x, z), x)

To see where these additional clauses come from, convert into clauses the statement "for *all* x and for *all* z (x is the uncle of z *if* and *only if* there exists a y such that (y is the father of z **and** y is the brother of x))". Although our overall recommendation is for the equality form for uncle, some situations call for the other form. As we indicated earlier, exceptions abound, and the decision-making is an art.

As for the second question, that concerned with harmful consequences of using as much unit representation as possible, too much of a good thing is still too much. Forcing, as much as possible, a unit clause form removes one criterion that can be used to classify information. The various properties of a clause, such as unit or nonunit, are useful aids for an automated reasoning program to base decisions upon. Such decisions include which clause is best to focus on next, which new clauses should be kept, and which list should a new kept clause be placed on. For example, all nonunit clauses can be classified as auxiliary—as information to be used when some unit clause is the focus of attention.

As seen in Chapter 14, Prolog requires that all facts be unit clauses, and considers all nonunit clauses to be part of procedures. By retaining certain information in a nonunit form, you are permitted the choice of using inference rules such as UR-resolution and hyperresolution for certain tasks. Cavalierly presenting, whenever possible, information to a reasoning program in unit clause form thus restricts the choices of inference rule. In addition, such action removes one criterion that can be used to separate information into various classes. Such criteria can be used to enable a reasoning program to schedule its activities. You will see more clearly what we mean when we discuss, later in this chapter, certain uses of demodulation.

Finally, in answer to the first question, we recommend that you represent much of a problem in unit clauses if the action seems reasonably natural. The more expert you become, the more risks you can take with the representation, even to the point of using the *or* function and the *not* function and the *and* function. By taking such risks, you may provide a means for an automated reasoning program to solve some otherwise unsolvable problem, and you may eventually contribute to the theory of representation in automated reasoning.

We recommend the use of unit clauses in part because of our preference for inference rules such as UR-resolution and paramodulation. For effective use of a reasoning program, we comment again that the choices for representation, for inference rule, and for strategy are best not made independently. A graphic illustration of how a reasoning program can be hampered by independent choices consists of representing a problem mostly in unit clauses with an equality predicate while employing binary resolution as the only inference rule.

For example, in the everyday situation in which you are told that Shorty and Jack are the same person and are also told that Shorty's great-grandfather is 80 years old, you immediately know that Jack's great-grandfather is 80 years old. A reasoning program could draw the same conclusion and in one step, given an appropriate representation in unit equality clauses and using paramodulation. On the other hand, given that representation but forced to use binary resolution, the program would require four steps to reach the conclusion. The extra steps in themselves are not the real problem, but rather the additional clauses they generate, which can cause more extra steps of an irrelevant nature to be taken, which in turn can result in an explosion of irrelevant information. We thus have yet another example of the complexity of reasoning, and not just automated reasoning.

As with the examples given earlier from everyday situations, we can also give examples from pure mathematics, from circuit design, and systems control to illustrate the complexity of making choices. Simply put, the art of automated reasoning is a difficult one to master, but practice does improve your skill. Examination of the material from the various chapters provides additional hints. Although many exceptions can be found for each of the proverbs and to each of our recommendations, the proverbs and recommendations do provide useful guidelines.

16.2.2 Equality Predicates

Besides readability and naturalness, why prefer a representation that emphasizes the use of equality predicates? With equality predicates present, an automated reasoning program can be instructed to use paramodulation as the only inference rule or as one of its inference rules. Paramodulation can focus directly on the appropriate term even when that term is found deep within a literal. Other inference rules are oriented toward the literal level, and not the term level. As seen in the preceding section, the fact that Shorty and Jack are the same person can lead to useful conclusions. Everything being equal, and of course it is hard to tell if that is the case, an automated reasoning program is more effective when permitted to focus directly on the target rather than approaching the target obliquely. In mathematics, for example, some action often takes place deep within an expression. The mathematician does not travel the circuitous path to the nested term, but makes the desired substitution directly. Paramodulation performs the same direct substitution. Thus, we recommend writing the associative law, as well as similar laws, as a unit equality clause, rather than as two clauses with four literals each that avoid using equality.

Are there any problems with a representation that emphasizes equality? As in the discussion of emphasizing the use of unit clauses, the same point of classification of information and control applies. If, as much as possible, all information is written as unit equality clauses, then a reasoning program may have a harder job separating information into classes that in turn can be used to make scheduling decisions.

For example, some tasks are best treated as asides, while others are best treated as primary. In the full jobs puzzle of Chapter 3, crossing off combinations of people and possible jobs they might hold is treated as an aside, dispatched automatically by using demodulation. By doing so, a reasoning program is able to concentrate on the acquisition of facts that are then used for crossing-off possibilities. Demodulation takes precedence over other processes; thus the automatic crossing off and corresponding updating of information is given the highest of priorities. Since this move clearly is one we recommended in the full jobs puzzle, perhaps as much as possible the instructions and representation to a reasoning program should be of this type.

If too many tasks are so relegated, then the scheduling virtue is simply undone. Rather than being able to schedule some tasks as asides and others as primary, all or most tasks will be merged into one class, and another means will be needed to classify tasks and aid in the scheduling problem. Thus we recommend against the attempt to represent everything in terms of unit equality clauses. As your skill increases, you can rely increasingly on the use of equality. Such heavy reliance gives access to more complex uses of demodulation and use of paramodulation. But demodulation can be used to the point of moving all tasks from the classes of primary and asides to the class of asides, thus destroying one criterion for scheduling. And paramodulation is more difficult to control than many other inference rules, but it is also a very powerful rule and very useful. A number of research questions exist concerning the control of paramodulation.

16.2.3 Shorter Rather than Longer Clauses

By a shorter clause, we mean a clause with fewer literals. The fewer the literals, the easier to produce a unit clause from it. In fact, the fewer the literals, the easier to use the clause successfully with others to obtain a conclusion. Each added literal presents a possible obstacle to completing a successful application of certain inference rules, such as UR-resolution and hyperresolution. When two or more nonunit clauses are directly involved in the attempt to draw conclusions, intuitively the reasoning program is performing a case analysis, but examining more than one case at a time. The fewer the cases being simultaneously examined, the more effective the analysis.

Is the case for shorter clauses this transparent? After all, the inclusion of literals to type various arguments makes a clause longer, but also decreases the likelihood of introducing an error in the problem formulation.

$$\neg PERSON(x) \mid \neg JOB(nurse) \mid \neg HASAJOB(x, nurse) \mid MALE(x)$$

With UR-resolution and the appropriate unit clauses, or with hyperresolution and the appropriate clauses, a reasoning program can still obtain the desired conclusions. So, at least for cases of this type, why not include such extra literals and glean the benefit of reduced likelihood of error?

The position as given has merit but, as usual, another side of the story can be told. The added clauses—needed because of the extra literals—must be placed in the axiom or assumption set, the special hypothesis set, or the denial set of input clauses. If placed in either of the last two sets, then a typical use of the set of support strategy will focus on those clauses and thus possibly explore areas of the space of clauses that would otherwise have been avoided. The decision to place such additional clauses in the set of support is justified when, for example, the rule for making such choices says to give support to everything about Roberta. This rule works quite well in certain classes of problem. This rule can, of course, be replaced by a more complicated rule, but one goal is to make the use of a reasoning program less complicated. In any event, placing the additional clauses in the axiom set still leaves the extra literals.

Extra literals in a clause can cause a reasoning program to bring the clause into play more often in its attempt to complete the application of an inference rule. If the attempt fails, then the effort has been wasted, and the ineffectiveness increased. Too many failures prevent a reasoning program from achieving the goal in a reasonable amount of time. If the attempt succeeds, often the result will duplicate an existing conclusion. Although subsumption removes such duplications, again time is required.

If you wish to exercise this extra care, include such typing literals. Ordinarily, we recommend in this case as well as the general case that shorter clauses are preferable to longer.

16.2.4 Implicit Argument Classifying

From the preceding remarks, you can see that we prefer to use implicit argument typing. We recommend in most cases using a notation that implicitly considers the argument in a specific position in a literal to give the type of the argument. If one clause had a person in the first argument of a literal and a job in the second, while another clause had them reversed, various problems could result. Examination of the output of a computer run usually exposes such inconsistent usage.

16.2.5 Dependent Information

When speaking of dependent information, we are focusing on a clause in the input that can be deduced from other input clauses. For example, the fact that 0 is a right identity is dependent on the facts that 0 is a left identity and that the operation in question is commutative.

EQUAL(sum(x, 0), x)
EQUAL(sum(0, x), x)
EQUAL(sum(x, y), sum(y, x))

The first of the three clauses can be deduced from the second two by paramodulating the third into the second. Such dependencies are common in mathematics. The usual set of axioms for group theory includes those of right identity and right inverse, each of which can be deduced from the remaining.

Similar dependent information is relied on in everyday situations and in reasoning that is not automated. Such added information, when not included in the input, often must be deduced to complete the assignment. Leaving it out can make the puzzle or problem much harder than need be. After all, the object of the reasoning is to deduce the needed facts that lead to the desired conclusion. All of the conclusions are of course dependent on the input clauses. Forcing a reasoning program to search for information you strongly suspect is valuable and you know is deducible impedes its progress. If you wish to exercise great care and check that the information claimed to be dependent is in fact dependent, a reasoning program can be used to prove the claim.

Why not have an automated reasoning program look for such valuable information? Indeed, one use of a reasoning program is just that—looking for basic facts that are general and that might be useful in many situations. However, a standard approach of having the program always look for such information on the way to solving a specific problem is not recommended. Such dependent clauses are often most easily derived by applying inference rules to clauses selected entirely from the set of axioms. Permitting a reasoning program to take such an action defeats the intent of the set of support strategy. The strategy is intended to prevent a reasoning program from exploring the theory in general, thus enabling the program to focus its attention on the problem under study. Thus, if you wish, you can have an automated reasoning program search for such basic notions in an early run, and then include them as part of the input for a later run.

We are not recommending including everything you know that you can deduce from the clauses that present a problem to a reasoning program. We recommend including only those dependent clauses that correspond to useful information as determined by your experience and intuition. Since we cannot define precisely what we mean by useful, we are obviously again illustrating what an art all of this is.

16.3 Inference Rules

Choosing inference rules is far less subtle and complex than representing information to an automated reasoning program. Although the choice of representation strongly dictates the good choice of inference rule(s), the choices of representation and of inference rule(s) should not be made sequentially. For that matter, the choice of strategy should not be postponed until the preceding two choices have been made. What works is the appropriate and simultaneous choices for representation, inference rule, and strategy, for the three are extremely interconnected and interdependent. Unless some specific reason exists, we recommend that the instructions to a reasoning program cause it to use a single inference rule when attacking the problem under study. Using more than one rule at a time often results in certain conclusions being made via distinct paths, or sometimes even from the same set of clauses. For example, both UR-resolution and hyperresolution produce the same clause from the following clauses.

> BROTHER(Rick, Brian)
> FATHER(Brian, Bob)
> ¬FATHER(y, z) | ¬BROTHER(x, y) | UNCLE(x, z)

If the clauses given to a reasoning program to describe the problem contain many unit clauses using some equality predicate(s), then paramodulation is indicated. If the clauses include many unit clauses using predicates other than equality, then UR-resolution is indicated. If few unit clauses are present to begin with, then hyperresolution is indicated. In most cases, avoid using binary resolution.

In addition to the choice for representation, the expected form of the conclusions also is a factor in deciding what inference rule(s) to use. If the steps leading to the goal are expected to require substituting terms for other terms, then paramodulation is the choice. This is especially true if the substitutions are expected to take place deep within some literal. If the needed information is expected to be in the form of unit clauses, then UR-resolution is the choice. If the expected form is that of positive clauses, then hyperresolution is the choice. If some step that is expected is not found and you strongly suspect that the choice of strategy does not mesh with the representation and choice of inference rules, then briefly employ binary resolution to get past the impasse.

How can such an impasse occur? The following set of clauses is inconsistent—a proof is derivable under the appropriate choices.

> HASAJOB(Roberta, teacher) | HASAJOB(Roberta, nurse)
> ¬HASAJOB(Roberta, teacher) | HASAJOB(Roberta, nurse)
> HASAJOB(Roberta, teacher) | ¬HASAJOB(Roberta, nurse)
> ¬HASAJOB(Roberta, teacher) | ¬HASAJOB(Roberta, nurse)

Next, assume that only the last of the four clauses is placed in the set of support. Let us analyze the possible choices of inference rule.

Paramodulation is of no value here. Even if all clauses were placed in the set of support, UR-resolution is useless—no unit clauses are present to begin the search for a proof. Hyperresolution is useless, for the set of support strategy requires that the fourth clause be used at the start. This fact, coupled with the requirements of hyperresolution, says that only the first of the four clauses can be considered with the fourth. Such a consideration produces two clauses, neither of which is positive. Thus, from among the standard inference rules, we are forced to employ binary resolution. In point of fact, negative hyperresolution would suffice. However, the example was chosen to illustrate easily why the preferred rules might not be enough.

Not even negative hyperresolution can help in the following example.

> ¬N(a) | ¬O(a) | P(a)
> ¬R(a) | ¬S(a) | T(a)

$\neg T(a)$

$N(a)$

$O(a)$

$Q(a)$

$S(a)$

$\neg P(a) \mid \neg Q(a) \mid R(a)$

The set of support consists of the last of these clauses.

Historically, binary resolution deserves an accolade, for it was the first breakthrough in the area of inference rules. Nevertheless, with few exceptions, we recommend avoidance of binary resolution. The steps taken with its application are too small. So often its application behaves like conducting a simultaneous case analysis, and sometimes with many cases at a time. In fact, in the same spirit, we caution you about causing a reasoning program to apply an inference rule to a set of clauses two or more of which are nonunit clauses.

16.4 Strategy

The difficulty of choosing the right strategy or strategies falls somewhere between the difficulty of choosing a good representation and the difficulty of choosing good inference rules. Without strategy, an automated reasoning program will drown in new information. With strategy, a reasoning program can sometimes perform as a brilliant assistant or colleague. Of all the easy-to-use strategies, the set of support is by far the most powerful. The recommended uses are two—either choose the special hypothesis combined with the denial, or choose the denial alone as the set of support.

The clauses that are present because of assuming the hoped-for result false are easily identified. When no such obvious clauses exist, a trick like that used in Chapter 3 in the full jobs puzzle might be necessary. On the other hand, the clauses that are special to the problem are not so easy to identify. In mathematics, they are the statements that are assumed true, but are not the axioms or the supplied lemmas. They are the statements that, so to speak, specify the theorem. Assumptions such as "the square of every element is the identity" are an example. When the problem is not of this nature, then you might look for the unusual information. In the full jobs puzzle, the facts about each of the four people are a candidate. Depending on the choices of representation and inference rule, we recommend deleting from this set the nonunit clauses.

While choosing a good set of support is often straightforward, choosing weights that assign effective priorities to the concepts is often not. We recommend that the weights reflect your experience in problem solving in the area under investigation, but also reflect your intuition about how the proof might proceed. Weights can be chosen to instruct a reasoning program to discard one class of information, to retain a second class but only to be used if all else fails, and to treat a third class as highly preferential. Fortunately, you are free to assign weights as you wish, so the typical notion of complexity can be discarded in favor of just the reverse. For example, you might wish to have a reasoning program retain information only if the clause has more symbols than some specified number. If your intuition so dictates, and especially if you have demonstrated an understanding of the particular field under study, follow your intuition.

In addition to using the set of support and weighting, we recommend using the unit preference strategy. Intuitively, since unit conflict is the usual objective, and since using a unit clause or clauses with one nonunit clause produces a clause with fewer literals than the nonunit clause, the unit preference strategy is oriented toward reaching the objective. This strategy matches well our preference for unit clauses and our preference for shorter clauses rather than longer. Even when a unit clause is not produced, at least shorter clauses are. When the strategy cannot find any unit clauses on which to focus, it chooses the shortest clause within the other constraints on which to focus. We warn you that cases of course exist in which the unit preference strategy does not mesh with the chosen set of support. In such cases, usually you should not change the set of support, but rather temporarily suspend using the unit preference strategy.

Our final recommendation for strategy is to include demodulators as part of the set of input clauses. With access to the appropriate demodulators, an automated reasoning program can sharply reduce the number of retained clauses during its attempt at solving a problem. Such demodulators permit a reasoning program to transform clauses that are syntactically different but semantically similar into a single clause. Clauses such as

EQUALP(brother(father(x)), uncle(x))

EQUALP(Shorty, Jack)

EQUAL(minus(minus(x)), x)

EQUAL(sum(0, x), x)

EQUAL(product(0, x), 0)

EQUAL(sum(sum(x, y), z), sum(x, sum(y, z)))

are usually valuable demodulators. With such clauses, a reasoning program maps distinct clauses that have the appropriate properties to identical copies, and then subsumption removes the extra copies. By removing the syntactically different versions of the same semantic information, those clauses are not available to produce other clauses, and the search can be speeded up greatly.

Just as you can use a reasoning program to find certain dependent information to then include in future uses, you can use a reasoning program to find valuable demodulators. The new demodulators can be added to the clause set and immediately used if the program is so instructed. You can establish the criterion on which a reasoning program bases its decision about which new unit equality clauses are to be classed as demodulators. The choice of the criterion, as well as the choice of demodulators supplied as part of the input, is an art.

In addition to the use of demodulation to remove syntactically distinct but semantically similar clauses, we also use it to perform "tricks". This use is highly nonstandard, and not to everyone's liking. The feature that disturbs some researchers is that certain uses are not sound—under certain conditions, conclusions can be reached that do not follow logically, and in fact may not be true. Nevertheless, we find it most convenient to have a reasoning program carry out tasks with demodulation that would otherwise require much more effort.

As one example of such a nonstandard and potentially unsound use of demodulation, we use demodulation to count symbols in an expression. Two demodulators can be supplied in the input that enable the program to find the correct counts of the symbol in question, say the function e.

EQUAL(count(e(x, y)), \$sum(\$sum(count(x), count(y)), 1))

EQUAL(count(x), 0)

To produce the correct count of the number of occurrences of the function e within a literal, the two demodulators must be used in the given order. After all, the second demodulator applies to any expression since the variable x is implicitly universally quantified. Even with this proviso, if the two demodulators are used as clauses, an unsound inference can result. Were they used with a version of transitivity of equality, and were the inference rule hyperresolution, then in effect the program would deduce that $1 = 0$. A deduction of this type can easily be termed questionable. Such unsound conclusions are easily avoided simply by placing the demodulators on a list whose elements are not allowed to be used with other clauses to draw conclusions.

Despite the potential unsoundness of using demodulation to perform such tasks as counting, we do recommend it, especially to the person who is rather skillful in using an automated reasoning program. We prefer this course to making such counts by hand, or to writing a separate program to take the output of a reasoning program and then make the counts. Uses of this type are procedural, and we employ a number of such procedures. Be warned that errors are easy to make when using such tricks. If you invent your own, carefully check the output of the reasoning program that is employing the new procedure based on demodulation.

Demodulation has one more important use, a use that depends on the fact that demodulation takes precedence and is applied immediately. In Chapter 3, solving the full jobs problem required continual updating of information, crossing off of possibilities for a person holding a job. Such updating is done automatically by a person working on this puzzle, and is treated as an aside. By treating it so, a potential distraction is removed from the main activity of acquiring new knowledge about the four people in the puzzle. In effect, solving this puzzle and problems in general involves scheduling of the various tasks and subtasks. An updating subtask is given high priority even though it is an aside. As you saw in Chapter 3, a reasoning program was provided with the means to do likewise. Without demodulation, such updating would have waited its turn, and the entire solution would have required much more time. Thus, demodulation can be used to dispatch certain tasks automatically as asides—and immediately.

Why not then relegate as much of the problem solving to demodulation as possible? Just as we pointed out that mapping too much of the information to unit clauses could remove an important criterion that a reasoning program might use for decision making, so it is with demodulation. For example, if everything were phrased as unit equality clauses, and if all such clauses were classed as demodulators, then the separation of tasks into primary and asides would be lost. After all, a reasoning program still proceeds serially. Thus the tasks would each be forced to wait its turn, and updating, for example, might be placed far down the list. We therefore recommend that demodulation, as is true for so much of automated reasoning, be given an important role, but caution and care must be exercised.

16.5 Bibliography

Having given various recommendations for the use of an automated reasoning program, we now turn to references to the literature. The discussion is organized, more or less, chapter by chapter. For the various concepts covered in the book, we cite certain papers and books for those who might wish to explore the topic more fully or read the original treatment. Of course we only sample the literature. We do include opinions about readability and importance for some of the citations. Finally, where possible, we give the reason you might wish to read a specific item. For example, where it is the case, we indicate that the paper contains actual problems that were solved with an existing program, or that the paper was the first to introduce a new concept. The inclusion in a paper of problems that were actually solved with a program distinguishes that paper from one in which the value of a concept is conjectured without evidence. If, in addition, a paper contains data that provides a measure of the difficulty of solving a problem with an automated reasoning program, such data can be used to evaluate the effectiveness of other reasoning programs.

You might be puzzled to find that the various citations do not often mention automated reasoning but instead refer to theorem proving, perhaps with some modifier. The explanation is that the designation "automated reasoning" has been used only since 1980. Prior to 1980, much of the research and many of the applications covered in this book under automated reasoning were discussed in terms of automated theorem proving. The difference between the two fields rests mainly with the way in which the corresponding software is used and with their scope. In automated reasoning, as we have illustrated in this book, the emphasis is on an active collaboration between the user and the program and on many uses you would not ordinarily consider to involve "proving theorems". Automated theorem proving is now a part of automated reasoning.

Among the references, four general books are included, three of which cover the field of automated reasoning as a whole, while the fourth provides a convenient source for a number of historically significant papers. The first of the three, *Symbolic Logic and Mechanical Theorem Proving* by Chang and Lee[16], is an introductory text that is very readable, although in a formal way. This book covers in detail the concepts illustrated in Chapters 2 through 5, reviewed in Chapter 6, and formalized in Chapter 15. Thus, it is a good reference for discussions of representation, inference rule, strategy, demodulation, and subsumption. If the book has a short-coming, it is its lack of guidance for choosing from among inference rules and strategies and the like. (However, when the book was written, little was known in that regard.)

The second book, *Logic for Problem Solving* by Kowalski[30], provides a reasonably informal introduction to a variety of topics in applied logic. In addition, this book introduces the general topic of *logic programming* and discusses the logic programming language Prolog specifically.

The third book, *Automated Theorem Proving: A Logical Basis* by Loveland[31], presents a complete and thorough treatment of the subject in a very formal manner. If you prefer the treatment of logic in Chapter 15 better than that found in Chapter 6 or in the earlier chapters, this book is the choice.

The fourth book, *The Automation of Reasoning: Collected Papers from 1957 to 1970* edited by Siekmann and Wrightson[1, 2], is a two-volume book consisting of a compendium of papers that are considered historically significant. The first of the two volumes contains a paper by M. Davis that gives the early history of automated theorem proving. The two volumes include a number of the papers we cite in this section. The second of the two volumes contains a paper by Wos and Henschen that presents a critical history of the field from 1965 to 1970 and includes evaluations of the trends that were current. With these general recommendations in hand, we now turn to citations specific to the individual chapters.

In Chapter 2, the two inference rules of UR-resolution and hyperresolution are introduced and, therefore, so also is unification. The paper in which unification first appears is "A Machine-Oriented Logic Based on the Resolution Principle" by J. A. Robinson[46]. That paper also presents a unification algorithm that is still in use in many automated reasoning programs. The algorithm is a straightforward left to right symbol matching algorithm, not including the table updating given in Chapter 15. The source for the inference rule of UR-resolution is the paper "Complexity and Related Enhancements for Automated Theorem-Proving Programs" by Overbeek, McCharen, and Wos[38]. The paper contains a number of problems from various fields of mathematics that illustrate the kinds of problem that can be solved with a reasoning program. The inference rule hyperresolution first appeared in the paper "Automatic Deduction with Hyper-resolution"[47]. However, the algorithm given in this paper for implementing hyperresolution is not the recommended one. For an algorithm that admits of a highly efficient implementation, consult the paper "An Implementation of Hyper-resolution" by Overbeek[43].

In Chapter 3, the inference rules UR-resolution, hyperresolution, binary reso-lution, and paramodulation are employed or mentioned. The chapter also introduces the concepts of unit clause, strategy, weighting, and demodulation. The references for UR-resolution and hyperresolution given in the preceding paragraph suffice. The reference for binary resolution is the "Machine-Oriented Logic" paper, also just given[46]. Paramodulation was first introduced in "Paramodulation and Theorem-proving in First-Order Theories with Equality" by G. Robinson and Wos[45]. To illustrate the potential power of paramodulation, the rule is employed to prove (not with a computer program) that if in a group the cube of every element is the identity, then $[[x, y], y] = e$, where $[x, y]$ is the commutator of x and y. The notions of unit clause and of strategy were introduced in "The Unit Preference Strategy in Theorem Proving" Wos, D. Carson, and G. Robinson[60], a paper that includes problems from various fields of mathematics. Evidence of the importance of unit clauses is presented in "The Unit Proof and the Input Proof in Theorem Proving" by Chang[17] and in "Unit Refutations and Horn Sets" by Henschen and Wos[27]. In those two papers, two classes of proof are discussed and proved equivalent. In the first of the two, conditions are given for applying a strategy that relies heavily on unit clauses.

The set of support strategy and the conditions for its being refutation complete, as well as the proof of that fundamental theorem, are given in "Efficiency and Completeness of the Set of Support Strategy in Theorem Proving" by Wos, D. Carson, and G. Robinson[61]. The paper includes evidence obtained from actual computer runs concerning the value of the strategy, where the problems are taken from various areas of mathematics. The strategy of weighting is introduced in "Complexity and Related Enhancements for Automated Theorem-proving Programs" by Overbeek, McCharen, and Wos[38]. This paper also includes evidence obtained from actual computer runs. The idea of demodulation was introduced in "The Concept of Demodulation in Theorem Proving" by Wos, G. Robinson, D. Carson, and Shalla[62]. The paper is based on results from actual computer runs.

In Chapter 4, the procedure of subsumption and the inference rule of paramodulation are discussed in detail. The concept of completeness for an inference rule and the inference rule of factoring are simply mentioned. The concept of subsumption was introduced in "A Machine-Oriented Logic Based on the Resolution Principle" by J. A. Robinson[46]. The concept of factoring was first discussed in "The Unit Preference Strategy in Theorem Proving" by Wos, D. Carson, and G. Robinson[60]. The reference for paramodulation was given in a preceding paragraph. The refutation completeness of paramodulation is proved in "Maximal Models and Refutation Completeness: Semidecision Procedures in Automatic Theorem Proving" by Wos and G. Robinson[64].

In Chapter 5, the important concepts are subsumption, demodulation, UR-resolution, hyperresolution, set of support strategy, and state. References for all of these except the concept of state have already been given. For the concept of state, see the book *Logic for Problem Solving* by Kowalski[30], which includes a number of examples and a discussion of state-space problems.

For the concepts of unification, binary resolution, the empty clause, and subsumption discussed in Chapter 6, the reference is "A Machine-oriented Logic Based on the Resolution Principle" by J. A. Robinson[46]. For unit clause, unit conflict, the unit preference strategy, and factoring, consult the paper "The Unit Preference Strategy in Theorem Proving" by Wos, D. Carson, and G. Robinson[60]. For a discussion of the distinctions between the axioms, the special hypothesis, and the denial of the theorem, and for an introduction to the set of support strategy including recommendations for its use, refer to "Efficiency and Completeness of the Set of Support Strategy in Theorem Proving" by Wos, D. Carson, and G. Robinson[61]. This paper includes experimental evidence for the potential value of the set of support strategy. The source for the inference rule of UR-resolution is the paper "Complexity and Related Enhancements for Automated Theorem-proving Programs" by Overbeek, McCharen, and Wos[38]. For hyperresolution, the paper "Automatic Deduction with Hyper-Resolution" by J. A. Robinson[47] is the source. From the viewpoint of implementation, the paper is "An Implementation of Hyper-Resolution" by Overbeek[43]. For paramodulation, the concept was first introduced in "Paramodulation and Theorem-proving in First-order Theories with Equality" by G. Robinson and Wos[45]. In this paper a proof of a somewhat difficult problem in group theory is given in terms of paramodulation. Although the proof given in that paper was obtained by hand, various proofs using paramodulation have since been obtained with an automated reasoning program, and thus the problem provides a valuable test case for such programs. The refutation completeness of paramodulation is given in "Maximal Models and Refutation Completeness: Semi-decision Procedures in Automatic Theorem Proving" by Wos and G. Robinson[64]. In "Paramodulation and Set of Support" by Wos and G. Robinson[63], the study of imposing the set of support strategy on paramodulation is fully discussed, and the required proofs are given relying on the use of the functional reflexive axioms. Unit resolution is covered in "Unit Refutations and Horn Sets" by Henschen and Wos[27]. Negative hyperresolution was introduced in "Automatic Theorem Proving with Renamable and Semantic Resolution" by Slagle[48]. Weighting is covered in "Complexity and Related Enhancements for Automated Theorem-proving" by Overbeek, McCharen, and Wos[38]. The reference for demodulation is "The Concept of Demodulation in Theorem Proving" by Wos, G. Robinson, D. Carson, and Shalla[62], and various problems and experiments with a program employing demodulation are presented. The only reference for the concept of environment and for any details concerning the automated reasoning program AURA is "Reference Manual for the Environmental Theorem Prover, An Incarnation of AURA" by B. T. Smith[49]. For a discussion of a software system for producing automated reasoning programs, the papers are "Logic Machine Architecture: Kernel Functions" by Lusk, McCune, and Overbeek[34] and "Logic Machine Architecture: Inference Mechanisms" by Lusk, McCune, and Overbeek[32]. The motivations for many of the implementation details can be found in "Data Structures and Control Architecture for the Implementation of Theorem Proving Programs", by Lusk and Overbeek[33]. If you wish to build a reasoning program utilizing the LMA package, you would read "Logic Machine Architecture Inference Mechanisms—Layer 2 User Reference Manual" by Lusk and Overbeek[35]. "An LMA-based Theorem Prover" by Lusk and Overbeek[36] is an introductory users manual for the interactive reasoning system ITP.

We turn now to references for the use of automated reasoning in specific application areas. For Chapter 7, one of the first papers that discusses the use of automated reasoning for logic circuit design is "Automated Design of Multiple-Valued Logic Circuits by Automatic Theorem Proving Techniques" by Wojciechowski and Wojcik[57]. This paper focuses on logic design using T-gates and gives the detailed methodology for using a reasoning program for circuit synthesis. This work is extended in "Automated Synthesis of Combinational Logic Using Theorem Proving Techniques" by Kabat and Wojcik[29].

In Chapter 8, the use of canonicalization techniques implemented via demodulation is described in "Formal Design Verification of Digital Systems" by Wojcik[58].

For Chapter 9, the reference for the concept of the set of support strategy and for the distinctions between axioms, special hypothesis, and denial of the theorem is that given in the references for Chapter 6. A discussion of the various types of strategy—ordering, restriction, deletion, and canonicalization—can be found in "Automated Theorem Proving 1965–1970" by Wos and Henschen[65]. For the concepts of hyperresolution, paramodulation, demodulation, weighting, and subsumption, the references cited for Chapter 6 suffice. The original paper, presenting the detailed method, for generating models and counterexamples with the assistance of an automated reasoning program is "Generation and Verification of Finite Models and Counterexamples Using an Automated Theorem Prover Answering Two Open Questions" by Winker[54]. This paper also includes a detailed discussion of the solution to the formerly open questions concerning ternary Boolean algebra. For a detailed account of the solution to the formerly open question concerning the possible existence of the semigroups focused on in Chapter 9, the paper is "Semigroups, Antiautomorphisms, and Involutions: A Computer Solution to an Open Problem, I" by Winker, Wos, and Lusk[53]. The corresponding minimality questions are discussed in a sequel to this paper, as yet unpublished.

For Chapter 10, two papers contain the appropriate information about the equivalential calculus, condensed detachment, and the use of an automated reasoning program to answer the formerly open questions discussed there. The first, "Questions Concerning Possible Shortest Single Axioms for the Equivalential Calculus: An Application of Automated Theorem Proving to Infinite Domains" by Wos, Winker, Veroff, B. T. Smith, and Henschen[66], emphasizes the viewpoint of the logician rather than the viewpoint of automated reasoning. The second "A New Use of an Automated Reasoning Assistant: Open Questions in Equivalential Calculus and the Study of Infinite Domains" by Wos, Winker, Veroff, B. T. Smith, and Henschen[59], emphasizes the role of the reasoning program and contains a very detailed account of how the program was used to answer the open questions. The references for UR-resolution, hyperresolution, demodulation, and subsumption are given among those for Chapter 6. For the concept of level, the paper is "Efficiency and Completeness of the Set of Support Strategy in Theorem Proving" by Wos, D.

Carson, and G. Robinson[61]. For a discussion of the demodulators used to classify and count, the paper is "Procedure Implementation through Demodulation and Related Tricks" by Winker and Wos[55].

The annunciator panel example of Chapter 11 came from the extended abstract "Automated Diagnosis of Multiple Alarms for Reactor Control Rooms" by Gimmy and Nomm[24]. The entire system is described in "Logic for Diagnosis of Multiple Alarms (DMA) System" by Hightower[28] and "Automated Diagnosis of Multiple Alarms for Reactor Control Rooms" by Gimmy and Nomm[25].

In Chapter 12, the symbolic execution of programs, the invariant assertion method of proving programs correct, and abstract programming are discussed. The invariant assertion approach to program correctness proofs stems from the paper "Assigning Meanings to Programs" by Floyd[22]. A good survey of the topic can be found in "An Assessment of Techniques for Proving Program Correctness" by Elspas, Levitt, Waldinger, and Waksman[21]. This paper discusses the method of Manna, which uses the unifications that occur when making deductions to carry out the substitutions necessary to change the program state. The book *Proving Programs Correct* by R. Anderson[6] is a good introductory work on program correctness. The book *The Craft of Programming* by Reynolds[44] discusses program development with an eye toward proof, as does "The Science of Programming" by Gries[26]. Both books include a thorough treatment of reasoning about arrays. Invariants and induction are discussed in the papers of Floyd and of Elspas, Levitt, Waldinger, and Waksman already cited, and also in "A Computational Logic" by Boyer and Moore[12]. Boyer and Moore's program prover incorporates mathematical induction as an inference rule. In "Computability and Unsolvability", Martin Davis discusses the ideas of partial and total correctness from the point of view of recursive function theory[20]. The paper by Elspas, Levitt, Waldinger, and Waksman also discusses these ideas. Topics related to abstract programming are discussed in "Can Programming Be Liberated from the von Neumann Style? A Functional Style and Its Algebra of Programs" by Backus[7], "Program Development by Stepwise Refinement" by Wirth[56], and "Program Adaptation and Program Transformation" by Boyle[13]. One of the earliest discussions of abstract programming methodology, including raising the level of program proofs and the relationship between abstract programs and correctness-preserving program transformations, is in "Knowledge about Programs: a Model and Case Study" by Gerhart[23]. A recent example of work in this area, including a formal development of an algorithm using the abstract programming methodology, is given in "Combining Algebraic and Algorithmic Reasoning: An Approach to the Schorr-Waite Algorithm" by Broy and Pepper[15]. An ambitious attempt to develop an abstract programming environment for writing programs for lattice gauge theory calculations is the GIBBS project of K. G. Wilson[52]. The automatic transformation of LISP-level abstract programs to FORTRAN-level concrete programs is discussed in "Program Reusability through Program Transformation" by Boyle and Muralidharan[14].

For Chapter 13, the reference for EMYCIN is *System Aids in Constructing Consultation Programs* by van Melle[39], which provides an introduction to the system. A collection of papers on expert systems is found in *Readings in Artificial Intelligence* edited by Webber and Nilsson[3].

As for Chapter 14, Kowalski's book cited earlier contains appropriate material. An introduction to Prolog that contains numerous example programs is provided in "Programming in Prolog" by Clocksin and Mellish[18]. Additional examples of Prolog are found in "How to Solve It with Prolog" by Coelho, Cotta, and Pereira[19]. Finally, for a discussion of implementation of Prolog, the papers "Implementing Prolog—Compiling Predicate Logic Programs" by Warren [50], and the paper "Prolog—The Language and Its Implementation Compared with Lisp" by Warren, Pereira, and Pereira[51] each give a detailed account. The reactor trip system described in Chapter 14 is a real one. It is described in the TREAT Upgrade Preliminary Safety Analysis Report[4].

For the concepts treated formally in Chapter 15, in addition to the various papers cited earlier in this section, the four books cited at the beginning of this section serve well as references. In addition, for a discussion of the lack of a lifting lemma for proving the refutation completeness of paramodulation and for a discussion of the functional reflexive axioms, the paper is "Paramodulation and Set of Support" by Wos and G. Robinson[63].

Chapter 16 is the only source we know of for actual advice on the use of an automated reasoning program.

For a set of problems and the corresponding discussion of using various inference rules, the paper is "An Interactive Theorem-proving Program" by J. Allen and Luckham[5]. For another set of problems and the results of the corresponding experiments, the paper is "Problems and Experiments for and with Automated Theorem Proving Programs" by McCharen, Overbeek, and Wos[37]. This paper contains the actual clauses used for the experiments.

For a different approach—that of natural deduction—than that taken in this book, the paper "Non-resolution Theorem Proving" by Bledsoe[11] and the paper "A Human-oriented Logic for Automatic Theorem Proving" by Nevins[40] are suggested. Related papers include "Splitting and Reduction Heuristics in Automatic Theorem Proving" by Bledsoe[8], "Computer Proofs of Limit Theorems" by Bledsoe, Boyer and Henneman[9], "A Man-machine Theorem-proving System" by Bledsoe and Bruell[10], "Plane Geometry Theorem Proving Using Forward Chaining" by Nevins[41], and "A Relaxation Approach to Splitting in an Automatic Theorem Prover" by Nevins[42].

16.6 Conclusion

The art of automated reasoning is complex and sometimes even obscure, with many and diverse aspects. By saying that we can only give guidelines and not rules and that exceptions abound, we may have caused you to wonder whether an automated reasoning program can really be used effectively as an assistant. After all, if effective use requires adding appropriate dependent information and requires strategy to prevent the program from being overwhelmed with numerous and unwanted conclusions, how valuable can a reasoning program be? For those who solved the open questions discussed in Chapters 9 and 10, an automated reasoning program proved invaluable. They relied heavily on the fact that it reasons logically, that all deductions are made explicit (including the precise history), and that it can be given astoundingly complicated assignments that it often completes. Acquiring a thorough understanding and a mastery of any powerful program that offers many options requires much practice and much experience. In the case of an automated reasoning program, we have found the price small when measured by the reward.

To begin acquiring an understanding and a mastery, you might start by representing very simple everyday problems to the reasoning program. Problems like the minipuzzle of Chapter 3 are a good choice. You might then move to problems like the full jobs puzzle of Chapter 3, followed by puzzles like the puzzle of 15 from Chapter 4, and finally ones like the checkerboard puzzle of Chapter 5. On the other hand, if you are quite familiar with some discipline such as circuit design or some area of mathematics, you might try some simple problems from that discipline. As you experiment with a reasoning program, look to the proverbs for guidance. Please heed the following warning.

You will encounter an exception to each of the proverbs.

Nevertheless, an automated reasoning program can be used as an invaluable assistant and colleague.

In addition to mastering the skills of representation, of the choice of inference rules, and of the use of strategy, you will encounter the need to develop axioms or assumptions that adequately characterize the particular domain of interest. The ascertaining of an adequate set of axioms may require patience and much experiment. No test exists in general for determining that a set of axioms (totally) characterizes a domain of inquiry. However, an automated reasoning program's output sheds much light on what may be missing. An examination of the conclusions being drawn is usually sufficient to find the problems that might exist with the chosen set of axioms. Such an examination also is useful in checking for inaccuracies in the representation and for suggestions about the inclusion of valuable information such as provable facts or lemmas. You can check your notion of how a problem might be solved against the derivation information supplied by a reasoning program, since the precise history is made explicit. Such checking sometimes uncovers a misconception in the problem formulation.

An automated reasoning program offers many features whose value can easily be underestimated. Unit clauses, for example, play a vital role in its use, but are also of much interest theoretically. They have been the subject of much research in various areas—unit proof, input proof, and the significance of Horn clauses.

Demodulation plays various roles—canonicalization, simplification, and procedural —and has been the focus of research in various contexts. Subsumption is the key to obtaining solutions to many problems and in an acceptable and often surprisingly small amount of computer time. Finally, an automated reasoning program gives you access to quite distinct inference rules and quite diverse strategies.

As in any art, automated reasoning presents a number of themes that occur in a number of forms. Many tapestries, many musical selections, and many works of fiction present themes that emerge, are modified, are placed in the background, and then reemerge in a slightly different form. These themes are often interwoven to the point that no clear separation can easily be found. The use of an automated reasoning program also has this property of themes occurring, recurring, being modified, and finally being interwoven into a complex pattern. Just as no procedure exists that can be followed to produce a beautiful picture or piece of music or work of fiction, as yet no procedure exists that can be followed to produce the "good" set of instructions to be given to an automated reasoning program. Nevertheless, an automated reasoning program can perform as a highly trained automated reasoning assistant.

We close by wishing you increased skill, understanding, and success in your use of an automated reasoning program. Even more, we wish you the excitement, zeal, and expectations we share. The field is young and progressing rapidly. If the next three years produce as much as the last three years, we shall meet again in the next book of this kind.

16.7 References

1. J. H. Siekmann and G. Wrightson (Eds), *The Automation of Reasoning: Collected Papers from 1957 to 1970, Vol. I*, Springer-Verlag, New York (1983).
2. J. H. Siekmann and G. Wrightson (Eds), *The Automation of Reasoning: Collected Papers from 1957 to 1970, Vol. II*, Springer-Verlag, New York (1983).
3. Nils J. Nilsson and Bonnie Lynn Webber (Eds), *Readings in Artificial Intelligence*, Tioga Publishing Co., Palo Alto, Calif. (1981).
4. *TREAT Upgrade Preliminary Safety Analysis Report*, SAREF/TU S3490-0001-YT-OB, Argonne National Laboratory (1981).
5. J. Allen and D. Luckham, "An interactive theorem-proving program" pp. 321–336 in *Machine Intelligence 5*, ed. B. Meltzer and D. Michie, American Elsevier, New York (1970).
6. Robert B. Anderson, *Proving Programs Correct*, John Wiley and Sons, New York (1979).
7. John Backus, "Can programs be liberated from the von Neumann style? A functional style and its algebra of programs," *Communications of the ACM* **21** (8), pp. 613–639 (August 1978).
8. W. W. Bledsoe, "Splitting and reduction heuristics in automatic theorem proving," *Artificial Intelligence* **2**, pp. 55–77 (1971).
9. W. W. Bledsoe, R. S. Boyer, and W. H. Henneman, "Computer proofs of limit theorems," *Artificial Intelligence* **3**, pp. 27–60 (1972).

10. W. W. Bledsoe and P. Bruell, "A man-machine theorem-proving system," *Artificial Intelligence* **5**, pp. 51–72 (1974).

11. W. W. Bledsoe, "Non-resolution theorem proving," *Artificial Intelligence* **9**, pp. 1–35 (1977).

12. Robert S. Boyer and J. Strother Moore, *A Computational Logic*, Academic Press, New York (1979).

13. J. M. Boyle, "Program adaptation and program transformation," in *Practice in Software Adaptation and Maintenance*, ed. R. Ebert, J. Lueger, and L. Goecke, North Holland Publishing Co. (1980).

14. J. M. Boyle and M. N. Muralidharan, "Program reusability through program transformation," in *Proceedings of the ITT Workshop on Reusability in Programming*, (1983).

15. M. Broy and P. Pepper, "Combining algebraic and algorithmic reasoning: an approach to the Schorr-Waite algorithm," *ACM Transactions on Programming Languages and Systems* **4** (3), pp. 362–381 (July 1982).

16. Chin-Liang Chang and Richard Char-Tung Lee, *Symbolic Logic and Mechanical Theorem Proving*, Academic Press, (1973).

17. C. L. Chang, "The unit proof and the input proof in theorem proving," *Journal of the ACM* **17** (4), pp. 698–707 (1970).

18. W. F. Clocksin and C. S. Mellish, *Programming in Prolog*, Springer-Verlag, New York (1981).

19. Helder Coelho, Jose Carlos Cotta, and Luis Moniz Pereira, "How to solve it with Prolog," Ministerio da Habitacao e Obras Publicas Laboratorio Nacional de Engenharia Civil, Lisbon (1980).

20. Martin Davis, *Computability and Unsolvability*, McGraw-Hill Book Co., New York, Toronto, and London (1958).

21. Bernard Elspas, Karl N. Levitt, Richard Waldinger, and Abraham Waksman, "An assessment of techniques for proving program correctness," *ACM Computing Surveys* **4** (2), pp. 97–147 (1972).

22. R. W. Floyd, "Assigning meanings to programs," pp. 19–32 in *Mathematical Aspects of Computer Science*, ed. J. T. Schwartz, American Math. Soc., Providence, R.I. (1967).

23. S. L. Gerhart, "Knowledge about programs: a model and case study," *Proceedings of the International Conference on Reliable Software*, pp. 88–95 (April 21–23, 1975).

24. K. L. Gimmy and E. Nomm, "Automatic Diagnosis of Multiple Alarms for Reactor Control Rooms," *Transactions of the American Nuclear Society* **41**, (June 1982).

25. K. L. Gimmy and E. Nomm, *Automatic Diagnosis of Multiple Alarms for Reactor Control Rooms*, DP-MS-81-91 June 1982.

26. David Gries, *The Science of Programming*, Springer-Verlag, New York, Heidelberg, and Berlin (1981).

27. L. Henschen and L. Wos, "Unit refutations and Horn sets," *Journal of the ACM* **21**, pp. 590–605 (1974).

28. N. T. Hightower, *Logic for Diagnosis of Multiple Alarms (DMA) System*, Savannah River Laboratory, June 20, 1983.

29. W. C. Kabat and A. S. Wojcik, "Automated Synthesis of combinational logic using theorem proving techniques," *Proceedings of the Twelfth International Symposium on multiple-valued logic*, pp. 178–199 (May 1982).

30. Robert Kowalski, *Logic for Problem Solving*, Elsevier North Holland, New York (1979).

31. Donald W. Loveland, *Automated Theorem Proving: a Logical Basis*, North-Holland, Inc., New York (1978).

32. E. Lusk, William McCune, and R. Overbeek, "Logic Machine Architecture: inference mechanisms," pp. 85–108 in *Proceedings of the Sixth Conference on Automated Deduction*, *Springer-Verlag Lecture Notes in Computer Science, Vol. 138*, ed. D. W. Loveland, Springer-Verlag, New York (1982).

33. E. Lusk and R. Overbeek, "Data structures and control architecture for the implementation of theorem-proving programs," pp. 232–249 in *Proceedings of the Fifth Conference on Automated Deduction*, *Springer-Verlag Lecture Notes in Computer Science, Vol. 87*, ed. Robert Kowalski and Wolfgang Bibel, (1980).

34. E. Lusk, William McCune, and R. Overbeek, "Logic Machine Architecture: kernel functions," pp. 70–84 in *Proceedings of the Sixth Conference on Automated Deduction*, *Springer-Verlag Lecture Notes in Computer Science, Vol. 138*, ed. D. W. Loveland, Springer-Verlag, New York (1982).

35. Ewing L. Lusk and Ross A. Overbeek, "Logic Machine Architecture inference mechanisms—layer 2 user reference manual," ANL-82-84, Argonne National Laboratory (December 1982).

36. Ewing L. Lusk and Ross A. Overbeek, "An LMA-based theorem prover," ANL-82-75, Argonne National Laboratory (December 1982).

37. J. McCharen, R. Overbeek, and L. Wos, "Problems and experiments for and with automated theorem-proving programs," *IEEE Transactions on Computers* **C-25** (8), pp. 773–782 (1976).

38. J. McCharen, R. Overbeek, and L. Wos, "Complexity and related enhancements for automated theorem-proving programs," *Computers and Mathematics with Applications* **2**, pp. 1–16 (1976).

39. William J. van Melle, *System aids in constructing consultation programs*, UMI Research Press, Ann Arbor, Michigan (1980).

40. Arthur J. Nevins, "A human-oriented logic for automatic theorem proving," *Journal of the ACM* **21**, pp. 606–621 (1974).

41. Arthur J. Nevins, "Plane geometry theorem proving using forward chaining," *Artificial Intelligence* **6**, pp. 1–23 (1975).

42. Arthur J. Nevins, "A relaxation approach to splitting in an automatic theorem prover," *Artificial Intelligence* **6**, pp. 25–39 (1975).

43. R. Overbeek, "An implementation of hyper-resolution," *Computers and Mathematics with Applications* **1**, pp. 201–214 (1975).

44. John Reynolds, *The Craft of Programming*, Prentice Hall (1981).

45. G. Robinson and L. Wos, "Paramodulation and theorem proving in first-order theories with equality," pp. 135–150 in *Machine Intelligence 4*, ed. B. Meltzer and D. Michie, Edinburgh University Press (1969).

46. J. Robinson, "A machine-oriented logic based on the resolution principle," *Journal of the ACM* **12**, pp. 23–41 (1965).

47. J. Robinson, "Automatic deduction with hyper-resolution," *International Journal of Computer Mathematics* **1**, pp. 227–234 (1965).

48. J. Slagle, "Automatic theorem proving with renamable and semantic resolution," *Journal*

of the ACM **14**, pp. 687–697 (1967).

49. B. Smith, "A reference manual for the environmental theorem prover, an incarnation of AURA", to be published as Argonne National Laboratory technical report.

50. D. H. D. Warren, "Implementing Prolog—compiling predicate logic programs," DAI Research Reports 39 and 40, University of Edinburgh (May 1977).

51. D. H. D. Warren, L. M. Pereira, and F. Pereira, "Prolog—the language and its implementation compared with Lisp," *Proceedings of the ACM Symposium on AI and Programming Languages, Rochester, N.Y.,* (August 1977).

52. K. G. Wilson, "The textbook model of program display and documentation: addendum to the GIBBS proposal", Newman Laboratory of Nuclear Studies, Cornell University, Ithaca, NY 14853 (1983) (private communication).

53. S. Winker, L. Wos, and E. Lusk, "Semigroups, antiautomorphisms, and involutions: a computer solution to an open problem, I," *Mathematics of Computation* **37** (156), pp. 533–545 (October 1981).

54. S. Winker, "Generation and verification of finite models and counterexamples using an automated theorem prover answering two open questions," *Journal of the ACM* **29** (2), pp. 273–284 (April 1982).

55. S. Winker and L. Wos, "Procedure implementation through demodulation and related tricks," pp. 109–131 in *Proceedings of the Sixth Conference on Automated Deduction, Springer-Verlag Lecture Notes in Computer Science, Vol. 138,* ed. D. W. Loveland, Springer-Verlag, New York (1982).

56. N. Wirth, "Program development through stepwise refinement," *Communications of the ACM* **14** (4), pp. 221–227 (April 1971).

57. W. S. Wojciechowski and A. S. Wojcik, "Automated design of multiple-valued logic circuits by automated theorem proving techniques," *IEEE Transactions on Computers,* (September 1983).

58. A. S. Wojcik, "Formal design verification of digital systems," *Proceedings of the 20th design automation conference,* (June 1983).

59. L. Wos, S. Winker, R. Veroff, B. Smith, and L. Henschen, "A new use of an automated reasoning assistant: open questions in equivalential calculus and the study of infinite domains" (submitted for publication).

60. L. Wos, D. Carson, and G. Robinson, "The unit preference strategy in theorem proving," pp. 615–621 in *Proceedings of the Fall Joint Computer Conference,* Thompson Book Company, New York (1964).

61. L. Wos, D. Carson, and G. Robinson, "Efficiency and completeness of the set-of-support strategy in theorem proving," *Journal of the ACM* **12**, pp. 536–541 (1965).

62. L. Wos, G. Robinson, D. Carson, and L. Shalla, "The concept of demodulation in theorem proving," *Journal of the ACM* **14**, pp. 698–704 (1967).

63. L. Wos and G. A. Robinson, "Paramodulation and set of support," *Proceedings of the IRIA Symposium on Automatic Demonstration, Versailles, France, Springer-Verlag Publ.,* pp. 276–310 (1968).

64. L. Wos and G. Robinson, "Maximal models and refutation completeness: semidecision procedures in automatic theorem proving," pp. 609–639 in *Word Problems: Decision Problems and the Burnside Problem in Group Theory,* ed. W. Boone, F. Cannonito, and R. Lyndon, North Holland (1973).

65. L. Wos and L. Henschen, "Automated theorem proving 1965–1970," pp. 1–24 in *The Automation of Reasoning: Collected Papers from 1957 to 1970, Vol. II*, ed. Jorg Siekmann and Graham Wrightson, Springer-Verlag, New York (1983).

66. L. Wos, S. Winker, R. Veroff, B. Smith, and L. Henschen, "Questions concerning possible shortest single axioms for the equivalential calculus: an application of automated theorem proving to infinite domains," *Notre Dame Journal of Formal Logic* **24** (2), pp. 205–223 (April 1983).

Index